SOUTH

FODOR'S TRAVEL GUIDES

are compiled, researched and edited by an international team of travel writers, field correspondents, and editors. The series, which now almost covers the globe, was founded by Eugene Fodor in 1936.

OFFICES
New York & London

FODOR'S SOUTH:

Area Editors: JEANIE BLAKE, EDGAR CHEATHAM, PATRICIA CHEATHAM, PHIL HALPERN, BERN KEATING, KAREN LINGO, JOHN D. PHILLIPS, WILLIAM SCHEMMEL, EDWARD J. WOJTAS
Contributing Editor: IRA MAYER
Editor: DEBRA BERNARDI
Editorial Associate: STEPHEN BREWER
Drawings: SANDRA LANG
Maps: DYNO LOWENSTEIN

SPECIAL SALES

SOUTH
1985

**ALABAMA
FLORIDA
GEORGIA
LOUISIANA
MISSISSIPPI
NORTH CAROLINA
SOUTH CAROLINA
TENNESSEE
VIRGINIA**

FODOR'S TRAVEL GUIDES
New York

All the following Guides are current (most of them also in
the Hodder and Stoughton British edition).

FODOR'S COUNTRY AND AREA TITLES:

AUSTRALIA, NEW ZEALAND AND SOUTH PACIFIC
AUSTRIA
BELGIUM AND LUXEMBOURG
BERMUDA
BRAZIL
CANADA
CANADA'S MARITIME PROVINCES
CARIBBEAN AND BAHAMAS
CENTRAL AMERICA
EASTERN EUROPE
EGYPT
EUROPE
FRANCE
GERMANY
GREAT BRITAIN
GREECE
HOLLAND
INDIA, NEPAL, AND SRI LANKA
IRELAND
ISRAEL
ITALY
JAPAN
JORDAN AND HOLY LAND
KOREA
MEXICO
NORTH AFRICA
PEOPLE'S REPUBLIC OF CHINA
PORTUGAL
SCANDINAVIA
SCOTLAND
SOUTH AMERICA
SOUTHEAST ASIA
SOVIET UNION
SPAIN
SWITZERLAND
TURKEY
YUGOSLAVIA

CITY GUIDES:

AMSTERDAM
BEIJING, GUANGZHOU, SHANGHAI
BOSTON
CHICAGO
DALLAS AND FORT WORTH
GREATER MIAMI
HONG KONG
HOUSTON
LISBON
LONDON
LOS ANGELES
MADRID
MEXICO CITY AND ACAPULCO
MUNICH
NEW ORLEANS
NEW YORK CITY
PARIS
ROME
SAN DIEGO
SAN FRANCISCO
STOCKHOLM, COPENHAGEN, OSLO, HELSINKI, AND REYKJAVIK
TOKYO
TORONTO
VIENNA
WASHINGTON, D.C.

FODOR'S BUDGET SERIES:

BUDGET BRITAIN
BUDGET CANADA
BUDGET CARIBBEAN
BUDGET EUROPE
BUDGET FRANCE
BUDGET GERMANY
BUDGET HAWAII
BUDGET ITALY
BUDGET JAPAN
BUDGET LONDON
BUDGET MEXICO
BUDGET SCANDINAVIA
BUDGET SPAIN
BUDGET TRAVEL IN AMERICA

USA GUIDES:

ALASKA
CALIFORNIA
CAPE COD
COLORADO
FAR WEST
FLORIDA
HAWAII
NEW ENGLAND
PACIFIC NORTH COAST
PENNSYLVANIA
SOUTH
TEXAS
USA (in one volume)

GOOD TIME TRAVEL GUIDES:

ACAPULCO
MONTREAL
OAHU
SAN FRANCISCO

CONTENTS

FACTS AT YOUR FINGERTIPS

When to Go 1; Planning Your Trip 1; Packing 2; Insurance 3; Hints to the Motorist 3; What Will It Cost 4; Hotels & Motels 6; Hotel and Motel Categories 7; Dining Out 9; Restaurant Categories 9; Summer Sports 10; Winter Sports 10; Roughing It 11; Tipping 12; Hints to Handicapped Travelers 12

THE SOUTH, STATE BY STATE

FACTS AT YOUR FINGERTIPS

 WHEN TO GO. All in all, spring is probably the most attractive season in this part of the U.S. Cherry-blossoms are followed throughout the region by azaleas, dogwood, and camellias from April into May and apple blossoms in May.

Seasonal and special events occur throughout the year. Numerically speaking, however, summer has the most, followed by spring, fall and winter in that order. Festivals (folk, craft, art and music) tend to come in the summer, as do sports events. State and local fairs come mainly in August and September, though there are a few in early July and into October. Historical commemorations usually have no connection with the seasons and are likely to occur at any time of the year. The temperature averages in the winter generally run in the low 40's in inland areas, in the 60's at southern shores. Summer temperatures, modified by mountains in some areas, by sea breezes in others, range from the high 70's to the mid-80's, now and then, the low 90's. And so summer is becoming increasingly popular as more and more travelers note the tempering effect of Atlantic and Gulf breezes. Nine states border on salt water, making for over 10,000 miles of coastline.

Fairs and festivals, art shows, parades, and fiestas beckon from January through May, from mid-September through October. Perhaps the most popular is the clamorous, swashbuckling *Gasparilla Pirate Days,* held at Tampa the second week in February. Biggest off-season drawing cards are, of course, *Mardi Gras* (day before Lent) in New Orleans, and that city's *Spring Fiesta,* held each April. And of course, the *Kentucky Derby* acts as a magnet in early May. Other off-season events of great interest include: Christmas parades, bowl games, Indian expositions and powwows, and flower festivals.

 PLANNING YOUR TRIP. In the *Practical Information* sections for each of the separate states you will find detailed sources for information on general tourism, national and state parks, tours, gardens, festivals, sports, museums, historic sites and monuments, and much more. If you don't want to bother with reservations on your own, a travel agent won't cost you a cent, except for specific charges like telegrams. He gets his fee from the hotel or carrier he books for you. A travel agent can also help those who would prefer to take their vacations on a "package tour"—thus keeping planning to a minimum; and in explaining the details of the "travel now, pay later" vacation possibilities offered by the nation's carriers. Various tour operators offer package tours to the South, most of them to five main destinations: Washington, D.C., New Orleans, Miami Beach, Walt Disney World and the Kentucky Derby. Here are a few suggestions: *Greyhound World Tours,* Greyhound Tower, Phoenix, Ariz. 85077; *Jefferson Tours,* 1206 Currie Ave., Minneapolis, Minn. 55440; *Trailways Tours,* 1500 Jackson St., Dallas, Tex. 75201; *Travel Services,* 501 4th Ave., P.O. Box 1319, c/o Stewarts, Louisville, Ky. 40201;and *Tour Service,* 507 West Ave., Austin, Tex. 78701.

If you don't belong to an auto club, now is the time to join one. They can be very helpful about routings and offering emergency service on the road. Two such are: the *American Automobile Association,* 8111 Gatehouse Rd., Falls Church, Va. 22047; and the *Amoco Motor Club,* 3700 Wake Forest Rd., Raleigh, N.C. 27609. In addition to its information services, the AAA has a nation-wide network of some 26,000 service stations which provide emergency repair service. The *Exxon Travel Club,* 4550 Decoma, Houston, Tex. 77092, provides information, low-cost insurance, and some legal services. The *National Travel Club,* 51 Atlantic Ave., Travel Building, Floral Park, N.Y. 11001 offers information services, insurance, and tours. Some of the major oil companies will send maps and mark preferred routes on them if you tell them what you have in mind. Try: *Exxon Touring Service,* 4550 Decoma, Houston, Texas 77092; *Mobil Travel Service,* 106 Hi-Lane Rd., Richmond, Ky. 40475; *Texaco Travel Service,* P.O. Box 538, Comfort, Tex. 78013. The practice of giving away free road maps at gasoline stations has almost entirely disappeared, and the most convenient place to get them now is bookstores. The three major road atlases for the U.S. are those published by Rand McNally, Hammond, and Grosset. Most states have their own maps, which pinpoint attractions, list historical sites, parks, etc. Write to the tourist services, in the state or states you plan to visit for copies of current maps. The precise addresses of the various state tourist services are given in the *Practical Information* sections for each state. City chambers of commerce are also good sources of information.

Plan to board the pets, discontinue paper and milk deliveries, and tell your local police and fire departments when you'll be leaving, when you expect to return. Ask a kindly neighbor to keep an eye on your house or apartment; fully protect your swimming pool against intruders. Have a neighbor keep your mail, or have it held at the post office. Consider having your telephone disconnected, if you plan to be away more than a few weeks. Look into the purchase of trip insurance (including baggage), and make certain your auto, fire, and other policies are up-to-date. The *American Automobile Association* (AAA) offers both group personal accident insurance and bail bond protection as part of its annual membership. Today, most people who travel use credit cards for major expenses such as gas, repairs, lodgings, and some meals. Put most of your trip money into travelers' checks. Arrange to have your lawn mowed at the usual times, and leave that kindly neighbor your itinerary (insofar as possible), car license number, and a key to your home (and tell police and firemen he has it). If you qualify for Senior Citizen discounts be sure to have the proper membership cards and identification along. (See below at the end of the Hotels and Motels section.)

 PACKING. *What to take, what to wear.* Make a packing list for each member of the family. Then check off items as you pack them. It will save time, reduce confusion. Time-savers to carry along include extra photo film (plenty), suntan lotion, insect repellent, sufficient toothpaste, soap, etc. Always carry an extra pair of glasses, including sunglasses, particularly if they're prescription ones. A travel iron is always handy, as are plastic bags (small and large) for wet suits, socks, etc. They are also excellent, of course, for packing shoes, spillable cosmetics, and other easily-damaged items. Fun extras to carry include binoculars, a compass, and a magnifying glass—useful in reading those fine print maps.

All members of the family should have sturdy pairs of shoes with non-slip soles. Keep them handy in the back of the car. You never know when you may want to stop and clamber along a rocky trail. Carry rain gear in a separate bag in the back of the car (so no one will have to get out and hunt for it in a downpour en route).

Women will probably want to stick to one or two basic colors for their wardrobes, so that they can manage with one set of accessories. If possible, include one knit or jersey dress or a pants suit. A full-skirted traveling dress will show less wear and wrinkling. For dress-up evenings, take along a couple of "basic" dresses you can vary with a simple change of accessories. That way you can dress up or down to suit the occasion.

If you go in spring or summer plan to dress as lightly as possible, but have along a light sweater for overcast days, cool evenings, and air-conditioned interiors. Women should have sleeveless dresses of cotton, linen, or synthetic fabrics that breathe. For men, tropical-weight suits of synthetic blends that breathe easily and are wrinkle-resistant are best. Cotton shirts are more absorbent than synthetics.

In the humid coastal areas and in heat-generating cities temperatures over 29°C (85°F) often build into thundershowers, so a lightweight raincoat that can double as an overcoat in cooler weather, or as a windbreaker over warmer clothes in winter, will be handy. November through March be prepared for cooler weather, especially as you go inland and into higher ground. Men will probably want a jacket along for dining out and a dress shirt and tie for the most formal occasions. Turtlenecks are widely accepted and are a comfortable accessory. Don't forget extra slacks.

Planning a lot of sun time? Don't forget something sufficiently cover-up to wear over swim suits en route to the pool, beach, or lakefront, and for those first few days when you're getting reacquainted with sun on tender skin.

INSURANCE. In planning your trip, think about three kinds of insurance: property, medical, and automobile. The best person to consult about insuring your household furnishings and personal property is your insurance agent. For Americans, he is also the person to ask about whatever special adjustments might be advisable in medical coverage while traveling. Foreigners visiting the United States should bear in mind that medical expenses in this country can be astronomical compared to those elsewhere, and that the kind of protection that some countries (Britain, for example) extend not only to their own nationals but to visiting foreigners as well simply does not exist here.

Every state has some sort of Financial Responsibility law establishing minimum and maximum amounts for which you can be held liable in auto accidents. Most states require insurance to be offered, and 17 states require you to have it in order to register a car or get a license within their jurisdictions. In any case, it is almost essential to have third party coverage, or "liability insurance," as claims can run very high for both car repairs and, particularly, medical treatment. Insurance premiums vary according to place and person; they are generally highest for males under 25 and for drivers who live in large urban areas.

One possibility is the *American Automobile Association* (AAA), which offers both group personal accident insurance (up to $7,000) and bail bond protection up to $500 as part of its annual membership. Foreigners should consider getting their insurance before leaving their own countries since short-term tourists will find it difficult and expensive to buy here. For the AAA, write to *AAA*, 8111 Gatehouse Road, Falls Church, Va. 22047.

If you are over 50, write to the American Association of Retired Persons/AIM, 215 Long Beach Blvd., Long Beach, Calif. 90802 for information about its auto insurance recommendations and other travel services.

HINTS TO THE MOTORIST. Probably the first precaution you will take is to have your car thoroughly checked by your regular dealer or service station to make sure that everything is in good shape. Second, you may find it wise to join an auto club that can provide you with trip planning information, insurance coverage, and emergency and repair service along the way. Thirdly, the *National Institute for Automotive Service Excellence,* which tests and certifies the competence of auto mechanics, publishes a directory of about 10,000 repair shops all over the U.S. which employ certified mechanics. It is available from *NIASE,* Suite 515, 1825 K Street N.W., Washington, D.C. 20006. The main highways of the South are great for high-speed driving. Speed limit is 55 miles per hour, to conform to gas conservation laws. However, highway hypnosis can be a decided danger on roads that stretch for miles without a break. It results from steady driving over long distances at set speeds. Principal symptoms are drowsiness and the inability to concentrate on what you're doing. The cure: Vary your speed occasionally, stop to stretch your legs, have a cup of coffee or tea, take a little exercise, take a brief nap.

If you get stuck on any kind of road, pull off the highway onto the shoulder, raise the hood, attach something white (a handkerchief, scarf, or a piece of tissue) to the door handle on the driver's side, and sit inside and wait. This is especially effective on limited-access highways, usually patrolled vigilantly by state highway officers. A special warning to women stalled at night: Remain inside the car with doors locked, and make sure the Good Samaritan is indeed what he seems. It is easier to find telephones along the major highways these days, since their locations are more frequently marked than they used to be. If you are a member of an automobile club, call the nearest garage listed in your Emergency Road Service Directory. Or ask the operator for help.

The mountains you will encounter in the South will present no particular driving problem. The roads are engineered for the ordinary driver, being well graded, normally wide, and safe. Observe the posted speed signs, particularly for curves. Keep to the right, again especially on curves. Use your engine in second or low gear on long descents, in order to save your brakes. If your car stalls, and your temperature gauge is high, it could mean a vapor lock. Cool the fuel pump with a damp cloth for a few minutes.

Budget your vacation driving time as carefully as you do your money. It's no fun to go sightseeing after a neck-and-shoulder-wearying day behind the wheel. In the wide open spaces, 250 miles a day is enough. In congested areas, make it 200. In most of the South, you'll be able to do the 250 miles comfortably. Stop occasionally to stretch your legs, walk the dog, buy a postcard, or give the kids a nature lesson in the woods or a roadside wiener roast. Save the big push for a business trip.

Traveling by car with your pet dog or cat? More and more motels accept them, but be sure to check *before* you register. Some turn them down, some want to look first, some offer special facilities. If it's a first-time trip for your pet, accustom it to car travel by short trips in the neighborhood. And when you're packing, include its favorite foods, bowls, and toys. Your dog may like to ride with its head out the window. Discourage this. Wind and dust particles can permanently damage its eyes. Dogs are especially susceptible to heat stroke. Don't leave your dog in a parked car on a hot day while you dawdle over lunch. Keep your dog's bowl handy for water during stops for gas; service station attendants are usually cooperative about this.

One tip for frequent motel stops along the road is to pack two suitcases—one for the final destination, and the other with items for overnight stops: pajamas, shaving gear, cosmetics, toothbrushes, fresh shirt or dress. Put overnight luggage into the trunk last, so it can be pulled out first on overnight stops. A safety hint: Don't string your suits and dresses on hangers along a chain or rod stretched across the back seat. This obstructs vision, and may cause an accident.

WHAT WILL IT COST? Two people can travel in the USA for an average of about $80 a day (not counting gasoline or other transportation costs), as you can see in the table below. Regionally, however, there are wide variations. The Northeast is the most expensive part of the country, followed by the Mid-Atlantic states, the Midwest, the South Central states, the Plains and Far West, and the Southeast, in that order. And within the South of course prices vary too. Mississippi is cheaper than Florida, West Virginia than Maryland.

In some areas you can cut expenses by traveling off-season, when hotel rates are usually lower. The budget-minded traveler can also find bargain accommodations at tourist homes or family-style YMCA's and YWCA's. Some state and federal parks also provide inexpensive lodging. And some 250 colleges in 41 states offer dormitory accommodations to tourists during vacations at single-room rates of $2-$10 per night, with meals from $1-$5. A directory of some 200 such bargains all over the U.S. is *Mort's Guide to Low-Cost Vacations and Lodgings on College*

Campuses, USA-Canada, from Mort Barrish Associates, Inc., Research Park, State Rd., Princeton, N.J. 08540.

Another way to cut down on the cost of your trip is to look for out-of-the-way resorts. Travelers are frequently rewarded by discovering very attractive areas which haven't as yet begun to draw quantities of people.

Typical Expenses for Two People	
Room at *moderate* hotel or motel	$35.00 plus tax
Breakfast, including tip	5.00
Lunch at *inexpensive* restaurant, including tip	8.00
Dinner at *moderate* restaurant, including tip	20.00
Sightseeing bus tour	6.00
An evening drink	4.00
Admission to museum or historic site	2.00
	$80.00

If you are budgeting your trip, don't forget to set aside a realistic amount for the possible rental of sports equipment (perhaps including a boat or canoe), entrance fees to amusement and historical sites, etc. Allow for tolls for bridges and super-highways (this can be a major item), extra film for cameras, and souvenirs.

After lodging, your biggest expense will be food, and here you can make great economies if you are willing to eat simply in your room and to picnic. It will save you time and money, and it will help you enjoy your trip more. That beautiful scenery does not have to whiz by at 55 miles per hour. Many states have picnic and rest areas, often well-equipped and in scenic spots, even on highways and thruways, so finding a pleasant place to stop is usually not difficult. Before you leave home put together a picnic kit.

Sturdy plastic plates and cups are cheaper in the long run than throw-away paper ones; and the same goes for permanent metal flatware rather than the throw-away plastic kind. Pack a small electric pot and two thermoses, one for water and one for milk, tea, or coffee. In other words, one hot, and one cold. If you go by car, take along a small cooler. Bread, milk, cold cereal, jam, tea or instant coffee, bouillon cubes and instant soup packets, fruit, fresh vegetables that need no cooking (such as lettuce, cucumbers, carrots, tomatoes, and mushrooms), cold cuts, cheese, nuts, raisins, eggs (hard boil them in the electric pot in your room the night before)—with only things like these you can eat conveniently, cheaply, and well.

Even in restaurants there are ways to cut costs. 1) Always stop at the cash register and look over the menu *before* you sit down. 2) Have a few standard items like coffee, soup, side dishes, etc. to test the price range. 3) Look around to see what other people are actually getting for their money. How big are the portions? Is there more than one slice of tomato in the salad? 4) Order a complete dinner; a la carte *always* adds up to more, unless you see someone with an enormous Chef's Salad and decide that's all you need. 5) If there is a salad bar or any kind of smorgasbord, fill up there and save on desserts and extras. 6) Ask about smaller portions, at lower prices, for children. Most places are providing them now. 7) Go to a Chinese restaurant and order one less main dish than the number of people in your group. You'll still come away pleasantly full. 8) Ask for the Day's Special, House Special, or whatever it's called. Chances are that it will be better, and more abundant, than other dishes on the menu. 9) Remember that in many restaurants lunch may be a better bargain than dinner. 10) Insist on *no ice* in your beverages; you'll get 30%-50% more to drink. 11) Drink half your coffee then ask for a refill; usually it won't be charged. 12) Below, in the section on restaurants we suggest some chains that offer good value for your money.

If you like a drink before dinner or bed, bring your own bottle. Most hotels and motels supply ice free or for very little, but the markup on alcoholic beverages in restaurants, bars, lounges and dining rooms is enormous, and in some states peculiar laws apply regarding alcohol consumption. And in any case, a good domestic dry white wine makes a fine aperitif and is much cheaper than a cocktail.

 HOTELS AND MOTELS. *General Hints.* Don't be one of those who take pot luck for lodgings. You'll waste a lot of time hunting for a place, and often won't be happy with the accommodations you finally find. If you are without reservations, begin looking early in the afternoon. If you have reservations, but expect to arrive later than five or six P.M., advise the hotel or motel in advance. Some places will not, unless advised, hold reservations after six P.M. And if you hope to get a room at the hotel's *minimum* rate, be sure to reserve ahead or arrive very early.

If you are planning to stay in a popular resort region, at the height of the season, reserve well in advance. Include a deposit for all places except motels (and for motels if they request one). Many chain or associated motels and hotels will make advance reservations for you at affiliated hostelries along your route.

A number of hotels and motels have one-day laundry and dry-cleaning services, and many motels have coin laundries. Most motels, but not all, have telephones in the rooms. If you want to be sure of room service, however, better stay at a hotel. Many motels have swimming pools, and even beachfront hotels frequently have a pool. Even some motels in the hearts of large cities have pools. An advantage at motels is the free parking. There's seldom a charge for parking at country and resort hotels.

Hotel and motel chains. In addition to the hundreds of excellent independent motels and hotels throughout the country, there are also many that belong to national or regional chains. A major advantage of the chains, to many travelers, is the ease of making reservations en route, or at one fell swoop in advance. If you are a guest at a member hotel or motel, the management will be delighted to secure you a sure booking at one of its affiliated hotels for the coming evening—at no costs to you. Chains also usually have toll-free WATS (800) lines to assist you in making reservations on your own. This, of course, saves you time, worry and money. In some chains, you have the added advantage of knowing what the standards are all the way. The insistence on uniform standards of comfort, cleanliness and amenities is more common in motel than in hotel chains. (Easy to understand when you realize that most hotel chains are formed by simply buying up older, established hotels, while most motel chains have control of their units from start to finish.) However, individuality can be one of the great charms of a hotel. Some travelers prefer independent motels and hotels because they are more likely to reflect the genuine character of the surrounding area.

Because the single biggest expense of your whole trip is lodging, you may well be discouraged and angry at the prices of some hotel and motel rooms, particularly when you know you are paying for things you neither need nor want, such as a heated swimming pool, wall-to-wall carpeting, a huge color TV set, two huge double beds for only two people, meeting rooms, a cocktail lounge, maybe even a putting green. Nationwide, motel prices for two people now average $37 a night; hotel prices run from $35 to $85, with the average around $52. This explains the recent rapid spread of a number of budget motel chains whose rates average $17.50 for a single and $21 for a double, an obvious advantage.

The main national motel chains are Holiday Inn, Howard Johnson's; Quality Courts, Ramada Inns, Sheraton Motor Inns, and TraveLodge. Alongside the style that these places represent, however, are others, less luxurious and less costly, at which rates run about one-half those of the bigger, "more luxurious" ones. Here are the main ones operating in the South: Best Western, P.O. Box 10203, Best Western Way, Phoenix, Az. 85064; Budget Host Inns, P.O. Box 10656, Fort

Worth, Tex. 76114; Days Inns of America, Inc., 2751 Buford Highway, Northeast, Atlanta, Ga. 30324 (various toll-free numbers); Downtowner Motor Inns, 622 Two-Mile Parkway, Goodlettsville, Tenn. 37072; Family Inns of America, P.O. Box 10, Pigeon Forge, Tenn. 37863; Friendship Inns International, 739 South Fourth, West, Salt Lake City, Utah 84101, call (800) 453-4511; Scottish Inns of America, 1152 Spring St., N.W., Atlanta, Ga. 30309; Econo Travel Motor Hotel Corp., 20 Kroger Executive Center, P.O. Box 12188, Norfolk, Va. 23502, call (800) 446-6900; Red Roof Inns, 4355 Davidson Road, Amlin, Oh. 43002; Thrift Inns Ltds., P.O. Box 2699, Newport News, Virginia 23602. These chains all publish free directories of their member motels.

Prices in the budget chains are fairly uniform, but this is not the case in chains such as Ramada, Quality, Holiday Inns, Howard Johnson's, and TraveLodge. Their prices vary widely by region, location, and season. Among the national non-budget chains the most expensive are Hilton, Marriott, and Sheraton; the middle range includes Holiday Inns, Howard Johnson, Quality Inns, and Trave-Lodge; and the least expensive are usually Best Western, Ramada, and Rodeway (mainly in the South).

HOTEL AND MOTEL CATEGORIES

Hotels and motels in all the Fodor guidebooks to the U.S.A. are divided into categories, arranged by price.

Although the names of the various hotel and motel categories are standard throughout this series, the prices listed under each category may vary from area to area. This variation is meant to reflect local price standards, and take into account the fact that what might be considered a *moderate* price in a large urban area might be quite expensive in a rural region. In every case, however, the dollar ranges for each category are clearly stated before each listing of establishments.

Our ratings are flexible and subject to change. We should also like to point out that many fine hotels and motels had to be omitted for lack of space.

Super Deluxe: This category is reserved for only a few hotels. In addition to giving the visitor all the amenities discussed under the deluxe category (below), the super deluxe hotel has a special atmosphere of glamor, good taste, and dignity and it will probably be a favored meeting spot of local society. In short, super deluxe means the tops.

Deluxe: The minimum facilities must include bath and shower in all rooms, valet and laundry service, suites available, a well-appointed restaurant and a bar (where local law permits), room service, TV and telephone in room, air conditioning and heat, pleasing decor, and an atmosphere of luxury, calm and elegance. There should be ample and personalized service. In a deluxe *motel,* there may be less service rendered by employees and more by machine (such as refrigerators and ice-making machines in your room), but there should be a minimum of do-it-yourself in a truly deluxe establishment.

Expensive: All rooms must have bath or shower, valet and laundry service, restaurant and bar (local law permitting), limited room service, TV and telephone in room, heat and air conditioning, pleasing decor. Although decor may be as good as that in deluxe establishments, hotels and motels in this category are frequently designed for commercial travelers or for families in a hurry and are somewhat impersonal in terms of service. Valet and laundry service will probably be lacking; the units will be outstanding primarily for their convenient location and functional character, not for their attractive or comfortable qualities.

Moderate: Each room should have an attached bath or shower. There should be a restaurant *or* coffee shop, TV available, telephone in room, heat and air conditioning, relatively convenient location, clean and comfortable rooms and public rooms. *Motels* in this category may not have attached bath or shower, may not have a restaurant or coffee shop (though one is usually nearby), and may have no public rooms.

Inexpensive: Nearby bath or shower, telephone available, clean rooms are the minimum.

Free parking is assumed at all motels and motor hotels; you must pay for parking at most city hotels, though certain establishments have free parking, frequently for occupants of higher-than-minimum-rate rooms. *Baby sitter* lists are always available in good hotels and motels, and *cribs* for the children are always on hand—sometimes at no cost, but more frequently at a cost of $1 or $2. The cost of a *cot* in your room, to supplement the beds, will be around $3 per night, but moving an *extra single bed* into a room will cost around $7 in better hotels and motels.

Senior citizens may in some cases receive special discounts on lodgings. The Days Inn chain offers various discounts to anyone 55 or older. Holiday Inns give a discount to members of the NRTA (write to National Retired Teachers Association, Membership Division, 215 Long Beach Blvd., Long Beach, Ca. 90802) and the AARP (write to American Association of Retired Persons, Membership Division, 215 Long Beach Blvd., Long Beach, Ca. 90802). The amounts and availability of such discounts change, so it is well to check their current status with either your organization or with the hotel chain. The *National Council of Senior Citizens,* 925 15 St. N.W., Washington D.C. 20005, works especially to develop low-cost travel possibilities for its members.

The closest thing America has to Europe's bed-and-breakfast is the private houses that go by the various names of tourist home, guest home, or guest house. These are often large, still fairly elegant old homes in quiet residential or semiresidential parts of larger towns or along secondary roads and the main streets of small towns and resorts. Styles and standards vary widely, of course; generally, private baths are less common and rates are pleasingly low. In many small towns such guest houses are excellent examples of the best a region has to offer of its own special atmosphere. Each one will be different, so that their advantage is precisely the opposite of that "no surprise" uniformity which motel chains pride themselves on. Few, if any, guest houses have heated pools, wall-to-wall carpeting, or exposed styrofoam-wooden beams in the bar. Few if any even have bars. What you do get, in addition to economy, is the personal flavor of a family atmosphere in a private home. In popular tourist areas, state or local tourist information offices or chambers of commerce usually have lists of homes that let out spare rooms to paying guests, and such a listing usually means that the places on it have been inspected and meet some reliable standard of cleanliness, comfort, and reasonable pricing.

In larger towns and cities a good bet for clean, plain, reliable lodging is a YMCA or YWCA. These buildings are usually centrally located, and their rates tend to run to less than half of those of hotels. Nonmembers are welcome, but may pay slightly more than members. A few very large Ys may have accommodations for couples but usually sexes are segregated. Decor is spartan and the cafeteria fare plain and wholesome, but a definite advantage is the use of the building's pool, gym, reading room, information services, and other facilities. For a directory, write to National Council of the YMCA, 101 N. Wacker Dr., Chicago, Ill. 60606, and the National Board of the YWCA, 135 W. 50 St., New York, N.Y. 10020.

DINING OUT. The Chesapeake Bay area has a rich culinary tradition. *Baltimore* is famous for its seafood, notably oysters and crab cakes. And Chesapeake Bay yields over 40 species of fish including grey trout, sea trout, bluefish, black and channel bass, white and yellow perch, rock shad, herring (also taken in the Potomac), catfish, sea robin, flounder, and menhaden.

Maryland in general is known for its fried chicken, terrapin soup, terrapin stew (use butter and sherry), steamed hard-shell crabs, and beaten biscuits; but along the *Eastern Shore* you will encounter the towns of Bivalve, Md. and Oyster, Va. as well as the villages of Oystershell, and Shell-town, and the "Seafood Capital of the World," Crisfield, Md., much of which is built on a huge mound of oyster shells. Finer distinctions arise; you may attend a crab "feast" but an oyster "roast." The *Delmarva Peninsula* also produces melons, tomatoes, and potatoes; these last (with the skillful addition of milk, butter, eggs, sugar, lemon, cinammon and nutmeg) are made into White Potato Pie, another regional specialty.

Virginia is another land of plenty overflowing with ham, spoonbread, fried chicken, crabs, and beef, if not milk and honey. It is said that a good *Tidewater* cook knows at least 20 ways to prepare a crab; and Crab *Norfolk*, seasoned with vinegar, salt, red and black pepper and baked en casserole, is but one of them. Nearby *Hampton* considers itself the Seafood Capital of Virginia (the world title being already taken, as noted above). At *Smithfield*, on the Pagan River, hogs are allowed to roam free in the fields until autumn and then are let into the peanut fields to fatten. It is the peanuts and the special method of curing that give the dark-red Smithfield hams their distinctive flavor. The state is also noted for Black Angus beef.

For evening dining, the best advice is to make reservations whenever possible. Most hotels and farm-vacation places have set dining hours. For motel-stayers, life is simpler if the motel has a restaurant. If it hasn't, try to stay at one that is near a restaurant.

Some restaurants are fussy about customers' dress, particularly in the evening. For women, pants and pants suits are now almost universally acceptable. For men, the tie and jacket remains the standard, but turtleneck sweaters are becoming more and more common. Shorts are almost always frowned on for both men and women. Standards of dress are becoming progressively more relaxed, so a neatly dressed customer will usually experience no problem. If in doubt about accepted dress at a particular establishment, call ahead. Roadside stands, turnpike restaurants and cafeterias have no fixed standards of dress. If you're traveling with children, find out if a restaurant has a children's menu and commensurate prices (many do).

When figuring the tip on your check, base it on the total charges for the meal, not on the grand total, if that total includes a sales tax. Don't tip on tax.

The restaurants mentioned in this volume which are located in large metropolitan areas are categorized by type of cuisine: French, Chinese, Armenian, etc., with restaurants of a general nature listed as American-International. Restaurants in less populous areas are divided into price categories as follows: *super deluxe, deluxe, expensive, moderate,* and *inexpensive.* As a general rule, expect restaurants in metropolitan areas to be higher in price, but many restaurants that feature foreign cuisine are surprisingly inexpensive. Limitations of space make it impossible to include every establishment, so we have listed those which we recommend as the best within each price range.

RESTAURANT CATEGORIES

Although the names of the various restaurant categories are standard throughout this series, the prices listed under each category may vary from area to area. This variation is meant to reflect local price standards, and take into account the fact that what might be considered a *moderate* price in a large urban area might be quite expensive in a rural region. In every case, however, the dollar ranges for each category are clearly stated before each listing of establishments.

Super Deluxe: This category indicates an outstanding restaurant which is lavishly decorated, must have a superb wine list, excellent service, immaculate kitchens, and a large, well-trained staff.

Deluxe: Many a fine restaurant around the country falls into this category. It will have its own well-deserved reputation for excellence, perhaps a house specialty or two for which it is famous, and an atmosphere of elegance, attentive service, and unique decor. It will have a good wine list where the law permits and will be considered one of the best in town by the inhabitants.

Expensive: In addition to the expected dishes, it will offer one or two house specialties, wine list, and cocktails (where law permits), air conditioning (unless locale makes it unnecessary), a general reputation for very good food and an adequate staff, an elegant decor and appropriately dressed clientele.

Moderate: Cocktails and/or beer where the law permits, air conditioning (locale not precluding), clean kitchen, adequate staff, better-than-average service. General reputation for good, wholesome food.

Inexpensive: The bargain place in town, it is clean, even if plain. It will have air conditioning (when necessary), tables (not a counter), clean kitchen and attempt to provide adequate service.

 SUMMER SPORTS. *Swimming* is excellent in the many lakes as well as along the golden beaches that edge much of this area (over 10,000 miles of ocean shoreline). *Water skiing* (equipment may be rented in many places) abounds on lakes and in sheltered salt-water areas (the *Masters Water Ski Tournament* is held annually at Pine Mountain, Georgia). *Skin- and scuba-divers* explore the fantasies not only of the salt-water world, but also of lakes and numerous outsize springs.

Tennis and golf are played virtually everywhere. *Shelling* is extremely popular on Gulf beaches; and *rockhounds* are particularly partial to northern Georgia. All forms of *boating* are highly popular throughout the region, as are races and boating *regattas;* and sailing ranks high in some areas (the *Gulf Yachting Races* are held in July at Gulfport, Miss.).

Fresh-water fishermen angle for bass, shad, perch, snook, etc., in the region's rivers, for trout, crappie, bream, muskie, walleye, catfish, bluegill, etc., in the many lakes and streams. Experts go after muskellunge in Georgia's Blue Ridge Reservoir. Fishermen will find *surf casting* in a number of areas, and fishing from piers and bridges lures literally millions at some seasons. Salt-water anglers go out after amberjack, cavalla, bluefish, king mackerel, grouper, red snapper, sea trout, etc., flats fishermen after the wily bonefish. Big-game fishermen go forth to do battle with tarpon, tuna, marlin, sailfish, etc. Vacationers will find tarpon and other big-game fishing tournaments in many areas. Everything from rowboats to cruisers is available for hire or charter almost everywhere.

Spectators flock to thoroughbred, harness, greyhound, and stock-car races.

To make certain you don't miss any of the exciting sports events in the areas where you are vacationing, read the local newspapers as you go along.

 **WINTER SPORTS.** On the whole, the climate in this region is so mild numerous sports may be enjoyed year-round. *Spectator sports* include rodeos, stock-car races, football (including Bowl games on Jan. 1st), greyhound racing, harness and thoroughbred racing, fast and fabulous jai alai games at frontons in half a dozen Florida cities. Many of the big-league *baseball* teams hold their spring training in Florida communities. *Horse shows* are held in various

areas; and *polo* is big in Florida and South Carolina (Aiken is called the Polo Capital of the South) during the first four months of each year. Both the *Masters Golf Tournament* in mid-April and the *Women's Titleholders Tournament* in mid-April draw large numbers of spectators to Augusta, Ga. Other important spectator events include the *races* held during February and March at the Daytona International Speedway and the *International Grand Prix Sports Car Race* at Sebring in March.

The range of *participant sports* is high, wide, and handsome. *Swimming* in midwinter is enjoyable only in the most southerly areas, as are *water skiing and skin- and scuba-diving.* But *boating* of all types is enjoyed throughout the area on a year-round basis, as is *golf. Horseback riding* and *skeet* and *trapshooting* are popular. *Hunters* trek out for deer, quail, grouse, goose, boar, turkey, rabbit, squirrel (open seasons vary within states, sometimes within areas). Exceptional waterfowl shooting is found along the Mississippi flyway.

Anglers angle for bass, perch, snook, etc., in the many rivers of this region, while lake and stream fishermen bait their hooks for bass, bream, crappie, trout, muskie, walleye, bluegill, and catfish. Piers and bridges are liberally sprinkled with casters throughout the winter; while out on the briny catches consist of amberjack, dolphin, king mackerel, cavalla, bluefish, grouper, sea trout, pompano, etc. Fishermen will find charter boats available in almost every area. Big-game fish here include tarpon, tuna, marlin, and sailfish. Bonefishing in the shallows has its many devotees, as does surf fishing.

 ROUGHING IT. More, and improved, camping facilities are springing up each year across the country, in national parks, national forests, state parks, in private camping areas, and trailer parks, which by now have become national institutions. Farm vacations continue to gain adherents, especially among families with children. Some accommodations are quite deluxe, some extremely simple. For a directory of farms which take vacationers (including details of rates, accommodations, dates, etc.), write to *Adventure Guides, Inc.,* 36 East 57 Street, New York, N.Y. 10022 for their book *Farm, Ranch & Country Vacations,* by Pat Dickerman ($10.50, including shipping, or $12, first class).

Because of the great size of the United States and the distances involved, youth hostels have not developed in this country the way they have in Europe and Japan. In the entire 3½ million square miles of the U.S. there are upwards of 160 youth hostels, and because they arc, in any case, designed primarily for people who are traveling under their own power, usually hiking or bicycling, rather than by car or commercial transportation, they tend to be away from towns and cities and in rural areas, near scenic spots. In the U.S. they are most frequent and practical in compact areas like New England. Although their members are mainly younger people, there is no age limit. You must be a member to use youth hostels; write to *American Youth Hostels, Inc.,* 1332 I St., N.W., Washington, D.C. 20005. A copy of the Hostel Guide and Handbook will be included in your membership. Accommodations are simple, dormitories are segregated by sex, common rooms and kitchen are shared, and everyone helps with the cleanup.

Useful Addresses: National Parks Service, U.S. Dept. of the Interior, Washington, D.C. 20240; *National Forest Service,* P.O. Box 2417, U.S. Dept. of Agriculture, Wash., D.C., 20013. For information on state parks, write *State Parks Dept., State Office Building,* in the capital of the state in which you are interested. Exact addresses of such agencies are given separately in the *Practical Information* section for each state in this book.

The *National Campers & Hikers Assoc.,* 7172 Transit Rd., Buffalo, N.Y. 14221, is an informal organization of camping enthusiasts. *American Camping Assoc., Inc.,* Bradford Woods, Martinsville, Indiana, 46151 is a commercial camping organization. Headquarters of the *Appalachian Mountain Club* is 5 Joy St.,

Boston, Mass., 02108. Also *Kampgrounds of America, Inc.,* PO Box 30558, Billings, Montana 59114.

 TIPPING. Tipping is supposed to be a personal thing, your way of expressing your appreciation of someone who has taken pleasure and pride in giving you attentive, efficient, and personal service. Because standards of personal service in the United States are highly uneven, you should, when you get genuinely good service, feel secure in rewarding it, and when you feel that the service you got was slovenly, indifferent, or surly, don't hesitate to show this by the size, or withholding, of your tip. Remember that in many places the help are paid very little and depend on tips for the better part of their income. This is supposed to give them incentive to serve you well. These days, the going rate for tipping on *restaurant* service is 15% on the amount *before* taxes. Tipping at counters is not universal, but many people leave at least 25¢ and 10% if it's anything over that. For *bellboys,* 25¢ per bag is usual. However, if you load him down with all manner of bags, hatboxes, cameras, coats, etc., you might consider giving an extra quarter or two. For one-night stays in most *hotels* and *motels,* you leave nothing. But if you stay longer, at the end of your stay leave the maid $1-$1.25 per day, or $5 per person per week for multiple occupancy. If you are staying at an *American Plan* hostelry (meals included), $1.50 per day per person for the waiter or waitress is considered sufficient, and is left at the end of your stay. If you have been surrounded by an army of servants (one bringing relishes, another rolls, etc.), add a few extra dollars and give the lump sum to the captain or *maître d'hôtel* when you leave, asking him to allocate it.

For the many other services you may encounter in a big hotel or resort, figure roughly as follows: doorman, 25¢ for taxi handling, 50¢ for help with baggage; bellhop, 25¢ per bag, more if you load him down with extras; parking attendant, 50¢; bartender, 15%; room service, 10-15% of that bill; laundry or valet service, 15%; pool attendant, 50¢ per day; snackbar waiter at pool, beach, or golf club, 50¢ per person for food and 15% of the beverage check; locker attendant, 50¢ per person per day, or $2.50 per week; golf caddies, $1-$2 per bag, or 15% of the greens fee for an 18-hole course, or $3 on a free course; masseurs and masseuses 20%; barbers, 50¢; shoeshine attendants, 25¢; hairdressers, $1; manicurists, 50¢.

Transportation: Give 25¢ for any taxi fare under $1 and 15% for any above; however, drivers in New York, Las Vegas, and other major resorts *expect* 20%. Limousine service, 20%. Car rental agencies, nothing. Bus porters are tipped 25¢ per bag, drivers nothing. On charters and package tours, conductors and drivers usually get $5-$10 per day from the group as a whole, but be sure to ask whether this has already been figured into the package cost. On short local sightseeing runs, the driverguide may get 25¢ per person, more if you think he has been especially helpful or personable. Airport bus drivers, nothing. Redcaps, in resort areas, 35¢ per suitcase, elsewhere, 25¢. Tipping at curbside check-in is unofficial, but same as above. On the plane, no tipping.

Railroads suggest you leave 10-15% per meal for dining car waiters, but the steward who seats you is not tipped. Sleeping-car porters get about $1 per person per night. The 25¢ or 35¢ you pay a railway station baggage porter is not a tip but the set fee that he must hand in at the end of the day along with the ticket stubs he has used. Therefore his tip is anything you give him above that, 25-50¢ per bag, depending on how heavy your luggage is.

 HINTS TO HANDICAPPED TRAVELERS. Two important sources of information are the books: *Travel Ability,* by Lois Reamy, published by Macmillan; and *Access to the World: A Travel Guide for the Handicapped,* by Louise Weiss, available from Facts on File, 460 Park Ave. S., New York, N.Y. 10003. *Rehabilitation International,* 1123 Broadway, New York, N.Y. 10010, publishes a 16-page International Directory of Access Guides, actually a bibliography of some 275 individual manuals of access possibilities at travel facilities all over the U.S. and Canada, plus three European countries. Another publication which gives valuable information about motels, hotels, and restaurants (rating them, telling about steps, table heights, door widths, etc.) is *The Wheelchair Traveler,* by Douglas R. Annand, Ball Hill Rd., Milford, N.H. 03055. Many of the nation's national parks have special facilities for the handicapped. These are described in *National Park Guide for the Handicapped,* available from the U.S. Government Printing Office, Washington, D.C. 20402. International Air Transport Association, 2000 Teel St., Montreal, Quebec, H3A 2R4, publishes a booklet *Incapacitated Passengers Air Travel Guide* to explain available special arrangements and how to get them. A central source of free information is the *Travel Information Center, Moss Rehabilitation Hospital,* 12th St. and Tabor Rd., Philadelphia, Pa. 19141. And you may also get information from the *Easter Seal Society for Crippled Children and Adults,* Director of Education and Information Service, 2023 West Ogden Ave., Chicago, Ill. 60612.

ALABAMA

Promise of Field and Factory

BY
CALEB PIRTLE

Caleb Pirtle, formerly Travel Editor of Southern Living Magazine, *has become one of the South's most eloquent and amusing spokesmen.*

Birmingham, Alabama's largest city, with a population of over 300,-000, is a good base for touring the state. Long known as the "Pittsburgh of the South," Birmingham's industrial past has given way to a modern look that has rising cultural overtones. Its symbol, however, remains a giant statue of Vulcan, readily seen if you approach the city from the south on US 31. Presiding over a beautiful countryside, this towering monument stands mounted atop a pedestal 124 feet high. Cast in the Birmingham locale, the fifty-five-foot iron statue, created by Giuseppe Moretti, made its first public appearance at the 1904 St. Louis "Louisiana Purchase Exposition." Thousands come to view this exceptional sight yearly, a monument to the memory of the 19th-century artist. You can take a glass-enclosed elevator to the observation deck at the base of the statue for a breathtaking view of Birmingham and surrounding Jones Valley.

Near Birmingham and Bessemer is the Tannehill State Park, where you can enjoy camping, fishing and hiking along the Cahaba River, as well as view the old Tannehill Iron Furnaces, standing today as mute evidence of the fiery raid which destroyed them in the closing days of the War Between the States. There are several hiking trails in the park,

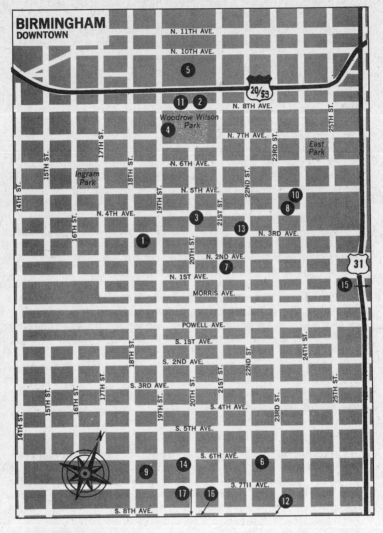

BIRMINGHAM
DOWNTOWN

Points of Interest
(Birmingham)

1) Alabama Theater
2) Art Museum
3) Birmingham Green
4) City Hall
5) Civic Center
6) Engineering Building (U. of Alabama)
7) Greater Birmingham Arts Alliance
8) Liberty National Building
9) Medical Center (U. of Alabama)

10) Miss Liberty
11) Municipal Auditorium
12) Red Mountain Museum
13) St. Paul's Cathedral
14) School of Dentistry (U. of Alabama)
15) Sloss Furnace
16) Southern Research Institute
17) Vulcan Statue

including the Tannehill Scout Trail, which is 10.5 miles and takes an average of five to six hours to complete.

Find your way to 331 Cotton Avenue SW, and you can visit Arlington Antebellum Home, an eight-room, two-story dwelling built in 1842 by William S. Mudd. It is a half-timber structure which used the property's own trees and incorporated the nails, beams, and bricks hand-fashioned by local slaves. It has over six landscaped acres for a scenic background and brims with original furniture of the 1800's: French, English, and American in design. Arlington was constructed thirty years prior to the founding of Birmingham in what was then Elyton, the seat of Jefferson County. Owned over the past century and a quarter by the Mudd, Whitney, DeBardeleben and Munger families, the house was purchased in 1953 by the city. It has a Civil War Museum.

Birmingham's Museum of Art is worthy of inclusion on your city tour. You will be able to view the nation's largest Wedgwood collection, as well as numerous Old World paintings, a great assortment of bronzes and silver, and other standard museum fare.

Your small fry will enjoy a visit to the Jimmy Morgan Zoo at 2630 Cahaba Road SW off US 280, where they can visit an aviary, a serpentarium and the large variety of hoofed creatures housed there.

Nearby in the wooded areas of beautiful Lane Park are Birmingham's Botanical and Japanese Gardens.

For a different look at Birmingham, visit the Red Mountain Museum. Here you'll find geological displays from the area, and you can take a walking tour along one side of the Red Mountain Cut, where the center of a mountain was torn away, revealing thousands of years of geological history in its layers.

Birmingham is noted for its beautiful displays of roses and dogwood, and if you visit the steel city during the height of the season, late April and early May, get the latest information from the chamber of commerce regarding location of the best blooms.

Environs of Birmingham

If you're in Birmingham during the spring, be sure to take in the city's Festival of Arts, which has skyrocketed to national prominence. Each festive day is packed with entertaining and informative activities—concerts, dramas, operas, ballets top off outstanding exhibits of painting, sculpture, and crafts. Each year the festival salutes a different country.

Also located in Birmingham, on the south side, is the University of Alabama Medical Center. The rapidly growing, multi-million-dollar complex covers more than sixty blocks and contains more than sixty health service facilities. It is considered one of the leading medical centers in the South, where patients come from all over the world for open heart surgery and, more recently, for organ transplants. Nearby is Southern Research Institute, where important cancer research is under way.

To begin a northern circle tour from Birmingham, follow US 78 northwest to Jasper. Nearby is Smith Lake, covering 21,000 acres, with 500 miles of wooded shoreline, formed by the Lewis Smith dam. At Jasper change to State 5 (also State 4 in this section), and proceed to the town named Natural Bridge. Nearby is Alabama's natural bridge. Slowly eroded by the perpetual abrasion of the stream, the sandstone fell away,

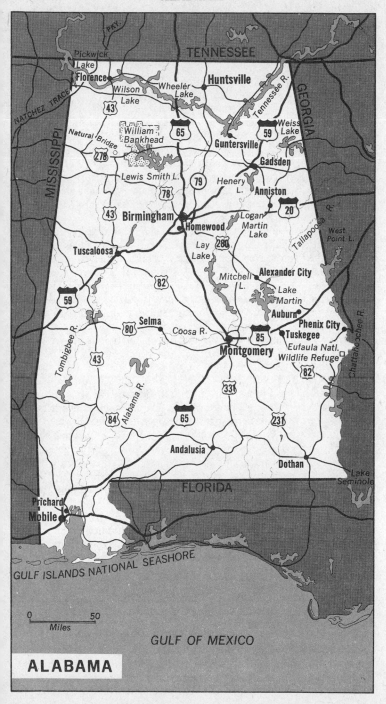

ALABAMA

leaving two large arches, one 148 feet long and 33 feet wide. Nearby, just outside of Hodges, is Rock Bridge Canyon with a major hiking trail that winds for about two miles through tunnels and unusual rock formations. Ball rock, Alabama's largest, is a huge hunk of sandstone rising 285 feet above the canyon.

Tuscumbia is the birthplace and early home of Helen Keller. "Ivy Green," built by her grandfather in 1820, is still there. Typically southern in architecture, its large square rooms have individual fireplaces. An office where the plantation books were kept was built in the yard near the house, and later a dressing room and porch were added. When Captain Keller brought his bride home, the ex-office-turned-residence was furnished for them. Here Helen Keller, a normal child, was born on June 27, 1880. Two years later, typhoid fever tragically deprived the little girl of both sight and sound, beginning the greatest drama in Ivy Green's long history. The story of how she overcame her handicaps has been an inspiration to millions the world over.

Much the same now as it was then, the many significant places and things—Whistle Path, the pump, her personal effects—have been kept intact for the visitor. Her story is retold each summer when William Gibson's play "The Miracle Worker" is staged at her birthplace.

Tuscumbia once was the site of an eighteenth-century Chickasaw town. During the 1830's, a canal was built around Muscle Shoals in the Tennessee River to aid navigation, and the first railroad west to the Allegheny Mountains was built from Tuscumbia to the boat landing. In Tuscumbia's Legion Park is the Big Spring. The copious flow of water attracted the Indians who located there and later it became the home of the first white settlers.

Sheffield (like Florence) can be reached easily from Tuscumbia. It's the principal railroad and industrial center of the Muscle Shoals areas. Your chief interest, however, will be the Wilson Dam, five miles northeast on State 133. Part of its powerhouse and an overlook are open free to the public. Its great bulk—4,500 feet in length, 137 feet in height and 101 feet thick at the base—creates Wilson Lake. The resulting miles of available shoreline make it a popular area for vacation activities, with the emphasis, of course, on aquatics.

Florence—third of the Tri-Cities—was settled in 1779 and has a population of 37,029. Florence was the birthplace of William C. Handy, famous Negro composer of "St. Louis Blues," and his home on W. Mobile St. has undergone restoration. Also in Florence is the largest Indian mound in the Tennessee River Valley, rising upward forty-two feet. The temple, which once stood atop the mound, was used for Indian ceremonials honoring the sun god. A modern museum, tracing the movement of prehistoric Indians through Northern Alabama, has been opened at the base of the mound. The city's other major attraction is restored Pope's Tavern, an early-day stagecoach inn. It was here that Andrew Jackson stopped for a night on his way to the battle of New Orleans.

Eighteen miles east of Florence on US 72, turn off on State 101 and, four miles south, you will reach Wheeler Dam, named for "Fighting Joe" Wheeler who served as a Confederate cavalry commander and with the U.S. during the Spanish-American War. Behind Wheeler Dam is Wheeler Lake on the Tennessee River. Another of the TVA dams, Wheeler backs the river up for seventy-four miles. Today Joe Wheeler State Park, opened on the north bank of the Tennessee River, offers an eighteen-hole championship golf course, a beach front swimming area, 116 campsites, a marina with 120 slips, a lavish 75-room resort hotel and restaurant. There are also a fishing pagoda, tennis courts, riding trails, biking and nature trails, and 25 family cottages.

Continuing south on State 101, you junction with Alternate US 72 which runs south of the lake. Heading east on 72A, it's a short drive to Decatur, a flourishing, industrial area thriving as a result of the TVA. Founded in 1820, it was later the scene of so many Civil War battles that when peace was declared all but five buildings had been reduced to rubble. In Decatur, Point Mallard, named for the ducks that come each winter to the adjacent Wheeler National Wildlife Refuge, is a family park, complete with the nation's first wave pool. Although Decatur is three hundred miles from the nearest ocean, its olympic-size pool provides three-foot-high waves just like the seashore. The 749-acre park also provides a 175-site campground, picnic facilities, and biking and hiking trails. There are an eighteen-hole championship golf course, paddle boats for use on the Tennessee River, and a playground for children.

Continuing east six miles on US 72A, you come to Mooresville. The first town incorporated in the state, it has a post office that still uses wooden call boxes of the last century, and still radiates a feeling of the early 1800's.

From cotton field to the moon might be a good description of your next stop—Huntsville, which likes to call itself "The Space Capital of the Universe."

Before Wernher von Braun and his space experts arrived on the scene, the city was a sleepy cotton town with a population hovering around 16,000. Today, a little over a decade later, Huntsville has a population of more than 308,000 and is one of the fastest growing cities in the country.

Most of the fantastic growth is due to the emergence of the Alabama Space and Rocket Center, located at Redstone Arsenal, just southwest off US 231.

Some of the most important experimental work in man's conquest of space has taken place here, and arrayed just inside the center and dominating the skyline are gleaming white models of numerous rockets.

The sprawling space flight center, set up at Redstone Arsenal in 1960, is also the home of the Army Missile Command and the Army's Missile and Munitions Center and School.

In the Space Orientation Center at Marshall, the history of rocketry and space exploration is recounted through the use of exhibits "from the early Chinese fire arrows to the V-2 rocket." Also on display is the Mercury capsule piloted by Commander Walter M. Schirra, Jr., on this country's third manned flight in 1962. You can also see exhibits illustrating the National Aeronautics and Space Administration's method for conducting a lunar landing, and an exhibit showing the late Lieutenant Colonel Edward H. White's "space walk."

To meet its fantastic boom, Huntsville now has under way several multi-million-dollar urban renewal projects which will give the old downtown section a completely new look. Already built are the city's gleaming new city hall, civic center, and probably the most modern and up-to-date courthouse in the South.

But the old still remains with such structures as the First National Bank, Alabama's oldest bank, on the downtown square, still standing. Rows of cotton may be seen too, planted along the city's traffic-laden Memorial Parkway, where numerous motels, restaurants, and shopping centers have sprung up practically overnight. All of the town's old textile mills have closed their doors, but farsighted leaders saw that they were put to good use. The offices of a number of space-oriented firms are now housed in one of the old cotton plants which was reconverted and is now known as the "Huntsville Industrial Center."

The city's research park, located near the University of Alabama at Huntsville campus, northwest of the city off US 231, also is a must for the tourist.

Huntsville's link to the past is Twickenham, a twelve-block, 300-structure district recently added to the National Register of Historic Places. In the area, 159 buildings are said to have historic and architectural significance, and twelve are listed in the Historic American Buildings Survey of 1935. Twickenham is the founding place of Huntsville and the cornerstone of Alabama.

Huntsville was the home of six Alabama governors, and is known for many beautiful old homes, located in the tree-shaded Twickenham District just a few blocks from downtown.

The Pope-Spragins Home, though not open to the public, was the abode of Confederate Secretary of War, LeRoy Pope Walker. It is noted for its classic portico—Mr. Walker for his command to bombard Fort Sumter.

Another TVA Creation

Guntersville, site of another huge TVA dam, is your next destination, via US 431. Originally an 18th century Indian village, Guntersville became a boomtown in the early 1820s with the coming of the steamboat and white settlers. Today it's just a sleepy Southern town, known mostly for its water recreation. Nearby Guntersville Dam and Lake provides 76 miles and 67,900 acres of fresh water for boating, fishing and swimming.

Two state parks are located near Guntersville. Buck's Pocket is 16 miles to the northeast via State 227 and county road 60. It has 55 campsites for tent or trailer, picnic facilities and 2,000 acres of rugged mountain scenery.

Lake Guntersville State Park, six miles northeast of Guntersville on State 227, features a luxury 100-room lodge, restaurants, 34 family-vacation cottages, swimming pool, 322-site campground, tennis, an 18-hole golf course, fishing and bicycles and canoes for rent.

Driving along State 79 north from Guntersville to Scottsboro, and then swinging northeast on US 72 headed for Bridgeport will roll you through some of Alabama's most mountainous terrain. Bridgeport is the gateway to the Russell Cave National Monument, which lies about eight miles northwest off US 72 via County 75 and 91. Originally a gift from the National Geographic Society, and now under strict supervision of the National Park Service Administration, the cave has a striking significance in that man has dwelled in it for some 8,650 years: a possible unparalleled continuity of cave life. The main cave area has been only partially opened; an immense, relatively unexplored cavern lies behind it. Near the Tennessee River where it passes the Cumberland Plateau, the Russell Cave National Monument takes up over three hundred acres. To gain added knowledge of how life was lived by prehistoric man, stop at the Visitors Center, and view the intriguing exhibits there.

Backtracking on US 72 a short distance to its junction with State 117, follow 117 to Hammondville. Five miles north are Sequoyah Caves, named for the unusual Indian who developed the Cherokee language in written form. Sequoyah Caves were probably inhabited about 500 B.C. and today, under private ownership, they may be explored daily.

Also near Hammondville—five miles east on State 117—is De Soto State Park, a 5,067-acre playground for outdoor-action devotees. Little River Canyon, said to be the deepest gorge east of the Rockies, runs twenty-seven miles within the park. A sixteen-mile road edges the canyon for scenic delights, and you may wish to view De Soto Falls which plunges 110 feet from a mile-long lake.

Within the state park, atop Lookout Mountain, is a 25-room lodge, 22 cabins (both chalet and rustic), restaurant, 82-site campground, hiking trails, fishing, bicycles for rent, and a country store. During May, the rhododendron and mountain laurel are abloom.

Out of Hammondville, you can take either US 11 or 1-59 to Fort Payne. Will's Town, an Indian community where Sequoyah lived, is nearby but more magnetizing is Manitou Cave right in Fort Payne. The cavern's attractions include rooms twenty to sixty feet from floor to ceiling plus a rock-formed span. Take a sweater, as the cave has a steady fifty-degree temperature. If traveling with children be sure to visit Canyon Land Park. They will love the miniature train ride and the chair lift to the bottom of the canyon.

To resume your meandering, head down US 11 for Gadsden to see Noccalula Falls about five miles north of the city on State 7. Noccalula was the despondent daughter of an Indian chief who, according to legend, pressed on by a broken heart, hurled herself from a ledge ninety-five feet high atop Lookout Mountain. At this drop, the mountain has wept ever since. Now gaiety prevails at the site's barbecue pits and picnic tables.

Beside the falls is a pioneer village, made up from old cabins hauled in to Gadsden from the surrounding rural highlands. Tying them all together is one of the state's best preserved covered bridges.

Gadsden has erected a monument, at Broad and First, to another girl, Emma Sansom. It is a memorial to the young girl who, during the War Between the States, used her intimate knowledge of the area to help Confederate troops under the command of General Nathan Bedford Forrest to safety. This, in turn, enabled one of the men to give early warning that the Northern army was advancing on Rome, Georgia, thus insuring the safety of the town's inhabitants.

Before heading for Birmingham, you can take a side trip south, via US 431, to Anniston. The Church of St. Michael and All Angels and its bell tower, noted for its architectural beauty, is worth a visit. Of interest also is the Regar Memorial Museum of Natural History. Not too far from

Anniston, at Fort McClellan, you can visit the Edith Nourse Rogers Museum, U.S. Women's Army Corps Center with permanent and temporary military exhibits. During the summer, all of Anniston is a stage at its annual Shakespeare Festival. Recently declared the State Theater of Alabama by the governor, this is the only professional resident repertory in the Southeast. Performances are given during July and August.

Traveling southwest from Gadsden toward Birmingham, two routes (US 11 and 411) lead to a junction with US 231. US 11 is the shorter. At US 231, proceed northwest toward Oneonta for a visit to the odd Horse Pens 40. On top of Chandler Mountain, they are between Oneonta and Ashville near where US highways 11 and 231 intersect. Named by John Hyatt, who climbed pathless Chandler Mountain in the 1870's, they are an unusual formation of rocks including a stone pen which he used as a corral. The "40" indicates the number of acres the rocky area comprises, and apparently Indians had also used them for penning horses. Today, little Horse Pens 40 has become a favored locale for art shows, Bluegrass Festivals, and folk fairs, focusing on the games and crafts from the past.

You can reach Cullman via US 231 to its junction with US 278, and then into town. Before you enjoy the city's nearby recreational areas, you might like to view the unusual Ave Maria Grotto, on the campus of St. Bernard College. Covering four acres, it consists of the handiwork of one Joseph Zoettl, a Benedictine lay brother, who for almost half a century labored over 150 diminutive duplicates of celebrated European and Middle Eastern cathedrals, shrines, and churches. They are masterpieces of stone and concrete and Brother Joseph even used marble, beads and jars during their construction. California missions, though not as striking, have been included. Beautiful gardens add spectacular luster to the attraction.

North of Cullman, six miles east on US 31, is Hurricane Creek Park. Among the many enticements—a nature trail of a mile and a half with a natural spiral staircase and stone sculptures wrought by the elements; waterfalls; swinging bridges. A small cable car can be used for rides out of a canyon which can also be viewed from an overlook. Picnic tables are provided.

Enroute to Birmingham, pull off at Warrior, a tiny town, if you'd like to roam through Rickwood Caverns State Park. They have an abundance of glittering stalagmites plus a lake. Camping facilities, picnic tables, a cafe and swimming pool are part of the cavern area's amenities.

South of Birmingham

For your swing south, take US 280 out of Birmingham to Childersburg.

Five miles east, via State 76, is DeSoto Caverns, the home of Kymulga Onyx Cave. The caverns, named for explorer Hernando DeSoto who trekked across the land that was to become Alabama, was believed by the Creek Indians to house fairies. These fairies, it was said, assisted the divine "Master of Breath" who gave the Indian life and let him live in the warmth of the sun, sustaining himself on corn. DeSoto is the oldest recorded cave in the United States, reported by an Indian Agent to President Washington in 1796.

Again moving south on US 280, you pass through Sylacauga, a town noted for its excellent marble. Two miles outside Sylacauga are the great quarries which have contributed their output to such buildings as the U.S. Supreme Court in Washington. Sylacauga, by the way, is at the western wedge of uniquely split Talladega National Forest.

From Sylacauga, stay on US 280 to Alexander City, springboard to the recreational complex of Martin Lake, formed by Martin Dam at Cherokee Bluffs. Wind Creek State Park is another aquatic park seven miles south of Alexander City on State 63. Open daily all year, it has nine acres of shoreline on Lake Martin, a marina, 1,400 acres of rolling hills, 400 campsites and a country store.

State 22 northeast from Alexander City leads to Newsite after 13 miles, and a short drive further, on State 49 south, puts you at the entrance to Horseshoe Bend National Military Park. A captain at the time, Andrew Jackson and his soldiers met the rebelling Red Stick (Upper Creek) Indians on March 27, 1814, in a short but bloody stand. The Battle of Horseshoe Bend ended the Creeks' power in the southeastern region and added territory comprising more than half of the present state of Alabama to the United States. It also started Jackson on the road that was to lead eventually to the White House.

You can tour the area by car.

Pick up State 49 again and, moving south, you'll rejoin US 280. Following the route, which dips southeast, you come to the twin cities of Opelika and Auburn. Auburn University's 2,105 acres are quite attractive and contain an agricultural experiment station. Though Opelika is also agricultural it has a number of well-known textile mills.

On to the Capital

Montgomery, Alabama's capital, should be your next goal. En route from Auburn on either I-85 or US 80, you may wish to divert briefly to Chewacla State Park, three miles southeast off US 29. Chewacla's 696 acres encompass a 26-acre lake popular with swimmers, as well as picnicking facilities, cottages, camping, riding trails and the like, all amid a valley as cragged as any below the Appalachians.

Another halt could be made en route to Montgomery at Tuskegee. Booker T. Washington founded Tuskegee Institute here in 1881. Part of the campus—1,800 acres—is the George Washington Carver Museum, among many buildings. At the museum, the African Negro's cultural enrichment of western civilization is illustrated through the use of dioramas while the history of the American Negro is vividly portrayed in the Chapel's stained-glass panes with religious genre folk songs as the theme. Washington was a leading researcher in agricultural chemistry, but he never took money for his discoveries. As a result, his fame was always greater than his fortune. His ambition was to teach people how to make fertile again that soil which overplanting with cotton had wasted away. And when the boll weevil ate out the cotton fields of 1910, he persuaded farmers to plant peanuts, then developed a staggering array of commercially practical synthetic products, using the shell as well as the nut, creating a new important industry.

Art and history behind them, hunters and fishermen may find more energetic enjoyment in nearby Tuskegee National Forest with its sizeable 10,777 acres.

Finally in Montgomery, you'll find a city of antebellum homes and, in some respects, an antebellum attitude, still proudly conscious of its deep Southern traditions: a heritage that emanates from every building and monument. Sacred, too, for Southerners, is the capitol edifice site where, on February 18, 1861, Jefferson Davis was sworn in as president of the Confederate provisional government. Later, the hope that there would be no Civil War was buried with the words—"Fire on Fort Sumter," the ominous orders from the capital of the Confederacy. Northerners are sometimes amused at Montgomery's long memory, but men here are as genuinely proud of their family's fight for independence as Bostonians are of theirs against the British, and jokes, on tour or just around town, are ill-placed.

Prime tour point is the historic State Capitol. Using the nation's capitol building as his inspiration, George Nichols is credited with this Alabama edifice, one of the Southland's most beautiful. Inside, the state's rich, historical background has been caught by an artist's brush in great, colorful murals. Conveniently across from the Capitol is the two-story First White House of the Confederacy. Built on Bibb Street, it is difficult to guess by looking at it that this handsome dwelling has been moved to a new setting. The capitol building is surrounded by other state office buildings including the Archives and History Building.

A reminder of the Union's eventual entry into Montgomery is Teague House, at High and South Perry street, noted since it was used by Northern General J. H. Wilson during Civil War days. St. John's Episcopal Church is another interesting structure. Built in 1855, it has a special gallery once set aside for slaves. Jefferson Davis also attended services there.

Most of Montgomery's outstanding historic homes are now in private hands or used by various establishments such as insurance firms or schools. Visits may be made, however, to the buildings not used for personal possession, and among the most important are the Lomax House, the Murphy Home, and the Seibel-Ball-Lanier Home, all built before 1860. The second, on the corner of Bibb and Coosa Streets, is an elaborate home built in 1851. During the Civil War the Union Army used it as headquarters. It now houses offices of the City Waterworks Board. Seibel-Ball-Lanier Home, 405 Adams St., an imposing Colonial house on a spacious, landscaped lawn, contains heirlooms, including carved marble mantels and ornate Regency mirror frames. Also restored and open to the public is the Old North Hull Historic District, which includes a tavern, church, log cabin, grange hall, doctor's office, and 1850's townhouse.

Eight miles north of Montgomery on US 231 are the lovely Jasmine Hill Gardens. Statues and fountains stud the flowering formal grounds, and green pines are prominent. Programs in performing arts are given in an amphitheatre during the summer months.

Montgomery does have modernity, most notable is its large Garrett Coliseum, its Museum of Fine Arts, and Maxwell Air Force Base. It was Wilbur Wright himself who founded the airfield but its name was bestowed in 1922 in honor of Lieutenant William C. Maxwell who was killed during the Philippine insurrections. Annual events that pack the Coliseum include the Southeastern Livestock Exposition and Rodeo in mid-March, and the South Alabama Fair in mid-October.

The W.A. Gayle Planetarium is interesting for adults and children alike. It has education programs for children, films and lectures. You can also buy astronomy and space science items.

Selma and Environs

Leaving Montgomery, you can ease out of the Civil War reminders surrounding you and drive seventeen miles northeast on US 231 to Wetumpka. Via State 9 just two miles south and then some three miles west on State 11, you encounter the site of Fort Toulouse State Monument. This marks the locale of a French fort erected in 1714 and successfully stormed by the British in 1763 and held by them until Revolution's end dictated surrender. Also close to Wetumpka is Lake Jordon, four miles north on State 11, a recreation region particularly popular with fishermen. Twenty-five miles north via US 31 is Clanton and ten miles further is Lake Lay for more outdoor activity, plus a possible free tour of Lay Dam's hydroelectric plant.

After such side trips you could return to Montgomery and take a fast trip to Selma, high above the Alabama River. It was the scene of frequent bombardment during the Civil War. But despite the ensuing destruction many architecturally attractive homes lend the town an aura of antebellum life even today. Sturdivant Hall, built in 1852, is among those with a neo-classic air. Reconditioned to its original state, the handsome mansion, designed by a relative of Robert E. Lee, is open to the public.

Twelve miles from Selma, southwest off State 22, is Cahaba, the state's first established capital. Now a moss-covered crumbling ruin is all that remains.

Much livelier is Paul M. Grist State Park, seventeen miles north of Selma and four miles northwest of State 22. This 1,080-acre playland has a primitive camping area for visitors who wish to stay overnight. Also available are opportunities to swim, fish and hike along wooded trails.

Continuing north on State 22 and 139, you come to Brierfield, site of Brierfield Ironworks Park, where the outdoor drama *Brighthope* by Kermit Hunter is performed June through August.

Moving west on US 80 from Selma, you can make a side trip on State 5 at Browns, turning north to visit the town of Marion. It is very small and famed for three people of historical significance who have lived there: Francis Marion, the "Swamp Fox," for whom it was named; Sam Houston who took for his bride a young woman who lived there—in fact, the wedding ceremony took place at her Green Street home, and Civil War teacher Nicola Marshall, who created both the uniform and the flag for the Southern Confederacy. A large segment of the small population (under 4,000) is made up of cadets who are enrolled in the Marion Institute, established twenty-nine years prior to the Civil War, and Judson College, Alabama's only non-coeducational institution of higher learning.

Returning to US 80 via either State 5 or 183 to Uniontown, drive on to Demopolis. Despite its name, with its proletarian implications, it was

French aristocrats—officers and courtiers—who colonized the government-given lands in the early 1800's. Straight from soft European court life, they struggled here vainly for three years and fell before the task. The land itself, with perfect growing soil, was waiting for tillage, which came with the advent of heartier native settlers. Responsive to their touch, great cotton plantations grew and with them, vast fortunes. Left behind as a testimonial to these times are many magnificent mansions. Among these is beautiful Gaineswood. Purchased by the state, it is open for tours.

Highlight: Tuscaloosa

Retracing your tour eight miles on US 80, you pass through Prairieville to track State 69 north to Greensboro. Here, Magnolia Grove, the ancestral home of Rear Admiral Richmond P. Hobson, is the main attraction. Hobson drew fame as the hero of the action that sank the *Merrimac* in Santiago Harbor to bottle up the enemy fleet in June, 1888, during the Spanish-American War. You can visit his home, representative of the 1800's.

Twenty-one miles to the north via State 69, you encounter a different facet of Alabama history at Moundville. It is Mound State Monument, a 325-acre park surrounded by forty Indian ceremonial hills ranging up to fifty-eight feet high. In the wings of the museum, excavated Indian burials are housed. The park graphically reveals how the Indian mound builders once lived, worked and worshipped. Nature trails by the river and picnic facilities add to the pleasantness of this site.

Sixteen miles north on State 69 is Tuscaloosa, home of the University of Alabama. Beginning in 1836, Tuscaloosa was the state capital for ten years until a collapsed cotton market instigated the government's move to Montgomery. The Civil War took its toll too but antebellum homes are nonetheless in evidence—at least a trio of them on the University of Alabama campus. Two merit special attention: The Gorgas House, dating from 1829, honors by name Dr. William C. Gorgas, whose work in Panama triumphed over yellow fever. With neo-Grecian architecture, the second of the pair is the 1840 President's mansion.

Filling the air of the campus with music both day and night are the bells of the Denny Chimes. From a carillon tower hymns are played and time is marked by the quarter hour. Named for Dr. George H. Denny, a onetime President and Chancellor of the University, the chimes are especially lovely.

At the university, a marker for students that fought Tuscaloosa invaders during the Civil War is located near the "Little Round House," once used as a sentry box. Smith Hall contains a Museum of Natural History.

From Tuscaloosa, you can return to Birmingham via US 11 and portions of I-20 and I-59. En route, pause at Vance. Just off US 11 lie the Bama Rock Gardens. Prehistoric Indian artifacts and rock houses are among some unusual natural formations.

Pioneer and Recreation Spots

Dedicated explorers will want to set off on another circle tour from Montgomery. This one would begin by heading southeast on US 82 through Union Springs to Eufaula on the banks of the Chattahoochee

River. In Eufaula is the famous "tree that owns itself." This oft-used phrase emanates from the fact that in 1936 the city commission deeded the land on which the tree stands to the tree itself. No legal challenge has ensued. Some locals feel that Eufaula is in for a boating boom due to formation of Walter F. George Lake by the same-name dam about twenty-five miles south, and that this will enrich the town as a springboard site. At any rate, you can reach the dam by following US 431 to Abbeville and there following State 10 to the structure on the Alabama-Georgia line.

If you pass through Eufaula in the spring, be sure to inquire about its Spring Pilgrimage of old homes. Most notable of these is the beautiful Shorter mansion.

Following this side trip, get back on US 431 and continue south to Dothan, a southeast Alabama trade center. In the 1880's when it was founded, it was a rough-and-tumble town that made mincemeat of any mild-mannered marshals but today, reasonably calmed by the benefits of its peanut production, life is much as elsewhere. Each October, Dothan is the scene of the National Peanut Festival, which adds pork to the annual playtime with a greased-pig contest as well as parades and similar festival adjuncts.

A drive up U.S. 231 to Troy brings you to the Pike Pioneer Museum, located three miles north of the city. It recreates a 19th century way of life through reconstructed buildings and antique furnishings.

Following State highways 87 and 167 south, you arrive at Enterprise, a town that has, in gratitude, erected a monument to an insect. That pest is the boll weevil, and Enterprise is delighted that it so ravaged its cotton that the town changed over to the production and processing of peanuts with a resultant surge of prosperity. Peanut butter plants are, in fact, the town's dominant structures.

Continuing west on US 84, you pass through Opp and Andalusia mainly to get to Conecuh National Forest's scenic splendors via US 29 and State 55. Alternatively, you could take State 88 sixteen miles south of Andalusia to Open Pond Recreational Area for leisure along the shores of its fifty-acre lake.

Evergreen, thirty-three miles west of Andalusia, is the map mark from which to swing southeast on State 29 for six miles to the Jay Villa plantation, site of the boyhood home of William Barrett Travis. On the grounds of this 135-year-old estate, Travis, one of the Alamo's heroes, played. It is not open to the public, but you can view from the outside the log cabin where young Travis lived while the plantation home was being built.

Near the little town of Belleville, ten miles west of Evergreen, the first clash of the Creek Indian War of 1813-14 occurred at Burnt Corn Creek.

Returning to Montgomery via US 31 or I-65, you go through Greenville, correctly dubbed The Camellia City. An antebellum mansion, White Columns, stands at nearby Camden on State 10. From there, you can get back to Montgomery either by returning to US 31 at Greenville or by taking State 21 from Camden directly to the capital.

Mobile, the Garden City

Deep-Alabama Mobile is another hub for sightseeing tours. This busy port city overlaps past and present on the western bank of the Mobile River at the top of Mobile Bay. Despite a raking by Hurricane Frederick in 1979, old mansions, grillwork balconies and lovely gardens abound, and belie the madness of the city's annual Mardi Gras for ten days preceding Shrove Tuesday. Its industrial endeavors are typified by the Alabama State Docks, capable of berthing some thirty ships at one time.

Fort Conde was the name the French gave the site in 1711, around which blossomed the first white settlement within what is now Alabama. For eight years it was the capital of the French colonial empire and stayed under their control after New Orleans became government headquarters, or until 1763.

Mobile today is noted for its tree-lined boulevards fanning out from Bienville Square at the center of the city. Many firms in town are in buildings dating prior to the Civil War, and the streets lead through flower-gardened residential sections.

At 350 Oakleigh Place and Savannah Street stands Oakleigh, built between 1833 and 1838. A half-timber house, Oakleigh is a splendid example of the period. Towering oak trees outside; fine furniture pieces inside. Owner James W. Roper was also its architect and today there is a museum on the lower floor.

Admiral Raphael Semmes is remembered as a Mobile resident, and for his fame during the Civil War, with a statue downtown and preservation of his house at 802 Government Street, given him by a grateful Confederacy.

Most highly publicized of gardens in the Mobile area is Bellingrath. This 800-acre spread is twenty miles south of town on US 90 and then Bellingrath Road, in the hamlet of Theodore. A river, the Ile-aux-Oies, laces through some sixty-five acres of gardens and forest, and Bellingrath's owners claim to have counted 250,000 azalea plantings comprised of two hundred different varieties.

Thousands of showy flowering shrubs and bushes are beautifully placed. Guides are on hand throughout the gardened vastness to assist or explain but a free map lets you plan your own flower-fringed strolls along paths as you will. Industrialist Walter D. Bellingrath began the nucleus of the noted section in 1917 when he and his wife bought a large tract as a hunting preserve. Their travels, however, prompted them to create, instead, a garden shrine rivaling some of the well-planned properties they had seen abroad. The Bellingrath-Morse Foundation has supervised the management of the gardens ever since his demise. Mrs. Bellingrath died in 1943, and their home, in the middle of the garden grandeur, is magnificently furnished, with objets d'art of all kinds and fine, old glassware.

In downtown Mobile, as a contrast to so many gardens, is the $2.2 million restoration of 18th century Fort Conde, whose remains were discovered when construction began on the I-10 interchange. I-10 now runs through a tunnel under the fort. In the early eighteenth century, the fort was the French administrative and military center for the Louisiana Territory. Many artifacts are on display there now.

Also of interest are the Phoenix Fire Museum on 203 S. Claiborne St., and the Mobile Art Gallery, Langan Park.

If you plan your visit to Mobile for February and March you will be in the right place to participate in the famed Azalea Trail Festival. Along Mobile's streets and in and around the city the Trail twines for thirty-five well-marked miles, showing off azaleas at their best. Scores of special events celebrate the yearly blossoming, from concerts to art exhibits and, of course, crowning of a queen—in this case, America's Junior Miss.

Don't let the fun, frolic and touring of the Azalea Trail Festival exhaust you, however, as there are still a couple or so side trips you should make from Mobile for full appreciation of Alabama's attractions.

Rewarding Side Trips

To reach Alabama's seashore area, take US 90 east through the Bankhead Tunnel that cuts beneath Mobile Bay. Then turn south on either US 98 or State 59. The latter is the only way to reach Pleasure Island, a thirty-mile region for romping along the Gulf of Mexico. It was a peninsula until the Intra-Coastal Waterway Canal cut across the land.

Before reaching Pleasure Island, though, you pay a call aboard the U.S.S. *Alabama*. She's berthed alongside a four-lane highway of the U.S.S. Alabama Memorial Park, created by dredging up enough of the bottom of Mobile Bay to spread out seventy-five acres. Public subscription saved the ship from being scrapped ignominiously after her heroic World War II service, which ranged from Scapa Flow to the South Pacific.

Indian Mounds and Industry

Other activity is underway at Gulf State Park, two miles east of Gulf Shores on State 182. Amid those 6,000 acres are a beach-front lodge with 100 rooms, restaurant, swimming pool, cabins, 322-site campground, two freshwater lakes large enough for skiing, canoes, sailboats, fishing boats, tennis, bicycles, a beach pavilion, and an 18-hole golf course. A white sand beach is lapped by the Gulf for two and a half miles, and a freshwater lake lures boaters. Pick your season: the park is open all year.

On the western end of the island is Fort Morgan, centerpiece of twenty-eight acres in a four-hundred-acre reservation, both under state control. With an extremely unique design, the construction of the fort began in the early nineteenth century. It was named after Daniel Morgan, an American Revolutionary hero. Both Confederate and Union relics and artifacts are housed in its museum.

Stone Age caves, Indian mounds, colorful caverns, antebellum homes, Space Centers, faded fortresses and rising resorts—such is the spectrum of sightseeing that greets the tourist in eye-opening Alabama.

PRACTICAL INFORMATION FOR ALABAMA

 FACTS AND FIGURES. In Choctaw Indian, *Alabama* means "vegetarian-gatherers" or "thicket-clearers." The state boasts two nicknames: the Cotton State and Yellowhammer State. Yellowhammer is also the state bird; camellia its flower; southern pine, its tree. Alabama's motto: *Audemus jura nostra defendere* ("We dare defend our rights"). "Alabama" is the state song.

Montgomery, the Confederacy's first capital, is the state capital. State population: approximately 3,800,000.

HOW TO GET THERE. *By air:* Birmingham may be reached on direct flights of American, U.S. Air, Delta, Eastern, Republic and United; Huntsville-Decatur on American, Republic and United; Mobile on Eastern, Air South, Texas International, and Republic; Montgomery on Delta, Air South and Republic; Dothan and Tuscaloosa on Republic.

By car: I-59 runs from Chattanooga, Tenn., to Birmingham, Tuscaloosa; I-20 from Atlanta, Georgia, to Anniston and Birmingham; I-65 from Tenn. passes through Decatur, Cullman, Birmingham and Montgomery and terminates in Mobile; I-85 comes from Atlanta, via LaGrange, Georgia, to Auburn and Montgomery; I-10 from New Orleans to Biloxi, Miss., Mobile and Pensacola and Jacksonville, Florida.

By bus: Greyhound and Trailways have good service.

By train: Amtrak trains go into Birmingham, Anniston, and Tuscaloosa.

HOW TO GET AROUND. *By air:* Local flights are provided by *Republic.*

By car: I-65 goes from the Tenn. state line to Mobile; US-80 crosses the state from the Georgia state line to the Mississippi state line; US 43 from the Tenn. state line through Florence, Tuscaloosa to Mobile.

Car rentals: Hertz, Avis, National, Econo Car, Budget Rent-A-Car, Dollar, Thrifty, Sears, and American International.

By bus: Greyhound, Basden Transportation, Thrasher Transportation, Capitol Trailways, Faith Bus Service, Gulf Transport, Ingram Transportation, Johnson Bus Service, Joiner, and Trailways operate.

By train: Amtrak.

TOURIST INFORMATION SERVICES. There are numerous sources of tourist information in Alabama. Among them are: Alabama Bureau of Publicity and Information, State Highway Bldg., Montgomery 36130; Alabama State Parks, State Administrative Bldg., Montgomery 36130; Alabama Travel Council, 660 Adams Ave., Montgomery 36130; Forest Supervisor, U.S. Forest Service, P.O. Box 40, Montgomery for detailed information on recreational facilities in national forests. Alabama Department of Conservation and Natural Resources, Information and Education Section, 64 N. Union St., Montgomery 36130, for fishing, hunting and camping. All local Chambers of Commerce. Alabama Mountain Lakes Association, P.O. Box 2222, Decatur 36501; DeKalb County Tourist Association, P.O. Box 316, Fort Payne 35967; Greater Birmingham Convention & Visitors Bureau, Suite 940, First Alabama Bank Building, Birmingham 35203; Gulf Shores Tourist Association, Gulf Shores 36542; Mobile Tourist Information Mobile Chamber of Commerce, P. O. Box 2187, Mobile 36601; Tallacoosa Highland Lakes Association, Rte. 1, P.O. Box 128, Sterrett 35147; Historic Chattahoochee Commission, P.O. Box 33, Eufaula 36027. For toll-free information from out-of-state (except Alaska, Hawaii), call 1-800-252-2262. In Alabama, call (800) 392-8096.

SEASONAL EVENTS. Because of its warmer climate, Alabama features outdoor events throughout the year. Some highlights are:

January. Mobile: Senior Bowl Football Game.

February. Mobile: Azalea Trail Festival, featuring 35 mi. of the beautiful blossoms, continuing into March; Mardi Gras. *Birmingham:* Camellia Show.

March. Fairhope: Arts and Crafts Week. *Mobile:* Tour of historic buildings. *Montgomery:* Southeastern Livestock Exposition and Rodeo. *Opp:* So. Alabama Rattlesnake Rodeo. *Selma:* Annual homes pilgrimage.

Spring. Birmingham: Festival of Arts.

April. Eufaula: Antebellum home pilgrimage. *Guntersville:* Civitan Horse Show. *Tuscaloosa:* Heritage Week Open House (mid-Apr.).

May. Birmingham: Annual sidewalk art show. *Eufaula:* Fresh Water Fishing Rodeo. *Ft. Payne:* Tours of homes (3rd weekend). *Mobile:* America's Junior Miss Pageant (usually early May). *May to Sept.: Talladega:* Alabama International Motor Speedway, car and motorcycle races.

June. Alexander City: Dixie Sailboat Regatta. *Tuscaloosa:* Charity horse show.

July. Bayou La Batre: near Mobile: Blessing of the Shrimp Fleet (1st Sun.). *Tuscumbia:* "The Miracle Worker," powerful drama depicting Helen Keller's heroic struggle with deafness and blindness. *Brierfield:* Outdoor drama "Brighthope," depicting the birth of Alabama coal and iron industries (early July–early Aug.) *Anniston:* Alabama Shakespeare Festival (early July–mid-Aug.).

September, Florence: North Alabama State Fair. *Montgomery:* National Championship Sports Car Race. *Selma:* Horse show (late Sept.); Central Alabama Fair (last week).

October. Birmingham: Alabama State Fair. *Dothan:* National Peanut Festival. *Mobile:* Greater Gulf State Fair. *Montgomery:* South Alabama Fair. Folk Festival and Bluegrass Festival, *Horse Pens 40.*

November. Montgomery: Southeastern Championship Horse Show.

December. Birmingham: Botanical Gardens Christmas Show. *Talladega:* state's biggest Christmas parade.

On the first Mon. and preceding weekend of every month you can witness "Barter Day" on Court House Sq. in *Scottsboro.*

Year-round (except January): Greyhounds race at Greentrack in *Eutaw* and at Mobile Greyhound Park.

 NATIONAL PARKS AND FORESTS. Oldest of Alabama's four National Forests is the *William B. Bankhead,* established in 1913, located in the northwestern part of the state. A wilderness area with hiking trails has been preserved and set up at *Bee Branch. Talladega National Forest* consists of two divisions—the *Oakmulgee,* located in the west-central part of the state, and the *Talladega* in the northeast part. In east-central Alabama is the *Tuskegee National Forest,* while *Conecuh Forest* lies on the Alabama-Florida state line.

There are various recreational facilities at 12 different locations. In the *Bankhead Forest,* the most complete facilities are provided at *Brushy Lake, Corinth* and *Sipsey River* recreational areas. There are two major areas in the *Conecuh Forest* located at *Blue* and *Open ponds.* In the *Talladega Forest,* Payne Lake, Lake Chinnabee, and Coleman Lake are the most complete. Additional facilities are being installed at *Houston Lake* in *Bankhead Forest.*

Alabama's National Military Park—Horseshoe Bend. The 316-acre site commemorates General Andrew Jackson's victory over the Creek Indians in the battle on the banks of the Tallapoosa River in March, 1814. The resulting peace treaty opened 23 million acres of land to white settlement. A Visitors' Center features graphic displays depicting events causing the Creek War of 1813 to 1814, Indian life, and the course of the battle. It's located on Rte. 49 and US 280, 12 mi. N of Dadeville, and 80 mi. SE of Birmingham. Closed Christmas.

The state's *Russel Cave National Monument* is located eight miles northwest of Bridgeport off US 72 via county roads 75 and 91. Oldest known cave-homes in southeast, where Stone-Age men lived, are here. A Visitor's Center provides information and displays depicting life of those prehistoric and historic cave dwellers. Closed Christmas.

STATE PARKS. Alabama has 24 state parks all equipped for the handicapped: *Blue Springs; Buck's Pocket; Roland Cooper; Cheaha* (highest point in Alabama); *Chewacla; De Soto, Little River Canyon* is the deepest gorge east of the Rockies, also has *De Soto Falls; Gulf; Joe Wheeler; Lake Guntersville; Monte Sano, Oak Mountain, Wind Creek; Bladon Springs; Chattahoochee; Chickasaw; Florala; Lake Lurleen; Lakepoint Resort; Paul M. Grist; Rickwood Caverns; Tannehill; Fort Morgan;* and *Fort Toulouse-Jackson.* There is camping and swimming at most. In addition *Gulf, Joe Wheeler* and *Lake Guntersville* also offer boating and fishing. Sun. open-air worship services at *Wind Creek.*

Family camping is possible in 14 of the parks. All provide picnic areas. Fishing tackle and rental boats are available from concessionaires at several parks.

In addition, Alabama has 23 managed, public, fishing lakes under the administration of the Department of Conservation. These lakes range in size from 13 to 250 acres. There's a daily fee of $1.50 per fisherman.

Anglers are required to have fishing licenses for Alabama waters. A seven-day, nonresident license costs $4.25. A nonresident annual license costs $10.25.

CAMPING OUT. Camping facilities for both those who enjoy living under canvas, and those who tow trailers are available in 14 state parks: *Blue Springs,* 6 miles E of Clio; *Buck's Pocket,* 2 miles N of Groveoak; *Roland Cooper,* 6 miles NE of Camden; *Cheaha,* 17 miles N of Lineville; *DeSoto,* 8 miles NE of Fort Payne; *Gulf,* 10 miles S of Foley; *Lake Guntersville,* 6 miles NE of Guntersville; *Lakepoint Resort,* 7 miles NE of Eufaula; *Lake Lurleen,* 12 miles NW of Tuscaloosa; *Oak Mountain,* 15 miles S of Birmingham; *Tannehill,* 12 miles SW of Bessemer; *Rickwood,* 4 miles N of Warrior; *Joe Wheeler,* 2 miles west of Rogersville; and *Wind Creek,* 7 miles SE of Alexander City. The number of campsites with hookups ranges from 41 at Roland Cooper to 468 at Gulf State. Family cottages are available at Cheaha, DeSoto, Joe Wheeler, Lake Guntersville, Oak Mountain, Roland Cooper, Chewacla and Monte Sano State Parks. Camping fees vary from park to park, ranging from $3 for primitive sites to $9 for full hookups. A waterfront site at Gulf State Park is $1 extra. Maximum occupancy is 8 persons per site. Two-week limit on stays.

Brushy Lake, 15 mi. S of Moulton, has 13 tent and camping sites; *Corinth Recreation Area* (open 4/1 to 10/31), 4 mi. E of Double Springs, has 74; *Lake Chinnabee,* 10 mi. S of Oxford, 14; *Taska,* 2 mi. E of Tuskegee, 6 for tents only; *Open Pond,* 15 mi. SW of Andalusia, 32; *Payne Lake,* 24 mi. W of Centreville, 84; *Pine Glen,* 2-½ mi. W of Heflin, 31; *Coleman Lake* (open 5/1 to 10/31), 8 mi. N of Heflin, 39. Fee is $2-$4 per day.

TRAILER TIPS. Alabama's trailer laws are similar to those of other states. Maximum over-all length of trailer and car is 50 feet. For 24-hour travel, widths are limited to 8 feet. Trailers up to 12 feet wide and 12-½ feet high can be moved on the highways between sunrise and sunset.

Trailer camping facilities are found in state parks and in the national forests. In addition, there are a number of private trailer parks.

KOA has trailer facilities on *Lake Eufaula* ($9 per night for two, 75¢ ea. additional person, $2 electric hookup); *Montgomery* ($10.50 for two, $1.50 each additional person, $8.50 tent, $2 electric hookup). Mobile: (off of I–10 and U.S. 90, $11.25 for two, $1.50 each additional person) *Valley Head,* adjacent to Sequoyah Caverns ($9 per night for two, $2 ea. additional person; a/c or electric heat $1.25 per day extra).

MUSEUMS AND GALLERIES. *Birmingham: Arlington Antebellum Home and Civil War Museum.* 331 Cotton Ave. SW. Built 1822. Gift shop. *Gulf Shores: Fort Morgan Museum.* Free. *Tuskegee: Tuskegee George Washington Carver Museum,* on campus of Tuskegee Institute. *Huntsville:* The Burritt Museum, built in the shape of a Maltese cross, contains works of local artists, historical articles. *Jacksonville:* Doctor Francis Medical Museum. *Montgomery:* Tumbling Waters Museum of Flags, 131 S. Perry St.

Art: *Birmingham: Museum of Art.* 2000 8th Ave., N. Modern as well as classical paintings. Free; *the Greater Birmingham Arts Alliance,* 2114 First Avenue North. Changing exhibits of area artists. Free. *Mobile: Mobile Art Gallery,* Langan Park. Free. *Montgomery: Museum of Fine Arts,* 440 S. McDonough St. Free.

Special Interest: *Anniston: Regar Museum of Natural History,* 1411 Gurnee. Features bird material—present-day and extinct birds in natural settings—and an excellent bird-egg exhibit. Free. *Birmingham:* Red Mountain Museum, 2230 15th Ave. S., Geological displays. Free. *Fort McClellan: Edith Nourse Rogers Museum,* U.S. Women's Army Corps Center, Permanent and temporary military exhibits. Mon. to Fri. Free. *Mobile: Bellingrath Home,* in Theodore. Open daily. *Phoenix Fire Museum,* 203 S. Claiborne. Free. *Tuscaloosa: Museum of Natural History,* Smith Hall, U. of Ala. campus. Free. *Tuscumbia: Ivy Green,* 300 W. North Commons. Helen Keller's birthplace. "The Miracle Worker" performed on Fri. and Sat., July & Aug.

Other: *Florence: Indian Mound Museum, Pope's Tavern, W.C. Handy Home. Old Tavern* in Tuscaloosa, a restored stagecoach stop in Alabama's old capital.

 HISTORIC SITES. The state was once heavily populated by Indian tribes. Famous battles of Indian wars and the Civil War are commemorated in many historic sites. Today, near *Atmore,* is Creek community, which the Indians retained through treaty with Andrew Jackson after the Battle of Horseshoe Bend. They live here on farms they own themselves. *Confederate Museum. Dadeville: Horseshoe Bend National Military Park,* Rte. 1, nr. Alexander City. Site of General Jackson's 1814 defeat of Creek Indians. Visitors' Center. Free.

Gulf Shores: Fort Morgan, twin fort defending the entrance to Mobile Bay, captured by Union forces during Mobile Bay campaign. *Civil War Museum.* Free. *Mobile: Oakleigh Home,* 350 Oakleigh Pl. *Monterey Home,* 1553 Monterey Place. *Fort Conde,* S Royal St. *Montgomery: First White House of Confederacy,* Washington & Union Sts., displays personal furnishings of Jefferson Davis and his family, preserved since their brief residency there over 100 years ago. *Capitol Bldg.* Free. *North Hull Historic District. Teague House* (State Chamber of Commerce Bldg.) Closed holidays. Free.

Moundville: 16 mi. S of Tuscaloosa on Rte. 69. State's largest ground of prehistoric *Indian mounds.* Also museum. *Selma: Sturdivant Hall. Tuscaloosa: Gorgas Home,* on U. of Ala. campus. Donations.

TOURS. The *Gray Line Tours,* part of a nation-wide system, offers a variety of package tours to Mobile's historic points of interest and famous gardens. Office is located in the Sheraton Inn at 301 Government Street.

 INDUSTRIAL TOURS. You can make a variety of industrial in-plant tours in Alabama at the following cities: *Albertville:* Reeves Rubber, Inc. (rubber floor tiles); *Anniston:* FMC Corp., Steel Products Div.; *Birmingham:* Astralloy-Vulcan Corp., the *Birmingham News* and *Birmingham Post-Herald; Coosa Pines:* Kimberly-Clark Corp.; *Decatur:* Amoco Chemicals Corp.; *Demopolis:* Gulf States Paper Corp.; *Gadsden:* Coosa River Garment; *Opelika:* Uniroyal

Tire Co.; *Prattville:* Bush Hog/Continental Gin; *Tuscaloosa:* BF Goodrich Tire. Reynolds Metal Co. (aluminum).

 SPECIAL INTEREST TOURS. *DeSoto Caverns,* nr. Childersburg. *Manitou Cave,* off US 11, Fort Payne. *Natural Bridge,* nr. Haleyville. *Alabama Space & Rocket Center.* On Rte. 20, Huntsville. Bus tour through the Space Flight Center. Closed Christmas. *NASA Bus Tour.* Space and Rocket Center Exhibits. *Horse Pens 40,* nr. Oneonta. *Sequoyah Cave Valley Head. Rickwood Caverns,* Warrior, nr. Birmingham. *St. Michael and All Angels Church,* 18th St. & Cobb Ave. Anniston. *Lay Dam,* Rte. 145, Clanton. Tour of hydroelectric generating plant. Free. *Ave Maria Grotto,* off US 278, on campus of St. Bernard College, nr. Cullman. Features 150 carved replicas of great religious buildings. *Wilson Dam,* Power House and Overlook, on Rte. 133, Sheffield. Free.

 GARDENS. The French, who came as colonists, brought to Alabama their architecture and their traditional azalea gardens. Mobile is the azalea center of the state, and houses Alabama's most famous gardens. Best known is *Bellingrath,* featuring hundreds of thousands of azaleas and magnificent displays of many other flowers. Located in Theodore, 20 mi. S of Mobile via US 90, on Bellingrath Road. Also, *Bellingrath Home. The Botanical & Japanese Gardens,* 2612 Lane Park Rd., Birmingham. Dawn to dusk. Free. *The Jasmine Hill Gardens,* Montgomery. Attractive garden with statuary. *Dismals Wonder Gardens,* Phil Campbell. *Bama Scenic Rock Gardens,* Vance.

MUSIC. The Mobile Symphony and Civic Music Association presents six concerts and two recitals each season. The season extends from Oct. to April.

 NIGHTCLUBS. *Birmingham:* A new night club scene has developed in Birmingham, on the south side, near the redevelopment of the old Five Points area. Popular spots include *Burly Earl's, Louie Louie, O'Hara's, Stage 5, The Stage Door, Barney's Tavern,* and *Rocky's Up 22nd.* Also popular are *Grundy's Music Room,* 1924 Fourth Ave. N., *The Polaris Lounge* in the Birmingham Hyatt House and *Reo's* in the Sheraton-Mountainbrook. *Montgomery: Wrangler's Club,* 113 S. Jackson, featuring country music. Western attire encouraged but not essential. Closed Sun. *Mobile: Chez Paree,* located in St. Francis Motel, US 90, 3 mi. W. Open six nights, closed Sun. Continuous live entertainment; *Club Oasis,* 3405 Moffat Road. Open daily. Live music, Wed. to Sun.; *Club Manor,* 3260 Halls Mill Road. Open daily. No rock 'n roll music.

 DRINKING LAWS. Liquor is sold by the drink in licensed hotels, restaurants, and clubs in the state. It is sold in miniatures (1/10 pint bottles) and 1-½ pints in restaurants and cocktail lounges, which also sell beer. Beer is sold for both on- and off-premises consumption. Liquor is also sold in state stores. No Sun. sales. Minimum age limit: 19 years. The state has some "dry" counties, but most of the metropolitan areas are "wet."

 **SPORTS.** Whether you're an armchair athlete or an active participant, you will find ample opportunity to satisfy your sports taste in Alabama. Due to its geographic location, there's little difference between summer and winter activities.

For the active man or woman, there are ample opportunities. *Fishing,* of course, is an important sport as a result of the numerous *fresh water rivers* and *lakes,* plus the *Gulf of Mexico* for *saltwater angling.* Anglers must have a license. Nonresident, sports licenses cost $4.25 for seven days; annual $10.25. The state has an open season the year round with no size limitation, but there are daily limits for various species.

With an abundance of water; *boating* is popular. Rental boats can be obtained in many state parks, and from marinas and fish camps located both on fresh and salt water.

Swimming and *water-skiing* are popular in some state parks, in many lakes and in the Gulf of Mexico.

Golf: Point Mallard G.C., Decatur, a public course with 10 water holes; *Jetport G.C.,* Huntsville, a municipal course with practice range; *Marriott Grand Hotel,* Point Clear, an excellent, tree-lined resort course; *Langan Park G.C.,* Mobile, a fine municipal course; *Lakepoint Resort,* Eufaula; *Gulf State Park,* Gulf Shores, with wide fairways and four lakes that make six water holes; *McFarland Park,* Florence, with 11 lakes and elevated greens; *Still Waters G.C.,* Dadeville, a private course with tight fairways; and *Olympia Spa & G.C.,* Dothan, a resort course with rolling fairways and several water holes; *Alpine Bay,* a first-class resort near Birmingham, also offers an 18-hole championship golf course, as well as tennis.

Hunting is excellent, exact dates for various types of hunting can be obtained from the *Alabama Department of Conservation, Game and Fish Division,* Montgomery. Nonresident hunting licenses cost $50 annually for all game and $15 for small game. A 5-day license for all game is $25 and for small game $10.

SPECTATOR SPORTS. If you like to watch rock 'em and sock 'em, *big-time football,* you have a full menu. The University of Alabama and Auburn University are rated among the top teams in the nation each year, and play heavy schedules dotted with intersectional games. Many of these are played in *Birmingham's Legion Field Stadium.* Seating 70,000, it is the largest stadium in the Southeast other than the Orange and Sugar Bowls. In addition, Alabama has two famous post-season games. The Hall of Fame Bowl in Birmingham in December, and the Senior Bowl Game, held each January in Mobile. Birmingham has professional *baseball, football,* and *stock car racing.*

Basketball thrills, too, are available via the college teams. *Horse shows* are held in *Guntersville, Anniston* and *Athens* during the late spring and early summer.

Water enthusiasts can watch *sailing regattas* and both *inboard and outboard races. Alexander City* stages the *Dixie Sailboat Regatta* in June. *Gulf Shores* stages an *Outboard Regatta. Guntersville* stages the *Dixie Cup hydroplane regatta* in August. For other races and regattas on Mobile Bay and lakes throughout Alabama, check local papers.

Although you're a long way from the wild and woolly West, you can watch *bronc riders* and other *rodeo acts. Montgomery* stages a *rodeo* in Mar. in connection with the *Southeastern Livestock Exposition. Opp* has the *South Alabama Rattlesnake Rodeo* in Mar. *Athens* is the site of the *state championship rodeo* in Aug., and you find other less publicized rodeos scattered throughout the state.

Action also at the *Alabama Intern. Motor Speedway,* featuring the famed *Winston 400* in May, Talladega.

WHAT TO DO WITH THE CHILDREN. Many of Alabama's attractions will appeal to the varied interests of children. Here are some of those most likely to win the applause of the younger generation. *Birmingham: Birmingham Zoo,* 2630 Cahaba Rd., off US 280. It features 11 major exhibit areas and a wide array of animals housed in ultramodern facilities, and miniature train.

Bridgeport: Russell Cave National Monument features caves where primitive men lived as long ago as 6000 B.C.—their oldest known home in the Southeast.

These caves were still used as dwelling places up to about 1650 A.D. Located 8 mi. NW of Bridgeport off US 72 via country roads 75 and 91.

Fort Payne: Canyon Land Park. Miniature train, ferris wheel, chair lift to the bottom of the canyon. *Manitou Cave,* off US 11. *Huntsville: Alabama Space & Rocket Center.* NASA bus tours.

Mobile: Bellingrath Gardens, one of the most famous gardens in the South. Located 20 mi. S in Theodore, via US 90 and Bellingrath Rd. *Bellingrath Home U.S.S. Alabama,* Battleship Parkway.

Montgomery: W. A. Gayle Planetarium, 1010 Forest Ave. Lectures, films, varied showtimes. *Tuscaloosa: Museum of Natural History,* on campus of the U. of Ala. Indian artifacts and geology exhibit. *Tuscumbia: Ivy Green,* birthplace of Helen Keller. *Ave Maria Grotto* at St. Bernard College. *Dismals Wonder Garden* at Phil Campbell.

 RECOMMENDED READING. A few good books include: *History of Montgomery with Pictures; Remember Mobile,* by Caldwell Delaney; *Story of Mobile,* by Caldwell Delaney; *Colonial Mobile,* by Peter Joseph Hamilton; *Mansions of Alabama,* by Ralph Hammond; and *History of Alabama,* by Albert James Pickett.

 **HOTELS AND MOTELS.** Most of the motels and hotels in Alabama, especially those along the Gulf Coast, boast swimming pools and various other forms of indoor and outdoor recreational facilities. Listings are in order of price category. Price categories, based on double occupancy, are approximate: *Expensive,* $30 and above; *Moderate,* $16-$30; *Inexpensive,* $10-$16. For a more complete explanation of hotel and motel categories see *Facts at Your Fingertips* at the front of this volume.

Albertville

King's Inn Motor Hotel. *Moderate.* Air-conditioned rooms on 2 levels. Pool. Restaurant adj. Coffee makers in rms.

Alexander City

Bob White Motel. *Expensive.* Small. Pool. Restaurant nr.

Horseshoe Bend. *Expensive.* On 280 Bypass, 1-½ mi. SW. Comfortable, attractive rooms. Pool, deli, with food to take to your room.

Anniston

Days Inn. *Expensive.* One of fine chain. Pool, play area, gift shop, gas station. *Tasty World* restaurant. Pets.

Downtowner. *Expensive.* Appealing. Restaurant, pool.

Holiday Inn. *Expensive.* Pool. Courtesy airport transportation. Pets accepted.

Ramada Inn. *Expensive.* Airport courtesy car. Well operated. Pool, color TV. Pets allowed.

Heart of Anniston. *Moderate.* TV, cafe; apartments available.

Van Thomas Motel. *Moderate.* Pleasant rooms. Air conditioning, TV, pool. Pets permitted for an additional charge.

Auburn

Heart of Auburn Motel. *Moderate.* A medium-sized motel near the University. Attractively furnished with restaurant and room service. Pool, pets allowed.

Birmingham

Birmingham Airport Motel. *Expensive.* Opposite air terminal. A large 3-story sound-proof motel with connecting units and day rates available. Restaurant, cocktail lounge. Free parking.

Birmingham Hilton. *Expensive.* 808 20thSt. S. 300 rooms. Dining room, swimming pool.

Beacon Park Inn. *Expensive.* 400 Beacon Pkwy. W. Live entertainment in lounge.

Days Inn. *Expensive.* 5101 Messer-Airport Hwy. Pool. Pets permitted for extra charge.

Holiday Inn. *Expensive.* Five locations. All have restaurant, pools and allow pets. **20th Place:** 420 20th St. S. **East:** 7941 Crestwood Blvd. **South:** 1548 Montgomery Hwy. Nicely located. Entertainment, dancing. Coffee in rms. **Civic Center:** 2230 10th Ave. N. Pool (heated). **Airport:** 5000 10th Ave. N.

Hyatt House. *Expensive.* 901 21st St. N. Hugo's is one of the city's finest restaurants. Lounge.

Primeway Inn. *Expensive.* 195 W. Oxmoor Rd. All facilities.

Sheraton-Mountain Brook. *Expensive.* Restaurant. Swimming pool. Lounge with live entertainment.

Tara House. *Expensive.* 2800 20th St. S. Restaurant, lounge with fine entertainment, some of the best in the city.

Motel Birmingham. *Expensive.* 7905Crestwood Blvd. Pleasant rooms; some family units and efficiencies. Coffee makers in rms. Restaurant nr. Pool, play area. Library.

Ramada Inn. *Expensive.* 951 18th S., convenient to the Univ. of Ala., Birmingham campus, and Medical Center. Pleasant location and rooms. Restaurant, entertainment, dancing. Pool.

Southern Motor Inn. *Expensive.* 1313 3rd Ave. N. All facilities.

Best Western Inn of Boaz. *Expensive.* Restaurant, pool, pets permitted.

Econo Lodge. *Moderate to expensive.* Two locations: 103 Green Springs Hwy. Cafe adjacent. 2224 5th Ave. N. Pool, restaurant, lounge.

Boaz

Passport Inn. *Moderate.* 8th Ave. S. at 11th St. Swimming pool. Restaurant, convenient to the campus of the University of Alabama in Birmingham.

ALABAMA
Cullman

Holiday Inn. *Expensive.* Indoor pool (heated). Free airport transportation. Pets allowed.

Anderson Motel. *Moderate.* Pool, restaurant, coffee shop.

Decatur

Decatur Inn. *Expensive.* Very attractive rooms. Restaurant. Huge pool. Pets permitted. Airport courtesy car.

Holiday Inn. *Expensive.* Two floors. Some studios. Restaurant. Pets allowed.

Ramada Inn. *Expensive.* Pleasant rooms. Airport courtesy car. Two swimming pools, restaurant.

Days Inn. *Moderate.* I-65 and U.S. 278. Pool, restaurant, coffee shop.

Nitefall. *Moderate.* Pool, playground, cafe next door.

Dothan

Days Inn. *Expensive.* Pool, restaurant.

Holiday Inn. *Expensive.* Free airport transportation. Appealing rooms. Pool. Pets permitted.

Olympia Spa and Country Club. *Expensive.* U.S. 231 S. Restaurant. Golf.

Ramada Inn. *Expensive.* Airport courtesy car. Very nice rooms, some studios. Restaurant, bar. Pool.

Sheraton Motor Inn. *Expensive.* TV, dining room, lounge with live entertainment, Pool.

Quality Inn Carousel. *Expensive.* Ross Circle. Pleasant. Some studios. Restaurants, bar. Pool.

Motel Leon. *Moderate.* 1621 E. Main St. Restaurant.

Heart of Dothan. *Inexpensive.* 314 N. Foster St. Restaurant two blocks away.

Eufaula

Holiday Inn. *Expensive.* Two locations. Restaurant. Pool. Pets allowed. Airport courtesy car.

Lake Eufaula Motor Lodge. *Moderate.* Coffee in room. Pool. Cafe opposite.

Florence

Master Host Inn. *Expensive.* Very nice. Restaurant, room service. Pool.

Tourway Inn. *Expensive.* Medium-size motel with restaurant next door.

Florence TraveLodge. *Moderate.* Attractive units. Air conditioning. TV, restaurant. Pool. Wheelchair ramps.

Florence-Muscle Shoals

Lakeview Inn. *Moderate.* Restaurant, pool, some kitchenette units, boat dock.

Fort Payne

DeSoto State Park Resort Inn. *Expensive.* Rte 1. In state park, with access to all facilities, including pool, hiking trails, restaurant.

Best Western. *Moderate.* Restaurant, pool.

Gadsden

Holiday Inn. *Expensive.* Airport courtesy bus. Attractive rooms; some studios. Restaurant. Pool. Pets allowed.

Holiday Host Motel. *Moderate.* Restaurant nearby.

Traveler's Inn. *Moderate.* Restaurant. Pets permitted.

Greenville

Holiday Inn. *Expensive.* Well managed; appealing rooms. Restaurant. Pool. Pets accepted.

Gulf Shores

Holiday Inn. *Expensive.* Beach front. Multi-stories. Restaurant, bar, dancing, entertainment. Pool. Seasonal rates.

Lighthouse. *Expensive.* Small motel with some apartments. Overlooks Gulf.

Riverside Inn. *Expensive.* Quiet, comfortable motel. Some efficiencies and family units. TV, air conditioning. Restaurant 5 mi. Coffee in rooms. Playground and outdoor games. Fishing pier on Bon Secour River, boats available.

Guntersville

Lake Guntersville State Lodge. *Expensive.* Resort inn, chalets, cottages, restaurant. All with magnificent view of Guntersville Reservoir. 18-hole championship golf course, hiking trails, and beach complex.

BelAir Motel. *Moderate.* Just across the river from an excellent seafood restaurant.

Huntsville

Barclay Motel. *Expensive.* Two locations: 2201 N. Memorial Pkwy.; and 3312 S. Memorial Dr. Restaurants, pools.

Best Western Carriage Inn. *Expensive.* 3811 University Dr. Very appealing rooms, some with balcony. Restaurant, entertainment, dancing. Airport courtesy car. Pool. Pets allowed.

Best Western Sands Motor Hotel. *Expensive.* 2700 Memorial Pkwy. Multi-storied. Large tastefully decorated motel. Restaurant, room service. Pool (heated).

Hilton Inn. *Expensive.* 401 Williams Ave. at Freedom Plaza. Restaurant, pool. Pets accepted. Airport courtesy car.

Holiday Inn. *Expensive.* 3810 University Dr. Airport courtesy car. Handsome rooms. Pool. Pets accepted.

Howard Johnson's *Expensive.* 2524 Memorial Pkwy. N. Some rooms with terraces. Restaurant. Pool. Pets allowed.

Ramada Inn. *Expensive.* 3502 Memorial Pkwy S. Appealing rooms. Restaurant. Pool.

Regency Inn Motor Hotel. *Expensive.* 1220 N. Memorial Pkwy. A large, very attractive motel. Restaurant, room service. Pool. Health club. Recently remodeled.

Sheraton Motor Inn. *Expensive.* 4404 University Dr. Large and comfortable. Specialty restaurant, entertainment, dancing. Pool.

Skycenter Hotel. *Expensive.* At airport. Large, attractive. Some studios. Restaurant, entertainment, dancing. Golf, pool. Free parking.

Tourway Inn. *Expensive.* 1304 Memorial Pkwy. N. Nice rooms; some studios. Restaurant. Pool.

Mobile

Best Western Admiral Semmes Motor Hotel. *Expensive.* 250 Government St. Large nicely decorated downtown operation. Some suites. Restaurant, room service, bar. Pool. In-room movies.

Best Western Battleship Inn. *Expensive.* Located across from battleship U.S.S. *Alabama.* Good seafood restaurant inside.

Holiday Inn. *Expensive.* Four locations: 3339 Government Blvd., 255 Church St., 850 S. Beltline Hwy., US 90/98 East. Restaurant, pool. Accept pets. Airport courtesy car. Entertainment.

Howard Johnson's. *Expensive.* 3132 Government Blvd. Appealing rooms, some with terraces. Pool. Restaurant, room service.

Malaga Inn. *Expensive.* 359 Church St. Excellent restaurant. Pool. In restored buildings with a courtyard.

Ramada Inn. *Expensive.* Two locations: 600 S. Beltline Hwy., and 1705 Dauphin Island Pkwy. Attractively furnished; some studios. Restaurant, room service. Pools.

Riverview Plaza. *Expensive.* 64 Water St. New. Restaurant, oyster bar, pool, sauna.

Days Inn. *Moderate.* I-65 & US 90. Member of popular chain. Pool, play area, gift shop, gas station. Pets for extra charge. *Tasty World* restaurant.

Taylor Motel. *Moderate.* 2598 Government Blvd. Comfortable rooms. Pool. Restaurant nr. Coffee makers in rooms.

Montgomery

Governor's House Motel. *Expensive.* 2705 E. Southern Blvd. Attractive rooms, many overlooking pool-patio area; some studios. Sauna, golf. Restaurant, bar, dancing. Airport courtesy car.

Holiday Inn. *Expensive.* Three locations. All have restaurant, pool and accept pets. **East:** I-85 & US 231. Entertainment. Airport courtesy car. **Midtown:** 924 Madison Ave. Some studios. Dancing, entertainment. **Southwest:** 4231 Mobile Hwy. (US 31). Airport courtesy car.

Howard Johnson's. *Expensive.* Two locations. Both have some rooms with balconies. Restaurant, bar, coffee makers in rooms. Pool. Accept pets. 1110 Eastern Bypass and 995 W. South Blvd.

The Madison Hotel. *Expensive.* 120 Madison Ave. New, with two restaurants and lounges, some suites, airport transportation. Within walking distance of Capitol, Civic Center.

Sheraton Riverfront Station. *Expensive.* 200 Coosa St. Restaurants, lounges, pool, free parking. Within walking distance of Capitol, Civic Center.

Days Inn. *Moderate.* Two locations. 1150 W. South Blvd. and S. Bypass & I-65. A good buy. Pool, play area, gift shop, gas station. Pets. *Tasty World* restaurant.

La Quinta. *Moderate.* 1280 East Blvd. Restaurant, cable TV, complimentary morning coffee.

Town Plaza Motor Hotel. *Moderate.* 743 Madison Ave. Two blocks from state capitol. Coffee in rooms.

Motel 6. *Inexpensive.* Pool. Cafe adjacent.

Opelika

Holiday Inn. *Expensive.* Comfortable, attractive rooms. Air conditioning, TV. Restaurant, coffee makers in rooms. Pool, large grounds.

Motel 6. *Moderate.* TV optional. Pool, restaurant nearby.

Travelers Inn. *Moderate.* Medium-size 2-story motel with restaurant. Pool.

Ozark

Best Western. *Expensive.* Some studios. Restaurant, bar, coffee makers in rooms. Entertainment. Airport courtesy car. Pool. Pets allowed.

Candlelight Motel. *Moderate.* Restaurant nearby. swimming pool.

Point Clear

Grand Hotel. *Expensive.* Large resort hotel with wide choice of accommodations —cottages, cabanas, suites, studio rooms—on Mobile Bay. TV in most rooms. Dining rooms, bar. Social program. Tennis, golf privileges, pool, beach, dock, rental boats & motors, fishing, water-skiing. With advance notice, trains and planes met. Seasonal rates, MAP and EP.

Selma

Holiday Inn. *Expensive.* Airport courtesy car. Restaurant, bar. Pool (heated). Pets allowed.

Plantation Inn. *Expensive.* Hwy. 80 E. Small motel. Restaurant, pool, pets accepted.

Selma Motel. *Moderate.* Nice rooms. Coffee makers in rooms. Pool. Pets allowed.

Tuscaloosa

La Quinta. *Moderate.* 4122 McFarland Blvd. E. Pool, restaurants nearby.

Stafford Inn. *Moderate.* 2209 Ninth St. The city's only hotel. Restaurant, pool.

Days Inn. *Expensive.* 3600 McFarland Blvd. E. One of the chain, pool, playground.

Holiday Inn. *Expensive.* Two locations: 2 miles N. on 82 bypass, and 3–½ miles S. at junction of 82 bypass, I-20 and I-59. Both have restaurant, pool and accept pets.

YOUTH HOSTELS. Mobile: *YMCA,* 61 S. Conception St.; *YWCA,* 1060 Government St. Montgomery *YMCA's* are: *Central Branch,* 761 S. Perry St; *East Montgomery Branch,* 3407 Pelzer Ave.; and *Cleveland Ave. Branch,* 1202 Cleveland Ave.

DINING OUT in Alabama leads one toward trying traditional Southern dishes, including Southern fried chicken, ham steak with red gravy, and chicken pan pie. You'll soon discover that virtually everything is accompanied by at least a side-dish of the ubiquitous grits. Along the Gulf Coast, you can try creole specialties, so be sure to ask for Gulf flounder, shrimp, and other special seafoods and gumbos. In river towns or nearby, you might try catfish caught fresh from the Tennessee River. For other worthwhile restaurants, re-check our hotel listings. Restaurants are in order of price category. Price categories and ranges for a complete meal are as follows: *Expensive:* $9.50 and up; *Moderate:* $6.50–$9; *Inexpensive:* $3.50–$6. For a more complete explanation of restaurant categories see *Facts at Your Fingertips* at the front of this volume.

Albertville

Food Basket. *Moderate.* 301 Martlin. Steaks and seafood served here. Closed Thanksgiving and Christmas.

The King's Restaurant. *Moderate.* Specialty, steaks and seafood. Closed Christmas Day.

Alexander City

Horseshoe Bend Restaurant. *Moderate.* A daily buffet with large selection of items.

Anniston

Annistonian. *Moderate.* Specialty: steaks, seafood.

House of Chen. *Moderate.* Chinese cuisine.

Morrison's Cafeteria. *Inexpensive.* One of fine chain.

Auburn

The Hungry Hunter. *Moderate.* Steaks, seafood.

Country's Barbecue Place. *Inexpensive.* Barbecue plates, sandwiches.

BIRMINGHAM

EDITOR'S CHOICES

Rating restaurants is, at best, a subjective business, and obviously a matter of personal taste. It is therefore, difficult to call a restaurant "the best" and hope to get unanimous agreement. The restaurants listed below are our choices of the best eating places in Birmingham, and the places we would choose if we were visiting the city.

HUGO'S ROTISSERIE   French Cuisine
The dining room, set atop the 14-story Hyatt House, is candlelit and elegant. The menu is ambitious, and the service first-rate. Dancing. *Expensive.* 21st Street N.

MICHAEL'S SIRLOIN ROOM   American/International
Top-notch steaks, seafood and "kabobs" serve as the best part of the menu. The atmosphere is subdued, and the food delicious. *Expensive.* 431 20th Street S.

SUMO   Japanese
Japanese hibachi-style cooking at table, with an all-Japanese staff. Food preparation is a show in itself. *Expensive.* 7767 Eastwood Mall.

JOHN'S   American
Specializing in fresh seafood, this restaurant has a relaxed atmosphere in which patrons are comfortable in casual dress. *Moderate.* 112 21st. St. N.S.

| **LLOYD'S**   American/Southern |
| Casual atmosphere, regionally popular. Specialty is barbecue, but limited |
| other dishes available. *Inexpensive.* 5301 Hwy. 280 S. |

Other recommended restaurants:

Rube Burrows. *Moderate.* 1015 20th S. Gourmet burgers, sandwiches, salads. Locally popular.

Gulas. *Expensive.* 7401 Atlanta Hwy. A varied menu specializing in steaks and chops. Live music and dancing.

The Cabana. *Moderate.* Hwy 31 S. at junction of State 149. Quiches, salads, sandwiches, in pleasant plant-filled atmosphere.

Cathay Inn. *Moderate.* 1926 29th Ave. S., Homewood. Specializes in Chinese cuisine, Mandarin and Szechuan.

Joy Young. *Moderate.* Brookwood Shopping Plaza. Restaurant with Chinese motif, specializing in Chinese and American food, 18 different menu selections. Open daily for lunch and dinner.

La Paree. *Moderate.* 2013 5th Ave. N. Specializes in lamb kebob, seafood and steak. Liquor served. Music.

Lovoy's. *Moderate.* 420 Green Springs Hwy. Italian food. Closed Sun.

Leo's. *Moderate.* 401 1st. Street N. Specializes in fresh seafood.

Rossi's. *Moderate.* 427 S. 20th. The emphasis is on Italian cooking.

Sarris. *Moderate.* 600 N. 31st St. Seafood with a Greek flavor. Lunch is cafeteria style. Ten blocks from Civic Center.

Mathews Cafeteria. *Inexpensive.* Formerly Britlings, at 2711 Culver Rd. in Mountain Brook Village.

Steve Leontis Smokehouse. *Inexpensive.* 2731 8th Ave. South. Barbeque deluxe with the spotlight on ribs.

Cullman

Holiday Inn. *Moderate.* Attractive dining room, overlooking an enclosed pool, provides relaxed dining. Buffet is featured.

All Steak Restaurant. *Inexpensive.* As you'd expect, steak is emphasized here, aged and in large portions, but they also offer seafood and chicken, plus rolls and pastries baked on the premises. Sun. buffet lunch. Children's portions.

Decatur

Lyon's Dining Room. *Moderate.* Specialty: steaks.

Gibson's. *Inexpensive.* Specialty is barbecue, but the Brunswick stew is popular also.

Dothan

The Conestoga. *Moderate.* Dinners only; specialty is steak.

King's Inn. *Moderate.* Popular locally. Dinners only. Children's portions. Entertainment. Closed Sun.

Eufaula

The Chewella Restaurant. *Moderate.* Steaks a specialty.

Town Terrace. *Inexpensive.* Specialty: steaks.

Florence

Dale's. *Moderate.* Steak served in pleasant atmosphere. Dinners only. Children's portions. Closed Sun.

The Hermitage House. *Moderate.* An inviting atmosphere with varied entrées, vegetables. Across from Pope's Tavern museum.

Lakeview Inn Restaurant. *Moderate.* Regional specialties, sandwiches. Children's portions.

Gadsden

The Embers. *Moderate.* Specializes in seafood and delicious home baking.

Greenville

Alabama Grill. *Inexpensive.* Steaks a specialty. Closed Sun.

Gulf Shores

Coconut Willie's. *Moderate.* Seafood; view of Gulf of Mexico.

Gulf Shores State Park Lodge. *Moderate.* Steaks and seafood are the specialties.

Lovoy's. *Moderate.* Italian cuisine, with emphasis on seafood.

Shrimp Boat Restaurant. *Moderate.* Specializes in fresh Creole-style seafood, with children's plates available.

Guntersville

Reid's. *Inexpensive.* Specialty is catfish, with fresh vegetables in season, and home baked desserts.

Huntsville

Rib Cellar. *Expensive.* Well-prepared beef and lobster specialties. You can dance here, too. Dinners only.

Fogcutter. *Moderate.* Locally popular after 5 P.M. Specializes in steaks and seafood.

T.P. Crockmier's. *Moderate.* Serves lunch and dinner. Specialty is seafood, with own baking.

Michael's. *Inexpensive.* Specializes in steak, with own baking. Serves all meals.

Jasper

White Way Restaurant. *Moderate.* Steaks and seafood. Check days closed.

S&F Restaurant. *Inexpensive.* Features general menu.

Mobile

Bernard's. *Expensive.* 407 Conti St. Steak and seafood, offered in French creole style. Pleasant decor.

The Pillars. *Expensive.* In old home, specializing in steaks and seafood.

The Back Porch. *Moderate.* In Fort Conde Plaza. Specialty is red beans and rice.

Constantine's. *Moderate.* 1500 Government St. An outstanding restaurant for gourmet dishes, both Continental and American. Emphasis is on seafood preparations with shrimp, oysters or crab. All meals served.

Eight Kings. *Moderate.* BelAir Mall. Fine European cuisine. Gracious atmosphere. Bar. Also informal Pub and inexpensive sandwich shop.

Malaga Inn. *Moderate.* 359 Church St. French/American menu. Lump crabmeat *pestalozie* and *escalopes de veau au parmesane* are specialties.

Wintzell's Oyster House. *Moderate.* 605 Dauphin St. If you like oysters, this is the place to find the best, prepared any way you want them, "fried, stewed or nude". Informal atmosphere and friendly service. Children's portions.

Morrison's. *Inexpensive.* 3282 Springdale Plaza. A regional chain of outstanding cafeterias, with good food, attractively displayed and served. A favorite for family dining. Children's portions.

Montgomery

Rotunda. *Expensive.* In Governor's House Motel. Specialties are beef, pastries; music to dine by.

Elite. *Moderate.* 129 Montgomery St. A Montgomery tradition. Specialties: Trout amandine, oysters and shrimp Athenean. Open breakfast, lunch and dinner.

Mr. G's Gourmet. *Moderate.* Prime rib, seafood, baking on premises. Chef-owned.

Sahara Restaurant. *Moderate.* 511 Edgemont. Music and pleasant decor provide a relaxing atmosphere in which to enjoy beef and seafood specialties. Children's portions. Closed Sun.

T.P. Crockmier's. *Moderate.* Specialty prime rib; seafood.

Morrison's. *Inexpensive.* 150 Lee St. Good food, attractively displayed. Children's portions. Open for lunch and dinner.

Oneonta

Little Joe's. *Inexpensive.* Family style meals.

Round The Clock. *Inexpensive.* Delicious, buffet-style lunch and dinner.

Opelika

The Greenhouse. *Moderate.* In old Victorian house. Chef-owned, baking on premises.

Morrison's. *Inexpensive.* Chain cafeteria with baking on premises.

Point Clear

Fram's *Moderate.* In Fairhope. Seafood, steaks, Lebanese specialties.

Grand Hotel Restaurant. *Moderate.* Specialty: steaks and seafood in the heart of a 4-star resort.

Yardarm. *Moderate.* Seafood.

Selma

The Crossing. *Moderate.* Located in 1859 building on historic Water Avenue. Steaks, seafood, children's plates available.

Tuscaloosa

The Lamplighter. *Moderate.* An inviting dining-out spot, charmingly decorated in a theme of the past. The menu items are today's favorites, however, including charcoal-broiled steak and seafood. Children's portions.

Nick's Filet House. *Moderate.* Small and cozy. A hideaway for steaks. Bar with restaurant.

Morrison's. *Inexpensive.* The usual good food and pleasant environment, in this regional chain cafeteria. Open for lunch and dinner.

Piccadilly Cafeteria. *Inexpensive.* One of regional chain. Features own baking.

The Waysider. *Inexpensive.* Specialties range from biscuits at breakfast to catfish for dinner. Locally popular.

FLORIDA

Where the Sun Spends the Winter

BY
FLORENCE LEMKOWITZ

Florence Lemkowitz, former travel editor of the Hartford, Connecticut, Times, is a freelance writer whose articles appear in a number of magazines and newspapers.

Exploring Miami and Miami Beach

Miami Beach has almost everything of a lively nature, and among these are visitors. Millions come to this little (7.2 square miles of land) island which lies just three miles across Biscayne Bay from mainland Miami. There is a permanent population of over 96,000, but the city can accommodate three times this many visitors. One-fourth of the hotels in Florida are situated here in a slender strip of architectural virtuosity.

Whereas the municipal limits show Miami Beach bounded on the south by Government Cut (the channel to Miami's port) and on the north by 87th Street, in truth the beach and the hotels extend northward more than a hundred more blocks. Surfside and Bal Harbour, plus some bayside towns, are immediately adjacent on the north, then comes the county's Haulover Park with a public beach, fishing pier, and a marina, and then the oceanfront motels—fancy, gaudy, pretty, monstrous, prim, ostentatious—side by side in a battle for attention almost all the way to the county line.

The entire string, top to bottom, should be seen at least once by every visitor. The tour can start at the top by taking A1A from Hollywood and

Hallandale, where it will be noted that such hotels as the *Diplomat* continue the fashion with vigor and decor.

Haulover Park, just south of motel row, is the largest along the strip and has beachside picnicking facilities. Across the four-lane highway, via a pedestrian underpass, is a large parking area and marina. Charter fishing craft, drift boat fishing, and sightseeing boat trips are available here.

A new beach, stretching as wide as 300 feet, is Miami Beach's newest production tabbed at $64-million. It all begins at 80th Street and proceeds north to Bal Harbour, and from the fishing pier north to the end of Haulover Park. Recently completed are 10½ miles of sugary, wave-washed sand beach from Government Cut at South Miami Beach to the northern end of Haulover Park. The sand is topped by dunes and sea oats. New bicycling paths have also been added.

A high bridge over the inlet to the bay takes you into Bal Harbour, a strictly zoned, plush little compound where neatness, building setbacks, and lawn maintenance seem supreme. Apartment houses and hotels of the fashionably expensive variety are on the oceanfront, and more apartments of the same rating are across the wide boulevard. The Sheraton Bal Harbour (formerly the Americana) at 97th Street and Collins Avenue, will be the first of the large, convention-oriented luxury hotels you will see. Across the street are some of the area's fancier shops.

Just south is Surfside, a small community known for its cleanliness, friendliness, and the personalized service at its motels.

Collins Avenue, for the next 87 blocks, is Miami Beach, the resort, in all its variety. Broken only by block-long oceanfront parks at 71st Street, 65th Street, 46th Street, and 23rd Street, plus the really better beaches along Ocean Drive in the Art Deco historical district of South Beach, the view is of hotels.

There are plenty of economical hotels in Miami Beach, and some are a real buy. Most are new since World War II.

The Row of Splendor

Across Collins Avenue from these hotels are other hotels, but of a less flamboyant caste. They do not have the ocean front. It is a matter of supreme importance to many visitors that they stay at an oceanfront hotel, whether or not they ever go near the ocean, and whether, in fact, the hotel has any actual beach remaining, erosion being a problem. Years ago, it was a similar mark of distinction to stay at "This Year's" hotel, which simply meant the fanciest, most expensive one built since the previous season.

New hotels continue to go up from time to time, but in truth, the Fontainebleau Hilton, on 1,000 feet of beachfront that was once the Harvey Firestone estate, has settled the issue. In late 1978, the legendary Fontainebleau became the Fontainebleau Hilton, a 1200-room vacation paradise. More than $30 million was spent to refurbish and improve the splendid resort. The old cabana club, torn down for an unobstructed view of the Atlantic, was replaced by a gorgeous freeform swimming pool with natural waterfalls, water slides, Grotto Bar. A lagoon, hot jacuzzi springs, an aquarium, lavish gardens and alfreso restaurants are adjacent. Along with new, rich decor, there are new boutiques, lively lounges,

Points of Interest

1) Aventura Mall
2) Bass Museum of Art
3) Bayfront Park; Auditorium; Torch of Friendship
4) Biscayne Kennel Club
5) City Convention Complex
6) Coconut Grove Exposition Hall
7) Fairchild Tropical Garden
8) Flagler Dog Track
9) Hialeah Park Race Course
10) Hotel Fontainebleau Hilton
11) Jai-Alai Fronton
12) Japanese Gardens
13) Lincoln Road Mall
14) Lowe Gallery
15) Marine Stadium
16) Miamarina
17) Little Havana
18) Theater of the Performing Arts
19) Miami Beach Garden Center and Conservatory
20) Miami Beach Ocean Front Auditorium
21) Museum of Science and Natural History, Planetarium
22) North Shore Open Space Park
23) Omni International Hotel
24) Orange bowl
25) Parrot Jungle
26) Planet Ocean
27) Seaquarium
28) South Florida History Museum, Arts Center
29) University of Miami
30) Vizcaya Art Museum
31) Calder Race Track
32) Metro Zoo

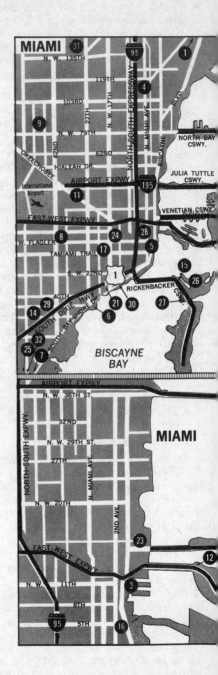

and a dramatic 22-foot glass dome in the lobby ceiling to let the sun shine in.

The newest and most elaborate hotels and apartments stretch northward from the Fontainebleau Hilton, at 44th Street and Collins Avenue, but the "older" hostelries south to Lincoln Road are still luxury hotels by any definition of the word.

South of Lincoln Road are the first-built, generally smaller hotels which offer good location and the same sun—plus a superior beach—at economy rates.

Hotel rooms, sand, and water do not a vacation make, of course—at least, not a Miami Beach vacation. The island is maintained like a garden to foster that euphoria which tends to make people want to stay a little longer. A million plants and flowers a year are grown in the city nursery to maintain elaborate displays along Alton Road, Pine Tree Drive, and the eight-block-long Lincoln Road Mall. The open-air mall has 180 stores along artistically decorated walkways decorated with luxuriant plants, shrubs, semi-tropical flowers and fountains. It was designed for strolling among the gardens en route to the boutiques, but an electric tram can also take you from one end of the traffic-free mall to the other. There are no "dead" times—flowers and shrubs are transferred to the viewing beds when they're in bloom, taken out and replaced by others as the blossoms fade. The three golf courses and two-hundred acres of recreational parks get similar attention. You shouldn't pick the flowers, of course—sometimes the city's justly proud gardeners volunteer to sit up all night and guard a particularly tempting display.

Entertainment Galore

The nightlife is considerable—everything from elaborately costumed showgirl reviews, to name-act comedians and singers, to impromptu amateur acts by the patrons of small bars. The big shows are in the big hotels, especially at the Fontainebleau Hilton, and the entertainment bill is big, too. Estimates of the cost of live performers run up to $10 million a year; an individual act may cost $25,000 a week and it is said one big name drew $60,000 for a week's work. Almost all the big oceanfront hotels have a cocktail lounge, supper club and late-night disco.

Some big names may be expected during the winter season. Depending on your appetite—and thirst—the tab for a table of four will run over $150 for dinner when one of the names is there to entertain.

Concerts by the Greater Miami Symphony and superstar touring groups are also held in the Miami Beach Theater of the Performing Arts.

Much of the lure of Miami Beach consists of other divertissements on the mainland. Causeways connect the two in seven places, from north to south at 163rd Street, 125th Street, 79th Street, 36th Street, 15th Street, and the newest—192nd St. All street numbers are for the mainland side; Miami Beach street numbers differ.

The Julia Tuttle Causeway at 36th Street (41st Street on the Beach) offers quick access to Miami and connects with the city's expressway system, while MacArthur Causeway, exiting at 13th Street in Miami, jogs south to the lower end of Miami Beach. MacArthur, Tuttle, as well as the 79th and 192nd Street Causeways are free; the Venetian Causeway at 15th Street and Broad Causeway at 125th Street have a small toll charge.

MacArthur Causeway was the first, and offers a bit of sightseeing as a bonus. It's bounded on the south by the channel to Miami's new seaport, which stretches for more than a mile parallel and across the channel from the Causeway; while on the north are symmetrical, man-made islands with fine homes and yachts "parked" in front. Al Capone lived here for a spell, on Palm Island.

Watson Island, near the west end of the Causeway, was the mooring spot for the Goodyear blimp, now moored at Pompano Beach. Helicopter and seaplane services are still available here. Just across the roadway in a small bayside city park is an authentic Japanese teahouse and garden. A Tokyo industrialist visited Miami some years ago and was so pleased with the place that he began sending gifts back to the city. He started with several hundred wild orchid trees, then a 300-year-old stone lantern, then an eight-ton statue of Hotei, Japanese god of good fortune. The teahouse was built in Japan, taken apart and shipped over, along with Japanese carpenters to put it back together. It's a delightful little spot—and free.

Just over the final bridge and on Miami's mainland, stretching north to the Venetian Causeway, is the *Miami Herald* building, which is one of the most modern newspaper plants in the world. Uniformed guides conduct tours daily both morning and afternoon.

Getting around in Miami by automobile is fairly simple, but can run into a lot of mileage. The street numbering system begins at Miami Avenue and Flagler Street, and is divided into quadrants from that point—i.e. northeast, northwest, southeast, and southwest. Streets run north and south, as do terraces. The avenues and places run east and west. There are sufficient exceptions to befuddle anyone, however; Coral Gables has its own system of Spanish named avenues and the like, which only a map and diligence can fathom. And Hialeah uses streets and avenues, but of a different and perplexing orientation. Everywhere else, overridding municipal borders, the basic system prevails generally—to 215th Street on the north, 360th Street on the south, and 217th Avenue on the west. If you want to get to Northwest South River Drive, or Southwest North River Drive, however, it's perhaps best to take a cab.

Downtown Miami

Biscayne Boulevard is the city's best-known thoroughfare and runs north and south. Since it is also US 1, it will wend you to Key West or Canada if you stick with it, but, in the main, it is the city's downtown "show" street. Stately royal palms line its eight traffic lanes, divided by four parking lanes, between Southeast First Street and Northeast Fifth Street. On the west are tall hotels and office buildings; on the east is Bayfront Park, sixty-two acres of tropical flora, statues, pools, shaded benches and walkways. On the north end of the park is the city's auditorium and an access road to the Dodge Island three-hundred-acre seaport, which hosts some two million cruise passengers yearly—No. 1 in the U.S. Cruise ships leave daily from ultra-modern $40-million Port of Miami for the most fascinating Caribbean ports. You can also catch a luxury liner to Mexico or Central America.

A stroll about a bit will reveal some 21,000 well-kept plants, plus annuals in flower beds as the seasons change. At the south end of the park, on a post, is a plaque marking the spot where President Roosevelt almost was assassinated in 1933. Farther south is the multi-million dollar Pavillon Hotel; a block west is the new Hyatt/City Convention complex.

Along the boulevard in the northern corner of the park is the Torch of Friendship, signifying Miami's ties with neighboring Latin republics. There is also a plaque memorializing President John F. Kennedy, and the official national seals, in bronze, of most Latin American nations. Colorful flags of the nations wave from atop the curved native stone wall with a gas-fed perpetual flame as the centerpiece. Regrettably, the entire area is now a hangout for panhandlers, so avoid it at night.

Just east, opening soon, is the $93 million 20-acre Bayside, a waterfront marketplace featuring specialty shops and entertainment spots.

In Miami, the Old Havana before Castro, has been reborn. It is called "Little Havana," not surprisingly, an exciting area of excellent restaurants, nightclubs, and shops. For the English-speaking visitor it provides the flavor and feel of a foreign country. Although there are several large sections of Miami in which Cubans are the dominant population, "Little Havana" is that region around S.W. 8th Street and W. Flagler Street where most of Miami's Cubans work and live.

Little Havana is no hybrid; it's a completely Cuban world. A familiar sign in store windows is: "English Spoken Here." English or Spanish, communication is easy in the hundreds of open front cafes, restaurants, oyster bars, bookstores, tobacco shops, and groceries.

Some famous Old Havana spots have established Miami counterparts —the Floridita where Ernest Hemingway used to drink daiquiris, the Zaragozana seafood restaurant, founded in 1832, was transported to Miami and emerged as two extravagant nightclubs, the *Flamenco* and the *Les Violins*.

Prices in Little Havana can be ridiculously low for good Cuban dishes in some of the smaller niches to downright expensive in such places as the two supper clubs just mentioned. There are also excellent Cuban-Chinese restaurants in the area.

Unfortunately, Little Havana is not as much fun as it used to be. Since boatloads of refugees from Cuba (and from other islands) arrived in 1980, there has been strife among the prosperous, older citizens and the impoverished arrivals. In addition, the 1980 Liberty City riots didn't help, but the situation is better now. Just be careful on the streets and don't walk alone at night or park in a deserted lot.

Close to downtown, at Northwest Third Street and 14th Avenue, is the Orange Bowl, where the Miami Dophins and University of Miami Hurricanes play their games. It's simpler to park downtown and take a special bus or cab on game days, for parking facilities are limited.

Also close in—only some twenty blocks south of Flagler Street via Brickell Avenue, US 1—is the Rickenbacker Causeway which for 75 cents will pass a car from the hurly-burly city to a very reasonable facsimile of a South Sea island. Key Biscayne, the ultimate destination was a coconut plantation for long before the postwar causeway was built and is a favorite of movie-makers for its tropical lushness. Parts of *Guadalcanal Diary* and *They Were Expendable* were filmed here.

Even the causeway itself is a park of sorts, providing wide parking areas adjacent to the four-lane road and handy swimming, boating and waterskiing areas.

Of Keys, Parks and Villas

The first real island reached will be Virginia Key, which in addition to a palm-fringed beach, offers the Seaquarium, a commercial attraction with an elaborate collection of sea life, including trained porpoises and seals, colorful reef fishes, sharks, barracuda, turtles, and the like. It's open until dark, and there's a monorail passenger car which circles the entire area. The monorail ride can be taken without paying to enter the Seaquarium itself, but you'll miss the real show in the viewing tanks and the like. Bird Island, which is part of the Seaquarium, was designated as a wildlife sanctuary by the Audubon Society in summer '78.

Also on Rickenbacker Causeway is Planet Ocean, the new $6-million attraction dedicated to exploring and explaining the mysteries of the seas. Visitors are encouraged to push buttons and activate exhibits with special effects, board a submarine and an iceberg, and explore 100 space-age exhibits or view the panoramic, multi-media shows.

Nearby is Miami's Marine Stadium, a modern, $2 million concrete structure providing 6,500 armchair seats for the viewing of boat races of all types, as well as convention sessions and cultural and religious activities, including Easter sunrise services. Many of the boating contests are recognized nationally; some are broadcast. The most prominent boating event is the Champion Spark Plug Regatta, which is the opening race of the international hydroplane schedule. The stadium has dock space for local boats and rents water sports equipment.

A New State Park

A bridge connects Virginia Key to Key Biscayne, which is, by all odds, the area's favorite recreation spot. The northern half of the 4½-mile long island is county-owned Crandon Park, which offers a marina, 2½ miles of uncluttered beach, landscaped parking areas, barbecue pits. Across the road is the top-notch Key Biscayne Golf Course. Its clubhouse lounge is a popular night spot.

The middle third of the island consists of privately owned homes, apartments, restaurants, and hotels. In 1967, the State of Florida opened the southern third—Cape Florida—as a state park. Once a haven for pirates and shipwreckers who lured sailing craft onto the reefs with false signals, the Cape also is the site of the aforementioned lighthouse attacked by Indians, not to mention by federal gunboats during the Civil War.

You'll have to retrace your route back to the mainland, but it won't cost anything to exit. Just a few blocks south (follow the signs) is another county facility, Villa Vizcaya, the former home of James Deering of the International Harvester fortune. Deering collected art works abroad for twenty years before beginning work in 1912 on what is, in reality, an Italian Renaissance palace. With up to one thousand craftsmen working, it took five years to complete the sixty-nine-room main palace and formal gardens. The latter cover ten acres with clipped hedges, fountains, reflecting pools, and statuary in seven separate garden areas. As a breakwater, offshore from the steps leading to Biscayne Bay, there is a stone version of Cleopatra's barge.

Inside the mansion, architects were faced with the problem of designing rooms to accommodate a frescoed ceiling here, a sideboard from a fifteenth-century Italian church there, or the tapestry that hung in Robert Browning's villa in Asolo, Italy, which the poet described in his "Childe Roland to the Dark Tower Came."

What it all cost, Deering didn't say, but estimates range up to $10 million hard, pre-World War I, pre-income tax dollars. A hundred million couldn't duplicate it today. You can see it all and enjoy what is now the Dade County Art Museum.

Across South Miami Avenue from the Vizcaya entrance is the Museum of Science, on original Vizcaya grounds. The Space Transit Planetarium at the east end of the museum aims to make every viewer feel like an astronaut; visitors blast off and go on a reeling simulated space ride. A sixty-five-foot dome makes it the third largest planetarium in the country.

Coconut Grove isn't a town anymore, but it was one before and in fact until Miami, it is alleged, pulled a sneaky annexation one summer while a lot of residents were vacationing out of town. But Coconut Grove is still a different place; part Greenwich Village and part Sausalito, with overtones of Tahiti. To reach it, go south on Miami Ave., which becomes Bayshore Drive.

It is arty hereabouts. There are some fine painters in residence, so it follows that bad painters will be here too in the hopes that buyers may know and buy what they like, even if it isn't good. There may be more ovens employed in the baking of ceramics than bread; perhaps more guitars are carried about than are really played, but it is not all sham. There is good theatre at the Coconut Grove Playhouse, where pre-Broadway bugs are worked out of the script, or touring companies perform.

The village atmosphere is conducive to shopping and dining. Some of the finest restaurants are in the Grove. The shopping is classy, especially at Mayfair, with its high-fashion merchandise. There are also numerous art galleries. A good way to look around is on a bicycle. You can rent one in the Grove, and there are bicycle paths to adjacent Coral Gables and down to Matheson Hammock, another pleasant county park with nature trails and a swimming lagoon.

Residential Gables

To get to Coral Gables city hall from US 1, look for S.W. 22nd St. (Coral Way) and head west. At 37th Avenue, you enter Coral Gables. Stick with it as you drive through a business area of shops and stores on a wide boulevard (this is Miracle Mile), and at the end of this section, dead ahead, will be the Spanish-towered and columned city hall. Inside they'll give you a map and notes for the self-guided tour.

Using the two, you can follow a series of self-guided tour signs on the street that will hit all the high spots for twenty rambling miles. With luck and close attention, you'll always know where you are.

Markers and the notes explain the what and wherefore about such as the Venetian Pool, the University of Miami, the villages (little compounds of homes in Dutch, French, and Chinese architecture), the plazas, and entranceways.

Coral Gables is not a tourist attraction, but rather an example of what can be done to keep a city's tone and appearance the way most of the residents want it. Every street was planned and plotted before a lick of work was done when it all began in the early '20's. George Merrick, the founder, wanted a certain sort of city for pleasant living, and he got it. Now as always, every new building must be approved by a board of architects and erected according to a strict zoning code. There are no billboards, no cemeteries, no trailer parks, and the only industry allowed must be clean, smokeless, and within a designated area. For most Americans, Coral Gables is something different.

For a guided group tour, including the history of Coconut Grove and Coral Gables, contact The Villagers, a non-profit organization dedicated to preservation and restoration. Tour includes downtown Miami. Call (305) 667-4246 or 595-1146, or write Marlies Tindall, The Villagers, Inc., 4900 Biltmore Dr., Coral Gables 33146.

Sports Paradise

The agenda of spectator sports in the whole Miami area is practically endless. Powerboat and sailboat races are weekly events, stock car racing, boxing, wrestling, annual Grand Prix car races, baseball (both minor league variety and major league spring training games), tennis tournaments, basketball, soccer, major golf tournaments and the pari-mutuel sports of horse racing, dog racing, and jai alai abound.

Greyhound racing continues the year around at one or more of the area's three tracks. Summer racing has been added to the thoroughbred horse racing scene in the Miami area with the completion of Calder Race Course. An air-conditioned grandstand and clubhouse prevents heat prostration among overexcited bettors. The Calder season runs for 132 days (May through November). Hialeah Park, March through mid-April, and Gulfstream Park, mid-January to March, just across the county line to the north, provide horse racing in the winter season. Tropical Park is run at the Calder Race Course, mid-Nov. to mid-Jan.

Summer or winter, Hialeah is a showplace worth seeing, and hundreds of thousands tour the elaborate racing plant each year with not a horse in sight. Forty groundskeepers keep things pretty, including some 1,200 stately royal palms and 95,000 other plants and flowers. The track is open to visitors and there's a tram ride around the 209 acres. The four hundred pink flamingoes nesting on the infield lake are free to leave whenever they want, incidentally, but nowhere else can they depend on a daily supply of free shrimp.

PRACTICAL INFORMATION FOR MIAMI AND MIAMI BEACH

HOW TO GET THERE. *By air.* You can reach Miami on direct flights from all major U.S. cities via American, Air Florida, Delta, Eastern, Pan Am, US Air, Ozark, Piedmont, Republic, Northwest Orient, TWA, United. Most of these airlines serve Miami from various cities within the state, since deregulation. Air Florida, an all-jet airline, is always adding service between the state's most important cities and other U.S. and foreign destinations.

Air Canada, Delta and Eastern have direct flights from Montreal; Eastern from Ottawa; Air Canada or Eastern from Toronto. There are connecting flights from Calgary, Edmonton, Halifax, Hamilton and Vancouver, via Air Canada, CP Air, Eastern Provincial, Nordair or Western.

By train: Amtrak has regular service. Even before streamlining by Amtrak, the *Seaboard Coast Line,* a Miami to New York run, was one of the last truly luxury trips by train still available in the U.S. Now it is even better. Coach fare is cheaper than by air; sleepers are much more expensive. Approximately a 24-hr. journey.

By car: From the northeast I-95 (almost complete now except for a confusing detour near Vero Beach) is your fastest route; A1A the beautiful, leisurely way.

By bus: Trailways or Greyhound will get you there.

By boat: The Intracoastal Waterway parallels the coastline and runs 349 mi. from Jacksonville to Miami.

 HOW TO GET AROUND. Take the airport limousine to your hotel, if it is a major one. Taxi fares in the Miami area are high and distances are long. Local bus service, however, is good, and local transport is even better now that the new monorail is operating. There's a lot of competition among car rental agencies, so shop around for a good buy.

TOURIST INFORMATION. Metro Dade Dept. of Tourism, 234 W. Flagler St., Miami 33130. Miami Beach Visitor and Convention Authority, 555 17th St., Miami Beach 33139.

 SEASONAL EVENTS. *January:* New Year's Day, *Orange Bowl Classic* football game. *International Travel Camping Show,* Miami. *Art Deco Week,* Miami Beach.
February: Doral Open Golf Tournament, late Feb. to early Mar., at Doral Country Club. *Sidewalk Art Show,* Coral Gables. More than 200 artists participate. Feb. 15 to 17. *Miami Grand Prix* auto race, *Miami Boat Show,* and *Coconut Grove Arts Festival,* all in mid-Feb.; also a *Film Festival; LPGA Golf; Museum of Science's Around the World Fair,* Tropical Park. *Vizcaya Art Show,* on grounds of old Deering estate, last Sun. in Feb.

March: Carnaval Miami, lavish Hispanic festival, first two weekends in March. *Exhibition games of the Baltimore Orioles,* mid-Mar. to Apr.

June: Poinciana Festival, early June.

July: Fourth of July Parade, Key Biscayne, old-fashioned parade, featuring floats, marching units, and bicycles. *Bowling Tournament of the Americas,* Miami. Amateur bowling champions from nations of the Western hemisphere vie for top honors. July 8 to 14.

November: Jr. Tennis Championships, Coral Gables, for youngsters 8 to 12, regarded as tune-up for Jr. Orange Bowl Tennis Tournament.

December: Orange Bowl Festival, one of the nation's most celebrated festival and sporting events. *King Orange Jamboree Parade* highlights New Year's Eve in downtown Miami, terminating with the football classic on New Year's Day. *Junior Orange Bowl* activities in nearby Coral Gables consist of sports tournaments attracting the finest young athletes in the world; outstanding parade. The Festival concludes with the renowned 10 K/Marathon races. Alberto Salazar and Bill Rodgers have competed here.

 MUSEUMS AND GALLERIES. Historical: *Cape Florida State Recreation Area,* 1200 S. Crandon Blvd., Key Biscayne. Seminole history. Restored Cape Florida Lighthouse. *Historical Museum of Southern Florida,* N.W. 2nd Ave. and 1st St., Miami. Maintained by nonprofit Historical Association of South Florida. Free. Closed Christmas.

Art: *Bass Museum of Art,* 2100 Collins Ave., Miami Beach. The John and Johanna Bass collection of paintings; sculpture; vestments and tapestries. Free. Closed Sun. & holidays. *Bacardi Art Gallery,* 2100 Biscayne Blvd. Exhibitions by local, national, and international artists. Free. *Dade County Arts Center,* N.W. 1st St. and 2nd Ave. *Lowe Art Museum,* 1301 Miller Dr., Coral Gables. Becoming one of the finer galleries in the South. Free. Closed New Year's, Thanksgiving and Christmas. *Metropolitan Museum and Art Center,* used to be in two locations; now combined in Coral Gables in the old Biltmore Hotel at 1212 Anastasia Ave. Free. Closed Fri. *Virginia Miller,* Coconut Grove. Fine art and artifacts. *Monastery Cloister of Saint Bernard,* 16711 W. Dixie Hwy., North Miami Beach. Built in Segovia, Spain, in 1141, it was disassembled and brought to the U.S.

Special Interest: *Museum of Science,* 3280 S. Miami Ave., Miami. Recently upgraded. Dynamic hands-on scientific exhibits and dioramas. Museum has extensive displays of Florida wildlife. Free Planetarium is adjacent to the Museum of Science. Afternoon and evening show daily. Weekly programs in Spanish. Programs changed every 5 to 6 wks. Closed Christmas. *Planet Ocean,* 3979 Rickenbacker Causeway, near Key Biscayne. An International Oceanographic Foundation $6-million showcase for "exploring" the mysteries of the seas. Visitors can climb into a submarine or upon Florida's only iceberg. More than 100 exhibits with special effects, including a new Weather Machine. Open daily.

Others: *Arch Creek Park/Museum.* Eight acres of natural flora and a museum with a nature center housing Indian and fossil exhibits. *International Design Center,* North Miami Ave. at 42nd St., Miami. A grouping of art centers that offer revealing glimpses of interior design and the technical construction of architectural and decorating innovations. Only building of its kind, they say, in the world. Full reference system, changing programs on "Centre State" which aim to dramatize the newest work of the finest designers.

HISTORIC SITES. *Vizcaya,* Dade County Art Museum, 3251 S. Miami Ave., Miami. An Italian palace, created by an American millionaire with a Hollywood imagination continues to be one of Miami's main attractions. Added to the $9 million worth of magnificence is a new Sound and Light show. *Art Deco Historic District.* 10-block long concentration of Art Deco structures, in South Miami Beach.

TOURS. *Nightclub tours: American Sightseeing,* 871-4992 or *A-1 Bus Lines,* 573-0550 or see the bell captain at your hotel.

By boat: The Island Queen makes a 2-hr. Great Circle Cruise of Biscayne Bay from Pier 5 at Bayfront Park in Miami. See Vizcaya and the millionaire estates. Luncheon and dinner cruises. 947-6105.

By air: Cruise a fine camera height in a *helicopter* from Gold Coast Helicopters, 15101 Biscayne Blvd. or 3000 Interama Blvd., or try *glider-sightseeing* from the Miami Gliderport, operating from Nov. to May and located on Krome Ave. and S.W. 162nd St. Flying instructions, also some air tours from Gene Simmons.

Everglades by airboat. Along the Tamiami Trail, on US 41 about 17 mi. W of downtown Miami, airboat operators will whisk you off on small craft with aircraft motors and guarded propellers. These were developed for fishing and hunting forays into the remote wilderness areas. Four to twelve persons can pile aboard and the normal sightseeing tour has only a nominal fee—perhaps $1.25 for adults and 50¢ for children.

Other tours: American Sightseeing Tours offers one-day and extended tours to Disney World, shuttle service, group sightseeing, special tours, school charters and race track service. 1000 N.W. LeJeune Rd. Call 633-0281, 448-1711 or 445-0098. *Burnside-Ott,* at the Opa Locka Airport, offers air tours with professional pilots and late-model aircraft. Call 685-5111. *Show Queen.* Nightly dining, dancing, and entertainment as part of a moonlight cruise. Crandon Marina.

Nikko Gold Coast Cruises offers good variety; call 945-5461. Do check at hotel desk, as new sightseeing cruises are added (or disbanded) each season.

INDUSTRIAL TOURS: The *Miami Herald Publishing Co.,* 1 Herald Plaza. Tours Mon. to Fri. *Bertram Yacht Corp.,* 3663 N.W. 21st St. Fiberglass boats, 20-38 ft. Tours.

 GARDENS. The Cloud Forest, part of the Miami Beach Garden Center and Conservatory (a rapidly building horticultural complex), is operated without admission charge by the city. On Washington Ave. 2 blocks N of Lincoln Road Mall (follow in to the west). The air inside the dome is changed very frequently, but it's so hot no visitor can stay too long. The Cloud Forest plants thrive in a droopy-hot atmosphere like that in the backwaters of the Amazon. This is a compact display with many rarities. The conservatory was recently gifted with one of the world's larger orchid collections. Closed Christmas.

Fairchild Tropical Garden, 10901 Old Cutler Rd., Miami, always open from sunrise to sunset and the "largest tropical botanical garden in America," holds the Fairchild Ramble in early Dec. It's a benefit bargain hunt with unimaginable goods—bobcat skin, a 90-year-old baby buggy, a Japanese party set that cost the lady who gave the party $2,500. The garden itself, founded by a tax attorney, is spread out on 83 acres south of Matheson Hammock Park. Leave US 1 at S.W. 112th St. and take a short jog on S.W. 57th Ave. before turning left on Old Cutler Road. Admission charge.

Other horticultural things to see: the *Miami Flower Show* is in mid-Mar. Women who go to the *Orchid Jungle,* 25 mi. S of Miami, receive an orchid as a gift. *Garden of Our Lord,* St. James Lutheran Church, 110 Phonetia, Coral Gables, with many exotic plants mentioned in the Bible. *Japanese Garden,* Watson Park, on the MacArthur Causeway, which features statue of Hotei, arbor, teahouse, stone lanterns, pagoda, ornate main gate, rock gardens, and waterfall lagoon. Free. *Redland Fruit and Spice Park,* 35 mi. SW of Miami, Homestead. Intersection of Coconut Palm Dr. (SW 248th St.) & Redland Rd. (187th Ave.). A 20-acre tropical showplace featuring fruit, nut, and spice-producing plants from around the world. Guided tours. Free. Lost Islands at the Miami Seaquarium has more than 100 varieties of palms, breadfruit trees, exotic plants in a jungle setting. In 1978, it was designated a Wildlife Sanctuary by the Tropical Audubon Society. Seabirds and migratory birds feed here. Between Miami and Key Biscayne.

 MUSIC. The *Opera Guild of Greater Miami* books important stars from the Continent, the Met, and elsewhere. Its seasonal openings bring out a socially conscious, conspicuously gowned and furred crowd. Rehearsals are year round, the chorus members are paid just as the stars are. The company keeps engagements as far off as Fort Lauderdale. Family operas are booked as late as spring and make a memorable musical occasion. A number of leading families lend their support to the Opera Guild. Call 854-1643 for up-to-date information. The Company usually appears at Dade Auditorium and Miami Beach Theatre of Performing Arts. Luciano Pavarotti is one of the superstars who has appeared here during the past two years.

Miami Beach also has a symphony, with a season extended into the warmer months with a *Summer Pops series.* Alberto Munar directs both the winter symphony and the summer program. The Miami Beach Theater of the Performing Arts box office at 1700 Washington Ave. will provide current information.

The *Youth Symphony of South Florida,* the *Chamber Music Society in Greater Miami,* the *Miami Little Orchestra* and dozens of other groups are active in the resort area. The Miami Herald is a good source for information on current performances.

STAGE AND REVUES. The Greater Miami area cannot yet compete with New York in legitimate theater, but it is doing quite well in its own right. Visitors who love theater will find a variety of excellent productions.

Coconut Grove Playhouse, 3500 Main Hwy., Coconut Grove, is the home of the *Players State Theatre,* where lesser-known Broadway shows and pre-White Way productions are staged. Aesthetically and technically, the theater is an improvement on many of Broadway's more famous houses, with fine seats, good acoustics, excellent restaurant service attached, and an upstairs art gallery. Coconut Grove, really a corner of Miami, is a semi-art colony with millionaires and artists living in close proximity.

The Miami Beach Theatre of the Performing Arts is the chief outpost of Broadway hits with major casts. Audiences, including many socialites, are attracted from all over the world. The $6-million facility also hosts outstanding concerts, ballets, and other cultural events. 1700 Washington Ave.

The *Ring Theater,* Univ. of Miami, offers presentations of such high quality they could compare with Broadway performances. Other area colleges also have good theater, especially Florida International University and Miami-Dade Community College.

The *Merry-Go-Round Playhouse and Drama Studio,* 235 Alcazar, Coral Gables, has continuous *Children's Theater;* also presents amateur Shakespeare and contemporary plays. Spanish plays may be seen at *Teatro America,* 2173 S.W. 8th St.; and *Teatro Avante,* 4601 W. Flagler St.

Ruth Foreman Theatre, Fla. International University, N.E. 151 St. and Biscayne Blvd., North Miami, presents both legitimate and children's theater, Sat. matinees.

Parker Playhouse, Fort Lauderdale, was created by Zev Buffman, former owner of the Coconut Grove Playhouse (he's now with the new Miami Beach Theatre of the Performing Arts) and run on the same principles. Most shows appearing at Miami Beach Theatre of Performing Arts go to the Parker next stop.

At the *Sunrise Theater,* West Commercial Blvd. and 95th St. in Sunrise, top celebrities such as Frank Sinatra, Barry Manilow and Dolly Parton are booked.

BARS. After the hot sun goes down, Miami and Miami Beach continue to sizzle with hot jazz, burning blues, and passionate country music. Many of the bars here are as big as nightclubs elsewhere; some nightclubs take on arena proportions. Check ahead for information on current acts, hours, and details of cover, minimum, or admission charges.

Topping the list is the famous *Regine's* in the Grand Bay Hotel. For combos providing music for listening and dancing, there are *Dancin' on the Roc,* 531-0000; *Daphne's* 871-3200; the *Forge,* 538-8530; *Cy's,* 358-9100; *Viscount,* 871-6000; *Airport Hilton,* 262-1000; *Doral,* 592-2000; and a piano bar at the *700 Club* in the David William Apartment-Hotel, 700 Biltmore Way, Coral Gables (445-7821) and at *The Toast,* 13675 Biscayne Blvd. (947-1514).

For disco, try any clubs of the *Big Daddy's* chain, found throughout Florida. Also try "Z", 1238 Washington (538-0888); *Stefano's* 24 Crandon (361-7007); *Fire and Ice,* 3841 NE 2nd Ave. (573-3473); *Rick's,* NW 103rd St., Palmetto Expressway (825-1000); and *Rainbows* 6600 Red Rd. (666-4641).

If it's jazz you're after, dial the jazz hotline number, 382-3938. Then try *Arthur's,* NE 15th St., Biscayne Blvd. (371-1444); *Grand Bay,* 2669 S. Bayshore (858-9600), *Pickford's,* 395 Giralda, (443-4376), *Ginger Man* at 3390 Mary St., Mayfair (448-9919), *Hemingways* in Hollywood at 219 N. 21st. Ave. (923-0500; it's a toll call from Miami). Other top spots are *Greenstreets,* 2051 LeJeune; *Monty Trainers,* 2560 S. Bayshore; and *Harbour Lounge,* 1335 79th St. Causeway.

NIGHTCLUBS. The headliners, who can make more money per minute by appearing in a nightclub than most people make in a week, have really only one complaint: they say that New York doesn't have the number of big dates for the top acts that are available in Miami Beach. Christmas season—really, Christmas Eve itself—marks the annual opening of the great star parade. Veterans and comparatively new entries—so long as they bear a famous name and have whipped up what is reputed to be a headline act—are brought on here. To "fill the big room"—for the rooms can be very big—tends to be an ultimate test of personal stardom.

On Miami Beach most of the important nightclubs are located in resort hotels. Most of the hotel nightclubs have developed a style—they go for revues, for smash action, or for intimacy. Prices often range from expensive to staggering but the cost can be softened up by paying a very nominal fee for a nightclub tour.

In Miami the most lavish, and the wildest, night spots are the Cuban supper clubs. The best are *Les Violins* and *Flamenco.* They're not cheap, of course, but the prices won't stagger you, as per the average Miami Beach lollapalooza. But money spent in a Cuban nightclub is never regretted—when the Cubans do a nightclub show, they tear off a good one. And the food is usually excellent. These classy Las Vegas revues spotlight extravagantly costumed girls, a real Rolls Royce driven on stage, gold cages hoisting dancers to the ceilings, free-flowing waterfalls and rainstorms on stage, and a full-sized ice rink. Fantastic! Another top club is *Copacabana,* 3600 S.W. 8th St. The *Little Havana* clubs of S.W. 8th Street (Calle Ocho) have proliferated in recent years and count many Anglos as appreciative regulars. Lively combos entertain for listening and dancing in the *Sonesta Beach Hotel and Tennis Resort* on Ocean Drive, Key Biscayne. Also on the Key, look into *Rogers on the Green.*

SPORTS. Because of the semi-tropical climate there is no division of sports activities into summer or winter in the greater Miami area. Instead, we will list them alphabetically.

Bicycling: There are about 120 mi. of well-marked secondary routes adjoining thoroughfares for safe, scenic cycling. Greynolds Park is a good starting point in the north part of the Miami area—bike paths wind through picnic grounds, around a lake with boat rides and fishing. Coconut Grove has excellent bike paths, winding through the oldest and most historic section of Miami. Route maps are provided by local chambers of commerce, the Coral Gables Community Development Dept. and Miami-Metro Dept. of Publicity and Tourism. Numerous shops offer loaners; bicycles can be included in some auto rental arrangements.

Boating: Miami has berthing for over 4,000 boats and takes anything up to a 180-ft. yacht. Miamarina is the city's newest and most modern marine facility with all the downtown advantages. It offers 178 slips for pleasure craft and space for 30 commercial craft, such as charter and sightseeing boats. There are circuit voyages out of Miami through the Keys, Fort Myers and Okeechobee Waterway. As for distance on the Intracoastal Waterway, Jacksonville to Miami is a 349-mi. trip; and it's 158 mi. inside the Keys from Miami to Key West. Competitive boating includes a speed classic at the Marine Stadium on Rickenbacker Causeway and, in mid-Jan., a 9-hr. endurance race. There's an 807-mi. race from Miami to Montego Bay and races from St. Petersburg to Fort Lauderdale and Miami to Cat Cay in late Feb. The Lipton Cup yacht race is considered by yachtsmen to be a warmup for the great Miami-Nassau race—both are held in Mar. The new Miami Beach Marina (south of Fifth St.) claims to be the largest marina in the southeastern U.S.

Fishing: Deep-sea fishing: You can charter boats for trolling, drift-fishing or bottom fishing. Charter boats vary in cost from about $80 for a half day to around $150 for a full day. Since they carry up to six persons, you can share the costs of the charter. The deep blue of the Gulfstream is their beat for the big gamefish, marlin, sail, wahoo, dolphin and tuna. Key Largo, south of Miami in Florida Keys, is great sport-fishing haunt. There are about 200 licensed fishing guides to take you to the Upper Keys and into the flats of Florida Bay.

Pier Fishing: Try your luck at Haulover Pier in Haulover Beach Park, north of Bal Harbour on A1A; Sunny Isles Pier, 167th St. and Collins Ave; Pier Park, Ocean Dr. and First St., Miami Beach; Children's Pier, adjacent to City Hall; Dinner Key, Miami.

Freshwater fishing: Most famous freshwater fishing in Greater Miami is the Tamiami Canal, extending from west edge of Miami along US 41. The canal is 50 ft. wide, 50 mi. long with plenty of parking and fishing spots along the banks. A freshwater fishing license is necessary. Skiffs and hired guides are available along the Tamiami Trail for trips into the Everglades. The Miami Herald's Metropolitan Miami Fishing Tournament, one of the world's largest, runs each year from mid-Dec. to mid-Apr. Despite the skill and knowledge of local anglers, a majority of the average annual 50,000 entries of fish contesting for citations and trophies are made by visitors from all parts of the world.

Golf: The greater Miami area has over 45 golf courses. Green fees are much less expensive on summer wkdays at most 18-hole municipal courses. Many courses offer reduced "twilight" rates, which go into effect daily between 3 P.M. and 6 P.M., depending on the season.

The *Doral C.C.,* Miami, is outstanding. Other excellent courses are: *Le Jeune G.C.,* with gently rolling terrain; *Vizcaya G. & C.C.,* nicely landscaped with palm trees; *C.C. of Miami,* a fine resort course; *Miami Lakes Inn & C.C.,* a challenging course; *King's Bay Yacht & C.C.,* a challenging, scenic course open to members and hotel guests; *Fontainebleau Hilton C.C.,* a Mark Mahannah course with seven lakes, rolling fairways (all in Miami). Also: *Miami Shores C.C.,* Miami Shores, for members and their guests only; *Miami Springs G. & C.C.,* Miami Springs, former site of the Miami Open; *Bay Shore Municipal,* Miami Beach, a municipal course with rolling fairways, mounds and lakes; *Key Biscayne G.C.,* Key Biscayne, a unique Robert Von Hagge course, with tough tests; *Palmetto G.C.,* So. Miami, a municipal course with 13 water holes; *Biltmore G.C.,* Coral Gables, a municipal course, with some tricky water holes; and *Normandy Shores G.C.,* Miami Beach, on the Isle of Normandy in Biscayne Bay. The plush *Turnberry C.C.* is the site of the yearly Ladies PGA tournament.

Shelling: For the best shelling in Florida, and in fact in the whole world, you'll have to go to Sanibel Island on the Gulf coast. But you'll find an occasional shell on Miami and Keys beaches, and there's good hunting in shell shops.

Water sports: Water-skiing schools, jumps, and towing services are located along beaches and causeways. *Skiing* lessons consist of approximately three 1-hr. sessions. Boats with tow equipment and fuel can be rented. *Surfing* is a practiced art in Florida, although the local surfers are a frustrated lot—the waves are seldom large enough. However they do their best at Haulover Beach Park and South Miami Beach, where there are special areas reserved for surfers. There are miles of sand beaches for *swimming:* Crandon Park and Cape Florida State Park on Key Biscayne; Haulover Beach on Collins Ave., north of Bal Harbour; Lummus Park on Miami Beach; Matheson Hammock, 2 mi. south of Miami on Old Cutler Rd; Tahiti Beach in South Miami, are among the many choice spots. Another favorite swimming spot is the Venetian Municipal Pool, 2701 DeSoto Blvd., formed from the coral quarry which is mined to build the city. The pool is reminiscent of a Venetian palazzo, with shady porticos, loggias and towers.

A number of local firms specialize in *scuba* and skin-diving instructions and excursions to sunken hulls, reefs and underwater gardens. Fowey Rocks Light area, just south of Key Biscayne, is among the best for *underwater photography.* Persons renting scuba diving equipment must have a card certifying that they are licensed divers. Other fine locations are Haulover, Elbow Light, Pacific Light, Carysfort Light and John Pennekamp State Park. Skin divers should observe State

Conservation laws regarding crawfish (Florida lobster) and other regulations on *spearfishing.* Crawfish may not be taken by spearing. There are no special restrictions on the use of spearguns in Dade and Broward Counties, but it is prohibited in Pennekamp Park and within one mile of US1 in the lower keys. Diver flags are required. *Windsurfing* is the new rage and most big resort hotels have rentals and schools on their beaches.

SPECTATOR SPORTS. *Baseball:* One of the first things sports-minded Florida visitors are interested in (especially if they're late vacationers) is the baseball training camps. In Miami, the Baltimore Orioles work out at the Miami Stadium, 2301 N.W. 10th Ave., beginning Feb. 15, with exhibition games starting Mar. 15. *Football:* The Miami Dolphins, under Coach Don Shula, won their first World Championship in 1973 and repeated in 1974. They play in the Orange Bowl, as do the Univ. of Miami Hurricanes.

Racing: There are 3 horse racing tracks and 1 harness racing track in South Florida. Hialeah Park, 4 E. 25th St., also features an aquarium, rare birds, flamingos, English carriages, riding regalia, snacks and souvenirs. You can take a tram ride. Gulfstream Park Race Track, US 1, Hallandale, is open mid-Jan. to Mar. Miami's Calder Race Course, N.W. 27th Ave. at 210th St., has two seasons: May to Nov. and Nov. to Jan. All three tracks are within easy reach of Miami and Miami Beach. While meets are in progress, buses run directly to horse and greyhound racing facilities. Special buses from Miami Beach to Pompano Beach for harness racing at Tourist Attractions, mid-Dec. to early April. The races may be watched from a terraced dining room in the spectacular 7-story grandstand. Dog racing (greyhounds, of course), a Florida staple, at Biscayne, 320 N.W. 115th St.; West Flagler, 300 N.W. 37th Ave.; Investment Corp. of South Florida Track in Hollywood.

Jai-alai: A dangerous combination of handball, tennis and lacrosse, jai-alai requires great nerve, endurance and savvy—and lends itself to betting. The sport derives from Spain and 17th-century Basques. Players use a pelota (virgin-rubber ball covered with goatskin) and a cesta (curved basket of imported reed) which straps to the wrist. At push *Dania Jai-Alai,* you may view the game directly or on closed circuit TV. Dec. To Apr. *Miami Fronton,* 3500 N.W. 37th Ave. is also served by bus from Miami Beach.

WHAT TO DO WITH THE CHILDREN. A number of sea zoos have been created in Florida. The largest and most famous is the *Miami Seaquarium* located beyond the Rickenbacker Causeway (follow US 1 to the sign with the circling shark), south of downtown. It has been there 18 years, and it is often so crowded that daddies should be prepared to hold the youngest on their shoulders for the show in the porpoise tank. But there are also the shark show, the killer whale show, the penguin-seal-pelican show (for this you sit in an inclining grandstand), and the show down below in the great tank when the divers vacuum the bottom and feed the ocean's biggest captive. The Seaquarium also includes Lost Islands, a bird sanctuary in a jungle-like setting.

Serpentarium, US 1, 126th St. and Dixie Hwy., South Miami. Cobras and other snakes, tortoises, crocodiles, galapagos, iguanas. Cobra venom extraction. *Parrot Jungle,* 11000 S.W. 57th Ave. White cockatoo named Butch has been in with all the big shots. He kissed Winston Churchill. Birds perform all kinds of tricks. Winding trails through natural hammock to Flamingo Park.

Planet Ocean is sort of an Expo of the Seas. Educational portrayal of mankind's dependence upon the oceans, but highly entertaining for kids and adults alike. On Key Biscayne just before Seaquarium. For details call 361-2186.

Monkey Jungle, about 20 mi. s. of Miami on US 1, features monkeys cavorting without being caged. Visitors are in the cage instead!

The new *Metrozoo* at 124000 S.W. 152nd St., Miami will be, its promoters claim, the world's largest zoo when it's complete. Many areas are already open including a replica of a temple in which tigers were found. Uncaged tigers roam free here today, and you'll find animals and birds throughout the zoo in freedom. (You're protected by little-noticed nets, fences, and ditches.) Admission charge.

Many of the better hotels, such as the Sonesta Beach and Fointainebleau Hilton, have all-day kiddy programs run by trained counselors.

A colorful two-story carousel is part of the whirl of fun in Treasure Island, part of the 10.5-acre hotel/shopping complex of the Omni International Hotel on Miami's Biscayne Blvd. at 16th St. The family entertainment center, one level below the lobby via the glass-bubble elevator, features games, a carousel, fortune tellers, pirates from Robert Louis Stevenson's famous adventures, etc.

 **HOTELS AND MOTELS.** The hotels of Miami Beach seem almost like one continuous city. The Flabbergast Hotel, as they have been called, are the prototypes of much of the resort architecture around the world.

What the hotels charge varies widely, coming to a peak in mid-December through Easter. The labels attached here have meaning mostly as a way of establishing one or another as a bit more expensive than its neighbor. Many modestly rated establishments are the equal in comfort and location of those that—usually because of a later construction date—have a higher standard price.

The lowest rates are in the summer, which usually begins in May and continues until Nov. 1. This is the period for bargain hunters, when you can acquire pleasing and even sumptuous accommodations for about $20 a day per person.

We have listed hotels and motels alphabetically in categories determined by double, in-season rates: *Deluxe,* $85 and up; *Expensive* $75–$80; *Moderate,* $50–$75; *Inexpensive,* under $50. For a more complete explanation of hotel and motel categories see *Facts at Your Fingertips* at the front of this volume.

The Greater Miami Hotel Association, Suite 618, 300 Biscayne Blvd. Way, Miami, Fla. 33131 will send you a list of member hotels. Also contact area tourism offices. For prices, write individual hotels.

Miami

Airport Hilton. *Deluxe.* 5701 Blue Lagoon. Swank facilities. Opened in '84.

Coconut Grove Hotel. *Deluxe.* 2649 S. Bayshore Drive. Pool, tennis, marina, saunas, swanky restaurant on 20th floor, garden, bar with dancing, entertainment. Strong Florida flavor in modern garden setting.

Costa Del Sol Golf & Racquet Club. *Deluxe.* Adjacent to Doral Country Club (N.W. 36th St. Exit). Two and 3 bedroom split-level villas. Restaurant, cocktail lounge. Mediterranean atmosphere. Daily, weekly, monthly, yearly rates.

David William Apartment Hotel. *Deluxe.* 700 Baltimore Way. A favorite with actors appearing at Coconut Grove Playhouse. Superb facilities. Great food.

Doral Country Club. *Deluxe.* 4400 N.W. 87th Ave. Elegant resort hotel that is almost a city in itself. Pools, play areas (with supervision during major holidays), tennis, golf, water sports, boating. Unmatched sports facilities. Night life.

Dupont Plaza. *Deluxe.* 300 Biscayne Blvd. Way. Pools, sauna, golf avail. Some kitchen units. Dining room, bar.

Four Ambassadors. *Deluxe.* 801 S. Bayshore Dr. Pools, sauna, play area. Marina. Golf, tennis avail. Fine restaurant, bar. Kitchen units avail.

Grand Bay. *Deluxe.* 2669 S. Bayshore. New and elegant. Shaped like a pyramid. Great food and night life.

Harbor Island Spa. *Deluxe.* More than just a place for overweights seeking slimness. Special "finishing school" plan for teen-age girls in summer. Pools, sauna. Full sports program. Planned entertainment. Closed Sept., Oct. 7900 Harbor Island.

The Hotel Mutiny at Sailboat Bay. *Deluxe.* 2951 S. Bayshore Dr. Closest to Coconut Grove business district, with sweeping view of Dinner Key Marina. Exotic fantasy décor in each room.

Hyatt Regency. *Deluxe.* 400 S.E. 2nd Ave. Superb new property.

Omni International Hotel. *Deluxe.* Biscayne Blvd. at 16th St. Outstanding resort-in-city complex. Variety of restaurants, lounges, entertainment. Lower level has international shopping-restaurant-entertainment area.

Pavillon. *Deluxe.* S.E. 1st St., Biscayne Bay. Exquisite in all respects.

Riverparc. *Deluxe.* 100 S.E. 4th St. Luxurious. All suites.

Sonesta Beach Hotel and Tennis Club. *Deluxe.* 350 Ocean Dr., Key Biscayne. Beachside pool. Bicycles, sailboats available. "Just Us Kids" program. Four unusual restaurants, bar. MAP avail., also fam. rates summers.

Key Biscayne Villas. *Deluxe.* 701 Ocean, Key Biscayne. Recently upgraded.

Airport Regency Hotel. *Expensive.* Near the airport at 1000 N.W. LeJeune Rd. In Fla (800) 432–0170. Elsewhere, (800) 327–0182. Restaurant, lounge, poolside snack bar. Rooms, suites.

Miami International Airport. *Expensive.* In terminal at N.W. 20th St. & Le Jeune Rd. Restaurant, bar. Rooms are soundproof, available for day use.

Miami Marriott Hotel and Racquet Club. *Expensive.* 1201 Le Jeune Rd. Restaurants, bars, dancing, entertainment. Tennis, lawn games. Pool. Golf avail.

Viscount & Kings Inn. *Expensive.* Olympic pool, sauna. Restaurants, bars, dancing, entertainment. Tennis, lawn games. Pool. Golf avail.

Sheraton River House. *Expensive.* At Miami International Airport (3900 NW 21st St.), opposite terminal entrance. Overlooks Miami River. Three lounges, gourmet restaurant (*Daphne's*), sports, boat docking. Heated pool.

Holiday Inn. *Moderate to Expensive.* Almost a dozen in Miami and Miami Beach areas: **Holiday Inn Central,** I-95, 79th St.; **Holiday Inn Civic Center-Airport East,** N.W. 12th Ave. (East-West Expressway); **Holiday Inn-Golden Glades,** 148 N.W. 167th St., North Miami; **Holiday Inn-International Airport** (one mi. n. of terminal entrance), Miami Springs; **Holiday Inn Crowne Plaza,** 10 blocks from airport; **Holiday Inn Airport Lakes** (about 3 mi. from entrance), 1101 N.W. 57th Ave.; **Holiday Inn at Calder Race Course,** 21485 N.W. 17th Ave.; **Holiday Inn of Coral Gables-Downtown,** 2051 LeJeune Rd.; **Holiday Inn of Coral Gables South,** 1350 S. Dixie Hwy.; **Holiday Inn N. Miami,** 11190 Biscayne Blvd.; at **Hialeah,** 1950 W. 49th St.; and **South Dade,** 10799 Caribbean Blvd. The new downtown **Holiday Inn on Brickell Ave.** is a 17-story showplace. For information call any Holiday Inn or (800) 238-8000.

Howard Johnson Key Biscayne (formerly Quality Inn). *Moderate.* 798 Crandon Blvd. All efficiency units. No restaurant so far, but conv. to restaurants. More Howard Johnson's: **HJ's Motor Lodge-Downtown,** 1100 Biscayne Blvd.; **HJ's Motor Lodge Plaza,** 200 S.E. 2nd Ave.; **HJ's Motor Lodge-Airport,** 1980 N.W. Le Jeune Rd.; **HJ's Motor Lodge-Airport West,** N.W. 36th St. (4 mi. from airport); **HJ's Motor Lodge-Broad Causeway,** 12210 Biscayne Blvd.; **HJ's Motor Lodge,** 4000 Alton Rd. Also in Coral Gables, Kendall, and Northwest.

Miami Airport Inn (Best Western). *Moderate.* 1550 N.W. Le Jeune Rd., 1 block S of International Airport. Color TV. Pool (heated). *Playboy Club* now housed here. Bar, dancing in season. Free airport transportation.

Miami Lakes Inn & Country Club. *Moderate.* N.W. 154th St. Pool. Restaurants. Bar, entertainment, dancing. Golf, tennis. Recently expanded.

Ramada Inn. *Moderate.* 2 locations: Airport: 3941 NW 22 St. Heated pool, dining room, cocktail lounge, entertainment. Also 7250 N.W. 11th St., about 5 miles from airport. Pool, sauna, restaurant, cocktail lounge.

Riviera Court. *Moderate.* 5100 Riviera Dr. (US 1), Coral Gables, 30 rooms, 14 efficiencies. Pool, patio. Opposite University of Miami. Nr. restaurants.

Town and Country. *Moderate.* 600 Coral Way. Heated pool. Attractive efficiency apartments. Garden setting. Across the street from public golf course.

University Inn (Quality Inn). *Moderate.* 1390 S. Dixie Hwy. Most convenient to the University of Miami's Coral Gables campus.

Miami Airways. *Inexpensive.* 5001 N.W. 36th St., Miami Springs. Pool. Restaurant, bar, music. In airport area.

Willard Garden. *Inexpensive.* 124 N.E. 14th St. "Do it yourself" hotel. Convenient location.

Miami Beach

Alexander. *Deluxe.* 5225 Collins. Luxurious—world-class facilities. All suites. Gourmet food.

Doral-on-the-Ocean. *Deluxe.* 4833 Collins Ave. Stunning high-rise, decorated like a Fellini set. Shares sports facilities with Doral Country Club & Hotel, and cosponsors Florida's biggest golf tournament. Pool, beach; 4 18-hole, 19-hole golf courses; tennis, baseball. Restaurants, nightclub, dancing, entertainment. MAP, suites avail.

Eden Roc. *Deluxe.* 4525 Collins Ave. Large, attractively furnished rooms. Pool, private beach Golf, tennis, boating, water sports. Restaurants, nightclub features name talent nightly. Penthouse suites, EP avail.

Fontainebleau Hilton. *Deluxe.* 4441 Collins Ave. Something of a legend. Vast resort hotel with multitude of accommodations ranging from single rooms to plush suites. The standard by which flamboyant hotels are measured. Pools, cabanas, private beach. Golf, tennis, boating. Restaurants, boutiques, cocktail lounges, nightclubs, disco. Newly redecorated and refurbished. Waterfalls, grottos and free-form swimming pool cover over 15,000 acres.

Konover Ramada Renaissance Hotel. *Deluxe.* 5445 Collins Ave. A grand ocean-front resort. Pool, wading pool, health club, theaters. Rooms with small refrigerators. Coffee shop, gourmet restaurant, cocktail lounge, entertainment, dancing.

Sheraton Bal Harbour (formerly Americana). *Deluxe.* 9701 Collins Ave., Bal Harbour. One of the leading resort hotels in Florida. Their biggest pool is not olympic, it's "lagoon-sized." Private beach. Golf and tennis privileges; lawn games, special children's programs; social director. Restaurants, nightclubs, dancing, entertainment. Tropical gardens and 2-story terrarium in lobby and an extra touch of glamour. MAP, suites avail.

Aztec Resort Motel. *Expensive.* 15901 Collins Ave. Pools, game room. Restaurant, bar, dancing, entertainment. MAP, kitchen units avail. Informal. Popular with French-Canadian tourists.

Beau Rivage Hotel (Best Western). *Expensive.* 9955 Collins Ave., Bal Harbour. Pools, beach, lawn games; golf & tennis privileges. Restaurants, cocktail lounge, dancing, entertainment. Solarium, sauna. Lively resort atmosphere. Children's & teen's program, many activities. Kitchen apts. MAP avail.

Colonial Inn. *Expensive.* 18101 Collins Ave. Pools, beach game area. Supervised children's teens' program. Restaurants, bars, dancing, entertainment. Very well-maintained and well-managed. Convenient to shopping. MAP, kitchen units avail.

Di Lido. *Expensive.* 155 Lincoln Rd. Pools, private beach. Special program for teen-agers. Restaurants, bars, dancing and entertainment. Popular with older tourists. MAP, penthouse suites avail.

Marco Polo Resort Motel. *Expensive.* 192nd St. & Collins Ave. Pools. Supervised program for children, teens. Golf & tennis nr. Casual and informal, for the young at heart. Restaurant, bar; dancing, entertainment. Lower level shopping arcade. Very lively atmosphere.

Palms Resort Motel. *Expensive.* 9449 Collins Ave. Pool, beach, boating, fishing, game area. Restaurant, bar, dancing, entertainment. Pets, MAP, kitchen units avail.

Newport Beach Resort. *Expensive.* 16701 Collins Ave. Outstanding resort facilities. Social program. Kids' activities. Restaurant.

Pan American. *Expensive.* 17875 Collins Ave. Pool, play area, private beach. Restaurants. Kitchen units avail. Tasteful decor, very well-maintained. Friendly service. You get money's worth here.

Quality Inn of Runaway Bay. *Expensive.* 1019 79th St. Causeway. On Intercoastal Waterway. Water sports. Nice hideaway.

Sans Souci. *Expensive.* 3101 Collins Ave. Pool, private beach. Golf, tennis nr. Game room. Restaurant, bar, night-club. Newly refurbished—great appearance! Very attentive service.

Seaview. *Expensive.* 9909 Collins. Pool, beach, superb cuisine. Fine hotel with fine service.

Seville. *Expensive.* 2901 Collins Ave. Pools, cabanas, private beach. Restaurants, bar. Game room. Nightclub with entertainment nightly. MAP avail.

Singapore Resort Motel. *Expensive.* Oceanfront at 96th St. Private beach, big pools, sundecks. Golf, tennis. Coffee shop, dining room, cocktail lounge. Cooperative packages with *Aztec Resort Motel* at 159th St.

Thunderbird Motel. *Expensive.* 18401 Collins Ave. Water sports, tennis; some efficiencies. Restaurant.

Versailles. *Expensive.* 3425 Collins Ave. Pool, cabana club, private beach. Pets. Supervised children's program during holidays, summer. Restaurants, bar, dancing, entertainment. Was a fancy hotel in the 1950's. MAP avail.

Alujo Motel (formerly Hawaiian Inn). *Moderate.* 17601 Collins Ave. Large 2-story motel. Pools, beach, boating, game area. Supervised children's program. Restaurant specializes in luaus. Bar, dancing, entertainment. New steak house; disco. Cheerful, informal atmosphere. Family favorite. MAP avail.

Barcelona Hotel. *Moderate.* 4343 Collins Ave. Pools, beach, health club. Pets. Restaurant, cocktail lounge, dancing, entertainment. Refurbished.

Beacharbour Resort. *Moderate.* 18925 Collins. Pool, beach, game room. Popular with Canadians.

Castaways Beach and Tennis Club. *Moderate.* 16375 Collins Ave. Pools, beach, boating, game area. Pets. Restaurant, bar, dancing, entertainment. Also hydrotherapy pool. Special French-Canadian night club. Lively atmosphere. MAP avail.

Chateau Resort Motel. *Moderate.* 19115 Collins Ave. Pools, beach, boating, game area. Restaurants, bar, dancing, entertainment in season. MAP avail.

Coronado Motel. *Moderate.* 9501 Collins. Pool, beach, restaurant. Friendly service.

Desert Inn & Motel. *Moderate.* 17201 Collins Ave. Pools, beach, game area. Restaurant, bar, dancing, entertainment. AP, kitchen units avail. A French-Canadian favorite.

Golden Nugget. *Moderate.* 18655 Collins Ave. Pool, beach, game area. Restaurants, bar; entertainment in season. MAP. Kitchen units avail. Very pleasant for family vacations.

Moulin Rouge Resort Motel. *Moderate.* 280 Arthur Godfrey Rd. Pools, beach, boating, fishing. Restaurant. Pets. Kitchen units avail.

Nichols Apt. Hotel. *Moderate.* 9585 Collins. Spacious rooms. Pools, beach.

Ocean Roc Resort Motel. *Moderate.* 19505 Collins Ave. Very pleasant. Spacious rooms with balconies (formerly a Holiday Inn). Tennis, heated pool, pool for children. Beach-view dining room, cocktail bar. Good value for families.

Olympia Motel. *Moderate.* 15701 Collins Ave. Pool, beach; efficiencies. Good location.

Rodney Motel. *Moderate.* 9365 Collins Ave. Oceanfront. Family-oriented. Kitchenettes available.

Sahara Resort Motel (Best Western). *Moderate.* 18335 Collins Ave. Resort motel with pool, beach, boating, game area. Restaurant, bar, entertainment in season. MAP avail.

St. Moritz Hotel and Motel. *Moderate.* 1565 Collins Ave. Pool, beach, game area. Restaurant open in season. Attracts older clientele—old fashioned hotel. MAP avail.

Suez Resort Motel. *Moderate.* 18215 Collins Ave. Pools, beach, game area. Restaurant, bar, dancing entertainment. Better maintained than most 1950's hotels on beach. Bright yellow-orange exterior. Lively disco, lounge. Tennis. Another French-Canadian favorite. AP avail.

Sea Breeze. *Moderate to Inexpensive.* 16151 Collins Ave. New ownership; attractive nautical Scandinavian decor. New air-conditioning in carpeted rooms. Renovated pool, sundeck. Terrific bargain.

Wakiki Resort Motel. *Moderate to Inexpensive.* 18801 Collins Ave. Near restaurants, shopping, amusements. Comfortable, neat rooms. Casual family atmosphere. Tennis courts. Lively, with groups of Canadian vacationers. Pools, beach, game area. Restaurant, bar, dancing, entertainment. Kitchen units avail.

Canadian Motel. *Inexpensive.* 9201 Collins. Pools, beach, play area. Sauna. Efficiency rooms with kitchenettes available.

Caravan Motel. *Inexpensive.* 19101 Collins Ave. Pets. Pool, beach, boating. Restaurant, bar. Patronized by French-Canadians. Fam. rates, kitchen units avail.

Pier House Inn. *Inexpensive.* 17451 Collins Ave. Formerly a Holiday Inn. Family games, heated pool on rooftop. (Views into the lobby from underwater portholes in pool.) Coffee Shop. Nr. restaurants.

Sea Isle Hotel. *Inexpensive.* 3001 Collins Ave. Pool, beach, game area. Restaurant, bar, dancing, entertainment. Interesting art-deco high-rise. About $500,000 spent for refurbishing. Attentive management, friendly staff. American and kosher cuisine. In good shape for a grand dame hotel. Nightly social program. Lower level has shops. MAP avail.

 DINING OUT. Of the several thousand places to dine in Miami and Miami Beach, the range is from gourmet restaurants to economical cafeterias, from hotels to sandwich shops. Some of the Cuban restaurants in Miami are among the finest anywhere, and offer dishes you won't find elsewhere. Stroll long "Calle Oche" (S.W. 8th St.) and order a many-layered meat-cheese-vegetable salad on crispy Cuban bread; refreshing "batidos" (fruit shakes); rich bean soups and South American specialties; hot, strong coffee and luscious pastry at a sidewalk café. The area offers a full range of foreign restaurants, with entrees running the gamut from sea foods to roast beef, turkey or steaks and lavish feasts.

Florida lobster, or crawfish, is a big favorite in these parts. You can dine on succulent Everglades froglegs, pompano or conch chowder. Stone crabs are a native south Florida delicacy, and fresh shellfish, lobsters and oysters are flown in daily. Tangy key lime pie is the dessert.

Restaurants are listed alphabetically by cuisine and price category. Restaurant price categories are based on a meal of soup or salad, entrée, and dessert, but do not include taxes, tips, and beverages. *Deluxe* meals will cost $20 per person and up; *Expensive,* $9.50–$20; *Moderate,* $5.50–$9; *Inexpensive,* under $5. Prices are based on an *average* main dish—not the lobster, not the vegetarian plate. For a more complete explanation of restaurant categories see *Facts at Your Fingertips* at the front of this volume.

EDITOR'S CHOICES

Rating restaurants is, at best, a subjective business, and obviously a matter of personal taste. It is, therefore, difficult to call a restaurant "the best," and hope to get unanimous agreement. The restaurants listed below are our choices of the best eating places in the Greater Miami area, and the places we would choose if we were visiting this area.

CAFE CHAUVERON
French Cuisine

New York City's loss was Miami's gain. Roger Chauveron pulled up stakes and moved his world famous establishment to a lovely waterside location, and if anything, the new restaurant stands out even more now than before. The diversity of the menu is enormous, and all dishes are cooked to order. There is real artistry at work here, and this restaurant ranks with the finest in the entire country. 9561 East Bay Harbor Drive (Bay Harbour Island, Miami Beach). *Deluxe.*

VINTON'S
Continental

A perennial award winner. Chef Rene, brother Hans, and his wife, Susan, serve up gastronomic delights that are consistently excellent and innovative. Every Monday a seven-course set menu is featured; these gourmet nights are the talk of the town. Small restaurant in old hotel (La Palma), 116 Alhambra Circle (Coral Gables). *Deluxe.*

JOE'S STONE CRAB
Seafood

A classic since Ragtime days, specializing in guess-what. But also serves memorable seafoods of all types, vegetables, breads. Closed Thanksgiving Day and May–September. No reservations, so wait may be long. Now also open for lunch. 227 Biscayne St., South Beach. *Expensive.*

PLACE FOR STEAK
Steak House

The name says it all, and it is wise to go with the house specialty. It is a fine piece of beef. The "house" salad dressing is also very good, and the cheesecake is truly special. Harbor Lounge often features fine jazz combos. 1335 79th St. Causeway (Miami Beach). *Expensive.*

THE STUDIO
Continental

The place for special occasions. Gourmet menu with huge salads and superb desserts. The atmosphere is of the same quality as food—the décor of each room centers on a different theme. The dinner music adds to the effect. 2340 S.W. 32nd Ave. (Miami) *Expensive.*

REFLECTIONS ON THE BAY
American

On the grounds of Miamimarina, this striking modern restaurant overlooks the Bay and has tasteful contemporary décor. Unusually well-prepared foods, attentive service. Informal Dockside Terrace is also part of complex. 301 N.E. Miamimarina Pkwy. Dr. (Miami). *Expensive.*

COURT OF TWO DRAGONS
Japanese/Chinese

Choice of exotic Japanese and Chinese gourmet cuisines. A feast for the eyes and taste-buds. Japanese dining room is simply beautiful. Chinese dining room has romantic, canopied booths with beaded curtains. Overlooking Japanese garden in Sonesta Beach Hotel, Key Biscayne. *Expensive.*

EL BATURRO
Cuban/Spanish

It is no surprise that a fine Latin American/Spanish restaurant should exist in this center of Cuban expatriates, and this is the place. Interesting items dot an extensive menu, and the specialties are the paella and the sauteed red snapper. Music is live. 2322 N.W. 7th St. (Miami). *Moderate.*

PORT OF CALL
Seafood

The owners are fishermen themselves, and it is partially their own catch that graces the tables. The decor is nautical in the extreme, and the entire dining area is festooned with ship's rigging, nets, running lights, and mooring lines. The bouillabaisse is something special. 14411 Biscayne Blvd. (Miami). *Expensive.*

TAURUS STEAK HOUSE
Steak House

Located in scenic Coconut Grove, near the Playhouse, it is popular with theatergoers and just plain diners alike. Steaks are the prime attraction, and there is also a popular cocktail lounge. 3540 Main Highway (Miami). *Expensive.*

FONTAINEBLEAU HILTON
Continental

Dining Galleries in the Fontainebleau Hilton. Supreme elegance, sublime dishes—especially the stuffed pompano. Luncheon buffet. Lucullan Sunday brunch. *Expensive to Deluxe.*

Other recommended restaurants:

Miami

American International

Brasserie de Paris. *Expensive.* 244 Biscayne Blvd. Informal, yet classic French spot. Extensive gourmet menu; desserts superb. Some say this establishment has the style of a New York restaurant; for many it brings to mind memories of Paris in the spring.

Csarda. *Expensive.* 13885 Biscayne Blvd., N. Miami. Humdinger Hungarian specialties, some flamed at your table. Gypsy music 5-10 nightly, except Monday.

Chez Vendome. *Expensive.* David William Hotel, 700 Biltmore Way. Fine French cuisine in elegant surroundings. Strolling musicians serenade diners. Piano bar.

Cy's Rivergate. *Expensive.* 444 Brickell Ave. Stone crabs and seafood are extra special on the lengthy menu. Always crowded because of excellent reputation for food and service. Terrific drinks at the very friendly, long bar. Lunch, dinner, late supper.

The Depot. *Expensive.* 5830 S. Dixie Hwy. (US 1 South). Elaborate railroad décor, indlucing a dine-inside reproduction of Henry Flagler's swanky dining car. Award-winning specialties, prime rib, seafood. Menu printed on replica of Florida East Coast Railway timetable. Limo service and helicopter from airport but make arrangements in advance. Closed Mondays.

King Arthur's Court. *Expensive.* Miami Springs Hotel, 500 Deer Run, Miami Springs. Pleasant old English atmosphere. Music. Fine, well-aged beef and stone crabs are their specialty. Closed Labor Day, Christmas Eve. Jacket required.

Le Festival. *Expensive.* 2120 Salzedo St., Coral Gables. As the name suggests, the entire room is festive. True French cuisine in friendly atmosphere. From Clams St. Tropez to chocolate mousse cake, you can't go wrong.

Prince Hamlet. *Expensive.* 8301 Biscayne Blvd. Scandinavian food in a chalet-like atmosphere. The salmon is a treat and they have a wide selection of other dishes.

Tuttles. *Expensive.* Biscayne Blvd., off Julia Tuttle Causeway. In Charter Club condominium. Dazzling supper club and disco, where harpist plays softly. Strawberry soup and lobster Julia are specialties. Wide, comfy chairs; mirror-top tables.

Kaleidoscope. *Moderate to Expensive.* 3112 Commodore Plaza. Coconut Grove. At least 20 entrées on interesting menu. Delicious crepes filled with King crabmeat. Delightful garden patio atmosphere.

Les Violins. *Moderate to Expensive.* 1751 Biscayne Blvd. Dinner and show are a terrific combination. Lunch was served with entertainment this past season, so check on this good bargain.

Mike Gordon's Seafood Restaurant. *Moderate to Expensive.* On Biscayne Bay at 79th St. Causeway. Serving New England-style seafood for over 30 years, and local fish, too. Try the red snapper.

Dockside Terrace. *Moderate.* At Miamarina, in downtown Miami. Filet mignon, skewered shrimp and beef, and a variety of fish dishes, plus a lovely view of the city's night skyline.

English Pub. *Moderate.* 320 Crandon Blvd., Key Biscayne. A fantasy of tropical plants, relaxed dining. Open for lunch, dinner.

My Apartment. *Moderate.* Miami Springs Hotel. Filet mignon served at "cook-it-yourself" tables. Jacket required. 6 to midnight. Closed Sun.

94th Aero Squadron. *Moderate.* 1395 N.W. 57th Ave. Nr. Miami International Airport. World War I aviation memorabilia décor is unusual. Supersize margaritas. Bird of Paradise salad, quiche, steaks on varied menu. Lunch, dinner. Very popular.

Piccadilly Hearth. *Moderate.* 35 N.E. 40th St. A glamorous pub located on Decorator's Row. Excellent Continental fare.

Tony Roma's. *Inexpensive to Moderate.* Five locations around town serve lunch most of the day and half the night. Baby back ribs, juicy burgers, barbecued chicken.

Biscayne Cafeteria. *Inexpensive.* 147 Miracle Mile, Coral Gables. Usual cafeteria fare. Be prepared for a wait during the winter season.

Hofbrau Bar. *Inexpensive.* 172 Giralda. Tasty sandwiches, lots of atmosphere.

International House of Pancakes. *Inexpensive.* 8110 Biscayne Blvd. Main dishes, sandwiches and lots of pancakes. Open 24 hours. Twelve locations in Greater Miami.

Sally Russell's Part I. *Inexpensive.* 68 W. Flagler. Downtown opposite the Dade County Courthouse. A varied menu of meat and fish. Red snapper is a good choice. Open for lunch and dinner.

Italian

Raimondo. *Expensive.* 4612 S. LeJeune Rd. Try the zuppa di pesce alla Peppino or stuffed veal Dante. Special orders only by advance notice. Intimate. Closed New Year's, Easter, Thanksgiving, Christmas. No credit cards.

Stefano. *Expensive.* 24 Crandon Blvd., Key Biscayne. Great northern Italy veal dishes. View of outdoor garden. Music.

Sorrento. *Inexpensive.* 3059 S.W. 8th St. You don't have to be Cuban to have a restaurant on "Calle Ocho." Family-owned, casual. Lunch, dinner. The Florentine chicken is a favorite.

Latin American

Juanito's Centro Vasco. *Moderate.* 2235 S.W. 8th St. Charming and intimate. Among the Spanish specialties, seafood à la Basque is a favorite.

Minerva Spanish Restaurant. *Moderate.* 265 N.E. wnd St. Convenient location downtown. Popular long before Cuban refugees arrived. Lunch, dinner.

La Tasca. *Moderate.* 2741 W. Flagler. Another longtime favorite. Paella Valenciana and red snapper Cataloman rate raves. Nr. Dade County Auditorium.

Oscar's. *Moderate.* 901 S.W. 8th St. Delicious black bean soup, Colombian stews. Dance off any calories in Oscar's Latin Disco—open until dawn.

Oriental

Japanese Steak House. *Expensive.* Miami Springs Hotel. Patterned after Misono Steak House in Tokyo. Specially built tables with stoves in center turn out superior steak with Japanese vegetables. Chopsticks are the order, although forks are furnished upon request.

Tiger Tiger Teahouse. *Moderate.* 5716 S. Dixie Hwy. Mandarin, Shanghai and Mongolian dishes. Jin jo shrimp and cashew chicken are specialties.

Polynesian

Rusty Pelican. *Expensive.* Off Rickenbacker Causeway, nr. Key Biscayne. Very atmospheric. Open hearth cooking. Succulent Polynesian spareribs.

Miami Beach
American International

Doral Roof Garden. *Deluxe.* Doral Beach Hotel. Lush garden ambience high above Miami Beach. Gourmet seafood and continental specialties. Impeccable European-style service. Live harp music.

Lalique. *Deluxe.* In Sheraton Bal Harbour Hotel. Art Deco design. Extensive menu from "land, sea, and air"—culinary creations from around the world in elegant formal surroundings.

Embers. *Expensive.* 245 22nd St. Settle for duckling, stone crabs and homemade pastries. Jacket & tie for dinner.

The Forge. *Expensive.* 432 Arthur Godfrey Rd. Prime ribs & steak in an intimate 1890's room. Ornately decorated. Extensive wine list (1,000 choices!). Dinner only. Disco entertainment until dawn in lounge.

Ma Folie. *Expensive.* 1045 95th St. Bay Harbor Island. Romantic setting in Garden Room with waterfall. Terrace dining also. Turbot en courte and chicken Josephine among nicely prepared dishes. Soft piano music. Reservations. Dinner only.

New York Steak House. *Expensive.* 191st Street and Collins Ave. at the Chateau Hotel. Only hand-picked, aged prime steaks and 3–6-lb. Maine lobsters.

Sea View. *Expensive.* Oceanfront at 99th St., Bal Harbour. Superb continental cuisine, candlelight, excellent service. Chops, steaks, and seafood. One of finest hotel dining rooms around.

La Fontaine. *Moderate.* Bay Harbor. Continental cuisine in a mecca for prominent sports figures and writers.

Newport Pub. *Moderate.* 167th St. and Collins Ave. Steak, chicken, ribs and seafood in pleasant, informal surroundings.

Old Key West Fishing Village. *Moderate.* 18288 Collins Ave. Lots of atmosphere. Casual, friendly. Dinner only.

Roney Pub. *Moderate.* 23rd St. and Collins Ave. Same management as *Newport.* Very generous servings of roast beef.

Coco's. *Inexpensive.* 9700 Collins Ave. Bal Harbour. In classy shopping area. Delightful salads, soups, sandwiches, omelets, and super hamburger Americain. Luscious desserts, good house wines.

French

Dominique's. *Deluxe.* 5225 Collins Ave. Same owner as Washington, D.C.'s famous restaurant of same name. Unique, exotic fare. Delicacies from around world.

Le Parisien. *Deluxe.* 474 Arthur Godfrey Rd. Authentic French cuisine. National award winner with sole meuniere, frogs' legs provencale, among many specialties. Closed Sun., early fall. Reservations required.

Henri's. *Expensive.* In Konover Hotel. 5445 Collins Ave. Dining and dancing to a continental orchestra. Good scallopini of veal Française, salade Henri, Peach Melba. Dinner only.

Italian

Gatti's Restaurant. *Moderate.* 1427 West Ave. Continental food with Northern Italian accent. Chicken a la tetrazzini a specialty. Closed Mon. and May 1 to Nov. 1.

Jewish

Wolfie. *Moderate.* 2038 Collins Ave. Stuffed cabbage, cheesecake, corned beef, smoked whitefish.

Bagel Garden. *Inexpensive.* 12886 Biscayne Blvd. N. Miami. Breakfast, lunch, dinner and snacks until the wee hours.

Rascal House. *Inexpensive.* 17190 Collins Ave. "Wolfie" Cohen, creator of the Wolfie delicatessen restaurants satisfies thousands daily with overstuffed sandwiches and hearty full-course meals. From breakfast to a pre-dawn feast.

Middle East

Middle East Restaurant. *Moderate.* 1764 Coral Way. Pass the pita while enjoying the gyrations of the in-house exotic dancer. Shish-kebab dinners, too.

Natural Foods

The Garden. *Inexpensive.* 17 Westward Dr., Miami Springs. Excellent vegetable soup, stuffed clams, shrimp tempura, broiled locally caught fish sauced with lemon and herbs. Mixed vegetable salads, just-squeezed fruit and vegetable drinks.

The Spiral. *Inexpensive.* 1630 Ponce de Leon Blvd., Coral Gables. Only foods free of preservatives and naturally seasoned are served. Tempting desserts sweetened with honey, maple syrup.

Oriental

Benihana of Tokyo Steak House. *Expensive.* 1665 N. E. 79 St. Causeway. Japanese décor. Steak, chicken, seafood dramatically prepared by chef at hibachi table. Cocktails, lunch, dinner.

Christine Lee's Gaslight. *Expensive.* 18401 Collins Ave. In Thunderbird Motel. Lobster Cantonese in a subtle sauce is among the 36 Chinese entrées. Or compromise and order sliced broiled sirloin garnished with Chinese vegetables. A Mandarin Feast for 4 diners is memorable. Exotic décor. Cocktails. Dinner only. A live combo entertains nightly.

Toshi. *Expensive.* 5759 Bird Rd. Unpretentious. Sit on floor or at tables for delicious Japanese food and efficient service.

Canton. *Moderate.* 6661 S. Dixie. Chinese. Huge portions, dependable food, reasonable prices.

Fu Manchu. *Moderate.* 325 71st St. 40-year-old institution. Menu has 166 selections. Steak kew a popular dish. Intimate; good service. Noon–10:30 P.M.

Exploring Florida

US 1, forerunner of the superhighway which first made possible a motor trip from the Canadian border to the tip of Key West, resumes its dreams of glory as it crosses the St. Marys River and enters northeast Florida. Suddenly the road is wide and handsome—if not very high—and seems to rush through the piney woods toward Jacksonville, forty miles away.

Jacksonville, affectionately called Jax, is the first city you'll see in Florida after entering from Georgia via I-95. There's a soaring downtown, more than 30 miles of pristine beach communities to the east, and myriad historic sites. Moreover, the city has its own symphony orchestra, ballet troupes, opera companies, and so many theater groups you'll always have a full calendar.

Don't, as most visitors do, pass up this vibrant city, except in the dead of winter when you'll find bonnier temperatures in the Keys. Jax is bustling and a bargain bonanza.

A rewarding one-day adventure, including time for ocean bathing, can be had by examining the area and coast northeast of Jacksonville—an unlikely looking spot for history but one that has seen French-Spanish scuffling over squatters' rights in the New World, a pirate fleet, a flamboyant slave-runner, a short-lived "Republic of Florida," and capture of the strip of land by the United States Navy from its "Mexican" ruler.

From Jacksonville, either US 17 or Interstate 95, north, will take you to Heckscher Drive, just across the Trout River from downtown Jacksonville. Turn right onto Heckscher, stopping at the free Jacksonville Zoo if the children demand, then continue along the north bank of the St. Johns to Fort George.

Fort George Island's most colorful resident perhaps was Zephaniah Kingsley, a squat little Scotch slave trader who picked the island as headquarters for his business because it was still Spanish territory and he expected the United States to forbid slave imports. The U.S.A. did just that in 1807, but Kingsley was already in action. He had expanded his operation into a combination plantation and training school for slaves by the time the U.S.A. acquired Florida from Spain in 1821. His activities then became illegal, of course, but more profitable as well.

Kingsley married the daughter of an African East Coast king, and she—as Ma'm Anna—oversaw the training of the slaves. Her full name was Anna Madegigine Jai, and she remained Kingsley's favorite despite his propensity for spotting other comely companions among the slave cargo.

The Kingsley plantation buildings are preserved in a state historical memorial and may be seen by taking a paved but unnumbered road from Fort George. The trip takes only a few minutes.

Heckscher Drive continues from Fort George to Little Talbot Island State Park, directly on the ocean, and here's the first chance for that swim. (There'll be another at Fernandina Beach.) On the island, your road becomes A1A and continues north, ending temporarily at Nassau Sound where a ferry will take you across to Amelia Island, named for Princess Amelia, sister of England's George II, by Oglethorpe in 1735.

At the north end of Amelia Island is Fernandina, named for Don Domingo Fernandez, who was given a huge tract of land by the Spanish government in 1783, when Florida was returned to Spain by the English after the success of the American Revolution. Spain had ceded Florida to England in 1763, and during the Revolution Florida remained loyal to the crown. Many loyalists from the colonies in the north fled to Amelia Island, eventually making a total of 16,000. All but a handful emigrated to the Bahamas, West Indies, and Nova Scotia when American independence came and the territory was ceded back to Spain by England.

Just across the American border, Fernandina became a haven for pirates, smugglers, and hijackers, and Highway A1A along the length of the island is called "The Buccaneer Trail."

The Republic of Florida

Shortly before the War of 1812, a band of two hundred Americans crossed the St. Marys from Georgia and captured Spain's Fort San Carlos, north of Fernandina, proclaiming a "Republic of Florida." The action had the actual support of the U.S. government, but failed after President Madison yielded to strong objections from the English and Spanish ministers. Spain regained possession, but weakened by an impending war with Napoleon, could do little to prevent the island from being usurped by one adventurer after another.

Gregor McGregor, another Scotsman, arrived with five ships and accepted the surrender of the Spanish in 1817, but left again when other Spaniards in Florida joined forces to do battle. Then Jared Irwin, a former Pennsylvania Congressman took over, recruited some help from the pirates who populated the port, and routed the Spanish again. But another pirate, Luis Aury, arrived with a superior force and claimed the island. He did allow Irwin to remain as "adjutant general," however. Aury, who had been governor of Texas under Mexican rule, raised the Mexican flag and declared the island "annexed" to the Republic of Mexico. The United States moved to break up such free-lance government when it sent the navy in and took possession "in trust" for Spain. Four years later, in 1821, the United States had all of Florida.

After all that, it would seem Amelia Island was past the point of fortification, but work began in 1847 on Fort Clinch, named after Gen. Duncan Lamont Clinch. However, the fort was neither finished nor equipped by the time the Civil War broke out and the Confederates, who quickly moved in, had to try to finish the job. The Third Florida Volunteers occupied the fort until 1862 when a strong Union Army force approached. The Northern forces kept Fort Clinch throughout the rest of the war.

Used briefly during the Spanish-American war, the fort was almost abandoned; but after being acquired by the city of Fernandina and the State for a park in 1935, it was used again during World War II for radar and Coast Guard details.

Today, the fort makes a pleasant sightseeing and picnicking spot. There are trails and camping areas, a lodge and a boat ramp. South of the Fort, at Fernandina Beach, is one of the finest bathing beaches anywhere, some fourteen miles long. At times, cars may be driven over the packed sands, depending on the tides.

To return to Jacksonville, you can either retrace your route, or, for a faster trip, take State 200 east to Yulee, then US 17 south to the city. Another option is to return south on A1A to catch the ferry that crosses the St. Johns to Jacksonville Beach on the south shore of the river.

South of Jacksonville

Inland, the St. Johns River wends its way north (one of the few anywhere to do so), offering a freshwater fishing paradise more than eighty miles long. US 17, south, skirts the western shore of the river and its by-product of lakes for much of the way. Along the route are some once-fashionable and still colorful resort towns. Green Cove Springs, for instance, was the stopping place for President Grover Cleveland back in the late 1880's when steamers from Charleston and Savannah came up the St. Johns to the spa. J. C. Penney of the chain stores and Gail Borden, condensed milk mogul, were regulars.

Palatka, twenty-seven more miles south, was also a popular tourist resort right after the Civil War, and one of the fancy hotels put its imagination to work Madison Avenue-style by listing on its menu "adolescent chicken."

The fisherman's route can be followed all the way to De Land, a pleasant college town (Stetson University) another fifty miles or so south, or a fairly quick connecting trip back to US 1 or A1A and the coast can be made at several points.

But for general touring the first southern stop should be at rustic, realistic Fort Caroline, just east of Jacksonville. The national monument is also on the way to St. Augustine, if you take the Jacksonville Expressway east out of the city to State 10 and follow the markers to the fort, directly across the river from the first day's northshore trip to Fort George.

The actual site of the original fort no longer exists, having been washed away after the river channel was deepened in the late nineteenth century. But the National Park Service has reconstructed the walls of the triangular fort, following a sketch by Jacques LeMoyne, artist and mapmaker for the Huguenot colony. On an overlook 110 feet above the river stands the Ribaut monument.

Returning to State 10, head east again to reach the ocean beaches, then turn south on A1A. Jacksonville Beach has thousands of guest accommodations, and, along with coastal cities southward for two hundred miles, actually it is more a summer resort for inland Southerners than a winter warming spot for chilled Northerners. The chill can be felt here, too, in the winter months.

A few miles of semicommercial congestion gives way to a relatively sparse assortment of beach houses and dunes south of Jacksonville Beach. First, though, there is sumptuous Sawgrass, a plush resort and inn, plus oceanfront cottages, a nationally famous golf course, tennis, a superb beach, and great restaurants.

Oldest City

An abrupt right turn, and A1A rejoins the mainland. Just as abruptly, you are in St. Augustine, the nation's oldest city, with history dripping from every overhanging balcony. For this, you'll need some time . . . and a guide book, for volumes have been done about this antique treasure without fully covering the subject. Recommended is *St. Augustine's Historical Heritage*, a publication of the St. Augustine Historical Society. There are numerous illustrations, an excellent map, and a well-written text. Try the information center on Castillo Drive as you near the city gates.

St. Augustine celebrated its 400th anniversary in 1964, but its fifth century should prove a lively one without getting too far away from the pageantry of the past. In midsummer a festival called Days of Spain has inhabitants out sword fighting (rather bloodlessly) in the streets. Along St. Geroge St.—in the evening—musicians and dancers cast spells. The *New York Times* has said that St. George St. "is losing all resemblance

to a modern street." That's about right. No light poles—lanterns from Seville light the way.

Another drama, with the traditional cast of thousands, can run concurrently in your mind as you walk (or ride in horse-drawn surreys) through the narrow streets, and see the restored area where eighteenth-century Spanish colonial houses are exhibited in a living-history atmosphere.

From the First Spanish period, the mission of Nombre de Dios, founded on the same day as the city when Father Francisco Lopez Mendoza Grajales stepped ashore with Don Pedro Menendez de Aviles and became the first parish priest of a nation-to-be. And at the mission, the Shrine of Nuestra Senora de la Leche, a tiny jewel of a chapel, coquina rock covered with ivy, as appealingly antique as any Old World shrine anywhere but actually built in 1918, following the design of the original.

Or The Cathedral of St. Augustine—from the second Spanish period —completed in 1797, restored after a fire in 1887; the Llambias House— English period—once owned by T. Llambias who was a member of the Minorcan colony brought to Florida by Dr. Andrew Turnbull to settle a grant at what he called New Smyrna, seventy miles south. Today, the house is called the Prince Murat House, after Napoleon Bonaparte's nephew who lived there. Ralph Waldo Emerson was a guest in 1827.

And the St. Francis Inn, once known as the Dummitt House, headquarters for Civil War spies, before that a jail just after Florida became a U.S. territory, before that a barracks for English soldiers . . . and before that the first church of the Franciscans, in 1577.

So it is an old town. With an Old Jail, an Oldest House, Oldest Schoolhouse, Oldest Store . . . and quite rightly for Florida, the oldest alligator exhibition, at the St. Augustine Alligator Farm founded in 1893.

But some new things, too. New motels, new attractions with a wide spectrum of taste displayed in both.

Among the new might be considered Castillo de San Marcos, the quadrangular, moated fortress just opposite the old city gates, for the Castillo isn't finished yet. It has been a national monument since 1924, and it now is being improved by restoration of some of the inside rooms together with the reconstruction of the Cubo Line, the ancient town wall which extended from the Castillo to the San Sebastian River.

FLORIDA

GEORGIA

St. Mary's R.

ATLANTIC OCEAN

Jacksonville

10

30

St. John's R.

St. Augustine

Gainesville

Ocala

40

Daytona Beach

95

19

75

Titusville

JOHN F. KENNEDY
SPACE CENTER
Cape Canaveral

Walt Disney
World

Orlando

Meritt Island

4

Melbourne

Tarpon Springs

Clearwater

Tampa

St. Petersburg

Tampa Bay

27

Fort Pierce

Sarasota

70

95

Venice

75

Lake
Okeechobee

1

Palm Beach

80

West Palm Beach

Cape Coral

Fort Myers

27

Boca Raton

Naples

84

41

Big
Cypress
Natl. Preserve

Fort Lauderdale

**Miami
Beach**

Miami

Biscayne
Bay

*EVERGLADES
NATIONAL PARK*

Cape Sable

Florida Bay

0   50

Miles

1   Florida Keys

Key West

Some 19th-Century Grandeur
St. Augustine is also the homesite of the fabled Ponce de Leon Hotel, now a college. Built by Henry Flagler in 1889 to house the nation's rich and famous as they helped him, and his railroad, establish St. Augustine as a *ne plus ultra* winter resort, it was a wondrous place.

South from St. Augustine into the newer Florida. Route A1A is the more scenic, and after a splash of modernity and neon along St. Augustine Beach, there's a souvenir reminder of the old city again, fourteen miles south at Matanzas Inlet. It was here that Menendez caught up with Jean Ribaut's hapless French fleet, which had sailed out of Fort Caroline to attack the Spanish, only to be caught in a hurricane while Don Pedro wiped out the fort by land assault. Helpless on the sands, the four hundred French were slaughtered in the cruel fashion of that time to give the inlet its name, Matanzas (slaughter).

The stone fort, built at the inlet in 1742 to protect the inland waterway approach to St. Augustine, is a national monument and a park ranger will give you information during the daily visiting hours of 8:30 A.M. to 5:00 P.M.

The Ormond-Daytona Complex
Only a couple of miles south is Marineland, a scientific, commercial, and interesting attraction presenting displays of marine specimens, porpoise acts, a performing whale, and below-the-water viewing ports of the ocean's creatures, some bizarre, some brilliantly colored. There are two restaurants and a razzle-dazzle new playground for the kids.

Half an hour more on A1A will put you in the first of the major tourist-oriented resorts on this route—the Ormond Beach-Daytona Beach complex, geared almost totally to entertainment of the fun-seeking tourists. If the automobile isn't king here, it is at least the royal godfather.

From Daytona Beach, it is sixty miles to Cape Canaveral directly down the coast along US 1, or it is sixty miles to Orlando, a bustling but attractive interior city which can be reached quickly by car via Interstate Highway 4, which cuts all the way across the state to St. Petersburg.

You may wish to sample some of Florida's inland lake country. Interstate 4 skirts past the towns of De Land and Sanford, but you will see some rich citrus and farm land, dotted by lakes. This is a ridge section dividing the state: the watershed flows north through the St. Johns; south by the Kissimmee River to Lake Okeechobee and the Everglades.

Around Orlando
Orlando was settled, after the Seminole Wars, by former volunteers who decided to stay with the land after the withdrawal of the regular army. Later, new blood was added by English settlers who bought land from the state and railroad interests for as little as $1 an acre. They came to grow citrus, but they also brought a way of life with them, and many built tennis courts and played cricket. They had organized a polo team by 1884. In 1975, Orlando celebrated its 100th birthday.

More than half the citrus growers abandoned their groves after a devastating freeze hit the trees in 1895, but many remained to rebuild or to take up new occupations. For many years Orlando, with its well-

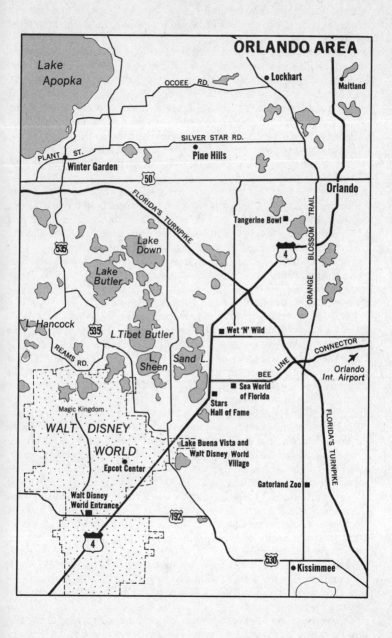

ORLANDO AREA

Lake Apopka

OCOEE RD.

● Lockhart

■ Maitland

SILVER STAR RD.

PLANT ST.

Winter Garden

● Pine Hills

50

Orlando

FLORIDA'S TURNPIKE

Tangerine Bowl ■

535

Lake Down

Lake Butler

4

BLOSSOM TRAIL

ORANGE

L. Hancock

535

L. Tibet Butler

REAMS RD.

L. Sheen

Sand L.

■ Wet 'N' Wild

BEE LINE

CONNECTOR

Orlando Int. Airport

■ Sea World of Florida

■ Stars Hall of Fame

Magic Kingdom

WALT DISNEY WORLD

● Epcot Center

Lake Buena Vista and Walt Disney World Village

Gatorland Zoo ■

FLORIDA'S TURNPIKE

Walt Disney World Entrance

192

4

530

● Kissimmee

ordered beauty, was a favorite winter vacation and retirement center for middle-aged or older people who found its climate, location, and atmosphere "just right."

Today, Orlando is having a hard time retaining that old atmosphere. As soon as the Space Age began, a booster was ignited under the city. Cape Canaveral is only sixty-five miles away, and Orlando qualifies as the nearest—or only—semilarge city within handy distance. Some 3,000 people a day commute to the Cape, and more than 4,000 work at the Glenn L. Martin Company's twenty-two-building plant on the outskirts.

Because of its location amidst the state's main and best highways, Orlando is an excellent hub for one-day touring in almost any direction. (A hotel/motel explosion since Disney World has added 20,000 new rooms.)

Twenty miles south, for instance, on four-laned US 17, is Kissimmee, and its sister city St. Cloud, now the heart of hotel-land for the Disney complex. Plenty of bargain rooms, many of them under $30 a night, and plenty to do when you tire of theme parks. This is bass country, and the fresh-water lakes also offer swimming, waterskiing, and boating.

There's Gatorland with endless walking trails, the Tupperware Museum with its collections of historic food containers, and lively livestock markets on Wednesdays. February and July, take in the Silver Spurs Rodeo. It's the state's oldest and largest.

Of course anyone who is in the Orlando area will want to visit Walt Disney's Magic Kingdom, which is as much a part of the Space Age as Cape Canaveral. You can spend a day or a week and still not see everything the Magic Kingdom has to offer. New in 1982 was EPCOT, a tomorrow-land that needs another day or two to explore. Located on US 192, just west of Interstate 4, Walt Disney World offers golf, boating, swimming, camping, hiking, waterskiing, horseback riding, canoeing, and night life as well as the thrills and excitements of the theme park. About a five-minute drive away, the almost 200 acres of Sea World also entice the visitor. Shamu, the star killer-whale, performs with porpoises, penguins, and mermaids. The Japanese Village, Hawaiian Village, waterski shows with Batman and Wonder Woman, and the Atlantis Theater all add to the excitement.

North of Orlando, within an hour's time, via US 441 to Eustis, then State 19, is the outdoorsman's jackpot: Ocala National Forest. There are thirty-one varied recreation areas within the forest's 362,000 acres of lakes and rolling hills, offering swimming, camping, trailer sites, fishing, and scenery by the mile.

In fact, there are sixty-five miles without a stoplight on State 19, which offers a north-south "vistaway" all the way from Palatka, north of the forest. Another state road, 40, is east-west and crosses 19 in the middle of the forest.

Two favorite spots in the forest are Alexander Springs, near the southern entrance, and Juniper Springs, near the crossroads. Alexander Springs bubble up a torrent of 76 million gallons of 74-degree water every day of the year, and there's a white sand beach, picnic area, refreshments, a bathhouse, boats for rent, nature trails and nearby camping and trailer sites, equipped with electricity, water, and sewers.

Juniper Springs offers the same, basically, but in addition there's a thirteen-mile (downstream) canoe rental trip available. One can just laze along, drifting through a subtropical forest, until reaching a waterway park back beside State 19. The Forest Service people take the canoe back by trailer.

Whenever you're ready, the return to Orlando can be made by taking either State 40 or 42 east to US 17, then south to get back on Interstate 4.

The final leg of the northeast-Florida tour takes you back to a history-laden coastline, but this time the history is only years old, instead of centuries, and could be as current as today's breakfast.

Missile Land

Cape Canaveral, the Merritt Island moon-launch site, Patrick Air Force Base Missile Test Center—all the jumping-off places for our epochal strides into space—are aligned along a forty-mile strip of until recently deserted sandpits. Mainland villages just a few years ago—Titusville on the north, Melbourne on the south, Cocoa in the center—pulsated with the excitement of heart-stopping suspense as giant, flame-spitting cylinders carried live men to the moon.

From Orlando, for instance, State 50, east, will take you twenty four-laned miles to a junction: south of State 520 for Cocoa and Cocoa Beach, or straight ahead on 50 for Titusville.

If there's no blast-off scheduled, you can tour the main launching area for the Atlantic Missile Range and the place from which astronauts are shot into space, and/or NASA's moon-launch area on Merritt Island. The only authorized guided tours of the area are Kennedy Space Center (KSC) Tours, operated and conducted by TWA Services, Inc. Tours depart regularly throughout the day from the Visitors Information Center from 8 A.M. until two hours before sunset. However, due to operational activity at the space center, the tours are subject to change. Because the VAB (Vertical Assembly Building) has been closed for future missile operations, everything is now concentrated in the Visitors Information Center, where all is free, including a series of fascinating movies. The KSC Tours are operating, too, of course. Handicapped persons may ask, a week in advance, for a guide at no extra charge to take them on the tour in their own car.

On Sundays you can drive your own car around Cape Canaveral Air Force Station, at no charge. Sometimes there are restrictions for the Sunday-only self-drive tours, due to the activity of the Space Shuttle program. It doesn't affect the KSC Tours or the Visitors Center. You can check ahead with Patrick Air Force Base, or from anywhere in Florida, you can call this toll-free number for information: (800) 432-2153. It operates 24 hours a day and also has information about upcoming launches from the Space Center. The Air Force Space Museum, with a display of 30 rockets, is near the south gate of KSC.

Before you leave the Cocoa Beach-Sebastian Inlet area and you like to fish, anglers report that fishing is "the hottest" here in the coldest months. Best surf-fishing includes bluefish and redfish. Or you can troll offshore for dolphin, king mackerel and sailfish. From the piers, you can fish for snook, flounder, whiting. Fishermen-in-the-know claim this is "the saltwater trout capital of the world."

In whatever manner you choose to visit this historic site, be sure to stop at the Visitors Information Center, located at the space center, six miles east of US 1, south of Titusville, which has splendid free exhibits, movies and detailed lectures on the space program.

For those who can't take the weekend tours, there's a display of missiles at Patrick Air Force Base, reached by A1A just south of Cocoa Beach.

Gold Coast Beaches

The first faint reflections of South Florida's Gold Coast show up slowly, then in a tumbling cascade as you proceed south from Melbourne along the south central coast. Included in the 120-mile strip to the Broward County line, just south of Addison Mizner's storied Boca Raton, are brand new oceanfront resorts, older fishing villages only barely retaining their quaintness, the great millionaires' playground of Palm Beach with its brawnier big brother, West Palm Beach, and a skinny megalopolis of side-by-seaside municipalities made up of motels, restaurants, shuffleboard courts and the almost unending beach.

But more, too. Giant jet engines are built at Pratt & Whitney's sprawling plant inland from West Palm Beach. The nation's winter vegetables spring from the rich black muckland surrounding Lake Okeechobee. Sugar mills send giant stacks upward to process tens of thousands of tons of cane daily. And the cowboys are Indians on the Brighton Reservation ranch.

Stick with A1A south from Melbourne for a relaxing drive. On the east will be the rolling surf of the Atlantic; on the west the Indian River. Pelican Island, a National wildlife refuge established by President Theodore Roosevelt in 1903, is washed over daily by the tides in the river, but thousands of pelicans are hatched here annually.

Sports fishing and agriculture offer both substance and diversion in the towns of Vero Beach, Fort Pierce, and Stuart. This is Indian River citrus country, yielding some of the state's tastiest oranges and grapefruit. Citrus packing houses are open for visitors from October through May. With luck, in one of the three towns you may be able to locate a glass of fresh orange juice, rather than the frozen concentrate sort.

But there'll be no trouble finding a place to fish. Offshore, the sailfish is much sought after—and found—by charter craft, while bay waters provide snook, channel bass, pompano, and sea trout. Freshwater catches are numerous and weighty in the St. Lucie River, which joins the ocean at Stuart.

Bridges and piers offer the pedestrian angler his chance, and Fort Pierce provides especially constructed balconies on either side of the bridge spanning the Indian River.

On the ocean at Vero Beach stands the well-nigh unbelievable Driftwood Inn, a rambling, unpainted conglomeration that has been variously described as "Florida's Most Fabulous Hostelry," and "The Junkpile by the Sea" in national publications. The late Waldo Sexton, owner, architect and scavenger, furnished the place with an unbelievable array of cast-offs, pickups, float-ins, and exotic bric-a-brac from everywhere. Sexton bought much of the leftover furnishings Addison Mizner had brought over from Europe for Palm Beach mansions, getting the discount price when the boom's bust halted construction. And he added to the collection thirty years later when many of the Palm Beach mansions that had been built were razed to escape taxes.

And at Jensen Beach, a tiny tongue of land between the St. Lucie and Indian River just east of Stuart, there's Frances Langford's Outrigger restaurant, plus villas and a yacht basin. You may remember Frances as the blond singer who spent a lot of World War II and the Korean War entertaining troops around the world.

The yacht basin, in case you're interested, can handle any craft up to 120 feet long. New in 1978, the luxurious Indian River Plantation Resort flaunts a challenging 18-hole golf course and 11 tennis courts, beautiful villas and restaurants. If you catch a fish, the chef will prepare it for free for your lunch or dinner in the Porch restaurant.

Directly east of Jensen Beach is Hutchinson Island, with protected beaches which offer the spectator sport of watching giant sea turtles, usually loggerheads, come ashore during the summer months to lay their eggs. Weighing up to two hundred pounds, the mother-to-be waddles up on the beach, usually at night, and starts digging a hole in the sand. Her flippers scoop out sand as far as she can reach, then she begins laying the eggs—pingpong ball sized. Her eyes begin to water as the count increases—she may lay up to 150—and some see the giant tears as indications of pain. Others suspect the digging has gotten sand in her eyes. She waddles back to the sea after covering the eggs, which hatch into baby turtles if they're lucky.

The turtles don't mind human witnesses, but turtle eggs are considered a delicacy by some and there are fines of $200 or more for disturbing the nests. Raccoons, however, have no respect for the law and devour up to ninety percent of the eggs. At the House of Refuge museum on Hutchinson Island a sea turtle hatchery rescues the eggs and protects them until birth. Green turtles, much desired for green turtle soup, once were numerous here, but diminished as human appetites grew. Now the nursery imports infant green turtles from Costa Rica in an effort to reestablish the species in this area.

The House of Refuge, however, wasn't originally established for the protection of turtles, but to give aid to shipwrecked sailors. It's now a museum, open daily for a token fee.

The Elliott Museum, nearby, is devoted to the evolution of wheeled vehicles and to examples of business shops near the turn of the century.

Superstar Burt Reynolds opened the Burt Reynolds Dinner Theater in Jupiter, his hometown, early 1979 and that, too, is attracting national attention.

Upper-Crust Palm Beach

The change won't be noticeable for a spell, but, after you cross the St. Lucie inlet proceeding south, you are in a very ritzy neighborhood. So ritzy, in fact, that the part-time residents of the Hobe Sound colony over on Jupiter Island consider Palm Beach a bit "gaudy."

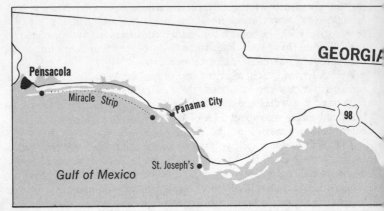

Don't bother taking a look, for Hobe Sound likes privacy. You can't see anything except high shrubs hiding estates. Roads, parks and even a post office have been fought off in the pursuit of nontourism.

It's more neighborly on Jupiter's south end, where the fishy Loxahatchee River snakes past the 106-year-old red brick Jupiter lighthouse. South into Palm Beach Country on A1A there's a nice view from atop an oceanside dune near Juno Beach.

Mr. Flagler's Dream Come True

To get to Palm Beach, you go to West Palm Beach, and that's just the way Henry Flagler wanted it. Palm Beach is an island, with Lake Worth giving it stylish distance from the mainland. Flagler saw the island in 1893, some fifteen years after a Spanish bark loaded with coconuts and wine went aground and broke up. The coconuts floated up on the beach, as did the wine-soaked crew, and before long the island had a new profile, with graceful coconut fronds undulating in the sea breezes.

The best was good enough for Philadelphia's Wideners, Stotesburys, and Wanamakers, who were early samplers, and spurred by such social acceptance Palm Beach was on its way, via Flagler's railroad, of course.

So was West Palm Beach, the town Flagler built for his "help," who would build and run the resort. There was no bridge connection with the eighteen-mile-long island back then, and for years no automobiles were allowed in Palm Beach.

Many of the great mansions—for example Mrs. E. L. Stotesbury's El Mirasol and Mrs. Horace Dodge's Playa Reinta—are gone now, victims of another age . . . and another tax scale. But the Via Mizner remains: a tiny, Old World shopping alley with some of the world's most fashionable—and expensive—goods. And the Everglades Club is still there (members only). And up on North County Road, behind a high wall, is the oceanfront villa where a young John Kennedy frolicked on the beach . . . and where he spent the last weekend of his life as President of the United States.

West Palm Beach, the city Flagler built for his help, has helped itself as well, and now is comfortably supported by a three-way economy: tourism, agriculture, and industry. Pratt & Whitney's research and development center is a bit outside the city limits, it's true, but the impact

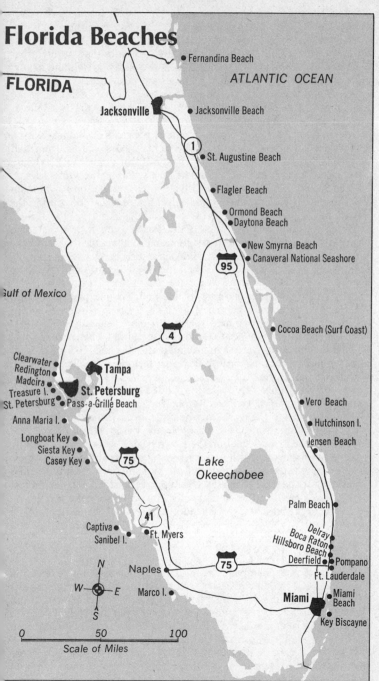

Florida Beaches

FLORIDA

ATLANTIC OCEAN

- Fernandina Beach
- **Jacksonville**
- Jacksonville Beach
- ① St. Augustine Beach
- Flagler Beach
- Ormond Beach
- Daytona Beach
- New Smyrna Beach
- Canaveral National Seashore
- 95
- 4
- Cocoa Beach (Surf Coast)

Gulf of Mexico

- Clearwater
- Redington
- Madeira
- Treasure I.
- St. Petersburg
- Pass-a-Grille Beach
- **Tampa**
- **St. Petersburg**
- Anna Maria I.
- Longboat Key
- Siesta Key
- Casey Key
- 75

- Vero Beach
- Hutchinson I.
- Jensen Beach

Lake Okeechobee

- Palm Beach

- Captiva
- Sanibel I.
- Ft. Myers
- 41

- Delray
- Boca Raton
- Hillsboro Beach
- Deerfield
- Pompano
- Ft. Lauderdale

- Naples
- 75
- Marco I.
- **Miami**
- Miami Beach
- Key Biscayne

N
W — E
S

0   50   100
Scale of Miles

is felt in downtown dollars. Minneapolis Honeywell, International Telephone and Telegraph, and RCA are closer in and near the airport.

The weather helps the resort trade perhaps a bit more here in winter, for the warming Gulf Stream comes closer to shore than at any other mainland Florida point. There are diversions aplenty: greyhound racing, polo, jai alai, fishing, a number of important boat races.

West Palm Beach may also be said to have the closest thing to casino gambling—the Lucayan Beach casino at Freeport in the Bahamas is directly east and only minutes away from the West Palm airport.

The area lacks not for cultural pursuits, either. West Palm's Norton Gallery has an almost priceless collection of jades, plus current and permanent art works. In Palm Beach, the Royal Poinciana Playhouse offers direct-from-Broadway legitimate theatre during the winter season, and the Society of the Four Arts with a garden entrance on Royal Palm Way has an art gallery, library, and film theatre. This, too, during the winter only.

Strung together south of West Palm Beach, each with a mainland business section and an offshore island beachfront, are the towns of Lake Worth, Lantana, Boynton Beach, and Delray Beach. All have everything Palm Beach has, except perhaps the ratio of millionaires and the flossy history.

Boca Raton, however, is next in line and has had plenty of both. Although the name came from a Spanish phrase, *boca de ratones,* meaning mouth of the sharp-pointed rocks, it is more generally agreed that Boca Raton means rat's mouth. And that sounds a lot better than some of the things investors were saying about it after the mid-'10's boom went blooey (among them, according to resort historian Cleveland Amory, was "Beaucoup Rotten").

The top-rated polo players in the United States play every Sunday, January through April, in Boca Raton. The only other polo teams with higher-rated men in the world are the Argentines. Prince Phillip's team in England is in the same class, but the fact is, the boys from Boca Raton have beaten the Prince's best on their own field. Polo is growing rapidly as a spectator sport, but still preserves vestiges of its aristocratic origins. Most of the players are members of old and still very wealthy families who can afford a stable of ponies. (Each player must have six ponies just to play one game.) And be careful when you order two cold ones as you are sitting in the bleachers—the vendor sells splits of champagne as well as beer.

The Lake of Plenty

From pâté and champagne to meat and potatoes—not to mention sugar, beans, corn, lettuce, celery, and twenty-six other vegetables—it's only about an hour's drive into the rich Lake Okeechobee area. From West Palm Beach, US 98 and 441 will deliver you into Belle Glade on the southeastern corner of the 730-square-mile lake, second largest fresh water body wholly within the United States.

It's worth the trip, especially during the winter growing season. More than 30,000 railroad carloads of vegetables are shipped each season from Belle Glade to frosty but hungry Northerners—and occasionally, Californians. In addition, there are lush grasslands by the hundreds of thousands of acres to support a growing cattle industry, including the Brighton Seminole Indian Reservation's 35,000 acres which will eventually field a herd of 44,000 cattle.

The secret of this whole area's success is the lake, which really was more of a swamp until the Herbert Hoover Dike was built along the southern edge beginning in 1930. The sixty-six-mile-long dike, plus a network of canals and pumping stations, make possible the water control that is the key to agricultural success. It also makes possible a cross-state canal from Stuart on the East Coast to Fort Myers on the West Coast. Belle Glade, Clewiston, Pahokee, South Bay, and the other towns around the edge are actually often below the level of the lake's waters.

Sports fishing is a primary diversion, and the lake, although rarely more than six or eight feet deep, is a contender for the best-fishing-in-America title. Guides and boats are available.

There has been a vast increase in the amount of sugar production in this area since 1959, when Castro came to power in Cuba, but the state had its first commercial sugar operation in 1767 at the Minorcan colony in New Smyrna. Present sugar operations in the Lake Okeechobee region began about 1923, and today there are eleven sugar mills serving a cane growing area of almost a quarter of a million acres. Half a million tons of sugar are produced each year.

As the oldest and largest sugar firm, U.S. Sugar Corp. laid out the town of Clewiston with an eye to spaciousness. And it also built and operates the Clewiston Inn, which has a dependably good hotel and restaurant. After all, that's where the company's executives stay when they come to town.

To return to the coast and your first glimpse of the golden tip of Florida, you can return to West Palm Beach on US 441, or angle south on US 27, then branch off east on State 84 to Fort Lauderdale.

The Golden Tip

Fort Lauderdale is not the Venice of America, despite its occasional use of this Chamber of Commerce slogan. Venice should be so lucky.

There are inland waterways—165 miles of them—but they connect areas of subdued prosperity rather than decaying grandeur. Here there are no waterlogged tenements, but manicured fingers of land, spread to let the warm blue waters lick along bulkheaded back yards.

The fortunate residents—some with an old automobile out front and a rowboat in back, others with two cars and a yacht—are pretty well-equipped to go anywhere they want. Many already have, for Fort Lauderdale is the home of a colony of the world's wealthy who have traveled near and far and have decided that this is a congenial place for their retirement years.

In Florida, a man of vision is one who turns out to be right sooner or later. Many dreamy developers who put in wide, concrete sidewalks through scrub pine woods to accommodate the "proposed" shopping center are long forgotten, for only the sidewalks ever came. But Fort Lauderdale's men of vision somehow saw that the city should have lots of clear, uncluttered beach and that there should be protected waters for the yachts.

In the case of the beach, the acquisitive city commissioners, who kept adding little chunks until there were six miles of it, were proved right when adjacent communities allowed hotels, motels, restaurants, and what-have-you directly on the oceanfront, shutting off public access.

Once, there seemed plenty of beach to go around, and the concessions to attract hotels and business may have seemed sensible, perhaps even visionary. But now, of course, Fort Lauderdale has been proved right and profits greatly because the hotels, apartments, shops, and the like are across a wide boulevard from the public's sands.

From US 1, you can get to where the boys were for several springtimes during the college vacation madness by taking one of three routes. On the north is Sunrise Boulevard, which connects with oceanfront A1A at the south edge of Birch Park; in the center is Las Olas Boulevard, and on the south S.E. 17th Street, which becomes Brook Memorial Causeway —locally called the 17th St. Causeway.

East Las Olas offers a fashionable shopping and browsing area from Federal Highway to 12th Avenue. Resort clothing is sold in branch stores of firms that operate in the summer in other resorts such as Nantucket and Blowing Rock. Grillwork, shutters, and a restrained use of signs give a pleasant air and there's even a French-style sidewalk cafe. Galleries, a museum, ballet studio, and plush furnishings shops add to the cultural effect.

Other noteworthy shopping areas are on North Federal Highway near Oakland Park Blvd. (which also will take you to the beach and a sumptuous hotel and high-rise apartment area) and a large, modern shopping center on Sunrise Blvd.

The 17th Street Causeway on the south offers a good view of Port Everglades, which is a port of call for many cruise ships as well as freighters. Alongside this causeway is Pier 66, an elaborate marina, restaurant-motel complex, and, just as the beachfront is reached, there is the world-famed Bahia Mar Marina and Resort.

After exploring Miami, head south to the Everglades National Park, some of the world's most productive farm land and the Florida Keys.

Bus tours are conducted both to the park and to Key West, and the Audubon Society conducts one- and two-day trips through parts of both, starting in Miami. If you prefer to drive, you can take old reliable US 1 south from Miami some twenty-five miles to Florida City and turn west on State 27. Ten more miles will put you at the Everglades Park entrance, connecting with the park's thirty-seven-mile road which ends at Flamingo at the southern tip of the park.

Tip: You can avoid much US 1 congestion in Miami by taking Old Cutler Road south until it rejoins US 1. Turn east from US 1 at LeJeune Road, which is 42nd Avenue, and keep going. You can stop at Fairchild Tropical Garden along the way and browse among the nation's largest collection of tropical plants. An estate area of fine homes and vegetable farms is also along this route.

The Everglades

The beauty of Everglades National Park escapes some people, but it wouldn't if they'd shift mental gears and slow down enough to really look at it. There are more than two thousand square miles in the park,

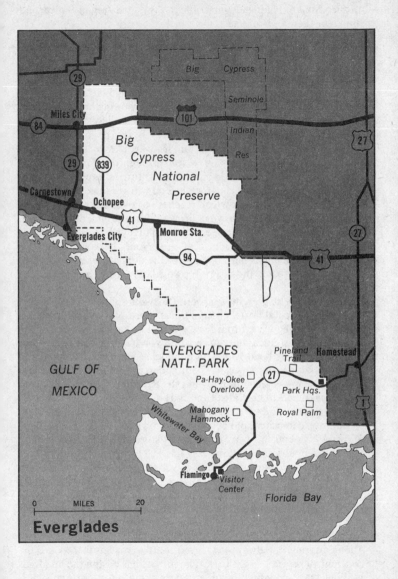

Everglades

making it the nation's third largest. At first, there seems a sameness, a monotony to the landscape. But the sameness isn't actual. There are subtle blendings of plant and animal life in cycles that began, ended, and began again thousands of years ago.

Near the park entrance, at the Royal Palm Hammock visitors' center, Park Rangers can tell you what to look for as you progress—and can show you what is there through exhibits and color movies. But the vastness, the variety, the shadings do not appear in miniature representations. You can only see them in their larger-than-life actuality.

Branching off from the main road are various viewing areas and trails which sample the complexity of the Everglades. Pa-hay-okee overlook is elevated to give you the perspective of a sea-of-grass panorama stretching endless miles. Gumbo Limbo trail leads you through a tropical density where you can see only a few feet through the dark foliage. At Taylor Slough, alligators, water birds, ducks, turtles, otter, deer, panther, black bear, and bobcats congregate. You will see some of them. The *Anhinga Trail* is a boardwalk which reaches out over a slough, in which the visitor can observe the everyday life and death drama of the glades.

About the time you have become convinced that you are near the outer limits of anthropoid civilization, that only you, the road, and your strange vehicle remain as outcroppings of the nonnatural universe, you will reach Flamingo and the surprising world of martinis and steaks and air conditioning.

Flamingo has a lodge, a dining room for two hundred, shops, a drug store, a marina, rental boats, groceries, gas, tires, oil—even houseboats you can rent by the week.From here you can go on to see more of the park—and there is much more to see than you have, to this point—but from here you go by boat. And with a guide, of necessity. Morning and evening excursion boat tours can accommodate the mildly curious; those with their own or rented craft may join the Saturday Ranger-conducted boat-a-cades which ramble along for sixty-five mile tours.

There are picnic and camping areas at Flamingo and Long Pine Key. The Flamingo campsites hold 60 mobile homes and 171 tents or trailers, at a charge of about $2 per car. A small store sells groceries, fishing supplies, and sundries. Long Pine Key has 108 camp units, each including a picnic table, cookout grill, and a paved strip for trailer or tent, with drinking fountains and comfort stations close by. The charge is about $1 per car. You can fish all year here and do pretty well. You won't even need a license for saltwater fishing. But no hunting of any kind at any time. (You may, of course, defend yourself against the mosquitoes, but they are the hunters in this case.)

A long, furious, not-always-low-keyed controversy has surrounded the "flood control project" in the park. The project has cost in the hundreds of millions and, according to conservationist and naturalist opponents, controls flooding only in a minor way. They consider it land reclamation in disguise; a publicly subsidized move, benefiting landowners and real estate men. They have raised fears that loss of water, without replenishment, could destroy the park and hurt tourism.

Unless you're traveling by boat, return to Florida City, US 1, and the turnoff point to the Florida Keys by the same way you went.

South from Florida City on US 1, the first twenty-mile leg of the journey to the Florida Keys may be considered the dreariest segment of landscape anywhere. There's nought but swampy grasslands on either side as far as the eye can see. Then come little ponds to help a bit, then a bay and the beginnings of civilization again. The last short hop over Jewfish Creek bridge puts you on Key Largo, northernmost and largest of all the keys.

To Key West

Curving southwestward in a one-hundred-mile scimitar are the keys, strung like a necklace along the highway that went to sea. The highway, of course, came by train more or less, because it follows the fabulous Flagler's route to Key West for much of the way and uses most the railroad's original bridges.

The terrible killer hurricane that swept the keys on Labor Day in 1935 signaled the end for rail service to Key West—and to Cuba—but opened the way for the highway. New bridges have doubled the highway's capacity.

There are forty-two bridges linking the keys, some little more than one hundred feet in length, several a mile or more, and one seven miles long. The scenery is almost all seascape, but among the world's most spectacular. This is the saltwater fisherman's happy hunting grounds, offering a choice of bonefish on the shallow flats or tarpon in Florida Bay and the Gulf of Mexico, plus the Gulf Stream's sporty smorgasbord.

Despite the plentitude of ocean, however, this is not beach and bathing territory; there are few beaches, except where they have been pumped up by man, and the water is shallow and surfless generally. Sharp coral rock discourages wading.

There are resort areas of every stripe along the way—from plush to primitive—plus a few commercial attractions and some, but only some, really good restaurants. Seafood is, naturally, a frequent specialty of the house, and green turtle steak, conch chowder, stone crabs, and Key lime pie are regional items worthy of being searched out. When ordering Key lime pie, be sure that it is yellow in color, not green. Real Key lime pie is yellow, and only establishments with no aesthetic sense will serve the artificial, dyed green variety.

Guides and boats are plentiful all along the keys, but spearfishing is allowed only along the southern portion of the route from Long Key to Key West. Skindiving, of course, is great sport the whole route, but perhaps at its very best near the beginning on Key Largo.

Stretching twenty-one miles parallel to Key Largo, and three and a half miles wide, is the John Pennekamp Coral Reef State Park, the nation's first continental underseas park, named for the associate editor of the *Miami Herald,* who had much to do with the park's establishment, plus that of Everglades National Park.

Glass-bottom boats embark from the park's 2,100-acre land base for viewing the only living coral reef along the Atlantic Coast. The crystal-clear water allows clear views to sixty-foot depths of the forty-one varieties of coral in colorful, flowerlike formations, with here and there the hulks of old sailing wrecks. Reef fish, giant turtles, barracuda, and sharks add an accent. A better view is possible, certainly, for those with diving equipment, but the glass-bottom views will suffice for most.

The park's headquarters on Key Largo also affords overnight camping facilities, boat docks and launching areas, trails through natural woods, and a bathing lagoon. An entrance fee is charged.

Along the way south you can stop and browse along the shore for driftwood, old bottles, or just a closer look at the busy marine life.

Eventually, you'll reach Key West, an old and different town with an air of its own. There are nearly 30,000 individualists living here, each proudly proclaiming himself a "Conch" (pronounced Conk), even though he may have moved in only last month. The original Conchs trace to Cockney English settlers in the Bahamas, their descendants moving to Key West in the early 1800's as marine salvagers and fishermen. Stir in some native Bahamians, a large portion of Cubans, some Yankee sailing men, and Virginia merchants and you have the basic blend.

In the 1830's, this mixture was assessed as the richest per capita citizenry in the United States. But a hundred years later, the depression left it perhaps the poorest. Eighty percent of the population was on relief. A state agency was created to bring the city back to life via tourism, and out-of-work artists and writers were set to work changing the town's appearance and image. One administrator decreed that all men should wear shorts, to appear picturesque for the tourists' benefit. All seemed to be going well until the '35 hurricane cut the umbilical to the mainland. Only World War II and the U.S. Navy really brought economic stability, although completion of the highway permitted postwar growth.

Today, the city's colorful past, it's every-man-for-himself architecture and some big names have made another blend that pulls the tourism in.

The best way to see Key West is via the Conch Tour Train or Old Town Trolley, trams that ramble some fourteen miles in a 1½-hr. viewing of such sites as Harry Truman's Little White House, Ernest Hemingway's home, Audubon House, the turtle kraals, the shrimp fleet, art centers, and all the seeable attractions.

Audubon House was the Geiger House when the artist stayed there in 1831-32 while sketching Keys birdlife. It's been restored and contains some of Audubon's work, plus a mixture of furnishings much like the original owner salvaged from shipwrecks.

Ernest Hemingway lived in Key West during much of his most productive writing period, working on *Green Hills of Africa, To Have and Have Not, Snows of Kilimanjaro,* and *For Whom the Bell Tolls.* Hemingway was attracted by the old (1851) house's grillwork. He furnished it heavily with Spanish antiques and rebuilt the kitchen to put all the appliances several inches higher and thus handier for him whenever he wanted to whip up a specialty.

A wealthy couple bought the house in 1961, intending to make it their home, but as they discovered more and more artifacts and Hemingway memorabilia they decided instead to make it a museum.

The town's atmosphere seems to stimulate writers. Tennessee Williams, John Dos Passos, and Robert Frost also worked here.

West of Key West in the Dry Tortugas is Fort Jefferson National Monument, an early venture in defense spending that never really defended anything. After almost twenty years of building with forty million bricks (at $1 each for the shipping alone), the massive fort never fired any of its 243 big guns. Nor did any foe test the five-foot-thick walls. The fort did manage to serve as a prison for Dr. Samuel Mudd after Lincoln's assassination.

The return to mainland Florida again is simple—US 1 north. And if you plan to continue the tour west across Florida on the Tamiami Trail, you can miss metropolitan Miami traffic by switching to US 27 at Florida City, then turn west on US 41.

The Tamiami Trail connects Miami with Tampa, sweeping through Everglades country for one hundred miles to the West Coast at Naples, then angling northward, generally inland from the "quiet coast" of Florida. The section from Miami to Naples, however, is more specifically known as "The Trail." It was built at a cost of $13 million during five hard years of the mid-'20's and changed the face and future of South Florida. What had been a two-day roundabout excursion became a two-hour jaunt, thanks to The Trail.

There is also a two-lane toll road from US 27 west of Fort Lauderdale to Naples, completed in 1967, but it is referred to as Alligator Alley by Miamians jealous of the intrusion on the Trail's place in history.

Along the Tamiami Trail

Aside from its purely transportational aspects, The Trail has long served as a recreational access route, both in reaching the West Coast beaches at Marco and Naples, and in supplying one of the world's longest fishing holes. The Tamiami Canal, which parallels the road on the north, was dug to supply fill for the roadbed and automatically presented prime freshwater fishing grounds the length of the route.

Here, too, are the Seminole villages—or at least the villages you are permitted to see. Most of them along The Trail are semitourist attractions, ranging in scope from a couple of elevated huts, called *chickees,* to an elaborate restaurant-marine-souvenir shop-filling station complex, erected via a government loan. Airboat rides are offered, and are exhilarating once one gets over the shock of skimming along over an inch or two of water or perhaps only some damp sawgrass.

Another thirty-five miles brings you to State 29 and a choice: to the south are Everglades City, a planned metropolis that didn't pan out but does offer the renowned Rod and Gun Club, which retains its regal air, and the village of Chokoloskee on a tiny island off shore. Smallwood's Store, a rustic former Indian trading post, is worth seeing.

Access to the western portion of Everglades Park is by boat from Everglades City. Birdwatchers will want to see this section, which includes Duck Rock, home of some 75,000 white ibis during the summer months.

Turn north on State 29 and you will reach the town of Immokalee, then Corkscrew Swamp Sanctuary, the National Audubon Society's six-thousand-acre preserve which features thousands of rare birds, elevated walkways through the heart of a jungle, and giant bald cypress trees seven hundred years old and 130 feet high. The Sanctuary also can be reached via State 846 north of Naples, if you prefer.

The third choice can keep you on The Trail to Naples, Naples isn't the end of The Trail, but it's the culmination of the tour of Florida's tip. Long a favorite with wealthy folks, Naples' aesthetic raw material has been pretty well protected. There's a seven-mile white sand beach, and a continuing fight to uphold strict zoning laws. The town's success in this matter may be measured by the fact that many longtime Miamians vacation in Naples and find it offers refined relief from the hurly-burly of bigtime resortery. With several dozen part-time resident millionaires, Naples has a sufficiency of smart shops. There are six golf courses. Sunset watching and beach strolling are the favorite "active" sports hereabouts except for the truly wild and woolly Swamp Buggy Races in November and February.

Another eight miles up US 41 is the turnoff point for Sanibel and Captiva Islands, which are the seashell fancier's idea of paradise because of the supply of left-handed welks, spiny periwinkles, large cockles, and coquina. Sanibel, connected to Captiva on the north end by a small bridge, was considered the ultimate in tropical splendor mixed with blessed privacy when only a ferry gave access to the mainland at Punta Rassa, but a toll causeway now makes the 3½-mile trip simple and quick. The $4 roundtrip toll, a concession to islanders who didn't want so many visitors after all, keeps the traffic down. The beaches are fine, accommodations range from simple but comfortable to the epitome of resort luxury.

Fort Myers is next, a pleasant city on the broad Caloosahatchee River and Thomas Alva Edison's choice for a winter home site. You can reach both via McGregor Blvd. from Punta Rassa. Edison had the home prefabricated in Maine, shipped it down by schooner, and used it well for fifty years. Now a museum, it's just as Edison left it, with such ahead-of-his-time Edison touches as an intercom system and automatic lights in the closets. His laboratory is intact, and you may note that they don't make light bulbs any more the way Edison did—some of his have been burning twelve hours a day ever since he made them.

Fort Myers also is bracketed by two of the large, complete-city housing developments designed to attract retirees. Some residents are tickled pink with their new life, others can't get used to the change. The area does not consist only of retirees, however; the 19–54-year-old age bracket has recently experienced explosive growth. Cape Coral is west of town, across the river. Lehigh Acres is east on State 82. And north on State 41 is Port Charlotte.

As US 41 bends westward to skitter along the Gulf Coast again, you may detect a subtle quickening, a feeling that something is going on up ahead. Indeed, lots of things are, for you approach Sarasota and its outrigger keys which extend north to south for thirty-five miles, and with all this casual living frontier there is also culture.

Culture-happy

Sarasota—and the term is used loosely to apply to the mainland and its companions north and south, plus Siesta Key, Lido Key, and Longboat Key—seems to be the place with a little something, or everything, extra. More space, more beach, more to see and do in more comfort and in a most scintillating atmosphere.

Whatever the combination, it's pulled in a lot of people who could live and work almost anywhere, yet they chose this place.

An early one was John Ringling, the circus magnate, who enriched the community and state with his collection of art, his mansion, and his appreciation of the stimulating good things of life. The John and Mabel Ringling Museum of Art, owned and operated by the state, contains one of the nation's outstanding collections of Baroque and Renaissance paintings, the Rubens collection being America's finest. Contemporary and modern art also are on display.

Near the museum is the state-acquired Asolo Theater, a magnificent eighteenth-century interior from the castle at Asolo, Italy, which is in almost constant use for appropriate presentations—opera, concerts, and an eight-month season of plays.

The grandiloquent Ringling mansion on Sarasota Bay, and Ringling Museum of the Circus, also are part of the overall museums, which may be entered separately or with a combination ticket for all.

The culture doesn't linger in the past, however. Such outstanding architects as Paul Rudolph and Victor Lundy have contributed greatly with churches, homes, shops, and schools, and I. M. Pei designed buildings for the Oxford-like New College, which had Dr. Arnold Toynbee on the faculty for the first handpicked class of ninety-four scholars.

Among the well-known writers who have worked here are the late MacKinlay Kantor, and John D. MacDonald. The well-known names in the artists' colony range from cartoonist V. T. Hamlin, organizer of *Alley Oop,* to Ben Stahl, Syd Solomon, and Philip Guston.

The intellectual life is contagious, of course. Little theater groups, art schools, concerts, and art shows permeate all strata of the population. And everybody shares the "regular" niceties of sun, beaches, fishing, golf, tennis, patio socializing, and the like. But a little bit more, this being Sarasota.

Bradenton is contiguous to Sarasota on the north, and you'll be into it without knowing you've left Sarasota. There's a little difference, but county and municipal lines spawn competing chambers of commerce promoting the same thing. Bradenton has its own offshore key, too, but this one's an island—Anna Maria—instead of a key. The terms are always interchangeable, of course. And in fact, Longboat Key, one of Sarasota's claims, extends well into Manatee County and the Bradenton sphere. A bridge connects Longboat to Anna Maria if you want to stick with the beach route.

At the mouth of the Manatee River, five miles west of Bradenton, is De Soto National Memorial Park and the spot whence de Soto began his ill-fated trek all over the south. Just across the river on US 41 or 301, turn east for a couple of miles to reach the Gamble Mansion, a plantation-style antebellum museum. Judah P. Benjamin, Confederate Secretary of State, hid out here briefly after the South lost the war and eventually made it to England where he became a successful barrister.

The Sunshine Skyway

Either 41 or 301 will take you to Tampa, but for a spectacular view and a quick entry into St. Petersburg and that burgeoning resort area, it's best to switch to US 19 north, or I-275, just outside Palmetto. This

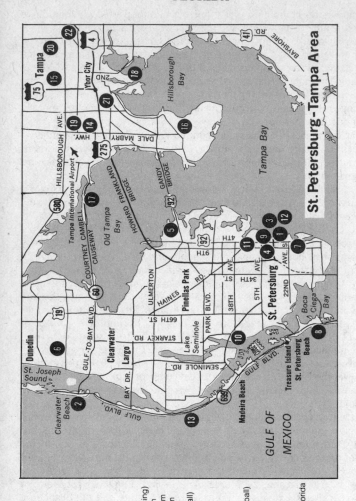

St. Petersburg–Tampa Area

Points of Interest

St. Petersburg
1) Bayfront Center
2) Big Pier 60
3) Bounty Exhibit
4) Al Lang Stadium
5) Derby Lane (dog racing)
6) Jack Russell Stadium
7) Salvador Dali Museum
8) London Wax Museum
9) Museum of Fine Arts
10) Payson Field (baseball)
11) Sunken Gardens
12) The Pier
13) Tiki Gardens

Tampa
14) Al Lopez Field (baseball)
15) Greyhound Track
16) Jai Alai Fronton
17) Municipal Beach
18) Shrimp Fleet
19) Tampa Stadium
20) University of South Florida
21) University of Tampa
22) Busch Gardens

will take you across the fifteen-mile Sunshine Skyway (Toll: $1 per car) and save some forty-five miles. The Skyway is part causeway and part bridge spanning Tampa Bay and replacing the old Bee-Line Ferry. High spot, in more ways than one, is the high-level main Skyway Bridge, four miles long and rising the equivalent of fifteen stories above the water. Although ocean freighters cruised underneath with plenty of room to spare, in 1980, a phosphate freighter slammed into the southbound span of the Skyway during a rainstorm and knocked a large chunk of the bridge into the water. Thirty-five persons, driving over the span, lost their lives. So far, there has been no decision about how to rebuild the lost portion. However, traffic is not impaired between Sarasota and St. Petersburg; it's all one-lane each way, via the causeway, and just takes more time. The destroyed part of the bridge has become a sightseeing attraction.

You enter St. Petersburg from the south, this way, and it doesn't look like an old resort town, for old people. It has, in fact, new life and pizzazz in fine shops, museums, good restaurants, billowing sails everywhere, and the new Dali Museums with the largest collection of Salvador Dali works in the world! If you're coming down from the north, I-75 will take you directly into St. Petersburg.

The ocean beaches north of Mullet Key (turn west onto State 699 if returning from Mullet Key) are known collectively as the Pinellas Suncoast, consisting of the eight Gulf of Mexico communities: Clearwater Beach, Dunedin, Holiday Isles, Madeira Beach, St. Pete Beach, St. Petersburg, Tarpon Springs, Treasure Island. The Holiday Isles include Redington Beach, Indian Rocks Beach and other small Gulf communities. All told, there are twenty-eight miles of beach—and beachfront accommodations ranging from luxury hotels and apartments to weathered frame beach houses that may be rented by the week or month.

St. Pete is connected to the mainland by Corey Causeway (free) and is a favorite place to stay, shop, and dine. Waterfront restaurants, chartered fishing boats, rental sailboats, and the wide expanse of sandy beach attract sun-seekers all the year-round. Serious shell-hunters comb the beach as early as 6 A.M.

Clearwater Beach connects with Clearwater, on the mainland, via Garden Memorial Causeway. Clearwater has a fine marina and a large sport-fishing fleet. As with St. Petersburg and Tampa, its major league spring training games help make it popular with baseball fans.

From Clearwater, a choice: south on US Alternate 19 you can reach downtown St. Petersburg, sampling en route the modern suburbs; west on State 60 will feed you into the north part of Tampa across the Courtney Campbell Causeway; or north on Alternate 19 gets you to Tarpon Springs, a mere fifteen miles away. En route, is Innisbrook Golf and Tennis Resort, considered one of the best in the country. A long, winding lane leads to the 900-acres of landscaped gardens, three championship golf courses, tennis courts, and the vacation villas.

Tampa is now Florida's third largest city and one of the nation's fastest growing, attracting diversified industry.

Busch Gardens, a public relations whim of the Anheuser-Busch ownership, is a man-planted tropical garden with one of the world's largest aviaries. Hundreds of colorful birds and animals live among the 150,000 trees, plants, and lakes on 300 acres. You can tour the Dark Continent complete with Moroccan Village, Claw Island, the Congo, Stanleyville, Serengeti Plain, etc. The beer is on the house. Recent additions are the frothy, exciting Congo River Rapids. A separate theme park is Adventure Island, with its pools, water slides, and beach. Plan to stay all day.

Drive north on 40th Street to Temple Terrace Highway, then west, to reach Busch Gardens. And, if you like, a few more blocks north on 30th Street to the Schlitz Brewery for a tour and complimentary brew.

On the way to, or returning from, Busch Gardens via 40th Street, a turn west onto Broadway will yield a sample of Ybor City and the Latin Quarter of Tampa. It's pronounced "E-Boe" City by folks hereabouts and offers Spanish architecture and some of the nation's best Spanish restaurants. Tampa has picked up mightily in recent years, and now has a $4½ million convention center and streamlined traffic system.

Mr. Plant's fine hotel still sits in the middle of town, just across the Lafayette Street Bridge, but now it's the University of Tampa. The thirteen Moorish minarets on this interpretation of the original Alhambra make it hard to miss. There's a museum in the south wing of the main building, and nearby on the well-kept grounds is the De Soto Oak, whereunder de Soto supposedly bargained with the Indians.

The city's biggest day of the year is the second Monday of February. School is out for Gasparilla Day, a festival keyed to the "capture" of Tampa by a modern "Jose Gaspar" and his crew of one-day buccaneers as they cruise up Hillsborough Bay in a flag-bedecked pirate-type ship to accept the city's surrender. The original Jose Gaspar supposedly buried some of his treasure in the area, although there's much dispute from some quarters that he ever existed at all. No matter, the excitement of Gasparilla Day is real. Best spot for watching is along Bayshore Blvd.

Winter Haven can be reached quickly from either Lakeland (via US 92) or Bartow (via US 17) and should. Not only because it's another pleasant, lake-dotted town with all the amenities, but because from Winter Haven it is only five miles to Cypress Gardens. Drivers needn't worry about the road number—plenty of signs direct the way.

Perhaps as much as any place in Florida, Cypress Gardens proves what imagination, promotion, and a pliant Mother Nature can do. What was once only a swamp well off the beaten track now has its own track, very well beaten by up to eight thousand tourists a day, and the swamp has been nurtured, prodded, drained, elevated, and manicured into 164 acres of botanical flamboyance, accented by pretty girls. Fabulous Cypress Gardens always has something in bloom and new things to do and see.

The amateur photographer may not be king here, but he will feel like one—even after the film is developed. Expert professionals give the proper camera settings for every shot, and it's very hard to take a bad picture under these circumstances. There's even a special grandstand for the picture takers (it costs a little extra to get in it).

But the gardens cannot be overshadowed—or perhaps oversplashed—once you're on the scene. Lagoons, moss-hung cypress, bougainvillea, banks of azaleas, and rare and exotic plants from around the world combine to present a series of "vistas" along the winding walkways and waterways (electric boats, a little extra charge). Millions were spent for new attractions in 1980 for the "Southern Cross Roads" and "Living Forest" exhibits, and a sky ride was added in 1983.

Entrepreneur Dick Pope, who started it all and has kept it going and growing for over forty years, with the assistance now of his son, Dick Jr., has even managed to make the parking lot outside into something different with a spiral "Palm Bowl" arrangement.

Anyone within reasonable distance should try to see Cypress Gardens —and bring the camera.

An Area of Sundry Attractions

Leaving Cypress Gardens, tourists may take State 540 east, cross US 27, continuing west on 540, and should be prepared for a surprise. Here, tucked away beside a little lake smack in the center of Florida is what appears to be a miniature European castle. This is Chalet Suzanne, which offers one of Florida's dining adventures. A big splurge is recommended for those who have the time and money.

There are also thirty guest rooms, furnished with an intriguing collection of antiques from throughout the world.

Lake Wales and the Bok Tower are only four miles south of Chalet Suzanne, by US 27.

Edward Bok, wealthy editor of the *Ladies Home Journal* and a Pulitzer Prize winner in 1920, established Mountain Lake Sanctuary on the slope of Iron Mountain (324 feet above sea level, the highest point in peninsular Florida) as a refuge for birds and man, as well as a proper setting for the carillon tower that now serves as his memorial. Lovely gardens surround the 205-foot tower, and there are "blinds" for visitors to observe or photograph the birdlife. A pool reflects the image of the tower, and carillon concerts are given several times weekly. There is no access for tourists to the tower's top. Serenity is the attraction.

Near the entrance to the Sanctuary is Spook Hill, a Lake Wales city street (5th Street at North Avenue) on which one may park, release the brakes and have the illusion that the car is rolling uphill.

Lake Wales is also the scene, from early February to mid-April, of the Black Hills Passion Play, presented four times a week in a 3,500-seat amphitheater with a stage more than one hundred yards wide. In 1977, the performers celebrated the 25th year of this annual event. Along with the fine cast of actors, a flock of 30 sheep, lambs, and two camels participate.

Thirty miles south of Lake Wales—again by US 27 or Alternate 27—is Sebring, famous for its annual twelve-hour speed and endurance sports car races, held in March. Located in the citrus belt, with its lemon, lime and avocado groves, is the Sebring Packing Co. Otherwise, Sebring is just a quiet spot for fishing, hunting, golf and outdoor pursuits. The nearby Highlands Hammock State Park has catwalks into a cypress swamp area, as well as a guided tour and small museum.

For variety, it's suggested that, if the trip south to Sebring from Lake Wales was on US 27, the return north should be via Alternate 27. Some nice panoramas present themselves, and at Babson Park, named for himself by economist Roger Babson when he bought the town of Crooked Lake in 1923, is Webber College. Webber, founded at Wellesley, Mass., by Mrs. Babson to teach rich young ladies how to take care of money, has a branch here. In 1959, the Babson Park branch began admitting males—day students only—perhaps to teach rich young men how to protect themselves from rich young ladies.

North Central Florida

The drive northward into the state's varied north central section can be that rare thing in this motorized age: simply a pleasant drive without too much traffic and with an interesting countryside unrolling past the windows. On US 27 north—this will be through the heart of the citrus area with trees of all sizes stretching to the horizon in exact lines like the dots on a sheet of graph paper—there are rolling hills, with little lakes in the valleys, and giant propellers sticking up above the groves to stir up chill air when frost threatens, or smudge pots to generate a layer of warm smoke over the tender trees. You are also in real cattle country, po'dner, between Lake Wales and Okeechobee at Yeehaw Junction. If you like to ride 'em, cowboy, and feast on delicious grub, a vacation is fun at River Ranch on 50,000 acres. A million-acre cattle ranch, the Kicco, was here long ago. Cookouts, square dancing, and rodeos are part of guest activities.

Just north of the town of Clermont is one of the state's two Citrus Towers (the other is at Lake Placid, also on US 27, fifteen miles south of Sebring). On a hill of 340 feet elevation, the Clermont tower rises an additional 226 feet to an observation platform reached in less than a minute by elevator. The view is spectacular, an expansion of what may be seen from ground level with hundreds of lakes and two thousand square miles of citrus land spreading in all directions. Admission is charged to the tower.

There are, of course, other excellent viewing routes north. If the swing into the interior of the state isn't taken, US 19 north from St. Petersburg offers a near-coastal route and access to Weeki Wachee and Homosassa Springs, two of the state's twenty-seven major producers of crystal clear waters. Accommodations and underwater viewing of freshwater fish— and freshlooking girls—are available at both. From Tampa, US 41 wends north through interesting lake and river country, with dependably excellent fishing and camping facilities. Rainbow Springs is near Dunnellon on this route.

A few miles north of Clermont, the Sunshine State Parkway offers superhighway connections to Wildwood. There is a toll for the approximately twenty miles, but then a connection with Interstate 75 at Wildwood for a rapid arrival at the Ocala interchange. An option is to stick with US 27 to Leesburg, in the middle of the bass fishing country. US 27 and 441 join here for a divided-highway approach to Ocala.

Southern Wild West

Ocala is in the middle of what used to be called rural Florida, but now it's pastoral. And in the pastures are some very high-class thoroughbred horses who live in $75,000 barns. All this is relatively recent—the biggest boost came when a locally bred dandy named Needles won the Kentucky Derby in 1956—but it all adds up to an additional tourist attraction for Ocala's already well-endowed bill of fare.

Other winners followed Needles, such as Carry Back with the 1961 Derby and Preakness, and Hail to All in the 1965 Belmont, but these are results, not causes, of the Florida horse farm boom.

The real and original causes are basic: limestone water, rolling hills and grassy knolls, the things Kentucky offered earlier in the game. Ocala adds the clement climate, and the mere presence of good horses brings others, breeding being a consideration.

As usual, the horsemen go first class, riding on a nationwide amalgamation of $2 tickets, with which the bettor pays all bills. The result is some 150 thoroughbred farms worth more than $20 million, and all kept parklike with white fences, green grass, and old oaks. Most of the farms welcome visitors, but the hours vary. However, in mid-Ocala, at the Chamber of Commerce, are free maps showing the location and hours for most of the showplaces.

Ocala was the stage for the beginning of the Seminole War in 1835 when Wiley Thompson, an Indian agent, called a meeting to explain just how the government was going to ship the Seminoles west to the Indian Territory. The Seminoles demurred with vigor, and Thompson cut off the sale of guns and ammunition. This upset Osceola, who said, in the more temperate parts of his little speech, "I will make the white man red with blood, and then blacken him in the sun and rain . . . and the buzzard shall live upon his flesh."

Some months after the Ocala confrontation, Osceola and his companions killed a Mikasuki chief who had been selling cattle to the white men, then scattered the chief's presumably ill-gotten profits to the winds. In December, two months later, Jumper and Alligator, allies of Osceola, ambushed and massacred Major Francis Dade and one hundred officers and men near Bushnell. On the same day Osceola appeared at Fort King to the north, two miles east of Ocala, and killed the Indian agent, Thompson, and an Army lieutenant. After that day the war was on in earnest.

It sometimes sounds like it's still on in this neighborhood, for only a mile or so away, on what is now State 40 east of Ocala, is an elaborate attraction called "Six Gun Territory," where shoot-outs in the street continue on schedule all day.

Six Gun Territory is a manufactured version of an old Western town, with some forty buildings and a wood-burning locomotive and train, which hauls the customers in at the rate of two thousand an hour. There is a Palace Saloon, naturally, and cancan dancers, wild Western Indians (but no wild Eastern Indians, like Osceola), an O.K. Corral, general store and the like, plus such anachronisms as a cafeteria, photo shop, coffee house, and a movie house showing only the oldest available films.

Just why a Western frontier town should be sitting here in the middle of Florida does not have an answer, except that the ownership started getting rich with the same sort of thing up in North Carolina.

Nearby, just a mile or so east on State 40 (again, it's unlikely anyone will miss seeing the signs), is Silver Springs and a veritable shopping center of attractions—all at a price, of course.

Silver Springs itself attracts close to two million visitors a year, and a complete motel and restaurant industry has been built up in the area to accommodate the viewers.

Glass-bottom boat guides describe the wondrous sights, starting with the main spring, a cavern twelve feet high, sixty-five feet long and sixty feet below the surface, from which gush 650 million gallons of beautifully clear water every day. This would keep such cities as New York well-supplied, unless perhaps a political water commissioner was in charge.

The trip continues over fourteen other springs or groups of springs, all colorfully named, plus visits to pools where friendly, or hungry, fish come up to nibble from the fingers of passengers. A viewing station eight feet below the surface offers a good chance for photographers at the trip's end.

Other attractions, with additional admittance charges, include the Jungle Cruise, a deer ranch with more than three hundred tame deer from around the world (the kids like to feed them), Ross Allen's Reptile Institute for those who are interested, an Early American Museum, and a Prince of Peace Memorial with religious themes in a series of small chapels containing dioramas illustrating the life of Christ. New arrivals are four one-year old, 450-pound zebras to keep about 700 other animals company in the natural settings. Wild Waters, opened in Spring '78, is an exciting $1 million, 10-acre attraction of flumes and surf-crested pools that is sure to bring more gold into Silver Springs.

Certainly there is enough going on here to keep everyone occupied the minimum of six hours the management recommends.

Another recommendation is that State 40 be pursued just three more miles east, where one can find sanctuary in the Ocala National Forest. The noncommercial springs and attractions here are noted in the tour of northeast Florida.

The gauntlet must be rerun returning to Ocala, but the thirty-five miles north to Gainesville from there is pleasant or fast, depending on the route. Interstate 75 is quickest, but bypasses almost everything inhabited and presents little to attract the eye. US 441, however, threads through some Old South towns and villages that possess a genteel charm. Especially is this so in the spring, which begins in early March hereabouts. Banks of azaleas, dogwoods, the fresh green leaves of oaks, sweetgum, and camphor trees make all this seem a thousand miles from the stereotype Florida of palms, sand and sunglasses.

Back to the Old South

Just north of Lake City on US 41, at White Springs, is the Stephen Foster Memorial on the Suwannee River. Carillon recitals from the two-hundred-foot tower feature the composer's work four times daily. Foster never even saw the Suwannee, of course, picking the name for its beauty. As it happened, he picked a good one—the rambling Suwannee, from the Georgia line to the Gulf, is a beautiful stream, and the 243-acre park at the Memorial sets it off well. The Florida Folk Festival, with two thousand or more folk dancers, singers, craftsmen and tale tellers, is held during the first week in May each year. A "Jeannie With the Light Brown Hair" contest is held in February, with Florida lasses of both beauty and musical talent competing for a scholarship.

Less than twenty miles east of Lake City, on US 90, is the Olustee Battlefield Memorial, where the only significant Florida battle of the Civil War occurred. A museum there has displays of the action, plus newspaper accounts of the battle, in which the Confederates entrenched east of Lake City.

The way west from Lake City on US 90 reveals a change in the terrain: instead of flat pinelands, the surroundings become rolling red clay hills, giant live oaks and other hardwoods taking over from the pines. Live oaks were once a national resource, and much of the area here was held in reserve by the government for use in building wooden naval ships. Timber cutters hereabouts were called "Live Oakers" by Audubon in the 1830's, but, when the area was opened to homesteading in the late nineteenth century, much of the forest was destroyed during land clearing.

There's a town of Live Oak on the route; a picture-pretty version of the sleepy Southern village, moss hanging from the giant trees along shady streets. This area now is cattle country, but it has also long been a producer of bright leaf tobacco.

West of Live Oak, the meandering Suwannee is encountered, and at its juncture with the Withlacoochee River (there's another Withlacoochee River farther south) is Suwannee River State Park. There are old Confederate earthworks near a picnic area, fresh springs, and nature trails. Overnight camping is allowed.

The farther west a traveler ventures along US 90, the deeper into the Old South he finds himself. There are such towns as Madison, founded by South Carolina planters in 1838 when Sea Island cotton was grown here. This was a Confederate stronghold during the Civil War, and the news of secession brought bonfires and speeches, bell ringing, and Southern songs.

Then there's Monticello, with a courthouse modeled after Thomas Jefferson's home, elaborate plantations, and the remains of even more elaborate ones. The town's school, built with slave labor in 1852, was integrated—calmly—in 1965.

Tallahassee, the Capital

West again, on US 90, ahead is Tallahassee, the state's capital some 650 miles from Key West. And beyond Tallahassee, more than two hundred more miles of another, and different, Florida.

Tallahassee (the name means Old Fields in Apalachee Indian talk) has one of the state's most spectacular floral extravaganzas at Maclay State Park, formerly Killearn Gardens, about five miles north of town on US 319. Given to the state by Mrs. Alfred Maclay in 1953, the gardens are maintained by the state and are open from October 15 to June 15. Spring is probably the best time to visit. There are 308 acres of garden and recreation area with pools, formal arrangements of flowers bracketed by blooming trees, a walled garden, and a Camellia Walk flanked by twelve-foot-high camellias. Adjacent in the recreation area are picnic shelters with grills, swimming, and a boat ramp.

Near the airport is the Tallahassee Junior Museum's Pioneer Village, which presents typical farm buildings and implements of Northwest Florida farm life, circa 1880. The kids will like this, and older folks will enjoy the country store's stock of 19th-century goods.

South on State Rd. 363, you can enjoy Wakulla Springs, with its glass-bottomed boats and refuge wildlife, and St. Marks, with its state museum. A turnoff a few miles south of Tallahassee takes you the short distance to the site of the Battle of Natural Bridge, where Confederate soldiers, bolstered by boys from the West Florida Seminary in Tallahassee, repulsed a Union march in 1865 to maintain Tallahassee's record as the only Confederate capital east of the Mississippi never captured by Union troops.

Westward from Tallahassee, remain with US 90, or I-10, being especially careful at Chattahoochee lest you drift over the adjacent state line into Georgia. The mile-long Jim Woodruff dam creates Lake Seminole here, and you will have access to excellent lakeside facilities at Three Rivers State Park, a mile north of the town of Sneads, a few minutes farther along. Set your watches back an hour after passing westward through Chattahoochee, for you'll be in the Central Time Zone.

The Miracle Strip

Just to prove to yourself that Florida has at least a little bit of everything, stick with US 90 the twenty-four miles to Marianna, then swing off to the north three miles on State 167 to reach Florida Caverns State Park. This must be one of the few cave complexes anywhere with its own golf course, but rest assured the golf course is outside the cave. A hook or slice is trouble enough without stalactites adding some funny bounces.

The caverns, with well-lighted underground tours, are not the whole show; the aforementioned golf course—a 9-holer modeled after St. Andrews Golf Course—picnic and camping areas, and nature trails fill out the bill.

But to get on with it, best start southward to reach Florida's greatest expanse of beach, one hundred miles extending from Apalachicola to Pensacola and modestly termed the Miracle Strip.

Nine miles west of Marianna on US 90, turn south on US 231 for a fifty-five-mile straight shot into Panama City, This is summer resort country, with excellent reason, and out-of-state visitors to the area make it among the state's most popular. The figures are a bit misleading, however, for Alabamans and Georgians can make the trip every weekend, and lots do.

Some come in the winter, too, for although the temperature runs five to ten degrees below that of South Florida, the rates for good accommodations take a deeper dip.

In truth, there is not only more beach to spread the throng, but there is better beach along the Miracle Strip: it's pure white sand, quartz variety, and the offshore formation provides a good surf.

Panama City qualifies as a sort of Southern Atlantic City, complete with roller coaster and convention hall, but the fishing is better than Jersey's. The city claims as its share twenty-three miles of beach, a portion of it in St. Andrews State Park, with a 450-foot fishing pier to help pedestrian anglers get out there with the bigger ones. Sports fishing of all types is a big attraction, and the city's $7 million marina is home port for a considerable fleet of charter craft.

US 98 is the east-west coastal route, and in truth the Miracle Strip extends eastward of Panama City all the way to Port St. Joe and Apalachicola. The latter towns, however, haven't joined the cooperative promotion efforts of Panama City, Fort Walton Beach and Pensacola, and are chopped off the end of maps you may pick up in the area.

It's a bit quieter, therefore, to the east, but Port St. Joe is there all right, and in fact has been for a long spell: the state's first constitutional convention was held there. Apalachicola is also there, twenty miles east of Port St. Joe, and perhaps it deserves a complimentary visit from grateful tourists if for no better reason than that this is where air conditioning got its start.

Dr. John Gorrie built an ice-making machine here in 1845 and used it to cool the rooms of fever-stricken patients, but he was never able to raise enough cash to get the invention into production. He died in 1885, four years after securing a patent, and is one of the few Floridians to be honored in Washington's Statuary Hall.

Oysters, shrimp, and other seafoods are also an Apalachicola industry, but couldn't be if ice were still floated in, ensconced in sawdust, by ship.

Nearby Apalachicola National Forest is prime hunting land, and there are supervised black bear hunts during September and October. The area is also easily reached from Tallahassee.

But back to the Miracle Strip. Westward from Panama City via US 98 there remain some relatively unpopulated seashore vistas, by Florida standards at least, but you will have little trouble finding accommodations almost anywhere along the route.

Fort Walton Beach is approximately midway between Panama City and Pensacola and has staked out twenty-five miles of the beach. The town itself is built on and around a huge Indian temple mound, which has yielded important artifacts that trace American Indian culture back for ten thousand years.

In the center of town is a museum displaying some of the pottery, tools, and idols found here, although many earlier discoveries are on display at the Peabody Museum in Boston. There is also a diorama illustrating how the area may have looked five hundred years ago.

Inland from Fort Walton Beach is Eglin Air Force Base, which serves as a proving ground for both planes and weapons and where a climatic hangar tests equipment for use in arctic conditions. This is where Jimmy Doolittle's men trained for the raid on Tokyo. The base's huge proving grounds cover eight hundred square miles, but a large part of the land is a game preserve, and managed hunts for deer and turkey are held. There are conducted tours of the base.

Another marine aquarium, the Gulfarium, with leaping porpoises and the like, is on the beach where US 98 resumes its westward trek to Pensacola.

Anchors Aweigh

The last city in the state of Florida and on this tour, Pensacola was almost the first, historically. Don Tristan de Luna and an expedition of 1,500 landed here in 1559—six years before the founding of St. Augustine—and called the place Santa Maria. A storm destroyed de Luna's fleet two years later, however, and the settlement was abandoned.

Pensacola Beach has been a postwar bonanza; before 1945 Santa Rosa Island and its fifty-five miles of virgin beach were held undeveloped by the government. Now, with good causeway connections and with Fort

Pickens State Park on the western tip overlooking the channel entrance to Pensacola, tourism has joined the city's economic standbys.

Driving from Fort Walton Beach on US 98, you can cross over to Santa Rosa Island on State 399 at Navarre and continue to Fort Pickens. This is another one of those brick salesman's dreams which never really saw much action. The Confederates, who held Pensacola, ordered the Federals to surrender Fort Pickens in 1862 or face the consequences. The Federals said no, so the Rebels said they didn't want the danged thing anyway. Like Fort Jefferson in the Dry Tortugas, it wound up as a sort of prison. Geronimo was among those jailed here.

To reach Pensacola itself, take State 399 to US 98 and enter the city via a four-lane bridge. The downtown area offers a few historic sites, among them the Plaza Ferdinand VII at Palafox and Ferdinand streets, where Spanish headquarters were situated; the Panton trading post at Barcelona and Main streets; and Old Christ Church, now City Museum.

The Naval Air Station (take Garden St. to Navy Blvd. from downtown) has its own attractions in a blend of new and old. Free Navy buses take you on tours of the station, plus visits to Fort San Carlos and Fort Barrancas.

Included are visits to the Naval Aviation Museum, Sherman Field, home of the Blue Angels, a precision flying team, the giant aircraft carrier U.S.S. *Lexington* (on holidays you can go aboard), and the Old Pensacola lighthouse, built in 1825 and still working.

Each summer, Pensacola erupts in what it calls the Fiesta of Five Flags. Auxiliary events such as fishing tournaments begin as early as April, but the parades, fancy-dress balls, coronation, a reenactment of Don Tristan de Luna's landing, and a treasure hunt are concentrated in a single week in June. The newest attraction in town is LaFitte's Landing, a theme park.

PRACTICAL INFORMATION FOR FLORIDA

 FACTS AND FIGURES. Florida takes its name from the Spanish *Pascua florida,* referring to the Easter Feast of Flowers. Its nicknames are Everglades State, Land of Flowers and Sunshine State. The state flower is the orange blossom; the state tree, the sabal palm; the state bird, the mockingbird. "In God We Trust" is the state motto. Stephen Foster's "Suwannee River" is the state song.

Tallahassee is the state capital. State population is over 9 million.

Miles of excellent white beaches border Florida's long Atlantic and Gulf of Mexico coastlines, and the seaside plus a mild climate have combined to make the state one of the nation's leading resort areas, with tourism the state's major industry. Most of Florida is flat coastal lowlands, with only a few low hills in the center of the state. Next to its beaches, Florida's most notable natural scenery is in the wild swamps of the vast Everglades National Park at the state's southern tip. The mild climate that attracts tourists also makes it possible for Florida to be the nation's leading producer of citrus fruit and some vegetables, and food processing is the state's leading manufacturing industry.

The famous Florida climate is also noted for being considerably wet, especially in late summer and early fall.

HOW TO GET THERE. *By air:* Numerous carriers, including the major ones, serve Daytona Beach, Gainesville, Jacksonville, Orlando, Panama City, Pensacola, Sarasota-Bradenton, Tallahassee, Tampa-St. Petersburg-Clearwater, Titusville, and West Palm Beach, depending on your point of origin. Air Florida, the all-jet inter-state carrier, has regular schedules to most of the important cities. Pan Am flies non-stop to Mexico from Tampa/St. Petersburg/Clearwater; Pan Am also flies to Frankfurt and Paris from Tampa/St. Petersburg/Clearwater.

Air Canada, Delta, Eastern fly from major cities in Canada to Florida's major airports, where you can connect easily to your destination within the state. New airlines and routes are being added at a dizzying rate.

By train: Amtrak has service to Orlando, Winter Haven, Tampa, St. Petersburg, W. Palm Beach, Ft. Lauderdale and Hollywood. You might want to look into the popular "Week of Wheels" package, which includes use of a car.

By car: The speedy way to penetrate to the main East Coast resort area and Central Florida from the northeast is I-95. Not yet completed, in some parts you will have to use US 301, 15 and 17, which will slow you down somewhat. The beautiful, leisurely way is A1A. The frustrating, stoplight way is US 1. If going to the west coast from the northeast, take I-95 to Daytona Beach, then I-4 through Orlando to Tampa and I-275 to St. Petersburg.

Car rentals are possible in all major cities.

By bus: Trailways and Greyhound provide good service.

HOW TO GET AROUND. *By air:* Delta, Eastern, Pan Am, TWA, U.S. Air, Braniff, Ozark, Republic, Piedmont, Air Florida or Commuter Airlines serve Daytona Beach, Eglin A.F. Base, Ft. Lauderdale, Ft. Myers, Gainesville, Lakeland, Melbourne, Ocala, Pensacola, Tampa/St. Petersburg/Clearwater, Sarasota/Bradenton, Jacksonville, Key West and other airports within the state. With deregulation, new routes are constantly added and more airlines fly in.

By car: Major routes, some still being perfected are: I-4 from Daytona Beach, on the eastern seaboard, to St. Petersburg, on the Gulf Coast; I-10 from Jacksonville to Alabama line projection. US 301 diverges from US 1 at Callahan, strikes off through Starke, Ocala, Wildwood, Dade City, passes Tampa, to Sarasota. State 60 goes cross-state from Clearwater, on the Gulf Coast, to Vero Beach, on the Atlantic Coast, taking Clearwater-Tampa Bay traffic. State 84 (Alligator Alley) is a toll shortcut from the lower west coast to the Ft. Lauderdale area—access 6 mi. east of Naples, running across the Everglades to US 27 at Andytown.

By boat: The intracoastal Waterway parallels the coastline and runs 349 mi. from Jacksonville to Miami. It is 8 ft. deep in the shallower southern portions. Canals abound, connecting to the ocean. Write: Florida Dept. of Natural Resources for *Florida Boating.*

By bus: In addition to Greyhound and Trailways, Gulf Coast Motor Lines offers service within the state.

TOURIST INFORMATION. Florida makes it easy for the tourist to get information with a proliferation of welcome stations for the motorist, friendly, helpful chambers of commerce and tourist bureaus in every city, and tourist conscious airlines, which are geared up to answer all sorts of questions.

Welcome stations, dispensing information, maps, and often a free glass of orange juice—as well as spacious parking areas and clean restrooms—are located at major entry points into the state.

Florida Division of Tourism, 126 Van Buren St., Tallahassee 32304; Florida Department of Natural Resources, 3900 Commonwealth Blvd., Tallahassee 32304.

Pinellas Suncoast Tourist Development, Suite 228, St. Petersburg/Clearwater Airport, Clearwater 33520. Tampa Tourist Information, P.O. Box 420, Tampa 33601.

Visitor Information Center, 75 King St., St. Augustine 32084.

Broward County Tourist Development Council, 314 S.E. 9th St., Ft. Lauderdale 33316.

Pensacola Tourist Information, 803 N. Palafox, Pensacola 32501.

 SEASONAL EVENTS. *January: Epiphany (Greek Cross Day),* Tarpon Springs; Epiphany rites begin with elaborate services at St. Nicholas Greek Orthodox Church, followed by a colorful "Diving for the cross" ceremony. *International Kite Flyoff,* Sarasota. *Old Island Days,* Key West; city pays tribute to its colorful past with elaborate celebration. Late Jan. through Feb. *Southwest Florida Championship Rodeo,* Fort Myers; parade, rodeo, horse show, gymkhana, dance, barbecue, and rodeo queen contest.

February: Old Island Days, Key West; city pays tribute to its colorful past with elaborate celebration. *Flagler Museum Open House,* Palm Beach. *Speed Weeks,* Daytona Beach; two full weeks of speed fare are offered at Daytona International Speedway. *National Sprints,* Tampa, spring car racing at Florida State Fair. *Edison Pageant of Light,* Fort Myers. *Ybor City Pirate Fiesta Days* (Gasparilla), Tampa; Tampa's Latin Quarter, Ybor City, has own special participation in the Gasparilla celebration. *Gasparilla Pirate Invasion,* Tampa; founded in 1904, Gasparilla has become one of Florida's most elaborate pageants. *Swamp Buggy Races,* Naples. *Black Hills Passion Play,* Lake Wales; reconstructs dramatic events of the seven last days in the life of Christ, mid-Feb. through Apr.; *Bach Festival,* Winter Park; unique musical experience attracts music lovers from around the country.

March: Daytona Motorcycle Classic, Daytona Beach, *Gatornationals,* Gainesville; national record holders and former national champions in drag racing gather for top-ranked competition. *Sidewalk Art Festival,* Winter Park. *Antique Car Show,* Tarpon Springs. *Winter Lightning Championships,* St. Petersburg; small sailcraft compete in annual regatta hosted by St. Petersburg Yacht Club. *Fun 'n' Sun Festival,* Clearwater; State Pram Regatta and National Records Power Boat Race, Pancake Festival, State Baton Twirling Contest. *Sebring* (twelve-hour) *Grand Prix,* Sebring.

April: Delray Affair, Delray Beach; sidewalks turned into a showplace for arts, crafts, flowers, and produce. *King Neptune Frolics,* Sarasota; landing of King Neptune, Queen Athena, and Y Mystic Krewe, fish fry, water-ski show, art displays, boat parade, tennis tournaments, horse show, sports car rally, and children's parade. *Blessing of the Fleet,* St. Augustine; traditionally held on Palm Sunday, the ceremony of blessing shrimp boats and power craft is held at the Yacht Pier on Matanzas Bay.

May: Eight Flag Shrimp Boat Races, Fernandina Beach, only race of its kind in Florida. *Cypress Gardens Festival,* Cypress Gardens; Florida State Delta Wing Kite Championships, Aquarama Pool Shows, sky diving demonstrations, and fashion shows. *Sunfish Regatta,* Cypress Gardens, *Dunnellon Art Show,* Dunnellon. *Blessing of the Fleet,* Destin; each year on Ascension Day (40 days after Easter), this picturesque fishing village on Florida's Miracle Strip presents its Blessing of the Fleet ceremony. *New College Music Festival,* Sarasota. South's only music festival of its kind; among nation's top forty. World-famous artists perform. Six public concerts from beginning of May through mid-June.

June: West Florida Rodeo, Pensacola. All the ride-'em-cowboy events plus western musical groups to entertain. *Fiesta of Five Flags,* Pensacola. Reenactment of 1559 landing of Don Tristan de Luna and Spanish colonists. Concerts, parades, sports activities. *Sea Turtle Watch,* Jensen Beach. Ancient sea turtles deposit eggs on beach. *Florida Theatre Festival,* Daytona Beach; full program of seminars and entertainment, open to the public. *Masters Barefoot Ski Tournament,* Cypress Gardens. World's top ten men, top five women compete. *"Cross and Sword,"* St. Augustine; outdoor drama by Pulitzer Prize winner Paul Green, Florida's official state play is based on the founding of St. Augustine by Pedro Menendez de Aviles in 1565, late June to Sept. *All-American Water Ski Championships,* Cypress Gardens. *Kissimmee Boat-a-Cade.* Go through the Chain of Lakes by boat or meet the flotilla by car for sightseeing, picnics, fishing, barbecues. *Jefferson County Watermelon Festival,* Monticello; Watermelon Queen Contest, parade and watermelon eating and seed-spitting contests.

July: Silver Spurs Rodeo, Kissimmee, 4th of July weekend. Florida's oldest; national points. *All-Florida Championship Rodeo,* Arcadia. Held since 1929. *Biggest All-Night Gospel Sing in the World,* Bonifay. *Apollo II Anniversary,* July 16, Cape Canaveral. Celebrities, speakers, fun. *Pensacola Shark Rodeo,* mid-July. Rod, reel, nerve, cash prizes. Also 4th of July hoopla in most communities.

August: Days in Spain Festival, St. Augustine. *Fun Day,* Wasau. Small northwest Florida town has day-long old-fashioned bullfrog races, possum auction, gopher races, cornpone baking, hog-calling, mule-rides, horse-wagon rides. *Fishathon,* St. Petersburg. Fishing event for boys and girls 12 years of age and younger. Cane poles and fishing gear provided—also cookies and cold drinks. Annually for over 30 years.

September: Bluegrass Festival, Live Oak. Continuous jam sessions, regional foods, hiking trails. *Ford Deuce Days,* Cypress Gardens. 1932 Fords from around the world. *International Worm Fiddling Contest,* Panacea. Blue crab, gospel sing, seafood dinners. *Regattas* in Jacksonville and Sarasota. *Pioneer Days,* Englewood, Labor Day weekend (most other communities also plan some sort of "do" this weekend, so check locally).

October: Western Roundup, Pensacola; six-guns and shoot-outs, stagecoaches, can-can girls, Indian ceremonies and dances; TV and movie personalities are special guests. *October Fishing Rodeo,* Destin, all month. First weekend *Destin Seafood Festival. Windsurfing Regatta,* Port Charlotte. *Rattlesnake Roundup and International Gopher Race,* San Antonio; bounties are paid on all rattlesnakes brought in during the Sept. 2 to Oct. 20 roundup, and prizes are awarded for both the heaviest and the largest number; activities include hourly snake shows, demonstrations of venom milking, first aid exhibitions, chicken dinner, pottery exhibit and appearance of former Indian Chief Osceola and family. The Gopher (Land Turtle) Races are presented in heat, semi-finals and International Championship run. *World's Chicken Pluckin' Championship,* Spring Hill. Miss Drumstick contest, performances by Masaryktown Czechoslovakian dancers, "chicken concertos," "plucking" concerts. Previous festival pluckin' records in *Guinness Book of World Records.* This small community northwest of Tampa is one of nation's leading poultry centers.

November: Winter Fishing tournaments, Pompano Beach and West Palm Beach. *International Boat Show,* Ft. Lauderdale features in-the-water boats. *St. Sophia Greek Festival,* Miami, first weekend. *Golden Age Games,* Sanford. *Antique Car Meet,* Ormond Beach. *"Turkey Trot" Drag Races,* Gainesville; draws contestants from throughout the Southeast.

December: Tangerine Bowl, Orlando; holiday bowl game for two top football teams from small colleges. *Gator Bowl Festival,* Jacksonville; the Gator Bowl football game, basketball tournament, boating regatta, and President's Ball. Many communities have glittering *Christmas boat parades.* Among them: DeLand, Ft. Lauderdale, Boca Raton, Madiera Beach, Pompano Beach. *Candlelight Processional,* Disney World.

NATIONAL PARKS. Warren F. Hamilton, former superintendent of *Everglades National Park*, said. "There is a subtle charm to the area unlike anything else in this country." Alligators, orchids, and stilt-walking birds are subtle? Well, it is subtle in the sense that the 'Glades' larger self creeps up on you like a wind rising rising. Only as your eyes become accustomed to the seeming sameness do you begin to glimpse the world within. Its grasslands, jungle hammocks, and mangrove forests bemuse the first-time visitor. To begin to *see*, in the Everglades, is to enjoy an unfolding more vital and strange than the opening of a great flower. Motorists en route to Flamingo, the civilized takeoff point for most ventures, have a better chance to understand all their journeys in the 'Glades if they are first briefed at the park entrance by a ranger.

When you get there, forget your first impression that nothing is moving in that great sawgrass marsh and look again for otter, bobcat, black bear, panther, whitetail deer, and 230 species of birds. Hammocks (small jungle islands which dot the 'Glades) are their natural habitat. The Park Service has established some elevated boardwalks so the visitor may peer down into the hammock itself. Here in their natural state are the tropical mixtures of orchids, mosses, and ferns imitated in the city gardens. No visitor, the rangers say, has been bitten by a poisonous snake, for the snakes mostly stay clear of inhabited sections. The Shark Valley Loop Road, south of the Tamiami Trail and the newest gateway to the park, provides a look at alligators, which sluggishly con the tourists for pretzels. An observation ramp over Shark Valley shows the Everglades nakedly to the eye from 35 feet up. Traveling speed on the Loop Road is 25 miles an hour; it has 21 stopping points, each with exhibits indicating the rocks, plants, animals and bird life to be found there.

The Visitor Center at Flamingo has a large dining room, cocktail lounge, a good-size motel, and a U.S. post office. The facilities include a large marina with dockside electric power, launching ramps for private boats, campgrounds, picnic areas, service station. Boats can be hired for fishing or sightseeing; there are also houseboat rentals and canoe trips into huge rookeries. Ranger naturalist lectures and excursions are free. Campsites continue to expand, with a growing corps of outdoor types springing up in the U.S. Admission to Everglades National Park is $2 per car and 50¢ on foot. Fees for campsites are $2 per car on improved sites and $1 for unimproved sites.

For *Apalachicola National Forest*, Tallahassee can be your take-off point. Silver Lake, one of the forest's chief attractions, is just 8 mi. W on Rte. 20 and three mi. S on Rte. 260. Many lakes and rivers lie in an extensive upper state area running to more than 500,000 acres. At Silver Lake, camping with tent or trailer is possible, and electrical and water connections are available for trailers—along with laundry, sewage, drinking water, and toilet facilities. Hitchcock Lake, 17 mi. N of Carrabelle and approached first on Rte. 67 and then a mile and a half east on Forest Service Road 125-B, has camping, with all the trimmings. Camel and Wright lakes are other main attractions. Wright Lake is two mi. S of Sumatra on Rte. 65 with a turn west for a mile and a half on Forest Service Road 101. Camel Lake is 5 mi. S of Bristol and Rte. 20, on Rtes. 67 and 379 and Forest Service Road 108.

In *Ocala National Forest*, private hunting and fishing camps mingle with a rather untamed semitropical wilderness managed by the Forestry Service. Canoe trips down Juniper Springs provide an exciting look at the inside of the forest. The recreation area at Alexander Springs has drawn attention of late from those who describe the camping glories of the state. What can you see here? If you know your way, there are glimpses of wild hog, alligator, otter, deer, even panther and bear. In the springs, water temperature is 74 degrees most days of the year, and a wide, white sand beach lures the bather. A paddlewheeler makes scenic trips down Spring Creek. Head for the Alexander Springs area on State 445. It's 48 mi. from Ocala, or 45 mi. from US 1 at Daytona Beach. Marjorie Kinnan Rawlings' much-read book, *The Yearling*, was set in the Big Scrub, which gives the forest its native character. The *Big Scrub Hunt Camp* is located at a junction of Forest Service roads 88 and 73, 12 mi. S of Central Tower and Rte. 40. Pens for hunting dogs are here, and a meat storage house for those who come in with game. Halfmoon Lake Campground, 20 mi. W of Astor on State 40 (south one and a quarter miles on Forest Service Road 79), sits on a large lake in a beautiful oak hammock. It has boat launching facilities.

In *Osceola National Forest*, the chief attraction is a 2,000-acre natural lake. To reach Ocean Pond go two and a half miles north of US 90 at Olustee. Lake City is also in the vicinity of the forest, which runs to 157,000 flattish acres. Hunters head for the nearby Osceola Game Management Area, where a special permit is required. Ocean Pond has 24 camping and picnicking units, and a boat dock.

Fort de Soto National Memorial Park is a prime 900-acre picnicking area near St. Petersburg. It has smooth roads and consists of five islands with white beaches, well dispersed picnic tables and charcoal grills. You can approach by boat. Take excursion craft from St. Petersburg, or drive in by toll causeway (65 cents total) from US 19 near Sunshine Parkway. Near the fort itself, at the southwest end, fishermen can cast from a 1,000-foot pier. Another long pier overlooks Tampa Bay. Fine facilities for tenters at St. Christopher Key. Units also are being developed on St. Jean Key.

Gulf Islands National Seashore, almost 76,000 acres, stretches from Destin all the way to Ship Island near Gulfport, Mississippi. Excellent beachfront camping, or by Fort Pickens. Admission fee to the Fort Pickens area. Ranger programs.

Canaveral National Seashore, encompassing 57,000 acres, is located north of the Kennedy Space Center. The Visitor Center is open every day from 7:30 A.M. to 7:30 P.M. Beautiful beaches for swimming; excellent fishing.

 STATE PARKS. Despite the often justified concern that Florida is rapidly becoming overdeveloped, there are many areas which remain in a natural condition. Happily, many of those areas shall remain so permanently, as state parks. Most state parks charge 50¢ per person admission (under 6 free), $5 nightly for camping, $6 in the Keys, $2 extra for electricity.

Anastasia is 3 mi. S of St. Augustine on A1A. 1,035 acres with facilities for camping, picnicking, boating, nature trails, skin diving and scuba diving.

Caladesi Island State Park, offshore Dunedin. Swimming, boating, fishing, skin diving, scuba diving, picnicking, 60-ft. observation tower.

Bill Baggs Cape Florida State Park, on the southern tip of Key Biscayne, historic *Cape Florida Lighthouse*, all sports and picnicking.

Collier-Seminole State Park is 12 mi. NE of Marco where Big Cypress Swamp joins the Everglades. Historically, the last refuge of Seminole Indians. Picnicking, boating, ramp, fishing, camping, and nature trails.

Falling Waters State Recreation Area is a 154-acre park 3 mi. S. of Chipley off Rte. 77A. Picnicking, camping, swimming, nature trails.

Faver-Dykes State Park, 752 acres of woodlands and marsh. Picnicking, camping, fishing, boat ramp, boating, and hiking. 15 mi. S. of St. Augustine.

Florida Caverns State Park, 3 mi. N of Marianna. Picnicking, camping, boating, swimming, skin diving and scuba diving, fishing, concession, nature trails, and youth camping area.

Fort Clinch State Park has museum exhibits, nature trails. On State A1A at Fernandina Beach; 1,086 acres, with picnicking, fishing barbecue pits, tent and trailer camps, recreation lodge. Union Army-uniformed Park Rangers staff garrison in Living History exhibit.

Fort Gadsden State Historic Site, south of Sumatra on State 65, has 78 acres cut with nature trails. Picnicking facilities and historical and recreational spots.

Mike Roess Gold Head Branch State Park has vacation cabins and barbecue pits with 1,338 acres of recreational park. 6 mi. NE of Keystone Heights on State

21. Fishing, boating, rentals, ramps, water skiing, swimming, skin diving and scuba diving, picnicking, concession, camping.

Highlands Hammock State Park is 6 mi. W of Sebring off US 98. Has 3,800 acres, including picnicking, fireplaces, shelters, concession, camping, nature trails.

Hillsborough River State Park is accented by a swinging bridge which spans the river. Picnicking, concession, camping, boating, rentals, skin diving and scuba diving, fishing. 6 mi. SW of Zephyrhills.

Hontoon Island State Park, 1,060-acre park 6 mi. W of De Land, accessible only by boat. Tent camping only, picnicking, cottages for rent, observation tower, boating, nature trails, marina, concession, boat rentals, fishing.

Ichetucknee Springs State Park, 16 mi. NW of High Springs, Rte, 47N, 238 W from Fort White. 2,241 acres, borders the Ichetucknee River. Especially popular for tubing, swimming, skin diving and scuba diving. Picnicking, fishing and boating. 8:30 to sundown.

John Pennekamp Coral Reef State Park is the first underwater park in the United States. 3 mi. NE of Key Largo. Part of only living coral reef formations in North America. It is a mecca for skin divers. Picnicking, swimming, fishing, marina, boat rentals, launching facilities, nature trails, concession and camping.

Jonathan Dickinson State Park is 3 mi. N of Jupiter on US 1 and has 8,923 acres. Picnicking, camping, concession shelters, playground equipment, cabins, swimming, fishing, boating, rentals, ramps, nature trails, bicycle rentals, horseback riding, guided tours.

Little Talbot Island State Park, 17 mi. E of Jacksonville on A1A. 2,500-acre island park with picnicking, swimming, museum, fishing, boating, sand dunes, bathhouse, playgrounds, concession, camping, thick forest, skin diving and scuba diving, and youth camping area.

Long Key State Recreation Area is 291 acres of island in the Florida Keys. Camping, picnicking, swimming, fishing, boating, skin diving and scuba diving, playground equipment, youth camping area and concession. Located on Long Key at Layington.

Manatee Springs State Park. 8 mi. W of Chiefland on Rte. 320. 1,799-acre site with camping, picnicking, concessions, swimming, skin diving, scuba diving, boat ramp, rentals, fishing, nature trails.

Myakka River State Park, nationally noted for variety and quantity of birds, 17 mi. SE of Sarasota, 28,875 acres. Picnicking, concession, fishing, boat rentals, cabins, camping, nature trails, nature museums, and backpacking trail.

Ochlockonee River State Park, 4 mi. N of Panacea. Heavily wooded land, with swimming, boating, picnicking, fishing, and camping.

O'Leno State Park, 9 mi. N of High Springs on US 41, has 1,717 acres. Picnicking, camping, swimming, skin diving and scuba diving, fishing, boating, well-equipped group camp, and nature trails.

Pepper Park State Park, E of Fort Pierce on State A1A. 32 acres of white sand beach with footbridge across the Indian River to 958-acre Jack Island. Picnicking, swimming, fishing, boating, skin diving and scuba diving, concession, guided tours. Museum of local history.

St. Andrews State Recreation Area has 1,022 acres, 3 mi. E of Panama City Beach. Camping, picnicking, concession, swimming, skin diving and scuba diving, fishing, boating, ramp, dock, museum exhibits.

St. Joseph Peninsula State Park has one of most beautiful beaches in Florida. 20 mi. W of Port St. Joe. Camping, swimming, fishing, boating, skin diving and scuba diving, picnicking, concession, playground equipment, boat rentals.

Suwannee River State Park has 1,838 acres of scenic, historical and recreation sites, 13 mi. W of Live Oak on US 90. Camping, picnicking, stoves, concession, fishing, boating, ramps, swimming, youth camping area, and nature trail.

Tomoka State Park, 2 mi. N of Ormond Beach, is an archeological park on 915 acres of land with scenic historical interest. Camping, picnicking, concession, shelters, playground, fishing, launching ramp, dock, nature trails and museum with exhibits.

Torreya State Park, on State 20, 4 mi. E of Blountstown. Confederate gun pits, old river boat landing. Fishing, picnicking, concession, barbecue pits, camping, and nature trails.

Wekiwa Springs State Park, E of Apopka on State 436. Picnicking, nature trails, fishing, swimming, boating, skin diving and scuba diving.

Wiggins Pass. 6 mi. S of Bonita Springs. Picnicking, swimming, saltwater fishing, boating.

Big Lagoon, 10 mi. SW of Pensacola, off State 292. Picnic, swim, fish, boat.

St. George State Park, 10 mi. SE of Eastpoint, off U.S. 98. Sand dune beaches on Gulf. Picnic, fish, boat, backback, primitive camping reached via 4-mi. trail.

Lake Talquin, 20 mi. E. of Tallahassee off State 20 and Vause Rd. Picnic pavilion for 200 guests, fishing, boating.

Stephen Foster State Folk Culture Center, White Springs, off I-75 and U.S. 41. Museum, picnicking, boat tours on Suwannee River.

Fort Foster Historic Site at Hillsborough River State Park. Fort is replica of original built in 1837 during Second Seminole War.

Ybor City State Museum, 1818 9th Ave., Tampa. Building on National Registry of Historic Sites. Exhibits tell story of immigrants who worked in cigar factories.

DeLeon Springs State Park, on U.S. 17 N of DeLand. Original Fountain of Youth, swimming, camping, picnics, peacocks roam free, nice flowering shrubs.

CAMPING OUT. Florida is a year-round affair, although the best times are winter (except in cold spells) and spring. Mosquitoes and rain are most likely to intrude in spring, summer or early fall. Florida state parks permit camping for $7 per day ($8 for parks in the Florida Keys only) on a 2-wk. permit issued by the park superintendent, for up to and including four people in one family. Additional campers using the site will be charged $1 per person (maximum persons per site is eight). Exceptions will be made for families with minor children. Fees for extra cars at a campsite are $2 nightly. More than 2600 campsites are available, with no additional charge for fishing, swimming, picnicking or boat ramps. Campsites may be reserved by telephone only directly to the parks. Many camp areas in the national forests permit 3-wk. stays; fees vary.

TRAILER TIPS. Here are just a few of the more elaborate sites available across the state:

Guernsey City. A mobile waterfront community at Tampa on the sandy beaches of Old Tampa Bay. 4851 Gandy Blvd. (write for brochure). *El Rancho Village.* At Bradenton. It's one of the larger Florida parks. Citrus trees and concrete patios. Door-to-door mail delivery. Beaches and fishing nearby. Adults only and no pets. Rte. 301 and Cortez Road. Write for color brochure. *Mobilemanor Inn.* They want the retired ("adults only") for this park at 2866 Okeechobee Road in West Palm Beach. Ten-minute drive to the ocean. Served by city buses. Fishing and boating on lake. Pool. One block to shopping center. Dog-racing, jai alai, baseball nearby.

Sarasota Mobile Home Park. In their air-conditioned auditorium, year-round dances. Free movies, too. Game nights. Big layout of shuffleboard courts. Calls itself "One of America's finest and oldest trailer parks." US 301 at Laurel St. *Shangri-La.* Dramatic pool under a tremendous screened enclosure. Putting green for golfers and lawn croquet. Mail at the door, sodded lawns, city water. On the West Coast, it's between Largo and Clearwater. *Crystal Bay Mobile Estates.* Between Clearwater and Tarpon Springs. Pool and marina (applications taken for membership in Crystal Bay Yacht Club). Recreation hall and shuffleboard courts. Reached on A19. 5 min. drive to Gulf fishing. *Whispering Creek Village.* At Fort Pierce on US 1 and Airport Road. Pool and party cook-out facilities with city sewer service, private phones, modern laundry, barber shop, hobby rooms, library lounge. *Colonial Acres.* Pool and putting green, recreation hall, planned activities. Barbecue and picnic area, twice weekly garbage collection, mail at the door, street lights. 9674 NW 10th Ave., Miami. *Rainbow Isles.* Pompano Beach waterfront setting at 751 S. Federal Hwy. Over a hundred spaces on the water. Patios and paved roads, city water, putting green, pool, luggage storage, free lawn maintenance. *Bay Pines Park.* Three private lakes stocked for fishing in a St. Petersburg setting at 1005 Bay Pines Blvd. A19. Ft. Myers has the *Red Coconut Park.* Trailer space in Florida is extremely tight, so stop early in the day. Better still, send ahead for confirmed reservations.

HOT SPRINGS. A year-round 87 degrees is the constant temperature of *Warm Mineral Springs,* 12 mi. below Venice on US 41. Approximately 10 million gallons flow daily. The Inn there has 29 units plus nearby cottages. It usually has a brisk business of arthritis victims testing the waters. The Inn is inexpensive. Ft. Myers also has a warm springs.

For sightseeing purposes, the cooler springs of Florida are unmatched in the nation, and many have been developed as tourist attractions.

Some places to go: *Silver Springs,* near Ocala on State 40. Its daily discharge is 834 million gallons. It's a famous resort, sought after by the outdoor-minded. *Rainbow Springs,* near Dunnellon on US 41, has a larger flow than any limestone spring in the U.S. and possibly the world (659 million gallons). Underwater glimpses here from submarine boats at exotic marine growths and browsing fish. *Homosassa Springs,* on US 19, and *Salt Springs,* 28 mi. E of Ocala on 19, both have saltwater fish swimming in them. Observatory portholes view directly on mangrove snapper, sea trout, snook, channel bass, sheepshead at Homosassa. It's called "Nature's Fish Bowl." In *Ocala National Forest,* campers go to *Juniper Springs,* off Rte. 40; *Silver Gleen,* on State 19; *Alexander Springs,* 14 mi. from Umatilla on State 19 and 445. "A virtual Eden" says the State Development Commission of Alexander Springs. Below Tallahassee at *Natural Bridge,* springs bubble in a river that appears and disappears. More remote springs (you boat in or have to go by winding, unpaved road) are *Cypress Springs* near Vernon, and *Ichatucknee Springs* near Hildreth on State 47 and State 238. A principal attraction: *Ponce De Leon Springs,* 8 mi. N of De Land, reached on US 17, at DeLeon Springs, formerly privately owned, is now a state park.

MUSEUMS AND GALLERIES. *Historical: Pensacola Historical Museum.* 405 S. Adams St. Housed in 1832 Old Christ Church. Closed Mon. Free.

St. Petersburg: Haas Museum & Grace S. Turner House & Village, 3511 2nd Ave. Antiques. Closed Mon., Sept.

Tallahassee: The capitol building, *Division of Archives, History & Records Management,* 401 Gaines St. Archeological history museum.

Tampa: Tampa Municipal Museum, in the south wing of the U. of Tampa's main building. Mon. to Sat. Closed Aug. Free.

Art: Daytona Beach: Museum of Arts and Sciences, 1040 Museum Blvd. Cuban paintings, F. Batista collection; U.S., Caribbean, and Central American fine and decorative arts. Closed nat'l. holidays. Free. Charge for planetarium.

Fort Lauderdale: Fort Lauderdale Museum of the Arts, 426 East Las Olas Blvd. Emphasis on American and European graphics of the 19th and 20th centuries. Southwestern American Indian ceramics and basketry, and collection of Japanese *Inro* and *Netsuke.* Special exhibitions Sept. to July. Closed Mon. and August. Free.

Gainesville: University Gallery, U. of Florida, S.W. 13th St. and 4th Ave. Study collection contains historic and contemporary prints and Oriental (India) paintings and small sculptures. Closed Sat., holidays and Sept. Free.

Florida State Museum on U. of Florida campus has outstanding historical exhibits and Mayan walk-through palace.

Jacksonville: Cummer Gallery of Art, 829 Riverside Ave. Western European art from 6th century B.C. to present. Free. Closed Mon. & nat'l. holidays; *Jacksonville Art Museum,* 4106 Blvd. Center Dr. Emphasis on 20th-century works by living artists and pre-Columbian art. Free. Closed Aug. and legal holidays.

Orlando: Loch Haven Art Center, Inc., 2416 North Mills Ave. Small collection 20th-century American paintings, graphics. Closed Mon. and holidays. Free.

Palm Beach: The Society of the Four Arts. Four Arts Plaza. Special exhibitions and performing arts events. Closed Sat. Botanic gardens: open all year. Free.

Pensacola: Pensacola Art Association, 407 S. Jefferson St. Graphics and regional paintings. Closed Mon. and nat'l holidays. Free.

St. Augustine: Pan American Building, 97 St. George St. Art gallery with South American paintings, sculptures and artifacts.

St. Petersburg: Museum of Fine Arts, 255 Beach Dr. N. 9 galleries, including 3 authentic English and French period rooms. Closed Mon., July. *Dali Museum,* 1000 3rd St. S. has world's largest collection of Dali works.

Tallahassee: Florida State University Art Gallery, Fine Arts Bldg. Temporary exhibitions of collections and special exhibitions. Free. Closed school holidays: *Le Moyne Art Gallery,* N. Gadsden St. Free.

Tampa: Florida Center for the Arts, U. of S. Fla., 4202 E. Fowler Ave. 25 art exhibitions presented annually. Free. Closed university holidays.

West Palm Beach: Norton Gallery, 1451 S. Olive Ave. Chinese jades and many collections. Free.

Winter Park: Morse Gallery of Art., Holt Ave., Rollins College. American and European art, glass, stained glass windows. Free. Closed holidays and school vacation.

 HISTORIC SITES. *Apalachicola: John Gorrie State Historic Memorial,* Ave. D & 6 St. Features exhibits of early local history. *Bradenton: DeSoto National Memorial,* 75th St. Free. *Bushnell: Dade Battlefield State Historic Site,* on US 301. Site of infamous Dade Massacre in 1836, which touched off Second Seminole War. Monuments mark the battlefield, museum contains exhibits and artifacts of the battle. 80-acre recreational site. Admission 25¢. *Cedar Key: Cedar Key State Memorial.* State 24. 19 acres of scenic and historical sights, including the St. Clair Whitman Museum. *Crystal River: Crystal River State Archeological Site,* off US 19, 98. One of the most spectacular and important pre-Columbian Indian sites in Florida. Museum houses Indian artifacts. *Ellenton: Gamble Mansion State Museum,* US 301, 4 mi. NE of Bradenton. *Fort Myers: Edison Home Museum,* 2341 McGregor Blvd. First prefabricated home built in Maine and brought to Florida by boat, housing Edison's inventions. *Homasassa Springs: Yulee Sugar Mill State Historic Site.* 5 mi. W of US 19 on State 490. Part of sugar-making machinery built by David Levy Yulee, Florida's first U.S. Senator and Confederate leader. Free. *Jacksonville: Fort Caroline National Memorial,* 12713 Ft. Caroline Rd. Free.

Key West: Audubon House, Whitehead & Greene Sts. Close to the Coast Guard Station, almost as far south as you can go. *New Smyrna Beach: New Smyrna State Historic Site,* 1 mi. W on Rte. 44. Remains of a large sugar mill destroyed by Indians during Seminole War. Free.

Olustee: Olustee Battlefield State Historic Site Museum, off US 90, 2 mi. E. *Port St. Joe: Constitution Historic Memorial.* On US 98. 12 acres of historical and scenic sights, museum exhibits.

Rattlesnake Island: Fort Matanzas National Monument, 14 mi. S of St. Augustine. Free.

St. Augustine: All of St. Augustine is, in fact, one enormous historic site, with the early days of American development written indelibly in crumbling or reconstructed stone. The Visitor Information Center has a free Visitor's Guide to help you decide which of dozens of historical buildings you want to see. The *Historic St. Augustine Preservation Board* has strip tickets to all the historic buildings. *Castillo de San Marcos,* located on site of an original Spanish fort. *St. Petersburg: Madira Bickel Mound.* 10-acre historic memorial located at Terra Cela Island off US 41 S of St. Petersburg. *Tallahassee: Natural Bridge State Historic Site* marks spot where Confederate forces repulsed a Federal force to prevent capture of the state capitol. Free. *Prince & Princess Mural Home of Bellevue.* Wknds.

 TOURS. *Gray Line Tours* and *American Sightseeing Bus Tours* operate all over the state. Seven of their most popular tours are Walt Disney World, Sea World, Kennedy Space Center, Cypress Gardens, Busch Gardens, Silver Springs, St. Augustine. Gray Line also conducts tours of major cities in the state, such as Miami, Fort Lauderdale, St. Petersburg, Tampa, and special tours to attractions within the cities. Tours of varying lengths (3½ hrs. to one day).

Florida Parlor Car Tours offers a seven-day Circle Tour from Jacksonville, which visits Silver Springs, Weeki Wachee Springs, St. Petersburg, Cypress Gardens, the Everglades, Miami Beach, Miami, Parrot Jungle, Key West, Fort Lauderdale, Walt Disney World, Marineland and St. Augustine among other places. *Tauck Tours,* departing from Jacksonville, has a similar nine-day Florida Circle Tour. *Greyhound, Continental,* and *Trailways* all offer special tours from cities around the country to various Florida locations and attractions. Greyhound also operates a good many local tours.

By Boat: The *Captain Anderson* features two-hour narrated cruises of the St. Pete Beach area, daily at 2 p.m. (except Sun.). Sunset dinner-dance cruises sail out at 7 p.m. and return at 10 p.m. Private charters available, too. Behind Dolphin Shopping Village on St. Petersburg Beach. From mid-Oct. to mid-May.

St. Augustine's sightseeing cruise takes 1½ hr., leaves from Municipal Yacht Pier, Avenida Menendez. In *Titusville* boat tours leave from Westlands Marina daily. *Winter Park* has a narrated tour of the canals and lakes to view estates, azaleas, Rollins College, etc. There's also a 2-hr. narrated cruise on the *Commodore II* leaving from Bill King's Marina in Marathon, Oct. to May and July to Labor Day. And at *Homosassa Springs,* US 19, there is a scenic boat trip.

Glass-bottom boats will open a whole new world. Silver Springs, Wakulla Springs.

You can rent a river cruiser on pontoons from *Sunshine Lines* in De Land. The fleet of 30 cruisers is available for the St. Johns River trip, which can go as far north as Jacksonville, about 130 nautical miles. Information at *Sunshine Lines,* P.O. Box 3349, De Land 32720. (800) 874-7004.

Key Largo has a 2-hr. boat trip to the coral reefs daily if the weather is good and *Key West* a 2-hr. reef cruise on the *Fireball* from the Gulf to the ocean daily, if clear, except for one week in May and in Oct.

Il Cristo Degli Abissi (Christ of the Abysses), a 9-ft. bronze replica of an Italian statue, can be glimpsed by sightseers who take a glass-bottom boat tour of the *John Pennekamp Coral Reef State Park.* Skeletons of old ships lie here with tropical fish swimming among them. The remarkably visible reef has 40 kinds of coral and is 21 mi. long. The trip lasts 2½ hrs.; leaves three times daily. Those who are willing to take the underwater tour can hire diving equipment on the spot—tank with air, masks, fins, snorkel.

Jungle Queen cruises, leaving from Fort Lauderdale's huge and beautiful Bahia Mar Yacht Basin, has two sailings daily. The Jungle Queen passes Venetian Isles, winds through Fort Lauderdale, takes in exotic gardens, tropical bird grounds, Seminole villages, Hollywood, Intracoastal Waterway, Port Everglades and Stranahan River. From mid-Jan. to May there are also dinner cruises with entertainment. The *Paddlewheel Queen* leaves from 1 blk. S. of Oakland Park Beach

Bridge on daytime and evening dinner cruises. The *Island Queen* operates out of Riviera Beach and the *Bay Queen* in Sanford on the St. John's River.

Everglades Jungles Cruises leaves from City Yacht Basin, Fort Myers, for a 3-hr. trip up Caloosakachee River to Everglades. Birds, rookeries, wild orchids and alligators can be seen. No cruises in Sept. or on Mon. from May to Aug. and Nov. to Christmas. Also other cruises of varying lengths. Call 334-7474 for details.

If you have the time, take a *Shanty Boat Cruise* on the *Lazy Bones* from Caloosahatchee River into Everglades. There's time allotted to explore by swamp buggy and air boat and to visit heron and egret rookeries. Departs on Mon. from Orange River Dock, Nov. to Apr. and July, returns Fri. No children under 16. For reservations write Rte. 29, Box 434, Fort Myers 33905, or tel. 694–3401.

At *Myakka River State Park,* on State 72, 17 mi. E of Sarasota, you can see an exciting variety of wildlife.

Island and Casino Tours. Cruise ships leave daily from Dodge Island port in Miami, and Port Everglades in Fort Lauderdale. The casinos at Freeport and Paradise Island are the favored destinations. Island life lures non-gamblers, also, to Nassau, and colorful Caribbean ports.

Check locally for more cruises. There are many—aboard boats large and small —throughout Florida.

By train. When you hit the Florida Keys, you can take the *Conch Train Tour* or Old Town Trolley; both are narrated. Fort Lauderdale has three train tours: *Voyager Train* leaves from Bahia Mar Yacht Basin for an 18-mi., 1½ hr. trip through the city, daily. There is also from the same location a Safari Tour, 25 mi., daily. The *Gold Coast Railroad,* 811 S.W. 34th St., offers a steam train tour Sun. The fee includes inspection of an armored car used by Presidents Roosevelt, Truman and Eisenhower, and a museum car with railroading souvenirs. *St. Augustine's* sightseeing train trip offers a 24-hr. ticket, stop-off privileges, and pkg. tours. The regular 7-mi., 1-hr. narrated trip leaves 3 Cordova St. daily, except Christmas, every quarter hr.

 SPECIAL INTEREST TOURS. *Wild life tours* can be arranged during the winter season into remote areas where the eagles and egrets fly. Contact the Audubon Center of Greater West Palm Beach Chamber of Commerce. Naturalist guides take nature tours through Okefenokee, Dry Tortugas and other spots.

The Florida traveler becomes a *bird watcher* in spite of himself. Tall water birds grace the canals and the lower coast has cowbirds among the sea cows. Only here and in Alaska can you see the bald eagle with his treetop nest. You'll see them in the Kissimmee River Valley, Everglades National Park and Ocala National Forest. At Myakka River State Park, 17 mi. E of Sarasota, a 30-ft.-high observation tower offers a glimpse of a great water bird rookery. Six miles of the road is in too bad shape for cars, you'll have to go by bus. An evening train tour leaves Tues. to Sat. at 7:30 (8:30 in summer). The frigate bird exists in great concentration on Bird and Kitchell keys, near Fort Myers. Southeast of Fort Myers a great nesting colony of wood storks inhabits Corkscrew Swamp at Immokalee. The pelican, celebrated for his beak, actually is most astounding in his diving habits. You can see his amazingly funny slop-plop into the water at Pelican Island, 15 mi. N of Vero Beach in the Indian River, where up to 3,500 pelicans hatch annually. Access is by boat only. The Cape Kennedy area has been called the best bird-watching territory in the country—and not for its "iron birds," either: *Suncoast Seabird Sanctuary.* Ralph Heath has received national fame for his tender, loving care to sick and injured land and seabirds. Open 7 days a week during daylight hours. Free. 18328 Gulf Blvd., Indian Shores, near St. Pete Beach.

Turtle watching: Female sea turtles come shoreward on a July night to lay their eggs in the sand. Local newspapers keep track, and can tell you which nights to stake yourself out on the shoreline. Mother digs a hole and lays up to 300 eggs in 45 min. She is jittery beforehand, but is not easily disturbed once she's embarked on egglaying. Try Jensen Beach in Martin County.

 GARDENS. Garden visiting in Florida is nothing like tulip time in the Netherlands. Enter a noted garden in this state (there are many, for its very name means "flowers"), and you will often find you have come not to a garden but a garden-jungle. Considerable commercial competition has been exerted by tropical planters trying to outdo each other. At Cape Coral a Mount Rushmore in miniature has taken shape in the gardens created for a pathway known as the *Avenue of Roses.* Many growers, not geared up to make sculptured mountains within their jungles, simply strive for the closest possible imitation of the more spectacular aspect of the tropical and subtropical forests.

One of the first to be seized with a desire to realize a true tropic garden was the inventor, Thomas A. Edison. Edison's Tropic Gardens, open to the public, are located within the laboratory he left at his winter home at Fort Myers. This botanical garden ("one of the most complete in America") must be much as he pictured it when he first began to plant. The two-inch banyan tree brought him from India in 1925 by Harvey Firestone is now more than 250 feet around the trunk. Edison found the materials of invention growing right out of the ground. The swimming pool he built in 1900 was reinforced with the same material he used for electric-light filaments—bamboo. It was a natural stand of bamboo that helped attract him to Fort Myers. His swimming pool has no leak as yet. The artesian well which fills it also supplies the underground irrigation for the gardens. Visit Edison Tropical Gardens.

Edison had the jump on most of those who now capitalize on Florida's rare propensity to throw up lush gardens on a quick schedule. But fabulous gardens abound. Here are a few of them:

Bok Singing Tower, southeast of Cypress Gardens, houses one of the world's largest carillons. The 205-foot tower is made of coquina stone and marble, surrounded by sub-tropical gardens and nature trails.

Busch Gardens— yes, they owe everything to Anheuser Busch and to Adolphus Busch, August A. Busch, Sr., and Adolphus Busch, III. Showmanship with birds mingles with a concentration of 150,000 trees and shrubs. Each fall 50,000 annuals are planted. Best of all, you'll get a chit that entitles you to a free Busch beer at one of the Gardens' restaurants or pubs. A monorail passes through "African veldt inhabited by hippos, rhinos, waterbuck, and wildebeest." As Horace Sutton says: "The drinking man's Disneyland." 3000 Busch Blvd., Tampa.

In the *Caribbean Gardens* at *Naples* winding paths take the visitor through an ordered jungle interspliced with lagoons. Waterbirds in great numbers; and there are several bird shows daily.

Cypress Gardens, east of Lakeland, a world-famous attraction of tropical plants and flowers, and water-ski shows of champions and aqua maids.

Marie Selby Botanical Gardens, opened in Sarasota in 1975, created for scientific research. Offers guided tours, lectures and botanical courses. Includes stroll through the Selby house, built in 1920s, and display greenhouse.

Merritt Island Tropical Nursery was called by Logan Owen, Jr., "a kind of United Nations of Tropical plants that grow naturally on the island plus scores of tropical and semitropical specimens from most of the countries in the torrid zone." Prospective purchasers only are invited to tour. Between the missile firing range at Cape Kennedy and the mainland.

Sarasota Jungle Gardens, highly accessible, is at 3701 Bay Shore Road, just off US 41. Cactus as well as tropical plantings grow along the jungle lake. Flamingos, swans, and other waterbirds flash in the sun-streaked waters.

Maclay State Gardens, 51½ mi. N of Tallahassee, planted as a private estate garden, has one of the South's finest azalea and camellia collections. The original

Aunt Jettyu Camellia—125 yrs. old—blooms there. Lake Hall picnic area is adjacent; open year round. Swimming, skin diving and scuba diving, boating, fishing, picnicking and concession. Open 9 to sunset all year.

Ravine Gardens. Palatka, is breathtaking at azalea time (early spring) and makes ruggedly beautiful walking any time. Brooks and steep ravines.

Tiki Gardens, Indian Rocks Beach (nr. St. Pete Beach), features a Polynesian Adventure Trail, a Mangrove Jungle Walk and a thicket of shops, as well as a pleasant restaurant with views of birds, beasts and fish while dining.

Washington Oaks State Gardens was originally a Spanish land grant to Bautesta Don Juan Ferreira in 1815. Nature museum, picnicking, nature trails and fishing. Three mi. S of Marineland. *Botanic Gardens* at the Society of the Four Arts, Palm Beach, is open daily. Free.

MUSIC. Among the many orchestras in the Sunshine State are the *Florida Symphony* (Orlando), *Fort Lauderdale Symphony, Hollywood Philharmonic, Jacksonville Symphony, Pensacola Symphony. Central Florida Community Orchestra* (Winter Park), *Palm Beach Symphony, Lakeland Symphony Orchestra.* All are active throughout the winter season, and a number give pops concerts in late spring and summer. The *Florida Gulf Coast Symphony Orchestra* performs regularly at McKay Auditorium, Tampa, Nov. to late Apr. and at Bayfront Auditorium, St. Petersburg, early Nov. to early May.

The *Asolo Opera Co.,* Sarasota, offers opera in English mid-Jan. to mid-Feb. Also in Sarasota, *Van Wezel Performing Arts Hall,* 777 N. Tamiami Trail, offers a varied program Sept. to June.

Outstanding annual musical events in Florida include the *Florida Folk Festival* at White Springs in early May, when over 2,000 performers present choral and dance works; *Winter Park's Bach Festival* (mid-Feb.); *Stephen Foster Week,* White Springs (mid-Jan.); *New College Summer Music Festival,* Sarasota, wkends in June. *Hollywood's Seven Lively Arts Festival* (mid-Feb.) offers everything from classic drama to jazz concerts.

STAGE AND REVUES. Popular plays are presented in winter at the *Royal Poinciana Playhouse,* Palm Beach. From early Feb. to mid-Apr. the *Black Hills Passion Play* can be seen at the Passion Play Amphitheater, nr. Lake Wales. Sarasota offers an 8-month season of plays at *Asolo Theater,* a gem of an Italian 18th-century theater. *Burt Reynolds Dinner Theater,* Jupiter, has good food, good theater. The *Players* is a Sarasota community theater group with nightly performances mid-Oct to mid-May at 838 N. Tamiami Trail. *Daytona Playhouse,* 100 Jessamine Blvd., presents drama, comedy and musicals in late Oct. to early June, as well as a musical in Aug. *Lake Worth's Playhouse* and *Lakeland's Theatre-in-the-Round* at Florida Southern College, schedule regular performances in winter. Broadway musicals and plays are presented in Orlando, Jacksonville, and St. Petersburg, late Dec. to late April. The *Sunrise Music Theater,* near Fort Lauderdale, has booked such superstars as Frank Sinatra. Now a National Historic Landmark, the ornate *Tampa Theater,* downtown Tampa, features live entertainment and film festivals. St. Petersburg's *Bayfront Center* offers an interesting program of Broadway plays, ice-skating revues, and personal appearances by entertainment celebrities.

CASINOS. The closest casino to Florida is in the Bahamas. Extralegal card games are common in south Florida, but powerful factions continue to defeat those who would make gambling go the Nevada way. The procasino element hasn't overcome the objections of Florida governors from nonresort counties; nor has it been able to sway objecting caterers, who fear the wrong kind of visitor. Palm Beach and West Palm Beach (as well as Miami and Miami Beach) have become, therefore, prime jumping-off spots for visitors lured by the promise of close action with a pair of dice. But there are also roulette and slot machines. The well-spoken, very young British croupiers are a pleasure to watch.

 NIGHTCLUBS. Resort area night life includes very high, and very low, quality clubs. Nearly all of those listed here will mean an expensive evening. But claims of "No Cover —No Minimum" don't necessarily mean a cheap evening. Know about cost before you order. A continuous effort is made to eliminate the B-girl from south Florida but the clubs are forever changing hands. There are clubs for the dignified and for the sport. In the more expensive nightclubs, a small card will often make a simple statement of minimum-per-person for dinner and drinks. It can be as much as $10, and good-sized tips are expected.

Some top south Florida nightspots:

Cafe Cristal at the Diplomat Hotel in Hollywood puts the most conspicuous names in American show business on its schedule. Besides guests from the hotel complex itself, the audience is likely to include guests from Palm Beach downward and Key West upward. Some come by yacht—why not? The Diplomat also has *The Tack Room,* a cocktail lounge, and *Les Ambassadeurs,* the dining room.

Mai Kai. A restaurant-nightspot between Pompano and Fort Lauderdale on US 1, where Miami Beach or Palm Beach visitors often drop in on a fun-excursion. Most perfectly realized of all the Polynesian places, its exterior architecture stuns the eye with torches, palms, wooden idols, exotic plants, small pools, thatched roofs, winding trails, and dugouts all blended into something that Polynesia itself has never seen.

The *Columbia* restaurant in Ybor City (Tampa) presents flamenco shows in a red velvet and crystal ambiente, and the Spanish food is delicious.

Chuck's Steak House in Ft. Lauderdale is a meeting place for the yachty set; good jazz at *Darryl's* in Jax; Country and Western is big everywhere. For a choice ranging from disco to country to Dixieland, go to the *Church Street Station* complex in Orlando. Sarasota has the *Old Heidleberg Castle,* and the St. Petersburg area also has a number of popular spots.

Most hotels in Florida have live music in the cocktail lounge or dining room, either to listen to or for dancing.

 BARS. Heartland in Palm Beach is Worth Avenue, and *TaBoo* is where the action is. The elegant bars in *The Breakers* are relaxing. *Sloppy Joe's* and *Captain Tony's* in Key West are hangouts of the old city's artists, writers, fishermen and assorted bohemians. Although everyone mistakenly thinks it was Sloppy Joe's, Captain Tony's was Ernest Hemingway's favorite watering hole back in the 1930s when he lived in Key West. In the resort area, it's not a bad idea to stick close to the bars in the well-established hotel or motel where you're stopping. If they're run as a subsidiary service, they're generally run well. The management holds them to a standard. St. Pete Beach and the adjoining Holiday Isles are dotted with waterfront bars, some with small discos. Most of the bars offer Happy Hour drinks, two for the price of one, with hors d'oeuvres. Just about every seaside community has a window-walled bar for drinking in the view with the martinis. Some, like *Pier 66* in Fort Lauderdale and the *Hiltons* on Clearwater Beach and St. Pete Beach, offer penthouse-seascapes.

DRINKING LAWS. City and county establish their own closing times for bars and nightclubs where liquor is sold. It's not unusual in the resort area to find establishments with licenses good until 4 or 5 A.M. In Fort Lauderdale city bars are open until 2; some in the county are open till 4. In the Miami area, the swingers can get service later yet (see Bars). Package liquor stores, common throughout the area, are under control of State Beverage Commission. Supermarkets can't sell wine 'til past 1 o'clock on Sundays. Under recent legislation, Florida now grants adult privileges to 19-year-olds.

 SPORTS. The state's subtropical climate makes sports possible throughout the year. For that reason, they are listed alphabetically here, and not grouped by season. Florida is high on participant sports—fishing, hunting, tennis, even boccie—and takes a nibble from the national sports scene, too. It is the great winter training ground for big league baseball. Snow sports aren't the style, although ice skating is a growing summer sport, and Bradenton throws an artificial blizzard every year (orange-colored snow). Skiers, in *conquistador* costumes, compete for the Florida State Skiing Championship, in mid-March. In addition, there are sports exotica for the tourist and the gambler—jai alai, polo, racing with dogs, horses, sulkies. And the state pleases the playboy set with some of the world's great sailing and powerboat events. Shuffleboard is everywhere, including perhaps, your motel. St. Petersburg's Mirror Lake Park has the world's largest shuffleboard court.

Boating: Florida beckons insistently to touring, sporting, and competing boatsmen. There are 8,426 miles of tidal shoreline, thousands of navigable lakes and rivers. South Florida has so many canals that babies must learn to swim as soon as they learn to walk—or live in constant danger. Under the out-of-state reciprocity system, Florida grants full recognition to valid registration certificates and numbers from other states for 90 days. Those staying longer must register their vessels with the county tax collector. You'll find ramps and berthing easily, but to be totally prepared write the Florida Department of Natural Resources, Crown Bldg., Tallahassee for a boating directory. This gives route maps, lists marine facilities, and tells where all ramps are located.

Tested trips include the circuit voyage—out of Miami to the Florida Keys, then northward to Fort Myers and across the state, via the Okeechobee Waterway, and down to Miami again. It has become a popular odyssey for the local and out-of-state boater. Your course depends on boat size. Larger yachts, after running south-ward to the Keys, go on to Islamorada before heading north via Nine-Mile, Oxfoot, and Schooner banks on the outside passage. The light-draft outboard, and many sterndrive craft, can go into Florida Bay; entry is by Jewfish Creek, via the Boggies. Aim for Naples going north. A 200-mi. sail from White Springs to the Gulf of Mexico takes 3 days, offers camping spots at Suwannee River State Park, near Live Oak, and Manatee Springs State Park, near Chiefland. The St. Johns River, famed for its bass fishing, is lush and lovely, perfect for cruising. Now you can rent fully furnished houseboats by the week. There is deep water from Sanford to Jacksonville, as well as lots of streams and coves to explore. Miamians have great weekends island hopping along Islandia Keys, an area which may become a national park. You'll find a 93-acre park at Elliott Key, where the pirate Black Caesar roamed. Look out for brownish colored water. It usually indicates a flat or exposed reef.

Distances on the *Intracoastal Waterway:* Jacksonville to Miami is a 349-mi. trip, with a marked channel depth of 12 feet to Fort Pierce, and 8 ft. from that point south to Miami. On the two charted routes, it's 158 mi. inside the Keys from Miami to Key West (limited to five-foot draft), and 152 mi. by way of Hawk Channel, on a buoyed passage between the outermost reefs and the Keys (limited to 10-ft. draft). Pensacola to St. Marks is 259 mi. with a 12-ft. depth-marked channel through protected harbors and the inland canal to Carrabelle (from Carrabelle, one route is across the Gulf and Apalachee Bay; the other through Crooked and Ochlockonee Rivers—channel depth limited to 3 ft.)

Distances on *main water routes.* On *Okeechobee Waterway,* it's 135 mi. from St. Lucie Inlet, near Stuart, across the State to Fort Myers. From below Welaka, where the Oklawaha flows into the St. John, it's 52 mi. upstream to dramatic Silver Springs. From Kissimmee to Lake Okeechobee, on the Kissimmee Waterway (via lakes Tohopekaliga, Cypress, and Hatchineha) it's 137 mi. You must, for river exploring, check for current water depths and conditions. Recent droughts have closed some waterways. It's 107-plus mi. from Apalachicola to Jim Woodruff Lock and Dam at Chattahoochee, traveling the 9-ft. channel from your takeoff on the *Apachicola River.*

Canoeists claim to paddle Florida's most unvisited waters and not suffer a mosquito bite—that's when beautiful tourists have lured all the mosquitoes to the resort cities. Take Rte. 445 to the *Alexander Springs* recreational area, in *Ocala National Forest.* The Alexander Springs canoe trail is one way, runs 6½ mi., and takes you through startling forest tunnels that open suddenly on broad shallows. A trip on the *Silver River* offers shades of early Tarzan movies. The Dept. of Natural Resources has designated 17 rivers as canoe trails. They will supply a booklet listing locations and length.

The so-called shantyboat or houseboat can be a thing of glory these days. It provides something different for the trailerite who thinks he ought to be on water or the boater who wants the comforts of land. Houseboat operations can be found in the Keys, De Land, and Jacksonville.

Marinas throughout the state offer information for the boater. On the Amena River, at Fernandina Beach, is a marine welcome station: a two-story octagonal building, with yacht and outboard parking space. It dispenses charts, maps and weather information.

Fishing: The question isn't where—because it's everywhere. Only shy Florida cities fail to claim fame as fishing capitals of one sort or another. Most deserve these self-conferred titles. You'll hear that tarpon have sometimes finned so thickly across the Boca Grande Pass, their bodies were like a bridge. There's great sport everywhere—but you need to know the habits of the fish you're after. No license needed for saltwater, but a freshwater license is necessary. You have the choice of fishing in canals, lakes, rivers, by ocean pier, or by ocean-going yacht. Canal fishing can provide a dinner; deep-sea fishing the fury and ecstasy Ernest Hemingway experienced to write *The Old Man and the Sea.*

Freshwater equipment may be used in saltwater, but must be cleaned afterwards to prevent corrosion. If you're able, buy big gear after arrival, when you know what you want to catch. Tackle shops are everywhere.

For saltwater quarry: Try for tarpon May to July anywhere, except for upper east coast. Sailfish, which make handsome mounts, are good prey winter and spring anywhere, and even in summer. Snook, a favorite of the fishing writers, are scattered in winter but go for the passes and tidal rivers in spring and summer. Try for snook and tarpon all along the Florida Keys bridges, and near Stuart on the east coast. Pompano and dolphin are supreme among the catchable-eatables. Other excellent eaters are: bass, flounder, bluefish, cobia, Nassau and red grouper, king and Spanish mackerel, mullet, porgies, red and yellowtail snapper, and wahoo.

For freshwater quarry: Ocean-running fish like snook, mangrove snapper, channel bass, sheepshead and tarpon turn up in freshwater as well. There are about 40 strictly freshwater species. Day's bag limits: 10 black bass; 15 chain pickerel; 50 panfish—bream, perch and red-finned pike individually or in aggregate; 6 sunshine bass; 6 striped bass (min. length 15 inches). Total possession limit: Two days's bag limit after first day of fishing. There are also special bag limits on certain lakes and rivers. For complete fresh and saltwater rules write: Game and Fresh Water Fish Commission, Tallahassee, Fla., 32304. The really big bass are in Lake Tohopelika, Lake George, Cypress Lake, Talsa Apopka, Orange Lake, the St. Johns River, and the Withlacoochee.

Spearfishing: Legal in saltwater except in the Pennekamp Coral Reef State Park, Collier County, that part of Monroe County from Long Key north to the Dade County line, and the immediate area of the following: all public bathing beaches; commercial or public fishing piers; bridge catwalks; jetties. It is illegal to spearfish in fresh water or for freshwater fish in brackish water except for rough fish in special areas designated by the Game and Fresh Water Fish Commission.

Water Sports: With aquatic adventurers abounding, Florida keeps pace, with water-ski schools, skindiving shops and surfing-supply houses. Dozens of local restrictions exist on where and when water skiers may be towed, and many areas are off limits to divers (too dangerous), so inquiries should always be made.

The *surfing* craze has created thousands of surfers and filled the beaches with wahinis and beach bunnies (surfing girls and nonsurfing girlfriends), but the Florida waves are rarely conducive to first-class sport. Mobile surfers spend hours, going from Miami to Fort Pierce, and higher, seeking the best water. Cocoa Beach is a favored spot. *Windsurfing,* an international sport, has caught on quickly on St. Pete Beach and Clearwater Beach, complete with schools for novices and rental boats. *Parasailing* is a fun sport on St. Pete Beach.

Lobster diving. Use only your hands—it's a state law. Spears and hooks aren't allowed, skin divers wear a mask, swim fins, cotton gloves, possibly a snorkel, to go after the lobsters. They're found at any depth from three feet on. In daylight, the lobster hides but can be spotted under logs or rocks by his antennae. Grabbed, the antennae break off; so the diver must get a grip on the front body shell. First he twists, then he pulls. Watch out for the moray eel, barracuda, and the black, pincushiony sea urchin.

Shelling: Even before Marco Island became the object of massive real estate development, in the Florida manner, it was considered excellent shell-hunting. Many tourists become passionate shellers the minute they hold the hard little cowries, shaped like disembodied jaws, and shining with colors no jewel can match. Other shellers become hooked by a visit to one of the tightly packed seashell novelty houses which dot the major highways. In these shops, you may painlessly, cheaply, and unwetly acquire a fine seashell collection, lacking only the *Canus gloria-maris Chemnitz,* the Glory-of-the-Seas, worth $1,200-per specimen. Many shellers frown on buying. They collect their own, some specializing in minute specimens. Some go into the Everglades to find fossilized shells from other eons (you can also find brilliant tree snails in the Everglades).

The sheller is best advised to search for specimens after a storm, when high tides have delivered new batches to the beaches. Still the champion shelling spot in Florida (and one of the world's better stalking grounds) is *Sanibel Island,* west of Fort Myers Beach via a toll bridge. It has the secluded tang of the South Seas. So does little Captiva Island, which neighbors it. A free shell fair at Sanibel Community House is held in early Mar. The excellent Branaham Shell Collection is part of the Shell Factory in North Ft. Myers. Other places: Coral and sand beaches along the Florida Keys down to Key West are good spots; so is the Cape Sable area—it has to be approached by boat. . . . Shellers also go to the beaches north and south of Naples; to the Sarasota area, including Longboat Key and Anna Maria Island; to beaches west of Bonita Springs; to Tarpon Springs, Clearwater, Pass-a-Grille Beach, and Cedar Key. The St. Petersburg Club offers the Smithsonian Award for year's top shell find.

Golf: Florida is a golfer's paradise, with some of the finest courses in the U.S. The *Seminole G.C.,* North Palm Beach, ranks among the best. *Pine Tree G.C.,* Delray Beach, is Florida's toughest. Some others: *PGC National G.C.,* Palm Beach Gardens, *Bay Hill Club,* Orlando; *Innisbrook G. & C.C.,* Tarpon Springs; *Disney World G.C.,* Lake Buena Vista. The three extraordinary courses at the Innisbrook Golf and Tennis Resort are among the finest in the state.

Other courses are located in: Jacksonville, Ponte Vedra Beach, Tallahassee, Pensacola, St. Augustine, New Smyrna Beach, Daytona Beach, Ormond Beach, Cocoa Beach, Titusville, two in Vero Beach, Ft. Pierce, Stuart, Port St. Lucie, Tequesta, Lost Tree Village, No. Palm Beach, four in W. Palm Beach, Palm Beach, Royal Palm Beach, two in Lake Worth, Lantana, two in Boynton Beach, two in Delray Beach, six in Boca Raton, Coral Springs, four in Pompano Beach, Plantation, Lauderhill, seven in Ft. Lauderdale, six in Hollywood, Homestead, Biscayne Village, No. Key Largo, Marco Island, four in Naples, Rotonda West, four in Ft. Myers, Cape Coral, two in Lehigh Acres, Englewood, two in Punta Gorda, Port Charlotte, No. Port Charlotte, two in Venice, Captiva Island, six in Sarasota, Palma Sola, Sun City, Lake Placid, two in Sebring, three in Clearwater, five in Tampa, Leesburg, several in St. Petersburg, Dunedin, Clearwater, two in Orlando, Sanford, Howey-in-the-Hills, Crystal River, Wildwood, Ocala, Amelia Island, and two in Panama City Beach.

Hunting: Hunting seasons are: deer, Nov. 13-Jan. 23 in northwest region, Nov. 13-Jan. 9 in northeast, central, south and Everglades; turkey, Nov. 13-Jan. 23 in northwest, Nov. 13-Jan. 9 in northeast, central south and Everglades; quail and squirrel, Nov. 13-March 6 in northwest, Nov. 13-Feb. 27 in other regions. Rabbit, no closed season. Statewide seasons for turkey gobblers, wildhog, and bear are more complicated. Best go get Game and Fresh Water Fish Commission's book of rules. Also, use that publication to check for sizes and hunting methods allowed, as well as those species that are protected. Florida has many species that are on endangered and threatened lists.

A sport on the upsweep here is hunting with bow and arrow. Archery season, statewide, is from Sept. 4 through Sept. 26. Legal game are deer of either sex, other than fawn; bear (in Baker and Columbia counties and on Tyndall AFB in Bay County); turkey (except in northwest region); quail, squirrel, rabbit, and wild hog. No open season in Broward or Dade counties or certain parts of Palm Beach, Hendry, Collier and Monroe counties.

Milder prey for the hunter include woodcock and snipe, ducks and doves, coots and geese. There's a forty-day season on ducks, geese and coots. It starts in late November and goes into early January. West Coast Florida is a natural flyway for ducks; and wild fowl, in general, are plentiful.

Riding: Florida's version of the Old West is Davie, 18 mi. W of Fort Lauderdale. You'll also find stables at Amelia Island Plantation, Seminole near St. Petersburg, Jonathon Dickinson State Park, and many other places. River Ranch Resort, Lane Wales, offers dude-ranch-type vacations.

SPECTATOR SPORTS. *Baseball:* Late vacationers can see some early baseball at the training camp cities, where major leaguers repair their rusty throwing arms. The Washington Senators tried Florida in 1888, and most teams since have followed suit. Two hundred exhibition games start early Mar. and continue for a month. Seventeen of 20 major league teams train on the lower coast—Winter Haven built a $300,000 stadium to catch a defector, the Boston Red Sox. The Houston Astros have just moved their "home" from Cocoa, where they had wintered for years, to Kissimmee. Bradenton's million-dollar stadium (for the Pittsburgh Pirates) has a winged canopy roof extending far out over the center seating section. *Home Bases:* Atlanta Braves and Montreal Expos at West Palm Beach; Chicago White Sox at Sarasota; Cincinnati Reds at Tampa; Detroit Tigers at Lakeland; Kansas City Royals at Fort Myers; L.A. Dodgers at Vero Beach; Minnesota Twins at Orlando; St. Louis Cardinals and New York Mets at St. Petersburg; New York Yankees at Fort Lauderdale; Phillies at Clearwater; Twins Farm Teams at Melbourne; Texas Rangers at Pompano Beach; Baltimore Orioles at Miami; Toronto Blue Jays at Dunedin. During Spring training, some exciting major-league games are played at the $3.5-million Al Lang Stadium near the bay in St. Petersburg. Or at Payson Field, not far from downtown St. Pete, you can watch the baseball stars play for free, while they train.

Car racing: The famous 12-hr. endurance race at Sebring in Mar. is still exciting. The world's finest compete, and spectators come here from around the globe. The Feb. Daytona 500 has attracted as many as 110,000 spectators. Short and long stock car events precede the 500. Drag and sports car races are held at Lakeland International Raceway. Auto races in Tampa, Mar. to Nov. Stock car races at W. Palm Beach, Feb. to Nov. Refer to Sports pages of St. Petersburg Times for schedule at Sunshine Speedway.

Dog racing: Slick greyhounds are champion performers at the no-children emporiums. At Daytona the dog track is close by the International Speedway. Other greyhound tracks are: St. Petersburg Kennel Club (Derby Lane); Sanford-Orlando Kennel Club at Winter Park; Orange Park Kennel Club at Jacksonville; The Jacksonville Kennel Club; Bonita Springs Track; Associated Outdoor Clubs at Tampa; Investment Corp. of Palm Beach, West Palm Beach; Jefferson County Kennel Club, Monticello; Keys Racing Assoc., Key West; Pensacola Greyhound Racing; Hollywood Dog Track; Ebro Dog Track, Panama City; Sarasota Kennel Club and Seminole Park in Castleberry.

Boat racing: powerboat racing is off to a zippy start in Jan. Several top events are scheduled as adjuncts to the Orange Bowl festivities. In early Feb. the bluewater racing season spawns a series of famed events, grouped under the Southern Ocean Racing Conference. There is an 807-mi. race from Miami to Montego Bay and races from St. Petersburg to Venice, St. Petersburg to Fort Lauderdale and Miami to Cat Cay (late Feb.). In late Feb. or early March is the Orange Cup Regatta on Lakeland's Lake Hollingsworth, where more than 100 limited hydroplane world speed records have been set, along with dozens of world skiing and ski-jumping records.

Horse racing: Tampa has mid-winter racing at Florida Downs, Jan. to Mar. No children. Gulfstream Park in Hallandale runs mid-Jan. to Mar. Post time 1:15 daily except Sun. No children. Harness horse racing is staged at Tourist Attractions at Pompano Beach, with races nightly except Sun. at 8, mid-Dec. to mid-Apr. There is quarter horse racing at Gator Down Racing, Pompano, June to Sept. In Hollywood the Calder Race Course has thoroughbred racing from May to mid-Nov.

Jai Alai is played at Dania, Daytona Beach, Tampa, W. Palm Beach, Winter Park, Ocala, Fort Pierce, Fern Park, Gadsden County, Melbourne, Miami, Orange Lake, and Quincy (near Tallahassee). There are winter and summer schedules.

Hydroplane races are held at Lakeland in Mar., also on Lake Maggiore, St. Petersburg, in Feb. and Aug.

Water-ski shows are given in Sarasota from Jan. to Mar. on Sun. afternoons.

Polo: The sport of princes is pursued and gaining popularity as a spectator sport in Boca Raton, where games are played every Sun., Jan. to Apr. Polo is also played in the Gulfstream Polo Field, West Palm Beach. Also, games at the new West Palm Beach Polo Club Resort complex.

 SHOPPING. A famous shopping street in Florida is Worth Avenue in *Palm Beach,* where Bonwit Teller, Saks and Elizabeth Arden mingle with shops as exclusive if not as nationally known. Worth Avenue's Spanish architecture, with its many arcades, alleyways, balconies, stairways, and nooks and crannies create a pleasant and relaxing European atmosphere. You can drive home in style after a stopoff at *Taylor Imported Motors, Inc.,* at 1314 S. Dixie in Palm Beach. Dealers in Rolls-Royce, Bentley, Jaguar, Ferrari, they have one of the country's more stunning collections of treasuries-on-wheels. . . . Florida has roadside stands everywhere specializing in products from the *orange groves.* A super-deluxe box (as packers call it) may cost as much as $24.50. That will be over a bushel and a half of oranges, grapefruit, pecan halves, candied fruits, coconut patties. To buy oranges, sample first. Quality varies. . . . Among the outstanding places to shop in St. Petersburg are downtown Beach Drive (elegant shops!), Tyrone Mall, Pinellas Park Mall; Clearwater Mall, Countryside Mall, Clearwater. *St. Armand's Key,* off Sarasota, has the beautiful and diverse *St. Armands Shopping Circle,* with over 100 individually owned and operated shops, services, restaurants, representing styles, architecture and exotic goods from around the world. Lake Buena Vista's *Shopping Village,* situated among trees and flowers on the banks of the Buena Vista Lagoon, offers 29 cedar-shingled shops and four restaurants. This Walt Disney World adjunct features such things as Toys Fantastique, European toys for children of any age; Posh Pets, with exotic animals such as albino skunks, besides the usual dogs and cats; and Port of Entry, with fashions, furniture and other goods from around the world. Of course, there are many shell shops in the resort areas, but the Shell Shop near Ft. Myers is certainly the largest. Even if you don't care for shells, you're sure to get "hooked" after a visit here. The *Old Marine Market Place* at Tin City in Naples is unusual, with 40 boutiques, craft and gift shops, snack bars, and the *Riverwalk Fish and Ale House.* Also in Naples, art galleries and shops line Fifth Avenue and on South Third Street, courtyards (Old Naples). *The Boatyard,* north of the St. Pete-Clearwater Airport, is a funky collection of boutiques, craftsmen, a fish market, and waterfront restaurants. Tampa and Jacksonville are booming cities and each is attracting new shopping centers daily.

 WHAT TO DO WITH THE CHILDREN. Marine shows are popular with children and their parents. One of the most developed sea shows is at *Marineland* of Florida, 18 mi. S. of St. Augustine. Six performances daily. The *Gulfarium,* E of US 98 on Okaloosa Island, nr. Fort Walton Beach, has fish and scuba diving shows in their reef tank; trained porpoises in the main tank. *Miami's Seaquarium* has a shark channel, killer whales, porpoise and sea lion shows. A monorail circles the 60-acre garden. At *Flipper's Sea School* in Key West you can see the porpoises at their lessons daily from 10 to 4.

The *Theater of the Sea,* in Islamorada, offers hr-long "bottomless" boat tours in addition to trained porpoise shows and the aquarium. You can also take a charter boat to visit underwater coral gardens and the wreck of a Spanish galleon, or take a 2-hr. glass-bottomed boat ride from Chesapeake Dock to view the reefs.

There's lots to see at Tarpon Spring's sponge docks. *Spongeorama,* 510 Dodecanese Blvd., gives sponge-diving exhibitions, shows movies and exhibits about the sponge industry.

On the other side of the nature-lover's coin are animal refuges. Tiny key deer, 25 in. high, can be photographed at the *National Key Deer Refuge* off Rte. 940 on Big Pine Key. Tame deer may be fed at *International Deer Ranch,* Silver Springs. The visitor is caged, the monkey free at *Monkey Jungle,* 3 mi. W of US 1 in Goulds, 20 mi. S of Coral Gables, not far from Metrozoo. In Tarpon Springs, visit *Noell's Ark Chimpanzee Farm,* US 19. Closed holidays. The *Jacksonville Municipal Zoo,* on Trout River off N. Main St., features animals and birds from many countries, with moated islands for bears and lions. Miniature railroad. Free.

Over 100 lions and other African wild animals roam at large in *Lion Country Safari,* on US 98 in West Palm Beach. You can rent an explanatory tape and tape recorder. "African Safari" at Caribbean Gardens in Naples is a 200-acre tropical garden with exotic birds, waterfowl, chimp shows and a lion and tiger training school. *Sarasota Jungle Gardens* has an awesome number of tropical plants in wild jungle and formal gardens, exotic birds, chimp acts and bird shows. 3701 Bayshore Rd. There's a bird walk, guided boat tours, a sundown train trip to a bird rookery and native wildlife at Myakka River State Park, 17 mi. E of Sarasota. *St. Augustine's Alligator Farms,* on Anastasia Island, has been in operation for over 75 years, features alligator wrestling, zoo of Florida wildlife. *Gatorland Zoo,* Kissimmee, features alligators, crocodiles, giant tortoises, zebras. Train ride.

Costumed Indians make dolls, do beadwork and make baskets at *Seminole Okalee Indian Village,* 6073 Sterling Rd., West Hollywood. There's an arts & crafts center, small zoo and alligator wrestling. Closed early Sept. to late Nov., Christmas and Easter. The Seminole Indian Reservation is on State 721, W. of Brighton. Exhibits at *Temple Mound and Museum,* US 98, Fort Walton Beach, tell story of Indian culture, religion.

Circus buffs will have a hey-day at the *Ringling Museums,* a complex of 4 bldgs. on 68 acres on US 41, 3 mi. N of Sarasota. The circus museum covers circus history from ancient Rome to the present day; with collections of handbills, posters, costumes, wagons, etc. The Ringling Residence is a fabulous Venetian Gothic building; the Museum of Art has both a fine collection of contemporary work and a renowned collection of baroque art; the Asolo Theater is a reassembled Venetian theater. Venice is winter quarters for *Ringling Bros.-Barnum & Bailey,* with a rehearsal hall and arena on Airport Ave. *Circus World* (at Haines City), near all the other fantasy worlds in Orlando, is fun for everyone. Kids and parents can walk the tightrope, swing from a trapeze, or perhaps be painted up like a clown. Panoramic screens bring circus life right to you. Older children who are movie and TV fans will enjoy *Stars Hall of Fame,* with lifesize, lifelike statues of the most famous celebrities in their best-known settings, such as *The Wizard of Oz.* Outdoor pavilion has footprints and fingerprints (even an earprint) of well-known headliners. Multi-vision movie features what show biz is all about.

One of Florida's major attractions is *Cape Kennedy.* The Visitor Center is on NASA Causeway nr. Titusville. There are lectures (Mon. to Fri.) and films (daily); except Christmas or morning of manned space launching.

There's no doubt at all that the kids will love *Walt Disney World.* The "Magic Kingdom" is divided into 6 sections: *Fantasyland,* with Cinderella Castle, Mickey Mouse revue and Captain Nemo subs; *Main St. USA*—a study in nostalgia; *Tomorrowland,* preview of the future; *Adventureland* with jungle cruises, tiki birds; *Frontierland,* a recreation of the Old West; *Liberty Square* with colonial shops, Hall of Presidents and a haunted house. There are motels, camping sites, tours, special package tours. The attractions are open daily. Write Disney World, Lake Buena Vista, Fla. 32830 for brochures. *River Country,* water-oriented adventure, located in Fort Wilderness campground. Contains two large flume slides 260 feet and 160 feet long into Old Swimming Hole. Also, you can plunge some rapids on inner tubes. There is a heated pool, nature walk, and play park.

Plan another day (separate admission) for *EPCOT,* Disney's World of Tomorrow with exhibitions of how your world will work in the future. *Sea World,* only a few minutes' drive away, almost upstages Mickey Mouse with Shamu, the performing killer-whale, and his all-star cast of porpoises, penguins, and mermaids. On beautiful landscaped acres, Sea World also has Japanese and Hawaiian Villages, water-ski shows, Atlantis Theater with star performers, observation tower, and restaurants. Orlando's *Mystery Fun House* has, among other surprises, magic floors and laughing doors.

Weeki Wachee Spring features underwater ballet by "mermaids" in a specially designed auditorium 16 ft. below the surface. A narrated boat cruise makes regular trips down the Weeki Wachee River. There's also an Exotic Trained Bird Show with macaws and cockatoos skating, playing cards and doing other unbirdlike tricks. The Springs are 12 mi. W of Brooksville at the jct. of Rte. 50 & US 19.

Fantasy Isles, Ft. Myers, has animated storybook shows and bird and animal displays.

Cypress Gardens, in Winter Haven, has water skiing, aquarama shows, boat tours of the canals and exquisite gardens. Garden is open daily from sunrise to sunset. The walkthrough aquarium and Living Legends of the South are just two of the new attractions added to Cypress Gardens in 1979.

Six Gun Territory, Silver Springs, is a recreation of an Old West Frontier town. Steam train, gondolas, rides, gunfights, Indian dances add to the fun. Daily June to Labor Day. Rides and shows are included in fee. *Petticoat Junction,* 10 mi. W of Panama City at Long Beach Resort, also features cowboy & Indian fights, steam engine rides. Mar. to Labor Day. Free. Children love to explore the Dark Continent at Busch Gardens, Tampa, complete with African animals grazing on the Serengeti Plain, a Moroccan Village, the Congo Jungle Cruise, an exciting Python ride, Stanleyville, and bazaars. Monorails, a sky-ride, and a Nairobi-style railroad take visitors around the vast, garden-bordered acres. A seperate Busch project is Adventure Island, a water park packed with wet and wild things to do. Plan to spend all day.

The famous *Goodyear Blimp* is now based in Pompano. Rides are no longer given; but you can see the huge airship and tour a museum.

Of interest to the pirate-adventure lover is MGM's replica of *The Bounty,* the mutiny ship, in St. Petersburg, adjoining Municipal Pier. Best free attraction is *Suncoast Seabird Sanctuary,* Indian Shores, near St. Petersburg. Open 7 days, 9 A.M. to dark. Over 500 seabirds of 40 species, most recuperating from injuries and free to fly away after rehabilitation.

There are many museums which will interest children. Among them: *South Florida Museum & Bishop Planetarium,* 201 10th St. W., Bradenton. *Museum of Arts and Sciences,* Jacksonville, 1025 Gulf Life Dr. Ecology, wild life, Timaqua Indians. Planetarium shows. Closed Sept. and major holidays. *John Young Museum and Planetarium,* 810 E. Rollins Ave., Orlando. Free. Planetarium shows Wed., Thurs., Sat., Sun. Admission charge.

The *Museum of Yesterday's Toys,* 52 St. George St., St. Augustine, displays over 1500 dolls, other toys and accessories. Guided tour of house, garden. Free. *Oldest Store Museum* in St. Augustine carries turn-of-the-century merchandise. The *Zorayda Castle,* 83 King St., St. Augustine, was inspired by the Alhambra in Spain. Daily mid-June to Aug. Kids will also appreciate the *Ripley's Believe It or Not Museum,* 19 San Marco Ave. In Winter Haven, the *Museum of Old Dolls and Toys* at 1530 6th St. displays 3-century-old dolls, mechanical banks. Sarasota's *Bellm's Cars & Music of Yesterday,* 5500 N. Tamiami Trail, has antique cars, mechanical music boxes.

Tallahassee's Junior Museum, 3945 Museum Dr., is a restoration of a pioneer farm with blacksmith shop, farm house, smokehouse, etc.; 4 museum bldgs, nature trails. Closed Easter, Thanksgiving, Dec. 23-New Year's Day. In Tampa, the *Junior Museum* features Seminole Indian culture, and a man in space display. Mid-Sept. to July. Free.

Newest fun things to do are the water worlds—winding flumes filled with flowing water, and then a plunge into the pool below. *Walt Disney World* has a Wet 'n' Wild watersport theme-park in River Country. There's the *Zoom Flume* in Panama City; *Water Boggan* in Pompano Beach; *Hawaiian Slip Waterslide* in Kissimmee; and *Okaloosa County Water Slide* in Fort Walton Beach. Silver Springs has a 10-acre aquatic park; and *Wild Waters,* with a 180-foot pool, almost four-foot-high waves, playpools, and three flumes. *Atlantis*—the world's largest theme park—is now open in Ft. Lauderdale. Wave pool, water slide, and rapids make for an exciting day. Check ahead—most close in winter. Largo has *Waterslide World.* And you can go summer ice skating in St. Petersburg's *Bayfront Auditorium.*

Also new is *Alligator Safari* in Kissimmee, an animal jungle compound; *Fort Meyers Wildlife Park* in Fort Myers (near the huge Shell Shop); *'Gator Jungle* in Plant City.

 INDIANS. If you know the Indian tongues well enough, you can learn a good deal about Florida simply by reading the names on the map. Oklawaha means "muddy or boggy," Palatka—"fording place," and Seminole (the name of the Florida tribe)—"wild man" or "runaway."

Outside influence on the tribes, as well as tribal influence on Florida, is detectable everywhere. At Boca Raton, in the chapel at *St. Andrew's Episcopal School for Boys,* the altar mural by Mary Osceola shows the Holy Family as Seminoles. (At Christmas, the Seminoles celebrate "Big Safe Day," as they like to call it.) The menfolk wear blue jeans these days and are abandoning the dugout for the airboat. They have automobile license plates—but special ones, for tribe members alone. Intermarried in the past with escaped Negro slaves and now put under a magnifying glass by those who would see them as they were, they contrive to be Seminoles still. Some of the spots where you can find traces of the tribe, both ancient and as their not-so-modern selves, are: The *Okalee Village* at Dania, a Seminole reservation; the *Indian Temple Mound* at Fort Walton Beach; the *Southeast Museum of the North American Indian,* at Marathon; the *Indian Burial Mound* at St. Augustine; the *Seminole Indian Village,* at Silver Springs; the *Tiger* and *Osceola Seminole Indian camps* on the Tamiami Trail. Ancient Florida, with artifacts from the Creek Indians of 200 B.C., is represented in the new *Indian Mound Museum* at Crystal River. It is situated on an 18-acre tract in western Citrus County.

When the Spanish came, four tribes, numbering perhaps 10,000, inhabited Florida. The Calusa in the southwest, the Tequesta on the east coast, the Timucuan in central and northeast Florida, and the semicivilized leading tribe, the Apalachee in the northwest. The Seminoles, runaways from the Creek tribes of Georgia, became important in the mid-18th century. They were forced to flee to the Everglades after Osceola fought, and lost, the Second Seminole War. (That war was declared over in 1938 when the Seminoles and the U.S. signed a truce.) Reduced to 208 tribe members in 1880, the Seminoles had quadrupled by the early 1950's. A council of five holds judicial power on the reservations; the *Green Corn Dance* (the first day after the first new moon of the vernal equinox) is their day of decision. *Bulow Plantation,* the wilderness kingdom where John Bulow defied the Mosquito Roarers and sided with the Seminoles during the Seminole War, is an extensive ruin and memorial. It is near St. Augustine, southeast of Bunnell on Old Dixie Highway—and it has boating and picnicking facilities.

Tours at Miami run to the exhibition village—the sights at Silver Springs are similar. The Dania Reservation is very accessible, but *Big Cypress* is far larger and more interesting. Deepwater alligator wrestling, most typical exhibition, is practiced at Okalee Village—reached via State 7. The arts and crafts shop at the village has carvings and brilliantly patterned skirts.

The *Miccosukee,* their chickees lining the Tamiami Trail between Naples and Miami, cling most firmly to the old ways. (The chickee is a thatched hut made from palmetto and cypress poles, with a sapling platform for sleeping.) These Trail Indians headquarter at Forty Mile Bent, and have a school and Cultural Center. The *Cow Creek Tribe,* at Brighton Reservation, is building a herd of mixed-stock Brahma cattle. The Bureau of Indian Affairs recently lent the Miccosukees over $100,000 to establish a service station-restaurant between Naples and Miami on the Trail. It is run by the Indians themselves and decorated with murals depicting their strange detainment in the Everglades.

In spite of these ventures, the Florida Indians remain shy and remote.

 **HOTELS AND MOTELS.** A Florida vacation means "which hotel" more than a sojourn in any other state, for your entire schedule of activities in the Sunshine State will probably revolve around where you stay. If you want active sports, you will want one kind of hotel; if you prefer to lounge on the beach, you will prefer another. Rule of thumb on prices: the farther from the ocean, the cheaper the room. Good buys can be found up and down US 1 on the east coast. Prices, of course, are always subject to change, but categories generally remain constant. In many locations, offseason prices are as much as 50 per cent cheaper, making an expensive hotel a summer bargain.

We have listed hotels and motels alphabetically in categories determined by double, in-season rates: *Deluxe,* from $85; *Expensive,* $75–$85; *Moderate,* $50–$75; *Inexpensive,* under $50. For a more complete explanation of hotel and motel categories see *Facts at Your Fingertips* at the front of this volume.

Amelia Island

Amelia Island Plantation. *Deluxe.* On A1A. Luxurious oceanfront resort with main hotel, private villas (some with own pools). Four miles of white-sand beach, 90-foot pool. Beach club, tennis center, championship golf course. Observation deck atop 50-foot sand dune. Restaurants, shops, marinas. Half-hour drive from Jacksonville Airport. Nr. Fernandina Beach airport. (904) 261-6161.

Apalachicola

A number of motels and cabins, some with kitchenettes, can be found along US 98 and in East Apalachicola. *Apalach Motel, Rancho Court and Gibson Hotel. Moderate.* Each has cabins and a restaurant. *Bay City Lodge and Restaurants. Sportsman's Lodge. Inexpensive.*

Apopka

Lake Page Motel. *Inexpensive.* On South Orange Blossom Trail. 9 units, several with kitchen. Pets. (305) 886-1010.

Auburndale

Chandler's Rainbow Drive Motel. *Inexpensive.* Cottages on lake. Beach, fishing, boats. Restaurant nr. (813) 967-1764.

Bartow

El Jon Motel. 1460 E. Main St. *Moderate.* Pool (heated), 18-hole golf. Restaurant nr. (813) 533-8191.

Belle Glade

Holiday Inn. *Inexpensive.* Between US 27 and 441 and Fl 80. Pool, restaurant. Nr. Lake Okeechobee, 2nd largest freshwater lake in U.S. 47 mi. to West Palm Beach.

Boca Grande

Gasparilla Inn & Cottages. *Deluxe.* Pool, private beach within walking distance. Games, rec. room, fishing. Golf, tennis. Dining room, bar. MAP. Area famous for tarpon fishing.

Boca Raton

Boca Raton Hotel. *Deluxe.* One of the most celebrated Gold Coast hotels. Rambling palace with villas avail. Golf courses, skeet & trap shooting, yacht dock, splendid beach, cabana club. Shopping arcade. Heated pools. Polo in season.

Holiday Inn. *Expensive.* 1950 Glades Rd. New in 1982, Spanish mission décor. Pool, restaurants, nr. I-95, executive airport, chic shopping. Also at US 1 (2901 N. Federal Hwy.), 3 miles to beach.

Sheraton. *Expensive.* I-95 at Glades Rd. Nr. shopping, interstate. Pool, lounge, entertainment, several very good restaurants.

Holiday Inn. *Expensive.* SR 808. Nr. beach and Florida Atlantic Univ. Pool (heated). Restaurant, bar.

Bokeelia

Useppa Island Club. *Deluxe.* Island hideaway. You can jet into Tampa, take helicopter to this tarpon-rich location. Launch transportation from Boca Grande or Bokeelia. Full sporting facilities. Off the coast of Captiva/Sanibel Islands.

Boynton Beach

Best Western Sage-N-Sand Motel. *Moderate.* US 1 S. Pool (heated), beach 1 mi. away. Play area. Coffee shop; wine & beer. Restaurant nr. Free tennis and golf 2½ mi. (305) 732-8196.

Bradenton-Bradenton Beach

Resort 66 Motel. *Expensive.* 6600 Gulf Dr. Holmes Beach. Pool (heated). Coffee shop. Private beach. Barbecue area. 15 mi. from Bradenton.

Aquarius Motel. *Moderate.* 105 39th St. Holmes Beach. On white sand beach. Heated pool, shuffleboard. Playground, fishing pier one block away. Efficiency apartments.

Harbor Lights Motel. *Moderate.* 1301 Gulf Dr. Private beach, heated pool. Picnic area. Fishing dock on bay. Kitchenette available.

Hoosier Manor Motel. *Moderate.* 1405 14th St. Walking distance to downtown, shops, restaurants. Picnic area. Game room, shuffleboard court. Efficiencies, cottages available. Continental breakfast included.

Days Inn. *Inexpensive.* US 41 and FL 301. A good operation. Pool, play area, gift shop, gas station. Popular *Tasty World* restaurant. Pets. Beaches 10 mi. Airport 7 mi.

Cape Coral

Country Club Inn. *Expensive.* 4003 Palmtree Blvd. Pool (heated), sauna. Pets. Restaurants, bar, entertainment, dancing. Golf, tennis.

Anchor Inn. *Inexpensive.* 1538 Cape Coral Pkwy. Pool; golf nr. Pets. Restaurant, bar, entertainment, dancing.

Colonial Resort. *Inexpensive.* Pets. Free coffee & rolls in motel units. Restaurant nr. Lawn games, free transportation to bus terminal. Kitchen units avail.

Captiva

South Seas Plantation. *Deluxe.* Lovely 1856 plantation, with private beach, heated pool, restaurants, bars, entertainment. Golf, marina, Steve Colgate's Offshore Sailing School, 16 tennis courts, Greg Parker Tennis School. Villa-style suites.

Cedar Key

Faraway Inn. *Moderate.* A very special fishing spot, catering to fishermen and honeymooners. Special hunting, fishing pkg. Free champagne for honeymooners. (904) 543-5330.

Island Hotel. *Moderate.* 2nd St., Box 460, Cedar Key. 904/543-5111. Favorite rendezvous for art colony. Bohemian atmosphere. Friendly bar is a famous landmark. Quaint rooms.

Clearwater

Belleview Biltmore. *Deluxe.* Resort hotel on 625 acres. Olympic-sized pool (heated). Two championship golf courses, tennis, play area. Supervised children's program during vacations. Cabana club on gulf, private beach. On Intracoastal

Waterway. EP avail. World's largest occupied frame structure, built by millionaire Henry Bradley Plant. On National Registry of Historic Places and Monuments. Closed summer.

Clearwater Downtown TraveLodge. *Moderate.* 711 Cleveland St. Heated pool, free in-room coffee. Restaurant, bar.

Clearwater Central-Best Western. *Moderate.* 100 US 19. Heated pool. Rooms or suites. Nr. beaches, attractions, restaurant, cocktail lounge. Nr. another Best Western at 2056 US 19 S.

Clearwater Beach

Gulf Sands TraveLodge. *Expensive.* 655 S. Gulfview Blvd. On private Gulf beach. Playground, heated pool. Restaurant, cocktail lounge. Guest privileges at Best Western Sea Wake Inn.

Sheraton Sand Key. *Deluxe.* 1160 Gulf Blvd. 390 waterview rooms. On beautiful beach. Pool, tennis, recreation room. Restaurant, penthouse Sky Lounge with nightly entertainment.

Aegean Sands Resort Motel. *Expensive.* 421 Gulfview Blvd. S. Opposite beach. Heated pool. Kitchenettes, efficiencies avail.

Adam's Mark Caribbean Gulf Resort. *Expensive.* 430 S. Gulfview Blvd. Lively resort hotel on Gulf of Mexico. Bar, disco, Calico Jack's restaurant, entertainment nightly.

Franzman Patio Apartments and Motel. *Expensive.* 17 Somerset St. Garden patio directly on white sand beach. Rooms, efficiencies, 1- and 2-bedroom apartments.

Gulfview Inn. *Expensive.* 504 Gulfview Blvd. S. Refrigerators, coffee-makers in every room. Heated pool, fishing dock. Direct access to beach.

Clermont

Holiday Inn. *Moderate.* US 27 at Exit 85 off Turnpike. Pool, kiddy pool. Efficiencies avail. Restaurant, gift shop. (800) 238-8000.

Howard Johnson's. *Moderate.* Fla. Tpke. and US 27 (exit 85). 8 mi. N. of Clermont, 14 mi. S. of Leesburg. Pool, playground. Coin laundry. Citrus Tower, 6 mi. Water-skiing, golf, 8 mi. Restaurant, cocktail lounge. Accommodations for handicapped. Nr. Disney World, Sea World (easy drive). (800) 654-2000.

Ramada Inn Northwest. *Moderate.* Rt. 2 Box 105G. 32711. (800) 228-2828. Restaurant, lounge with entertainment Fri. and Sat. nights. Pool, all rooms have wheelchair access.

Cocoa

Howard Johnson's. *Moderate.* 860 N. Cocoa Blvd. Pool. Pets. Restaurant (24 hr.). (800) 238-8000.

Days Inn. *Inexpensive.* I-95 and Hwy. 524. Nr. beach, zoo, Kennedy Space Center, shopping. *Tasty World* restaurant.

Cocoa Beach

Holiday Inn Merritt Island. *Moderate.* 260 E. Merritt Island Causeway. (800) 238-8000. Tennis court, pool. Nr. fishing, beach. Full service dining room, lounge with Happy Hour and snack menu. Nr. information center for Space Center.

Ocean Landings Resort and Racquet Club. *Deluxe.* 900 N. Atlantic Ave. 32921. (305) 783-9430. Tennis courts, pools, lounge, restaurant, shopping 2 blocks.

Polaris Motel. *Moderate.* 5600 N. Atlantic Ave. 32931. (305) 783-7621. Beach, restaurant, lounge, entertainment, pool, 2 blocks to shopping.

Crystal River

Plantation Inn and Golf Resort. *Moderate.* Just off US 19. Special vacation packages. PGA golf course, newly resurfaced tennis courts. Marina. Cocktail lounge. Dining rooms also open to public. Fishing and scuba diving arranged. Social programs. Live entertainment.

Cypress Gardens

Quality Inn. *Inexpensive.* P.O. Box 7, S.R. 540. 33880. (813) 324-5950. Handy to Cypress Gardens. Bar, entertainment, pool, shops 2 blocks. Restaurant.

Daytona Beach

Daytona Hilton. *Deluxe.* 2637 Atlantic Ave. Luxurious oceanfront resort and convention center. All rooms with bar, refrigerator. Pool, tennis courts, putting green, games. Exercise room, sauna. Boutiques, beauty salons. 5 mins. from golf course, charter boats. Rooftop restaurant, cocktail lounge. Also *Sunroom Café* and *Islander Lounge.*

Acapulco Inn. *Deluxe.* 2505 S. Atlantic Ave. Oceanfront. Efficiencies avail. Heated pool, children's pool. Playground, game room, gift shop, restaurant, lounge.

Mayan Inn. *Expensive.* Oceanfront. 103 S. Ocean Ave. Efficiencies avail. Kiddy pool, game room. Coffee shop, Aztec Lounge with entertainment. Handy to boardwalk, shops, restaurants, fishing pier.

Treasure Island Inn. *Expensive.* 2025 S. Atlantic Shores. Oceanfront. Rooms, efficiencies, penthouses. 2 pools, game room, putting green, shuffleboard. *Billy Boone's Tavern, Barefoot Bar, Galley Restaurant.* Entertainment.

Pirate's Cove. *Expensive to deluxe.* 3501 S. Atlantic Ave. Heated pool, beach, play area. Kitchen units avail. (800) 874-6996.

TraveLodge/Daytona Oceanfront. *Expensive.* 3135 S. Atlantic Ave. Heated pool, beach, play area. Kitchen units avail. Private balconies.

De Land

Chimney Corner Motel. *Inexpensive.* 1727 South Blvd. Pool, with closed circuit TV viewing. Pets. Restaurant. Opp. Stetson Univ.

Quality Executive Inn. *Moderate to inexpensive.* West of town on S.R. 44 near I-4. Pool, laundry, good restaurant, lounge with live entertainment.

Delray Beach

The Barrington. *Deluxe.* 1875 S. Ocean Blvd. Pool (heated), beach. Kitchen apartments in 2-story hotel. Restaurant nr.

Talbot House. *Deluxe.* 125 N. Ocean Blvd. Resort hotel with kitchen units. Pool (heated), beach, play area. Restaurant nr. Closed May–Oct.

Wright by the Sea. *Deluxe.* 1901 S. Ocean Blvd. Pool (heated), beach, play & barbecue area. Restaurant nr. Kitchen units avail. Closed June–Sept. 20.

Bermuda Inn. *Expensive.* 64 S. Ocean Blvd. Beach nr. Kitchen units avail. Pets. Restaurant.

Holiday Inn. *Expensive.* 2809 S. Ocean Blvd. Pool (heated), beach, play area. Restaurant, bar.

Disney World (Lake Buena Vista)

See also Kissimmee (5 min. from gate), Orlando, Clermont, St. Cloud and Altamonte Springs.

Buena Vista Palace. *Deluxe.* On lake's shore. 27-story, 825-room hotel is central Florida's tallest. Views of EPCOT Center from balconies. Rooftop restaurant, casual restaurants, lounges. A beautiful complete resort, with marina.

Contemporary Resort. *Deluxe.* In Disney World, right on monorail stop. Lakeside, beach, marina. Canoes, water-skiing, 2 heated pools, wading pool. Health club, sauna. Playground, game room, supervised children's activities. Lighted tennis courts, bicycles, golf, horseback riding. Gorgeous vistas from several dining rooms, cocktail lounges. Nightly entertainment, dancing. 24-hour snack bar.

Polynesian Village Resort Hotel. *Deluxe.* In Disney World. On lake. Exotic South Seas-style, tropical gardens, lagoons. Beach, marina. Heated pool, wading pool, playground. Supervised children's programs. Same sports as Contemporary Resort. Sauna. Boutiques, beauty shop. Luxurious suites. Coffee Shop, restaurant, cocktail lounge with entertainment.

Treehouse Villas. *Deluxe.* Walt Disney World Resort Community Shopping Village nrby. The 60 hideaways are nestled among trees at the 17th fairway of golf course. Beautiful views from picture windows. Completely equipped kitchen, dining-living room (2 bedrooms have 2 bathrooms). Nr. 7 restaurants, including *Empress Lilly Riverboat.* Nr. *Village Lounge.* Shuttlebus to Disney World's Vacation Kingdom.

Everglades

Flamingo Inn. *Moderate.* Pool, play area. Bicycles avail. Great bird watching in park.

Rod and Gun Club Lodge. *Moderate.* Presidents have stayed here! Great for hard-core fishermen. Chef will grill your catch. Charter boat and skiff fleet. Dock. Pool; golf nearby.

Captain's Lodge. *Inexpensive* to *Moderate.* At western water gateway to Everglades National Park. 16 motel rooms, 44 1-bedroom apartments, 7 2-bedroom apartments. Full-service marina.

Fort Lauderdale

Bahama Hotel. *Deluxe.* 401 N. Atlantic Blvd. Oceanfront. Pool (heated), play area. Golf nr. Restaurant in season. Bar, entertainment in season, dancing.

Bahia Mar Hotel. *Deluxe.* 801 Seabreeze Blvd. At Bahia Mar Yachting Center. Pool (heated), play area, yachting, fishing. Golf nr. 2 dining rooms, coffee shop, lounge. Also *Patricia Murphy's Candlelight Restaurant.*

Fort Lauderdale Marriott Hotel and Marina. *Deluxe.* Overlooking Intracoastal Waterway. Outstanding new resort complex. Pool, whirlpool, sauna, tennis. Excellent Riverwatch restaurant. Vacation packages for one day or longer.

Bali Hai Polynesian Resort Apartments. *Expensive.* 149 Isle of Venice. Hotel rooms with refrigerators, 1- and 2-bedroom apartments, large efficiencies. Heated pool, putting green, games. Barbecue grills, fishing dock, sundeck. Nr. restaurants, shopping.

Bahia Cabana. *Moderate.* 3001 Harbor Dr. Heart of the high-price area but small and owner-operated. Dining room, poolside bar. Motel rooms have refrigerators, efficiencies and apts. have full kitchens. Private terraces, heated pools.

Imperial Apartments. *Moderate.* 3054 Harbor Dr. Fully furnished apts, 1 or 2 bdrms., day or week. Half block to ocean, restaurants, boating, shopping.

Lauderdale Beach Hotel. *Moderate.* 101 S. Atlantic Blvd. Outside Fla. (800) 327-7600. All rooms have 2 doubles; kids under 16 free in parents' room. 2 economy restaurants, 2 new lounges.

Spindrift Motel. *Moderate.* 2501 N. Ocean Blvd. A1A. About 150 yards from beach. All rooms have refrigerators, also efficiencies and 1-bedroom apartments with fully equipped electric kitchens. Coin laundry. Large heated pool. Sundeck, shuffleboard courts. Barbecue area with gas grills. On city bus line.

Fort Myers

Days Inn. *Inexpensive.* 2 locations: 1099 N. Cleveland. Popular, budget chain. Pool, play area, gift shop, gas station. Pets OK. Restaurant. 5499 US 41 S. 121 rooms, pool, restaurant. Nr. airport, Edison Mall.

Fort Myers Rodeway Inn. *Inexpensive.* 4811 Cleveland Ave. Heated pool. Roman baths available. Restaurant, lounge. Nr. airport.

Fort Myers Beach

Island Towers. *Deluxe.* 4900 Estero Blvd. Pool (heated), play area. Kitchen apts. Overlooking gulf.

Caribbean Beach Club. *Expensive.* Pool (heated), fishing pier, beach. Pets. 7600 Estero Blvd. Restaurant nr. Cook-out facilities.

Kahlua Beach Club. *Expensive.* 4950 Estero Blvd. Pool (heated), play area. Restaurant nr. Beachfront. Coin laundry.

Sandpiper Gulf Resort. *Expensive.* 5550 Estero Blvd. Pool (heated), play area. Beach. Restaurant nr. Kitchen apts. with private patios or balconies.

Fort Pierce

See Port St. Lucie for listing of famed Sandpiper Bay Resort.

Holiday Inn. *Expensive.* 7151 Okeechobee Rd. 33450. (800) 238-8000. Nearest airport is Melbourne, 52 miles. Restaurant, room service, lounge, entertainment, pool. Nr. Exit 56, Turnpike. I-95 ends about 2 blocks from hotel. Also one at 2600 N. A1A.

Fort Walton Beach/Destin

Ramada Inn. *Deluxe.* Hwy. 98E. 13-acre complete resort. Balconies facing Gulf. Pool, wading pool. Beautiful revolving roof dining room and cocktail lounge.

Sandpiper Cove. *Moderate to Deluxe.* Villas with 1, 2, and 3 bedrooms, fully furnished kitchens. Nightly, weekly rates include housekeeping linens. Yacht Club Restaurant open to villa guests. Pools, tennis, golf, boating, fishing, private beach.

Bluewater Bay. *Inexpensive to Deluxe.* Niceville. Outside Fla. call (800) 874-2128. 1,500-acre leisure community. Villas, homes by night, week, month. Fazio-designed, 18-hole golf course, tennis, pools, forested setting. On ICW, marina, fishing.

Dolphin Point. *Expensive.* Holiday Isle. 1,000-ft. private lagoon beach, family-oriented resort. Dock, fishing, pools, tennis.

Sandestin Resort Inn (formerly a Sheraton). *Expensive.* On Florida Gulf. Championship golf course, nine tennis courts. Fishing in Choctawhatchee Bay or Gulf of Mexico. Two pools. Private half-mile beach. Restaurants, lounge with entertainment. Limo service available from Destin/FWB private airport (6 mi.) and Okaloosa County Airport (25 mi.). Bus station within 18 mi.

Aloha Village. *Moderate.* 860 Scallop Court. Pools. Restaurant. Cheery condo's on beach, full kitchens.

Beachmark. *Inexpensive.* 573 Santa Rosa Blvd. On Gulf beach, 2 pools, game room, 2 lounges, 2 restaurants. Rooms, eff's, apts. Pets extra.

Gainesville

Gainesville Hilton. *Expensive.* 2900 S.W. 13th St. 208 Mediterranean-style rooms overlooking lake. Heated pool, recreation area. Adjacent to University of Florida. Restaurant, lounge, nightclub.

Best Western Gainesville Inn. *Moderate.* 1900 S.W. 13th Ave. Pool. Restaurant, *Mardi Gras Lounge* with shows. Also at 7616 Newberry St.

Howard Johnson's. *Moderate.* 2 locations, 2830 N.W. 13th St, I-75 and State Rd. 26. Both have outdoor pools, restaurant, lounge.

Bambi Motel. *Inexpensive.* 2119 S.W. 13th St. Cozy. Pool.

Days Inn. *Inexpensive.* 6901 N.W. 8th Ave. One of popular chain. Pool, play area, gift shop. *Tasty World* restaurant.

Haines City

Grenelefe. *Deluxe.* This Radison Resort may be difficult to find at first, but it is worth the search for this vacation hideaway. One- and two-bedroom fully-furnished suites with patio or balcony. Championship golf, two heated pools, fishing, playground, tennis. Dining room, coffee shop, cocktails. On acres of landscaped gardens, 6 mi. E of US 27 on SR 544. Convenient to Cypress Gardens, Circus World, Sea World, and Disney World. (813) 422-7511.

Hallandale

Sunaqua. *Deluxe.* 1945 S. Ocean Dr. Pool, play area, dock. Restaurant. Cook-out facilities. Kitchen units avail.

Holiday Beach Motel. *Moderate.* On A1A. Friendly atmosphere. Pool, play area, beach. Restaurant with piano bar, dancing.

Hialeah

Sheraton Americas. *Moderate.* Palmetto Expressway & N.W. 103rd St. Ultra-modern facilities.

Hillsboro Beach

Barefoot Mailman. *Expensive.* 1061 Hillsboro Mile, just north of Pompano Beach. Newly decorated rooms. Docking facilities on Intracoastal Waterway. 18-hole golf course. Sundeck. Private 4-mile beach. Gourmet Mary Celeste dining room. Transportation to and from Ft. Lauderdale Airport.

Hollywood

Diplomat. *Deluxe.* Resort hotel on 600 acres. Pools (heated), beach, golf, tennis. Play area. Supervised children's program. Coffee shop, dining room. Bars with name entertainment, dancing. Excellent service. One of Florida's premier resorts.

Fond du Lac Apartment Hotel. *Inexpensive.* 1723 Johnson St. 1 block E of N. Federal Hwy. Efficiencies, 1-bdrm. apts. Weekly rates.

Homosassa Springs

Riverside Villas Resort Motel. *Moderate.* Pool. Tennis, fishing, boating. Golf nr. Kitchen units, wkly rates avail. Homosassa River views.

Sheraton-Homosassa Springs Inn. *Moderate.* Overlooks Pepper Creek. At US 19 and 98. Heated pool. Tennis, playground. Restaurant, cocktail lounge. Entertainment.

Indian Shores

Holiday Villas III. *Moderate.* 18610 Gulf Blvd., near St. Pete Beach and Clearwater. On beautiful beach. One- and two-bedroom apartments with kitchens, living rooms. Rent by day, week, month. Near restaurants, shopping, fishing. Friendly, attentive management.

Islamorada

Cheeca Lodge. *Deluxe.* US 1. 25-acre resort with 1,100-foot ocean beach, 525-foot illuminated fishing pier, par-3 nine-hole golf course. Once a rich man's hideaway; now a year-round resort.

Jacksonville

Jacksonville Hilton. *Deluxe.* 565 S. Main St. Pool (heated), play area, marina. Restaurant, bars, entertainment. Overlooks city, river. There is also a Hilton at the airport.

Sheraton St. Johns Place. *Deluxe to Expensive.* 1515 Prudential Dr. Overlooking river. $20-million, 350-room hotel, opened late 1980. Pool, tennis courts, two restaurants, lounges with entertainment.

Holiday Inn. *Moderate.* (800) 238-8000 all locations. **Airport** inn has room service, lounge, entertainment, pool and kiddy pool, lighted tennis court, restaurant. **West** inn at 555 Stockton St. 32204 has pool, restaurant, lounge, room service. **South** at 3233 Emerson is near sports stadiums, shopping; and **Orange Park,** US 17 at I-295, has 2 lounges.

Admiral Benbow Inn. *Inexpensive.* 820 Dunn Ave. Pool (heated), play area. Pets. Restaurant, bar, dancing. Free airport transportation.

Days Inn. *Inexpensive.* I-95 & State 102, Airport Rd.; I-95 & University Blvd. Many family efficiency suites; 5929 Ramona Blvd. Pool, play area, gift shop, gas station and *Tasty World* restaurant at all addresses. Pets allowed. (800) 241-3400.

Jacksonville Beach

Howard Johnson's. *Expensive.* 1515 N. 1st St. On the beach. Pool, whirlpools. Game room. Coin laundry. Tennis, golf, fishing nearby. Accommodations for handicapped. 24-hr. restaurant, cocktail lounge.

Sheraton Jacksonville Beach. *Moderate.* 11th Ave. S. at Ocean. Pool, volleyball, croquet. Golf nearby. Restaurant, lounge. Entertainment nightly. Tennis.

Key Biscayne

Key Biscayne Hotel & Villas. *Deluxe.* Pool (heated). On private beach, with Sunfish avail. Tennis, play area. Supervised children's program in summer & holidays. Restaurant, bars, dancing.

Sonesta Beach Hotel & Tennis Club. *Deluxe.* Resort hotel on private beach. Luxurious villas also available. Pool (heated), play area, tennis, sailing & bicycles avail. Supervised children's program in summer, vacation period. Restaurants, bars, entertainment, dancing. MAP avail., fam. rates avail. in summer.

Key Colony. *Expensive.* Pool (heated), private beach. Tennis, play area. Cookout facilities. Restaurant nr. Golf.

Royal Biscayne. *Expensive.* Pools (heated), beach, tennis, sailing, scuba diving, play area. Restaurants, bar. Kitchen units, fam. rates avail.

Key Largo

Holiday Inn. *Moderate.* US 1. Pool, marina, tennis. Kennel. Restaurant, bar.

Howard Johnson's. *Moderate.* Gulf-front, 2-story motel. Pool (heated). Restaurant, bar. Suites, studio rooms avail.

Key West

Key Wester Inn. *Expensive.* A1A at the Ocean, 33040. (800) 432-7413 in Fla.; (800) 327-7072 elsewhere. Lighted tennis court, pool, boating, snorkeling, fishing, entertainment, lounge, shopping, room service, restaurant. Efficiencies, villas avail.

Ramada Inn. *Expensive/Moderate.* 3420 N. Roosevelt. 33040. (800) 228-2828 all locations. Restaurant, room service, bars/lounges, pool, tennis, miniature golf, 2 blocks to shop. Across street from Gulf. Wheelchair rms. avail.

Marriott's Casa Marina Resort. *Deluxe.* Formerly the palatial Casa Marina Hotel, built by Henry Flagler in 1920. Declared an Historical Structure. Popular with celebrities in the '30s and '40s. Refurbished and expanded to 250 rooms, 200-seat restaurant, 150-seat cocktail lounge, cabana bar, pool, tennis courts, gym. About 1,000 feet of Atlantic beachfront. On 6.5 acres.

Pier House and Beach Club. *Deluxe.* Harborfront in picturesque old section of town. A landmark. Everybody meets here. Fortune spent in 1980–81 on improvements, refurbishing. Balconies, patios. Some efficiencies. Boating, waterskiing arranged. Interesting restaurant.

Kissimmee

Orlando Hyatt Hotel World. *Deluxe.* 6375 W. Highway 192. Resort world with 8 pools, playgrounds, 3 lighted tennis courts. Shuttle to Disney World. 960 rooms! 1.3 mile-free Fit-Trail jogging course on property with 12 "exercise stations," basketball courts, "electric" game room. Helicopter rides. Exhibit hall, convention facilities. Coffee Shop, *Limey Jim* dining room, cocktail lounge, entertainment.

Hilton Inn Gateway. *Expensive to Deluxe.* 7470 W. Highway 192. Only 1 mile from Disney World. 360 rooms with 2 queen-sized beds in each, 3 studios, 10 suites. Covered garden terrace dining area, 2 pools, 18-hole par 54 putting course. Playground, coin laundry. Game room. Boutiques. Convention facilities. Restaurant, cocktail lounge, entertainment. (See listing for 2 Hilton Inns, Orlando.)

Holiday Inn. *Expensive.* Three locations. **East:** 5678 Space Coast Pkwy. **West:** 7300 Space Coast Pkwy. **Kissimmee:** 2145 E. Vine St. Each with pool, wading pool, playground, tennis, coffee shop, restaurant, cocktail lounge, entertainment.

Rodeway Inn at Eastgate. *Expensive.* 5245 W. Highway 192. One mi. west of Disney World entrance. Heated pool, playground. Coin-operated laundry. Restaurant, cocktail lounge. Game room.

Colonial Motor Lodge. *Moderate.* 815 W. Highway 192. Apartments avail. with kitchens. 2 pools. Nr. restaurant. Pets.

Days Inn. *Moderate.* 3 locations: 5840 W. Highway 192, 7980 E. Highway 192, and 2095 E. Highway 192, St. Cloud. Inns are a couple of mins. from Disney World. All have pools, restaurant, playground. (See listing of 6 Days Inns under "Orlando," Altamonte Springs, Clermont, Sanford.)

Larson's Lodge. *Inexpensive.* 2 locations: 6075 W. Highway 192 and 2009 W. Vine St. 128 rooms in each. Heated pool, sundeck. Family game room, playground. Dining room, cocktail lounge. Nr. tennis, golf.

Lake City

Holiday Inn. *Moderate.* P.O. Drawer 1239, 32055. (800) 238-8000. Intersection I-75 and US 90. Lounge, entertainment, pool, restaurant, lighted tennis court, miniature golf, room service.

Days Inn. *Inexpensive.* I-75 at US 90, 32055. (800) 241-2340. Restaurant open 6 A.M. to 9 P.M. Pool.

TraveLodge. *Inexpensive.* U.S. 90 at I-75. P.O. Box 1238, 32055. Tel. (904) 752-7550. Restaurant, lounge, pool, snorkeling, fishing. Rental equipment avail.

Lakeland

Holiday Inn. *Moderate.* 3 locations with usual amenities: **North:** I-4 and Fl 33; **Central:** 910 E. Memorial Blvd.; **South:** 3405 S. Florida Ave.

Huntley Inn (formerly the Hilton). *Moderate.* I-4 and US Hwy. 98. One of the city's newest. Spanish-style structure has 40-by-50-foot L-shaped swimming pool, sun terrace and play area. Covered promenade connects dining room, lounge and meeting room. 5 mi. from Lakeland Civic Center. Near 18-hole golf course.

Days Inn. *Inexpensive.* On I-4 and US 98 (3223 N US 98). Usual good value at this chain. About 40 mi. from Disney World, 35 mi. from Busch Gardens.

Lake Wales

Chalet Suzanne Resort Inn. *Deluxe.* Pool (heated), play area. Fine restaurant. Kitchen units, cottages avail. Each room is decorated differently with objets d'art from around the world. Arab dhow moored in lake.

River Ranch Resort. *Moderate.* Route 1, Box 400. Hayrides, cookouts, square dances, rodeos, and dude-ranch diversions. Lighted tennis court, rental equipment, boating, fishing, shopping 2 blocks. Resort has own landing strip. Riding, golf, trap, and skeet.

Emerald Motel. *Inexpensive.* Pool. Pets. Restaurant nr. (Superior Motels chain.)

Howard Johnson's. *Inexpensive.* US Rt. 27 N. Pool, play area, fishing, boats. Private freshwater lake. Restaurant Open 24 hrs.

Marathon

Sombrero Reef Club (formerly Bill King's Sombrero Resort). *Expensive.* Pool (heated), sauna. Restaurant, bar, dancing, entertainment occasionally. Fishing, boat ramp. Cook-out facilities. Free airport transport. Kitchen units, cottages avail. (305) 743-5526.

Buccaneer Lodge. *Moderate.* US 1. Private beach, lagoon, pools. Tennis, fishing, boat ramp. Restaurant, cocktail lounge, entertainment. (305) 743-9071.

Faro Blanco Marine Resort. *Moderate.* Salt-water pool. Play area. Golf, tennis nr. Dock, charter boats avail. Cook-out facilities. Kitchen units avail. (305) 289-0821.

Marco

Port of the Islands (formerly Remuda Ranch). *Expensive.* Route 41. On Gulf of Mexico. Newly refurbished Southern-style resort with outstanding, relaxed decor. Y-shaped pool, six lighted tennis courts, marina with charter boats, landing strip. Own airline (Royal Airways) for charter to Miami (75 mi. away) or other points. About 250 rooms. 16 mi. from Marco Island.

Marineland

Marineland Quality Inn. *Inexpensive.* Pool (heated). Beach, pools, marina. Tennis, putting green. Rest. cocktails. Free return passes to Marineland exhibit.

Melbourne

Holiday Inn. *Moderate.* Multiple locations. **2600 AIA** is on ocean with indoor-outdoor pool, jacuzzi, game machines. Nr. tennis, golf, racquetball. Restaurant, lobby bar, pool bar. Entertainment and dancing in lounge. **Midtown** location is at 440 S. Harbor City Blvd, on ICW and US 1. Pool, game machines. Nr. golf and tennis. Steakhouse Restaurant, live entertainment in Yesterday Lounge. **Holiday Inn West** is at 10900 W. New Haven near FIT campus, easy access to S.R. 192 to Disney. Nr. golf, tennis. Pool, 24-hour gas. Restaurant, lounge, room service.

Naples

Beach Club Hotel. *Deluxe.* 851 Gulf Shore Blvd. Pool (heated), beach, golf, tennis. Play area. Free airport transportation. Golf pkg., EP, kitchen units avail.

Beach & Tennis Club. *Deluxe.* Hickory Blvd., Bonita Beach (at Naples). 7 mi. Gulf beach. 10 clay tennis courts. Fishing, boating, family recreation center.

Cove Inn. *Deluxe.* Pool (heated), play area. Boats avail. Golf nr. Kitchen units avail. Restaurant, bar. Free transportation to bus terminal, golf.

La Playa Beach and Racquet Club. *Deluxe.* 9891 Gulfshore Blvd. Beautiful 5-mile white sand beach. Heated pool. Fishing. Nr. golf. Penthouse suites available. Gourmet restaurant, lounge.

Sheraton Edgewater Beach Inn. *Deluxe.* Gulfshore Blvd. Pool (heated), play area. Golf nr. Private beach. Kitchen units, fam. rates avail. Free transp. to terminals. Swank, statue-decorated entrance; small, attractive lobby.

Best Western Buccaneer Inn (formerly Buccaneer Red Carpet). *Moderate.* U.S. 41 N. Heated pools with garden area. Pretty view from rooms. Very well-maintained.

Naples Motor Lodge. *Moderate.* 250 9th St. Heated pool. 5 min. from beach. Nr. fishing pier, fishing boats, golf.

New Smyrna Beach

Best Western Islander Beach Lodge. *Moderate.* 1601 S. Atlantic Ave. Heated pool, playground, restaurant, lounge. Wading pool, putting green. Indoor whirlpool, sauna. Miniature golf.

Smyrna Motel. *Inexpensive.* 1050 N. Dixie Freeway. Play area. Restaurant nr. Pets. (904) 248-2495.

Ocala

Holiday Inn-West. *Moderate.* I-75 at S.R. 40. (800) 238-8000. Restaurant, room service, lounge, heated pool. Staff speaks Spanish, English, German, Iranian.

Sheraton-Country Inn. *Moderate.* Pool, play area. Restaurant, bar, dancing, entertainment wknds.

Days Inn. *Inexpensive.* I-75 and FL 40. Usual good standards. Pool, play area, gift shop, gas station. Pets. *Tasty World* restaurant. (800) 241-3400.

Orlando

Orlando Marriott Hotel. *Deluxe.* 6700 Sand Lake Rd. (formerly Sheraton Olympic Villas). A multimillion-dollar renovation encompassing 652 rooms, 264 full kitchen suites. 11 separate 2-story buildings on 35 acres. 2 Olympic heated pools, 6 lighted tennis courts with pro, 2 playgrounds, putting green, miniature golf, shuffleboard. Golf courses nearby. Restaurants, live disco, cocktail lounges, snackbar gazebo. 24-hr. coffee shop. Boutiques, pro shop. Big convention facilities.

Sheraton-Twin Towers Hotel. *Deluxe.* 5780 Major Blvd. Suites avail. Heated pool, whirlpool, Sauna, gymnasium. Shuttle to Disney World. Restaurant, coffee shop, cocktail lounge, entertainment.

Colonial Plaza Motor Inn. *Expensive.* 2801 E. Colonial Dr. Nr. U.S. Naval Training Center. Suites, kitchenettes available. Heated pool, therapeutic pools. Nr. golf, restaurants. *Wooden Nickel* cocktail lounge.

Gold Key Inn. *Expensive.* 7100 S. Orange Blossom Trail. Heated pool, tennis arranged. Putting greens. Suites, also. Popular *Picadilly Restaurant* and cocktail lounge.

Sheraton Orlando International Inn. *Moderate to Expensive.* Convenient to airport. 9301 S. Orange Blossom Trail. Heated pool, popular restaurant, lively lounge.

Sheraton World. *Expensive.* 10100 Intl. Dr., next door to Sea World. Beautiful resort complex; heated pool, restaurants, cocktail lounge with entertainment. Wading pool, miniature golf. Two lighted tennis courts. Shuttle to Disney World.

Holiday Inns. *Moderate.* 6515 International Dr. **(resort);** 929 W. Colonial Dr. **(downtown);** 4049 S. Orange Blossom Trail, **nr. expressway.** I-4 at SR 436; SR 50 & **Fla. Turnpike;** 626 Lee Rd. (800) 238-8000 for all. All have pool, restaurant, bar.

Howard Johnson's Motor Lodge. *Moderate to Expensive.* Seven of 12 locations, each with full amenities of this reputable chain: **Sea World:** State 528 at I-4; **Airport:** 8820 S. Orange Blossom Trail; **Downtown:** 304 W. Colonial Dr.; **Florida Center:** Kirkman Rd.; **North:** 603 Lee Rd.; **South:** 4201 S. Orange Blossom Trail; **West:** 2014 W. Colonial Dr.

Ramada Inn. *Moderate.* 3 locations. West Highway 50. Pool, wading pool, playground. Lighted tennis. Shuttle for Disney World, Stars Hall of Fame, Mystery Fun House, Wet and Wild. Gift shop. Restaurant, cocktail lounge. Also at 4919 West Colonial Dr.; 8700 S. Orange Blossom. Accommodations for handicapped at two—not at Colonial Dr.

Red Carpet Inn O'Wizard. *Moderate.* 6301 International Dr. Heated pool, wading pool, playground. Wet and Wild flume attraction across the street. Coffee shop, restaurant, cocktail lounge. Nr. golf, shops.

La Quinta Motor Inn. *Inexpensive to Moderate.* Located next to Quality Inn High Q 5825 International Dr. Heated pool, wading pool. 2-story Spanish inn style. Good for families on a budget—rooms accommodate up to 6 persons. Restaurant adjacent to Quality Inn's La Trattoria.

Davis Bros. Motor Lodge. *Inexpensive.* 6603 International Dr. Heated pool, wading pool. Cafeteria. (Also Davis Bros. Motor Lodges and Cafeterias in Ocala, Ormond Beach, Bartow.)

Days Inns. *Inexpensive.* At 720 S. Orange Blossom Trail, 2323 McCoy Rd., 650 Lee Rd., 1221 W. Landstreet Rd., 606 Lee Rd. Information, (800) 325-2525. All have restaurant, pool.

Ormond Beach

Georgian Inn. *Expensive.* 759 S. Atlantic 32074. (904) 677-6043. On beach. Restaurant, room service, 7:30 A.M. to 1:30 P.M. Pool, 2 blocks radius shopping. On AIA, 1½ mi. S of S.R. 40.

Biltmore Beach Lodge. *Moderate.* 187 S. Atlantic Ave. (A1A). Pool (heated), play area, golf nr. Beachfront, restaurant, lounge. (800) 874-0552.

Days Inn. *Moderate.* 839 S. Atlantic. Pool (heated), play area, beach. Golf and tennis nr. Kitchen units. All the amenities of this top-rated, family-oriented chain.

Palm Beach

Brazilian Court Hotel. *Deluxe.* 300 Brazilian Ave. TV on request. Fine restaurant, bar. Breakfast free. AP avail. Closed Apr. to mid-Dec.

Breakers Hotel. *Deluxe.* Large, elegant resort hotel on private beach with cabana club. Pool (heated), golf, tennis, riding. Social director, planned activities. Dancing, entertainment. Restaurant, bars.

Colony. *Deluxe.* 155 Hammon Ave. Pool (heated), sauna. Golf nr. Restaurant, bar, dancing. Closed late Apr. to Thanksgiving.

Hyatt Palm Beach. *Deluxe.* 630 Clearwater Park Rd. Full service hotel with two restaurants; lounge and pool.

Holiday Inn. *Expensive.* 2770-2830 S. Ocean Blvd. Pools, sauna, play area, beach, tennis. Restaurant, bar, dancing. Kitchen units avail. A resort complex.

Howard Johnson's. *Expensive.* 2870 Ocean Blvd. Pool (heated), beach. Pets. Restaurant, bar. Exceptionally attractive balconied rooms.

Pensacola

Holiday Inns. *Moderate.* **University Mall** at 7200 Plantation Blvd., **Bay Beach;** **Gulf Breeze** on Hwy. 98 S.; Holiday Inn **North** on US 29. All have pools. (800) 238-8000 for reservations all Holiday Inns.

Holiday Inn Resort. *Moderate.* Pensacola Beach. Racquetball, golf, sailing, boating, surfing, tennis, nr. marina with fishing charters. Nightlife in lounge. Babysitting, game room, gift shop, restaurant.

Days Inn. *Inexpensive.* I-10 and US 29. Branch of this dependable budget chain. Pool, play area, gas station, restaurant. Pets.

Lenox Inn. *Inexpensive.* 710 N. Palafax St. Pool, restaurant, bar, suites avail.

Pompano Beach

Sea Garden Beach Tennis Resort. *Deluxe.* 615 N. Ocean Blvd. Beautiful tropical gardens, oceanfront. Rooms, efficiencies apartments. 2 pools (heated), putting green. Tennis arrangements. Restaurant, lounge.

Worlds of Palm Aire. *Deluxe.* 2501 Palm-Aire Dr. N. (800) 327-4960. Spectacular sprawl of golf, pools, trails, tracks, and luxurious spa catering to notables. Three fine restaurants offer diet or regular gourmet menus.

Beachcomber Lodge and Villas. *Inexpensive to Moderate.* 1200 S. Ocean. Efficiencies avail. Private beach, pools, dining, lounge, putting green.

Ponte Vedra Beach

Sawgrass. *Deluxe.* (904) 285-2261. Luxury destination with famous golf, beaches, dining. Villas, homes, hotel-type accommodations available. Parcours, tennis, pro shops, daily activities. If you fly in (JAX), rent a bike or use resort transportation to get around the grounds.

Port St. Lucie

Sandpiper Bay Resort. *Moderate to Expensive.* On banks of St. Lucie river (just off U.S. 1). Award-winning resort on 1,000 acres. 11 tennis courts, tennis clinic; 45 holes championship golf. Marina with powerboats, sailboats. Terrific restaurant, coffee shop, lounges. All accommodations are attractive suites. Vacation packages.

Riviera Beach

Hilton Inn. *Deluxe.* 3800 N. Ocean Dr. Pool (heated), private beach. Tennis, sauna, children's pool, play area. Restaurant, bar, entertainment, dancing. Kitchen units avail. Golf privileges. (305) 848-5502.

Seaspray Best Western. *Expensive.* 123 Ocean Ave. Pool (heated), play area, beach. Restaurant, bar, entertainment, dancing in season. Barbecue facilities. Kitchen units avail.

Sheraton Ocean Inn. *Expensive.* 3200 N. Ocean Dr. Attractive oceanfront resort. Heated pool. Restaurant; cocktail lounge with entertainment. Some suites. (305) 842-6171.

Tahiti on the Ocean. *Expensive.* 3920 N. Ocean Dr. Pools (heated), private beach. Cook-out facilities. Restaurant nr. Kitchen units avail. Picnic grills and tables. Nine-hole putting green; playground.

St. Augustine

Ponce de Leon Lodge & Country Club. *Expensive.* Resort style motel on 350 acres. Pool, play area, golf, tennis. Restaurant, bar, entertainment, dancing Sat. MAP, suites avail.

Best Western Inn. *Moderate.* Jct. I-95 and FL 16. Pool, wading pool. Play area. Cocktail lounge.

Holiday Inn. *Moderate.* 2 of 3 locations, each with pool, restaurant, bar, dancing, entertainment in season: I-95 at State 16; US 1, 1300 Ponce de Leon Blvd.

Candyland Red Carpet Inn. *Inexpensive.* I-95 and FL. 16. Pleasant 2-story motel. Pool. Pets. Restaurant.

Kenwood Inn. *Inexpensive.* A New England-style inn in the historic district. Gracious old home, some rooms with fireplace, some share baths. Antique furnishings. Bed and breakfast.

St. Augustine Beach

Holiday Inn By The Sea. *Expensive.* On SR A1A. Beachfront. Pool. Tennis arranged. Some kitchenettes. Restaurant, cocktail lounge, entertainment.

La Fiesta Motor Lodge. *Moderate.* Pool, play area, private beach. Coffee shop.

Sea Shore Motel. *Inexpensive.* A1A at 12th St. Kitchenettes, weekly rates avail. Convenient to restaurant, laundromat.

St. Pete Beach Area

Don CeSar Beach Resort Hotel. *Deluxe.* 3400 Gulf Blvd. A big, pink towered and turreted Spanish-style villa in the grand manner, completely modernized. 300 rooms, suites, penthouses. Private beach, tennis, health club, playground. Restaurants, lounge, entertainment. Boutique shops, ice-cream parlor. Designated a National Historic Landmark.

Dolphin Resort. *Expensive.* 4900 Gulf Blvd. On long stretch of beach. Heated pool, play area. Kitchen units avail. Restaurant, cocktail lounge, entertainment, dancing.

Holiday Inn. *Expensive.* 5300 Gulf Blvd. Gulf-front large rooms, some efficiencies. Golf, tennis, resort. Popular restaurant, live entertainment.

Normandy Beach Resort. *Expensive.* 5606 Gulf Blvd. On beautiful white sand beach. Small, friendly, family-oriented resort. Garden apartments, efficiencies. Children's supervised activities. Large heated pool. Coin laundry.

St. Petersburg Beach Hilton Inn. *Expensive.* 5250 Gulf Blvd. Unusual octagonally shaped tower on beach. Outside glass bubble elevator to revolving rooftop restaurant and cocktail lounge. Polynesian specialties. Entertainment. Coffee shop, boutique.

Sandpiper Resort Inn. *Expensive.* 6000 Gulf Blvd. Three penthouse apartments, lanai suites, balconied rooms. Kitchen units avail. Heated pool and patio, children's pool, new glass-enclosed, climate-controlled pool with sundeck. Supervised children's programs. Tennis, private beach. Gift shops. Snack shop. *Brown Derby* restaurant and *Luv Pub* nr. entrance.

Howard Johnson's Motor Lodge. *Moderate.* 6100 Gulf Blvd. Beachfront, heated pool, restaurant.

Odyssey Gulf Resort. *Moderate.* 5400 Gulf Blvd. Pleasant, small resort with comfortable efficiency units, garden apartments, heated pool, wading pool. Right on wide, white sand beach. Coin laundry. Pets. Coffee shop. Inter-resort children's supervised activities. Nice for families.

St. Petersburg

Bayfront Concourse (formerly Hilton). *Expensive.* 333 First St. on Bayfront. Extensively refurbished. Lobby bar, Greenhouse restaurant, New Playboy Bunny Club opened mid-1981; bring your Playboy Club keys, members! Convention-oriented. Nr. Municipal Marina, sightseeing attractions, shopping.

Sheraton-St. Petersburg Marina & Tennis Club. *Expensive.* 6800 34th St. At Sunshine Skyway bridge entrance. Pools, play area. Marina, fishing. Restaurant, cocktail lounge, entertainment. Kitchen units avail.

Holiday Inn. *Moderate to Expensive.* 4 locations: **north, south, Madiera Beach,** and **St. Pete Beach.** Call (800) 238-8000 for reservations and details.

Albermarle Hotel. *Moderate.* 145 Third Ave. N.E. Family-owned for over 40 years. Public rooms furnished with gorgeous antiques. Elegant atmosphere. Heated pool. TV in lounge. Social program. Dining room. Open winter season only.

Quality Inn (formerly Save Inn). *Inexpensive.* I-275 and 54th Ave. N. A budget bargain. Pool, play area, game room. Very good restaurant; cocktail lounge.

Sanford

Holiday Inn. *Moderate to Expensive.* Two locations: I-4 at SR 46 and 530 Palmetto Ave. (800) 238-8000. Pool, restaurant, room service, lounge, entertainment. Menus avail. in English, Spanish. Handy to interstate, Orlando.

Sanibel Island

Casa Ybel. *Deluxe.* Villa-style accommodations on site of island's first resort. Interval-ownership plan also. Excellent restaurant. Outstanding beach.

Island Inn. *Deluxe.* Pool (heated), beach, play area, tennis. Dining room with box lunches avail. MAP, fam. rates, kitchen units avail.

Shell Harbor Inn. *Deluxe.* 937 Gulf Dr. Pool (heated), beach, dock. Free in-room coffee. Kitchen units avail. Cook-out facilities. Tennis. golf nr.

Song of the Sea. *Deluxe.* 863 E. Gulf Dr. Pool (heated), beach, boats avail., play area. All accommodations (studios to apartments) have fully equipped kitchen, screened balcony. Cook-out facilities. Restaurant nr.

Sundial Beach Hotel. *Deluxe.* 1246 Gulf Dr. Heated pool. Gulf front villas. Putting green, tennis courts, bikes. Shuttle to Sanibel Inn restaurant.

West Wind Inn. *Moderate.* Gulf Dr. Pool (heated), play area, beach, tennis. Restaurant nr. Kitchen units avail.

Sarasota

Colony Beach & Tennis Club. *Deluxe.* 1620 Gulf of Mexico Dr. Longboat Key. National headquarters for U.S. Professional Tennis Association (over 21 championship courts and stadium court). Pool (heated), beach, tennis, play area. Restaurant, bar, dancing, entertainment.

Far Horizons. *Deluxe.* 2401 Gulf of Mexico Dr., Longboat Key. Pool (heated). Golf, tennis, play area. Beach with thatched cabanas. Kitchen units, suites avail. Closed Labor Day–Oct. 1.

Longboat Key Hilton. *Deluxe.* 4711 Gulf of Mexico Dr. Luxurious beachfront resort. Heated pool, tennis. Scuba, sailboats avail. *Banyan Tree* and *Pineapple Place* restaurants, *Tree House* cocktail lounge, entertainment.

Sarasota Hyatt House Hotel. *Deluxe.* 1000 Blvd. of the Arts. Four lighted tennis courts, marina, pool. Gourmet restaurants, cocktail lounge. Near Van Wezel Hall and Asolo Theatre.

Sheraton Sandcastle. *Deluxe.* 1540 Ben Franklin Dr. Lido Beach. Restaurant, cocktail lounge. Pool (heated); beach with thatched shelters. Golf nr. Sprawling resort complex with variety of accommodations.

Azure Tides Hotel. *Expensive.* 1330 Ben Franklin Dr. Lido Beach. Pool (heated), beach, fishing, play area. Restaurant, bar. Kitchen units avail.

Buccaneer Inn. *Expensive.* 595 Dream Island Rd. at Yacht Harbor. Longboat Key. Pool (heated), beach nr., boating, fishing, tennis, play area. Restaurant, bar, entertainment. Kitchen units avail.

Ramada Inn. *Expensive.* 6545 N. Tamiami Trail. Pool (heated), play area, Thatched shelters on beach. Golf nr. Kitchen units avail. Restaurant, bar, dancing in season.

Econo Lodge. *Inexpensive.* 5340 N. Tamiami Trail. Walk to Ringling Museum, Asolo Theater, restaurants. 3 blocks to airport. Near Jungle Gardens, greyhound track, golf, beaches. Heated pool. Efficiencies avail. No pets.

Best Western Royal Palms. *Inexpensive.* 1701 N. Tamiami Trail. Pool (heated), play area. Restaurant.

Days Inn Sarasota. *Inexpensive.* 4900 N. Tamiami Trail (Hwy. 41). New, $2 million two-story, 122-room inn. On five-acre site nr. Sarasota-Bradenton Airport. *Daybreak* restaurant, pool.

Stuart

Indian River Plantation Resort. *Deluxe.* On 195 acres on southern end of Hutchinson Island. Beachfront on Atlantic Ocean. 120 villa-style accommodations in two 4-story lodges. Each with private balcony overlooking beach. Fully equipped kitchens in all 1- and 2-bedroom apartments, 2 swimming pools, 11 Har-Tru tennis courts, 18-hole executive golf course, bicycle paths. Tom Falkenburg, Director of Tennis; PGA member Bob Erickson, Golf Pro. Sailboat rentals, charter fishing nearby. Direct access to beach via boardwalks, sand dunes. Porch Restaurant, cozy, relaxed. Open from early breakfast to late dinner. Hotel guests who catch fish may have them prepared and served. Small conference center.

Tallahassee

Tallahassee Hilton. *Moderate.* 101 S. Adams St. Pool (heated). Pets. Restaurant, bar, entertainment, dancing. Golf & tennis nr.

Tallahassee Motor Hotel (Master Hosts-Red Carpet Inn). *Moderate.* 1630 N. Monroe St. Playground. Restaurant. Rooms for handicapped.

Tampa

Hilton. *Deluxe.* Two Locations: 200 Ashley Dr. and 2225 Lois Ave. Convenient to all activities. Good food and night life. Fine properties.

Tampa Hyatt Regency. *Deluxe.* 2 Tampa City Center. Restaurants and lounges. Heated pool, health club, golf, and tennis. All watersports nearby.

Tampa Marriott Hotel. *Deluxe.* In Tampa's showcase International Airport. Luxurious rooms. Special Executives' Sixth Floor, with complimentary cocktails, champagne, and European services. Lobby Seafood Bar, cocktail lounge with backgammon games, pool, disco, coffee shop, revolving CK's penthouse restaurant. There is another superb Marriott at 1001 N. Westshore.

Bay Harbor Inn. *Expensive.* 7700 Courtney Campbell Causeway. Heated pool. Small beach, rental sailboats. Playground. Restaurant, entertainment.

Causeway Inn. *Expensive.* Courtney Campbell Causeway, 33607. (800) 237-2555 outside Fla.; (813) 884-7561. Resort but nr. airport. Two restaurants, pool, lighted tennis courts, room service, pool, lounge with entertainment.

Admiral Benbow Inn. *Moderate.* 1200 N. Westshore Blvd. Heated pools, sauna. Dining room, cocktails, lively entertainment. Meeting rooms. Nr. airport.

Days Inn. *Inexpensive.* 3 locations. 2901 E. Busch Blvd. nr. Busch Gardens; I-75 (701 E. Fletcher Ave.); E Tampa at I-4 and FL 579N. (800) 241-2340.

Howard Johnson's. *Inexpensive.* 2 locations, with pool, restaurant: **Airport:** 702 West Shore Blvd.; **North:** 720 E. Fowler Ave. At the E. Fowler motor lodge, guests can pick their own fruit (it's free!) in season from the citrus grove with 19 different trees.

Tarpon Springs

Innisbrook Golf and Tennis Resort. *Deluxe.* US 19. 900 landscaped acres. Villas, lodges. Top-rated championship golf courses. Golf pro, tennis pro. 5 heated pools. Clubhouse dining rooms. Fishing, boating, biking. Wildlife sanctuary. Children's program. Special package rates. Entertainment nightly. Guests can pick oranges, grapefruit from private groves. Deluxe Australian Tennis Institute opened June, 1981. Great summer bargain: family of four, about $13 each per day!

Tierra Verde

Tierra Verde Hotel Yacht and Tennis Club. *Deluxe.* Opened late 1977, after being completely refurbished. Las Brisas casual restaurant. *Le Jazz Hot* cocktail lounge with entertainment; *Le Club* for romantic dining and dancing to live orchestra on special nights of week and weekend. Coffee shop. Huge swimming pool. (813) 867-8611.

Titusville

Econo Lodge. *Inexpensive.* 3655 Chaney Hwy. Junction I-95 and Rt. 50. Pool, restaurant, barbecue. Open 24 hours.

L-K Motor Lodge. *Inexpensive.* 3755 Chaney Hwy. (I-95 at Hwy. 50). Pool, restaurant, lounge. Game room, shuffleboard, scheduled transport into town. Horseshoes. 10 mi. to Space Center. (800) 848-5767.

Vero Beach

Aquarius. *Moderate.* 1526 S. Ocean & 3544 N. Ocean. Motel rooms, efficiencies, apts. Pool, shuffleboard. Friendly accommodations.

Reef Ocean Resort Motel. *Moderate.* Pool (heated). Pets. Restaurant, bar, dancing, entertainment. On ocean with private beach.

Sheraton Regency Resort Motel. *Moderate.* SR A1A. Oceanfront. Beach, indoor and outdoor heated pools. Pets. Restaurant, lounge with entertainment.

Landmark. *Inexpensive.* US 1 at 17th St. Heated pool. Restaurant nr. Pet dep. required. Family plan all year.

Wesley Chapel

Saddlebrook. *Expensive to Deluxe.* New golf and tennis resort, about half-hour from Tampa Intl. Airport. Beautifully appointed suites, patios or balconies (villa style). *Little Club* restaurant, lounges. On 400 acres, surrounded by southern woodlands. Pools, six tennis courts, 18-hole championship golf course. Beauty salon, barber shop. 40 suites completed; 300 total by end of 1982.

West Palm Beach

Palm Beach Polo and Country Club. *Deluxe.* 13198 Forest Hill Blvd. On over a thousand acres. Golf, tennis and equestrian-polo villages with swimming pools. 18-hole championship golf course, 19 tennis courts (9 illuminated); polo fields, stables. Restaurants, lounges. About 15 mi. from beach and Palm Beach.

PGA Sheraton. *Deluxe.* 400 PGA Blvd. W of Turnpike exit 44. (800) 325-3535 exc. Mo. Exciting resort wrapsaround 3 championship golf courses. Tennis, racquetball, solar pool, lap pool, lake, fitness center. Gourmet dining at the Explorers Club, grill at Colonel Bogey's. Packages, MAP avail.

Ramada Inn. *Expensive.* Pool (heated). Free in-room coffee. Restaurant, bar, entertainment, dancing. Free airport transportation. Tennis. Golf.

Sheraton Inn-West Palm Beach. *Moderate.* Six-story inn with restaurant, pool (heated). Golf opposite; tennis nr.

Martinique Motor Lodge. *Inexpensive.* 801 S. Dixie Hwy., Lake Worth. Free morning coffee in season. Shuffleboard, heated pool.

Parkview Motor Lodge. *Inexpensive.* 4710 Dixie Hwy. Friendly, family-owned. Neat, quiet rooms. Nr. beaches, golf, shopping. Lion Country. Palm Beach International Airport 5 mins.

Winter Haven

Ranch House. *Moderate.* Pool (heated), play area. Boating, fishing, swimming in Lake Ina. Kitchen units avail.

Banyan Beach Motel. *Inexpensive.* Pool (heated). Pets. Dock, boats, fishing.

Best Western Landmark. *Inexpensive.* At US 17. Pool (heated), sauna. Restaurant, bar. Kitchen units avail. Shuffleboard. Nr. Cypress Gardens, Singing Tower. Disneyworld 25 mi.

Winter Park

Alabama Hotel. *Moderate.* 800 Palmer Ave. Built in the 1920s, typical of resort of that era. Nostalgia has been preserved. Now open all yr. Rates for overnight or all winter. Public dining room.

Best Western Mt. Vernon Motor Lodge. *Moderate.* Pool. Pets. Restaurant, bar.

Holiday Inn North. *Moderate.* Pool (heated). Pets. Restaurant.

Langford Resort Hotel. *Moderate.* Pool (heated), play area. Handsomely decorated restaurant, bar, dancing, entertainment. Kitchen units avail.

DINING OUT. Eating your way across Florida may not be good for the waistline—or the budget—but what fun you can have hopping a boat to *Cap's Place* in Lighthouse Point for turtle steak and hearts of palm salad, as well as a little history about rum-running days or the time Winston Churchill sampled Cap's cooking during a secret wartime conference! Or maybe the treat will be an old-fashioned farm feed at *Branch Ranch,* just off I-4 between Lakeland and Tampa. Or how about watching the shrimp boats come home as you dine in Florida's southernmost fish house, the A and B Lobster House in Key West? It's all mighty fine fare, and it's hard to find a city without at least one superior eating place. Restaurant categories reflect the cost of a medium-priced dinner at each establishment. Included are hors d'oeuvres or soup, entree and dessert. Not included are drinks, tax and tip. Price ranges for Florida are *Deluxe,* $20 and up; *Expensive,* $9.50–$19; *Moderate,* $5.50 to $9; and *Inexpensive,* below $5. For a more complete explanation of restaurant categories see *Facts at Your Fingertips* at the front of this volume.

Boynton Beach

Bernard's. *Expensive.* 1730 N. Federal Hwy. Worth the splurge. Price of entree includes seafood coquille or soup du jour, fresh bread, unusual vegetable platter, salad, coffee and dessert! Wine, no liquor. Gorgeous gardens. Reservations required. 737-2236.

Scotch and Sirloin. *Expensive.* 601 S. Federal Hwy. Steaks and seafood; excellent prime rib; different specials daily.

Bradenton

Piccirilli's Italian Restaurant. *Expensive.* 2½ mi. n. of Sarasota-Bradenton Airport on U.S. 41. 6713 14th St. W. Pillared villa in garden setting. Gourmet Italian specialties, also chops, brochette, steaks, seafood. Dinner only.

Pete Reynard's. *Moderate.* 5325 Marina Dr. Fisherman's platter, roast duckling, steak & prime ribs. Music. The revolving dining room overlooks bay. Beautiful cocktail lounge. Arrive by car or boat (turn in at Inland Waterway Marker 62 and follow markers.) Lunch, dinner.

Pewter Mug Steak House. *Moderate.* 108 44th Ave. E. (Cortez Rd.). Just off U.S. 41. Famous for steaks, 2 lb. prime rib, lobster tails, crab legs, teriyaki chicken. Big salad bar and imported cheese dressings included. Classy, beamed ceiling atmosphere. Cocktail lounge. Dinner only. Another Pewter Mug in Venice, 1485 So Tamiami Trail.

The Pier. *Moderate.* Foot of 12th St. downtown. On historic Bradenton Memorial Pier, overlooking Manatee River. Key West 1920s nostalgia décor. Menu includes prawns-on-a-skewer, swordfish steak, beef. Double cocktail Happy Hour, lunch, dinner.

Cape Coral

Cape Coral. *Expensive.* Country Club Inn. Nicely-prepared continental dishes. Dancing & entertainment nightly in bar. Closed Mon.

Willy's. *Inexpensive.* German-American specialties, beer & wine. Closed Sun.

Clearwater

(Attractive Clearwater Mall and Countryside Mall, both US Hwy 19, have excellent snack shops, small restaurants.)

Siple's Garden Seat. *Expensive.* 1234 Druid. Prime ribs, roast duckling, steak, shrimp. Music. Overlooks garden and bay.

Kapok Tree Inn. *Moderate.* 923 McMullen Booth Rd. Palatial estate named for 100-year-old tree. Gardens and fountains inspired by Villa d'Este near Rome. Seating for 1,700 in resplendent dining rooms. Long wait for tables, so stroll through the gardens.

94th Aero Squadron. *Moderate.* Near St. Pete-Clearwater Airport. Normandy farmhouse on landscaped acres. World War I nostalgia theme. Lunch, dinner, late and light supper. Bar with theater showing old movies, if you have to wait for tables. Adjoins Boatyard (designed as old fishing village) with *Crab Cooker* restaurant—seafood grilled over mesquite wood fire.

Tio Pepe's. *Moderate.* 2930 Gulf-to-Bay Blvd. Spanish-villa atmosphere. Baked shrimps with almonds the specialty. Lunch and dinner.

Morrison's Cafeteria. *Inexpensive.* 1315 Cleveland. Roast beef, shrimp, homemade soup.

Clearwater Beach

Pelican. *Expensive.* Seafood, delicious baked goods. Stuffed shrimp a specialty. Closed Mon., late-Aug. to early-Sept.

Heilman's Beachcomber. *Expensive.* Steak, skillet-fried chicken, fresh seafood. Music.

Flagship. *Inexpensive.* 20 Island Way. Seafood platters and fish are specialties. Cocktails, too. Lunch, dinner. Artistically decorated.

Cocoa

Dixie. *Moderate.* Forrest Ave. Their Greek salad is renowned. Dancing. Closes only for Christmas.

Neptune Restaurant. *Moderate.* Florida Ave. Seafood, shrimp, pastries. Children's portions. Closed Sun., hol.

Duff's. *Inexpensive.* Byrd Plaza. Smorgasbord. Extras don't cost extra.

Cocoa Beach

Bernard's Surf. *Expensive.* S. Atlantic Ave. Fresh seafood, steak. Candlelit dining. Children's portions. A family restaurant for 30 years. If you dare, try whale meat or alligator steak.

Pelican Point Inn. *Expensive.* 2200 S. Orlando Ave. On scenic Banana River. Unusual turf and surf combinations. Own fishing fleet to catch seafood. Baked rock shrimp stuffed with crabmeat a winner. Delicious quail, steaks. Terrific Salad Bar, corn fritters. Don't miss dining here!

Hong Kong House. *Moderate.* 5450 N. Atlantic Ave. 783-7600. Chinese favorites; liquor avail. Open for lunch and dinner, 7 days.

Pedro's Capri. *Moderate.* 260 N. Orlando. Homemade Italian/Latin food. In operation for more than 20 years.

Alma's Pizza and Italian Restaurant. *Inexpensive.* 306 N. Orlando Ave. Special pasta dinners. Take-out, too. Cocktail lounge.

Mousetrap. *Inexpensive.* On A1A. At Polaris Motel. Lunch, dinner, cocktail Happy Hour with hors d'oeuvres table. Sun. dinner only. Dancing, entertainment. Known for beef and salad bar dinners.

Dania

Chef Tonton/Never on Sunday. *Expensive.* 129 N. Federal. Charming old house. Dine on duck, seasoned rabbit, beef Wellington.

Tobbler's Swiss Restaurant. *Expensive.* 1605 N. Federal Hwy. Chalet atmosphere. Swiss casseroles, fondues, German delicacies. 35-year-old institution.

Daytona Beach

Chez Bruchez. *Moderate.* 304 Seabreeze Blvd. Try the roast filet nivernaise or frogs' legs provencale. French or American food. Attentive service. Beer, wine. Chef-owned. Everything is extra special.

Gringoes. 201 N. Atlantic. Mexican food by candlelight.

Tony and Jerrie's. *Moderate.* 15 N. Coates St. Italian cuisine. Villa atmosphere.

Anchor Inn. *Inexpensive.* 608 W. Dunlawton Ave. at Port Orange Shopping Center. Not easy to find but well worth the search. Chef-owned. Delicious Florida seafood dishes (chicken and steak for landlubbers). Children's plates. Beer, wine.

Morrison's. *Inexpensive.* 200 N. Ridgewood. You can always count on this excellent chain for good food at low prices. Take-out service, too.

Deerfield Beach

Riverview Restaurant. *Expensive.* E. Riverview Rd., end of Intracoastal Bridge. Rustic atmosphere, old pine and cypress packing house. with Intracoastal Waterway view makes this a favorite among locals. Boaters can tie up at dock.

Pal's Captain's Table. *Expensive.* All the best from the sea. Baking done on premises.

Marcello Ristorante. *Moderate.* 718 S. Federal Hwy. Gourmet dining, with a family atmosphere. Northern Italian cuisine.

Bagel Break. *Inexpensive.* 1177 S. Federal. Wholesome meals.

De Land

Hush Puppy. *Moderate.* West on S.R. 44 (New York Ave.). Watch for the sign east of the bridge over the St. Johns River. Rustic setting, big selection of fresh seafood from saltwater and sweet water.

Karling's Inn. *Expensive to Moderate.* North on Hwy. 17, find the Inn on the N. side of the road just S. of DeLeon Springs. Continental, majoring in German specialties.

Delray Beach

The Bridge. *Expensive.* 840 E. Atlantic Blvd. Waterfront setting where you can try such continental specialties as sweetbreads Normandy.

Patio Delray. *Expensive.* 714 E. Atlantic Ave. Steak, chops and king crab. Pianist, patio dining. Lunch, dinner, Sun. brunches.

Le Petit Chalet. *Expensive.* 2519 N. Federal Hwy. French cusine. Great dining. Popular spot.

Boston's. *Expensive to Moderate.* 40 S. Ocean. They fly in fresh scrod from Boston, live Maine lobster. Live entertainment nightly, 9:30–1:30.

Little Italy. *Inexpensive.* 1911 S. Federal Hwy. Family restaurant.

Dunedin

Bon Appetit. *Moderate to Expensive.* On scenic Marina. Superbly-prepared seafood, veal, beef, chicken. Delicious cocktails, fine wines. Classy service. Music in lounge. Beautiful seascapes from window walls. Breakfast, lunch, dinner.

Fernandina Beach

The Sandbar. *Moderate.* A beach roadhouse serving seafood in a fun way, like roasted oysters on a tin tray, shrimp on a towel. Overlooking Amelia River at Fernandina Beach.

Palace Saloon. *Inexpensive.* Florida's oldest (1878). Historic antiques on display. Player piano, copper still, artistic murals. Famous spicy boiled shrimp with hot tomato sauce only food served. Great drinks, especially the 22-ounce Pirate's Punch.

Fort Lauderdale

Casa Vecchia. *Deluxe.* 209 N. Birch Rd. An Italian palazzo on the waterway. Each room is lovely, as is the food. The best of Northern Italy, French Riviera cuisine. Spectacular wine list. Award-winning establishment.

La Bonne Auberge. *Expensive.* 4300 N. Federal. Award-winning restaurant with extensive French menu. Charming, rustic decor.

Charcoal Pit. *Expensive.* 825 E. Sunrise Blvd. Open only for dinner. Excellent wine list. Lovely patio-garden setting. Season only.

Christine Lee's Northgate. *Expensive.* 6191 Rock Island Rd. Special Oriental cusine.

Dante's. *Expensive.* 2871 N. Federal Hwy. Dover sole chablis and veal cordon bleu recommended. Great charcoal-broiled beef. Dressy atmosphere. Reservations suggested.

Down Under. *Expensive.* 3000 E. Oakland Park Blvd. On the ICW, with place to dock your boat. Varied menu includes unusual dishes such as rabbit. Continental, bustling, fun.

Jimmy's. *Expensive.* Early bird specials. 1200 N. Federal Hwy. Open 7 nights to 2 A.M. Live music, dancing. Chicken, lobster, steaks, veal. Non-smoking section.

La Ferme. *Expensive.* 1601 E. Sunrise Blvd. Rated as one of the top French restaurants in Fort Lauderdale. Excellent food; simple décor.

Le Cafe de Paris. *Expensive.* 715 Los Olas Blvd. Small, with intimate atmosphere. Fine French cuisine for over 10 yrs.

Bon Appetit. *Moderate to Expensive.* 3051 E. Commercial. Celebrated for modestly priced French cuisine, fresh vegetables, soups, Charming atmosphere, 4 rooms.

The Caves. *Moderate to Expensive.* 2205 N. Federal Hwy. (US 1). Cave men and cave girls in leopard skin togas serve in romantic, black plush caves. (Caves for non-smokers also.) Steaks, Alaskan king crab legs, snapper Dijon and other entrées served with soup, rice pilaf and selections from the Sterling Silver Salad Bar. Even a fur bar with stalactites in the lounge! Dinner only.

Cafe de Geneve. *Moderate.* Authentic Swiss fondues. Frog legs top the 24 dinner choices. Casual, friendly. Lunch, too.

Golden Spike Restaurant. *Moderate.* 6000 N. Federal Hwy. Lunch in the Mug Cellar is different, surrounded by tagged antiques, curios in this replica of an 1800 baggage room. Upstairs, there's Gold Rush atmosphere, candlelight and a continental menu.

New River Storehouse. *Moderate.* Part of Marina Bay hotel resort. Looks like dockside warehouse, but dining is elegant. Try the rock shrimp and "Tropical Pye." Dinner only.

94th Aero Squadron. *Moderate.* At Executive Airport. World War I flying aces are honored in this unusual theme restaurant. Oversize Margaritas. Good steaks, brochette, quiche. Very popular and crowded.

Patricia Murphy's Candlelight Restaurant. *Moderate.* In Bahia Mar Yachting Center. Intracoastal Waterway views. Lunch, dinner, cocktails.

Lauder-Deli. *Inexpensive.* Hearty delicatessen sandwiches and other combinations. Breakfast, business luncheon specials, dinner. Nr. airport.

Fort Myers—Fort Myers Beach

The Shallows. *Expensive.* On College Parkway. You may not get beyond the sumptuous salad bar. If you do, try the snapper with special crab-bearnaise sauce.

Veranda. *Expensive.* Broadway and Second. Downtown. Old-fashioned mansion tastefully decorated with antiques of historical Florida. New Orleans cuisine served in dining room or garden. Dinner only. Entertainment nightly in adjoining, attractive cocktail lounge.

The Holmes House. *Expensive.* 2500 Eastero Rd. Creative chef highlights 10-page menu with fresh seafood casserole, wild rice stuffed pheasant, chateaubriand. Two salad bars. Cocktails. Fancy coffees. Dinner only.

Mike's Landing. *Expensive to Moderate.* At Page Airport, Danley Dr. Reservations recommended for this locally popular spot. Frog legs, corn on the cob, french-fried vegetables.

Brown Derby. *Moderate.* 1800 College Pkwy. One of the Florida chain, best known for steaks and best salad bar in town. Lively lounge.

Gainesville

Cathay Tea House. *Expensive to Moderate.* 3226 S.W. 35th Blvd. 372-7772. Chinese favorites at lunch and dinner. Occasionally on Mondays or Tuesdays there is a cooking show, and audience eats a meal of 5 to 7 courses. Chinese gourmet banquet available on advance notice.

Sports & Courts Ltd. *Moderate.* 1430 SE 13th St. 377-0348. Open 11 to 11, serving 8 kinds of specialty burgers. Oyster bar.

Sovereign Restaurant. *Moderate.* 12 S.E. 2nd Ave. Old carriage house converted to New Orleans-style restaurant with courtyard patio. Continental cuisine.

Down to Earth. *Inexpensive.* 625 W. University Av. Natural foods breakfast house. Pancakes, herb omelets, huevos rancheros, freshly squeezed juices, etc.

Islamorada

Conch. *Moderate.* Good eating, specializing in seafood, conch chowder, stone crabs, steak. Player piano. Bar. On US 1.

Green Turtle Inn. *Moderate.* Highly recommended for chowder, turtle steak, rum pie and Key lime pie. Entertainment. On US 1.

Jacksonville

Alhambra Dinner Theater. *Expensive.* 12000 Beach Blvd. Includes superb Broadway fare. Flashy buffet, cocktail lounge, drinks available during play. Reservations essential. 641-1212.

Patti's East. *Moderate.* 7300 Beach Blvd. Italian and American food. Try the *chicken à parmigiana.* Beer, wine.

Stricklands. *Moderate.* Mayport, near Jacksonville. Rustic fishing-village atmosphere. On banks of St. Johns river. Just-caught red snapper, sheepshead, flounder, bass, shad, sea trout, and seafood. Seating for over 300.

Jensen Beach

Frances Langford's Outrigger Restaurant. *Moderate.* Polynesian decor and cuisine. Shrimp with "outrigger sauce" is a winner. Pert Miss Langford was one of the top pop-singers of the 1940s.

Key Largo

Marker 88. *Moderate.* Federal Hwy. Beachfront at "Marker 88," nr. Plantation Key. Interesting, creative menu. Lots of atmosphere. Dinner only. Very popular. Reservations necessary.

Key West
Pier House. *Deluxe.* 1 Duval St. 294-9541. Unsurpassed luncheon buffet and Sunday brunch. Dinners a la carte. Your choice of oysters, seviche, terrine, bisque. Inspired salads, masterful main dishes, tart Key lime pie.

Claire. *Expensive.* 900 Duval St. Good American cooking with a touch of Thai, plus fresh seafood. Try the conch chowder, yellowtail snapper, chocolate-banana cake.

Henri's. *Expensive.* In the Casa Marina. Look out over the ocean while delving into fabulous tastes. Sunday brunch extravaganza.

Spanish restaurants abound in Key West. Best are *La Lechonera* on Catherine St., *4th of July* on White St., *El Cacique* and *Gringo's,* both on Duval.

Kissimmee
Limey Jim's. *Deluxe.* In the Hyatt Hotel at 6375 W. Hwy. 192. Posh service, surroundings, fabulous appetizers include cruditees with curry dip. Homemade pastas. Veal Oscar, fresh catch.

Spinelli's. *Expensive.* 1200 Pennsylvania Ave., St. Cloud. One of Florida's finest restaurants. Vintage wines, Italian classics, quail, veal, steaks. Reservations, 892-2435.

Lakeland
Brown Derby. *Moderate to Expensive.* South edge of town. 646-5029. View of peacocks and wild birds as you dine. Sumptuous salad bar has oysters on the half shell in season. Early-diner specials, attentive service.

Lake Buena Vista
Walt Disney World Village (at Lake Buena Vista) has good eating establishments among the 30 boutiques. Everything from freshly shucked oysters in a waterfront lounge *(Cap'n Jack's Oyster Bar), Heidelberger's Deli* and *Lite Bite* for sandwiches, *Village Restaurant* for complete meals, and the *Empress Lilly* for elegant dining. Prices vary.

Empress Lilly Riverboat Restaurant. *Expensive.* At Walt Disney World Shopping Village. Gourmet seven-course meals in The Empress Room. Fisherman's Deck and Steerman's Quarters for seafood and steaks. Baton Rouge Lounge is a good-time show bar.

Great Ceremonial House. Papeete Bay Veranda. *Moderate to Expensive.* In Polynesian Resort Hotel. South Seas lagoon and garden artistic atmosphere. Breakfast buffet, lunch buffet, dinner. Children's prices for breakfast, lunch. Oriental-influenced dishes for enjoyable exotica. Nightly entertainment in *Captain Cook's Hideaway Lounge.* Reservations essential for dinner.

Lake Wales
Chalet Suzanne. *Expensive.* US 27 North. Pleasant surroundings. Fantastic soups, entrées, desserts. No two tables decorated alike.

Madeira Beach
Gene's Lobster House. *Moderate.* 565 150th Ave. On Intercoastal Waterway. Seafood; childrens' menus; lounge.

Richards (formerly Kapok Tree). *Moderate.* 5001 Duhme Rd. Acropolis-style statuary, lavish gardens, and lagoons. Ornate dining rooms, but low prices.

Captain's Galley. *Inexpensive.* Near Madeira Shopping Mall. Broiled grouper a specialty. Excellent strip steaks. Cozy dining room with water views. A longtime favorite with locals, the small restaurant is busy with the "overflow" from the nearby Santa Madeira restaurant.

Naples

The Chef's Garden. *Expensive.* 1300 Third St. S. Selected as one of Top Ten Florida restaurants by *Florida Trend* magazine. Features creative interpretations of continental cuisine in both indoor and outdoor setting. Extensive wine list.

Fujiyama Steak House. *Expensive.* 2555 Tamiami Trail. Communal seating, 8 to the table, so it's not the spot for business conspiracies or romantic secrets. Everyone enjoys the chef's show, special cocktails, superb Japanese specialties.

St. George and the Dragon. *Moderate.* Fifth Ave. S. Beef is the specialty, but there are many other selections on the menu, conch chowder and red snapper among them. Setting is amidst nautical memorabilia.

Ocala

Coach N Paddock. *Expensive.* 2677 N.W. 10th St. (US 27). Lunch, dinner, entertainment during dinner. Live Maine lobster.

Golden Corral. *Moderate.* 2426 E. Silver Springs Blvd. Entertainment during dinner. Open 7 days, 11 A.M. to 10 P.M. Senior citizen discount.

Orlando

Maison & Jardin. *Expensive.* 430 S. Wymore Rd. Altamonte Springs, near Orlando. Beautiful garden-surrounded villa. Prize-winning continental and American dishes. Romantic dining.

Piccadilly. *Expensive.* 7100 S. Orange Blossom Trail. Just like being in London with prime ribs and Yorkshire pudding, shrimp in beer batter, kidney pie. All this and French pastries, too.

Al E. Gator's. *Moderate.* In Florida Festival across from Sea World. Famous for chicken coco-banana, conch sandwiches, and Reuben made from swamp cabbage. Continuous entertainment after 6.

Brazil's. *Moderate.* 701 Orienta Ave., Altamonte Springs. Voted best new restaurant of 1980 in newspaper poll. New York steaks, fresh seafood. Entertainment Tues.–Sat. Free hors d'oeuvres Mon.–Fri. 4:30-7.

Casa D'Antonios. *Moderate.* New location, 1336 Orange. Ave., Winter Park. Pastas, veal specialties. House specialty is Fruitti Di Mare. Closed Sunday.

Gary's Duck Inn. *Moderate.* 3974 S. Orange Blossom Trail. Good place for French-fried jumbo shrimp.

Lili Marlene's Aviators' Pub and Restaurant. *Moderate.* Church St. Station complex. Turn-of-century nostalgia, with oak paneling, brass fans, stained-glass windows. Delicious wiener schnitzel, creole gumbo, stone crab claws, coffee praline parfait, fresh-baked cheesecake.

Palm Beach

Petite Marmite. *Very Expensive.* 309 Worth Ave. Definitely worth the big splurge for lunch or dinner. Excellent service. Reservations necessary. Extremely well-dressed clientele.

Bentley's. *Expensive.* N. Palm Beach (730 US Hwy. 1). Romantic candlelight, stained-glass windows, terraced gardens. Well-prepared veal, steak, duckling, chicken, fish. Lunch, dinner, Sun. brunch.

Capriccio. *Expensive.* 336 Royal Poinciana Plaza. Opp. Playhouse. Fine dining in an elegant setting. Mostly Italian and French specialties. Long wine list. Lunch, dinner.

Charley's Crab. *Expensive.* 456 S. Ocean. Steamers, raw bar, soft-shell crab, charcoal grilled catch of the day. Dinner only.

Chez Guido. *Expensive.* 251 Royal Palm Way. Tropical rattan and floral décor but the menu is strictly European. Superb flaming dishes. Reservations. Lunch, dinner.

Ta-Boo. *Expensive.* 221 Worth Ave. Celebrity rendezvous for over 30 years. Imaginative décor with tropical fruit lights! Seafood, steaks, canneloni, veal picata are menu favorites. Lunch, dinner, Sun. brunch. Dancing nightly in lounge. Jackets required.

Testa's. *Expensive.* 221 Royal Poinciana Way. Family-owned for over 50 years. Varied menu, principally Italian specialties, seafood. Sidewalk cafe, patio dining and tropical orchid greenhouse.

Hamburger Heaven. *Inexpensive.* 314 S. County Rd. Fat and fancy burgers festooned with a feast of toppings.

Palmetto

Pelican Point Sea Hut. *Moderate.* Snead Island Rd., or arrive by boat at Pelican Point Marina. Southern fishing village decor in secluded atmosphere. Very casual at lunch. Delicious fish, shellfish—steak, too. Crab is a specialty. Nr. Bradenton, Sarasota.

Panama City and Panama City Beach

Angelo's Steak Pit. *Expensive.* Hickory broiled ribs, steak, chicken. Apple pie is delicious. Children's portions. Longhorn saloon.

Boar's Head Restaurant and Tavern. *Expensive.* 17290 W. 98A. Medieval English atmosphere with lanterns, beams, armored knight displays. Hearty servings. Prime ribs, Yorkshire pudding, steaks, seafood, chicken. Super salad bar. Irish-style coffee in 20-ounce goblet. Live entertainment, generous drinks in cozy tavern. Dinner only from 4 P.M.

Foxfire Restaurant and Tavern. *Moderate to Expensive.* 4500 W. Hwy. 98. Red Fox Room with $4.95 entrees including salad bar (snapper, stuffed shrimp, barbecued ribs, etc.). *Torch Room* with gourmet dining. Special cocktails in souvenir glasses. Entertainment. Dinner only.

The Treasure Ship. *Inexpensive to Expensive.* Treasure Island Marina. 3605 Thomas Dr. 17th-century, 3-masted sailing galleon 200 feet tall. 4 decks of restaurants, gift shop, game room, wharf with raw bar, sandwiches, cocktails. Second deck main dining room. *Pirate's Pleasure* ice cream parlor third deck, *Top of Ship* for elegant dining. The *Brig* disco. Open 5:30 A.M. to 2 A.M.! No charge to board. *Top of Ship* dinner reservations (904) 234-8881.

The Hearty House. *Inexpensive to Moderate.* 3210 Thomas Dr. Delicious locally caught catfish, jumbo shrimp. Apalachicola oysters, Panamanian seviche appetizer, extra special. Steaks, too. Cocktails, wine, beer. Lunch and "to go" for fishermen. First call for breakfast 4:30 A.M.! 7 days a week. At the lagoon.

Pensacola

Charleyo's. *Moderate to Expensive.* In the University Mall Holiday Inn. Steak, seafood, Maine lobster.

The Greenery. *Moderate to Expensive.* Bay Beach Holiday Inn, Maine lobster, gourmet burgers, omelettes.

Apple Annie's Courtyard, Coppersmith Galley, Lili Marlene's World War One Pub, Oyster Bar, Rosie O'Grady's, Phineas Phogg's Disco. *Inexpensive.* Seville Quarter. Imaginative casual restaurants in historical, restored Spanish square. Phineas Phogg's took two years to plan, 15 months to construct. High point is 6-foot-high copper-brass balloon with gondola. (Also see *Orlando* listings.)

Plant City

Branch Ranch. *Moderate.* This restaurant, which grew out of Mrs. Branch's inviting a few friends to dinner, is worth the drive from Tampa—or anywhere. Serves chicken, ham, chicken-ham combination. Vegetable dinner has chicken pot pie as side dish. Everything is home grown. Antique shop upstairs.

Lani Purcell's 1776 Restaurant and Lounge. *Moderate.* Interstate 4 at SR 39 (12 mi. E. of Tampa). Gulf shrimp, Apalachicola oysters among appetizer selection. Florida frog legs, steak, Maine lobster, combination seafood platter, good salad bar. Senior Citizens' menu. Children's menu. Entertainment, dancing nightly. Open 7 days. Consecutively voted Number One Holiday Restaurant in the world.

Pompano Beach

Cap's Place. *Expensive.* Turtle steaks, Florida lobster tails, broiled catch-of-the-day, hearts-of-palm salad. Roosevelt and Churchill dined here. Across from Intracoastal Waterway. Park at Lighthouse Point Marina on 28th Court, flip light switch on dock, and shuttle boat-taxi will come to fetch you. Dinner only.

Bobby Rubino's Place for Ribs. *Moderate.* 2501 N. Federal Hwy. Barbecued baby back ribs, chicken, steak and seafood. 4 other locations in county. Popular.

The French Place. 3600 E. McNab Rd. *Moderate.* Still to be discovered by the masses. Excellent food well-served in a homey, French country atmosphere. Beef tournados, veal.

Norris Catfish Restaurant. *Moderate.* Casual restaurant offering all you can eat of fried catfish. 2 locations, S.R. 7 in **Margate** and another on **Atlantic Blvd.**

Sarasota

L'Auberge du Bon Vivant. *Expensive.* 7003 Gulf of Mexico Dr. Long Boat Key. Currently an "in" place for dinner. Two couples own it; the men are chefs, the wives, hostesses. Coquille St. Jacques Sauce Mornay just one of the gourmet selections. Good wines and beers. Less than 100 seats, so reservations necessary. Dinner only.

Buccaneer Inn. *Expensive.* Buccaneer Inn, 595 Dream Island Rd. Pirate theme in relaxed atmosphere. Charbroiled beef. Bar. Arrive by car or boat.

Cafe L'Europe. *Expensive.* St. Armand' Circle. Flower-filled, continental ambience in Sarasota's perpetual prize-winning restaurant. Crepes, duck l'orange, and international specialties. Lunch, dinner.

Columbia Restaurant. *Moderate.* St. Armand's Circle. Excellent Spanish and American dishes. Same family as famous Columbia in Tampa.

The Sawmill Inn Restaurant. *Moderate.* 33 Crossroads Shopping Center. Imaginative, attractive rustic setting. Delicious food, everything from soup and sandwiches to great steaks, Veal Cordon Bleu and seafood. Lunch, dinner. Dinner only Sat., Sun. Cocktail lounge, entertainment.

Oyster Bar. *Inexpensive.* 7250 S. Tamiami Trail. Always good seafood at very low prices in this popular chain. King crab salad a favorite, also seafood platters. Lunch, dinner, cocktails.

St. Augustine

Chart House. *Deluxe.* 46 Avenida Menendez. Ages-old hospitality in a historic house. Lounge, best beef. Dinner only.

Clam Shell. *Expensive.* North on AIA at Commanche Cove Marina. Plenty of steak and seafood, and the oysters come either raw or roasted. 7 days.

St. Petersburg

Peter's Place. *Deluxe.* 208 Beach Dr. downtown. Bayfront continental café. Exquisite crystal, linens. Imaginative entrées: Roquefort quiche, Pork loin with brandied pineapple, Bananas Foster. Prix fixe dinner about $22 per person (wines, tax, tip extra). Open Tues.–Sat., dinner only.

Isla del Sol Club House. *Expensive.* 5000 Sun Blvd. On the Bayway. Part of Isla del Sol Golf and Racquet Club complex. Varied dinner menu of steaks, seafood, continental dishes. Cocktails. Lunch, moderate, featuring crepes, sandwiches, salads, prime ribs, seafood.

Bradford's Coach House. *Moderate.* 1900 4th St. N. Popular place with a large selection of good food.

Pepin. *Moderate.* 4125 4th St. N. Popular Spanish restaurant. Children's Menu. Cocktails.

PierSide. *Moderate.* On fourth floor of showplace. Five-story, unique inverted pyramid building on downtown St. Petersburg's waterfront. Wonderful views from window walls. Seafood specialties, but varied menu. Cocktail lounge.

Seaman's Cove. *Moderate.* U.S. 19 at Maximo Moorings Marina. Scenic waterfront dining at yacht-lined harbor. Shrimp scampi the specialty. Varied menu. Window-walled dining room.

Sea Ketch. *Moderate.* 800 Bay Pines Blvd. No. Beautiful bay views from window walls. Superlong bar. Almond shrimp a specialty. Same management as Fish House. Lunch, dinner.

Athenian Gardens. *Inexpensive.* 2066 Tyrone Blvd. Crossroads Shopping Center. Friendly Greek atmosphere for souvlaki, shish kebab, moussaka, stuffed grape leaves and famous gyro sandwich. Delicious Greek salads and soups. Lunch, dinner. Beer, wine.

Aunt Hattie's. *Inexpensive.* 625 1st St. S. (Next door to *Uncle Ed's* for sandwiches, salads, beers.) Chicken & dumplings, seafood. Victorian decor. Childrens plates.

Tampa

Bern's Steak House. *Expensive.* 1208 S. Howard Ave. Serves superb steaks. 5,600 wines on hand, raises own vegetables in organic garden, ages own cheeses, roasts own coffee. Food cooked to order. Chef-owned. Entertainment.

Columbia Restaurant. *Expensive.* In Ybor City, Tampa's famous Latin Quarter. Winner of *Holiday* magazine's award for excellence. Spanish and American cuisine. Exciting floorshows nightly except Sun., plus strolling musicians.

CK's. *Expensive.* Atop Tampa Marriott Hotel, high over Tampa International Airport. CK was a legendary aviator of unusual exploits, but the delicious specialties in this revolving glass-walled penthouse are for real. Prize-winning menu. Bar. Impressive vistas.

Selena's. *Expensive.* 1623 Snow Ave. French cuisine and excellent service. Home-style recipes. Becoming the "in" place in the area.

Verandah. *Expensive.* 5250 W. Kennedy Blvd. Tampa's newest and most elegant dining experience, which manages to maintain a relaxed atmosphere.

Crawdaddy's. *Moderate to Expensive.* 2500 Rocky Pt. Rd. Old fish-house atmosphere. Unique décor, including old-fashioned bloomers in bar-discotheque. 7 levels for dining, with Tampa Bay vistas. Lobster Whisky, Rum Runner Steak, all unusual entrées. Huge margaritas. Lunch, dinner, late supper.

The Embassy. 2801 E. Busch Blvd. *Moderate.* Relaxed establishment with Mediterranean decor and a varied menu.

Mullet Inn. *Inexpensive.* 6415 Courtney Campbell Causeway. Casual place for Suncoast's smoked mullet. Unusual smoked shrimp.

Oyster Shanty. *Inexpensive.* 5421 W. Hillsborough SR 80. Real atmosphere with newspapers over plastic tableclothes for enjoying steamed crabs (all you can eat), shrimp steamed in beer, steamed clams, smoked mullet. Seafood combination plates, salads, chowders, desserts. Smoked chicken. Beer, wine. Lunch, dinner.

Tarpon Springs

Louis Pappas Riverside Restaurant. *Moderate.* On the sponge docks. Flavorful Greek and American foods. Chef's salads and fish delicacies. Bar. Family-owned for more than half a century.

Mullet Boat. *Inexpensive.* 701 N. Pinellas. Specializes in the smoked fish the Gulf coast so adores. Steamed clams, raw oysters, beer, wine, takout.

Tierra Verde

The Good Times. *Moderate.* 1130 Pinellas Bayway, Tierra Verde. Rostbraten Esterhazy, Veal Roast Florentine, roast duckling, old-fashioned soups, and steaks are popular. Delicious desserts. Lunch, dinner, but check ahead for special serving hours. About 20 min. drive from St. Petersburg en route to DeSoto Park.

Titusville

Sand Point Inn. *Moderate.* 801 Marina Rd. 30 mi N. of Titusville. Seafood specialties in an attractive weathered-wood building, jutting out over Indian River. Owned by Ponce Seafoods, own fishing fleet. Rock shrimp, scallops, quail, steaks, salad boat are great! Worth a special trip.

Treasure Island
Careless Navigator. *Moderate.* 11595 Gulf Blvd. Nautical décor. Homemade soups, breads. Seafood, veal, steaks, chops. Lounge. Dinner only.

Robby Pancake House. *Inexpensive.* 10925 Gulf Blvd. Popular for Sunday brunch, snacks, light meals, pancakes.

Vero Beach
Driftwood Inn. *Expensive.* 3150 Ocean Dr. Local landmark fashioned from wood, driftwood, and chips off old blocks. Gourmet dining.

Restaurant Forty-One. *Expensive.* 41 Royal Palm Blvd. Fresh food and flaming desserts.

Wellburn
Stephen Foster Colonial Inn. *Moderate.* At the gate of the Foster Memorial. Beer only.

West Palm Beach
The Gathering. *Moderate.* 4201 Okeechobee Blvd. Well-prepared food served in pleasant surroundings. Well-decorated with early-American memorabilia.

New England Oyster House. *Moderate.* Seafood, Maine lobster. Buffet lunch. Children's portions.

Winter Haven
Christy's Sundown Restaurant. *Moderate.* Ave. K and 3rd St. W. Neat, attractive dining room, varied selection, featuring charcoal steaks and seafoods. Cocktail lounge. Entertainment nightly. On US 17 S.

Coach Light Buffet. *Inexpensive.* All you care to eat at lunch and dinner "groaning boards," including Friday night seafood buffet. Also soup, salad, and beverage specials for calorie-counters. 2601 Havendale Blvd.

Winter Park
La Belle Verrier. *Expensive.* 142 Park Ave. S. 645-3377. Reservations. French specialties at lunch and dinner. Cocktails avail.

Musicana Dinner Theater. *Expensive.* 665 N. Orlando Ave. 628-8700. Includes show. Fun and feasting. Cocktails avail. Reservations essential.

Pizza Inn. *Moderate.* 415 Semoran Blvd. 678-1655. Choose your toppings, and savor your pizza with your favorite beer or wine.

GEORGIA

Pacesetter of the New South

BY
CAROLYN CARTER

Carolyn Carter, a native Georgian, was a staff writer and photographer for The Atlanta Journal and Constitution Sunday Magazine. *She now is a freelance writer specializing in travel.*

Revolving lounges atop two hotels in Atlanta provide a view from which you can *almost* see the city grow. New buildings are springing up at every compass point; old ones are being removed to make way for progress. A few years ago the Atlanta newspapers published a photograph of the skyline in the early '60's—another, of the same spot in the '70's. Two entirely different cities.

Atlanta is running ahead, pacing the South, just as she has since early Reconstruction days following the Civil War when most of her residences and businesses were devastated, but she came up with a determination to win—and she has.

Scarlett O'Hara said: "Atlanta is full of pushy people." Pushy, ambitious, determined—whatever the word—Atlanta had a winning combination which came through and is still excelling.

Much of the charm of legendary southern hospitality is tenaciously guarded, cherished. New tides of energy are surging everywhere, but the past remains as real as the present and will continue to color the future.

Businessmen regard the Georgia capital as a "national city" and its economic influence goes far beyond regional confines. The business community is aggressive, competitive. More than 400 of the Fortune 500 companies have headquarters or offices here. Atlanta is growing rapidly. Unemployment is half the national average. Bank deposits are well above average for cities of like size. Five Points (Decatur, Peachtree and Marietta Streets) is known as the heart of Atlanta's financial business district. The Peachtree Center Complex consists of a modern living center renowned for its architectural uniqueness. It includes office buildings, the country's second largest merchandise mart, and several new hotels. Headquarters for the Sixth Federal Reserve District are in Atlanta. Hartsfield Atlanta International Airport is the largest passenger terminal in the world. The Atlanta State Farmer's Market, ten miles south on I-75, is a large wholesale fresh fruit and vegetable distribution center.

Cultural leaders say the renaissance of art throughout the nation is nowhere more truly reflected than in Atlanta. Everything termed "cultural" has a way of thriving in the Georgia city. Visitors find rich treasures of music, drama and visual arts for their enjoyment and edification. The Robert Woodruff Arts Center contains the Atlanta Symphony Orchestra, Atlanta College of Art, and two live theaters. The new High Museum of Art, next door, is a masterpiece of modern architecture, housing collections of European, American, and African art.

Atlanta also supports a diversity of repertory drama and musical theater and books many of the major national road attractions in theater, opera, ballet and concert soloists. Noteworthy literary shrines are those connected with Joel Chandler Harris and *Uncle Remus,* and with Margaret Mitchell and *Gone with the Wind.*

The Atlanta Civic Center is an auditorium complex for conventions and music events. The Center contains a 70,000-square-foot exhibit hall, as well as a 4,600-seat auditorium where the Metropolitan Opera plays.

The Georgia World Congress Center, adjacent to the giant Omni megastructure, contains facilities for national and international meetings. It has a 2,000-seat auditorium, meeting rooms, and the largest single room of its kind on one level in the United States (650,000 sq. ft.).

The Cyclorama, famous three-dimensional panoramic painting of the Battle of Atlanta located at Grant Park, has been restored and reopened to the public. The Swan House (Atlanta Historical Society, 3099 Andrews Dr. NW) has an interesting collection of mementos from Georgia's past housed in the former Edward H. Inman residence. Adjacent is the Tullie Smith farmhouse which looks essentially as it did in 1840's. Georgia's governor resides in a new mansion located at 391 West Paces Ferry Road, a show place, opened for tourists several times each week.

Six Flags Over Georgia, a family entertainment park, covers 331 acres, has over 100 attractions, rides and live shows—all for one admission price. Rides include the Dahlonega runaway mine train, the log flume and the Jean Ribaut riverboat adventure. The park has sections, one for each of the six flags which have flown over Georgia—French, Spanish, English, Confederacy, United States and Georgia. The park boasts two hair-raising roller coasters, including the triple-loop "Mind Bender." "Thunder River," added in 1982, is an exciting raft trip on a white-water river. One of the most popular rides is "The Great Gasp," a 40-foot free-fall parachute drop that ends with a slow and controlled perfect landing and a "great gasp" of relief from partakers. Six Flags is popular with people of all ages and is kept scrupulously tidy. It's open from April through November.

The Metropolitan Atlanta Rapid Transit Authority (MARTA) commuter trains are a practical attraction. Trains are fast and luxurious, and stations are brightened by original artworks.

The Toy Museum of Atlanta (2800 Peachtree Rd.) has a rare collection of antique dolls and doll houses, model trains, boats, soldiers—13 rooms.

Atlanta Botanical Garden, Piedmont Park at the Prado, is located on 63 rolling acres dedicated to educating people about plants and plant culture.

The Bank Museum, in the Federal Reserve Building, displays Dahlonega gold coins, other rare coins, and has exhibits explaining how money is made.

Archives, 330 Capitol Avenue, houses history of the State of Georgia; research, displays, exhibits.

A visit to the Martin Luther King, Jr., District should begin at the Information Center, 413 Auburn Avenue N.E., and include his birthplace, tomb, and the church where Dr. King pastored.

The Center for Puppetry Arts, 1404 Spring St., N.W., has exhibits, shows, lectures, classes, workshops.

Stone Mountain

Stone Mountain, the world's largest mass of exposed granite, is surrounded by a 3,200-acre park that attracts nearly 4 million persons each year. A massive Confederate carving features General Robert E. Lee with General Stonewall Jackson and Confederacy President Jefferson Davis. Lee's likeness is 138 feet from the top of his head to his horse's hoof. His face measures twenty-one feet, his nose, five feet. The stars on his collar are bigger than dishpans and the sword, measuring fifty-eight feet in length and four feet in width, weighs one hundred tons. The giant granite dome, which rises 825 feet above the surrounding plain, stands about twenty miles east of downtown Atlanta and is visible from the top of many of the city's larger buildings. A cable-car lift rises from the base of the mountain to the summit 2,600 feet distant. Two glass-enclosed cars, each carrying fifty passengers, afford a superb view. A replica of the famous Civil War locomotive, "The General," pulls vintage coaches along a railroad that circles the base of the mountain. The seven-mile ride gives an idea of how massive the granite giant really is. A Memorial Building contains a museum featuring Sherman's famous "March to the Sea," depicted in a sixty-foot relief map. Magnolia Hall, an authentic antebellum plantation, was moved from its original site at Dickey, Ga., carefully furnished and restored. There is an antique automobile museum, a steamboat operating on an adjoining lake, a marina, a carillon with concerts daily, fishing, horseback riding, golf and camping.

Fifth Avenue South

Fashion-conscious shoppers deem Peachtree Street the Fifth Avenue of the South. Added to Georgia-based stores that have been style pacers for almost a century are many leading fashion firms from other parts of America that have opened Atlanta branches in suburban shopping de-

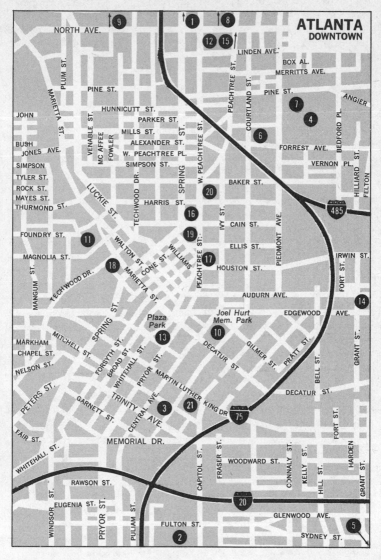

ATLANTA
DOWNTOWN

Points of Interest

1) Atlanta Historical Society
2) Atlanta Stadium
3) City Hall
4) Civic Center
5) Cyclorama
6) Emory University School of Dentistry
7) Exhibition Hall
8) Fox Theater
9) Georgia Institute of Technology
10) Georgia State University
11) Georgia World Congress Center
12) High Museum of Art
13) Five Points Rapid Rail Station
14) Martin Luther King grave
15) Memorial Arts Center
16) Merchandise Mart
17) Georgia-Pacific Center
18) Omni Hotel and Megastructure
19) Peachtree Plaza Hotel
20) Hyatt Regency Atlanta Hotel
21) State Capitol

velopments. Strollers along the avenue which Margaret Mitchell popularized through her novel are noted for their beauty and their chic attire.

Whether you want souvenirs from the Civil War Period, an antique from Vining's, an emerald from Tiffany's or furs from Sak's, Atlanta has some.

Educators consider Atlanta a mecca. In the area there are nineteen degree-granting institutions of higher learning, twenty-four business schools, ten vocational training schools, six two-year schools equivalent to junior colleges, and over 400 elementary and high schools.

Architecturally Atlanta is a city to see because of its famous residential area and its vast assortment of downtown office buildings.

As a sports center, Atlanta has an $18-million, 58,000-seat stadium, home of the Braves baseball and Falcons football teams. Its $17-million, 17,000-seat coliseum, the Omni, is home of the Hawks basketball team. Atlanta International Raceway, I-75 at Hampton, a 1½-mile oval track, has two Grand National race events annually, plus Indy car races, motorcross and other motor sports.

There's golfing for every handicap in the city that produced one of the greatest golfers, Bobby Jones. The country's largest lawn tennis association is in Atlanta, and racquet ball is moving in significantly.

A short distance from Atlanta is sprawling Lake Lanier, a paradise for water sportsmen. The 1200-acre family recreation resort area includes: an island for picnics, a white sand beach, bathhouses, golf course, rental houseboat fleet, rental sailboats, kyaks, canoes, pontoons, catamarans, paddle boats, fishing, trout ponds, riding stables, boat launching ramps, mini-golf course, and a 430-foot water slide.

The annual July 4 Peachtree Road Race attracts 25,000 runners at the starting line for the six-mile run.

The state capitol, its dome plated with gold leaf from Dahlonega, Ga., contains a Hall of Fame consisting of famous Georgians and a State Museum of Science and Industry. Both are open to the public. Tours are available on request. The museum contains Indian artifacts, rock minerals and industrial products.

Fernbank Science Center houses the third largest planetarium in the world. Performances change frequently and are accompanied by music ranging from Chopin to the Beatles. The center includes one of the largest observatories housed within a major city, a seventy-acre virgin forest, a "see and touch" museum as well as an electron microscope lab, a meteorological lab and supporting service areas. The planetarium, forest and observatory are open to the public year round.

Annual events include the Atlanta Dogwood Festival each spring, the Peach Bowl (football) late in December, the Atlanta Arts Festival at Piedmont Park each May, the Atlanta Golf Classic at the Atlanta Country Club in early June or late May. Two events at the Atlanta International Raceway south of Atlanta are the "Atlanta 500" in the spring and the "Dixie 500" in late summer.

PRACTICAL INFORMATION FOR ATLANTA

HOW TO GET THERE. *By air:* Atlantic Southeast, Bahamasair, British Caledonian, Delta, Eastern, Frontier, KLM, Lufthansa, Ozark, Northwest, Piedmont, Republic, and Sabena.

By Car: I-85, I-75, and I-20 will all get you to Atlanta.

By train: Atlanta may be reached by Amtrak with passenger service between New Orleans and Washington, D.C.

By bus: Greyhound, Trailways and several other companies come into Atlanta.

HOW TO GET AROUND. *By air:* Delta, Eastern, Republic. serve cities within the state.

By car: I-75 comes in from the northwest and goes south through Atlanta; I-85 from the northeast and also continues south through the city; I-20 runs across the city east to west; I-285 comes in from the north, cuts across I-75, I-20 and I-85 and continues east.

By bus: The Metropolitan Rapid Transit Authority operates the bus system in Atlanta and the suburbs. The fare is 60¢, transfers free. Maps may be obtained from the Chamber of Commerce, 34 Broad St. MARTA is building a 57-mile train system. The first phase opened in 1979. Fare is 60¢.

Especially for the handicapped: Airports in Atlanta, Savannah, Columbus and Augusta have special accommodations for the handicapped, with parking areas designated for users of wheelchairs, and ramps and special restrooms. The Georgia Welcome Centers have similar facilities.

MUSEUMS. *Georgia Dept. of Archives and History,* 330 Capitol Ave. SE. Displays, exhibits. History of Georgia depicted in lovely stained-glass windows. *Cyclorama* is huge canvas depicting 1864 Battle of Atlanta. Now being refurbished. To reopen mid-1982. *Swan House,* 3099 Andrews Dr. NW. Period rms. on first floor. *Governor's Mansion,* 391 W. Paces Ferry Rd. Federal furnishings in elegant home. Free. *Emory Museum.* Bishop's Hall, Emory Univ., S. Oxford Rd. NE in Druid Hills. Far Eastern, African, Near Eastern, American Indian artifacts. Closed school vacations.

Art. The dazzling, new *High Museum of Art,* Peachtree at 16th Sts., has extensive permanent collections and major traveling exhibitions.

Special Interest. *Georgia State Museum of Science and Industry,* 4th fl. State Capitol Bldg. Displays, dioramas. Free. *Fernbank Science Center,* 156 Heaton Park NE. Observatory, exhibit hall, forest & reference library. Third largest planetarium in the nation. Open daily.

HISTORIC SITES. *Wren's Nest,* 1050 Gordon St. SW. Home of Joel Chandler Harris, creator of Uncle Remus stories. Mon. to Sat. *Dr. Martin Luther King, Jr.* is entombed beside the Ebenezer Baptist Church, 413 Auburn Ave. NE. *Zero Mile Post,* nr. Decatur St. under Central Ave. Bridge, marks the southwestern terminus of the Western & Atlantic Railroad, and is the "birthplace" of the City of Atlanta.

TOURS. *By bus:* Tours range from 3 to 5 hours and include downtown, Georgia Tech, Peachtree St., Lenox Square, Emory University, Cyclorama, Druid Hills, State Capitol, Stone Mountain. Operators are American Sightseeing, Gray Lines, Arnel, Tour Gals, Atlanta Convention Planners, Presenting Atlanta Tours, and Guidelines.

MUSIC. The *Atlanta Symphony Orchestra* brings in many guest artists and guests conductors during its annual concert series from around Nov. 1 to Apr. Supplementing the symphony are the top stars—popular and classical— brought to Atlanta, Columbus, Savannah, Augusta, Macon and Athens by Famous Artists, and the classical attractions booked by the civic-minded *Atlanta Music Club,* which formed the symphony more than fifty years ago.

 STAGE AND REVUES. *Theatre of the Stars* presents its summer season at Civic Center Auditorium, winter season at Peachtree Playhouse, 1150 Peachtree St. NE. *Academy Theatre,* 581 Peachtree St. N.E., presents dramas and musicals year round. *Alliance Theatre Company,* in Memorial Arts Center, professional productions mid-Jan. to mid-May. *Upstairs at Gene's & Gabe's,* 1578 Piedmont Rd., presents upbeat cabaret revues.

 NIGHTCLUBS. Atlanta nightlife offers something for everyone. The *Hyatt Regency, Hilton,* and other downtown hotels have live entertainment and dancing. *Walter Mitty's* on N. Highland Ave. and *Dante's Down the Hatch* on Peachtree Rd. have top-flight jazz. *Moonshadow Saloon* is a cavernous forum for rock and pop. The sleek *Limelight* disco attracts chic locals and visiting celebs.

 SHOPPING. *Rich's,* the South's largest store, has downtown stores of six stories and four stories, which cover two city blocks. A full-line department store, with restaurants, cafeterias, coffee shop. A genuine tourist attraction. *Neiman Marcus* has a branch at Lenox Square. *Phipps Plaza,* across from Lenox Square on Peachtree and Lenox, has branches of *Lord & Taylor, Saks Fifth Avenue, Tiffany's, I. Miller* and *Mark Cross. Perimeter Mall* (I-285 and Ashford Dunwoody Rd.), *Northlake Mall* (I-285 and La Vista Rd.), *Park Aire* in Sandy Springs (corner Roswell Rd. and Johnson Ferry) and *Southlake* (near Airport), are new shopping centers, each containing fine specialty shops. Other fine stores: *Leon Frohsin.* A smart shop for business, party clothing, furs. *Peachtree Center,* just beyond Davison's and at Lenox Square, 3393 Peachtree Rd. NE. *Muse's.* Moderate to higher-priced men's fashions, notions. 52 Peachtree NW, 630 Peachtree NE, 3393 Peachtree Rd. NE, at Lenox Square. *Spencer's, Ltd.* Exclusive men's store features British imports only. 693 Peachtree St. NE. The Virginia/ Highland neighborhood, around the corner of Virginia and N. Highland Aves., about three miles northeast of downtown, has come back to life with many one-of-a-kind shops, pubs, and small, trendy restaurants, such as Milo's, see "Dining Out," below. Little Five Points, Moreland and Euclid Aves., is another area for dining, pubbing, and browsing for books, funky clothes, and antiques.

 **HOTELS AND MOTELS.** Atlanta's accommodations should prove pleasant for even the most discriminating traveler, and cover a wide, diverse range. Listings are in order of price category. Based on double occupancy without meals in the peak season the ranges are as follows: *Deluxe,* $80–$100; *Expensive,* $55–$80; *Moderate,* $35–$55; *Inexpensive,* $20–$35. For a more complete explanation of hotel and motel categories see *Facts at Your Fingertips* at the front of this volume.

Atlanta Hilton. *Deluxe.* 255 Courtland St., downtown. The 1,250-room Hilton is crowned by *Nikolai's Roof,* a sumptuous, glass-enclosed restaurant with a Franco/Russian menu and a huge wine list. The hotel also has meeting rooms, tennis courts, a health club, and a variety of cafés and lounges.

Atlanta Marriott Hotel. *Deluxe.* (763 rooms) Courtland & International. Excellent, lavish hotel with in-rm. movie avail. Pool, golf & tennis nr. Saunas, health clubs. Restaurant, bar, dancing, entertainment.

Colony Square. *Deluxe.* Peachtree and 14th St. Part of a contemporary office/residential/shopping complex, the hotel has 500 beautifully appointed guest rooms, several restaurants and lounges.

Hyatt Regency Atlanta. *Deluxe.* 265 Peachtree St. NE. The Southeast's largest, with 1,358 guest rooms. In-rm. movies avail. Pool. Restaurants, bars, revolving Polaris dining rm. and bar atop roof with panoramic view. Spectacular 23-story atrium is heart of this splendid hotel.

Peachtree Plaza. *Deluxe.* Peachtree at International Blvd. World's tallest hotel (73 stories). A truly breathtaking hotel: seven-story atrium lobby with half-acre lake, greenery, tapestries, sculpture.

Ramada Renaissance Hotel. *Deluxe.* At Atlanta Airport. New, with 505 luxury rooms, suites, restaurants, lounges, shops, health club.

Ritz-Carlton. *Deluxe.* Two magnificent new hotels now bear this proud name: Ritz-Carlton Buckhead, uptown at 3434 Peachtree Rd., and Ritz-Carlton Atlanta, downtown at 181 Peachtree St. Guest rooms, dining, and service are the ultimate in taste and elegance.

Stouffers Waverly Hotel. *Deluxe.* I-75 & US 41 NW. Luxurious suburban hotel has fine restaurants, complete health club, meeting facilities.

Terrace Garden Inn. *Deluxe.* 3405 Lenox Rd., across from Lenox Square Shopping Center. 354 rooms.

Tower Place Hotel. *Deluxe.* 3340 Peachtree Rd. 220 rooms.

Atlanta Airport Hilton. *Expensive.* 1031 Virginia Ave. 400 rooms.

Guest Quarters. *Expensive.* Two locations. 7000 Roswell Rd. (US 19); I-285 at Ashford-Dunwoody Rd. All deluxe suites with complete kitchens.

Habersham Hotel. *Expensive.* 330 Peachtree St. Tasteful, European-style hotel. 94 rooms.

Marriott at Perimeter Center. *Expensive.* I-285 at Ashford-Dunwoody Rd. Pool, tennis, restaurants, bars. 307 rooms.

Northlake Hilton Inn. *Expensive.* 4156 La Vista Rd., Tucker. Pool. Restaurant, bar, dancing, entertainment.

Radisson Inn. *Expensive.* (400 rooms) I-285 at Chamblee Dunwoody Rd.

Radisson Inn and Conference Center. *Expensive.* I-75 at Howell Mill Rd. Extensive meeting facilities, 700 guest rooms.

Ramada Inn Central. *Expensive.* 1630 Peachtree St. NW. Pool, tennis. In-rm movies avail. Restaurant, bar, dancing, entertainment.

Sheraton. *Expensive.* Six locations. Sheraton-Atlanta (501 rooms), 590 W. Peachtree St.; Sheraton-Cumberland (132 rooms), 1200 Winchester Pkwy., Smyrna; Sheraton-Emory, (113 rooms), 1641 Clifton Rd.; Sheraton-Century Center (279 rooms), I-85 and Clairmont Rd.; Sheraton-Airport (362 rooms), 1325 Virginia Ave.; Sheraton-Northlake (164 rooms), I-285 and La Vista Rd.

Holiday Inns. *Moderate to expensive.* More than a dozen Metro Atlanta Inns offer a variety of accommodations. Consult the Yellow Pages.

Admiral Benbow Inn. *Moderate.* 1470 Spring St. NW; (190 rooms); Airport, 1409 Virginia Ave. (253 rooms); I-285 and Buford Hwy. (250 rooms). Pool, with poolside service. Restaurant, bar, entertainment, dancing.

Atlanta American Motor Hotel. *Moderate.* (350 rooms) Spring & International Blvd. Pool. Restaurant, bar, dancing, entertainment. In-rm. movies avail.

Atlanta Cabana Motor Hotel. *Moderate.* 870 Peachtree St. Restaurants, lounges, pool in lively midtown shopping/dining area.

Atlanta Central TraveLodge. *Moderate.* (70 rooms) 311 Courtland St. NW. Pool (heated). Restaurant nr.

Capitol Airport Inn. *Moderate.* (300 rooms) 1200 Virginia Ave.

Days Inn Hotel. *Moderate.* 300 Spring St., downtown. Adjacent to Apparel Mart.

Falcon Inn & Conference Center. *Moderate.* I-85 N., Suwanee. Meeting rooms, 100 guest rooms, restaurant, lounge. Adjacent to Atlanta Falcons training center.

Hotel York. *Moderate.* 683 Peachtree St. Beautifully restored old hotel. 155 rooms.

Howard Johnsons. *Moderate.* Eight Atlanta area motor hotels and lodges offer a variety of accommodations. Consult the Yellow Pages.

Ramada Capitol Plaza Hotel. *Moderate.* 450 Capitol Ave., near Atlanta Stadium & State Capitol.

Ramada Inn. *Moderate.* Three of 6 locations, each with pool, restaurant: **Airport:** 845 N. Central Ave. Hapeville. Bar, dancing, entertainment; **Six Flags:** 305 Industrial Circle. Bar, dancing, entertainment; **Stockbridge;** 3509 Hwy. 138, Stockbridge.

Red Carpet Inn. *Moderate.* Two locations: I-75 S., at Locust Grove, and I-20 W., at Six Flags.

White House Motor Inn. *Moderate.* (219 rooms) 70 Houston St. NE.

Bed & Breakfast Atlanta. *Inexpensive.* Referral service for accommodations in private homes. Phone: 378–6026.

Days Lodges. *Inexpensive.* Six locations: I-75 south; I-85 at Clairmont; I-285 and Old Dixie Highway; Buford Hwy. & Beverly Hills Dr; Buford & Old Stone Mtn. Rd; Shallowford Rd. Each has pool, play area, pets welcome, restaurant.

DINING OUT in Atlanta can mean the usual fine fare to be found in most large American cities, but it can also mean good Southern cooking—often in re-created rural surroundings. Restaurants price categories are as follows: *Deluxe,* $25 and up; *Expensive,* $20–25; *Moderate,* $12–20; *Inexpensive,* under $12, for a complete dinner, excluding drinks. A la carte meals will bring the tab up. For a more complete explanation of restaurant categories see *Facts at Your Fingertips* at the front of this volume.

EDITOR'S CHOICES

Rating restaurants is, at best, a subjective business, and obviously a matter of personal taste. It is, therefore, difficult to call a restaurant "the best" and hope to get unanimous agreement. The restaurants listed below are our choices of the best eating places in Atlanta, and the places we would choose if we were visiting the city.

TROTTERS   Northern Italian
A nostalgic 1920s country club setting, enriched by Currier and Ives prints and harness racing silks, is the stage for sumptuous Northern Italian style pastas, some blended imaginatively with seafoods, outstanding veal, and deluxe pastries. 3215 Peachtree Rd. *Deluxe.*

MARY MAC'S TEA ROOM   Southern Cooking
An Atlanta landmark for authentic Southern homecooking. This maze of cheerful dining rooms is renowned locally for its golden brown fried chicken, country-fried steak, slowly simmered fresh vegetables, breads, and cobblers. 228 Ponce de Leon Ave. *Inexpensive.*

DARCY'S: AN AMERICAN CAFE   American
Small, charming restaurant in a former residence does wonderful American things with duck, veal, pastas, seafood, and beef. Chocolate dream—mousse in a chocolate shell—is a delicious house dessert. 3081 E. Shadowlawn Ave. *Expensive.*

Other recommended restaurants:

Bugatti. *Deluxe.* Omni International Hotel. Specialties from Northern Italy as well as American and Continental fine foods. Italian Sunday brunch.

Coach and Six. *Deluxe.* 1776 Peachtree Rd. NW. Steaks, chops, seafood and veal.

Hedgerose Heights Inn. *Deluxe.* 490 E. Paces Ferry Rd. Outstanding European dishes; elegant setting.

La Grotta Ristorante Italiano. *Deluxe.* 2637 Peachtree Rd. One of Atlanta's most outstanding restaurants. Exemplary Northern Italian cuisine; superior service; refined atmosphere.

Michelle's. *Deluxe.* Georgia-Pacific Center, downtown. Sumptuous French *nouvelle cuisine,* wines, in an exciting greenhouse setting.

The Midnight Sun. *Deluxe.* 225 Peachtree St. Creative French/continental cuisine in a spectacular Scandanavian-modern setting.

Nikolai's Roof. *Deluxe.* Atop Atlanta Hilton Hotel. Floor to ceiling wine vault and outstanding French/Czarist menu. Beautiful rooftop setting overlooking city. Reservations required.

The Abbey. *Deluxe.* 163 Ponce de Leon Ave. Deluxe French/continental cuisine in a converted church.

Red Barn Inn. *Deluxe.* 4300 Powers Ferry Rd. A strong local favorite. Steaks, seafoods in a cozy former stable. Fireplaces and equine décor.

The Old Vinings Inn. *Expensive.* 3020 Paces Mill Rd. Superb country French dishes in a restored clapboard cottage.

Petals of Jade. *Expensive.* Stouffers Waverly Hotel, I-75 & US 41, NW. *Haute* Chinese cuisine in a regal setting of Oriental art works, with gracious service.

Savannah Fish Company. *Expensive.* Peachtree Plaza Hotel. Fresh seafood in a beautiful, sophisticated setting.

Sidney's. *Expensive.* 4225 Roswell Rd. Eclectic French, Jewish, Hungarian menu; great wines, service.

Aunt Fanny's Cabin. *Moderate.* 2155 Campbell Rd., Smyrna. Traditional Southern cooking in an old plantation atmosphere.

Cafe des Amis. *Moderate.* 1428 Peachtree St. Chic little cafe with an outdoor patio serves innovative continental entrees, desserts.

Joe Dale's Cajun House. *Moderate.* 370 Maple Dr. Jambalaya and seafood dishes from Louisiana's Cajun Country.

Dante's Down the Hatch. *Moderate.* 3380 Peachtree Rd. Located in building used as hospital during Civil War, later as candy factory. Specialties: cheese trays, fondue; jazz. Lunch and dinner only.

Gene and Gabe's. *Moderate.* 1578 Piedmont Ave. N.E. Veal is the prime attraction (scaloppina al marsala is irresistible), and the spices are lightly applied.

Herren's. *Moderate.* 34 Luckie St. N.W. Long-established restaurant with its own art gallery. Excellent American cuisine, exemplary service.

The Pleasant Peasant. *Moderate.* 555 Peachtree St. N.E. Built in 1800's as an ice-cream parlor. Country French cuisine and lavish desserts. Dinner only.

The Colonnade. *Inexpensive.* 1879 Cheshire Bridge Rd. American and Southern cooking.

King and I. *Inexpensive.* Spicy, exotic dishes from Thailand make this a big local favorite.

Mary Mac's Tearoom. *Inexpensive.* 224 Ponce de Leon Ave. NE. Where Atlantans go for fried chicken and Southern-style vegetables.

Milo's. *Moderate.* 1026 Virginia Ave. Imaginative American/continental menu, in a lively revived midtown neighborhood.

Morrison's. *Inexpensive.* Numerous Atlanta area locations. Attractive cafeteria with background music. Fish amandine and roast beef are specialties. Children's portions. Eight other locations in the area.

Peking. *Inexpensive.* 3361 Buford Hwy. (Northeast Plaza). Outstanding Szechuan, Mandarin-style Chinese cooking.

El Toro. *Inexpensive.* Eight locations. The city's best Mexican food.

Touch of India. *Inexpensive.* 979 Peachtree St. Excellent curries, tandooris, Indian breads.

The Varsity. *Inexpensive.* 61 North Ave. N.W. Large fast-food drive-in next to Georgia Tech. Chili dog, frosted orange, onion rings. Lunch and dinner.

Exploring Georgia

Georgia has "Visitor Information Centers" at every major entry into the state, and all these facilities are staffed by friendly, knowledgeable receptionists who are happy to assist travelers with current information and who are happy to assist travelers with current information and are eager to suggest various tours through the state. All centers, except the one at the Atlanta Airport, have park-like areas with landscaping and picnic tables. At appropriate times of the year cotton may be found growing in the yard.

Receptionists suggest events and fun places to visit while in Georgia. They tell how to travel the most picturesque or the most expeditious route—as you choose—and they tell what to see and do at your chosen points of visitation. Information available includes the latest materials on golfing, hunting, fishing, camping, state and national parks, big league sports, special events, conventions, historical sites, scenic and guided tours, mountains and lakes, Golden Isles and other beaches and family fun attractions.

The Centers are located near Savannah on I-95 for tourists entering from South Carolina; Lavonia, I-85, one-half mile Southwest of the South Carolina line; Sylvania, US 301, one-half mile Southwest of the South Carolina line; Augusta I-20, one-half mile west of the South Carolina line; Columbus, intersection of US 280 and 27 for motorists coming into Georgia from Alabama; Ringgold, I-75, two miles south of the Tennessee line; Valdosta, I-75, two miles north of the Florida line, I-95 near Kingsland, just north of Florida line; on I-85 near West Point and on I-20 near Tallapossa for motorists coming from Alabama; at Plains on US 280; and at the Atlanta airport.

A stop at one of these Centers immediately upon arrival in Georgia can make your trip more meaningful, more enjoyable. Suggested routes are many, and the following are typical:

Colonial Georgia Route

Colonial Georgia route will take you along US 17 and portions of I-95 through Savannah, Midway, Darien, Brunswick and the Golden Isles, Kingsland and St. Marys.

In 1732, General James E. Oglethorpe brought his English colonists and settled the area named for his king, George II. An awareness of

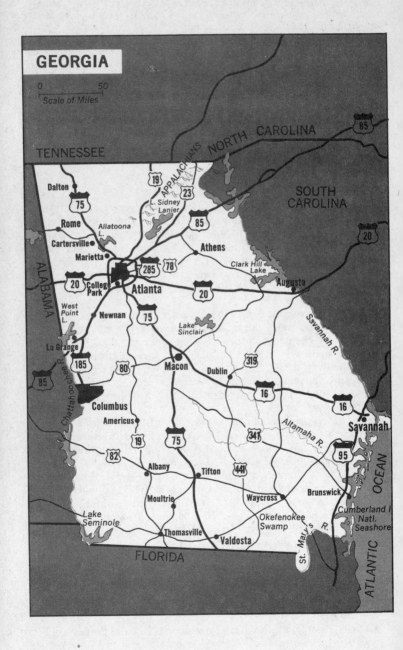

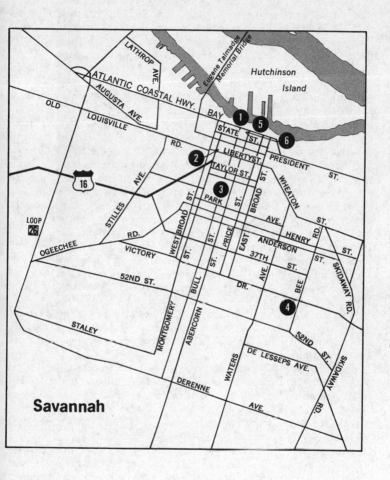

Savannah

Points of Interest

1) City Hall
2) Civic Center
3) Forsythe Park
4) Grayson Stadium
5) River Street shops, restaurants, taverns
6) U.S. Custom House

history, an appreciation for its preservation and perpetuation is everywhere evident.

Downtown Savannah remains essentially as General Oglethorpe planned it. For monuments, go to Johnson Square with its monument to Nathanael Greene; Wright Square, which contains a boulder honoring Indian Tomo-Chi-Chi, the Yamacraw Indian chief who befriended Oglethorpe's colonists; and Chippewa Square with its monument to Oglethorpe created by Daniel Chester French, designer of the Lincoln Memorial in Washington.

Historic houses include Owen-Thomas, designed by William Jay in 1818-19 and considered one of the purest examples of Regency architecture in America; Davenport House (1820), an excellent example of Georgian architecture; Telfair Academy of Arts and Sciences, site of the royal governor's mansion; Green-Meldrim Home, headquarters of General Sherman during his Savannah occupation and the birthplace of Juliette Gordon Low, founder of Girl Scouts. Savannah has 1,100 structures termed worthy of preservation. More than 90% of them have been saved and refurbished in the last 15 years. A 1-square-mile section of Victorian homes adjacent to Forsyth Park is being surveyed for restoration. Included are about 400 homes.

Spring is Savannah's most glorious season. Millions of azaleas and dogwood bloom, and many historic private homes are open to visitors. The city's St. Patrick's Day celebration is one of America's largest and most exuberant. Visitors may stay in a variety of historic inns and guest houses.

Marked tours of historical and scenic areas of the city are designed for do-it-yourself touring, but two bus companies have daily sightseeing trips originating at motels, hotels, and the Chamber of Commerce. Bike tours are marked also.

Five forts may be visited in the Savannah area: Fort Jackson, Fort Wayne, Fort Screven on Tybee Island, Fort McAllister, ten miles east of Richmond Hill off US 17, and Fort Pulaski, east of Savannah, now operated by the National Park Service. Built from 1829 to 1849, Pulaski was Robert E. Lee's first engineering assignment after graduation from West Point.

Savannah was the center of a struggle for power during the Revolutionary War, most of which it spent under English occupation. Count Casimir Pulaski, the great Polish patriot, gave his life during an attempt to retake it. Today Pulaski is honored along with Sargeant William Jasper, an Irish-American warrior who lost his life in the same battle. The city regained its important role as a center for export to Europe and served as a supply center for the Confederacy during the Civil War until the fall of Fort Pulaski in 1862. Fort Pulaski, a monumental engineering feat, guarded the city from the sea from a perch overlooking the Savannah River, while Fort McAllister, a huge earthwork fortress, defended the south. Surviving seven attacks by the Union Navy, Fort McAllister finally fell to Sherman on his march to the sea. In evacuating the city in the face of Sherman's advance, Confederate General Hardee spared the city the battering and burning Sherman had given Atlanta.

Savannahians observe Georgia Day each year on February 12, the anniversary of Oglethorpe's establishment of the Colony. Other annual events are a tour of homes and gardens late in March; a St. Patrick's Day Parade; the Savannah Arts Festival early in April; Designers Showcase in April, when local architects, decorators, landscape designers re-do a home; Garden Tour in April; Night in Old Savannah in spring; Blessing of the Fleet in June.

South from Savannah is Midway with its beautiful old church dominating the view from the highway. The church was erected in 1792. The old slave gallery and high pulpit remain unchanged. From its congregation that never numbered more than 150 came two signers of the Declaration of Independence, two Revolutionary generals, and a U.S. Senator. The church and historic cemetery may be visited at any time. Keys are available free at a nearby service station. The Midway Museum next to the church, is an Historic Site. The museum is built in raised-cottage style and displays furniture, artifacts, documents from early eighteenth to mid-nineteenth century.

Darien, a colonial Georgia town, has Fort King George, southernmost outpost in 1721 and an important Spanish site prior to that time. A museum depicts various periods of occupation by Indians, Spanish and English.

The route continues through Georgia's pine belt, producer of vast naval stores. Brunswick, a busy port, is noted for its shrimp. Fleets operating off the coast bring in as much as ten million pounds annually.

The Lanier Oak, just north of the town, is a living tribute to Georgia's most famed poet, Sidney Lanier, who immortalized the area in his epic, "The Marshes of Glynn." (The Marshes of Glynn are the largest salt marshes on the American east coast. An overlook park in Brunswick gives a fine view of their ever-changing beauty.) Plaques mark the tree under which he is said to have been inspired to write many poems. Another famous tree, giant Lover's Oak in downtown Brunswick, is believed to be nine hundred years old, measures thirteen feet in diameter three feet from the ground, at which point it branches into ten limbs, each measuring from twelve to thirty inches in diameter. Gulf and inland fishing as well as tours of the area are popular.

Brunswick is the gateway to Georgia's Golden Isles. Sea Island is home of the world-famed Cloister, a year-round vacation complex of luxuriously privately owned cottages, flower-bordered streets that run the entire north-south length of the island, a beach club, miles of flawless sand beach for beach walking or bathing. Classic cuisine is featured in the hotel dining areas.

St. Simons is the largest of the islands. Here is Fort Frederica National Monument from which Oglethorpe's troops marched off to defeat the Spanish at the Battle of Bloody Marsh. Foundations of the old settlement have been recreated as they were in the early 1700's. Christ Church is the historic frame building where John and Charles Wesley, the founders of Methodism, preached to Indians and settlers. The current structure was built in 1884 upon the site where they preached.

St. Simons Lighthouse was rebuilt in 1871. The lighthouse has been made into a museum. Ruins of Retreat Plantation may be visited on St. Simons; now a frontispiece for the Sea Island Golf Club. Hotels, motels and cottages along the excellent beaches are available at rates varying from luxury to economy.

Jekyll, now state-owned, once was a favorite for such millionaires as J. P. Morgan, William Rockefeller, William Vanderbilt and Joseph Pulitzer. The entire ocean side is beach, 9½ miles long. Rockefeller's twenty-five-room "cottage" is a museum. Faith Chapel, a small interdenominational church of English design, was one of the original buildings. The island's facilities are extensive. Many conventions are held each year and a permanent colony of several thousand persons reside on the island, many of them retirees. Georgia purchased the property in 1948 and developed it as a year-round vacation area. Four noted golf courses are located on the island—two of championship lengths and one a nine-hole seaside links designed after the sand dune courses of Scotland.

South from Jekyll and off the main route at Kingsland is Crooked River State Park, the only inland park in Georgia with saltwater fishing. Santa Maria Mission has outstanding tabby ruins. At the southernmost point is the old sea town of St. Mary's with its Presbyterian Church, one of the state's oldest. Ferries leave from St. Marys for the Cumberland Island National Seashore.

South to the Wilderness

Entering Georgia on US 301 from South Carolina, motorists are greeted at the state's first tourist information center. Available here are free literature, free directions and free picnic areas.

The nearest town is Sylvania. Ten miles east is Brier Creek Battle Site, and breastworks from this Revolutionary War battle are still visible. Dell House is the only remaining structure in once- busy Jacksonborough, six miles north.

An interesting side junket may be made to Waynesboro (north on State 24), then to Millen (south on US 25) into 301 at Statesboro. Waynesboro, named for General "Mad Anthony" Wayne, once was a part of the plantation belt. About five miles away is Shell Bluff, an unusual geological formation. Here, high above the Savannah River, are many giant oyster fossils twelve to fifteen inches long. The bed is said to have been formed when the coastal plains of Georgia were submerged beneath the sea.

Located near Millen is a $70,000 fish palace—an aquarium that displays freshwater game and fish native to the area, a few specimens of tropical fish, turtles, eels and alligators.

On State 17 is Jones Plantation at Birdsville considered to be the oldest plantation in Georgia lived in continuously by the family who built it. The rambling, romantic house was built in the 1780's. It is open to tourists by appointment.

North of Statesboro on a country road at Clito is Marsh Hunting Preserve, one of Georgia's many privately owned quail preserves where managed hunts may be arranged.

The route continues through agricultural areas, planted timbers and fields of peanuts and tobacco. Statesboro is trading center for naval stores and farm products.

Cake baking is major tourist attraction at Claxton where more than six millions pounds of quality fruit cakes are produced each year. Signs along US 301 invite motorists to visit the plant (three miles off the main route). As many as 150 to 200 cars stop each day.

A country-wide rattlesnake roundup is held each year in mid-March in Claxton. Contestants vie for the honor of catching the most rattlesnakes as well as the largest.

Giant oak trees shade the streets of Jesup, another agricultural town. Chief products are livestock, corn, cotton, timber, naval stores and milled lumber. The Lovers' Oak, one of the state's oldest, has a spread of 150 feet. The Altamaha River nearby offers excellent water activities including fishing, water-skiing and swimming. Cherokee Lake is approximately two miles northwest of US 301.

Driving through the piney woods and wiregrass section motorists next reach Nahunta. A frequent sight along the highway are giant log trucks enroute to sawmills.

Folkston is one of two eastern entrances to the famed Okefenokee Swamp. Visitors may enjoy the quiet natural surroundings on boat tours of the primitive wilderness area or visit a center where flora and fauna are explained in exhibits. An observation tower and many bird walks and nature trails are featured. There are boat tours, canoe liveries and special waterways where visitors are permitted without guides.

Westward twenty-three miles is Waycross and the entrance to the Okefenokee Swamp Park, which features wildlife shows, boat trips (ten-mile, two-hour guided boat trips or all-day excursions by advance reservations). There is an Interpretative Center, an Ecology Center and Pioneer Island exhibits. Visitors may even pick orchids as they stroll paths that pierce the almost forbidding growth of moss-strewn live oak, long leaf pine, hammocks, sweet gum, red bay, magnolia, water oak, hardwoods, and hollies of incredible size. The swamp is the headwater of both the Suwannee River and the St. Mary's, and Stephen Foster State Park, on State 177 north of Fargo, pays tribute to the famed composer. Because of the genuine peril from alligators and more than a dozen varieties of snakes, as well as the danger of becoming lost, no visitor is permitted in the park after dark. The park is open daily 8 A.M. to sunset. The area has the Waycross State Forest Game Management Area consisting of 37,500 acres of timberland. Hunters may take deer, rabbits or squirrels. Hunting is regulated by the Department of Natural Resources.

Annual events include a Forest Festival at Laura Walker State Park in early May; Okefenokee Holidays in late November, Fall Festival in mid-October and the Water Lily Festival in early June, all at Okefenokee Swamp Park; Haunted House, a Jaycee project in an old school house in Waycross in October.

The Satilla River Canoe Trail, about three miles north on US 82, begins its 149-mile trip to Woodbine, Ga. There are campsites, boat ramps, fish camps along the trail.

A Tour of Historic Houses

Entering Georgia from South Carolina via I-20, US 25 or US 1, Augusta looms up as the industrial giant of the Savannah River. A thriving textile city, its industry also includes the nearby Savannah River Project of the Atomic Energy Commission and the multi-purpose Clark Hill Dam located twenty miles upriver.

Golfing is king at Augusta where the Masters Tournament is played each spring. Former President Dwight Eisenhower had a cottage adjoining the course.

St. Paul's Episcopal Church, founded in 1735 and rebuilt four times, is a historic must-see. Its rear door to the river afforded escape for many officials during the Revolutionary War when the fort was the capital of Georgia.

Another landmark is Meadow Garden, which was a part-time residence of George Walton, one of the Georgia signers of the Declaration of Independence. It is a curious house that George Washington and Marquis de Lafayette visited, now a museum operated by the Daughters of the American Revolution. The Harris-Pearson-Walker House (pre-1750) is the oldest house in town. Thirteen American patriots were hanged in the house by a British officer during the Revolution.

The Augusta National Clubhouse was the antebellum home of P. J. Berckmans, a noted experimental horticulturist from Belgium who planted the avenue of magnolias leading up to the clubhouse. The Gertrude Herbert Institute of Art, a three-story frame built in 1818, is a showcase for local and nationally famous artists. The Signers' Monument is dedicated to the Georgia signers of the Declaration of Independence—George Walton, Lyman Hall and Button Gwinnett.

The route from Augusta is via US 278 or I-20 to the Crawfordville turnoff. At Crawfordville is the home of Confederacy Vice-president Alexander H. Stephens and a state park named for him. His home, Liberty Hall, is focal point of the shrine and a museum displays mementoes relating to Stephens and the Confederacy.

Continue north on State 47 to Washington, a gracious old city dating from the late eighteenth century and untouched by Civil War destruction. A list of forty antebellum homes dating back to 1790 is obtainable from the Chamber of Commerce. It is possible to visit a few homes from time to time. Many are open during the spring home tour. The Washington-Wilkes Historical Museum is a rambling eighteen-room building dating back to 1835. Thirteen doors open to the outside. Displays are Civil War relics.

From Washington take State 17 north to Elberton, the greatest monument-granite quarrying area in America. Free tours of granite quarries and plants in the area are available.

Continue north on State 77 to Hartwell, a light manufacturing city and site of Hart State Park, a day use area with picnic facilities, bike trails and points of historical interest. The Hartwell Reservoir, built for flood control and power generation, has as its by-product recreation—boating, camping, water sports.

The route then leads through an agricultural area with many cattle, cotton and chicken farms. Textile and garment manufacturers, pulpwood and poultry-processing plants may be viewed at Commerce.

Athens is home of the first chartered state university. It also is distinguished for its antebellum homes, where Greek porticoes with pediments and impressive Doric columns make up the dominant architectural theme. The romantic tradition of the Deep South lives amid early boxwood gardens, oaks and elms grown stately with age, and white-blossomed magnolias.

Points of interest at the University include the Georgia Arch, main entrance, placed in 1856; Demosthenian Hall completed in 1824, home of the university's first literary society; the Chapel, completed in 1832, has large painting of interior of St. Peter's in Rome; Phi Kappa Hall, 1836; Old College, a three-story red brick structure of post-Colonial design, completed in 1805 and modeled after Connecticut Hall at Yale.

Athens-of-Old Tours begin at 280 E. Dougherty St., in a federal style house built in 1820, which serves as Athens Welcome Center—considered the city's oldest surviving residence. Information on do-it-yourself tours of over 50 local historic sites. See the science center, Art Museum and the only double-barreled cannon in existence. The cannon was designed to fire two balls simultaneously, but failed because the chain linking them spoiled the trajectory and accuracy. In Watkinsville, on US 129 and 441, is the Eagle Tavern, a former stagecoach stop and store.

Madison is the town Sherman refused to burn. When Federal forces marching from Atlanta approached Madison, U.S. Senator Joshua Hill, who did not vote for secession, rode out to meet General Sherman whom he had known in Washington. Sherman favored Hill's plea that the city be by-passed. Some damage was done to the town, however, when General Slocum's troops came through. During this raid a silver service was taken from the Presbyterian church. After the war, General Slocum returned it, and today the service is still treasured and used.

Historic homes abound in Madison, a city chartered in 1809 and located on an old stagecoach road. Owner-maintained antebellum homes may be seen by visitors with the use of a map-keyed brochure. There are tours of homes and gardens in December and spring.

In Eatonton there's a monument to a rabbit. This town, where Joel Chandler Harris lived as a boy, has a statue of Br'er Rabbit, the famous character of Uncle Remus tales.

Rock Eagle 4-H Center is the world's largest youth camp of its kind. The Rock Eagle effigy is a huge rock formation made from milky quartz. The Indian-made effigy measures 102 feet from head to tail and 120 feet from wing tip to wing tip.

Milledgeville has the old State Capitol used from 1807 to 1867, now rebuilt and a part of the Georgia Military College. The Old Governor's Mansion served as the home of ten Georgia governors for some forty years. Built in 1838, the mansion is a superb example of Greek Revival architecture. It was restored in 1967.

Macon, a picturesque blend of Old South culture and New South progress, is six miles from the geographical center of the state. Modern settlement dates from 1806 when the Federal government established Fort Benjamin Hawkins on the east side of the Ocmulgee River. A reproduction of the original structure has been erected on the site and is open Sunday afternoons.

Ocmulgee National Monument traces the evolution of the Southeastern Indian cultures from 8000 B.C. to the present in one of the South's largest archeological museums.

The world's first college chartered to grant degrees to women, Wesleyan, is located in Macon.

Notable houses are the Hay House, a twenty-four-room antebellum villa of Italian Renaissance style, and the Old Cannonball House, a

Greek Revival built in 1853 and struck by a cannonball during the Federal attack on Macon in 1864. The Grand Opera House has the largest stage in the United States. Mark Smith Planetarium is housed at Macon Museum of Arts and Sciences.

Shunpike to Cherokee Nation

The Dixie Highway from Chattanooga to Atlanta (US 41) winds through the green Appalachian Valley, heart of the Cherokee nation until 1838. Shunpikers entering Georgia from Tennessee on I-75 may obtain routing from the Visitor Center at Ringgold. The Dixie Highway closely follows the route taken in 1864 by General William T. Sherman in his Dalton-to-Atlanta campaign, but few marks of the devastation of war remain. In their stead are evidences of the fresh, productive energies of this vibrant section. Dalton is the carpet capital of the world and easily earned the title since there are more than 160 carpet mills in the town.

From Dalton take US 76 to Spring Place and Chatsworth. Spring Place is location of the Vann House, an outstanding example of Cherokee Indian wealth and culture. Built in 1804 by James Vann, the house features hand carving inside and out. Bricks for the house were made on Vann's plantation, and hinges were produced in his own blacksmith shop.

At Chatsworth is Fort Mountain State Park. This park derives its name from an ancient fortification, the ruins of which stand on the high point of the mountain. Speculation regarding its origin includes reference to Spanish conquistadors hunting gold, twelfth-century Welsh adventurers and to the "moon-eyed people," mysterious white tribesmen.

From Spring Place take State 225 back into US 41/I-75 at Calhoun, old-time center of the Cherokee nation. Named for John C. Calhoun, the town has bedspread factories and cotton mills. A memorial arch and statue pay tribute to Sequoyah, the Dutch-Cherokee who gave the Cherokees their alphabet, which was used to publish their own newspaper, the *Cherokee Phoenix*. In happier days, the Cherokees set up a government in the area patterned after the U.S. Government. New Echota, three miles northeast on State 225, served as the capital of the Cherokee Indian Nation from 1825 to 1838. A thriving community of stores, homes, a print shop, and government buildings comprised the original settlement. The nation prospered until a treaty banned the Cherokees from the state. It was ruled unconstitutional by the U.S. Supreme Court, but President Andrew Jackson's defiance of the court forced the Cherokees to abandon their lands and set off for Oklahoma on the infamous "Trail of Tears." The village has been partially restored.

South from Calhoun by I-75 or US 41 is Cartersville, an exceptionally rich and varied mineral community with many workers engaged in mining and processing limestone, talc, manganese, barite, potash, ochre, shale, bauxite, cement and slate.

Etowah Indian Mounds, three miles south on marked route, are the most significant Indian settlement in the Etowah Valley. The burial grounds and copper, shell and stone relics from a village that thrived here two thousand years ago may be seen. The museum has artifacts and displays.

Nearby is Lake Allatoona, a vast federal flood control project on the Etowah River. The lake provides numerous recreation areas including campsites, fishing, sand beaches, swimming, boating and water-skiing.

Lowry Covered Bridge (or Euharlee Creek Bridge) is six miles west via State 113 and two miles north on the county road to Euharlee. The bridge was constructed in 1886 after high water swept a previous one downstream. It is one span wide, 116 feet long and of town lattice design. Numbers still legible on the bridge timbers indicate that such structures often were assembled in a nearby field to assure perfect fit, then rebuilt over the stream.

Scenery Plus Civil War

Rock City, atop Lookout Mountain on the Georgia side, is within sight of Interstates 24, 59, and 75. It has ageless rock formations, a sweeping panoramic view of the Appalachians and colorful flowers and foliage. Youngsters delight to the artistry of Fairyland Caverns and Mother Goose Village.

Continue to Chickamauga and Chattanooga National Military Park on US 27, the scene of a Confederate victory during the Civil War. A Union victory at the Battle of Chattanooga, however, shattered the South's hopes of winning the war. The oldest and largest of the national military parks, this one commemorates the heroic soldiers of both North and South. The park features an eight-mile driving tour, restored Brotherton House, specific battlelines, museum and numerous state monuments erected in memory of the state troops that fought in the battle. The park is operated by National Park Service and it's free.

Cloudland Canyon, off State 143, near Rising Fawn, covers 1,699 acres and is part of the old Cherokee Indian territory. According to legend, there is a secret and fabulously rich lead mine in the vicinity. When the first white settlers built a trading post here, the Indians were able, with just a few hours notice, to deliver lead to the settlers to make bullets. The Indians never revealed the location of their mine and it has never been found.

Rome is located on US 27 and 411. Like its Italian namesake, it is located on seven hills, from which it exerts a dominant industrial influence over the fertile Coosa Valley. A prominent statue of the Capitoline Wolf nursing Romulus and Remus is a famous gift from the Italian city. Rome is the seat of diversified industry—more than one hundred manufacturers turn out items ranging from textiles to chemicals.

The Chieftains was the home of John Ridge, Chief of the Cherokees, and was the scene of the U.S.-Cherokee Treaty that removed the Cherokees to Oklahoma. It is open to visitors. Oak Hill, north on US 27, was the gracious home of Miss Martha Berry, founder of Berry Schools. Miss Berry once traveled by horse and buggy to teach young people in the north Georgia mountains. The campus includes 30,000 acres of Berry-owned fields and forest, and it now has a senior college. Martha Berry Museum and Art Gallery exhibits Berry memorabilia, and it has a court of honor, a small theatre and art gallery. Rome was also the home of Ellen Axson, the first Mrs. Woodrow Wilson. She is buried in Myrtle Hill Cemetery on Broad Street.

Take US 441 to Cartersville, back onto US 41, and then to Kennesaw Mountain where a national Battlefield Park is located. Commemorated is the Battle of Kennesaw Mountain, decisive during the Civil War. The museum has slide presentations and exhibits, eighteen miles of hiking trails, picnic facilities. Kennesaw, known for many years as Big Shanty (for the still of the same name), was scene of the first major engagement in the Dalton-Atlanta campaign. The mountain has an altitude of 1,809 feet; the park covers three thousand acres.

Lockheed-Marietta Aircraft and Dobbins Air Force Base are near. Lockheed has seventy-eight acres under one roof with much work space underground as a result of World War II when the plant, then making Bell bombers, was bomb-proofed. The highway passes Marietta National Cemetery, twenty-four acres of lavishly landscaped grounds containing the graves of more than ten thousand Union soldiers and many veterans of other wars. Large oaks, magnolias, hollies, evergreen shrubs and a profusion of rose bushes surround the mansion-like main building overlooking the cemetery from atop a hill. A Confederate Cemetery lies about a half-mile from the Marietta city square. It has about three thousand slabs, most of them nameless.

From Marietta turn east eleven miles to Roswell on Ga. 120, a community gradually being enveloped by the suburban Atlanta complex. This town was laid out in 1835 by Roswell King, a Connecticut banker who managed the Pierce Butler plantation on St. Simons Island, almost 350 miles to the south. Envisioning a mountain retreat for himself and his friends from the summer heat of the Sea Islands, Mr. King set up about a dozen homes in the community. One of his neighbors, Martha Bulloch, married the senior Theodore Roosevelt there in 1835. One of their sons was the future president; another was the father of Eleanor Roosevelt. Barrington Hall, built by the town's founder in 1842, housed Union troops during the Civil War. Fourteen Doric columns and wide-planked floors are outstanding features, along with original antique furniture. It is shown by special arrangement. Roswell has a number of privately owned antebellum homes that visitors may see while driving through the town. Mimosa Hall (1846) is Greek Temple style. A tour of homes and gardens is scheduled each spring.

Mountains Where There's Gold

Georgia has mountains (one almost a mile high) and some with gold. In fact the expression "Thar's gold in them thar hills" originated at Dahlonega, site of America's first gold rush.

If you enter Georgia from South Carolina over I-85, a Visitor Center at Lavonia can direct you. Or you may choose a few days in the mountains following a stay in Atlanta.

Starting at the Lavonia Center, the first stop should be at Toccoa, which was on the stage coach routes of old. Traveler's Rest, six miles east on US 123, served as a plantation house, tavern, trading post and post office. It has authentic furnishings. One of Georgia's remaining relics of the road.

Toccoa Falls is two miles northeast off State 17 on grounds of Toccoa Falls Institute. The drop is 186 feet. Lake Yonah, a Georgia Power

Company facility, eight miles north on State 184, is one of Georgia's most beautiful remote, uncrowded mountain lakes.

Tallulah Gorge on US 23 is believed to be the oldest natural gorge in North America. It is one and a half miles long and reaches a maximum depth of two thousand feet. There are five waterfalls in the bottom of the gorge; however, the main water supply has been diverted for hydroelectricity. A 1,100-foot cable, used by Karl Wallenda in his historic tightwire walk across the gorge, spans the chasm. A thirty-minute movie explaining the erection of the cable, the daring walk and two famous headstands by Wallenda can be seen daily during the summer at Tallulah Point. A nature trail follows a portion of the gorge's rim. There is also an overlook.

A Mountaineer Festival is held in Clayton each year honoring the contributions of mountain folk to the American way of life. Events include buck and square dancing, a wood cutting contest, greased pole climbing, horse show, and baby contest.

The Bartram Trail attracts hikers who visit this area. Quaker naturalist William Bartram first blazed this route over 200 years ago. Midpoint of the trail (which extends about 40 miles) is 3 miles east of Clayton at Warwoman Dell.

Rabun Bald Mountain has a trail to an elevation of 4,663 feet and offers a panoramic view of the surrounding Chattahoochee National Forest.

In the downtown area of Cornelia, there is a Big Red Apple monument honoring the area's major crop. A Memorial Tower one mile from downtown has a fire observation station at the summit of Tower mountain, a memorial to men of the Forest Service killed in World War II.

Over 100,000 visitors go to Hiawassee each August for the Mountain Fair which lasts for ten days. This is an old-fashioned country fair with a wondrous variety of exhibits including quilting parties, wood carving, soap and hominy making, and "hawg rifle" shoots. There are no commercial exhibits but many special events.

Whitewater rafting on the Chattooga River near Dillard is popular. Sky Valley Ski Area, northeast of Dillard on State 246, has excellent snow-skiing facilities including beginner, intermediate and expert slopes. Equipment is available for rent or purchase. A lodge and double chair lift are also available.

Brasstown Bald, south of Blairsville via US 129 and 19, then east via State 180 to State 66, is the highest point in Georgia—4,784 feet. A visitors center is open May 1 to October 31.

Richard Russell Scenic Highway extends fourteen miles through the state's most beautiful mountain areas. The Appalachian Trail crosses the road at Tessnatee Gap, highest point on the highway. Elevations range from 1,600 feet to almost 3,000 feet.

Camping facilities are extensive throughout the mountain area. One at Lake Winfield Scott covers twenty-six acres in the Chattahoochee National Forest. Another is located at Track Rock where rock hounds delight in several soapstone boulders bearing many carved figures of unknown origin. According to Cherokee legends, the petroglyphs had been placed here by an earlier people before the first Cherokee entered the region. There are camp sites in Vogel State Park where (legend has it) fabulous treasures were buried and bloody battles fought between Creek and Cherokee Indians. The southernmost point of the Appalachian Trail is nearby.

Architecture is the key to the charm of Helen, an Alpine-type village. The buildings, redesigned in recent years to add appeal to visitors, feature gingerbread trim and face paintings. Unique shops, stone streets, and a picturesque setting make this Bavarian town a "must" for visitors to Georgia.

Anna Ruby Falls is one of the most beautiful waterfalls in the area, one and a half miles north of Unicoi Recreational Experiment Station. A covered bridge three miles north of Helen on Ga. 255 at Stovall Mill, is a seventy-five-year-old, forty-foot span across Chickamauga Creek.

Cleveland has a Fall Leaf Festival each year during the October peak of the season. Events take place in the downtown area, dominated by the Old White County Court House, built from 1857-59 and in continuous use until 1965. It now houses a local historical society.

Dahlonega's courthouse dominates the town square also. It is a museum and commemorates the exciting era when the nation's first major gold rush took place here in 1828, bringing scores of prospectors into the area. A branch of the United States Mint was located here in 1838, and more than $6 million of Georgia gold was coined during the twenty-three-year life of the mint. Crisson's Gold Mine, three miles north of the city on Wimpy Mill Road, has gold-panning and picnicking from April to November. Blackburn Park, five miles south on State 9E, is a site of early gold discovery. There are a nature museum, archery range and gold mine.

Steele's Covered Bridge (1897), eighty-four feet long, is near Dawsonville.

Lake Sidney Lanier, with a 540-mile shore line, extends around Gainesville, Cumming, Buford; it is the most visited U.S. Corps of Engineer impoundment in the United States. Fishing, boating, waterskiing are available.

Road Atlanta, ten miles south of Gainesville off State 53, is an SCAA-sanctioned road course for Grand Prix road racing.

Fountains, Flowers, FDR

The Columbus Visitor Center, located on US 27, is the first spot tourists from Alabama visit when they enter Georgia. Attendants suggest tours around Columbus, to Callaway Gardens, Roosevelt's home at Warm Springs, and through Pine Mountain areas into Atlanta.

"Fountain City" is an appropriate description for Columbus because fountains can be found in public parks, at office buildings, or gracing lawns in residential areas. The Springer Opera House is a restored Victorian theater where Edwin Booth and Franklin D. Roosevelt appeared. Performances are from mid-September to late May. Columbus has a Museum of Arts and Crafts where Yuchi Indian materials, paintings, a children's museum and prehistoric Indian artifacts are housed.

At the Fort Benning Infantry Museum the evolution of the Infantry is traced from the French and Indian War to the present. Fort Benning is the Free World's largest infantry training center, covering 282 square miles of varied terrain. An open reservation, it welcomes visitors.

Confederate navy ships are displayed at a museum on US 27. Included are the hull of the iron-clad *Muscogee*. The Ladies' Defender Cannon is displayed here, too. It was made from brass articles donated by the women of Columbus during the Civil War. Ladies gave up brass beds, cooking utensils, jewelry and door knobs to be made into this unusual field artillery piece.

A heritage tour of historic points is scheduled regularly. It originates at the Georgia Visitor Center, US 27, and lasts for two hours, visiting four house museums and the Springer Opera House.

Pine Mountain is home of the famed Callaway Gardens, a 2,500-acre resort noted for its wildflowers of the Southern Appalachians. There are miles of scenic drives, walking trails and display greenhouses, sixty-three holes of golf, a 175-acre fishing lake, horseback riding, quail hunting on a 1,000-acre preserve and skeet and trap shooting. From April through September a mile-long beach is open with rides for the entire family. The Florida State University Circus performs throughout summer, and a children's recreation program is provided free for children staying in motel or cabins.

Now managed by the nonprofit Callaway Foundation, the Gardens are engaged in a constant improvement program, in which as many as 75,000 plants may be planted in a single year. Pathways wind through banks of azaleas, rhododendrons, camellias, gardenias, boxwoods, hollies and magnolias. Grapes from the Gardens' arbors go into Pine Mountain muscadine sauces and jellies, sold at the Country Store and served in the Gardens' restaurants. The store features stone-ground corn meal, hickory smoked hams, guinea hens, banana nut breads and locally produced condiments.

Across the road from the Country Store is the entrance to Franklin D. Roosevelt State Park, established in honor of the wartime President who died at nearby Warm Springs. President Roosevelt chose the Pine Mountain area for his home because of the curative qualities of the mineral waters at Warm Springs and because of the peaceful atmosphere. A spot called Dowdell's Knob, on the mountain road from Callaway's to Warm Springs, was visited often by the President when he drove around the Georgia countryside. Mr. Roosevelt went to Warm Springs in 1924 for treatment of his infantile paralysis. He built a modest white frame house where he died in 1945. The Little White House has been operated as a shrine for thirty years and remains just as President Roosevelt left it. The furnishings are spartan. Displayed is the unfinished portrait of him that was being painted when he was fatally stricken. Native stones and flags line the walkway leading from a memorial fountain to the museum. A twelve-minute movie is shown.

In La Grange is Bellevue, home of U.S. Senator Benjamin H. Hill who acquired it in 1853. He was arrested in this home by Federal forces. On a more festive occasion, Jefferson Davis was entertained here. It is open Tuesday–Sunday. A Callaway Memorial tower is also located in La Grange. It is patterned after the famous Campanile of St. Mark's Square in Venice, Italy, and was built in 1929 as a tribute to the memory of Fuller Callaway, Sr.

Newnan was named for General Daniel Newnan of War of 1812 fame. It is a center of manufacturing and peach orchards. The town is noted for its springtime beauty when great clouds of purple wisteria, clusters of multi-colored tulips and banks of golden daffodils burst forth in its many gardens. Three red brick buildings on College Street served as a hospital for Confederate and Union soldiers. Buena Vista, an elegant old home of double porches and massive white columns, served as local headquarters for Confederate General Joe Wheeler. Antebellum homes are found throughout the city. Although privately owned, they may be seen on a driving tour of residential areas.

Power's Crossroads Country Fair and Arts Festival is held early each September about ten miles west on State 34.

A glimpse of Georgia's agricultural cash register is afforded motorists who come into the state from Florida via I-75, then shunpike over US 82 from Tifton to Georgetown near the Alabama line.

Turpentine is a major industry, and miles of pine forests may be seen from all sections. Hunting is excellent in acres of low-lying timberland. Deer, quail, dove, rabbit and squirrel hunting is regulated by state laws.

Crescent House is the garden center of Valdosta, built in 1898 with a ballroom that seats three hundred. The Withlacoochee River Canoe Trail starts two miles west for a fifty-five-mile journey south. Valfestiva Festival of the Arts takes place each April.

Take I-75 to Tifton, one of the state's leading tobacco markets. Farmers sell more than nine million pounds of tobacco at this market in a typical year. Visitors are welcomed at the sales in July and August. Soil is king in Tift county. Vegetable plants from this section are sent to major markets throughout the United States. Pecans are prominent, and bees raised here are shipped to apple orchards as far north as Canada in order to increase the fruit yield. The Abraham Baldwin Agricultural College is adjacent to the Coastal Plains Experiment Station where farmers and students study better methods of producing beef cattle, hogs, grasses and legumes, blueberries and muscadine grapes. The Georgia Agrirama off I-75 at Tifton is a living historical museum depicting a rural community of the 1800s. Over 25 authentic restorations—gristmill, sawmill, cotton gin, farmhouse, rural village.

The route is hewn from planted timberlands; it runs alongside tobacco fields and through peach and pecan orchards. Motorists see the money crops, which gained prominence as Georgians phased out the one-crop cotton economy.

Albany and Andersonville

US 82 leads through Sylvester to Albany, Georgia's newest metropolitan area. This brisk town was settled by Nelson Tift (for whom Tifton was named), a Connecticut Yankee who laid out the broad palm-bordered avenues which dominate the city today. During the slavery period, Albany was a leading cotton market with the Flint River serving as a major artery of transportation. Now it is the paper-shell pecan capital of the world with orchards of 700,000 trees, covering more than 60,000 acres.

Four miles south is Radium Springs, the largest natural spring in the state, maintaining a constant temperature of 68 degrees.

Albany also has excellent quail shooting with several preserves offering hunting privileges by prior arrangement. Chehaw Wild Animal Park on Ga. 99 off US 19 bypass is a 100-acre preserve where exotic animals roam free in their natural habitats, separated from visitors who stroll along protective trails and elevated walkways. Banks-Haley Museum, on Slappey Boulevard, is home of the Southwest Georgia Art Association. Exhibits change monthly. Thronateeska Museum, Heritage Plaza, is housed in a 1910 train depot and includes the McIntosh Indian collection of arrowheads and artifacts.

Andersonville National Historic Site is on State 49, north from Americus. A Confederate military prison was established here in 1864 and used for fourteen months. Many states have placed monuments. West of Americus on US 280 is Plains, the home of President Jimmy Carter and a center of Georgia's peanut country.

Westville is a recreated, functioning rural village of 1850 just a half-mile from Lumpkin. Authentic buildings were moved to the site, restored and furnished. Working craftsmen demonstrate the skills of yesteryear. In the town of Lumpkin, on the square, is Bedingfield Inn, a restored 1836 stagecoach inn that also served as a family residence. It is furnished with authentic period appointments. Providence Canyon State Park is Georgia's "Little Grand Canyon." The central basin of this octopus-shaped cavern covers more than three thousand acres, and the chasm is some three hundred feet wide and two hundred feet deep. Erosion began almost a century ago. Red clay, blue marl, shell and a yellow clay have crumbled away, and the giant erosion, having eaten into a layer of chalk, seems as insatiable as ever. Trees, leaning outward and awry, cling precariously to the steep walls. Small islands rise from the bottom of the vast fissure, and on these a few small pines struggle to survive.

Turn south on US 27 to Cuthbert, located on a fertile plateau between the Flint and Chattahoochee rivers. It was one of the earliest settlements in this area after the Lower Creek Indians were expelled. Many antebellum houses of the Classic Revival design may be seen, including: the McWilliams house with pedimented porch and square columns in center of the front; Key house, one story with colonnade on front only; Toombs house (1850), one of the first two-frame houses in town; McDonald house with its immense McDonald pecan tree, said to have been started from a Texas seedling nut planted in 1846.

Continue south on US 27 to Blakely and the Kolomoki Indian Mounds. Archeologists are still searching this key village of the ancient Mound-builders of Georgia. Two museums display their findings, but the huge burial mounds, built over five thousand years ago, are the most intriguing aspect of the old village. The Mounds are in a State Park where swimming, family camping and fishing are available.

There's a flagpole on the Court House Square, the last of the Confederate ones, erected in 1861; and there's a monument to the peanut, which serves as a constant reminder of the product's importance to this area's economy.

Next is Bainbridge where the fisherman, camper and swimmer may enjoy the bounty of sprawling Lake Seminole at Seminole State Park.

Take US 84 east from Bainbridge to Cairo (pronounced Kay-ro), a city bathed year round with blossoms. The fields around Cairo yield more cane sugar than any other area in the United States, and the spring-flowering tung tree is tapped for extensive supplies of tung oil used in paints, varnishes and as a dyeing agent. A huge pickle plant is one of the town's chief attractions.

If there is any modern parallel to the image of sprawling Southern plantations shaded by magnolias and sweet with the scent of many flowers, it would have to be Thomasville, Georgia's home of the roses. A Rose Festival takes place each April, and the Rose Test Gardens are one of twenty-five such gardens in the United States used for experimenting with development of new types of roses. The Test Gardens are open from mid-April to mid-November.

The most imposing single attraction of the town is the Big Oak, a sprawling live oak almost three hundred years old that has attained a magnificent spread of 155 feet; it is 65 feet high and the trunk is 22 feet in circumference.

Out beyond Pine Tree Boulevard are the great plantations maintained as winter retreats by many of America's leading industrialists, including former Secretary of the Treasury George M. Humphrey, a frequent host of former President and Mrs. Dwight Eisenhower and one of a long line of plantation owners with ties to the late Mark Hanna of Cleveland. A demonstration of the political power that made Hanna a formidable foe or ally is evident in the fact that William McKinley was his guest at Thomasville's Mark Hanna house when McKinley was nominated for the presidency.

There are many plantations in the area. The most noted is probably "Greenwood," the 140,000-acre quail hunting preserve maintained by Mr. and Mrs. John Hay (Jock) Whitney. The main house was constructed of heavy, hand-hewn timbers cut from the estate in 1835, and the architect personally carved an immense magnolia blossom and laurel wreaths on the front gable. Magnolias grace the lawn and Lady Banksha yellow roses surround the balconies in the spring.

Hedges of Cherokee roses border the highway alongside the large Dutch Colonial, Melrose, one of three plantations bought by the Hanna family, and now owned by Hanna's daughter. Plantation buildings are painted to match the hard, coral-colored clay and white oyster shell roads, and the elegant home boasts a swimming pool, motion picture theater, and a collection of antique cars. Ichauway Plantation, Pebble Hill (another Hanna estate), Hickory Grove, Pine Bloom, and Iris Court are other standouts among the thirty great plantations. Alas, they can only be seen from outside, and the great quail hunting is by invitation only.

PRACTICAL INFORMATION FOR GEORGIA

FACTS AND FIGURES. Georgia was named for King George II of England. It has a long string of mostly less august nicknames: Buzzard State; Cracker State; Goober State; Peach State; Empire State of the South. The state flower is the Cherokee rose; the state tree, the live oak; the state bird, the brown thrasher. "Wisdom, Justice, Moderation" is the state motto. "Georgia on My Mind" the state song.

Atlanta, the state's biggest city and the leading business center of the Southeast, is the state capital. Population of the state is over 5 million.

The furthermost reaches of Georgia are the string of offshore island resorts in the Atlantic, among them the tiny and fashionable Sea Island. From its Atlantic coastline, a flat coastal plain of swamps, pine forests and gracious old antebellum towns like Savannah, the land rises to the low hills of the central Piedmont district and in the north to the mountains and lake region of the southern reaches of the Appalachians. Georgia's economy has progressed since the '30's, when cotton reigned as the state's single crop and major source of income. Industrialization and agricultural diversification have brought great improvements in the state's finances.

 HOW TO GET THERE. *By air:* Atlanta may be reached by Bahamasair, British Caledonian, Delta, Eastern, Frontier, KLM, Lufthansa, Northwest Orient, Ozark, Piedmont, Republic, and Sabena. Delta, Eastern, Republic, and Atlantic Southeast offer service to Savannah, Columbus, Albany, and other cities.

By car: I-95 enters Savannah from South Carolina and continues along the east coast south to Florida. I-85 comes in from Anderson, South Carolina, continues to Atlanta, then goes southwest to Alabama. I-75 enters Georgia from Tennessee, goes through Atlanta and continues south to Florida. I-20 comes into Augusta from Aiken, South Carolina, west to Atlanta and on to Alabama. US 84 enters from Dothan, Alabama, and goes east to Bainbridge, Valdosta and Waycross. US 441 comes in from North Carolina, goes south through Athens and Dublin to Florida. I-16 extends from Macon to Savannah; I-185 connects Columbus with I-85 a short distance out of Lagrange.

By train: Amtrak serves Atlanta from New Orleans, Washington, and New York, and Savannah and Brunswick from Florida and the east.

By bus: Greyhound and Trailways.

 HOW TO GET AROUND. *By car:* I-95 goes from Savannah south to the Florida state line; I-16 runs from Savannah northwest to Macon; I-20 goes from Augusta west to Atlanta and on to Alabama; I-85 comes in from South Carolina, proceeds southwest to Atlanta, La Grange and continues to Alabama; I-75 enters from Tennessee, goes south to Atlanta, southeast to Macon and Valdosta and continues south to Florida; US 84 comes in from Alabama and goes east to Bainbridge, Valdosta and Waycross; US 441 enters from North Carolina, goes south to Athens and Dublin and on to Florida. I-16 extends from Macon to Savannah; I-185 connects Columbus with I-85 a short distance out of Lagrange.

Car rental: You will find Avis, Hertz, National and Budget rental offices throughout Georgia.

By bus: Southeastern Motor Lines, Inc., services cities within the state, in addition to Greyhound and Trailways.

By train: Amtrak has trains to Atlanta, Savannah, Thalman, Waycross and Valdosta.

 TOURIST INFORMATION. Visitor Information Centers, operated by the Tourist Division of the Georgia Dept. of Industry and Trade, offer information on facilities and routing advice. Hours: 8:30 A.M. to 7:30 P.M. Locations: Savannah—Intersection I-95, Lavonia—I-85, ½ mi. SW of South Carolina line; Columbus—Intersection of US 280, US 27; Ringgold—I-75, 2 mi. S of Tennessee line; Sylvania—US 301, ¼ mi. SW of South Carolina line; Valdosta—I-75, 2 mi. N of Florida line; Augusta—I-20, ½ mi. W of South Carolina line, I-95 at Kingsland; I-85 at West Point; Atlanta—I-20 near Tallapoosa, east of Alabama line, Atlanta Airport.

Additional information: Game & Fish, Dept. of Natural Resources, 270 Washington St. S.W., Atlanta 30334; Division of State Parks and Historic Sites, 270 Washington St., S.W., Atlanta 30334; Ga. Chamber of Commerce, Commerce Bldg., Atlanta 30334; Tourist Division, Georgia Dept. of Industry and Trade, P.O. Box 1776, Atlanta 30301; U.S. Forest Service, Box 1437, Gainesville 30501 (camping areas).

 SEASONAL EVENTS. Many Georgia cities take advantage of the natural beauty of dogwood, peach, camellia and azalea blossoms in the spring to showcase their finer homes. Augusta and Savannah sponsor camellia shows in January, early February. Home and garden tours are held in Augusta, Columbus, Washington, Newnan, Madison, St. Simons and Savannah in March and April. Thomasville's Rose Festival is held in April.

Summer: Georgia Mountain Fair at Hiawassee draws over a hundred thousand visitors to view the quiltmaking, woodcarvings, soap making, hog rifle shoots. 10 days, early Aug. Watermelon Festival in Cordele; frequent watermelon cuttings at Agrirama, Tifton. Buggy Days in Barnesville; Mule Day at Cairo and Dahlonega.

Fall: In this traditional time for harvest fairs, Lawrenceville has an Apple-Picking Rodeo, Stone Mountain, a Yellow-Daisy Festival; Helen, an Oktoberfest. *Powers Crossroads Country Fair & Arts Festival,* in early Sept., is the South's largest arts & crafts festival fair. *Dahlonega's Gold Rush Days* features country music, costumed citizens, pioneer floats, mule races. 3 days, Oct.

Winter: Several towns have Christmas celebrations: In Pine Mountains, Callaway Gardens has a 3-wk. Christmas program. Fitzgerald's civic clubs decorate the town parks with modern and traditional decorations. Westville has special Christmas events.

 NATIONAL FORESTS. Georgia has two national forests, the *Chattahoochee* and the *Oconee.* The Chattahoochee National Forest covers 687,000 acres in northern Georgia, and the Oconee comprises more than 100,000 acres in the central part of the state. Both contribute substantially to the state's timber production and share their wealth of natural, unspoiled, preserved beauty with vacationer and tourist alike. There are scenic hiking trails, mountain streams and lake fishing and ample camping facilities. The Chattahoochee has 31 recreation areas; the Oconee, four. For information about admission permits, write to U.S. Forestry Service, P.O. Box 1437, Gainesville.

 STATE PARKS. Georgia's State park system contains parks distributed throughout the state. Facilities vary from simple picnicking areas to highly developed recreation and overnight accommodations for families.

Georgia has been divided into seven areas to add thrust and to unify tourism programs. State parks in each sector tend to meld historic and geographic identities.

In the Big A (Atlanta) sector are Chattahoochee River State Park near Altanta, Indian Springs at Indian Springs, John Tanner at Carrollton, Sweetwater Creek at Lithia Springs, Panola Mountain, and Franklin D. Roosevelt State Park at Pine Mountain.

The Classic South has Alexander H. Stephens at Crawfordsville, Bobby Brown at Elberton, Elijah Clark at Lincolnton, Fort Yargo at Winder, George L. Smith II at Twin City, Hard Labor Creek at Rutledge, Magnolia Springs at Millen, Mistletoe at Appling, Watson Mill Bridge at Comer, and Will-a-Way (especially for handicapped persons) at Winder.

Three parks are in the Heart of Georgia region: High Falls at Jackson, Little Ocmulgee at McRae, Hamburg at Mitchell.

The Colonial Coast has Crooked River at Kingsland, General Coffee at Nicholls, Laura S. Walker at Waycross, Richmond Hill at Richmond Hill, Skidaway Island at Savannah, and Stephen C. Foster at Fargo.

The Northeast Georgia Mountains have Amicalola Falls at Dawsonville, Black Rock Mountain at Mountain City, Hart at Hartwell, Moccasin Creek at Clarkesville, Tugaloo at Lavonia, Unicoi at Helen, Victoria Bryant at Royston, and Vogel at Blairsville.

In Pioneer Territory (the northwest) are Cloudland Canyon at Rising Fawn, Fort Mountain at Chatsworth, James H. Floyd at Summerville, and Red Top Mountain at Cartersville.

Plains Country has George T. Bagby at Georgetown, Georgia Veterans Memorial at Cordele, Kolomoki Mounds at Blakely, Providence Canyon at Lumpkin, Reed Bingham at Adel, and Seminole at Donaldsonville.

All state parks are open year round. Many provide rental cottages and/or mobile homes. Campgrounds open at 7 A.M. and close at 10 P.M. No reservations accepted. Rental cottages and mobile homes are completely furnished, including linens and blankets. All reservations for cottages and mobile homes must be made through the superintendent of the park you wish to visit.

There are regulation golf courses in three of the parks—Victoria Bryant, Hard Labor Creek and Little Ocmulgee. One—Georgia Veterans Memorial—has an airplane landing strip. "Dream Boat" rentals are available at Vogel, Franklin D. Roosevelt, Indian Springs, and Georgia Veterans. There are tennis courts at Georgia Veterans and Little Ocmulgee.

For additional information and descriptive folders listing all parks and their facilities, write State Parks, Department of Natural Resources, 270 Washington St. S.W., Atlanta 30334.

CAMPING OUT. The U.S. Forest Service, U.S. Corps of Engineers, State Parks Commission and private owners operate many campgrounds. Campers in state parks are served on a first-come basis, and must obtain a permit from the park superintendent before setting up. Campsites for recreation vehicles cost $6 per night; tent and pop-up trailers, $5. The State Parks Dept., 270 Washington St., Atlanta 30334 and Georgia Campground Owners Assoc., P.O. Box 5487, Columbus 31902 have pamphlets, maps.

MUSEUMS AND GALLERIES. Historical: *Thronateeska Heritage Museum* in Albany has a permanent collection of Indian artifacts; changing nature, science, history & art exhibits. *Augusta Museum,* 540 Telfair St., has archeological, historical, natural science exhibitions, is open Tues. to Sun. *Harris-Pearson-Walker House,* 1822 Broad St., Augusta, is the site of a Revolutionary War battle. Eighteenth-century furnishings, Indian artifacts, Revolutionary relics. Tues. to Sun. Closed major holidays. *Midway Museum,* on US 17, commemorates the Midway Society, descendants of Puritans who came to Georgia as missionaries to the Indians in 1752. Period rooms, records, historical library. Tues. to Sun. *Salzburger Museum,* 6 miles from Rincon off Ga. 21 on Savannah River, commemorates 18th Century settlement of Salzburgers.

In Columbus is the *Confederate Naval Museum,* 101 4th St., May to Oct., Tues. to Sun. The *U.S. Army Infantry Museum* has exhibits covering the French & Indian War to present. Tues. to Sun. *Chattahoochee Promenade* is an outdoor historical museum developed during the National Bicentennial. Fitzgerald has the *Blue and Gray Museum,* with Civil War momentos; open Wed. and Sun. by appointment. A memorial museum to Jefferson Davis is north of Irvinville on a country road. Savannah's *Factor's Walk Military Museum,* 222 Factor's Walk, houses Civil War mementos. In Washington, *Wilkes Historical Museum,* 308 E. Robert Toombs Ave., displays Confederate records, antebellum furnishings. Closed major holidays. In Valdosta, the *Children's Museum,* N. Patterson St., displays 40 exhibits relating to science and history plus five color slide presentations. In Jefferson, the *Crawford W. Long Museum* sits on the site where Dr. Long performed the first operation using ether.

Art: *Georgia Museum of Art,* on campus of U. of Ga., Athens, has permanent Holbrook and Kress collections. Closed August & part of Sept., academic and legal holidays. Free. *Augusta Museum,* Old Richmond Academy Bldg., 504 Telfair St., built 1802. History, Art, Military, Archeology and Natural Science collection. Free. The *Columbus Museum of Arts and Crafts,* 1251 Wynnton Rd., offers changing exhibits as well as Indian collection. Regional contemporary art, as well as scientific exhibitions, are on display at the *Macon Museum of Arts and Science and Planetarium,* 4182 Forsyth Rd. Closed major holidays. *Telfair Academy of Arts & Sciences,* 121 Barnard St., Savannah, was established in 1875, and its main bldg. was designed by William Jay. Fourteen galleries display paintings from eighteenth century to present.

If you're fascinated by Indian history and culture, you'll want to spend a lot of time at *New Echota* nr. Calhoun. The restoration of a 220-acre site includes *Worcester House,* original home of a missionary to the Cherokee nation, *Print Shop, Courthouse, Vann Tavern,* all furnished authentically. Closed major holidays. Be sure to see the Indian museum in *Kolomoki Mounds State Park* near Blakely. Eighteen exhibits interpret artifacts and culture of moundbuilders. *Etowah Mounds Archaeological Area,* 3 mi. S of Carterville, also has a museum. Closed major holidays. Nr. Eatonton is a 10-ft. high mound of milky quartz called Rock Eagle, shaped like an outstretched bird with a 120-ft. wingspread, created approx. 6,000 yrs. ago. At *Indian Springs State Park* is the home of Creek Indian chief William McIntosh. Ten thousand yrs. of Indian settlement are reviewed at *Ocmulgee National Monument* nr. Macon. The museum is open daily. Cherokee history can be further studied at *Chieftain Museum.* 100 Chatillon Rd., Rome. Feb. to mid-Nov.

Special Interest: *Science Center,* U. of Ga., Athens, has 6-ft. relief globe of the world, planetarium, and 24″ reflector telescope. *Crawford W. Long Medical Museum,* US 129, in Jefferson, commemorates the first use of sulphuric ether as an anesthetic. Diorama, exhibits. *Savannah Science Museum,* 4405 Paulsen St., Savannah, has habitat groups of plant & animals; salt water & tidal aquariums, regional animals and planetarium lectures. Closed major holidays.

Others: *Dahlonega Courthouse Gold Museum* with exhibits from this country's first gold rush. *Uncle Remus Museum,* in Turner Park, Eatonton, has dioramas of 12 Uncle Remus stories, slave cabins, mementos. *Jekyll Island Museum,* 329 Riverview Dr., Jekyll Island, displays Edwardian Era (1901-10) furnishings. *Ships of the Sea Museum,* 503 E. River St., Savannah, displays ship models depicting the history of this early American port. Though not a museum, *The Mark of the Potter,* on Ga 197 near Clarkesville, is a landmark for unique mountain pottery and other handicrafts.

 HISTORIC SITES. Most famous—or infamous—is undoubtedly *Andersonville National Historical Site,* a Confederate prison where many Union soldiers died of exposure, hunger and inadequate medical care. On the grounds are Providence Spring, Sundial Monument commemorating Clara Barton's work, and adjoining, Andersonville National Cemetery. Rte. 49, 11 mi. NE of Americus. Free. One of the fiercest battles of the Civil War was fought at *Chickamauga,* nr. the Tennessee border. Part of Chickamauga and Chattanooga National Military Park is in Georgia, the rest in Tennessee. Visitor Center, on US 27, is open daily. Closed Christmas. At *Kennesaw Mountain National Battlefield Park,* US 41, 2 mi. N of Marietta, the Visitor Center has exhibits and a self-guided walking tour. *Fort Pulaski,* 15 mi. E of Savannah off US 80, was built during colonial days, demolished, rebuilt again 1829-47. It was captured and manned by Union forces, serving effectively in the blockade of the South. *Fort Frederica,* 12 mi. NE of Brunswick on St. Simons Island, was planned by James Oglethorpe in 1734. It was destroyed by fire in 1758, and the town abandoned soon after.

Fort McAllister, 17 mi. S of Savannah, off US 17 on the banks of the Ogeechee River, an earthen fortification withstood heavy naval ordinance during the Civil War. *Fort King George* at Darien, constructed in 1721 to protect against Spanish and French aggression, was first settlement in what is now Georgia.

Among the houses restored and maintained as State Historic Sites are *Eagle Tavern,* 8 mi. S of Athens on US 129 at Watkinsville; Chief Vann House at Spring Place; Jarrell Plantation near Macon; Lapham-Patterson House at Thomasville; Midway Museum, *Meadow Garden,* 1320 Nelson St., Augusta, was restored by the state DAR; *"Liberty Hall,"* home of Alexander H. Stephens at Crawfordsville.

Traveler's Rest, 6 mi. NE of Toccoa, off US 123, is a restored plantation house & stagecoach inn. *Callaway Plantation,* W of Washington on US 78, has restored houses, hewn log kitchen with utensils, craft demonstrations, working farm. The *Little White House,* Warm Springs, is preserved as it was during Pres. Franklin D. Roosevelt's occupancy. Museum, free movie.

FAMOUS LIBRARIES. *Margaret Mitchell Library,* adj. to original Fayetteville Academy, between Rte. 85 and Lee St. in Fayetteville, has over 14,000 author autographed books, and an extensive Civil War reference collection.

TOURS. *Columbus:* Two-hour *Heritage Tour* leaves from Georgia Visitor Information Center, Victory Dr., covers 5 historic houses and Springer Opera House. *Athens, Macon, Madison, Savannah, Fort Gaines,* and *Sparta* offer do-it-yourself maps of historic sites. *Thomasville* Chamber of Commerce sponsors tours of plantations, historic homes and gardens of the immediate area, daily. Tours of *Okefenokee,* ranging from 2-hr. trips to 8-hr. trip into the interior, are available at the Suwannee Canal Recreation Area, 7 mi. SW of Folkston. Electric boat tours at Okefenokee Swamp Park, Waycross.

A number of sightseeing companies provide several tours of Atlanta and the surrounding areas.

GARDENS. The *All-America Rose Test Garden,* 1840 Smith Ave., Thomasville, is open to visitors from Apr. 15 to Nov. 15 daily except Sun. morning. *Callaway Gardens* at Pine Mountain, US 27, offers miles of scenic drives and walking trails through wildflower and cultivated gardens and flowering shrub displays. The Green House exhibits native and tropical flower arrangements. *Founder's Memorial Garden,* Babcock Dr. and Lumpkin St., Athens, is the site of the first garden club in the country. *Garden Center,* 598 Telfair St., Augusta. *National Camellia Society Headquarters,* Massee Lane Farms, 5 miles south of Ft. Valley on Ga. 49. *Trustee's Garden,* East Broad near Bay St., Savannah, America's first public experimental garden.

MUSIC. Macon's annual *country music festival* is held early in April. *Carillon* concerts at 12 & 4 daily, Sun. 1, 3, 5, June to Sept. at Stone Mountain. Augusta's *symphony season* is active in both fall and spring.

STAGE AND REVUES. Macon's *Little Theater,* 4220 Forsyth Rd., presents musicals every summer. Write Box 7171, Macon 31204, or call 477-3341, for schedule. Albany's *Little Theater,* Pine Ave., presents four plays annually in restored, pre-Civil War home. *Springer Opera House,* Columbus, is a restored Victorian theater, with museum, tours, performances year round. Box 1622, Columbus 31902 for schedule. Jekyll Island has a music theater in summer.

DRINKING LAWS. Min. age is 19. Liquor stores are generally open from 8 A.M. to 11:30 P.M. daily except Sun. and election days. You can buy a drink during the same hours. State law prohibits the purchase of more than two quarts of liquor at a time. It is far easier to buy package liquor or beer and wine in those towns allowing it than to buy it by the drink.

SUMMER SPORTS. The active outdoorsman thrives in Georgia in the summer. Actually he can pursue his interests almost all of the year. Water-skiing, fishing, swimming and sailing are the chief participant activities in summer. Golfing is good all year. Atlanta International Raceway's summer schedule of stock and big car races, Callaway Gardens' Masters Water Ski Tournament and the Augusta National's Masters' Golf Tournament are the big ones. The Atlanta Braves play major league baseball at 50,000-seat Atlanta Stadium.

Fishing: The fisherman can find a challenge in many mountain lakes and streams as well as at Lake Lanier, above Atlanta, and Lake Allatoona, just south of Lanier. Clark Hill, Hartwell, and Savannah Bluff reservoirs near Augusta are fished extensively for bass, trout, crappie and other varieties. Bait, tackle and fishing boats are readily available in all areas. Lake Seminole near Blakely, West Point Lake, and Lake Sinclair near Macon offer anglers many challenges. Bass are particularly plentiful in these areas.

Golf: Since the first Scottish immigrants introduced the sport to the state at Darien in 1736, Georgians have taken their golf seriously. Mild temperatures and layouts ranging from the gently rolling greens of north Georgia to the windswept seaside courses of *Jekyll* and *St. Simons Island* permit golfing almost the year round. Private airstrips at Callaway Gardens and Jekyll-St. Simons have made golfing weekends a standard diversion for big city businessmen. There are 104 public courses and a host of private ones, the most famous of which is the *Augusta National,* home of the Masters Tournament and rated in the first ten of America's 100 greatest golf courses. Peachtree Golf Club, Atlanta, ranks among the fourth 10; Atlanta County Club and Sea Island Golf Club, St. Simons Island, among the second fifty. *Atlanta,* home of legendary Grand Slam Champion Bobby Jones, has a trio of excellent public courses.

WINTER SPORTS. *Skiing.* Georgia's newest winter spot is found at *Sky Valley Ski Area,* northeast from Dillard on Rte. 246. Facilities include beginner, intermediate and expert slopes. Equipment is available for rent or purchase. A lodge and a double chair lift are also available. It is open daily during the season.

Hunting: Game is abundant in the vast woodlands and includes quail, ruffled grouse, rabbit, 'coons, foxes, deer, 'possums and an occasional brown bear or wild boar. The twenty-two public preserves range from federal wildlife areas to small quail fields stocked and operated by farmers. Dogs, guides, transportation and dressing of game are available at moderate fees. Overnight facilities are available or may be arranged.

SPECTATOR SPORTS: The *Atlanta Falcons* brought professional football to football-mad Georgians. They play in the Atlanta Stadium and bring a special extra to gridiron enthusiasts, who ardently follow the *Yellow Jackets* from Georgia Tech and the *Bulldogs* from the University of Georgia. Atlanta now has professional basketball. The *Hawks,* of the NBA, play in the city's the Omni Coliseum downtown.

WHAT TO DO WITH THE CHILDREN. Pan for gold with the kids at Crisson's, 3 mi. N of Dahlonega on Wimpy Rd., Apr. 12-Nov. 7. *Fairyland Caverns* and *Mother Goose Village* is open daily yr. round at Rock City. *Big Shanty Museum,* Kennesaw, see "The General," famous Civil War locomotive; *Ocmulgee National Indian Monument,* Macon, is site of Georgia's first Indian settlement; at *Chehaw Wildlife Park,* Albany, see animals face to face, including jaguar and ant-eater; Visit Okefenokee Swamp, at Waycross. *Stone Mountain Park,* 16 mi. E of Atlanta on US 78, is a 3,800-acre recreation park with game ranch, antebellum plantation, skylift, lots more. Combination ticket available. *Six Flags over Georgia,* on I-20 outside of Atlanta, is an amusement park with six distinctive areas representing periods of Georgia's history. Rides, live entertainment. *Atlanta Zoo,* in Grant Park, southeast Atlanta, is the largest zoo in the state.

HOTELS AND MOTELS in Georgia run the gamut from the deluxe resort on Sea Island to the inexpensive, but attractive, motels found along many of the state's major highways. Accommodations are listed according to price categories, based on double occupancy in the peak season, without meals: *Deluxe,* $80-100 and up; *Expensive,* $55-80; *Moderate,* $35-55; *Inexpensive,* $20-35. For a more complete explanation of hotel and motel categories see *Facts at Your Fingertips* at the front of this volume.

Adel

Days Inn. *Moderate.* I-75 at Hahira-Barney exit. Restaurant, pool.

Quality Inn of Adel. *Moderate.* I-75 at Moultrie Exit.

Albany

Downtowner. *Moderate.* 732 Oglethorpe Blvd. (220 rooms). Pool. Pets. Restaurant, bar, dancing, entertainment. Rms. have refrigerators, snack dispensers.

Holiday Inn. *Moderate.* 422 W. Oglethorpe Blvd. Pool. Pets. Restaurant, bar. Free airport transportation.

Quality Inn. *Moderate.* 2 locations, each with pool: **Merry Acres:** 1500 Dawson Rd. Restaurant, bar; **Town House:** 701 Oglethorpe Blvd. Cafeteria across street.

Ramada Inn. *Moderate.* 2505 N. Slappey Blvd. (118 rooms). Pool. Restaurant, bar, dancing, entertainment.

Sheraton Motor Inn. *Moderate.* 999 E. Oglethorpe Expw. (150 rooms). Pool (heated), pets. Restaurant, bar, dancing, entertainment.

Oglethorpe Motel. *Inexpensive.* 941 Oglethorpe Ave. 34 rooms.

Americus

Americus. *Moderate.* US 19S. Pool, restaurant near.

Best Western. *Moderate.* US 19S. Pool, restaurant.

Eight Inn. *Inexpensive.* US 19S.

Athens

Downtowner Motor Inn. *Moderate.* 1198 S. Milledge Ave. Pool. Restaurant, bar.

Holiday Inn Downtown. *Moderate.* (191 rooms) 2 restaurants, 3 bars. Broad at Hull St. Pets. Restaurant, bar. Nr. Univ. of Georgia.

Howard Johnson's. *Moderate.* 2465 W. Broad. Pool. Restaurant. Fam. rates avail.

Quality Inn History Village Inn. *Moderate.* (113 rooms) 295 East Dougherty St.

Bulldog Inn. *Inexpensive.* US 441N. Pool. Pets. Restaurant nr.

Augusta

Augusta Hilton. *Expensive.* (216 rooms) 640 Broad St.

Telfair Inn. *Expensive.* 349 Telfair St. Charming colonial-era inn. Restaurant.

Continental Airport Hotel. *Moderate.* (92 rooms) Bush Field on State 56, opp. airport terminal. Pool, sauna, play area. Pets. Free in-rm. coffee. Restaurants, bars, entertainment, dancing. Golf nr.

Days Inn. *Inexpensive.* 3026 Washington Rd.

Holiday Inn. *Moderate.* (175 rooms) 1602 Ft. Gordon Hwy. (US 1, 78). ¼ mi. W of US 25. Pools. Restaurant, bar, entertainment, dancing. Terminals transportation avail. **Holiday Inn Augusta** at 1075 Stevens Creek Rd.

Horne's Motor Lodge. *Moderate.* (143 rooms) 1520 Ft. Gordon Hwy. at jct. US 1, 25, 78, 278. Pool. Golf nr. Restaurant, bar. Terminals transportation avail.

Howard Johnson's Motor Lodge. *Moderate.* (61 rooms) 1238 Ft. Gordon Hwy. Pool. Golf nr. Restaurant, bar with dancing Wed. to Sat. Pets.

Quality Inn. *Moderate.* 3 locations, each with pool: **Miles:** 2077 Old Savannah Rd. Restaurant; **Embassy Towers:** 444 Broad St. Restaurant; **Warrick.** 441 Broad St. Bar, entertainment.

Ramada Inn West. *Moderate.* 3023 Washington Rd. Pool, restaurant, lounge. Suites available.

Terrace Plaza Inn. *Moderate.* 919 15th St. Restaurant, sauna, handball court.

Bainbridge

Holiday Inn. *Moderate.* Hwys. 27 and 84. (80 rooms). Pets. Restaurant, bar.

Bainbridge. *Inexpensive.* 710 Scott St. Pool. Restaurant.

Charter House Inn. *Moderate.* US 27 and 84. Pool, restaurant, bar.

Blairsville

Young Harris Motel. *Inexpensive.* Pool, cafe.

Brunswick

Holiday Inn. *Moderate.* 2 locations I-95 at US 341; 2307 Gloucester St., each with pool, restaurant, bar, dancing & entertainment.

Howard Johnson's. *Moderate.* 341 at I-95. Pool, play area. Restaurant, bar. Pets.

Quality Inn. *Moderate.* 2 locations: Palms, andon I-95 at 490 New Jesup Hwy. each with pool, restaurant nr.

Ramada Inn. *Moderate.* 2 locations: East at 3241 Glynn Ave. (US 17); and US 341 at I-95. With pool, play area, restaurant, bar, dancing and entertainment.

Days Inn. *Inexpensive.* I-95 at US 341.

Knights Inn. *Inexpensive.* I-95 at US 341.

Palms Motel. *Inexpensive.* 2715 Glynn Ave.

Calhoun

Holiday Inn. *Moderate.* I-75 at Red Bud exit. Restaurantand pool.

Ramada Inn Calhoun. *Moderate.* I-75 at GA 53. Restaurant, heated and wading pools.

Cartersville

Best Western Crown Inn. *Inexpensive.* US 41 N. Small motel with pool.

Pioneer Inn. *Inexpensive.* I-75 exit 127.

Ramada Inn. *Moderate.* I-75 and 411.

Chatsworth

Cohutta Lodge. *Moderate.* On Ga. 52, atop Ft. Mountain. Resort inn on dramatic mountain top, with dining, recreational facilities.

Chief Vann Motel. *Inexpensive.* Pool. Restaurant nr.

Clayton

Heart of Rabun. *Moderate.* Pool (heated). Restaurant. Fam. rates avail.

Dillard Motor Lodge. *Moderate.* Main Street. Pool nearby. Rooms have mountain views from private patios. Free-in-room coffee. Seasonal rates available.

Cleveland

Gateway Inn. *Moderate.* (30 rooms). Pool (heated). Pets. Restaurant.

Columbus

Columbus Hilton. *Expensive.* 800 Front Ave. New, with restaurants, lounges shops. Adjoining convention center.

Holiday Inn. *Moderate.* Two locations: **Airport** (173 rooms), 2800 Manchester Expwy; **Columbus South** (172 rooms), 3170 Victory Dr. Pool, play area. Pets. Restaurant, bar.

Marriott Courtyard. *Moderate.* Manchester Hwy. New in '84. 128 guest rooms, restaurant, lounge.

Quality Inn of Columbus. *Moderate.* (180 rooms) 1011 4th Ave. Pool (heated). Restaurant, bar, dancing, entertainment. Pets.

Days Inn. *Inexpensive.* 3452 Macon Rd. 24-hr. restaurant; outdoor pool. Nr. airport.

Nora Faye Motel. *Inexpensive.* 2921 Warm Springs Rd.

Commerce

Holiday Inn. *Moderate.* Pool, play area. Kennel. Restaurant.

Quality Inn-Davis Bros. *Moderate.* Pool (heated), play area. Cafeteria open for bkfst, lunch, dinner.

Bulldog Inn. *Moderate.* Pool. Pets. Restaurant.

Days Inn. *Inexpensive.* Pool, play area. Pets. Restaurant.

Cordele

Holiday Inn. *Moderate.* (200 rooms) I-75. Pool (heated), play area. Pets. Restaurant. Golf nr.

Ramada Inn. *Moderate.* (102 rooms) I-75 and US 280. Pool. Pets. Restaurant; beer & wine served in taproom, dancing. Free airport transportation. Golf nr.

Colonial Inn. *Inexpensive.* I-75 at exit 36. Pool. Cafeteria. Pets.

Days Inn. *Inexpensive.* I-75 and Tremont Rd. Pool, play area. Restaurant.

Dalton

Best Western. *Moderate.* 2306 Chatanooga Rd. Pool. Pets. Restaurant.

Convoy Inn Motel. *Moderate.* I-75 at Carbondale Rd.

Davis Bros. *Moderate.* Pool, play area. Pets. Free morning coffee & rolls. Restaurant.

Holiday Inn. *Moderate.* I-75 and Walnut Ave. (200 rooms). Pool. Pets. Restaurant, serving beer & wine only.

Howard Johnson's Motor Lodge. *Moderate.* 2007 Chattanooga Rd. Pool. Restaurant. Free airport transportation. Pets.

Lee's Inn. *Moderate.* 2201 Chattanooga Rd. (103 rooms). Pool. Restaurant, serving beer and wine. Pets limited.

Quality Inn. *Moderate.* I-75 and Ga. Hwy. 3.

Knight's Inn. *Inexpensive.* 2208 Chattanooga Rd.

Passport Inn. *Inexpensive.* 1519 Walnut Ave.

Rodeway Inn. *Inexpensive.* 1518 W. Walnut Ave.

Dillard

Dillard House. *Moderate.* Restaurant specializes in homegrown vegetables.

Dillard Motel. *Moderate.* Mountain view. Restaurant. Seasonal rates.

Dublin

Holiday Inn. *Moderate.* I-16 and US 319/441. Restaurant and lounge with entertainment; pool.

Eastman

Stuckey's Carriage Inn. *Moderate.* US 23 and 341 (40 rooms). Pool, play area. Restaurant. Pets.

Folkston

Howard Johnson Motor Lodge. *Moderate.* Pool, play area. Restaurant.

Quality Inn Tahiti. *Moderate.* Hwys. 1, 23 and 301 S. Pool, play area, restaurant.

Forsyth

Best Western Inn. *Moderate.* I-75 and Ga 42.

Davis Bros. *Moderate.* Pool (heated). Complimentary morning coffee & rolls. Restaurant. Pets.

Holiday Inn. *Moderate.* I-75 and Juliette Rd. (120 rooms). Pool (heated), play area. Pets. Restaurant, serving beer.

Howard Johnson's. *Moderate.* Pool, play area. Restaurant. Pets.

Days Inn. *Inexpensive.* Pool, play area. Pets. Restaurant.

Days Lodge. *Inexpensive.* Pool, play area. Pets. Restaurant.

Economy Inn. *Inexpensive.* Pets. Restaurant nr. Simple, but comfortable.

Gainesville

Days Inn & Lodge. *Moderate.* US 129 and Ga 365. Cafe. Pool. Pets.

Holiday Inn. *Moderate.* US 19/41 and Lucky St. Pool (heated), play area; tennis & golf nr. Kennel. Restaurant, bar, entertainment. Free airport transportation.

Hazelhurst

Friendship Village Inn. *Moderate.* 312 Coffee St.

Helen

Helendorf Inn. *Moderate.* (34 rooms) 305 Main St.

Unicoi State Park Lodge & Conference Center. *Moderate.* Comfortably rustic lodge in a beautiful mountain setting.

Jekyll Island

Buccaneer Motor Lodge. *Expensive.* (210 rooms) 85 Beachview Dr. Pool, play area. Golf & tennis nr. Restaurant, bar.

Holiday Inn Beach Resort. *Expensive.* 200 Beachview Dr.

Jekyll Island Hilton. *Expensive.* 975 Beachview Dr.

Villas-by-the-Sea. *Expensive.* (338 rooms) 1175 N. Beachview Dr.

Jekyll Estates Motel. *Moderate.* (35 rooms) 721 Beachview Dr.

Ladha Island Inn. *Moderate.* 60 Beachview Dr. S.

Wanderer. *Moderate.* 711 Beachview Dr.

Seafarer. *Moderate.* Pool, play area, beach opp. Pets. Restaurant nr.

Jesup

Holiday Inn. *Moderate.* US 301 and 341. Pool. Pets. Restaurant, bar. Free airport transportation.

Lake Lanier Islands

Stouffer's Pineisle Resort. *Expensive.* (256 rooms) Golf adjoining. Lake and boating.

Lake Rabun

Lake Rabun Hotel. *Inexpensive.* Stone and wood lodge, on a serene mountain lake. An idyllic hideaway.

Macon

Macon Hilton. *Expensive.* First and Walton Sts. Pools, restaurants, convention facilities.

Davis Bros. *Moderate.* Chambers Rd. I-475 at US 80. Pool. Cafe. Pets.

Holiday Inn. *Moderate.* 2 locations with all the amenities typical of this chain: **Warner Robins:** 2024 Watson Blvd. 7 mi. E of Warner Robins-Centerville exit; **West:** 4775 Chambers Rd. at Jct. of US 80 and I-75.

Howard Johnson's. *Moderate.* 2 locations each with pool, play area: **North:** 2566 Riverside Dr.; **West:** Romeiser Dr.

Quality Inn. *Moderate.* 2 locations: North at 2720 Riverside Dr.; South at I-75 and Hartley Bridge Rd.

Ramada Inn. *Moderate.* 2 locations, each with pool, restaurant, bar: 1440 Watson Blvd., dancing, entertainment; North 2400 Riverside Dr.

Marietta

Northwest Atlanta Hilton and *Marriott Interstate North. Expensive.* Both located at I-75 and Windy Hill Rd. Restaurant, lounges, pools.

Best Western Bon Air. *Moderate.* 859 Cobb Pkwy. (US 41). Pool, playground, cafe.

Holiday Inn. *Moderate.* I-75 at Delk Rd. Pool, restaurant, bar.

Squire Inn Northwest. *Moderate.* I-75 at Windy Hill Rd. Pool, bar, restaurant.

McDonough

Davis Brothers Motor Lodge. *Moderate.* I-75 and Ga. 155.

Holiday Inn. *Moderate.* I-75 and Ga 155. Pool. Restaurant. Kennel.

Days Inn. *Inexpensive.* I-75 and Ga. 20.

Scottish Inn. *Inexpensive.* I-5, exit 68.

Milledgeville

Holiday Inn. *Moderate.* US 441 N. Pool, restaurant, bar.

Newnan

Holiday Inn. *Moderate.* I-85 and US 29 (132 rooms). Pool (heated). Pets. Restaurant; bar,serving wine, beer.

Perry

Holiday Inn. *Moderate.* I-75 and US 341. Pool, play area. Pets. Restaurant, serving beer, wine. Entertainment, dancing. Kennel.

Howard Johnson's. *Moderate.* I-75 and US 341. Pool, play area. Golf nr. Restaurant. All rms. have patios or balconies. Pets.

New Perry Hotel and Motel. *Moderate.* 800 Main St. (56 rooms). Excellent dining room.

Quality Inn. *Moderate.* Pool, play area. Pets. Free airport transportation. Spacious, lovely grounds. I-75 and US 341 (77 rooms).

Bel-Aire. *Inexpensive.* Pool. Golf nr. Restaurant. Laundry facilities free. Free airport transportation. Pets limited.

Georgian Inn. *Inexpensive.* I-75 and US 41.

Travelers 8 Inn. *Inexpensive.* Pets. Restaurant nr.

Travel Host Motel. *Inexpensive.* 101 Marshallville Rd. Pool. Restaurant.

Pine Mountain

Callaway Gardens. *Expensive.* Pools, heated, play area. Kennel. Restaurant. Free admission to Gardens & facilities. AP, MAP, seasonal, pkg. rates avail. (365 rooms).

Callaway Cottages. *Moderate.* A family recreation park with kitchen cottages supervised recreation program, entertainment, free admission to Gardens and its facilities. Fee for TV. Restaurant. Fam. rates only with 1-wk min., 2-wk max. in summer; S & D daily rates Sept. to June. No liquor on grounds. Free terminal transportation.

Richland

Kay-Lynn Kourt. *Inexpensive.* Pool, play area. Pets. Restaurant nr.

Rome

Holiday Inn. *Moderate.* Pool. Golf nr. Pets. Restaurant, bar. Fam. rates avail. 707 Turner McCall Blvd. (155 rooms).

Roman Inn. *Moderate.* US 411. Pool. Restaurant, bar. Pets.

Sheraton President Inn. *Moderate.* 840 Turner McCall Blvd. Pool, restaurant, bar.

St. Marys

Riverview Hotel. *Inexpensive.* 105 Osborne St. Attractive small hotel with restaurant, bar, across from Cumberland Island ferry docks.

St. Simons Island

Sea Palms Golf & Racquet Club. *Deluxe.* (150 rooms.) Frederica Rd. Resort hotel with kitchen units & villas. Pools (heated); supervised program for children. Golf, tennis, riding, fishing. Entertainment, dancing. Restaurant, bar. Free airport transportation. Seasonal rates.

King & Prince Beach Hotel. *Deluxe.* Arnold Rd. (94 rooms). Resort hotel on ocean. Pool, play area. Golf, tennis, sailing. Restaurant, bar, entertainment, dancing. Cottage, seasonal rates avail.

Sea Gate Inn. *Expensive.* 1014 Ocean Blvd. (32 rooms). Pool, play area. Pets. golf nr. Cook-out facilities. Restaurant nr. Kitchen units, seasonal rates avail.

Queen's Court. *Moderate.* 437 Kings Way. Pool. Free in-rm. coffee. Golf nr. Restaurant, bar.

Savannah

Central reservations number for **historic inns** and **guest houses:** (912) 233–7666.

Ballastone Inn. *Deluxe.* 14 Oglethorpe Ave. Beautifully restored inn in 19th-century townhouse.

Sheraton Savannah Inn and Country Club. *Deluxe.* 612 Wilmington Island Rd. Resort hotel with villas & cottages on Wilmington River. Pool, sauna, play area. Golf, tennis, riding, hunting, fishing, boating, marina. Restaurant, bar, dancing, entertainment. Seasonal, family, golf pkg. rates avail. (208 rooms).

DeSoto Hilton. *Expensive.* Liberety & Bull St. Rooftop pool (heated). Golf nr. Free in-rm. coffee. Restaurant, bar. (250 rooms).

Hyatt Regency Savannah. *Expensive.* Bull and Bay Sts. 350 deluxe rooms. Restaurants, lounges, sauna.

Stoddard-Cooper House. *Expensive.* 19 W. Perry St. Luxurious garden suites with fireplaces, kitchen in historic home.

Best Western Riverfront Motor Inn. *Moderate.* 412 W. Bay St. 200 rooms.

Days Inn. *Moderate.* 201 W. Bay St. 196 rooms. New, tastefully furnished. 24-hour restaurant.

Downtowner. *Moderate.* 201 Oglethorpe Ave. Pool. Restaurant, bar. Pets. (204 rooms.)

Holiday Inn. *Moderate.* 2 locations, each with pool, restaurant, bar: 121 W. Boundary St. just S of Talmadge Bridge; at Jct US 17 & I-95.

Howard Johnson's. *Moderate.* 2 loations, each with pool, restaurant: **Downtown:** 224 W. Boundary St. 232–4371; **West:** Rte. 204 at I-95. Bar. Golf nr.

Mary Lee Guest Accommodations. *Moderate.* 117 E. Jones St. Restored historic home. 3 guest suites.

Ramada Inn. *Moderate.* US 17 at I-95.

Sharaton Oasis Village. *Moderate.* 1 Gateway Blvd., 15 mi. SW on GA 20 at I-95 Abercorn exit. Pool. Pets. Cafc.

Days Inn. *Inexpensive.* Two locations: US 17, Richmond Hill; and 114 Mall Blvd. (GA 204). Pool, play area. Restaurant. Pets.

Savannah Beach

Ramada Inn. *Expensive.* Pool. Restaurant. Fam. rates.

Days Inn. *Inexpensive.* Pool. Pets. Kitchen units avail.

Tides Motel. *Inexpensive.* Tybee Island

Sea Island

The Cloister. *Deluxe.* One of the most glamorous, exclusive resort hotels. On 5 mi. private beach. Pools (heated), play area. Supervised play, golf, tennis, riding, boating, fishing. Bar. Dancing, entertainment. AP. Seasonal rates. (237 rooms).

Statesboro

Bryant's Best Western. *Moderate.* 461 S. Main St. Pool. Pets. Cafe.

Holiday Inn. *Moderate.* 230 S. Main St. Pool. Golf nr. Restaurant, bar. Kitchen & studio units avail. Kennel.

Quality Inn Downtown. *Moderate.* 109 N. Main St. Pool; restaurant adjacent. Golf and tennis nearby.

Stone Mountain

Stone Mountain Inn. *Moderate.* Ante-bellum style hotel inside state park, overlooking Confederate memorial carving on mountainside.

Sylvania

Paradise. *Moderate.* Pool, play area. Restaurant nr. Secluded, in 14-acre pecan grove. Pets.

Thomasville

Downtown Motor Inn. *Moderate.* Restaurant, bar.

Holiday Inn. *Moderate.* US 19 (140 rooms). Pool (heated), play area. Restaurant.

Days Inn. *Inexpensive.* (120 rooms). Pool, play area. Restaurant. Pets.

Tifton

Davis Bros. *Moderate.* I-75 and W. 8th St. Pool, play area. Morning coffee & rolls free. Fine cafeteria.

Quality Inn of Tifton. *Moderate.* I-75 at 2nd St. exit. Pool, play area. Free in-rm. coffee. Free airport transportation.

Ramada Inn. *Moderate.* (100 rooms) I-75 & US 82. Pool. Pets.

Thunderbird Motel. *Moderate.* I-75 at W. 2nd St. Pool (heated). Restaurant nr.

Village Green (formerly Howard Johnson's). *Moderate.* I-75 and US 41. Pool, cafe, tennis.

Days Inn. *Inexpensive.* Pool, play area. Restaurant. Pets.

Toccoa

Quality Inn. *Moderate.* I-75. Pool, restaurant.

Valdosta

King of the Road. *Moderate.* (137 rooms). I-75 at Hwy 94. Pool, lounge, restaurant.

Holiday Inn. *Moderate.* I-75 exit 5. Pools, play area. Pets. Restaurant, bars, dancing.

Howard Johnson's. *Moderate.* I-75 and Ga. 94. (88 rooms). Pool, play area. Restaurant. Pets.

Sheraton Valdosta Motor Inn. *Moderate.* (75 rooms) I-75 and US 84. Pool, play area. Restaurant, bar. Free airport transportation.

Best Western Outpost. *Inexpensive.* I-75 S. at exit 2. Pool and playground; golf course and 24-hr. restaurant adjacent.

Davis Bros. Quality Inn North. *Inexpensive.* 1209 St. Augustine Rd. Pool; cafeteria.

Days Inn. *Inexpensive.* I-75 S. at Lake Park exit. Pool. Pets. Restaurant.

Jolly Inn. *Inexpensive.* I-75 exit 5. Pool. Pets. Restaurant nr.

Quality Inn South. *Inexpensive.* I-75 and US 84.

Waycross

Holiday Inn. *Moderate.* (103 rooms) 1725 Memorial Dr. Pool, play area, putting green. Pets. Restaurant, serving beer & wine.

Pine Crest. *Moderate.* Pool, play area. Free morning coffee. Restaurant.

Palms Court. *Inexpensive.* Pool, play area. Golf nr. Restaurant nr. Pets.

Woodbine

Stardust Lodge. *Moderate.* Pool, play area. Pets. Restaurant nr.

DINING OUT in Georgia can mean fine Southern-style foods in a rural atmosphere or charming plantation house, or sophisticated French cuisine in an elegant urban dining room. Many worthwhile restaurants may be found at the hotels we have listed. Our price categories are for a complete dinner: *Expensive,* a complete dinner may run over $20 per person, excluding drinks; *moderate,* $10–20; *inexpensive,* under $10. A la carte meals will, of course, bring the bill up. For a more complete explanation of restaurant categories see *Facts at Your Fingertips* at the front of this volume.

Albany

Gargano's East. *Moderate.* 1640 E. Oglethorpe Ave. Steaks, seafood, pastas.

Athens

Martel's. *Expensive.* 325 N. Milledge Ave. French cuisine, wines in an elegant setting.

Augusta

Calvert's. *Expensive.* 475 Highland Ave. Handsome, sophisticated place with a varied continental menu.

Town Tavern. *Moderate.* 17 7th St. Popular, attractive. Bar. Children's portions.

Bainbridge

Jack Wingate's Lunker Lodge. *Inexpensive.* GA 310 at Lake Seminole. Excellent fresh seafood, barbecue. Locally very popular.

Brunswick

Kody's. *Inexpensive.* 300 Gloucester St. Very popular place for fresh, local seafoods, Southern cooking.

The Wharf. *Inexpensive.* 901 Bay St. Seafood, steaks.

Clarkesville

La Prade's. *Inexpensive.* Hwy 197 N. on Lake Burton. Specializes in mountain trout, country ham. Closed winer months.

Columbus

Goetchius House. *Expensive.* 405 Broadway. Gourmet food and drink in historic home of restoration district.

W.D. Crowley's. *Moderate.* 3111 Manchester Hwy. Trendy place with convivial bar and menu ranging from steaks to salads.

Morrison's Cafeteria. *Inexpensive.* In Cross Country Plaza Shopping Center.

Dahlonega

Smith House. *Inexpensive.* Old-fashioned mountain boarding house serves all-you-can-eat family style.

Dillard

Dillard House. *Inexpensive.* Fine family-style restaurant, serving fresh, home-grown vegetables, fruit, fried chicken, country style ham.

Helen

Sautee Inn. *Inexpensive.* Located in an old hotel that dates to turn of century.

Jasper

Woodbridge Inn. *Moderate.* Continental cooking, lovely great rooms in a rustic mountain setting.

Macon

Beall's 1860. *Moderate.* 315 College St. Prime rib, seafood, chicken in a restored old home.

Len Berg's. *Moderate.* Centrally located in Post Office Alley, ½ blk off US 41. Well established, popular meeting place. Beer served only with evening meal.

St. Simons Island

St. Simons Café. *Expensive.* Convivial café features imaginative, continental ways of preparing fresh, local seafoods.

Bennie's Red Barn. *Moderate.* Steak, seafood in rustic atmosphere. Drinks. Children's portions.

Savannah

Pirate's House. *Expensive.* 20 E. Broad at Bay St. in historic Trustee's Garden. 17 dining rms. Serving regional specialties, Oysters Savannah among them.

Elizabeth on 37th. *Moderate.* 105 E. 37th St. at Drayton St. Fresh seafoods in lovely old mansion.

Johnny Harris. *Moderate.* 1651 Victory Dr. Great fried chicken, barbecue. A Savannah landmark.

Spanky's. *Moderate.* 317 E. River St. Stone walls constructed from ballast of 18th-century sailing vessels. Pizza, chicken fingers, exotic drinks.

Crystal Beer Parlor. *Inexpensive.* W. Jones and Jefferson Sts. Comfortable old tavern famous for beer, hamburgers, and fried-oyster sandwiches.

Mrs. Wilkes. *Inexpensive.* 107 W. Jones St. Excellent Southern cooking served boardinghouse style.

Williams Seafood. *Inexpensive.* 8010 Tybee Island Rd. Simply prepared fried and broiled seafoods. Very popular.

Soperton

Sweat's Barbecue. *Inexpensive.* Ga 29, just off I-16. Landmark of great barbecue, Brunswick stew.

Statesboro

Vandy's Barbecue. *Inexpensive.* Has served pit-cooked BBQ for over 50 years.

Sylvania

Treado's Town House. *Inexpensive.* US 301 N. Attractive, well-run, small-town restaurant specializes in steaks, seafood, southern dishes.

Thomasville

Plaza. *Inexpensive to moderate.* 222 S. Broad St. Steaks, seafood, and Greek dishes.

Waycross

Sir Henry's. *Moderate.* 1506 Memorial Dr. Prime ribs, steaks, seafoods, dancing.

LOUISIANA

Romantic Outpost of the Old World

New Orleans is the home of a unique attraction: the French Quarter, or *Vieux Carré* ("Old Square"), which comprises the original town laid out by the French. There is nothing quite like the atmosphere of these narrow streets with their lovingly restored old buildings, flower-filled patios, antique shops and coffee bars. And for a change of pace after browsing among the Quarter's architectural charms, there are world-famous restaurants, the honky-tonk strip along Bourbon Street, and a few remaining places where authentic New Orleans jazz is still played.

The old buildings of the Quarter are built flush with the *banquette* (sidewalk), with flower- and shrub-crowded patios and courtyards to the rear. Many of these may be visited. In spring, wisteria twines its heavy, grape-like clusters of flowers over wrought-iron balconies, while the courtyards blaze with hedgerows of red, pink, and white azaleas.

A good place to refresh oneself is in the coffee bars of the French Market (toward the end of the walking tour given below). The specialties here include Creole or French (dark-roasted, chicory-flavored) coffee drunk with milk *(café au lait)* and the puffy square French doughnuts *(beignets)*.

Walking Tour of French Quarter

Walking in the oldest part of New Orleans is much more fun than driving. It's also more practical. You can go at your own pace, pausing to browse and enjoy. Allow about three hours for the tour or longer, if you wish to stop at those sites that are open to the public.

In case you wish to take an abbreviated tour, Items 14–16 and 18–25 are recommended as especially representative of the French Quarter.

A good place to start is at the Visitor Information Center of the Greater New Orleans Tourist and Convention Commission (1) at 334 Royal Street. Here you can have a cup of coffee, pick up brochures and enjoy looking at the building that was the Old Bank of Louisiana. Completed in 1826, this building and the others at this intersection comprised the financial hub of New Orleans.

What distinguishes the Quarter from the rest of the city is that within its area of about a square mile, strict legal ordinances have preserved its original character. Not only are the facades the original ones of French and Spanish design, they are painted in the original colors. This experiment in maintaining historic charm has insured that after over two hundred years the harmony of fanciful iron grillwork, intimate courtyards, and classic French and Spanish lines remains undisturbed.

Neatly bounded by Decatur Street and the Mississippi River on one side, and by Canal, North Rampart, and Esplanade on the other three, the Quarter is just the right size for a walking tour. In this way, the original creation of architects Latrobe, the Galliers, the De Pouillys, and the Dakins can be examined in the course of one leisurely walk.

Picking up the walking tour, cross Royal to 339 Royal Street (2). The Old Bank of the United States was built in 1800. Its balcony railings are exceptionally good examples of hand-forged (wrought) ironwork.

Cross Conti Street to 403 Royal Street (3) to the Old Louisiana State Bank. Note the bank's monogram ("LSB") in the delicate wrought iron of the balcony railing. The Louisiana State Bank, which opened for business in 1821, was designed by Benjamin H. Latrobe, one of the architects of the U.S. Capitol at Washington.

The large white building across the street is the New Orleans Court Building, 400 Royal (4). Erected in 1908-09, this marble edifice occupies a square of ground formerly covered by buildings from the Spanish era. It houses the Louisiana Wildlife and Fisheries Museum.

Across the street at 417 Royal Street (5), Casa Faurie is now Brennan's restaurant. This mansion was built soon after 1801 for the maternal grandfather of the French Impressionist painter Edgar Degas. In 1805 the newly organized Banque de la Louisiana bought the property, and the bank's monogram ("LB") was added to the balcony railing. In 1819 the bank passed out of existence, and the building became a social center of the city. When General Andrew Jackson visited New Orleans in 1828 he was entertained at several lavish banquets at this house. Later it was sold to Judge Alonzo Morphy, whose son Paul was the chess champion of the world by the time he was 21.

The cross street ahead of you is St. Louis. Turn left and go a block and a half to 820 St. Louis Street (6). This is the Hermann-Grima House, built by Samuel Hermann, a well-to-do commission merchant, about 1823. He sold it to Felix Grima, a prominent attorney and notary in 1844. Today it is owned by the Christian Women's Exchange and open to the public.

Retrace your steps to Royal and turn left. In the middle of the block is 520 Royal Street, Maison Seignouret (7). Originally built in 1816, it was occupied by François Seignouret, a noted furniture maker. It was later owned by the Brulator family, hence the name "Brulator Court." It now houses the radio and TV station WDSU. The patio is open to the public.

Across Royal is 533 Royal Street, Merieult House (8). This building, constructed in 1792, was one of the few that escaped the fire of 1794. It now houses the Kemper and Leila Williams Foundation's Historic New Orleans Collection of maps, prints, drawings, documents and artifacts.

Cross the street to 536 Royal (9). Casa de Comercio is an excellent example of Spanish architecture in New Orleans.

Recross Royal to 537 Royal and 710 Toulouse Streets (10), Court of Two Lions. Much of the novel *Anthony Adverse* was based on the life of Vincent Nolte, who bought this property in 1819 from Jean François Merieult. The Casa Hove House, 723 Toulouse Street, is an excellent example of early Spanish architecture. The Hove Perfume Shop, located on the ground floor, has created perfume for men and women since 1932.

Return to Royal. Walk one block to St. Peter. Turn left and go to 714 St. Peter Street (11), LeMonnier House. Built in 1829 for Dr. Yves LeMonnier, this house was acquired in 1860 by Antoine Alciatoire, its most notable occupant. Antoine operated a boarding house, and his fame for preparing succulent dishes eventually led to his opening the restaurant that today is known as Antoine's.

Only a few steps away is 718 St. Peter Street (12), Maison de Flechier. It is thought to have been built by the planter Etienne Marie de Flechier just after the disastrous fire of 1794. Pat O'Brien's now occupies both the building and the magnificent courtyard.

Return to Royal. At the opposite corner is 640 Royal Street (13), Maison LeMonnier, known as the "first skyscraper." The four-story structure was built in 1811.

Now turn off Royal into St. Peter. A little more than half a block along is the Spanish Arsenal at 615 St. Peter Street (14). During the years of Spanish dominance this was the site of the prison, or *calabozo*. The Arsenal, which is open during special exhibits, is entered through the Cabildo on Chartres Street. Next to the Arsenal is the Jackson House, 619 St. Peter Street. It is open during special exhibits only. Both buildings are part of the Louisiana State Museum complex.

Turn on the short Cabildo Alley, next to Jackson House, then right into a long passageway. This is Pirate's Alley (15). Legend has it that Jackson conferred here with freebooters Jean and Pierre Lafitte about the forthcoming defense of New Orleans, but the Alley simply did not exist at that time. It was cut sixteen years later in 1831. Nobel laureate William Faulkner lived at 624 Pirates Alley. It was here that he wrote his first novel, *Soldier's Pay*.

Now walk toward Royal Street. On your right is the Cathedral Garden (16). It is also called St. Anthony's Square in memory of one of the most beloved individuals in the colony's history—Antonio de Sedella, a Capuchin priest, who came to the Louisiana colony in 1779.

Cross Royal to Orleans and walk half a block. On your right is a hotel (717 Orleans Street). In the section above the main entrance is a substantial portion of the Orleans Ballroom, or Salle d'Orleans (17). Erected in 1817, this fine ballroom was the setting for the naughty-nice quadroon balls, where mothers would offer their virginal golden-skinned daughters to the aristocratic white men of the city. Each mother hoped that a wealthy man would choose her daughter to be his concubine, setting her up, often for life, in a little house in a special section of the city a few blocks from the ballroom.

Go back to Royal and turn left. On the far side of the Cathedral Garden from Pirate's Alley is Père Antoine's Alley (18), bounded by Royal and Chartres streets and the Cathedral and the Presbytère. This passageway was cut in 1831.

Follow this passage to its far end (Chartres Street). As you emerge, turn left. The large gray building with iron fence in its arches is The Presbytère (19). The first edifice on this site, a small Capuchin monastery, was destroyed by fire in 1788. In 1793 rich Don Andres Almonester Roxas began construction of what he called a Casa Curial, which in French is a Presbytère, or residence for the clergy serving the parish church. In 1794 fire swept through the structure again. The U.S. took over the Territory in 1803 and completed the building in 1813. But never did it serve as either Casa Curial or Presbytère. In 1853 the city purchased it from the wardens of the Cathedral, and it is now part of the Louisiana State Museum.

As you face the front of the Presbytère, to your left is St. Louis Cathedral (20). This is the oldest active Cathedral in the United States and the third church on this site. The present building dates from 1789-94. In 1964 Pope Paul VI designated it a minor basilica.

Next door, again to the left, is the Cabildo (21). During Spanish rule this structure housed the governing council, or Cabildo, of the colony. The first structure on this site was erected in 1770 but burned in 1788. What you see was built during the period from 1795 to 1799. The balcony railing has been called the finest work from the Spanish period in New Orleans. From this building France, then Spain, then France again, then the United States, the Confederate States and finally the United States again, have governed. On the second floor in 1803 France ceded the territory of the Louisiana Purchase to the U.S. Today a part of the Louisiana State Museum, the Cabildo displays such important items as the "founding stone" of the colony (1699) and the death mask of Napoleon Bonaparte.

Presbytère, Cathedral and Cabildo face the green oasis called Jackson Square (22). Established in 1721 as a drill field, it was known for more than a century as the Place d'Armes (under the French flag) or the Plaza de Armas (under Spain). The plaza acquired its current name in 1848. The statue of General Jackson on his rearing horse was the work of sculptor Clark Mills and was put in place in 1856. It is the world's first equestrian statue with more than one hoof unsupported.

Bordering Jackson Square on two sides you will see the Pontalba Buildings (23). Micaela Almonester de Pontalba, daughter of the colony's richest man in the Spanish period, built the great twin buildings which bear her name. Her plan was to offer luxury apartments and fine ground floor offices and shops. Work was begun in 1849 and both buildings were completed in 1851. The City of New Orleans now owns the St. Peter Street building; the St. Ann Street side of the Pontalba is owned by the state.

At about the middle of the Pontalba Building on St. Ann Street is 525 St. Ann, the 1850 House (24). Here a three-story section of one of the two Pontalba Buildings has been beautifully restored to present a typical New Orleans dwelling of 1850.

As you leave the 1850 House go to your left on St. Ann. At the first corner (Decatur Street) that long, low structure across the street is part of the French Market (25), across from Jackson Square. The French Market dominates a bend of the Mississippi River that forms the waterfront perimeter of the historic French Quarter. Its buildings are distinguished by graceful arcades and stately colonnades that have been a vibrant part of the New Orleans scene for more than 160 years. The French Market is anchored at its downriver end by the popular farmers' market area of open sheds filled with fresh fruits and vegetables. In the Market are longtime shopkeepers as well as many new shops, bistros, coffee stands and craft stalls.

On Ursuline Street, turn and walk one block to Chartres. At the corner you will find the Old Ursuline Convent, 1112 Chartres Street (26). This is one of the oldest structures in the Mississippi Valley. The Sisters of St. Ursula moved into the building in 1749. Theirs was the first nunnery in Louisiana, and they conducted the first Catholic school, the first Indian school, the first Negro school and the first orphanage. The sisters taught the colony's daughters at this site until 1824, then moved to another location outside the city. Scheduled tours of the convent and gardens are conducted Wednesday afternoons.

Across Chartres at 1113 Chartres Street is LeCarpentier House, or Beauregard House (27). A New Orleans auctioneer named Joseph Le-Carpentier built this handsome residence in 1827 on land he bought from the Ursuline nuns. With him lived his daughter and her husband, attorney Alonzo Morphy. Here, during the bleak winter of 1866-67 following the end of the Civil War, Confederate General P.G.T. Beauregard, "the Great Creole," rented a room. In recent years the house and garden were the property and residence of the prolific novelist Frances Parkinson Keyes, who adopted New Orleans as her home and wrote many books about the region. Open to the public.

In the same block is Soniat House at 1133 Chartres Street (28.) About 1829 wealthy, aristocratic planter Joseph Soniat duFossat built this place as a townhouse. In the 1860s the wrought iron with which Monsieur deFossat had embellished his home was torn away and replaced by the admirable castiron lacework it now wears.

Proceed to Governor Nicholls Street and turn left to the Clay House at number 618-20 (29). This is a residence built about 1828 by John Clay for his wife. Clay's brother was the famous statesman Henry Clay. Another building was added after 1871, which in the 1890s was used by Frances Xavier Cabrini—now St. Frances Cabrini—as a schoolhouse.

At the next corner (Royal Street), on your left is a tall building of considerable interest: LaLaurie House at 1140 Royal (30). This is the city's most infamous private residence, constructed before 1831 by Louis Barthelemy de MacCarthy. One of his five children, Delphine LaLaurie, acquired the house from her father in August 1831, and it became the scene of brilliant social events. But there was talk about the house: why did the servants seem so broken in spirit and physically emaciated? In

1833 a neighbor accused the glamorous Delphine LaLaurie of merciless-ly lashing a small slave girl. Madame LaLaurie was merely fined. Then, on the night of April 10, 1834, a fire broke out. Neighbors attempting to save the contents of the house crashed through a locked door and found seven wretched, starving creatures chained leg and neck in the most painful positions, unable to move. A newspaper the next day suggested that Madame LaLaurie herself had set the fire. Citizens began to mass outside the unhappy house. Suddenly a carriage burst out of the gate and raced away, with the LaLauries in the back. The crowd proceeded to tear down the house in anger. The wrecked building was later restored, but the LaLauries never returned. Not alive, that is. After she died in Europe some years later, Delphine's body was brought back and buried secretly. Ever since, some say, the house has been haunted by groans, screams and the savage hissing of whips.

Cross Royal and enter Governor Nicholls Street again. On your right is Thierry House, number 721. (31). This house, erected in 1814 for Jean Baptiste Thierry, embodies as much of the spirit of ancient Greece as its nineteen-year-old architect, Henry Latrobe, was able to give it, concentrating chiefly on the portico. This modest place started the Greek Revival that so influenced Louisiana architecture.

Go back to Royal. Turn right. On your left will be the Gallier House, 1132 Royal Street (32). James Gallier, Jr., was one of the most illustrious in a long line of notable architects in the city. In 1857 he bought a lot here, then designed and built this residence (1857 or 1858). It has been lovingly restored, presenting an excellent opportunity to see how the wealthy people of New Orleans lived just after the middle of the last century. Open to the public.

As you come out of the Gallier House, turn left, then right at Ursulines Street. Walk one block to Bourbon. Turn left for another block, reaching St. Philip. On the far corner of Bourbon and St. Philip is LaFitte's Blacksmith Shop (33) at 941 Bourbon Street. Just when this place was built or by whom is unknown. The oldest record of ownership dates back to 1772. Legend has it that this was a smithy operated by the dashing brothers Lafitte, the "hero" pirates of New Orleans.

Now return to Royal and turn right. In the middle of the block at 915 Royal stands the Cornstalk Fence (34). The old edifice that once stood here burned, but its most interesting feature remains—a cast-iron fence representing stalks and ears of corn intertwined with morning glory vines and blossoms. There is only one other like it in the city (at 1448 Fourth Street). The fence was cast in Philadelphia by the Wood & Perot foundry and shipped by sea to Dr. Joseph Secondo Biamenti, who bought the house in 1834 and placed the fence around it.

Across the street and a few steps to your right are the Miltenberger Houses, 900-906-910 Royal Street(35). The Widow Miltenberger built the houses in 1838 for her three sons.

Continue on Royal to Dumaine. Turn left. About a third of a block from Royal, on the opposite side of Dumaine, is a raised house with a recessed gallery, reminiscent of what is known as West Indian architecture. This place is "Madame John's Legacy," 632 Dumaine Street(36). Many researchers insist it is the oldest building in the Mississippi Valley. The great fire of Good Friday, 1788, which almost totally destroyed New

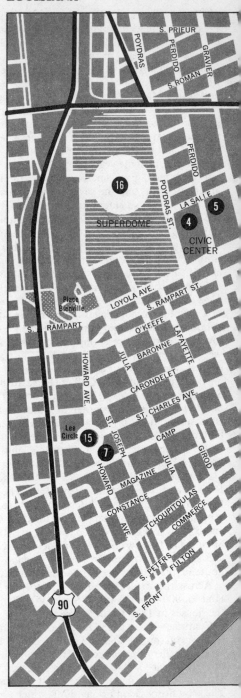

Points of Interest

1) Greater New Orleans Tourist Commission
2) U.S. Mint
3) Cabildo
4) City Hall
5) Civic Center
6) Theater for the Performing Arts
7) Confederate Memorial Hall
8) Louis Armstrong Park
9) Ursuline Convent
10) French Market
11) Hermann-Grima House
12) Madame John's Legacy
13) International Trade Mart
14) Municipal Auditorium
15) Lee Circle
16) Superdome

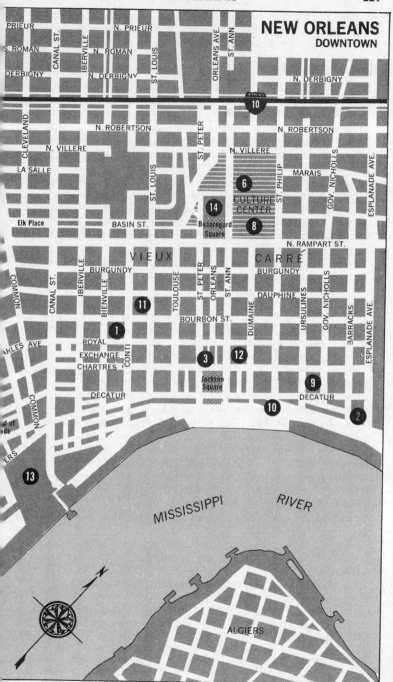

NEW ORLEANS
DOWNTOWN

Orleans, also burned this house, but it was soon rebuilt. There have been many owners. The current one is the Louisiana State Museum, which renovated the place and fitted it with furniture of the period. The name "Madame John's Legacy" was given to it in a fictional story, *Tite Poulette,* by George Washington Cable. This ends your walking tour. Now you're on your own.

Beyond the French Quarter

The Garden District, which is bounded by Magazine Street, St. Charles Avenue, Louisiana Avenue and Jackson Avenue, offers an interesting contrast to the French Quarter. Instead of buildings fronting the sidewalk with courtyards or patios hidden from the public in the rear, this area has old mansions, most in Greek Revival style, built on spacious grounds abounding with shade trees, shrubbery and flowers.

A free ferry across the river leaves every twenty minutes from the foot of Canal Street and offers a good view of the St. Louis Cathedral and Jackson Square. A fifteen-minute drive away from the Quarter is Longue Vue House and Gardens, an exquisite city estate, operated by the Longue Vue Foundation and open to the public. This estate features a series of cloistered gardens around the spacious greensward and topiary art of the Spanish Court.

The Louisiana Superdome, opened on August 3, 1975, is the world's largest enclosed stadium-arena covering 52 acres and reaching 27 stories high. It seats more than 80,000. Tours are conducted daily, except during certain events.

The New Orleans Museum of Art at City Park has permanent collections of 19th and 20th century French paintings and sculpture, and a distinquished pre-Columbian art collection.

The old cemeteries of New Orleans are intriguing; most burial is in tombs aboveground, because of the once-high water table in the swamp surrounded city. St. Louis No. 1, the city's most famous and oldest, is located at Basin and St. Louis. Famed voodoo queen Marie Laveau is buried here. It is recommended that visitors go in groups.

Louis Armstrong Park on Rampart Street features a complex of four historic buildings, surrounding a courtyard, an arcade and tower, all of which are landscaped and enclosed by a cast iron fence.

For exploring without a car, try the St. Charles Ave. streetcar. It runs under live oaks and past old houses with leaded glass doors, along the edge of the Garden District, past Tulane and Loyola Universities, to the place where the avenue meets the Mississippi River levee. Check bookshops for *Trolley Tours,* a sightseeing guide to the streetcar route.

PRACTICAL INFORMATION FOR NEW ORLEANS

HOW TO GET THERE. *By air:* New Orleans is served by Continental, Delta, Eastern, American, Republic, Northwest Orient, Lacsa, Royale, Aviateca, Northwest, Sahsa, Taca, Southwest, Pan-American, Ozark, British Airways. There are direct flights to New Orleans from many cities within the U.S. and from many other countries such as Mexico, Honduras, Guatemala, Puerto Rico and Venezuela to mention some. The airport at New Orleans has many of its facilities adapted to the handicapped and elderly, including available medical service. It is easy to get into, and then get around in once inside, and restroom facilities for the handicapped (wheelchairs included) are available.

By car: I-10 connects with Baton Rouge, Lafayette, Houston, Tex., and points west with New Orleans; I-10 also comes in from Mississippi to the east; I-55 connects New Orleans with Jackson, Miss., Memphis, Tenn., and points to the north; I-59 also comes into New Orleans from Mississippi.

By train: Amtrak to New Orleans from Chicago, New York, and Los Angeles.

By bus: New Orleans is served by Trailways and Greyhound bus lines. These lines make connections with many other bus lines. Charter buses from all over the country come into New Orleans regularly.

By ship: Passenger and cargo liners from all parts of the world make calls.

HOW TO GET AROUND. There is limousine and bus service from the airport.

By car: American International, Avis, Budget, Dollar, Econocar, Hertz, National, Thrifty all have offices at or near the airport.

By bus: The "Streetcar Named Desire" has been replaced by a bus.

By streetcar: Streetcars still run on St. Charles and Carrollton, starting from Canal St. It is an economical and fun way to go from Canal Street to Uptown.

SEASONAL EVENTS. In March, the Italians parade through the French Quarter for St. Joseph's Day, and the Irish have St. Patrick's Day celebrations in the Irish Channel. *Carnival* climaxes on *Mardi Gras* (Shrove Tuesday), which varies annually as the 41st day before Easter Sunday, not counting Sundays. Two-week *Spring Fiesta* is held beginning first Friday after Easter, during which tours of the French Quarter, Garden District and plantation homes are arranged. Parade, street dancing and outdoor art show add to fun. Spring Fiesta headquarters are at 529 St. Ann St., New Orleans 70116. *Jazz and Heritage Festival* celebrates crafts, food and music in mid-Apr. There are jazz, ragtime, gospel, blues, country, and cajun music concerts, parade, river cruise. Write Festival, P.O. Box 2530, New Orleans 70176.

MUSEUMS AND GALLERIES. The *Historic New Orleans Collection,* 533 Royal St. The *Louisiana State Museum,* housed in the Presbytere, 751 Chartres Street, is a complex of eight historic buildings, seven of which are open to the public: Cabildo, Presbytere, 1850 House, Madame John's Legacy, U.S. Mint, Jackson House, and the Arsenal.

Art: New Orleans *Museum of Art,* Lelong Ave., City Park. Free. Closed Mon. and holidays. *Gallier House,* 1118–32 Royal St. Decorative art museum, housed in 1857 Gallier House located on the site of the New Orleans Vieux Carre. Closed Mon. and holidays.

Special Interest: Louisiana's Maritime Museum, located in the International Trade Mart, closed Sunday and Monday, is dedicated to the preservation of Louisiana's maritime heritage. *Pharmaceutical Museum,* Chartres St. Built in 1847 for druggist Louis Dufilho, the museum reflects early history of New Orleans medicine. Open year round. *Confederate Museum,* 929 Camp St. Relics pertaining to military history; Civil War memorabilia. Closed Sundays. *Louisiana Wildlife Museum,* 400 Royal St. Natural history museum. Closed Sat. and Sun.

Others: Musee Conti Museum of Wax, 917 Conti St. Period settings of local history. Open daily except Mardi Gras and Christmas.

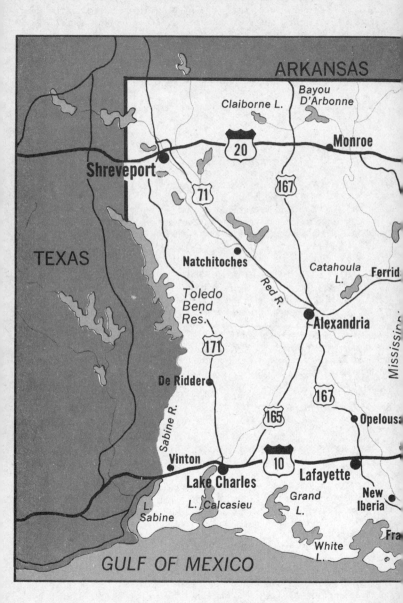

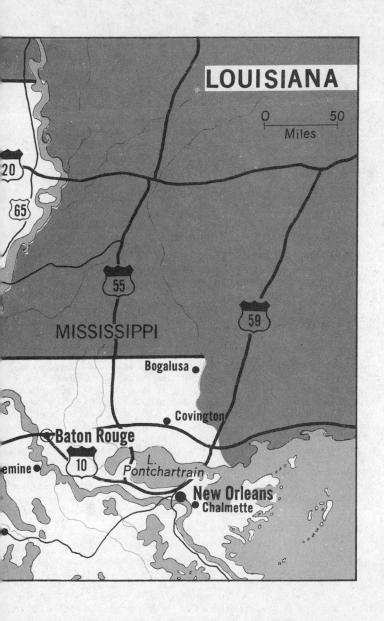

HISTORIC SITES. In New Orleans the *Vieux Carre* (Old Square) represents a concentration of historic sites, with the apex at Jackson Square, where the old *St. Louis Basilica* has housed the Catholic See of New Orleans continuously since 1794. It was around this square that Bienville had engineers lay out the city in 1718. For over two and a half centuries the city's history has centered here. Uptown, the *Garden District's* great homes are still maintained as showplaces of the antebellum period. *U.S. Custom House,* 423 Canal St. 4-story 1849 building of granite. The site was once occupied by Fort St. Louis. Used as an office by General Benjamin F. Butler during the Union Army's occupation of New Orleans. Closed wknds. and holidays. Free. *Chalmette National Historical Park,* St. Bernard Highway, State 39. Site of the Battle of New Orleans in the War of 1812. Open daily but closed Mardi Gras.

Historic Houses: Pitot House, 1440 Moss Street, on Bayou St. John near City Park, an 18th-century plantation furnished in the Federal style. Open Wed. through Sat.

TOURS. *Bus.* Gray Line offers six tours covering various sections of the city as well as nightlife tours. A wide range of fees, with some special tours including a meal. Tours include French Quarter, Jackson Square, French Market, plantation homes and River Road, Garden District, parks, Mississippi River, bayous, Lake Pontchartrain, old cemeteries, Superdome, Bourbon Street and nightclubs. Hotel pickup and return. Other tour companies such as Southern and Dixieland also run regular tours. Destinations Unlimited offers tours with foreign-language-speaking guides in Limousines. Medicab of New Orleans offers sightseeing trips for the disabled including those in wheelchairs.

Boat. MV Voyageur leaves from foot of Canal St. for cruise into Intercoastal waterway, Bayou Barataria, and return through Harvey Canal. 5 hrs. Harbor cruise to Chalmette Battlefield, 2 hrs. *Mark Twain,* diesel-powered replica of sternwheeler steamboat, leaves Canal St. Dock for bayou trip, 5 hrs.; also a nightly dinner-dance cruise of 3 hrs. *S.S. President,* large sidewheel steamboat, offers a daily 2½ hr harbor cruise, leaving Canal St. dock. Sat. night cruise with jazz band, drinks, dancing. The 1600-passenger sternwheeler *Natchez* leaves from Toulouse St. Wharf at Jackson Square at 11:30 A.M. and 2:30 P.M. for two-hour cruises on the Mississippi from Chalmette Battlefield to Huey P. Long Bridge. Moonlight dance cruise Sat only. Dining rooms, cocktail lounges, snack bar. The *Commodore* leaves three times daily for a 2-hr. cruise to Chalmette National Historical Park. The smaller *Cotton Blossom* makes 1 daily 5½ hr. trip into bayou country.

On foot. The Friends of the Cabildo in conjunction with the Louisiana State Museum offers walking tours at 9:30 A.M. and 1:30 P.M., Mon. through Sat. from the Presbytere on Jackson Square. Free walking tours of the French Quarter are given daily from the Pontalba Unit of the Jean Lafitte National Historical Park, 527 St. Ann Street.

GARDENS. During the blooming time of camellias (late Nov. to Mar.) and azaleas (late Feb. to Apr.) New Orleans becomes a huge garden, with concentrated displays in almost all parks. Along the country roads of St. Tammany Parish, across the causeway from New Orleans, the tung trees and azaleas bloom profusely in late March. *Longue Vue House and Gardens,* 7 Bamboo Road, is an eight-acre city estate featuring a 20th-century mansion and magnificent gardens. Open to the public. Closed Mondays. *City Park* has a conservatory featuring bromeliads and formal gardens built during the depression, now under renovation.

STAGE AND REVUES. The burlesque queens and strippers of *Bourbon Street* are world famous, and they bring back memories and images of New Orleans' notorious Basin Street red-light district. *Saenger Performing Theater,* 1111 Canal Street, offers regular performances. *Le Petit Theatre du Vieux Carré,* 616 St. Peter St., is one of the oldest community theater groups in the country. Tulane, Loyola, and the University of New Orleans also present meritorious productions during the school year. *One Mo' Time,* a musical based on performances at the old Lyric Theater—destroyed in 1927—is presented every night, except Tuesday, at the *Toulouse Street Theater,* 615 Toulouse Street.

 NIGHTCLUBS. On Mardi Gras day the whole downtown area and French Quarter are turned into a mammoth party, with drinks (only in paper cups) on the streets and plenty of entertainment from the maskers. Throughout the year, along Bourbon St., at least every third door is a nightclub, with entertainment varying from the predominant bumps and grinds of energetic stripteasers to the music of *Pete Fountain* (New Orleans Hilton, Poydras St. and the Mississippi).

Fat City was never planned—it just happened. The area's high density of apartment dwellers fostered the first lounges more than 10 years ago. In 1972 several nightclub owners were driving around the area trying to create a name for the location. They saw a snowcone stand on the corner of Severn and 17th Sts. where the Lakeside Plaza sign now stands. The two boys had painted the name "Fat City" on it, to mean "you have arrived." Just minutes from downtown New Orleans, the area is headquarters for dining and nightlife in Metairie. It's bounded by Veterans Blvd., North Causeway, West Esplanade and Division Sts. Fat City consists of more than 70 shops, boutiques, restaurants and night spots. Morning Call, one of the French Quarter traditional stops for *café au lait* and *beignets,* has moved to Fat City and is open 24 hours daily.

 SHOPPING. Royal Street in the French Quarter is as filled with antique shops as Bourbon Street is with bars and nightclubs. The best American antiques may be found in the Magazine Street section. Souvenir shops are all over the French Quarter. And don't forget the delectable Creole pecan pralines. Unique local shops include *You Boutique,* 8131 Hampton St., which specializes in elegant and unusual hats, and *Town and Country,* 8131 St. Charles Ave., where the local debutantes buy their ball gowns. The most exciting shopping center is the one at Canal Place, where *Brooks Bros., Saks Fifth Ave., Gucci,* and *Laura Ashley* are located.

 SPECTATOR SPORTS: New Orlean's *professional football teams,* the *Saints* and the *Breakers,* and Tulane University's football team play at the Superdome.

 **HOTELS AND MOTELS.** Minimum night stays are required at Carnival (and during the Sugar Bowl football and sports events at the New Year) than at any other time of the year. Almost all the better hotels and motels in New Orleans have French- and Spanish-speaking staff members. Many people in South Louisiana are bilingual, speaking English and French.

Listings are in order of price category. Based on double occupancy without meals price categories and their ranges are as follows: *Superdeluxe,* $110 and up; *Deluxe,* $95–$110; *Expensive,* $70–$95; *Moderate,* $55–$70; *Inexpensive,* under $55. For a more complete explanation of hotel and motel categories see *Facts at Your Fingertips* at the front of this volume.

Fairmont. *Superdeluxe.* University Pl. Restaurant, coffee shop, bar, top entertainment, color TV, sitter list, 24-hr. rm. service.

Hotel Inter-Continental. *Superdeluxe.* 444 St. Charles Ave. In the heart of the Central Business District. This 480-room hotel has a health spa and a French restaurant.

Hyatt Regency. *Superdeluxe.* Poydras St. Plaza. Opened 1976. Adjacent to Superdome. 1200 rooms & suites, 5 restaurants & lounges including revolving rooftop lounge, pool, garden patio. Spectacular indoor garden lobby 21 stories high.

International Hotel. *Superdeluxe.* 300 Canal St. Lounge, bar, restaurant, terrace dining room. Pool, sauna.

Maison de Ville. *Superdeluxe.* 727 Rue Toulouse. 18th-century building, furnished with antiques. Complimentary breakfast, coffee, tea, soft drinks. Suites with kitchens available. Small pets permitted. Pool.

Marie Antoinette Hotel. *Superdeluxe.* 827 Toulouse St., in the French Quarter. Attractive rooms. Suites, dining room, dancing in the lounge. Pool.

Marriott Hotel. *Superdeluxe.* 555 Canal St. Dining rooms, coffee shop, lounges with entertainment. Beauty parlor, barber shop. Pool with service at poolside. List of sitters.

New Orleans Hilton. *Superdeluxe.* Located by New Orleans cruise terminal on the Mississippi. You can get oysters on the half-shell in the lobby. Very plush and new. Everything from atrium cafes to rooftop disco.

Pontchartrain Hotel. *Superdeluxe.* 2031 St. Charles Ave. This famous luxury hotel has a superior restaurant. This is THE hotel for New Orleans' social elite.

Royal Orleans Hotel. *Superdeluxe.* Royal & St. Louis Sts. This plush hotel has a fine restaurant, cocktail lounge with jazz, and coffee shop. Second lounge and pool on rooftop.

Royal Sonesta. *Superdeluxe.* 300 Bourbon St., in the French Quarter. Well-appointed rooms. Dining rooms, pool with service at poolside. Barber shop.

Saint Ann (formerly French Quarter Inn). *Superdeluxe.* 717 Conti St. Luxury accommodations in the French Quarter. Suites. Pool. Restaurant.

St. Louis Hotel. *Superdeluxe.* 730 Bienville St., in the French Quarter. Suites; some refrigerators. Restaurant. Continental breakfast.

Sheraton New Orleans. *Superdeluxe.* 500 Canal. Pool, two lounges, disco, 24-hour café.

Windsor Court Hotel. *Superdeluxe.* 300 Gravier St. All of the 330 guest rooms are suites that include complete kitchens and minibars.

Bienville House. *Deluxe.* 310 Decatur St. In French Quarter. European atmosphere with iron balconies and courtyard. Restaurant, pool.

Bourbon Orleans Ramada. *Deluxe.* 717 Orleans St. In the French Quarter. Very nicely furnished rooms. Refrigerators in some. Restaurant. Pool.

Dauphine Orleans Motor Hotel. *Deluxe.* 415 Dauphine St. in the French Quarter. Continental breakfast. Bagnio Lounge. Pool, pets.

Downtown Howard Johnson's. *Deluxe.* 330 Loyola Ave. in the business district. Restaurant, pool, indoor car park.

Holiday Inn-Chateau Le Moyne. *Deluxe.* 301 Dauphine St. in the French Quarter. Restaurant, lounge with entertainment. Pool, sauna, health spa.

Holiday Inn-French Quarter. *Deluxe.* 124 Royal St. Member of the chain. Complimentary coffee. Kennel. Pool. Restaurant, lounge with entertainment.

Maison DuPuy. *Deluxe.* 1001 Toulouse St. in the French Quarter. Furnished in French Provincial style. Restaurant, cabaret with live entertainment.

Monteleone Hotel. *Deluxe.* 214 Royal St. Lobby-entrance garage. Rooftop terrace with pool.

New Orleans Airport Hilton Inn. *Deluxe.* Airline Hwy., opp. Airport. Putting green, shuffleboard. Free airport transportation.

Le Pavillon. *Deluxe.* 833 Poydras. In the business district. Pool, saunas, dining room, bar. Spacious and luxurious. Near the Superdome.

Prince Conti. *Deluxe.* 830 Conti. In the French Quarter. Continental breakfast, bar, elegantly furnished suites.

Chateau Motor Hotel. *Expensive.* 1001 Chartres. In French Quarter. Patio and poolside cafe. Pets allowed.

Corn Stalk Hotel. *Expensive.* 915 Royal St. in the French Quarter. Continental breakfast. Antiques in rooms.

Place d'Armes Motor Hotel. *Expensive.* 625 St. Ann St. in the French Quarter. Pool, restaurant, patio.

Provincial Motel. *Expensive.* 1024 Chartres St., in French Quarter. Very pleasant rooms with antiques as part of the decor. Restaurant, pool, list of sitters.

St. Charles Hotel. *Expensive.* 2203 St. Charles St. Restaurants and lounge. Barber, beauty and other shops. Babysitters.

Sheraton Inn International Airport. *Expensive.* 2150 Veteran's Memorial Blvd. Restaurant, lounge with entertainment. Large pool, tennis, sauna and health spa. Airport transportation.

Columns Hotel. *Moderate.* 3811 St. Charles Ave. Uptown. Continental breakfast. The bar here is a local favorite.

Fountain Bay Club Hotel. *Moderate.* 4040 Tulane. Three pools, coffee shop, dining room, cocktail lounge, entertainment.

Holiday Inn. *Moderate.* There are six branches in the New Orleans area: **East-Highrise:** US 90 & I-10; **Fat City:** Causeway Exit South at I-10; **Airport:** 2929 Williams Blvd.; **Gretna:** 100 West Bank Expwy.; **Slidell:** I-10 & US 190; **Hammond:** US 51 at Jct. I-55 & I-12. All have restaurant, lounge, pool.

Howard Johnson's Motor Lodge. *Moderate.* At two locations: **East:** 4200 Old Gentilly Rd. & I-10 at Louisa St. exit; **Airport-West:** 6401 Veterans Memorial Blvd., Metairie. Restaurant, cocktail lounge, pool.

Lafitte Guest House. *Moderate.* 1003 Bourbon St. in the French Quarter. Has only 14 rooms. Continental breakfast.

LaMothe House. *Moderate.* 621 Esplanade Ave. across from the French Quarter. Antique furnishings, quaint atmosphere. Continental breakfast served in charming dining room.

Park View Guest House. *Moderate.* 7004 St. Charles Ave. Uptown. Wonderful location, adjacent to Audubon Park and across from Tulane and Loyola universities. Continental breakfast.

Patio Motel (Best Western). *Moderate.* 2820 Tulane Ave. in midtown. Babysitters, family plan. Putting green, 2 pools, free parking. Washerteria.

Le Richelieu Motor Hotel. *Moderate.* 1234 Chartres St. in the French Quarter. Coffee shop.

St. Charles Inn. *Moderate.* 3636 St. Charles Ave. Continental breakfast.

Scottish Inn. *Inexpensive.* 6613 W. Bank Expwy. (at Garden Rd.); and I-10 and US 190 in Slidell. Attractive place with pool, café, bar.

TraveLodge West. *Moderate.* Five locations in the area: **Downtown:** 1630 Canal; **East:** 5035 Chef Menteur; **Airport:** 2240 Veterans Blvd.; **Lake Forest:** 101000 I-10 service road; **West:** 2200 Westbank Expwy. All are moderate except Downtown, which is expensive.

Rodeway Inn. *Inexpensive to Moderate.* At four locations: 851 Airline Hwy. (airport); 930 West Bank Expwy. in Gretna; 6322 Chef Menteur Hwy. Downtown, 1725 Tulane. Restaurant, cocktail lounge, pools.

Maisonnette. *Inexpensive.* 1130 Chartres St. in the French Quarter. Rooms overlooking patio. No restaurant.

 DINING OUT. Fine creole cooking is a treat in New Orleans, but other cuisines can also be found here. Classic French fare is also a specialty. See the previous hotel listings for some other good restaurants. Price categories and ranges (for a complete dinner) are as follows: *Deluxe,* $30 and up; *Expensive,* $20–$30; *Moderate,* $10–$20; *Inexpensive,* under $10. Listings are in order of price category. For a more complete explanation of restaurant categories see *Facts at Your Fingertips* at the front of this volume.

EDITOR'S CHOICES

Rating restaurants is, at best, a subjective business, and obviously a matter of personal taste. It is, therefore, difficult to call a restaurant "the best" and hope to get unanimous agreement. The restaurants listed below are our choices of the best eating places in New Orleans, and the places we would choose if we were visiting the city.

LE RUTH'S
French Cuisine

Chef Warren Le Ruth owns and operates this remarkable establishment, and the limited French menu perfectly complements the intimate environment. The restaurant is three miles south of the center of the city, across the Mississippi River. Specialties include stuffed soft-shell crab, frog's legs meuniere, and a noisette of lamb for two. Excellent appetizers include Crabmeat St. Francis, and the bread is baked on the premises daily. Franklin St. (Gretna). *Deluxe.*

GALATOIRE'S
French/Creole

This old-fashioned, traditional dining room accepts no reservations, but patrons don't seem to mind standing in line watching the passing scene on Bourbon St. Excellent seafood includes Trout Marguery, Trout Meuniere Amandine, and broiled pompano. Excellent appetizers are topped by Shrimp Remoulade, and the Creole gumbo is in a class by itself. 209 Bourbon St. *Deluxe.*

CARIBBEAN ROOM
Continental/Creole

Located in the Pontchartrain Hotel, this pleasant establishment provides leisurely dining in its inviting dining rooms and patio. The menu is eclectic, and specialties include Shrimp Saki, Trout Veronique, Steak Diane, and a crepe souffle that must be ordered in advance. Mile-high ice cream pie provides a perfect dessert. 2031 St. Charles Ave. (Garden District). *Deluxe.*

ANTOINE'S
French/Creole

This is dining in the opulent, old tradition, and regular customers even have their own personal waiters. The large wine cellar is open to the public and worth a visit. This restaurant can accurately be described as a local landmark, and specialties include Oysters Rockefeller, Pompano en Papillote, and the Tournedos. Crepes Suzette are a favorite sweet, and the menu is full of dishes that are specifically associated with this exceptional establishment. 713 St. Louis St. *Deluxe.*

COMMANDER'S PALACE
French/Creole

Choose between indoor or patio dining at this Garden District landmark, which blossoms with the grandeur of the 1880s. If you order crayfish Etouffe or crabmeat Imperial, you may give up your landlubbering ways forever. The town turns out in force for the Sunday jazz brunch. Musicians stroll and stomp, and no two corners of the restaurant are on the ground at the same time. Eggs Basin Street make the perfect jazz accompaniment. 1403 Washington Avenue. *Expensive.*

BROUSSARD'S
French/Creole

A grand New Orleans tradition has been reopened. Most attractive interiors and the famous Bonaparte Patio. Cuisine is excellent and prices most reasonable in the Vieux Carre. Specialties are Duck Nouvelle Orleans, Chicken Ratatouille, Oysters Gresham, Trout Conti and caramel custard. 819 Conti. *Expensive.*

Other recommended restaurants:

Andrew Jackson. *Expensive.* 221 Royal St. Elegant service and atmosphere. Tour the kitchen to see the chef prepare trout Meuniere, lump crabmeat or Creole gumbo. Family-owned and operated.

Arnaud's Restaurant. *Expensive.* 811 Bienville St., at Bourbon St. World renowned French restaurant in the French Quarter. Wide selection of delectable dishes on their menu. Specialties: oysters Bienville, shrimp Arnaud and filet mignon Clemenceau. *The Richelieu Room* requires black tie. Children's portions.

Brennan's. *Expensive.* 417 Royal Street. Breakfast has gained renown, but lunch and dinner merit equal attention. Buster crabs Bernaise or poached pompano could make a seafood fancier out of anyone.

Christian's. *Expensive.* 3835 Iberville. French and Creole cuisine. Stuffed trout and Shrimp Madeleine are especially recommended.

Corinne Dunbar's. *Moderate.* 1617 St. Charles Ave. Creole dishes served in a lovely antebellum home with period furnishings. The set menu changes daily. Reservations required. Closed Sun. and Mon.

Court of Two Sisters. *Expensive.* 613 Royal St. French and Creole menu. In the French Quarter, in a beautiful garden setting.

Etienne's. *Expensive.* 3100 19th St., Metairie. French and Creole menu features trout meuniere and roast chicken.

La Louisiane. *Expensive.* 725 Iberville St. Steak, Italian dishes. Established 1835.

Lucky Pierre's. *Expensive.* 735 Bourbon. Delights include oysters in champagne sauce and catfish in crayfish sauce. This popular nightspot has recently undergone a fantastic renovation.

Bon Ton. *Expensive.* 401 Magazine St. Creole food. Excellent turtle soup and bread pudding.

Masson's. *Expensive.* 7200 Pontchartrain Blvd. An elegant suburban place to dine. The quiche is special and so is the seafood, especially the sauteed crab "fingers."

Mosca's. *Moderate.* On Highway 90 in Waggaman. Little atmosphere but the food is something else. Loyal crowd patronizes this restaurant.

Rib Room of the Royal Orleans Hotel. *Expensive.* Royal & St. Louis Sts. Specialties: rib roast and extensive English and American cuisine. Good wine cellar. Unusually attractive decor.

K. Paul's Louisiana Kitchen. *Expensive.* 416 Chartres St. Specialties include Blackened redfish and Cajun Popcorn, which is deep fried crayfish claws. Expect to wait in line at this very trendy spot.

Casamento's. *Inexpensive.* 4330 Magazine St. Oyster "poorboys" are terrific. Closed middle of June to middle of September.

Felix's. *Moderate.* 739 Iberville St., between Bourbon and Royal Sts. Seafood is their specialty. The oyster bar is a stopover for everyone. Closed Sun., Christmas, Mardi Gras.

Indulgence. *Moderate.* 1501 Washington Ave. A changing menu that is always delightful. Open for lunch and dinner.

Kolb's. *Moderate.* 125 St. Charles. Authentic Bavarian decor. Schnitzel à la Kolb, imported draft beer. Est. 1899.

Tujagues. *Moderate.* 823 Decatur St. Est. 1856. Well-prepared Creole and French dishes served family style. There is no menu choice.

Camellia Grill. *Inexpensive.* 626 So. Carrollton Ave. Pecan waffles are a local favorite.

Joe Petrossi's. *Inexpensive.* 901 Louisiana Ave. Locals go here for their seafood.

Riverbend. *Inexpensive.* 734 So. Carrollton Ave. Wonderful soups and quiches.

 COFFEE HOUSES. Across the square from St. Louis Basilica and down the street are the outdoor coffee houses of the French Market. Although the famed *Morning Call* coffee house has moved to Fat City, the *Cafe Du Monde,* next to the entrance to the Moon Walk (here you can watch the ships and barges make their way along the Mississippi), and the *Cafe Maison,* located a few shops over, offer the weary tourist some of that special New Orleans coffee *(café au lait)* and mouth-watering *beignets* (square, puffy doughnuts always freshly made). Open 24 hours a day the year-round. The French Market has recently undergone a renovation, and in addition to the Moon Walk park area and a parking lot for cars, there are a dozen shops and boutiques. In one shop you can watch pralines being made daily and can purchase cookery equipment and spices. There's a candle shop, a toy store and several snack spots, as well as a seafood house and the Farmer's Market, where shopping for fresh fruits and vegetables has been a tradition since New Orleans' earliest days. On weekends, the area next to the Farmer's Market is the Flea Market and attracts thousands of tourists and locals. Scattered through the French Quarter are countless other small coffee houses and pastry shops. Locals go to *La Marquise Pastry Shop,* 625 Chartres St. and the *Gumbo Shop,* 630 St. Peter St. for breakfast.

Exploring Louisiana

Travel in Louisiana was once determined by its waterways; the vast, serpentine Mississippi and the state's innumerable lakes, rivers, and bayous. (A bayou, by the way, is a marshy inlet or tributary; the word comes from the Choctaw *Bayuk*—"small stream.") The first roads were the navigable streams. Early French explorers followed the great river south as it tumbled the silt of the east down-country toward the Gulf of Mexico. French, German, Acadian, Spanish, and American pioneers followed in time to establish settlements. Frontier river outposts became great cities and picturesque towns, and vast industrial complexes now cover ground where Indians once hunted.

Today, this watery network has been supplanted by a fine highway system, and there is a wide choice of routes for the traveler to explore. For example, if you should be driving southward through the state to New Orleans, it is possible to stop at as many as forty magnificent mansions, gardens, and plantations.

The route described in this guide begins at New Orleans and ends at Shreveport; but if you wish to return to New Orleans, it is possible to do so without retracing your path. This is because the route, in order to give the most complete coverage, outlines the shape of an hourglass, with its corners near the state's four corners and its waist at the state's central city of Alexandria.

The first leg of the journey crosses the state from New Orleans in the east to Lake Charles in the west, taking in Baton Rouge and Lafayette and lingering along the way among the charming and unique attractions of southern Louisiana. Next the route swings up on a long diagonal to Monroe in the northeast, and finally west across to Shreveport, the state's northern industrial center. As will be clear by tracing this itinerary on a map, the "hourglass" may be completed, if you wish to return to New Orleans, by striking southeast on the corresponding long diagonal from Shreveport to New Orleans.

From New Orleans

There are three ways to reach Baton Rouge by car. One way is by Airline Highway (US 61). A faster and more scenic route is along I-10. One elevated portion goes above a corner of Lake Ponchartrain and over the Bonnet Carre Spillway flood control area. The spillway does just what its name suggests; its 350 weirs provide an outlet through which, at high flood stages, the rampaging Mississippi waters may be diverted to Lake Pontchartrain. Since its construction in 1927, the spillway has saved New Orleans from floods several times.

By following the winding River Road (State 48) the visitor will travel along the Mississippi and see a procession of stately antebellum plantation homes, remnants of the class of wealthy planters before the War Between the States.

The first of these are Ormonde (not open to the public) and Destrehan (open daily), both late-18th-century plantation homes.

The River Road changes to State 44 at LaPlace, where crawfish bisque at Roussel's is a good idea if you're hungry.

See San Francisco (open daily), an authentic restoration of mid-19th-century architecture, a Gothic gem, covered with scrolls, fluted pillars and carved grillwork.

Further toward Baton Rouge, there is a free ferry at Lutcher, where you might want to take a detour across the Mighty Mississippi to see Oak Alley (open daily), with its overhead canopy of interlaced branches of huge oaks, one of the state's most famous plantation homes.

North of Oak Alley, on the River Road 2 miles north of White Castle, is Nottoway Plantation, the largest (64 rooms) and most impressive of the antebellum homes. Limited overnight accommodations. Reservations a must.

Come back across the river at Lutcher and continue on State Highway 44 to pass Manressa, a superb columned group of buildings, now a Jesuit retreat for laymen.

All along the River Road there are many south Louisiana-style, small, charming homes and stores amidst the many chemical plants that add to the industrial economy of Baton Rouge and New Orleans.

At Burnside, the River Road changes to LA 75. Continue to Houmas House (open daily), a magnificent restoration of home and gardens. Further on you'll pass Bocage (private), L'Hermitage (private) and Ashland Belle Helene (open and interesting, but not in good condition).

At Geismar, turn off for LA 30 and continue into Baton Rouge.

Baton Rouge

The Indians called it *Istrouma*—a tall cypress, its bark stripped to expose the ruddy wood beneath, adorned with freshly killed game. Set on the bluffs overlooking the river, it marked the boundary between the Houma and Bayougoula tribal hunting grounds. In 1699, someone in the

Iberville-Bienville party pushing up the Mississippi marked the spot on his map: *le baton rouge* ("the red staff"). The name stuck.

A good place to take a first look at Baton Rouge is from the observation platform atop the thirty-four-story capitol building (open daily) dating from 1932 and the gubernatorial term of Huey Long. Three years later the colorful and unscrupulous Long, then a U.S. Senator, was assassinated in the same building. His grave and monument now face the capitol.

Amid the twenty-seven acres of formal gardens on the capitol grounds is a curious structure called the Old Arsenal Museum (closed Tuesday). The building is thought to have been used for different purposes in various eras, most recently as a Civil War prison. That it was originally a Spanish arms storehouse is suggested by details such as four-foot thick walls and winding air vents to keep out stray bullets. It is now filled with exhibits on the theme "Louisiana Under Ten Flags."

The Old Capitol, downtown at St. Philip and North Boulevard, has been fondly preserved with its hand-wrought iron fence, spiral staircase, and stained glass skylight. An unusual blend of Norman, Gothic, and Moorish styles, the building was the object of both praise and criticism upon its completion in 1847. Mark Twain called it "the Monstrosity of the Mississippi" and recommended dynamite!

The Old State Capitol, now on the National Register of Historic Places, is open daily and has information hostesses to help you.

Across the street from the Old Capitol is the Louisiana Arts and Science Center Riverside, located in a remodeled railroad station (open daily except Mondays). Here you can find exhibits of art, natural history, anthropology, a gift shop, tea room and such, plus a marvelous viewing area of the port of Baton Rouge.

The Louisiana Arts and Science Center, at 502 North Blvd., was originally the official Governor's Residence. It has been restored and houses Louisiana Governor artifacts and excellent historical exhibits (open daily except Mondays). There is a planetarium next door.

One and one-half miles south of downtown Baton Rouge, on LA 30, is Magnolia Mound Plantation House, a French settler's cottage of 1791. It is open daily (except Mondays) and is an authentic restoration with superb furnishings and interesting out buildings and grounds.

Just south of Magnolia Mound, also on LA 30 is the LSU campus. The school's campus covers more than 200 acres; here and there are Indian mounds estimated to be over 750 years old. There are pleasant lake areas to relax in and a number of museums. The library has a collection of the "elephant folio" prints by Audubon.

The Anglo-American Museum in the Memorial Tower is a gem of a small museum, well worth seeing. LSU Rural Life Museum (Essen Lane at I-10) is a collection of 19th century buildings, including typical plantation buildings.

Two miles south of LSU is Mount Hope Plantation, 8151 Highland Road, a magnificent restoration of an early Louisiana home (1817) with West Indian influence (open daily). Limited overnight accomodations.

Southern University, the nation's largest predominately black university, is located on the bluffs overlooking the river (5 mi. north via US 61).

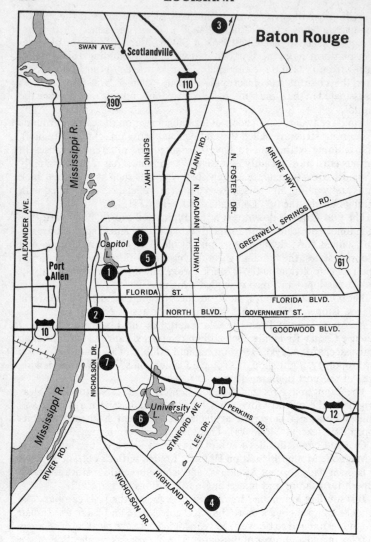

Points of Interest

1) Arsenal Museum
2) Old State Capitol
3) Cohn Memorial Arboretum
4) Mount Hope Plantation
5) Governor's Mansion
6) Louisiana State University
7) Magnolia Mound
8) State Capitol

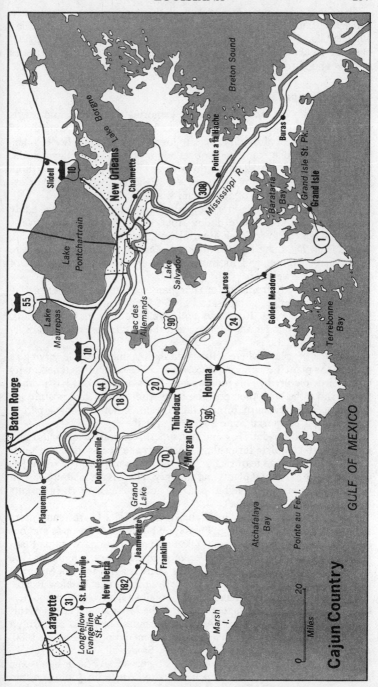

Cajun Country

There is a zoo some distance from the center of town that covers a 140-acre expanse, with walkways through forest settings for more than 500 animals. Cohn Memorial Arboretum (Foster Rd. off Comite Drive) has over 16 acres of rolling terrain covered by more than 120 varieties of trees and shrubs.

Baton Rouge Side Trips

The city may be used as a base for exploring the historic old towns of the surrounding country and the Atchafalaya Basin. Roughly 45 minutes to the west of Baton Rouge, following Interstate 10, lies Henderson, La. where one can arrange boat tours of the Atchafalaya Basin. Contact Mrs. Barbara Hanks at the McGee's Landing. To the north lie the handsome parishes of East and West Feliciana, which must be explored to get the flavor of antebellum Louisiana.

Clinton, thirty-five miles north of Baton Rouge via St. 67, has a stately white-columned courthouse dating from 1838. Facing it is Lawyer's Row, a block of five Greek Revival buildings dating from 1825-30. Scenes from *The Long Hot Summer* and *The Sound and the Fury* were filmed here. Clinton and its outskirts are an antiquarian's dream of pre-Civil War dwellings.

Jackson (State 10 from Clinton) has many old churches and attractive buildings. Further along on State 10 is St. Francisville and a cluster of fine plantation homes. Rosedown and Oakley are the most significant. Propinquity, Asphodel, the Myrtles, and the Cottage offer limited overnight accommodations.

Oakley is the place where artist-naturalist Audubon, while serving as tutor to the plantation children, observed, collected, and sketched many of the birds pictured in his monumental *Birds of America*. His method was to shoot the bird, then position it on wires in a lifelike posture for sketching. The excellently furnished and restored home is now a part of the Audubon Memorial State Park. Open daily.

Rosedown (open daily) is another superb restoration of house and grounds with complete furnishings, paintings and accessories. It's a distinguished showplace featuring a 30-acre garden inspired by Versailles, containing rare Oriental plants and statuary. There is a house and garden tour (children are welcome but must be accompanied by their parents to be admitted to the house).

North a few miles from St. Francisville, on US 61, are many more plantation homes. The Cottage Plantation has tours of grounds and out buildings, and provides overnight guest accommodations. Catalpa Plantation, open daily except during December and January, is a manor-type home with original antique furnishings. There is a free ferry at St. Francisville for river crossings, and it is worth taking to get to New Roads. This pleasant town lies on False River, actually not a river but a boomerang-shaped lake that eons ago was part of the Mississippi. (Lakes of this shape are called oxbow lakes.) About three miles northwest of town on the River Road is Labatur, an architectual gem dating from about 1800. A mile further west is another old home, Stonewall.

State 1 follows False River, on whose banks survive such handsome plantation homes as Parlange (open daily) and Austerlitz (not open; can be viewed from road). The road connects with US 190, which can be taken west to Opelousas, one of the state's oldest settlements and a very attractive town. Frontiersman Jim Bowie lived here in his youth. The food here is good, particularly the gumbo at Dedee's Restaurant. In the fall Opelousas holds a yam festival.

Magnolia Ridge, built by a Confederate officer and later commandeered as a Union headquarters, is six miles north of Opelousas on State 10.

Four miles north of town on State 182 is the quaint little town of Washington. In the same neighborhood is Arlington Plantation. Perched over its entrance is an unusual dormer wing, once a classroom for the owner's children.

From Opelousas, US 167 swings southward toward Lafayette, the "hub of Acadiana." Grand Couteau, near Sunset, has two fine old structures dating from the 1830's. St. Charles College now serves as a Jesuit novitiate, while the Sacred Heart Academy is still a girls' school. Both are beautifully landscaped with gigantic oaks and flowering shrubs.

Acadian Lafayette

Lafayette, a fast-growing city that bills itself as the "Capitol of French Louisiana," is a good base from which to explore the surrounding attractions of Acadiana.

This city, which now boasts a multimillion-dollar Oil Center, was once part of the territory of the Attakapas Indians. Tourist information can be obtained from the city's tourist bureau at 16th St. and the Evangeline Thruway.

At University Ave. and Johnston St., the handsome campus of the University of Southwestern Louisiana covers more than eight hundred acres. There are horticultural laboratories, and a Maison Acadienne dedicated to the perpetuation of French and Acadian traditions.

On Mardi Gras, Lafayette's carnival celebration is second only to New Orleans' gala pre-Lenten festival, drawing upwards of 100,000 people. The popular Festivals Acadiens takes place during the third weekend in September, and features Acadian food, music, arts, crafts, and dramatic and literary presentations.

If it is the right weekend in spring for the biennial Crawfish Festival (held in even-numbered years), those who enjoy eating this shrimplike food might want to visit Breaux Bridge, nine miles northeast of Lafayette, for the celebration. Several area restaurants offering country French cuisine serve special dinners of crawfish prepared every possible way, from bisque to boiled to étouffée.

Located off Ridge Road in the southwestern part of the city is the Acadian Village and Gardens. Ten acres of landscaped grounds surround the village, which presents an authentic vision of 19th-century Acadian society.

Southeast of Lafayette is St. Martinville, one of the oldest and most charming small places in Louisiana. In the early days of French and Spanish rule it was known, after the name of the regional tribe, as Poste des Attakapas. Settled in the 18th century by Acadian and French royalist refugees, the town became an early center of culture and elegant living where richly dressed nobles attended luxurious balls and operas; often it was spoken of as "Le Petit Paris."

Later, when the United States took over the Teche country, tensions between the two cultures were expressed in laws which forbade, among other things, biting off ears. The French replied by suspending municipal government until the U.S. came to terms.

St. Martin de Tours Church on Main Street is the oldest Catholic Church in Louisiana that is still in use. Exhibited inside are a baptismal font said to have been bestowed on his royalist friends by Louis XVI before his career was ended by the French Revolution, an oil painting of St. Martin, and a replica of the Lourdes grotto. Completing these unusual mementos is a statue of Evangeline, the Acadian heroine made legend in Longfellow's narrative poem, in a little cemetery outside the church. The life-size seated bronze statue was the gift of actress Dolores del Rio, who lived in St. Martinville during the filming of the movie about Evangeline.

The Evangeline Oak, on the banks of Bayou Teche at the foot of Port Street, is the most popular tourist attraction in town. Across the street is the Convent of Mercy, a very old building, once a trading post, now a school run by the Sisters of Mercy.

At the edge of St. Martinville is the attractive Longfellow-Evangeline State Commemorative Area. In this pastoral setting the Acadian Plantation House, an excellent example of a Louisiana raised cottage, dates from about 1765 and contains rustic frontier furnishings of the 18th and 19th centuries. Cajun crafts of weaving, palmetto work, and basketry are displayed and sold in the Acadian Handicraft Shop. Picnic shelters with tables and grills are available in the park; however, camping is no longer allowed on the grounds.

About two miles out of St. Martinville on the Catahoula Road stands Oak and Pine Alley, once the site of the Durand plantation. The story is that Durand, seeking to celebrate his daughter's wedding with something unheard-of, imported giant Chinese spiders to festoon the trees with webs. The great webs were sprinkled with silver and gold dust, it is said, to form a gauzy, glittering archway for the wedding guests.

Further to the northeast is Lake Catahoula, sacred pool of the Attakapas, where there is crabbing, fishing, and a seasonal crawfish harvest.

Fourteen miles south of St. Martinville on Highway 31 is New Iberia, first settled by Spaniards from the Canary Islands who named it Nuevo Iberia ("New Spain"). The town, billed as "Queen City of the Teche," has a variety of attractions.

Shadows-on-the-Teche, a stately mansion in the heart of town, now the property of the National Trust for Historical Preservation, was built in 1830. Stately moss-draped trees and a formal garden of roses, camellias, azaleas, and other flowering shrubs adjoin a handsome lawn sloping to the banks of the Bayou Teche. Open to the public.

There is an Acadian Regional Tourist Information Center for the town, quartered in a plantation cabin built of native cypress about 1880 (US 90 at State 14). At 541 E. Main is the Gebert Oak, a magnificent specimen shading almost an entire lawn with its limbs overgrown with fern and Spanish moss. It was planted in 1831 by Mrs. Jonas Marsh over the grave of her son.

At Weeks and St. Peter streets is a seven-foot, white marble statue of the emperor Hadrian, created in Rome about 130 A.D.

Three miles east of New Iberia on the Loreauville Road (State 86) is the Justine Plantation and Bottle Museum. The house, built by slave labor in 1822, was moved by barge some fifty miles up the Bayou Teche to its present location. It is built of native cypress and has a Gothic stairway and honeycolored woodwork. The bottle museum is a quaint country store displaying a collection of rare and unusual bottles, from flasks to inkpots to Mason jars.

Six miles further east on State 86 is the Heritage Village Museum in Loreauville. Open limited hours or by appointment. This is a complex of buildings and artifacts spanning three centuries of territorial history. They range from burial-mound objects to the Attakapas Indian Trading post to a turn-of-the-century village complete with log-cabin school, saloon, and country store. (If it's not open when you stop by, knock on the front door of the house in front of the museum, and chances are they'll open it up just for you.)

Seasonal festivals include the fall Sugar Cane Festival in New Iberia, featuring pageants, sports, and dances, and the annual Delcambre shrimp festival and fair. Delcambre, fifteen miles west of New Iberia on State 14 on the old Bayou Carline, is the home port of a colorful 150-vessel fleet of shrimpboats and seafood docks. Deep sea fishing trips are available with prior notification.

Jefferson Island (which, like Avery and Weeks, is not really an island at all) is seven miles southwest of New Iberia. Besides its underground caverns of salt (the eight hundred-foot shaft is no longer open to visitors) Jefferson Island has a horticultural paradise called Rip Van Winkle's Live Oak Gardens. It was once a hideout of Lafitte, and legends of buried booty were substantiated when in 1923 a treasure of gold and silver coins in three pots was uncovered near the Lafitte Oaks.

After the Civil War, the island was bought by Joseph Jefferson, famous 19th-century actor who portrayed Rip Van Winkle in the dramatic adaptation of Irving's story. The big house built by Jefferson in 1870 from native cypress shows a mixture of Hispano-Moorish, Gothic, and Southern architecture. (Not open to visitors.) The opulent gardens cover twenty acres of woodland, footpaths, fountains, and formal and informal plantings. Two-thirds of the gardens were ruined in 1980 when a lake and its shoreline fell into a subterranean salt dome. The area, still undergoing renovation, is temporarily closed.

Using New Iberia as a base for further forays, a drive nine miles south will take you to Avery Island, a stately showplace developed as a private preserve by the late E.A. McIllhenny. The "island" is a salt dome pushed up from sea-level marshland, producing rock salt from its mine, oil from its wells, and the world-famous Tabasco sauce from its pepper fields. For a fee, the tourist may drive through the two hundred-acre Jungle Gardens, landscaped with native and exotic plants, trees, and flowering shrubs. A giant statue of Buddha stands in a Chinese garden along the route. Bird City refuge attracts nesting egrets and herons in spring.

Weeks Island, another salt mine, is nine miles farther south; and another nine miles south is Cypremort Point, where there is swimming, fishing, and boating on West Cote Blanche Bay, an arm of the Gulf of Mexico.

Before leaving New Iberia to resume the westward journey, you might want to spend some time enjoying the town's own forty-five-acre park on the north bank of the bayou. It has tennis courts, picnic shelters, a pool, and boat-launching ramp beneath centuries-old oak trees.

From New Iberia it is best to return to Lafayette before proceeding. From there, Interstate 10 runs straight west to Lake Charles. (If you wish to curtail touring at this point, there is a choice of retracing your route to Opelousas and from there heading north to Alexandria, or striking north on State 13, further along I-10, after Rayne.)

Frog Festival at Rayne

Rayne, near I-10 and the first stopping place after Lafayette, is known as the Frog Capital of the World. There is a frog festival in the fall, celebrating the town's export of this delicacy to gourmet establishments around the country.

Crowley, eight miles further on, is the center of the country's rice production and home of the October Rice Festival. Irrigation systems transform the vast fields on either side of the highway into lakes each spring, later turning to endless acres of grain. The Chamber of Commerce can arrange visits to rice mills and to a rice experimental station.

Five miles southwest of Crowley off State 13 is the Blue Rose Museum. Built of cypress more than one hundred years ago, the building has the original pegged construction, cypress paneling, handmade bricks, and mud and moss walls. Collections of fine china, cut glass, silver, and antiques are on display. Rice cookbooks and souvenirs are sold.

Lake Charles, Louisiana's third seaport, is the center of an important petro-chemical empire. The port offers a busy scene of American and foreign ships loading and unloading. Visitors are often allowed on board. Lake Charles is the home of McNeese State University (Country Club Road, leading into University Drive). Once a neutral buffer zone between Spanish Texas and American Louisiana, this area sheltered pirates and smugglers. The early May Contraband Days, a festival featuring a water sports carnival, commemorates this tradition.

The Imperial Calcasieu Museum, Sallier and Ethel Streets, has historical exhibits with mannikins in furnished settings and a collection of original Audubon prints. The Sallier Oak is on the grounds; it was planted long ago by Charles Sallier, after whom the city is named.

About 12 miles north of Lake Charles off LA 378 is the 1,068-acre Sam Houston Jones State Park. Located on the Calcasieu River amid pine-clad hills, the park's facilities include camp and picnic grounds, stone cabins, and boat facilities with launching sites. Children will enjoy the wild deer compound.

Alexandria-Pineville

Striking north from I-10 some miles east of Lake Charles, US 165 leads toward Alexandria. The drive is about seventy-five miles.

Alexandria and its twin city Pineville on the opposite bank of the Red River mark the geographical center of the state, where the earth shades from red clay to moist black. The first settlements in the area were established in the mid-1700s when a French outpost was placed on the Pineville side of Red River, which separates the two towns. They called the area "Les Rapides" because of the rapids located just above the outpost. Just above the city is the site of Bailey's Dam, an outstanding engineering achievement of the Civil War. When the fall of the Red River trapped the Union fleet above the rapids, its destruction appeared certain until Lieutenant Colonel Joseph Bailey constructed a dam which raised the water sufficiently for the Union warships to navigate the shoals.

The old national cemetery in Pineville is the resting place of war dead from the Indian, Mexican, Civil, Spanish-American, and later wars. Also in Pineville is Mt. Olivet Church, built in 1853. It escaped burning during the Civil War because it housed Union troops.

Each of the twin cities has an institution of higher learning, Louisiana College at Pineville and a branch of LSU at Alexandria.

The Alexandria Museum, open daily, is housed on the Rapides Bank Building, constructed in 1898, at the corner of Main and Murray Streets.

There is a choice of side trips to be made from Alexandria before proceeding northeast to Monroe. Some thirty miles southeast on State 1 is the Marksville Prehistoric Indian Park, containing a number of Indian mounds and a museum of Indian life and art. There are also barbecue pits. A short distance north are the ruins of Fort DeRussy, a Confederate mud fort which fell to Union forces during the 1864 Red River campaign.

All of Alexandria and many plantations and homes in the outlying area were burned during the War Between the States. However, still standing and open to the public is the Kent House, completed in 1800. It was built by the father of one of the members of the board of directors of the Louisiana Seminary of Learning, which opened in 1860 with William Tecumseh Sherman as director. Union troops also spared Rosalie Plantation and Tyrone Plantation, both owned by men serving on the Seminary board of directors.

The seminary burned in 1868 and was moved to Baton Rouge, later becoming Louisiana State University. The site, marked by signs and a few stones, is on Hwy. 71 north.

Some 14 miles northwest of Alexandria, on Bayou Rapides Road, is Hot Wells Health Resort, where mineral waters flow from the ground at a temperature of 113 degrees. There's a motel and restaurant, as well as camping grounds, but the bath house is currently closed.

From Alexandria the most direct route to Monroe is US 165 north. However, if time permits, a westward swing to Natchitoches on State 1 allows more sightseeing. Beyond Natchitoches one can proceed east and north on State 6, US 84, and (at Winnfield) State 34.

If using this longer route, you will find places to visit near Cloutierville. Little Eva plantation is here. Robert McAlpin, a New Englander, was rumored to be the model for Simon Legree in Harriet Beecher Stowe's *Uncle Tom's Cabin.* During the Chicago World's Fair of 1893 one of the plantation's cabins was exhibited as the original home of Uncle Tom. A replica of the cabin along with the "graves" of Uncle Tom and Legree are nearby.

The Bayou Folk Museum in the same area has period furniture and displays depicting the history of the Cane River country. Those who are familiar with the work of Kate Chopin, distinguished author of *The Awakening,* will want to stop here, for the museum was once her home.

North of Cloutierville are Cane River plantations Beau Fort and Oakland.

Natchitoches

Natchitoches, a charming river town and farm center, is the oldest town in the Louisiana Purchase territory. It was established in 1714—four years before New Orleans—by Louis Juchereau de St. Denis, who built Fort St. Jean Baptiste here as a French outpost and trading center. A replica of Fort St. Jean Baptiste, finished in 1981, is open to the public.

Front street on Cane River provides the most charming prospect of any town in Louisiana. Many old buildings and antebellum homes remain along the river and side streets. The attractive campus of Northwestern State University dates from the 1880's. Melrose Plantation, 16 miles south of Natchitoches, is a typical Louisiana-style plantation, built in 1833. The grounds surrounding the plantation feature the Yucca House, the original main house built in 1796, and the African House, c. 1800, a strange-looking construction reminiscent of the straw-thatched huts found in the Congo.

Once the largest trading post in the South, the quaint town holds an historical tour every fall, when many of the private homes are opened to the public. For sightseers, Natchitoches is a miniature New Orleans. It was here that the El Camino Real (King's Highway) originated, winding westward and southward all the way to Mexico City.

The Cane River Country is the home of Clementine Hunter, sometimes called "the black Grandma Moses," whose bright and gay paintings in the style of the primitive school have attracted national notice.

Visitors who reach Natchitoches during the Christmas season will find themselves winding among a fairyland of lights, for streets, buildings, riverbanks, and bridges blaze with over 140,000 lights.

Between Natchitoches and Winnfield are a complex of lakes and bayous which abound with black bass, bream white and yellow bass, crappie, catfish, and pickerel. Fishermen will have Black Lake, Black Lake Bayou, Clear Lake, Prairie Lake, Saline Bayou, Saline Lake, and Chee Chee Bay to choose from.

Continuing to Winnfield, US 84 leads through a division of Kisatchie National Forest, a huge preserve for wildlife with uncommon species of birds and plants.

Winnfield itself is the center of timber production and the scene, each fall, of the State Forest Festival. For this event the town becomes one huge lumber camp, with the townsfolk dressed in lumberjack gear. Huey Long was born on Maple Street in Winnfield, and practiced law here for several years before entering politics.

From Winnfield, State 34 north leads to Monroe. Monroe on the Ouachita ("Washitaw") River is one of Louisiana's oldest settlements, established in 1785 as Ouachita Post. Later, when the post was stockaded against Indians, it was called Fuerto Miro after the Spanish governor of Louisiana. Its present name came about after the time in 1819 when the steamboat *James Monroe* tied up here. Evidently the visit was so convivial that the townsfolk decided to commemorate it by renaming the town.

In the 19th century, Monroe was a center of cotton production and export. After the discovery that the entire parish of Ouachita rested upon a vast pool of natural gas, Monroe and West Monroe (across the river) became a thriving industrial region.

Attractions in Monroe include Rebecca's Doll Museum, 4500 Bon Aire Drive, and the Isaiah Garrett House, 520 South Grand Street. The Masur Museum is an attractive art gallery with educational and cultural exhibits, and there is a Little Theatre housed in the Strauss Playhouse. The Louisiana Purchase Gardens and Zoo has a one hundred-acre park with formal gardens, moss-laden oaks, and winding waterways. The zoo uses natural settings. *Louisiana Legend,* an outdoor drama in Kiroli Park, is presented on Saturday evenings in July.

Northeast Louisiana University's campus has an art gallery, and in Hanna Hall there are geological exhibits and displays of Indian, Latin American, and African artifacts.

If there is time for an excursion to the east before heading west for Shreveport, take US 80 east, stopping first at Rayville. A dozen miles south of Rayville on State 135 is Alto, where in 1916 a gas well caught fire. It burned for fifteen years. The crater, three hundred feet across and sixty feet deep, was filled with water to create a swimming pool.

Sixteen miles east from Rayville on US 80 is Delhi, legendary hideout of Frank and Jesse James. The Carpenter House, a stagecoach inn during the 1850's, still stands here.

Poverty Point

About twenty miles from Delhi is the significant prehistoric Indian site of Poverty Point. The route is by State 17 north to Epps about sixteen miles and then right on State 134 for about five miles. A state park with a museum is located at Poverty Point.

The Poverty Point Indianas, numbering perhaps as many as six thousand, built their community on terraces more than 2,700 years ago. Although for years Indians relics had been found in the neighborhood, it was not until relatively recently that excavations showed the area's importance. Dr. James A. Ford of the American Museum of Natural History said of it: "Poverty Point is in every way one of the most remarkable sites in the Americas. . . . It is undoubtedly the earliest site yet discovered in the Lower Mississippi Valley and is the most complex and interesting I have seen in this country."

Twenty miles east of Delhi on US 80 is Tallulah, not far from the Mississippi border. It has an interesting courthouse and several plantation homes.

Returning to Monroe, you can now complete the last lap of the "hourglass" tour by heading east toward Shreveport on I-20.

The route passes Ruston, a charming town and the seat of Lincoln Parish, named for Abraham Lincoln in 1873. This area was settled by emigrants from Georgia and the Carolinas who flocked here after the Louisiana Purchase in 1803. Grambling College and Louisiana Tech, an engineering school, are located here. The Kidd-Davis House, 609 N. Vienna Street, now the home of the Lincoln Parish Museum and the Lincoln Visitor Bureau, is one of the oldest homes in Ruston. The two-story house was built shortly after 1874.

If it is spring, travelers who value scenic routes might want to take a northerly detour at Minden in order to enjoy the eighteen-mile Dogwood Trail Drive. Six miles northeast of Minden you can stop to see a restored Germantown community. One of the communal villages which were started in hundreds of places throughout the country during the 19th century by various religious and progressive groups, this one dates from 1836. A few of the original buildings still remain, along with the cemetery. The experiment lasted from 1836 to 1871.

To reach the Dogwood Trail Drive, head north on State 7 about four miles west of Minden. At Springhill, the Drive winds west on State 157 to Plain Dealing. It is a drive through the state's highest hills, among flowering dogwood, redbud, and wild flowers.

Shreveport

The earliest settlers in Shreveport were the Caddo Indians, who built dome-shaped straw houses in circular communities on the bluffs overlooking Red River and its tributaries.

In 1832, modern Shreveport was founded by a group including Captain Henry Shreve, an American trader and steamboat builder. Development of the area was hindered by the presence of a logjam in the Red River, where driftwood, snags, and treetrunks had accumulated for a century and a half. Then Captain Shreve invented a battering-ram type vessel to clear away the "Great Raft," as the log jam was called, cutting a navigable channel through it. In 1835, the town was purchased from the Caddos for $80,000.

Shreveport is situated in the center of the Ark-La-Tex (the combined corners of Arkansas, Louisiana and Texas).

There are three major annual events at Shreveport. In fall, the State Fair attracts half a million visitors during its ten-day run with music (the city considers itself a Country-Western capital), auto races, rodeo exhibitions, arts and crafts displays, carnival rides, band concerts, and fireworks. Adjacent to the fairgrounds is the Louisiana State Exhibit Museum with its doughnut-shaped exhibit building containing dioramas, an art gallery, historical murals, archeological relics and planetarium.

Another big event is the ten-day Holiday in Dixie each April. It is a round of flower shows, sports competitions, an air show, carnival, treasure hunt, pet show, two fancy-dress balls, and a grand finale parade. The city's brochure promises ten days "packed with a sort of leisurely frenzy!"

Then there's the Red River Revel, held in fall, which is "a celebration of the arts" on the riverfront.

Civil War students will be interested in the site of Fort Humbug, whose weapons were hollowed logs blackened to simulate cannon. This "defense" was set up during the Red River Campaign of 1864 to dissuade Union General Banks from attacking. However, since Banks never reached Shreveport, having been routed in the battles of Mansfield and Pleasant Hill, Fort Humbug was never called upon to fire its unfireable cannon.

There is a branch of LSU and Southern University at Shreveport, and Centenary College, oldest liberal arts college west of the Mississippi, is here, too. A Methodist institution, Centenary was founded in 1825. The

Marjorie Lyons playhouse presents dramas throughout the year. Community Theatre has always been active in Shreveport. Besides the Shreveport Little Theatre, there's also the Gaslight Players and a Gilbert and Sullivan Society. With its own symphony orchestra, concerts and opera performances are common occurrences. Famed pianist Van Cliburn makes his home in Shreveport.

The R. W. Norton Art Gallery, on Creswell Ave. in a forty-acre wooded and landscaped park, with azalea gardens, has thirteen exhibition galleries containing European and American painting, tapestries, sculpture, and silverwork. It has a double-elephant folio edition of Audubon's *Birds of America.*

A fascinating display of France's Jean Despujols paintings and drawings of Indochina, which he did between 1936 and 1938, are housed in the Meadows Museum of Art on the Centenary College campus.

The Barnwell Cultural Center, near the city's business district, is an imposing modern structure dedicated to art and horticulture. Plantings are sheltered in a 7,850-square-foot domed conservatory.

Cross Lake, at the city's western edge, offers fishing, hunting, boating, and water sports.

KRMD broadcasts weekly performances of the Louisiana Hayride. The broadcast originates at Hayride USA near Bossier City. Hank Williams, Elvis Presley, and Johnny Cash, just to name a few, have performed at the Hayride. A live show and dance is held every Saturday night.

The American Rose Center, with its Windsound Carillon Towers, is also located west of Shreveport. Rustic paths wander through 118 acres of water, trees and breathtaking roses in various garden settings.

For entertainment, you might try Shreve Square, a cluster of nightclubs, restaurants, and shops, in Shreveport, or the "Bossier City Strip" in nearby Bossier City.

Bossier City is home of Louisiana Downs thoroughbred racetrack, with its completely glass-enclosed, air-conditioned club house, grandstand and several restaurants. Track season runs late spring into fall.

The "hourglass" tour is now complete, although, as mentioned before, it is possible to return to New Orleans by a different southerly route, taking in such sights as the Mansfield Battlepark and Museum, four miles southeast of Mansfield on LA 175, and Hodges Gardens, south of Many and north of Leesville on US 171. The 4,700-acre Hodges Gardens, the "Garden in the Forest," is one of the South's most famous and features scenic drives and walkways, spectacular greenhouse displays, waterfalls, and lakes with excursion boats. Adjacent to the Gardens is the Toro Hills Golf and Tennis Resort, with golf course and tennis courts. Many is just a few miles to the east from Toledo Bend Lake, a bass fisherman's delight that extends north and south along the Louisiana-Texas border. Mansfield is the site of one of the most famous battles ever fought on Louisiana soil. Both sides claimed victory in this bitter battle during the War Between the States, a battle that involved 30,000 men and left thousands dead or wounded. But whether or not you continue, you will have savored during your trip an extraordinary range of flavorsome contrasts: such is the many-layered richness of Louisiana's cultures, histories, and ambiences.

PRACTICAL INFORMATION FOR LOUISIANA

 FACTS & FIGURES. Louisiana was named for Louis XIV of France. Its nicknames are *Bayou State, Sportsman's Paradise, Pelican State.* The magnolia is the state flower; bald cypress, the state tree. The brown pelican is the state bird. "Union, Justice, and Confidence" is the state motto. *Give Me Louisiana* and Jimmy Davis' *You Are My Sunshine* are the state songs.

Baton Rouge is the state capital. The state population is 4,203,972 (1980 census).

With the exception of some low hill country in the northern part of the state, Louisiana is flat, low Mississippi Delta country. The extreme southern area is a watery region of swamps, marshes, and bayous, the home of trappers, fishermen, and oil (Louisiana is second only to Texas in petroleum output). It is also the second largest mineral producer in the country and first in the annual fur catch. Fishing, both salt and fresh water, is important both to the state's economy and to its sportsmen. Timber is another important source of revenue, and tropical and subtropical crops flourish. Cotton, rice and sugar-cane fields line the fertile banks of the broad Mississippi, which courses down the state to the great port of New Orleans and the Gulf of Mexico. The climate is one of mild winters, hot summers and high humidity. Louisiana is a frequent victim of tornadoes, and the coastal areas lie in the tropical hurricane belt.

 HOW TO GET THERE. *By air:* New Orleans may be reached from cities within the U.S.A. on direct flights of: Continental, Delta, Eastern, Ozark, Southwest and United airlines. Baton Rouge on direct flights of Delta, Royale, and Republic; Monroe on direct flights of Royale and Republic; Alexandria on Delta and Royale; Lake Charles on Royale; and Shreveport on Delta and Royale.

To New Orleans: Delta has direct flights out of Caracas, Venezuela; Aviateca and Taca have direct flights out of Merida, Mexico; Sahsa flies to Honduras and El Salvador; Aviateca has a direct flight to Guatemala City.

By car: From Picayune, Miss., you can get to New Orleans via I-59. I-55 will take you from McComb, Miss., south to Kentwood and Hammond. I-20 comes in from Vicksburg, Miss., and cuts through the state west to the Texas state line. I-10 enters the state at Vidor, Texas, and goes through the state to Slidell. In the northern part of the state I-20 comes into Shreveport from Texas and continues east. US 71 comes in from Texarkana, Ark., goes south to Shreveport and then southeast to Alexandria and New Orleans. US 61 enters the state at Woodville, Miss., goes south to Baton Rouge and then east to New Orleans. Note: H'way I is best way to go from Shreveport to Alexandria.

By train: Amtrak trains enter the Union Passenger Terminal in New Orleans.

By bus: Greyhound and Trailways provide the most frequent service, tying in with other major lines. Several other smaller bus lines operate around the state.

 HOW TO GET AROUND. *By air:* Delta, Royale, and Republic airlines service cities within the state. Aircraft charter and rental services, including helicopter, are available.

By car: I-55 will take you from Kentwood to Hammond. I-20, in the north, runs west from Monroe, Ruston, Minden to Shreveport. On I-10 you can go from Slidell east through New Orleans, Baton Rouge, Lafayette, Jennings to Lake Charles. I-12 leads from Baton Rouge east to Hammond and Covington. US 61 goes from New Orleans west to Baton Rouge, then US 190 west to Opelousas. There is no interstate running from north to south through the state. To go from Shreveport to New Orleans, take US 71 to I-10. However, I-10 and I-12 are connected with I-20 by I-55 out of New Orleans through Mississippi, connecting at Jackson, Miss.

Car Rental: You can rent an *Avis, Hertz, Budget* or *National* car in Baton Rouge, Lafayette, Lake Charles, Monroe, New Orleans and Shreveport. Hertz and National also have rental offices in Alexandria, Morgan City, New Iberia and Opelousas.

By bus: Greyhound and Trailways, as well as Arrow Coach, Central Texas Bus Lines, Inc., Great Southern Coaches, Inc., Orange Belt Stages and Salter Bus Lines serve some cities within the state.

By ferry: The Mississippi River may be crossed by ferry at New Orleans, Plaquemine, White Castle, Reserve, Luling, Belle Chase, St. Francisville or at Lutcher.

TOURIST INFORMATION SERVICES. The Greater New Orleans Tourist and Convention Commission at 334 Royal St. will help you plan. The Chamber of Commerce at 334 Camp St., 527-6900, is also helpful. For the rest of the state, inquiries to specific chambers of commerce of cities and towns and to the Louisiana Tourist Development Commission, Box 44291, Baton Rouge 70804, with its 12 information centers around the state, will bring desired information.

Louisiana Wildlife & Fisheries Commission, 400 Royal St., New Orleans 70130, will supply fishing & hunting regulations.

Forest Service, Southern Region, 50 Seventh St., N.E., Atlanta, Ga. 30323, offers information on national forests.

SEASONAL EVENTS. There are more than 230 festivals and fairs held in Louisiana every year. For a complete listing, write the Louisiana Office of Tourism in Baton Rouge.

Spring: Mardi Gras is the most famous seasonal event in the state, with all-out, 2-wk. celebration in *New Orleans; Shrove Tuesday* celebration in *Houma* and *Lafayette.* In March, *Lafayette* annually observes the *Azalea Trail; Lake Charles* has a *House & Garden Tour; Spring Fiesta* in *New Orleans* features tours of homes in the French Quarter and the Garden District. Lake Charles celebrates *Contraband Day* late May to early June with a water sports carnival.

Summer: The Morehouse Rodeo takes place in *Bastrop* in June, while *Ruston* celebrates its *Peach Festival* late in the month. *Many* has its *Arts & Crafts Festival* and Lafayette has its *Food Fest* in June.

Fall: This is the time of harvest festivals: *La. Sugar Cane Fair & Festival, New Iberia,* Sept.; *Festival Acadiens, Lafayette,* Sept.; *International Rice Festival & Frog Derby, Crowley; Sauce Piquante Festival* and *Pirogue Races* in *Raceland; Yambilee Festival* in *Opelousas* all take place in Oct. *Natchitoches* offers its *Historic Plantation Tour* the 2nd weekend in Oct. *Louisiana State Fair,* Shreveport, Oct. Zwolle's *Hot Tamale Festival* is also in Oct.

Winter: Sugar Bowl Festival begins right after Christmas, culminating in Sugar Bowl Football Classic on New Year's Day. *Battle of New Orleans* is celebrated in January at *Chalmette National Historical Park.* The *Christmas Festival* in *Natchitoches* begins on the first Saturday in December and runs through New Year's Day.

NATIONAL PARKS AND FORESTS. Campsites and trailer space, as well as picnicking facilities are available throughout the nearly 600,000 acres of the *Kisatchie National Forest* in central and northwest Louisiana. Eleven recreation centers, open year round. Most are located on lakes or streams; and all have grills and sanitary facilities. A nominal charge is made for fishing, for duck hunting, and for boats. Reservations should be made through the Forest Service, U.S.D.A., Box 471, Alexandria 71360.

Chalmette National Historical Park, E of New Orleans on State 46, commemorates the last battle of the War of 1812. The American victory here assured westward expansion, and Gen. Andrew Jackson became nationally known. Beauregard House, an antebellum mansion, serves as information center, with exhibits and audio visual program concerning the battle of New Orleans. The 1-mi. battlefield tour road begins at Chalmette National Cemetery. Closed Shrove Tuesday, Christmas.

 STATE PARKS. There are 29 state parks and commemorative areas in Louisiana. All the parks, except Locust Grove and Kent House, allow picnicking.

Audubon Memorial State Park, nr. *St. Francisville* on State 965, is the site of Oakley Plantation House, a museum of Audubon memorabilia, with period furnishings. Formal garden, picnicking, hiking trails. *Bogue Falaya Wayside Park, Covington,* has a natural beach, picnicking on its 13 acres. *Fort Jesup State Monument,* 6 mi. E of *Many* on State 6, is the site of the antebellum garrison. *Fort Pike State Monument,* US 90, 30 mi. E of New Orleans. Picnicking. *Lake D'Arbonne State Park,* off Rte. 33 W of Rte. 15 nr. *Farmerville,* 90-acre wooded lakeside area with picnicking, boating, water skiing. *Longfellow-Evangeline State Park,* 3 mi. NE of *St. Martinville* on Rte. 31, on banks of Bayou Teche, has restored Acadian house, kitchen garden, craft shop, replica of Acadian cottage.

 CAMPING OUT. Nine of the state parks provide campsites.

Chemin à Haut State Park, 522 acres E of Rte. 139, 10 mi. N of *Bastrop,* is portion of road used by Indians. Picnicking, swimming, boating, fishing, camping. Rental cabins available. *Chicot State Park,* 6,500 acres in Evangeline Parish, 6 mi. N of *Ville Platte* on State 3042, features an artificial lake, picnicking, fishing, camping, swimming, water sports. Rental cabins available. *Fairview Riverside Park,* 2 mi. E of *Madisonville* on State 22, is 98-acre woodland on banks of Tchefuncte River. Picnicking, camping, fishing, swimming. *Fontainebleau State Park* in *Mandeville* on US 190, has nature trails, camping, picnicking, water sports. *St. Bernard State Park,* 18 mi. SE of New Orleans on LA 39, encompasses 350 acres on the Mississippi River. Camping, fishing, picnicking.

Grand Isle State Park, on State 1, in *Jefferson Parish,* is a 140-acre site with access to Gulf of Mexico. Beach, fishing, jetties, camping facilities, picnicking. *Lake Bistineau State Park,* E of State 163 nr. *Doyline.* 750-acre pine forest. Picnicking, swimming, camping. Rental cabins available. *Lake Bruin State Park,* E of US 65 nr. *St. Joseph.* 50 acres, with picnicking, swimming, camping, boating, fishing. *Lake Claiborne State Park,* 7 mi. SE of Homer, on State 146. 97-acre woodland area, with picnicking, swimming, camping, fishing.

Sam Houston Jones State Park, 12 mi. N of *Lake Charles* on State 378. Densely wooded, 1,068-acre tract with lagoons, nature trails. Picnicking, boating, fishing, water skiing, camping. Rental cabins available.

For a brochure on the state parks, write to Department of Culture, Recreation and Tourism, Office of State Parks, P.O. Drawer IIII, Baton Rouge 70821.

TRAILER TIPS. The Federal forest area, *Kisatchie,* provides trailer space at six of its recreational areas, but no connections.

Of the state parks listed above, all but Grand Isle have water and electricity hookups with dump stations. Because Louisiana is an outdoors state, commercial campsites complete with all hookups can be found around the state, not only on the main highways and interstates, but in interesting places off the beaten path. Permits for trailers over legal size may be obtained from the Division of State Police, Permit Section, P.O. Box 1791, Baton Rouge. Oversize are those with length over 60 feet; width of 8 feet; and height of 13 feet, 6 inches. Others require no permits.

MUSEUMS AND GALLERIES. *Lafayette Museum,* 1122 Lafayette St., *Lafayette,* was home of Gov. Alexandre Mouton. Furniture, historical documents, portraits, Indian artifacts. Tours. Closed Mon. & holidays.

Imperial Calcasieu Museum, 204 W. Sallier St., *Lake Charles,* contains Victorian period furnishings, Gay Nineties barber shop, glass, crystal. Tour. Closed New Year's, Easter, Christmas wk. Free. *Bayou Folk Museum,* off State 1 in *Cloutierville,* nr. Natchitoches, displays an extensive collection of period pieces, artifacts and memorabilia of the area. Sat. & Sun. only.

Louisiana State Exhibit Museum, 3015 Greenwood Rd., *Shreveport,* tells history of state through murals, dioramas. Glass, china, paper money, Indian artifact collections. Free.

In *Baton Rouge,* the *Old Arsenal Museum* houses historical exhibits in bldg. used by Federal troops during Civil War. The *Rural Life Museum,* Burden Research Center on LSU campus, is comprised of blacksmith shop, general store, overseer's cottage typical of 18th- & 19th-century plantation life.

Hanna Hall at *Monroe's* Northeast Louisiana U. campus, houses American Indian, Latin American and African artifacts.

Heritage Village Museum, 9 mi. NE of New Iberia in *Loreauville,* is a 40-unit village and farm, telling history of territory for the past three centuries.

Art Exhibits. *Art Center for Southwestern Louisiana,* Girard Park Dr., *Lafayette.* Permanent and changing exhibits. Closed New Year's, Mardi Gras, Thanksgiving, Christmas.

R. W. Norton Art Gallery, Creswell Ave., *Shreveport,* features a large collection of Remington and Russell works, also has fine permanent collection of American, European paintings and sculpture. Closed Mon., holidays. Free.

Meadows Museum of Art on Centenary College campus, has a collection of paintings and drawings of Indochina by Jean Despujols.

In *Monroe, Masur Museum of Art* has regular exhibits, and *Byran Hall Art Gallery,* Northeast Louisiana U. campus, sponsors shows by American and foreign artists, students and faculty during the school year. Free.

Special Interest Museums. In *Baton Rouge, LSU's Geoscience Museum, Museum of Natural Science,* Foster Hall. *Louisiana Arts & Science Center & Planetarium,* 502 North Blvd., houses paintings, sculpture, cultural, historical, scientific exhibits. Closed Mardi Gras, holidays. Planetarium shows: late May to Labor Day. *Wedell-William Memorial Aviation Museum* in Patterson. This museum was named after two of Louisiana's most famous aviation pioneers, Jimmy Wedell and Harry Williams, and is dedicated to the preservation and exhibition of Louisiana's aviation history.

HISTORIC SITES. Throughout Louisiana are numerous antebellum homes, many open to the public. *Oakley Plantation,* on Hwy. 965, east of *St. Francisville,* is where Audubon became acquainted with the wildlife of the Feliciana countryside. It is now the 100-acre Audubon Memorial State Park. *Rosedown,* on State 10, E of *St. Francisville,* has antique furnishings, 17th-century gardens. *The Cottage Plantation,* on US 61, 9 mi. north of *St. Francisville,* was started in 1795. On grounds are smokehouse, school, slave cabins. In White Castle, *Nottoway Plantation,* the largest plantation house in the South, has overnight accommodations. Reservations a must. *Destrehan Manor House,* the oldest remaining plantation home on the lower Mississippi, is on River Road, 8 mi. above the New Orleans International Airport.

Derbigny Plantation is a fine old Louisiana cottage on River Road (LA 541) near Oak Avenue, above *Westwego. Marksville Prehistoric Indian State Monument,* nr. *Marksville* on State 5, is site of Indian settlement of 2,000 yrs ago, and of Civil War ammunition supply point.

St. Martinville, E of New Orleans on US 90, is center of legends surrounding Longfellow's *Evangeline.* In the churchyard of *St. Martin of Tours Catholic Church,* 133 S. Main St., is the grave of the poem's heroine, Emmeline Labiche. The *Evangeline Oak* still stands at the end of Port St. *Evangeline Museum,* 429 E. Bridge St.

Edward Douglass White Memorial, 5 mi. N of *Thibodaux,* on State 1, includes restored homestead of Chief Justice of Supreme Court.

Oak Alley, on River Rd. near *Vacherie,* is a Greek Revival mansion, built in 1830's. Live oaks line a corridor from the house to the river.

Parlange Plantation, on LA 1, 5 mi. S of *New Roads,* was built in 1750.

Houmas House, on LA 942 in *Burnside,* is a magnificent Greek Revival mansion.

Near *Franklin* are two outstanding houses. *Oaklawn Manor,* 5 mi. off US 90, has a large grove of live oaks and lovely gardens. *Albania Mansion,* nr. *Jeanerette,* 14 mi. from Franklin on US 90, features a 3-story spiral staircase.

In *Natchitoches, Roque House,* Riverbank Dr. nr. Keyser Ave. Bridge, is an excellent example of pioneer Louisiana construction. *Shadows on the Teche,* 117 E. Main St., *New Iberia* is a gracious 2-story, 16-rm. townhouse set among live oaks. *Justine,* originally built in Franklin in 1822, was added to twice and moved to New Iberia by barge.

In *Reserve, San Francisco Plantation* house is 2 mi. upriver on State 44. 18th-century furnishings, landscaped grounds.

Bayou Folk Museum, off LA 1 in *Cloutierville,* is a charming home built in the early 1800s and the former residence of author Kate Chopin. It now belongs to Northwestern State University.

 FAMOUS LIBRARIES. Several million manuscript items of Louisiana are in the *Archives of the Louisiana State U.* at Baton Rouge, open daily 8 A.M. to 10 P.M. Also on display here are four Audubon folios, as well as about 150 framed sheets from other folios. Notable manuscripts of Lafcadio Hearn and others are available for short periods daily at *Tulane University Library* in New Orleans.

 TOURS. *Louisiana Lagniappe Tours* offers tours of Baton Rouge and nearby plantations. *Delcambre,* 15 mi. W. of New Iberia on Rte. 14, offers tours aboard paddlewheeler *Cajun Belle. Passe Partout Touring Co.,* 329 Beverly Dr., Lafayette, offers special interest & offbeat tours in Acadian country. *Old Natchitoches Tours* offers city and Cane River Plantation Tour and cruises on the *Cane River Belle.*

 SPECIAL INTEREST TOURS. *Annie Millier of Houma,* the lady who "talks to alligators," gives swamp and marsh tours.

Carville Hospital, approx. 20 mi. S of Baton Rouge on LA 141, is one of the only hospitals in the continental U.S. which cares for victims of Hansen'sDisease (leprosy). Walking tours are conducted daily free of charge.

Tours of *Atchafalaya Basin,* Louisiana's great swampland wilderness, leave from McGee's Landing in Henderson.

GARDENS. Avery Island's *Jungle Gardens,* off State 329 via a toll road, is a 300-acre paradise, with camellias blooming Nov. to April, iris Mar. to July, azaleas late Feb. to late Apr. Also featured are tropical plants, sunken gardens, a Chinese garden with a centuries-old Buddha, and a bird sanctuary where egrets nest.

Hodges Gardens, 15 mi. S of *Many* on US 171, is a 4,700-acre garden in a forest. There are experimental areas, wildlife refuge, wild and cultivated gardens in bloom yr. round. In Dec. there's a Christmas Light Tour. Picnicking, boating, swimming and fishing also avail.

Rip Van Winkle's Live Oak Gardens (temporarily closed) on *Jefferson Island,* is a very traditional English garden, featuring azaleas, camellias, wisteria, oleanders, as well as a fountain walk and Alhambra Garden. Self-guiding trails, picnicking. There are greenhouses displaying orchids and other tropical plants, some of which can be purchased seasonally.

Rosedown Plantation and Gardens, St. Francisville, is a magnificently restored antebellum home with 17th-century style French formal gardens.

In *Monroe, Louisiana Purchase Gardens is a* 140-acre garden and zoo with over *8,000 plants and 800 animals.*

Briarwood Gardens, on LA 9 in Saline, is set in a 120-acre pine forest, once the homesite of famous naturalist Caroline Dormon.

Walter Jacobs Nature Trail is open to the public.

Bossier's Cypress-Black Bayou Recreation Area has a 1½ mile hard surface nature trail for the handicapped and elderly.

Acadian Village and Garden, just south of LA 342 on Mouton Road in Lafayette, features a horticultural walking tour of the world's warm weather areas.

Afton Villa Gardens, N. of Baton Rouge, has a Gothic gate house, beautiful gardens and a great oak alley.

Longue Vue House and Gardens, 7 Bamboo Rd. in New Orleans, an eight-acre city estate series of varied gardens complemented by statues, pebbled walkways, patios and graceful fountains.

MUSIC. In *Shreveport* music enthusiasts can attend a number of concerts and musical offerings ranging from classical to country. The *Community Concert Association* brings major symphony orchestras. Metropolitan Opera stars and instrumentalists. The *Shreveport Symphony* brings guest artists, presents two performances a month during its season. The *Civic Opera Society* also brings in guest stars for its productions. Country & western fans will want to check out the *Louisiana Hayride,* broadcast over KRMD every Sat. night, followed by a big dance. *Centenary College Choir* is internationally known, regularly appears at the Convention Center, Hodges Gardens and on local TV stations. Pop band concerts are held at Centenary College's Hargrove Amphitheatre during the summer.

STAGE AND REVUES. You can hear Country and Western music in the "Grand Ole Opry" style, with Joe Woods and the Wilderness Express, at the *Dixie Theater* in Ruston every Saturday night. Centenary College's *Jongleurs* regularly presents plays at Marjorie Lyons Playhouse.

The *Monroe Civic Center* brings Broadway plays, leading entertainers, ice shows and the circus regularly.

DRINKING LAWS. Liquor sold by package and drink at stores or establishments with a license. Sunday sales optional in some locations. None may be imported from another state. The minimum age is 18.

SPORTS. *Fishing,* both fresh- and salt-water is a year-round sport. Spanish and king mackerel, jewfish, marlin, bluefish, cobia, speckled trout, pompano, red snapper and common jack are found in the coastal areas and Gulf of Mexico. Tarpon fishing below Houma and Grand Isle is becoming increasingly popular. Crawfish are found inland and are a popular food in Louisiana. Many consider Louisiana a bass fisherman's dream because of all the lakes to be found around the state. Many are manmade, which means there are lots of brush and tree stumps left, making for good bass fishing. Crappie fishing is also popular. Boats, tackle and bait are available everywhere. Nonresident fishing license costs $6; a 7-day license, $3. No license is required for salt-water fishing.

Hunting, concentrated generally during the winter, requires a non-resident license for 3 days, $10; for a season, the fee is $25. Visitors who are residents of Arkansas, Texas, Mississippi, Alabama, and Florida must pay an even higher fee. Turkey, squirrel and deer inhabit the pine hills and swampland.

Licenses and information available from Wild Life and Fish Commission, 400 Royal St., New Orleans 70130.

Swimming is available at the following recreation areas: Bogue Falaya Wayside, Covington; Chemin-A-Haut, nr. Bastrop; D'Arbonne Lake, Farmerville; Fontainebleau, Mandeville; Grand Isle, off Rte. 1; Lake Bistineau, S of Doyline; Lake Bruin, NE of St. Joseph; and at Cotile Reservoir, 20 mi. W of Alexandria.

Golf is popular throughout the state. *Alexandria: Bringhurst Park,* off Masonic Dr., 9 holes. *Lafayette: City Park Golf Course,* Mudd Ave. & 8th St. *Shreveport: Andrew Querbes Park,* Gregg & Fern Sts. *Lakeside,* Milam St., *Huntington,* Pines Rd.; *New Orleans: Lakewood Country Club* sponsors Greater New Orleans Open every spring.

SPECTATOR SPORTS: New Orlean's *professional football team,* the *Saints,* and Tulane University's football team play at Superdome. LSU's athletic teams play major competitors at Baton Rouge.

Racing: Thoroughbreds at *Evangeline Downs,* Lafayette, from early Apr.-early Sept. *Fair Grounds Race Track,* New Orleans, was established in 1872. Late Nov. to late Mar. *Jefferson Downs Race Track,* 44th St. & Williams Blvd., Kenner, has night races April to Nov. (with a short interruption during the season). Quarterhorses and thoroughbreds race at Delta Downs in Vinton for much of the year. Thoroughbreds run at Louisiana Downs, Bossier City, from late spring into the fall.

WHAT TO DO WITH THE CHILDREN. *Louisiana Purchase Gardens and Zoo,* off I-20, *Monroe,* exhibits rare animals in modern buildings, some glass-fronted, some moated. Nocturnal animals are shown under red lights. The entertainment section has a Lewis & Clark Railroad, boat rides, and other amusement rides. Baton Rouge and Alexandria also have zoos, with children's rides at Alexandria.

In *Shreveport, Ford Park* at Cross Lake on S. Lakeshore Dr., open May to Oct., daily. *Hamel's Park* is a small but good amusement park with nine outside rides, including a train and a roller coaster, and another half-dozen or so rides inside for rainy days. There's a Frisbee golf course on Clyde Fant Parkway.

INDIANS. Only one Indian reservation still exists in Louisiana. It is located nr. Charenton, about 4 mi. from Baldwin, 25 mi. W of Morgan City on US 90. Only a few Chitimacha Indians live there. A small settlement of Houmas is located nr. Kraemer (Rte. 20 and 307 N from Thibodaux), where they have their own chapel and school. The Koasati maintain their own trading post

3 mi. N of Elton. Their charmingly designed baskets, decorated with alligators, armadillos, frogs and turkeys, make fine souvenirs of the piney woods. The Tunica-Biloxi Indians maintain a trading post nr. Marksville, selling beadwork, basketry, wood carvings and metal work.

There are many ceremonial mounds in Louisiana. Among the more notable are: Poverty Point, West Carroll Parish. One of the largest in the state, believed to have been built by one of the oldest cultures in the Northern Hemisphere: Tensas Parish's Lide Mounds, off Rte. 605; Balmoral Mounds, off US 64, Newellton; Marksville's Prehistoric Indian Museum and Park; Brannin Mound in Franklin Parish, 240 ft. long, 130 ft. wide, 22 ft. high; Little River Mounds, LaSalle Parish, evident along river.

 **HOTELS AND MOTELS.** Most of the state's establishments are less expensive outside New Orleans. There are many "chain" motels along I-10 and I-12. One practical note: many of the motels in Baton Rouge are along US 61 from New Orleans north and US 190, which runs east-west. Both of these routes pass along the edge of the city on US Bypass 190. A few hotels and motels are within the downtown or capitol area. An Airline Highway address in Baton Rouge is located along the US 61 and 190 bypass.

Based on double occupancy without meals, price categories and ranges are as follows: *Deluxe,* $60 and up; *Expensive,* $45–$60; *Moderate,* $30–$45; *Inexpensive,* less than $30. Listings are in order of price category. For a more complete explanation of hotel and motel categories see *Facts at Your Fingertips* at the front of this volume.

Alexandria

Howard Johnson's Motor Lodge. *Expensive.* Free library. Olympic pool, nightly entertainment, free local calls.

Ramada Inn. *Expensive.* Pool, free saunas. Restaurant and cocktail lounge.

Rodeway Inn of America. *Expensive.* Pool. Restaurant and cocktail lounge adj. Free parking.

Sheraton Inn. *Expensive.* 2716 MacArthur Dr. Cafe, bar, entertainment, pool.

Alexandria TraveLodge. *Moderate.* Lounge and restaurant. Pitt Grill and shopping area nr.

Holiday Inn. *Moderate.* Member of chain. Restaurant and bar.

Baton Rouge

Baton Rouge Hilton. *Deluxe.* I-10 at College Drive. In Corporate Square, a 21-store enclosed mall. 3 restaurants, 2 cocktail lounges, nightclub with live entertainment. Tennis courts, pool, health spa. Fully stocked bars in rooms.

Sheraton Baton Rouge Hotel. *Deluxe.* 2728 Constitution Ave. Large motor inn. Suites. Restaurant, lounge with entertainment, coffee shop. Pool (heated). Golf nr.

Capitol House. *Expensive.* 201 Lafayette St. (downtown). Roof deck pool over Mississippi River. Elegant cocktail lounge and restaurant. Free lobby-entrance garage. 24-hr. cafe.

Prince Murat. *Expensive.* 1480 Nicholson Dr. Nicely decorated rooms. Pool, dining room, coffee shop, bar.

Ramada Inn. *Expensive.* 10330 Airline Hwy. Pool and kiddie pool, restaurant, bar.

TraveLodge. *Moderate.* 427 Lafayette St. (downtown). Some rooms have river view. Pool, café, coin laundry.

Bellemont Motor Hotel. *Moderate.* 7370 Airline Hwy. Restaurant, coffee shop, bar, and pool.

Best Western Inn. *Moderate.* 5955 Airline Hwy. 5 miles to downtown, 7 miles to LSU.

Holiday Inn. *Moderate.* At three locations: 10455 Reiger Rd. **South:** 9940 Airline Hwy. **West:** I-10 & State 415. Coffee shop, pool, bar, free airport transportation. Kennel.

Howard Johnson's Motor Lodge. *Moderate.* 2365 College Dr. Babysitter list, restaurant, pool, shuffleboard.

Oak Manor Motor Hotel. *Moderate.* 8181 Airline Hwy. Luxurious rooms and suites on 14 acres of landscaped grounds. Old English Manor restaurant. Bar, pool, free parking.

Rodeway Inn. *Moderate.* I-10 and S. Arcadian Thruway. Pool, restaurant, cocktail lounge, live entertainment.

Days Inn. *Inexpensive.* I-10 & State 415. Pool, restaurant, play area.

Lafayette

Best Western-Evangeline Inn. *Expensive.* Restaurant, pool, lounge with entertainment.

Holiday Inn. *Expensive.* At two locations: **South:** US 90E. Airport 1 mi. Free transportation. **North:** on US 167 at jct. I-10, lounge, entertainment. Restaurant, bar, pool.

Howard Johnson's Motor Lodge. *Expensive.* Attractive rooms, color TV. Pool with service at poolside, play area. Restaurant, lounge.

TraveLodge. *Expensive.* At two locations: **Center:** 1101 Pinhook Rd. **North:** 251 Frontage Rd. (US 167) at Willow St. Restaurant, pool, lounge with entertainment.

Rodeway Inn. *Expensive.* 24-hour restaurant, lounge with entertainment. Pool. Transportation to airport.

Sheraton Town House Motor Hotel. *Expensive.* Nice rooms, 3 dining rooms, cocktail lounge with dancing and live entertainment nightly. Pool.

Ramada Inn. *Moderate.* Restaurant, lounge with entertainment. Pool.

Imperial '400' Motel. *Inexpensive.* Pool. Business center.

Lake Charles

Downtowner Motor Inn. *Expensive.* On beautiful Lake Charles. Pool, restaurant, bar.

Howard Johnson's Motor Lodge. *Expensive.* Restaurant, bar, pools, play area. Children under 12 free.

Sheraton-Chateau Charles Motor Inn. *Expensive.* Children free. Pool. Restaurant with first-class French cuisine.

Holiday Inn. *Moderate.* Pool, restaurant, cocktail lounge.

Many

Toro Hills Hotel. *Expensive.* At entrance to the 4,700-acre Hodges Gardens. Spacious rooms overlooking pool and patio. Fine restaurant. Tennis courts and pro golf courses; private club.

Monroe

Holiday Inn. *Expensive.* Restaurant, pool.

Howard Johnson's Motor Lodge. *Moderate.* Across from Civic Center. Pool, play area, restaurant nr.

Ramada Inn. *Moderate.* Restaurant, grill, bar, pool, free saunas.

Rodeway Inn. *Moderate.* Glenwood Dr. in West Monroe.

Natchitoches

Holiday Inn. *Expensive.* Very pleasant rooms with color TV. Suites. Restaurant, lounge with live entertainment. Kennels. Free airport transportation.

Fort Claiborne Guest House. *Moderate.* 801 Second St., in the heart of Historic District. Kitchenettes.

New Iberia

Holiday Inn. *Expensive.* Decor follows railroad theme in Park Station Restaurant and Railhead Lounge.

Acadiana Motor Lodge. *Moderate.* Restaurant, bar, pool. Entertainment.

Opelousas

Downtowner Motor Inn. *Inexpensive.* Pool, restaurant, and bar.

Ruston

Holiday Inn. *Moderate.* Pool and restaurant. Kennel.

Shreveport

Chateau. *Deluxe.* 201 Lake St. Cafe, bar, entertainment, pool. Free in-room movies. Free airport transportation.

Hilton Inn, Bossier. *Deluxe.* I-20 at Airline Exit. Restaurant, lounge, disco.

Regency. *Deluxe.* Spring and Lake. Free airport transportation. Restaurant, lounge.

Sheraton Inn-Bossier. *Deluxe.* 2015 Old Minden Rd., Bossier City. Attractive rooms, some with king-size beds. Suites. Restaurant, lounge with dancing and entertainment. Pool with service at poolside. Free airport transportation.

Ramada Inn. *Expensive.* 5116 Monkhouse Dr. Pool, restaurant, and cocktail lounge with dancing.

Sheraton Inn-Shreveporter. *Expensive.* 3880 Greenwood Rd. Children free; play area and pool. Luxurious rooms.

Holiday Inn. *Expensive.* Three locations. **West:** 4900 Greenwood Rd. N off I-20. **North:** 1906 N. Market St. US 71 & State 1. **Bossier City:** 150 Hamilton Rd. (off I-20). All with restaurant, bar, pool, color TV and free airport transportation.

Howard Johnson's Motor Lodge. *Expensive.* 5101 Monkhouse Dr. Pool, kids playground; restaurant and lounge. Local calls are free and there is a free library and morning paper. Rates increase during State Fair.

Palace Inn. *Expensive.* 1968 Airline Dr., Bossier City. Pleasant rooms. Complimentary coffee. Babysitter list. Restaurant. Pool.

Days Inn. *Moderate.* Two locations: 4935 W. Monkhouse Dr. and 200 John Wesley Blvd., Bossier City. Pools, restaurant.

Western Hills Inn. *Moderate.* 3515 E. Texas St., Bossier City. Restaurant, lounge, and pool.

 DINING OUT in Louisiana often means the same fine creole cooking you can experience in New Orleans, as well as seafood specialties and the ever-present steak houses, fried chicken emporia, and occasional oriental establishments. Because of Louisiana's proximity to our southernmost neighbor, there are also many places featuring Mexican-style cuisine. For other worthwhile restaurants, check our hotel listings.

Restaurants are listed in order of price category. Price categories and ranges, for a complete dinner, are as follows: *Expensive,* $15 and up; *Moderate,* $7–$15; *Inexpensive,* under $7. For a more complete explanation of restaurant categories see *Facts at Your Fingertips* at the front of this volume.

Alexandria

Don's Seafood. *Expensive.* Excellent French cuisine.

Rapides Cotton Gin. *Expensive.* 3807 Prescott Rd. Located in an old cotton gin. Steaks, seafood. Dinner served daily from 5:30 P.M.

Herbie K's. *Moderate.* Specialties: oysters on half shell, other seafood, Cajun dishes, and steaks. Children's portions. Closed Sun.

Plantation Manor. *Moderate.* Seafood, steak. Crab-stuffed eggplant is great. Chef owned.

Piccadilly Cafeteria. *Inexpensive.* At two locations: 1400 MacArthur Dr., in MacArthur Village Shopping Center; and 3451 Masonic Dr., in Alexandria Mall Shopping Center. Try their spaghetti and meatballs. Children's portions. Closed on Christmas.

Baton Rouge

The Chalet Brandt. *Expensive.* 7655 Old Hammond Hwy. French cuisine is featured. Swiss Chalet decor. Choose wine to complete your dinner from their excellent wine list. Chef-owned. Medaillons de veau are a favorite. Pastries made on the premises. Closed Sun.

Mike and Tony's. *Expensive.* 10270 Airline Hwy. Tempting steaks and seafood à la Louisiane highlight the menu. Children's portions. Closed Sun.

Ralph and Kacoo's. *Expensive.* 7110 Airline Hwy. Open daily. Specializes in seafood—crawfish, crab, shrimp, trout meuniere, catfish. Also in New Orleans.

The Village. *Moderate.* 8464 Airline Hwy. Excellent Italian cuisine. Pasta and pastries are homemade. Dining room has pleasing decor. Children's portions. Closed Mon.

Piccadilly Cafeterias. *Inexpensive.* Five locations: 332 S. Sherwood Forest Blvd.; Cortana Mall, 8953 Florida Blvd.; Delmont Village, 5179 Plank Rd.; Westmoreland Village, 3164 Government St., Mid City. Excellent food for the price. Wide variety of food on the menu. A la carte.

Lafayette

Chez Pastor. *Expensive.* 1211 Pinhook Rd. Cuisine with a flavoring of Cajun and a touch of Creole.

Jacob's Fine Foods. *Expensive.* 1600 Cameron St. Very popular in the area. Relaxed and friendly atmosphere. Acadian and French cuisine. Seafood is their specialty. (shrimp de la Teche is very special). Children's portions. Closed Christmas and New Year's Day.

Chez Marcelle. *Expensive.* 102 N. St. Julien Rd. in Broussard. Excellent Creole food.

Vermillionville Café. *Expensive.* 1304 Pinhook Rd. Lafayette cuisine.

Lake Charles

Chez Oca. *Expensive.* 815 Bayou Pines Dr. Owned by a former New Orleans chef. Coat and tie for evening requested. Wine cellar.

Plantation House. *Expensive.* Seafood (crayfish in season and crabmeat Imperial lead the list), own baking. Chef owned.

Monroe

Bamboo Restaurant. *Moderate.* Hwy 80 East. Specializes in Chinese and American dishes.

Piccadilly Cafeteria. *Inexpensive.* In the Twin City Shopping Center. Extensive and varied menu. Closed Christmas.

Natchitoches

Lasayone's. *Inexpensive.* 622 Second St. Nationally known for its Natchitoches meat pies.

New Iberia

The French House. *Moderate.* Cajun dishes are featured at this pleasant dining spot. Try the crawfish, gumbo or other seafood as well as their steaks. Closed first 2 weeks in July; Christmas, New Year's Day; Labor Day.

Opelousas

Palace Cafe. *Moderate.* 167 W. Landry St. Gumbo, crawfish, seafood and steaks are specialties at this restaurant. Creole and Cajun menu. Family-operated since 1927.

Shreveport

Don's Seafood and Steak House. *Expensive.* 3100 Highland Av. Cajun dishes, seafood and steaks. Other Don's in Baton Rouge, Metairie, and Lafayette.

Ernest's Supper Club. *Expensive.* 612 Commerce St. Downtown. Known for its seafoods. Live entertainment.

Firenze. *Expensive.* 1846 Fairfield. A very fine, plush restaurant featuring Northern Italian and French cuisine in the Florentine manner. Adjacent lounge with live entertainment.

Sansone's. *Expensive.* 701 E. Kings Hwy. Steak, Italian and seafood dishes highlight the American, Continental menu here. There is a combo and vocalist for your listening and dancing pleasure nightly, except Sun. Children's portions. Bar is closed on Sun.

Smith's Crosslake Inn. *Expensive.* 5301 Lakeshore Dr. Seafood, steak and Crosslake catfish attract locals as well as visitors.

Cypress Inn. *Moderate.* A catfish restaurant featuring Atchafalaya catfish and char-broiled steaks. Located in nearby Benton. Closed Sunday and Monday.

Nanking Restaurant. *Moderate.* 614 Milam. In downtown Shreveport. Specializes in Chinese and American dishes. Open until 4 A.M. Closed Sundays. Local nightime gathering place of entertainers and night people.

MISSISSIPPI

White Pillars and Magnolias

BY
BERN KEATING

Exploring Mississippi is easy via north-south or northeast-southwest routes. From these you can reach every point of interest in the state. The three tours usually follow United States routes, in some cases portions of interstate highways.

Mississippi has four interstate highways: I-55, entering the state from Tennessee on the north and running south through Sardis, Grenada, Jackson and McComb into Louisiana; I-20, crossing the state from Meridian to Vicksburg; I-59, entering the state from Alabama near Meridian and running diagonally southwest through Laurel, Hattiesburg and Picayune into Louisiana; and I-10, paralleling the Gulf Coast from Alabama to Louisiana.

South from Tennessee
You begin the easternmost of the north-south tours by entering the state from Tennessee via US 45. Your first stop is at Corinth, first named Cross City when two railroads selected it as a junction point and later given the Grecian name. This was a vital crossroads during the Civil War. It was to Corinth the Confederates withdrew in April, 1862, after the bloody Battle of Shiloh, twenty-one miles to the north in Tennessee. The Confederates evacuated the town in May, 1862, and in October failed in an attempt to recapture the rail junction under General Van Dorn.

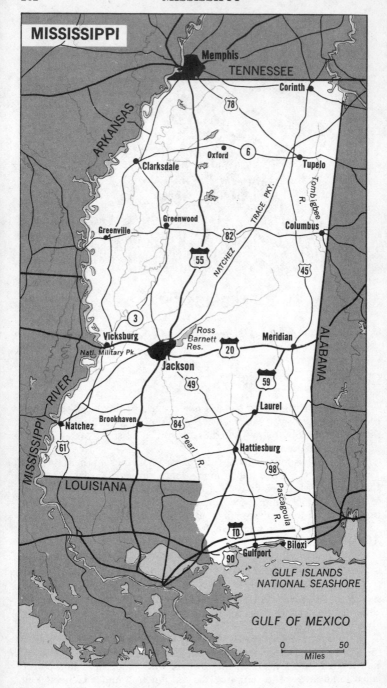

MISSISSIPPI

Memphis
TENNESSEE
Corinth
ARKANSAS
78
Oxford
6
Tupelo
Clarksdale
Tombigbee R.
Greenwood
82
TRACE PKY.
Columbus
Greenville
55
NATCHEZ
45
3
Ross Barnett Res.
Meridian
Vicksburg
20
Natl. Military Pk
Jackson
ALABAMA
49
59
MISSISSIPPI RIVER
Brookhaven
84
Laurel
Natchez
Pearl R.
61
Hattiesburg
98
LOUISIANA
Pascagoula R.
10
90
Gulfport
Biloxi

GULF ISLANDS
NATIONAL SEASHORE

GULF OF MEXICO

0   50
Miles

One mile east on Cemetery Street, you will find the Corinth National Cemetery, established in 1866 to provide a burial place for Union soldiers who died in the vicinity. There are 5,763 graves, of which 3,993 bear no names. The soldiers represented 273 regiments from fifteen states.

Taking US 72 east from Corinth to Iuka, you can visit the J. P. Coleman State Park, 12 miles northeast of Iuka and three miles east of State 25. The 1,468-acre park, situated on a bend in the Tennessee River, affords some of the most beautiful national scenery found in the state. You can watch passing tugboats and their tows for twelve miles on the river. Modern facilities include eight air-conditioned, duplex cabins, picnic areas, tent and trailer camping sites, and a boat launching ramp. Hiking, fishing, and swimming are popular on Pickwick Lake, formed by the dam of the same name across the state line in Tennessee.

Returning to Iuka, which was the site of a Civil War engagement in 1862, you continue south thirteen miles on State 25 to explore Tishomingo State Park. Named in honor of a great Chickasaw chief, it's located three miles east of the little town of the same name. The 1,400-acre park is divided by Bear Creek, which flows into the Tennessee River. Haynes Lake and Bear Creek are noted for excellent fishing, but be prepared to man the oars—no motors are allowed.

Tupelo and Its Battlefields

Continuing south on State 25 to Fulton, and there turning west on US 78, you can reach Tupelo, a town built on what were Chickasaw lands, ceded by the Indians in the Treaty of Pontotoc in 1832. In addition to its historical importance, Tupelo also is noted as the birthplace of Elvis Presley, and for the less momentous annual birth of some three million gamefish at the Federal Fish Hatchery. The hatchery, located at 101 Elizabeth Street, is one of the oldest in the Federal system, dating back to 1902. Covering seventeen acres with fifteen ponds, it produces largemouth black bass, bluegill, redear, sunfish and channel catfish. Annually 3,000,000-odd fish are distributed for use in management of ponds and reservoirs in twenty-four counties in northern Mississippi.

Within a radius of less than twenty-five miles of Tupelo are three national battlefield sites. Oldest is Ackia Battleground National Monument, a forty-nine-acre tract, between US 78 and State 6 on the old Natchez Trace. In 1736 the Battle of Ackia was fought on this site, once the location of an Indian village. In the eighteenth century, the French had widely separated centers of influence in North America, scattered from Canada through Illinois to the lower Mississippi Valley (New Orleans and Mobile). The Chickasaws, allies of the English, occupied a strategic area separating the French positions. Bienville, governor of Louisiana, in 1736 led an expedition from New Orleans against the Chickasaws, hoping to remove them as a menace to French lines of communication. His force failed to meet with another French expedition from Illinois, and in separate attacks, both failed to defeat the Chickasaws. Bienville's forces were so badly defeated at Ackia that he was forced to withdraw to Mobile, and France's position was badly weakened during her struggle with the English in the French and Indian Wars.

Approximately 20 miles northwest of Tupelo and six miles west of Baldwyn is the Brice's Cross Roads National Battlefield site, honoring both the Blue and Grey who fought here on June 10, 1864. As was the case with Rommel during his desert campaign, Sherman overextended his supply line when he invaded Georgia during 1864. Having been informed of General Forrest's plan to attack him, Sherman attempted to gain the element of surprise and had a detachment from Memphis move to engage Forrest. The Union force of some 8,000 men encountered Forrest's 4,800 at Brice's Cross Roads. After a daylong battle, the Federals were defeated, Forrest capturing all of the Federal supplies. Brice's Crossroads Museum, housed in a log-cabin pioneer home, features relics of Americana, Indian artifacts and interesting articles from the Civil War.

Nearest Tupelo is the third of the battle sites, the Tupelo National Battleground, one mile west of the downtown section of the city. The engagement here was the climax of the series of operations designed to protect Sherman's flank as he attacked Atlanta. Not content with having attacked Atlanta, the Union Army chased after General Forrest into Mississippi, ordering the expedition to "follow him to death, if it costs 10,000 men and breaks the Treasury."

The Union force of 14,000 men, which made a column fifteen miles long on the march, after fighting off Confederate raids for nine days, reached Harrisburg (today, within the Tupelo town limits) on July 13. Forrest attacked the following morning. Three assaults failed, and, low on ammunition, the Federals withdrew four miles. Forrest attacked this encampment but was driven off. The Union forces again withdrew, the Confederates following, but there were no more major attacks. Although an indecisive engagement, it served the purpose of keeping Forrest from attacking Sherman's supply line to Atlanta. After the Georgia capital fell, Sherman no longer depended upon his supply line, as he began his famous March to the Sea through Georgia, living off the land and leaving a path of destruction in his wake.

Near Tupelo also is the site of de Soto's winter camp in 1540-41. But seven miles east-southeast on State 6 is a more exciting spot. Tombigbee State Park, covering 822 acres, is famous as a fisherman's haven with its 100-acre lake. Facilities include tent and trailer camping sites, swimming area and a nature trail. Each summer, a fishing rodeo for children is held, and often the youngsters surpass their elders.

Columbus, Old Possum Town

Heading south again on State 45W, you reach Okolona, headquarters of the 65,232-acre Tombigbee National Forest, reached by either State 41 or 32. Davis and Choctaw Lakes are the two favorite recreational areas in the forest. The facilities offered are seasonal hunting and fishing, water sports and picnicking.

Continuing south on State 45W, you come to the junction with US 82. By turning east, you can visit Columbus, noted for its tree-shaded streets and beautiful, antebellum mansions. The first week in April a pilgrimage is held through nineteen of the houses. The program includes a Friendship Cemetery Observance and Parade, Candlelight Dinner, Junior Auxiliary Pageant and Ball, and tours of the city, the Air Force Base, and the campus of Mississippi University for Women. The latter, founded in 1847 as the Columbus Female Institute, was the first state-supported school in the nation to offer education exclusively for women. The home of the famous Confederate General Stephen D. Lee is now a museum containing his papers and personal belongings.

Columbus' past stretches back to the time of de Soto. The Spanish conquistador is believed to have entered what is now Mississippi in the vicinity of Columbus, in 1540. Columbus was an early stopover on the Military Road ordered built by Andrew Jackson between New Orleans and Nashville, at first being called "Possum Town," a name apparently the product of local Indian wit. In 1821 educators established the first public school in the state, while the following year Tombigbee River was the site of a historic event, the arrival of the first steamboat at Columbus.

Columbus' Friendship Cemetery was the site of the first Memorial Day observance on April 16, 1866, when the women of Columbus gathered to decorate both Confederate and Union graves. (This date is still Confederate Memorial Day in Mississippi, Alabama, Florida and Georgia.)

Heading west from Columbus on US 82, it's a short drive to Starkville, once an antebellum center of plantation life, now noted for its proximity to Mississippi State University. Established in 1878 and formerly known as Mississippi Agricultural and Mechanical College, MSU is located 1½ miles south of Starkville in the little town of State College. The 750-acre campus includes an agricultural experimental station, which utilizes much of the 4,000-acre tract assigned to the university.

Heading south on State 25, you pass through a portion of the southern section of the Tombigbee National Forest, and into Louisville. Here, change to State 15 and continue to Philadelphia, center of Mississippi's Indian country. This is the headquarters of the Choctaw Indian Agency, and the majority of the few Indians—less than 2,000—in the state live in this region. At Nanih Waiya Historic Site, 15 miles northeast off State 21, you can see the Indian facet of Mississippi history. The state park includes the Nanih Waiya Mound, the Nanih Waiya Cave, and the site of the Dancing Rabbit Treaty, which opened the state to white settlement. Currently it's a day-use area, undergoing expansion. East of Philadelphia via State 16 and 39 is Shuqualak, on US 45, one of the several Mississippi sites for bird dog National Field Trials. Southwest of Philadelphia eighteen miles on State 21 is another state park—Golden, affording swimming, fishing, picnicking, camping and canoeing.

Memorials in Meridian

Taking State 19 southeast from Philadelphia, you can reach Meridian, one of the leading industrial cities of the state, located in a region of abundant raw materials for wood and pulp industries and for textile manufacturing. The town is the site of the Jimmie Rodgers Memorial honoring one of America's most famous folk singers, grandfather of today's country music. Annually top stars in the music world gather to honor this outstanding entertainer.

Merrehope, in Meridian, is one of less than half a dozen residences left standing after the burning of the city during General William T. Sherman's fiery campaign of 1864. Included on the National Register of Historic Places, Merrehope has been restored and opened by the Meridian Restorations Foundation. During the Christmas season, Merrehope displays Christmas trees decorated in the styles of different nations.

The most direct route from Meridian to Laurel is via US 11. However, by taking a slightly longer route, US 45 to Quitman and State 512 to its junction with US 11, you can visit Clarkco State Park, a short distance north of Quitman. The 792-acre park is named for Clarke County, in which it is located. This is gently rolling land, featuring woodlands of loblolly pine, mixed with red and white oak, redbud and dogwood. Facilities include rental cabins, swimming, boating, fishing, picnicking, playfields, nature trails and tent and trailer camping.

Two sawmill men built Laurel in the piney woods of southeastern Mississippi after the Reconstruction, naming the town for the abundant flowering shrub in the area. But despite its pretty name, Laurel was a rough lumber camp for years. It began to bloom after an eastern company took over the mill and encouraged workers to buy houses. The state's first garden club was organized here in the 1890's. In contrast to its rough beginning, Laurel today has an unusual library—the Lauren Rodgers Library and Museum of Art, featuring permanent collections of American and European paintings, including works by Homer, Whistler, Corot, De Hoog and Daumier, Japanese prints, sculpture, pottery, glass and Indian relics.

Heading south from Laurel to Hattiesburg, you can sample Mississippi's I-59 interstate freeway—excellent for fast driving, but like others in the nation, not designed for sightseeing. However, you miss nothing of great import even at freeway speeds. You zip through Jones County, where, at Ellisville, nonslave-owning farmers elected a delegate to vote against secession. He didn't, and they burned him in effigy. Then they conducted guerrilla operations against the Confederates throughout the war.

Hattiesburg is another of the lumber towns in the longleaf pine belt of southern Mississippi. Only a few miles from both sections of the 500,240-acre de Soto National Forest, it still produces lumber and naval stores, but unlike many smaller neighbors which disappeared with the end of the lumber boom in the 1920's, Hattiesburg long ago diversified its industries. It is the site of the University of Southern Mississippi, specializing in teacher training. The university occupies an 840-acre campus. The town also is the site of William Carey College (founded in 1906).

Eight miles south on US 49 is the 805-acre Paul B. Johnson State Park. Tent and trailer camping sites are provided. There is a 225-acre lake, where fishing is excellent, in addition to three small ponds. Facilities for swimming, boating, picnicking and water-skiing are also available.

Twenty-two miles west of Hattiesburg via US 98 is Columbia, a small town noted for being the three-month capital of the state. The scenic Pearl River Valley is the location of the picturesque little town of Sandy Hook, situated on State 358, where the 19th-century John Ford homestead and its excellent collection of antiques and memorabilia can be seen. Throughout the years it has been used as an inn and post office. History reports that Andrew Jackson stayed here overnight on his way to the Battle of New Orleans.

From Hattiesburg, you can take four-lane highway US 49 directly into Gulfport, heart of Mississippi's sixty-five-mile seaside playground on the Gulf of Mexico.

Midstate North to South

You can begin your midstate north-to-south trip in Mississippi from several points on the Tennessee line on I-55. Probably a more interesting means of beginning your exploration can be experienced by entering the state either via US 78 from Memphis, Tenn., or via State 7. Both routes converge on Holly Springs, one of the state's antebellum jewels and once known as the Athens of the South.

Owners of many large plantations in the Carolinas and Virginia, well aware of the rich soil conducive to growing cotton in the Holly Springs vicinity, migrated to the area and settled the town in 1835. While there is much doubt as to the first settler, William Randolph from Virginia is generally considered to be the town's founder.

During this period the inevitable conflicts between cotton dynasties resulted, and legal practitioners found this the ideal place to open business. Because of this rapid growth, the town blossomed overnight into a resplendent community, with columned porches and wide lawns accenting the wealth of the plantations. Even today the restored mansions reflect the gracious living which characterized this time, and visitors from many states come to view many of the homes during the Holly Springs Pilgrimage in April.

The touch of the Civil War did not escape Holly Springs, despite her opulence, for it was here that over sixty-one minor skirmishes were fought, and in 1862, Confederate General Van Dorn dealt a crushing blow to the Union by destroying a supply base with a value estimated by General Grant at almost one million dollars. This one act stalled the attack on Vicksburg and lengthened the war by six months. The North was forced to regroup and reorganize supply lines before pressing on.

The Kate Freeman Clark Art Gallery in Holly Springs has been maintained as a memorial to one of the noted painters of the day, and visitors can see hundreds of her paintings on display here. Living a semisecluded life from 1923 until her death in 1963, Miss Clark kept many of her paintings in her home, and in later years provided funds for their display at the gallery.

A short distance south of Holly Springs on State 7 is 855-acre Wall Doxey State Park featuring lake swimming, fishing, boating, both developed and primitive camping.

Ole Miss and Oxford

Twenty-seven miles south of Holly Springs is Oxford, site of the University of Mississippi (Ole Miss). Borrowing its name from the Old World, as did many other towns, it rallied to the bugle when the Civil War broke out, sending many men to battle for the South, with the university contributing the famous regiment the Grays.

Oxford, too, was the home of one of the nation's great writers, the late William Faulkner, who lived near the university at 900 Garfield Street. Oxford is the "Jefferson" featured in so many of Faulkner's novels. In St. Peter's Cemetery is the grave of Lucius Quintus Cincinnatus Lamar, who drafted the Ordinance of Secession which was adopted by the Mississippi Convention on January 9, 1861. By a quirk of historical fate, he later became a U.S. Supreme Court Justice (1888-1893) and was noted for his work in reconciling the North and South before his death in 1893.

On Ole Miss campus in the Mary Buie Museum, founded by descendants of General Nathanael Greene of American Revolutionary War fame, are interesting displays of historic relics as well as medals and prizes awarded to Faulkner, 1949 Nobel Prize winner for literature.

Both Holly Springs and Oxford lie east of your main north-south route, but you can rejoin it (and I-55) either by taking State 4 from Holly Springs to Senatobia, or State 6 from Oxford to Batesville. If you take the first route to Senatobia, you can visit the Arkabutla Reservoir. North on I-55 is Hernando, one of several sites in Mississippi where U.S. and National Bird Dog Field Trials are held annually. Another site is at Shuqualak.

Between Senatobia and Batesville along I-55 is Sardis, near Sardis Lake and Dam. The dam is several miles east on State 315. Its water has created a thirty-mile-long lake, part of the Yazoo Basin flood control project, from the Little Tallahatchie River. John W. Kyle State Park covers 740 acres, for primitive and developed camping, with laundry facilities.

Proceeding south on either I-55 or US 51, you reach Grenada, on the eastern edge of the famous Mississippi-Yazoo Delta. Cotton always has been an economic mainstay, and now is joined by livestock raising, lumbering and nylon manufacturing. Chartered in 1836, the city developed from an important early trading post. Line Street marks the division between the old towns of Pittsburg and Tulahoma, founded by rival companies. Tired of competing and feuding, the two towns merged in 1836, celebrating the marriage of a Pittsburg man and Tulahoma maiden. Grenada was the headquarters of General Pemberton during Grant's second campaign against Vicksburg. The Grenada Historical Museum is on Poplar St.

Near Grenada are two state parks, both on the 64,000-acre Grenada Reservoir, three miles northeast of the town. Hugh White Park, located on State 8, covers 1,500 acres and features boating, swimming, fishing and camping, both primitive and developed. White also has a trailer area and a restaurant.

South of Grenada, US 51 begins to curve gradually southwestward as it heads for Jackson, the capital named in honor of Old Hickory. Near Durant, you can visit the 463-acre Holmes County State Park. It features fishing, swimming, boating, nature trails, rental cabins and camping.

Jackson, the capital, is your next stop, and well worth careful investigation. Jackson was laid out as the capital before it was even settled. In 1821, the legislature, which previously had met in Natchez and Washington, appointed a commission to select a site within twenty miles of the geographic center of the state, in the territory sold to the U.S. by the Choctaw Treaty of Doak's Stand in 1820. The commission chose Le Fleur's Bluffs, where French Canadian Louis Le Fleur had set up a trading post in 1792. The new capital was named for Andrew Jackson, and designed on a checkerboard plan with alternate squares reserved as commons. Surviving attempts to move the capital to Clinton and Port

Gibson, Jackson slowly grew and was firmly established by 1850. By the time of the Civil War, it was not only the center of state government, but also an important rail junction.

After the legislature passed the Ordinance of Secession in 1861, Miss Amanda Hilzheim produced a blue silk flag with a single star for the occasion. An Irish actor, Harry McCarthy, who was playing in town, wrote and sang three verses of the "Bonnie Blue Flag" as Mississippi withdrew from the Union. The capital played an important role in the Confederacy until 1863, when the Federal Army, commanded by General W. T. Sherman, besieged and captured it. Sherman's forces burned and looted it, but the legislature and state officials were safe, having fled previously to Columbus. Scars of the war remain. A Battlefield Park features a chain of Civil War entrenchments.

During rebuilding Jackson had to contend with hordes of Carpetbaggers, indicative of the problems of the entire South. It was here, in 1884, that Jefferson Davis last spoke to the vanquished South, and six years later the State Convention drafted the present charter.

Buildings connected with the past and present state government are important attractions for visitors to Jackson. The governor and other state officers can be located in the new state capitol, built over sixty years ago. It also houses the state Hall of Fame. The Governor's Mansion, set on grounds covering an entire block, has an exterior resembling the White House and dates from 1842. The Governor's Mansion has been restored, filled with American antiques that date from 1785 to 1840, and opened to the public. It is a National Historical Landmark. In 1908 the mansion was almost razed to make way for a commercial development. But the question was raised: "Will Mississippi destroy that which Sherman would not burn?" And the legislature voted no.

You can spend hours in the State Historical Museum, located in the Old Capitol. This aging structure, begun in 1833 and occupied by the Mississippi Legislature from 1839 until 1903, is an excellent example of Greek Revival architecture. Used later as an office building, the Old Capitol was completely restored (1959-61) at a cost of $1,600,000, excluding the cost of the furniture. The building originally cost $400,000.

During the restoration, rooms that had been modified in converting the Old Capitol to an office building were returned to their original state. Mississippi's history is capsuled by four dioramas in the building, depicting the discovery of the Mississippi River by de Soto in May, 1541; the Treaty of Doak's Stand in October, 1820, by which some 5,500,000 acres of land were opened to white civilization; the landing of the first steamboat at Natchez, December, 1811; and the running of the Confederate batteries at Vicksburg by Yankee gunboats in April, 1863, prelude to the capture of the city.

You can also inspect the restored governor's office with its ornate, authentic period furnishings, and the historic Hall of Representatives, where such important events occurred as the passage of the first law in America giving property rights to married women (1839); Andrew Jackson's address (1840); the passage of the Ordinance of Secession (1861); the Constitutional Convention of 1865, first in the South after the fall of the Confederacy; the overthrow of carpetbag government by the legislature of 1876; and Jefferson Davis' last address to the legislature (1884).

Also on the grounds is the Archives and History Building, which houses the State Department of Archives and History collections and valuable books and manuscripts.

Lovers of the outdoors will be interested in the Museum of Natural Science maintained by the State Game and Fish Commission. One feature of the museum is the excellent collection of state animals on display. There are approximately 25,000 specimens. The zoological park in Jackson is gaining one of the finest reputations in the country. A decade ago it was a sad collection of wild animals in a run-down setting. The present inventory, however, lists 748 specimens, ranking Jackson's zoo in the top 50 of the nation.

The Jackson City Hall, one block south of the Capitol on President Street, managed to survive the burning of the town by General Sherman's troops.

East of Jackson on US 80, at the edge of the Bienville National Forest, is Roosevelt State Park, covering 562 acres. It's three miles south of Morton. Facilities are similar to those in other Mississippi State Parks.

Continue south via I-55 and US 51, and in less than a hundred miles, you're approaching Louisiana. At McComb, a small railroad and manufacturing city, you can make a side trip to Percy Quin State Park, five miles southwest on State 24. Second largest in the state system, it comprises 1,680 acres, including a 675-acre lake. It provides group camping facilities, as well as rental cabins, boating, swimming, fishing, nature and bridle trails.

The Historic Mississippi River Country

No portion of the state is richer than the Mississippi River country, extending through the Delta section. Here the state's history began when de Soto first saw the mighty Father of Waters, and here French explorers cruised. Here, too, the Spanish were briefly in control, and here were fought some of the most important battles of the Civil War.

US 61, entering Mississippi from Memphis, Tennessee, provides a natural route to explore this most historic section of the state. Clarksdale is your first stop. Named for an Englishman, John Clark, it was founded after the Civil War (1868). However, it has a Civil War connection, for ten miles north is Yazoo Pass, through which General Grant attempted unsuccessfully to attack Vicksburg via inland waterways. De Soto first glimpsed the Mississippi River, in 1541, somewhere between Clarksdale and Memphis.

You have two routes south from Clarksdale. If you want to see Mississippi's big cotton market, then take US 49 and later the US 49E fork to Greenwood, which is particularly interesting during the cotton harvesting season, August to December. By taking US 61 south from Clarksdale and US 82 east from Leland, you can head for Greenville. (You also can reach Greenville by going west on US 82 from Greenwood.)

Mississippi's largest river port is not even on the river. Greenville, from its rebirth after being burned to the ground during the Civil War, steadily lost its riverfront streets to the river's currents that gnawed off great chucks of paved streets and two-story buildings. During the great flood of 1927, most of the city was under water for 70 days. Armed with a promise from the Corps of Engineers that dredges would keep open a year-round channel 9-feet deep, city fathers permitted the corps to close off the upstream opening of the branch of the river that flowed by the city, forcing all the stream into the other branch on the far side of an island facing the city. The corps left open the lower end of that chute, so that Greenville stands on a slack-water arm of the river, connected with the main channel but free of destructive currents. To take advantage of that slack water, many towboat companies and shipbuilding firms have made Greenville a kind of Liberia of the river trade.

Greenville has produced an uncommon number of writers for so small a city, among them William Alexander Percy, whose autobiography has remained in print as a standard explanation of the Old South through more than a score of printings and many decades; Hodding Carter, who won a Pulitzer Prize for his editorials defending civil rights for blacks; Shelby Foote, a prominent novelist and historian; Dave Cohn, a brilliant humorous, essayist and social historian; Ellen Douglas, a novelist who has won national awards; Bern Keating, author of 25 nonfiction books; Walker Percy, novelist and winner of the National Book Award; and Charles Bell, poet and novelist. Here you can also visit the Winterville Indian Mounds Museum and State Park. The museum has collections of archeology and Indian artifacts. At least 23 mounds are indicated in the area, 13 within the park itself. Arranged in an oval, they form two plazas, an unusual feature distinguishing Winterville from lesser sites. Development of the mounds, archaeologists say, began soon after the year 100. Winterville is a primary temple mound that ranks in size and importance with just a half dozen others in the country.

If you want to drive along the levees as close to the Mississippi River as possible, you can follow State 1 south from Greenville. An alternate route south is to follow US 82 east to Leland and then turn south on US 61. Both routes give you good views of the Delta country.

Between State 1 and US 61 west of Hollandale is the largest of the Mississippi parks, 2,441-acre Leroy Percy, with facilities similar to other major parks, plus the most spectacular natural display of live alligators in North America. Visitors view the giant beasts from a boardwalk over a swamp and wallowing hole. Because the hole is fed by hot springs, the gators are active year-round. Continue south on State 1 and take an 8-mile dogleg east on State 14 to Rolling Fork. Turn south on US 61 toward Vicksburg. However, if you want to sample further the Delta National Forest area, you can make a side trip via State 3 from Redwood to Yazoo City. You travel through low, flat, moist hardwood country bordering the 59,288-acre forest. This area is noted for fishing and squirrel, turkey, and waterfowl hunting. Near Yazoo City the first oil field in the state was discovered, the beginning of oil production in 1939 spurring a rapid industrial development. Now the city's economic base rests upon chemicals, oil refineries and cottonseed oil, as well as agriculture. It's the market center for a large farming area producing some $3 million worth of beef cattle, hogs and soybeans, corn and oats, annually.

Vicksburg and the Civil War

It's only eleven miles from Redwood to Vicksburg, the site of one of the greatest battles of the Civil War, the siege of Vicksburg. It's easy to get information about the city. There are two Tourist Information Centers, one on Washington Avenue and one across from the entrance to the military park.

Vicksburg's history stretches back to the early eighteenth century, when the French arrived (1719) and built a fort as protection against the Yazoo and Tunica Indians. The Spanish were in control in 1791 when they established Fort Nogales, but were replaced by the Americans in 1798. However, Vicksburg didn't really get started until the early nineteenth century, when, in 1812, Methodist preacher Newitt Vick and his followers arrived and established what became Vicksburg. The town was incorporated in 1825, and despite the usual river town problems resulting from an unwanted number of gamblers, highwaymen, rough flatboatmen and other unsavory characters, developed rapidly. The Mississippi became an ever more popular artery of travel in the first half of the nineteenth century.

Vicksburg's rough character can be realized easily when it's noted that the first five editors of the *Tri-weekly Sentinel,* established in 1837, died violently. Gamblers didn't like adverse comments. But the early violence was only a prelude to the Civil War, which, today, is Vicksburg's chief tourist asset.

You're impressed immediately with the fact that few cities live more intimately with the past than does Vicksburg. Today, the National Military Park surrounds it, just as the battle lines did more than a century ago, and as you tour the park in your car, you can almost visualize the battle scenes.

The Vicksburg National Military Park is not new, for it was established by Congress in 1899, when the 1,330 acres were set aside as a permanent memorial to the heroes of the Blue and the Gray. It covers the battle area of the actual siege and defense of Vicksburg (May 18 through July 3, 1863). The city surrendered on July 4, on the same day the Confederacy reached its high tide at Gettysburg. The National Cemetery here is even older than the Military Park, having been established in 1866.

The park, shaped like a great crescent, slips peacefully along the rolling hills and timbered thickets of the Mississippi River. From its visitor's center, a self-guided automobile tour winds back along the ditches and trenches where men once fought, and died, to possess control of that mighty river. Cannons, originals from the War Between the States, stare emptily out across the terrain, lining the ridges that once blocked the road to Vicksburg.

The tour passes the Louisiana Monument and Great Redoubt, the largest fort on the Confederate line; the oak tree where Grant and the Southern General, Pemberton, met to negotiate surrender, the Shirley House—the lone surviving wartime building in the park, the Third Louisiana Redan, where Federal engineers constructed a mine and exploded 2,200 pounds of powder in an attempt to blast through the Confederate stronghold, an equestrian statue of General Grant that marks his headquarters, and the National Cemetery, the final resting place for almost 17,000 Union soldiers. Thirteen thousand of them are unknown.

By June 1863, with the exception of the earthworks at Port Hudson, Vicksburg then was the only Confederate stronghold left on the Mississippi. As long as the South held this citadel, free passage of the river by the Union forces was impossible, and supplies, arms and men could be brought from Louisiana, Arkansas and Texas and sent to the Confederate armies in the East. This, then, was the stage for the Federal campaign to capture Vicksburg.

Located on the high bluffs overlooking a hairpin turn in the Mississippi, Vicksburg presented a formidable target. It was not until General Grant moved his army through the Louisiana swamps and marshes west of the river to a point thirty miles south of Vicksburg, and then crossed to the eastern side of the river that conquest was possible. His earlier attempts to approach the city from the north on the Mississippi shore had failed.

He was aided by daring maneuvers of the Federal fleet which ran under the Confederate guns on the bluffs, and, getting south of the city, was able to provide transportation for Grant's troops across the river. Porter's running past the Vicksburg guns was one of the outstanding naval operations of the war.

Operating without a base of supplies, Grant kept two Confederate armies apart, and eventually laid siege to Vicksburg. For forty-seven days and nights, the Federals and Confederates bombarded each other. Then, with no prospects of reinforcement, with few supplies and little ammunition, the Confederate garrison surrendered on July 4, 1863, and the fate of the Confederacy was sealed, although it was two years before Lee and Grant met at Appomattox Courthouse.

As you look down upon the Mississippi from the bluffs, you marvel that any gunboat could run the batteries successfully. Regarding the steep, trench-topped hills, you understand why the direct Union assaults failed. Hunger and lack of supplies, however, didn't fail, and the city fell.

If you take time to examine the numerous statues, monuments, memorials and signs, you will have a comprehensive knowledge of what took place. The detail with which the campaign is outlined is amazing. There are 898 historical tablets, 274 markers, and 230 monuments commemorating the various military organizations engaged here. As you stand reading each marker, you face in the same direction as the troops who long ago manned the position. There are also nine beautiful memorials, three equestrian statues and 150-odd busts and relief portraits. If you're interested in the ordnance of the period, examine the 128 cannons of various types mounted in the park.

The battlefield is a green, carefully manicured area now, a marked contrast to the shell-pocked terrain of the last century. But as you stand at these vantage points, it doesn't seem nearly as long ago as when you read about it in history books. It's an integral part of America, even today.

The Old Courthouse and Other Landmarks

Probably Vicksburg's most historic Civil War site is the Old Courthouse, once a favorite target of Union guns. It is now a museum containing Confederate memorabilia dealing with life in the South. There are eight display rooms featuring not only weapons of the Civil War, but also silver, glass and early handwritten documents such as receipts for slaves.

Anyone interested in flood control can learn much by visiting the U.S. Army Engineers Waterway Experiment Station on Hall's Ferry Road.

Miniature reproductions of different methods of controlling water are simulated here, and in this way scientists gain an insight into water management, whether it be for power or recreation. The working models vary in size and there are more than fifty of them to examine.

Among the antebellum houses in Vicksburg, three are of particular interest—Planters Hall, McRaven and Cedar Grove. McRaven, located at the eastern end of Harrison Street, developed from a frontier cottage built before 1797, with additions in 1836 and in 1849, the year during which it developed into its present Neo-Greek style with living wing stairway, exquisite plaster wall moldings, ceiling medalions and graceful marble fireplaces. Caught in a crossfire during the siege of Vicksburg, the house still bears shell marks visible both inside and out. John Bobb owned McRaven when General U.S. Grant came marching into Vicksburg. And on a morning in 1864, he glanced out the window and saw Federal troops in his yard. He ordered them to leave. They refused. So Bobb picked up a brick and threw it at them. When the troops returned they were carrying muskets and as Bobb walked alone in his garden, he was shot to death. It marked the first recorded incident of violence against the civilian populace during the Union occupation of Vicksburg. Grant, outraged, had the soldiers courtmartialed and hanged.

Cedar Grove, another antebellum home being restored as a civic project, is located at 2200 Oak Street. It was constructed between 1840 and 1858 by John A. Klein, prominent plantation owner and banker. Cedar Grove, too, bears Civil War scars. Mute testimony of the siege of Vicksburg can be seen in the walls, where Federal warships attempted to level the house with cannonballs but failed.

Planters Hall, at Main and Monroe streets, the third antebellum showplace in Vicksburg, has had a varied career. It was erected in 1832 as a bank, and contained a special second-story apartment for the bank president. The bank prospered until President Andrew Jackson ordered gold or silver payments for government land instead of bank notes. Banking became difficult, and operations ceased in 1848. The building was bought by the McRae family, and converted into a residence. They in turn sold it to the Vicksburg Council of Garden Clubs, who have maintained it as a museum dedicated to the true South.

Vicksburg is at the southern tip of the Delta country, from which you can cross the Mississippi into Louisiana via a large bridge. However, to complete your Mississippi state tour, you'll want to continue southward. US 61 takes you into Port Gibson, a town with a Civil War past closely linked to Vicksburg's. Port Gibson, remembered as the town Grant called "too beautiful to burn," is thirty miles south of Vicksburg and dates from 1788. US 61 enters the city along a wide thoroughfare lined by seven churches, the most famous and most photographed being the First Presbyterian, with its gold-lead, metal hand pointing skyward.

The tombstones in Port Gibson's cemeteries tell interesting tales of American history. In the Protestant Cemetery are the graves of Sam Gibson, founder of Port Gibson, and of Harmon Blennerhasset, associate of Aaron Burr in the Burr Conspiracy. Blennerhasset came to Port Gibson after his acquittal and established a plantation here. In the Catholic Cemetery is the grave of Resin P. Bowie, inventor of the famous bowie knife, first used by his brother, Jim, of Alamo fame in Texas history.

You'll want to make two side trips from Port Gibson. On Old Rodney Road, ten miles from town, are the ruins of Windsor. Built in 1861, and consisting of five stories and an observatory, it was one of the most extravagant antebellum mansions of Greek Revival style in the state. Because of sniping, General Grant was going to burn Windsor, but was dissuaded by the sweet-talking hostess. The mansion did burn in 1890. Nearby is the ghost town of Rodney—a town the river moved away from.

No town in the state felt the blows of the Civil War more than Grand Gulf. The Confederates fortified it to harass the Federals controlling the river. Beginning in May, 1862, the Union Navy bombarded Grand Gulf in reprisal for the Confederate attacks. In June, a landing party torched much of the town. The Confederates returned, and the Federals finally sent a strong column inland after landing at Bayou Pierre. During the march, the Federals were fired upon by a field gun mounted on a railroad flatcar and protected by bales of cotton, a forerunner of the armored trains of later wars. The Federals again occupied Grand Gulf and destroyed what was left.

War returned to the area in 1863 when General Pemberton had the Confederates throw up defenses against General Grant's forces, which he feared, correctly, would bypass Vicksburg. Rebuffed in his efforts to get at Vicksburg from the north, Grant marched his army southward on the Louisiana shore in late March, intending to cross the Mississippi and capture Grand Gulf. By April 29, the Union forces were ready to attempt the crossing. Admiral Porter's ironclad squadron began a sustained attack for five hours. By then, one Union vessel had been disabled, and one of the two Confederate forts silenced, but the big guns at Fort Wade, the second fort, still boomed. The Federals called off the attack, and the next day crossed the Mississippi at Bruinsburg with little opposition. After crossing, Grant moved north to begin his siege of Vicksburg.

A four-room cottage from the early days of Grand Gulf has been reconstructed to serve as a museum. Two rooms house Civil War displays, including large naval shells hurled into the forts by gunboats, drawings of the battle by actual participants, and colorful dioramas. Scattered through the 104-acre park are the remains of Forts Cobun and Wade, including some of the best preserved, original Civil War trenches and gun emplacements existing anywhere. What's left of the town of Grand Gulf is just outside the park boundaries.

Antebellum Natchez

Natchez, only a short distance farther south on US 61, is your introduction to an antebellum town where time seems to have stood still. Don't, however, despite the flood of promotional literature, assume you're going to see nothing but antebellum mansions, ladies in hoopskirts and men in frock coats. They're for publicity picture purposes only. The town treasures its antebellum past with greater intensity than most communities, however, and profitably so, for the antebellum is its prime tourist appeal. It's also a manufacturing town, and modern buildings

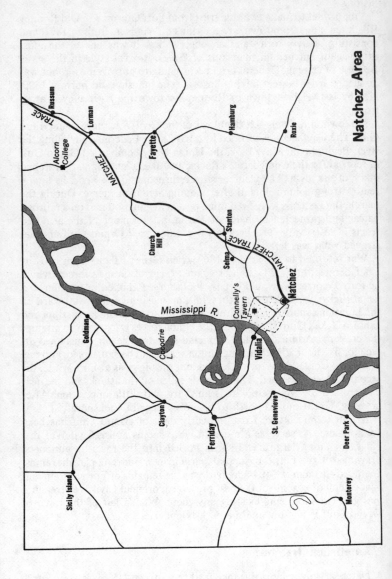

Natchez Area

mingle with the dominating eighteenth and nineteenth-century structures.

There's a lesser-known side to Natchez, however. Its history of bear-grease trapping, the role of the Indians for whom it was named, and the days of Natchez-under-the-Hill which was known far and wide as a den of iniquity, remained hidden subjects of conversation, while Natchez-on-the-Hill was developing as a wealthy, dignified city.

Its history is interwoven with that of the entire Mississippi valley. La Salle visited here in 1682, as did the enterprising Bienville, who established a fort in 1716. In 1729, the Natchez massacred everyone in the settlement. Later, the French, with the aid of the Choctaws, drove the Natchez Indians from the area. Spain held control briefly, the Americans taking over in 1798. Here, in 1797, the American flag was raised for the first time in the lower Mississippi Valley, a year before the Spanish left.

After the Civil War, steamboating continued to bring some prosperity to Natchez, but the loss of the slaves from the huge plantations was a blow stunting development. Natchez was the home of Captain Tom Leathers, who built several steamboats, all named *Natchez,* including the one which ran the famous race with the *Robert E. Lee* in 1870. The prize was $20,000. And Cap'n Leathers lost because he waited in a fog bank for six hours rather than endanger the lives of his passengers. So he returned to his home, Myrtle-Terrace, broke but proud.

Undoubtedly more people visit Natchez during the annual Spring Pilgrimage (March and April) than at any other time. The Pilgrimage was established during the Great Depression of the 1930's by the more farsighted ladies of the town. Since then, it has achieved national stature, and the old has become almost a way of life. In all, thirty antebellum homes are open to the public in Natchez. Many of the houses are open daily, some only during the Pilgrimage. The complete list can be obtained from the Natchez-Adams County Chamber of Commerce, which will tell you which ones are open during your visit, and tours can be arranged.

Many of the homes have their own stories to tell. Memories of Union looters still haunt Lansdowne. But even so, many of the original furnishings remain. Green Leaves houses such treasures as letters from Jefferson Davis and a saber from the Battle of Waterloo. The Briars, an old plantation home, was the girlhood home of Varina Howell who married Jefferson Davis. The Burn served as headquarters and hospital for northern forces during the occupation of Natchez. And Melrose has the only landscape ever painted by John James Audubon.

Natchez-Under-the-Hill is nothing more today than a ghost town in the heart of a city. Once it had the reputation of being the Devil's own personal workshop, a hard-drinking, always-fighting sort of place. During those lusty times, it was said that the only thing cheaper in Natchez than a woman's body was a man's life. Developers are beginning to restore the site. Already there are a tavern and a restaurant specializing in catfish dinners. The jazz orchestra from the steamboat *Mississippi Queen* often gives an impromptu concert at the tavern when the boat ties up at the wharf only 100 yards away.

On Ellicott's Hill can be seen Connelly's Tavern, which is one of the most interesting historic buildings open to the public. Its rules were simple. Fourpence a night for bed, sixpence with supper. No more than five to sleep in one bed. No boots to be worn in bed. Organ grinders to sleep in the washhouse. No dogs allowed upstairs. No beer allowed in the kitchen. No razor grinders or tinkers taken in. And it was inside these walls that former Vice-president Aaron Burr planned his defense against the charge of treason.

Another antebellum mansion, probably the most lavish remaining in Natchez, is Stanton Hall, built in 1851, and now owned by the Pilgrimage Garden Club. Located at Pearl and Monroe Streets, it's an imposing white structure set beneath towering oaks. Among its outstanding features are carrara marble mantles, bronze chandeliers, enormous mirrors from France, and a 72-foot ballroom.

Another interesting mansion is Longwood; its architecture has been described as Moorish, Egyptian, Byzantine, and bizarre. But it was the home and the dream of Dr. Haller Nutt, a Union sympathizer. He even raised the American flag above Longwood during the war. So Confederate soldiers burned his cottonfields. He fed and clothed Union troops, then watched in dismay as they marched away and put the torch to his cotton gin, three plantations and sawmill. Suddenly, Dr. Haller had nothing left in this world. He died of a broken heart and Longwood was never finished.

A side trip from Natchez via US 84-98 takes you to the Homochitto National Forest (189,072 acres), in one of the finest natural timber growing areas in the United States. Camping, picnicking, swimming and fishing are available.

You're less than fifty miles from the Louisiana line when you head south from Natchez. You can cross into Louisiana at Vidalia via the bridge at Natchez, but more than likely you'll prefer to continue southward. The Woodville area boasts two little-known sites connected to Mississippi and American history.

The Natchez Trace

For the motorists who abhor traffic, there's the Natchez Trace, leading southwest across the state from Tupelo to Natchez, and making accessible many historical points and accommodations.

Three state parks, with lodges, cabins and campsites available, are near the parkway entrance at Tupelo, on US 45 just north of town. Heading south you will find historic sites indicated by markers, with picnic spots nearby. There's the Old Chickasaw Indian Village, a French-Indian battleground and a nature trail just four miles from the parkway entrance. Twelve miles further you'll see where de Soto crossed the Trace enroute to the Mississippi River and camped in the winter of 1540-41. Past the Chickasaw Agency, relax at Davis Lake recreation area, located twelve miles off the Trace. Farther south is another similar spot, Choctaw Lake recreation area, eighteen miles off the Trace.

At Jackson, you'll find excellent accommodations. Outstanding attractions have been described in earlier pages of this chapter. Back to the Trace via State 18, you'll find Port Gibson, Windsor, and Rodney (also described on previous pages), not far from the Trace.

The Natchez Trace, following the trails of Indians and wild animals, became the link for communication between the Mississippi Territory and Washington, D.C. But it wasn't an important frontier highway until Thomas Jefferson, in 1801, ordered the U.S. Army to clear the road and, seven years later, appropriated $6 million for improvements.

The Natchez Trace Parkway doesn't pretend to follow the exact route of the original trail, yet all along the way you can find, and hike back along, depressions that once were the wilderness road. Markers have been erected every few miles to point out historic sites. Some are still visible: Emerald Mound, the crumbling ghost town of Rocky Springs, restored Mount Locust, an early pioneer hostelry and Tupelo Bald Cypress Swamp.

Along the Gulf Coast

Mississippi's sixty-five-mile stretch of coast bordering the Gulf of Mexico runs from the Alabama line to Louisiana and affords the state its own playground in the sun. I-10 and US 90, a four-lane highway from Pascagoula to Bay St. Louis, follows the Old Spanish Trail that ran from St. Augustine, Fla., to the missions in California. Today, there's scant evidence of the Spanish era, but the conquistadors are as much a part of the area's history as the French, English and Americans who also ruled here.

Along the blue waters of the gulf and its bayous grow colorful flowers, the dense green foliage hinting of the tropics. Moss-bearded giant oaks grow everywhere in profusion. A mixture of antebellum with twentieth-century recreation, the coast offers sun-kissed beaches and plenty of water sports—swimming, water-skiing, fishing and boating.

Entering Mississippi from Alabama via US 90, your first stop is Pascagoula, a shipbuilding center that boomed during World War II. Dating from 1718, Pascagoula has had a long and colorful history, one of the main centers of attraction being the Old Spanish Fort. Designed by the Frenchman, Joseph Simon de la Pointe, the structure is a monument to the creativity of its builders. The fort was constructed from fallen trees, mud, and even sea shells. Cited as the oldest building in the area, it is now used as a museum and is filled with artifacts of historical significance. The thick mud walls even today could withstand the onslaught of cannon balls.

No one can visit Pascagoula without hearing the legend of the singing river. The Indians have lent a touch of color to the area as well, for here is the Singing Pascagoula River which emits a low humming sound. While scientists have two or three possible answers which attempt to explain the oddity, none of them are as colorful as the Indian legend. Apparently, a young warrior of the Pascagoula tribe fell in love with a princess from the powerful Biloxi tribe. He managed to spirit her away much to the anger of the Biloxis, who attacked the Pascagoulas. Upon realizing that they were outnumbered and could not win, the Pascagoulas walked into the river and drowned themselves, their death song to this day clinging to the water. Thus, the legend persists, adding color to local literature.

In this region of former French-Spanish domination, it's not surprising that Mardi Gras is a big event. Here it takes the form of an eight-week carnival ending on Shrove Tuesday. As in New Orleans and Mobile, there are parades and other festivities, the schedule growing a bit longer each year.

With numerous antebellum homes, Pascagoula has joined the growing number of cities having spring pilgrimages sponsored by garden clubs. Exact last-minute details and dates can be obtained by writing the Chamber of Commerce.

Proceeding westward on US 90, you come to Ocean Springs, original site of Biloxi when d'Iberville made his settlement in 1699. There was some question as to whether this was the site of the original settlement, but the discovery of weapons from warships in the shallow bay dispelled the doubt. For a period of over 150 years, the town did little more than exist, then the influx of tourists about the turn of the century transformed it into a resort area, and it has grown to nationwide popularity over the past years.

Neighboring Biloxi, a short distance west, is one of the key points on the Mississippi sun-and-sand strip. Founded when the original settlement of Ocean Springs was shifted here, it has been a resort since the middle of the nineteenth century when the cotton planters first indulged in seaside recreation. Biloxi is not only a beach resort, the area is also noted for the quantity of seafood it has produced since the 1870's. Since 1883, shrimp has been one of the major products, and today, the seafood industry is an important part of the city's economic life.

Twelve miles across Mississippi Sound is Ship Island, part of the Gulf Islands National Seashore and site of ruined Fort Massachusetts. Because the sound is shallow, seagoing vessels from the early days of the French colonists landed first on Ship Island. The most popular cargo was eighty maidens sent from France in the early eighteenth century to be wives of the bachelor pioneers.

Fort Massachusetts was built by orders of Jefferson Davis while he was Secretary of War. Ironically, its only military use was as a prison for Confederate captives. The British fleet and army that assaulted New Orleans during the War of 1812 was based on Ship Island. The body of their leader, Sir Edward Pakenham, felled by one of Andy Jackson's sharpshooting riflemen, was packed into a barrel of rum for shipment home. Scheduled boat service connects Ship Island with both Gulfport and Biloxi. Also lying offshore are Deer Island, only half a mile from East Beach Boulevard in Biloxi, and Horn and Cat islands. The latter, actually closer to Gulfport than Biloxi, was named Cat Island because the French explorers, unfamiliar with raccoons, mistook them for large cats.

The area around Biloxi is filled with natural beauty and the streets of the town are accented with brilliant blooms and the majesty of tall trees shading the sidewalks, while strands of Spanish moss reach down from the limbs. With its long past, it's only natural that Biloxi has numerous historical points of interest. The dyed-in-the-wool Southerners undoubtedly are most proud of Beauvoir, the Jefferson Davis Shrine and Memorial Gardens, five miles west on US 90 (W. Beach Boulevard). This was the home of the Confederate president for the last twenty-two years of his life, after his release from a Federal prison in Virginia. After Davis died in 1889, the building was converted into a home for Confederate soldiers. Later, it was converted into a Confederate shrine, including a museum housing various Davis and Confederate relics. You can see the little white cottage Davis used as his library. Here, he wrote the *Rise and Fall of the Confederate Government.* There's also a Confederate cemetery.

In the same vicinity, along US 90, is the Biloxi Lighthouse, now operated by the United States Coast Guard. Upon the death of Lincoln it was painted black, but now is white. Before automation the light was tended for sixty-two years by a mother and daughter team.

Driving along US 90, you begin to realize the tremendous extent of the beach. The highway separates the sand strip from the hotels, motels, restaurants and other appurtenances of a beach resort, affording a twenty-six-mile stretch of sand and surf. North of Biloxi on State 15 (also north of Gulfport on US 49) is the de Soto National Forest, a cool place in summer.

Between Biloxi and Gulfport occurred a famous bit of heavyweight boxing history. Here was held the bare knuckles, heavyweight championship fight in which John L. Sullivan beat Paddy Ryan, on February 7, 1882. (The last bare knuckles, heavyweight championship bout was also held in Mississippi. John L. Sullivan defeated Jack Kilrain in seventy-five rounds on July 8, 1889, at Richburg, defying the governor, who had called out the state militia to prevent the match.)

Gulfport, a short distance west, was chosen as a port site in 1887, but it was 1902 before the plans matured. When the railroad was completed through the sparsely settled sections in the southern part of the state, Gulfport became a major lumber shipping port. The town turned to the resort business in the 1920's, as a result of the Gulf and Ship Lines being purchased by the Illinois Central Railroad in 1925. The boom soon collapsed, however. After World War II, the town developed rapidly as a resort city, and today, recreation is a vital part of the economy. The deep-sea harbor extends gulfwards from a junction of US 49 and 90. On its edge is the world's most modern banana terminal, where ships can unload 9,600 stems hourly. The port, quite naturally, is used mainly by Latin American carriers.

West of Gulfport and halfway to Pass Christian is Long Beach, another of the resort communities, featuring a municipal pier. Pass Christian was a seaside resort long before the Civil War and proudly claims the South's first yacht club, founded here in 1849. Settled in 1704, Pass Christian has been a favorite vacation area for six presidents—Grant, Jackson, Theodore Roosevelt, Taylor, Truman and Wilson. It, too, has a Mardi Gras, with carnival parade and ball. Several historic homes and gardens are open to the public during the annual Garden Club Pilgrimage.

At Bay St. Louis, US 90 swings inland to cross the Louisiana border eighteen miles to the west. Bienville is credited with exploration of the area, and also with naming it after Louis IX. During the War of 1812, it was the scene of a naval engagement involving five American gunboats, which attacked a British fleet of sixty vessels in an effort to protect New Orleans. Bay St. Louis was a favorite vacation spot with wealthy planters long before the War of 1812.

Nearby, at the western end of Waveland, is Buccaneer State Park. Covering 400 acres of land, with a mile-long beach area, it was designed to be Mississippi's finest, with camping, swimming pools, tennis and shuffleboard courts, and a basketball court, as well as picnic pavilions.

Ten miles north on Jordan River, you can visit Holly Bluff Gardens, a natural woodland of giant Spanish moss-draped oaks interspersed with cypress, pine, maple and gum trees.

North and south, east and west, Mississippi offers a fascinating blend of history, mixed with modern twentieth-century hospitality, creating a vacation area of great interest. Moreover, it's Southern to the core.

PRACTICAL INFORMATION FOR MISSISSIPPI

FACTS AND FIGURES. Mississippi is a tortured spelling of a simple Algonquian Indian word misi sipi, that means "big water." The state's nickname is the Magnolia State, and, naturally, the magnolia is both the state flower and state tree. The state bird is the mocking bird. *Virtute et Armis* ("By valor and arms") is the state motto. "Go, Mississippi" is the state song.

Jackson is the state capital. The state's population of about 2.5 million people is roughly divided equally between urban and rural. Only slightly more than half that population is white; the rest is mostly black, with a scattering of Chinese in the Delta region and a band of Choctaw Indians near Philadelphia.

The tail end of the Appalachian foothills gives the northeast and some of the central areas rolling contours. In the so-called Prairie along the Alabama border and in the Mississippi-Yazoo Delta from Memphis to Vicksburg along the big river are two billiard-table-flat, tremendously fertile farmlands.

Cotton has been the major crop for most of the state's history, but recently soybeans have surpassed the old king both in acreage and dollar return. Mississippi summers are long, hot and humid. Winters are mild, but an occasional ice and snow storm is not unheard-of.

HOW TO GET THERE: *By air:* American, Delta and Republic have direct service into many cities in the state. Royale serves New Orleans and Memphis, with stops at Natchez, Jackson, Greenwood and Oxford.

By car: I-55, US 45 and US 61 go from north to south; US 82, I-20, US 84, I-10 and US 90 run from east to west.

Car rental: Avis, Hertz, Budget and National in major cities.

By train: Amtrak from Chicago to New Orleans runs over Illinois Central Gulf rails from north to south. Amtrak officials plan a high-speed commuter rail line from Mobile and the other Gulf cities to New Orleans for the World's Fair.

By bus: Greyhound and Trailways.

By ferry: From St. Joseph, La., to Port Gibson.

HOW TO GET AROUND: *By air:* Republic for local service; Royale from Jackson and Natchez to New Orleans.

By car: I-55, US 45 and US 61, north to south; US 82, I-20, US 84, I-10 and US 90 east to west.

By train: Amtrak over the Illinois Central Gulf system north to south.

By bus: Greyhound and Trailways statewide; Gulf Transport from Mobile through eastern Mississippi to St. Louis.

TOURIST INFORMATION. Contact the Mississippi Department of Tourism Development, PO Box 22825, Jackson, 39205; the Mississippi Park Commission, 717 Robert E. Lee Bldg., Jackson, 39201; individual city chambers of commerce; Natchez-Adams County Chamber of Commerce, 300 N. Commerce St., 39120, for antebellum houses open to public.

 MUSEUMS AND GALLERIES: Brice's Cross Roads Museum, Baldwyn. Winterville Indian Mounds Museum & State Park, Greenville. Grenada Historical Museum, Grenada, State Historical Museum, in the Old Capitol, Jackson; Old Spanish Fort, Pascagoula. Natchez Trace Parkway, Visitor Center, Tupelo. Park Museum Vicksburg National Military Park.

Art: Kate Freeman Clark Art Gallery, Holly Springs; Municipal Art Gallery, Jackson. Mary Buie Museum, Oxford, Museum of Art, Meridian. The Lauren Rogers Memorial Library and Museum of Art at Laurel deserves special mention for it houses many canvasses of the Great Masters, including Homer, Whistler, Corot, de Hoog and Daumier.

Special Interest: Mississippi Museum of Natural Science, Jackson. Military Museum, Port Gibson. Dunn-Seiler Museum (geology), Mississippi State University, Starkville. Art Center Planetarium, Jackson.

Others: Old Country Store, Lorman, River Museum and Hall of Fame, Vicksburg. Florewood River Plantation State Park, Greenwood. Grand Village of the Natchez Indians, Natchez.

 SEASONAL EVENTS. In every section of Mississippi *Annual Spring Pilgrimages* are held in early spring (Mar.-Apr.). Hoopskirted attendants greet visitors to the pre-Civil War mansions—filled with rare antiques and treasures of the antebellum past. These Pilgrimages can be enjoyed in the following cities: Aberdeen, Carollton, Columbus, Hattiesburg (homes featured here were built during the first years of the 20th century); Holly Springs, Jackson, Kosciusko, Monticello, Natchez, Oxford, Port Gibson, Raymond, Sardis, Vicksburg, Woodville. The *Gulf Coast Pilgrimage,* held during mid-March, covers 11 coastal cities. Tours are marked and are free. The Pilgrimage is sponsored by the Mississippi Gulf Coast Council of Garden Clubs.

February: Dixie National Livestock Show and Rodeo, Jackson. 2nd week.

March: During this month there are brilliant celebrations of *Mardi Gras* at Biloxi, Pascagoula, Pass Christian, and Natchez. From early March to Sept. the *Dixie Showboat Players* present melodrama in Vicksburg.

April: Greenwood Arts Festival with literary lions, all-day jazz, exhibits.

May: Armed Forces Day, Keesler Air Force Base, Biloxi. *Atwood Blue Grass Festival,* Monticello; *Jimmie Rodgers Festival,* Meridian.

June: Biloxi Shrimp Festival, the *Blessing of the Fleet,* and the *Shrimp King & Queen Pageant* (1st week).

July: Yachting Regatta, Biloxi. *Yachting Regatta,* Pass Christian (July 4th). *Mississippi Deep-Sea Fishing Rodeo,* Gulfport. 1st wk. of July. *Miss Mississippi Pageant,* Vicksburg Municipal Auditorium, Vicksburg. *Choctaw Indian Festival,* Philadelphia.

August: Outdoor Fishermen's Club Fishing Rodeo, Pass Christian (all month). *Faulkner International Conference,* Oxford. *Neshoba County Fair,* Philadelphia.

September: Delta Blues Festival, Greenville.

October: Invitational Golf Tournament, Pass Christian. *Mississippi State Fair,* State Fairgrounds, Jackson (2nd wk.). *Gumbo Festival,* Necaise Crossing.

November: Bird Dog Field Trials, Holly Springs (late Nov.). *Frost-Bite Regatta,* Pass Christian (early Nov.). *Antique Forum,* Natchez.

December: Shrimp Bowl Football game: Delta Band Festival & Winter Carnival.
Greenwood (early Dec.). *Trees of Christmas,* Meridian. *Christmas at Florewood,*
Greenwood. *Christmas at Natchez.*

NATIONAL PARKS AND FORESTS. Bienville National Forest, US 80, east of Raworth, is a place where you
will find all necessary camping and picnicking facilities,
while fishing and hunting in season are two reasons for the
influx of many campers. DeSoto National Forest is in southern Mississippi, in the
Biloxi area. Again, hunting and fishing draw sportsmen from all over the state.
You can also visit one of the largest tree farms in the country here. Holly Springs,
Delta, and Homochitto National Forests all have good camp sites and picnic areas
for the visitor. Fishing and hunting are permitted in all three. Vicksburg National
Military Park, in Vicksburg, is something truly different for the traveler. As you
enter the park, the Visitor Center offers you a pictorial display of the Battle of
Vicksburg, fought on the site of the present park. As you walk over the surrounding countryside, dotted with memorial markers, you can see evidences of the lines
of battle. Half-covered trenches mark the Union and Confederate emplacements,
batteries of authentic cannons, restored earthworks and redans are mute testa-
ment to the battle that won the war. The Natchez Trace Parkway is the longest,
skinniest park in the federal system, a two-lane blacktop highway that retraces
the ancient frontiersman's route from Nashville to Natchez. Landscaping con-
ceals signs of industrialization in nearby towns; roadside billboards are forbidden.

STATE PARKS. Over 16,000 acres in Mississippi have
been set aside for camping and recreation. The cost of
staying at one of the state areas runs according to the
activities in which you want to take part. If you want to
camp overnight, you will be pleased to find that there are toilet and running-water
facilities in all fourteen camps. In some cases, rental cabins are available, but these
are generally filled early.

Some of the better parks are: *Clarbco State Park,* US 45, south of Meridian,
is an excellent place for those interested in nature study. The large freshwater lake
offers facilities for all types of water sports. *Leroy Percy State Park* is on Rte. 12,
west of Hollandale. If you are interested in camping but want something more
modern than a bed of pine needles, you will enjoy the cabins and the lodge, both
of which have good accommodations.

Percy Quin State Park, off Rte. 24 west of McComb, features water sports, with
the major area of interest centering around the large lake in the Tangipahoa River.
Roosevelt State Park, south of Morton on State 13, has all the facilities for
enjoyable camping. Swimming and boating are just two of the many recreational
activities you may enjoy here. *Wall Doxey State Park,* State 7, south of Holly
Springs, is where you may test your piscatorial skills. Some of the best fishing
waters in the state are located on this 800-acre tract.

CAMPING OUT. The state parks, though high in acreage,
have relatively few campsites (5-30 per park). Open all
year, the length of visit is unrestricted. Small charge.
Trailer space is available everywhere but in *Carver Point*
and *Roosevelt Park.*

Hunters are drawn to the rugged timberland of Mississippi's six national forests
and although quail and small game abound, campsites do not. Of the 109 available, *Davis Lake* (Tombigbee) and *Clear Springs* (Homochitto) each have 26
sites. The *Big Biloxi National Forest* campground area is very popular.

Clustered in the northwestern corner of the state, the four Corps of Engineer
Lakeside parks have created the greatest number of camp sites. *Lakes Arkabutla*
(500), *Sardis* (300), *Enid* (435) and *Grenada* (455) are open year round, charge

no fee and have trailer space. Visit need not be limited to two weeks if permission from reservoir manager is obtained.

Magnolia State Park at Ocean Springs has all facilities, plus a boat launching ramp and a channel into the Gulf.

HISTORIC SITES. The history of Mississippi seems to center around the War Between the States, whereby much that was the Old South was reduced to a memory, with large plantations made into crumbled ruins and elegant lace into faded rags. However, in many areas of the state you will find that there are places which have been restored or preserved. In these spots you may capture some small idea of the graciousness and charm of the South before the Civil War.

Baldwyn: Brice's Cross Roads National Battlefield Site, off Rte. 370. Daily. *Biloxi: Beauvoir,* on US 90, last home of Confederate president Jefferson Davis, now a shrine and museum. *Biloxi Lighthouse,* West Beach Blvd. *Columbus: Friendship Cemetery,* origin of the first National Memorial Day observation. *Corinth: Corinth National Cemetery,* the Blue and the Gray, who died in the battle of Corinth lie side by side in this first official U.S. Cemetery. *Ship Island: Fort Massachusetts* can be reached by excursion boats twice daily from Biloxi and Gulfport. *Tupelo: Tupelo National Battlefield.* Open year round.

Vicksburg: The town teems with memorabilia of the war, including the *Vicksburg National Military Park & Cemetery.* Daily. Free. *Cedar Grove,* 2200 Oak St. 1842 mansion located at the site of the siege of Vicksburg. Open year-round. *McRaven,* 1503 Harrison. Pre-Civil war home. Opening hours vary. *Rosemont Plantation,* the boyhood home of Jefferson Davis near Woodville. Guided tours are available. Closed Jan.–Feb.

TOURS. *By boat: Sailfish Tour Boat,* 1½-hr. shrimping and oystering expedition. Leaves Biloxi, Small Craft Harbor, April–Labor Day. *Island Trader.* Harbor tour from Biloxi. April–Labor Day. Excursion boats make two round trips daily, leaving Biloxi and Gulfport to historic Fort Massachusetts on Ship Island. April–September. *Spirit of Vicksburg* paddlewheeler makes 1½ hour cruises for sightseeing in the afternoon and dinner in evening. From April through Labor Day. River canoe trips from Pascagoula leave Old Spanish Fort morning and afternoon, May–November.

SPECIAL INTEREST TOURS. *Keesler Air Force Base,* largest technical station of the U.S. Air Force, Biloxi. *John S. Ford House.* On State 35 in Sandy Hook, nr. Columbia. Sat., Sun.

National Space Technology Laboratory in Hancock County near Waveland. Monday through Friday at 1:15 P.M.

Mississippi Petrified Forest, in Flora. Only petrified forest in the eastern U.S. Open year round 8 to dark.

Old Country Store, on US 61, Lorman. Operating since 1875. Daily.

Jimmie Rodgers Memorial, Highland Park, Meridian. Year round.

Grand Gulf Military Park, Port Gibson: Open daily to sunset. *The Ruins of Windsor,* Old Rodney Rd. Remains of 4-story mansion destroyed by fire in 1890. The town of Rodney, once a bustling river port, now a ghost town.

Elvis Presley Birthplace, Tupelo. Year-round except major holidays; spring-fall 9–5; winter 12–5.

In *Vicksburg: U.S. Army Engineer Waterways Experiment Station,* Halls Ferry Rd. Mon. to Fri. 1½-hr. guided tours. Closed holidays. *National Military Park,* handsomely landscaped battlefield and museum. Year-round except Christmas.

GARDENS. *"Beauvoir,"* Jefferson Davis Shrine and Memorial Gardens, Biloxi. 50 acres of landscaped grounds.

Mynelle Gardens, 4738 Clinton Blvd., Jackson. One of the South's finest gardens. Year round, dawn to sundown. Adults $1; under 12 free. Also on the grounds is the colonial home (Old Greenbrook) of Mrs. Mynelle Hayward, with exhibits of fine antique silks and art treasures. *Wister Gardens,* Belzoni. 14 acres, 8,000 azaleas, 1,000 roses, 5,000 tulips. Swans, flamingos. Year-round, free.

Palestinian Gardens. 12 mi. NW of Lucedale. 6 mi. N of US 98.

MUSIC. Jackson is the home of Opera/South, the only professional black opera company in the U.S. Also based there is the Mississippi Opera Association that presents grand opera with a mixed cast of gifted local amateurs and big name professionals. The Delta Blues Festival is held in Greenville in September, and Meridian has the Jimmie Rodgers Memorial Festival in May. Meridian also has a Lively Arts Festival in April. Jackson has a symphony orchestra and full-time professional ballet troupe. Greenville has a symphony orchestra that presents four concerts a season.

STAGE AND REVUES. Southern Exposure is presented Tuesdays, Thursday, Saturdays and Sundays during the Natchez Pilgrimage; the Confederate Pageant is presented on Mondays, Wednesdays, Fridays, and Saturdays.

DRINKING LAWS. Privately owned package stores and bars in hotels and restaurants are legal on a local option basis. Store hours 10 to 10, bars 10 A.M. to midnight. Certain designated resort area bars stay open past midnight. No Sunday sales of liquor. The drinking age is 21 for liquor, 18 for beer.

SPORTS. *Swimming:* The world's longest man-made beach is from Biloxi to Henderson. There are also beaches at Pascagoula, Ocean Springs, Bay St. Louis, Waveland and others on the offshore islands, reached only by boat.

Boating: Most towns have launching ramps. There is powerboating in the Mississippi Sound, Escatawpa River, Pascagoula River, Bluff Creek, on Biloxi Back Bay, Ft. Bayou, Tchoutacabouffa, Biloxi, Wolf and Jordan Rivers and many bayous. Small sailboats available for rent along the beachfront at Biloxi; races on weekends.

Fishing: There is year-round freshwater, saltwater and deep-sea fishing coastwide, as well as hard and soft-shell crabbing. No license or limit on saltwater fishing. Fishing for freshwater fish requires a non-resident license. There are fishing camps on all waters in the 3 coastal counties. Deep-sea fishing rodeos are held in Biloxi, Gulfport and Pass Christian.

Deep-sea charter fishing boats are available on the Gulf at an average of $300 for parties up to six, $25 per extra head.

Aqua-planing, waterskiing, skindiving all along the coast.

Horseback riding at the Gulf Hills Riding Stables, Ocean Springs.

Hunting: Fox, coons, possums, rabbits, squirrels, deer, quail, ducks, geese and turkeys are to be found. U.S. and National bird dog Field Trials are held at Shuqualak and Hernando.

Golf: With the warm climate, golf has long been a major sport in the state. There are lush, well-planned courses to try the golfer's skill: *Gulf Hills C.C.,* a resort course, with gently rolling fairways; *Edgewater Gulf C.C.,* Biloxi, a resort course; *Broadwater Beach G.C.,* Biloxi, a tough sun resort course; *Pass Christian C.C.,* a private course, open to guests of members only; *Hickory Hill C.C.,* Pascagoula, a semi-private Earl Stone course, with seven holes dominated by water; *Sunkist C.C.,* N. Biloxi, a semi-private course with level fairways and smallish greens; *St. Andrews,* a resort course in Ocean Springs; *Banyon Views C.C.,* a municipal course with three water holes and a driving range; *Diamondhead G.C.,* Bay St. Louis, a resort course with long tees, roller-coaster greens.

Tennis: Courts in Biloxi, Gulfport, Ocean Springs and Pascagoula, on the Gulf; and since the tennis boom, courts have mushroomed in dozens of inland cities.

SPECTATOR SPORTS. *Football:* The Shrimp Bowl Football game is held at Biloxi in early Dec., but college football is king throughout the state all fall.

Golf: Big-name golfers compete in the Magnolia Golf Classic PGA tour stop at Hattiesburg in April. The oldest tournament in the state is at Greenwood.

WHAT TO DO WITH THE CHILDREN. Here in Mississippi is the opportunity for youngsters to see first hand one of the most famous sites of the War Between the States. *Vicksburg National Military Park* and the Park Museum are teeming with mementos of the battle. You will find models, maps, and displays showing the course of the battle and the influence of the terrain. After seeing the museum, take the children around the park so they may actually see the trenches and barricades restored to their natural condition.

Those curious about Southern life before the war get an accurate picture from the exhibits and pictures on display in the *Old Courthouse Museum* in Vicksburg.

Eight Flags, Biloxi. Old West atmosphere. Visitors may feed and pet tame deer. Open June-Sept.

Marine Life Aquadome, Gulfport. 6 shows daily. Interesting exhibits. Apr. to Labor Day.

National Fish Hatchery, on US 11, Meridian. Free.

National Fish Hatchery, Tupelo. Summer fishing rodeo for children. Tombigbee National Forest. Free.

Harbor Tour Train, Gulfport. A 25-minute narrated tour along the ocean front.

RECOMMENDED READING. *Historic Architecture in Mississippi,* by Mary Wallace Crocker, published by University of Mississippi Press (1973), Jackson, Miss. 39205; *Mississippi, A Guide to the Magnolia State,* by the Federal Writers (Project), published by Somerset, New York; *History of Mississippi* (2 volumes), editor R. A. McLemore, published by the University of Mississippi Press (1973), Jackson, Miss. 39205; *Boy in Rural Mississippi,* by S. G. Thigpen, Box 819, Picayune, Miss. 39466; *The Mighty Mississippi,* by Bern Keating, published by the National Geographic Society, Washington, D.C. (1971); *Antebellum Natchez,* by James D. Clayton, published by the Louisiana State University Press (1968), Baton Rouge, La. 70806; *Mississippi,* by Bern and Franke Keating, University of Mississippi Press, Jackson, Miss. (forthcoming).

HOTELS AND MOTELS. The Gulf Coast of Mississippi boasts several fine resort establishments and a wide selection of excellent motels on or near the Gulf. Inland, the state has a more narrow range of accommodations, there being no super deluxe hostelries in the grand tradition. But these are more than compensated for by the abundance of comfortable, more modest accommodations. We have listed hotels and motels alphabetically in categories determined by double-occupancy, in-season rates. Family rates are available at almost all listings. Rates will be $3-$4 higher during Pilgrimages. *Expensive:* $50 and up; *Moderate:* $35–$50; *Inexpensive:* under $35. For a more complete explanation of hotel and motel categories see *Facts at Your Fingertips* at the front of this volume.

Biloxi

Broadwater Beach. *Expensive.* West Beach Blvd. (US 90). This large resort has all the facilities, including deep-sea fishing, heated pool, golf, tennis, but if none of them appeal, you can spend a quiet afternoon walking over the thirty-odd acres of terraced grounds. Free airport transportation. In-room coffee. Restaurant. Cocktail lounge with entertainment in evenings, dancing. Supervised play area.

Buena Vista. *Expensive.* 710 Fred Haise Blvd. Classic seaside hostelry.

Hilton Resort Hotel. *Expensive.* 300 Deluxe rooms, gourmet dining room, show lounge, lighted tennis courts, 18-hole championship golf course.

Royal D'Iberville. *Expensive.* 3634 W. Beach Blvd. (US 90) Pools (heated). Restaurant, cocktail lounge, entertainment, dancing.

Quality Inn Emerald Beach. *Moderate to Expensive.* 3717 W. Beach Blvd. Restaurant, bar. Limousine, tour service.

Ramada Inn. *Moderate to Expensive.* 3719 W. Beach Blvd. (US 90W). Restaurant, coffee shop, bar, dancing. Pool (heated).

Admiral Benbow. *Moderate.* 3910 W. Beach Blvd. On beach. Restaurant; cocktail lounge with entertainment. Heated pool.

Holiday Inn. *Moderate.* 92 W. Beach (US 90). Free airport transportation. Restaurant, bar, dancing. In-room coffee. Play area. Pets welcome.

Oak Manor Motel. Member of Best Western. *Moderate.* 626 Central Beach Blvd. Pool, restaurant nr.

Sun-N-Sand. *Moderate.* W. Beach Blvd. (US 90). For those who are interested in saltwater swimming, fishing and boating, this is the place. A large resort with pools. Play area. Restaurant, bar, dancing. Free airport transportation. Beautician.

Sun Tan Motel. *Moderate.* 200 Central Beach Blvd. A well-run medium-sized motel which offers many opportunities for both relaxing and sightseeing. Pool. In-room coffee. Restaurant nr.

Clarksdale

Clarksdale Uptown Motor Inn. Member of Best Western. *Inexpensive.* Central location. Restaurant, bar.

Holiday Inn. *Inexpensive.* Restaurant, bar. Free airport transportation. Pool.

Columbus

Hilton. *Moderate.* 1200 Hwy. 45 N. Four-story, landscaped atrium lobby. Close to downtown. Restaurant, lounge, disco. Pool.

Holiday Inn. *Moderate.* Two locations on US 45. Restaurant, bar. Pets welcome.

Ramada Inn. *Moderate.* US 45N. Pool. Pets allowed. Restaurant, cocktail lounge, entertainment.

Chief Econo Inn. *Inexpensive.*

Columbus. *Inexpensive.* This well-maintained medium-sized motel seems to cater to the family vistors. Restaurant nr. Pool.

Corinth

Ramada Inn. *Moderate.* US 45 bypass. Entertainment. Beauty shop.

Holiday Inn. *Inexpensive.* Free airport transportation. Pools. Pets welcome. Restaurant, bar.

Econo-Lodge. *Inexpensive.* On Highway 72. Brand-new.

Travel Inn. *Inexpensive.* Newly remodeled with restaurant and lounge.

Greenville

Best Western Regency. *Moderate.* US 82E. Indoor pool, sauna.

Coachman's Inn. *Moderate.* Pool, play area. Pets allowed. Restaurant nr.

Ramada Inn. *Moderate.* Pool, play area. Bar, entertainment.

Gilhara. *Inexpensive.* Large well-furnished rooms will add much to your comfort while you stay at this spacious motel. Pool. Pets allowed.

Holiday Inn. *Inexpensive.* Restaurant, bar. Pool. Play area.

Riverview Inn. *Inexpensive.* Restaurant, bar. Pool. Central location.

Greenwood

Holiday Inn. *Moderate.* Entertainment, dancing. Heated pool. Pets allowed.

Ramada Inn. *Moderate.* Dancing, entertainment.

Grenada

Best Western. *Inexpensive.* Swimming pool. Restaurant.

Comfort Inn. *Inexpensive.* No frills but complete comfort.

Holiday Inn. *Inexpensive.* Restaurant, bar. Pool (heated). Pets allowed.

Hilltop Motel. *Inexpensive.* Restaurant, pool.

Gulfport

Best Western. *Moderate.* Overlooks Gulf. Restaurant, bar, entertainment, dancing. Pool (heated). Pets allowed.

Holiday Inn. *Moderate.* Pools. Pets allowed. Free airport transportation. Bar, entertainment, dancing.

Moody's Fountainhead. *Moderate.* Fishing trips arranged. Restaurant, bar. Pool. Play area. Family units offered by this large motel-cottage combination. Seasonal rates.

Ramada Inn. *Moderate.* Entertainment, dancing. Heated pool. Pets allowed.

Sheraton Gulfport. *Moderate.* Heated pool, shuffle board. Entertainment, dancing.

Alamo Plaza Hotel Courts. *Inexpensive.* Large well-maintained operation, with rooms on Gulf. Family units with kitchens, outdoor barbecue facilities. Pool. Restaurant nr.

Worth. *Inexpensive.* Heated pool, tennis, putting green, shuffleboard.

Hattiesburg

Carriage Inn. *Moderate.* Restaurant nr. In-room coffee.

Holiday Inn. *Moderate.* Two locations. Both have restaurant, lounge, entertainment, pool, coffee makers in room. Kennels.

Quality Inn. *Inexpensive.* Restaurant, pool.

Ramada Inn. *Moderate.* Pool (heated). Restaurant, bar, entertainment.

Jackson

Sheraton Regency. *Expensive.* Central location. Mini-suites with in-room safes, huge desk-work areas, free *Wall Street Journals.*

Coliseum Ramada Inn. *Moderate to Expensive.* 400 Greymont St. Pool (heated), play area. Bar, entertainment. Pets welcome.

TraveLodge-Airport. *Moderate to Expensive.* Jackson Municipal Airport above terminal blvd. Restaurant.

Admiral Benbow Inn. *Moderate.* 905 N. State St. Restaurant, bar, entertainment. Pets allowed.

Holiday Inn. *Moderate.* Four locations. All have restaurant, entertainment, pool. **North:** 155 N. Frontage Rd. **Southwest:** 2649 US 80W. **Downtown:** 200 E. Amite. **Medical Center 2375 N. State.**

Howard Johnson's Motor Lodge. *Moderate.* I-55 at McDowell Rd. Restaurant, bar. Pool. Pets allowed.

Jackson Downtown Travelodge. *Moderate.* 550 W. Capitol St. Central location of this medium-sized motel helps account for its popularity. Excellent staff. Restaurant. Pool.

Jacksonian Master Hosts Inn. *Moderate.* US 51N, 5 mi. Ideal location for the sportsman, with bowling, golf, other sports to test his skill. Restaurant, bar. Wide choice of accommodations and rates. Pools. Play area.

Ramada Inn. *Moderate.* 2275 US 80W. Pool. Restaurant, bar.

Rodeway Inn. *Moderate.* 3720 I-55N. Restaurant, bar, entertainment. Pool. Pets allowed.

Sheraton Motor Inn. *Moderate.* US 51N, I-55. The large dressing rooms will add much to your pleasure while staying here. A good-sized motor hotel with an excellent restaurant, bar, entertainment. Pool. In-room coffee.

Walthall. *Moderate.* 225 E. Capitol. Central location, rooftop pool (heated). Restaurant, bar, entertainment.

Sun-N-Sand Motor Hotel. *Inexpensive.* 401 N. Lamar St. Restaurant, cocktail lounge, entertainment. Pool (heated). Pets allowed.

Stonewall Jackson Motor Lodge. *Inexpensive.* 1955 US 80W. Gracious staff. Medium-sized establishment. Restaurant, bar. Pool.

Laurel

Holiday Inn. *Moderate.* Free airport transportation. Bar, entertainment. Pets welcome.

Ramada Inn. *Moderate.* Typical chain operation. Sawmill Rd.

Town House. *Moderate.* This medium-sized motel is a favorite among the local gentry. The accommodations are better than average, so is the service. In-room coffee. Restaurant nr. Pool.

Long Beach

Ramada Inn. *Moderate.* Free in-room movies.

McComb

Holiday Inn. *Moderate.* Free airport transportation. Restaurant, bar. Pool. Pets welcome.

Meridian

Best Western. *Moderate.* Restaurant, bar. Pool, play area. Pets allowed.

Howard Johnson's Motor Lodge. *Moderate.* Restaurant, bar. Pool (heated).

Days Inn. *Inexpensive.* Swimming pool. Restaurant.

Holiday Inn. *Inexpensive.* Two locations. Both have restaurant, bar, free airport transportation and pool.

Natchez

Eola Hotel. *Expensive.* Splendidly restored post-W.W. I hotel.

Montmouth Plantation and The Burns Mansion. *Expensive.* Restored antebellum bed and breakfast.

Holiday Inn. *Moderate.* Restaurant, bar. Pool, play area.

Prentiss Motel. *Moderate.* Restaurant, cocktail lounge, entertainment. Pool (heated).

Ramada Hilltop. *Moderate.* Swimming pool. Restaurant. Superb view.

Ocean Springs

Royal Gulf Hills Resort and Country Club. *Expensive.* This is Mississippi's only first class resort, with tennis, golf, swimming pool, and horseback riding.

Oxford

Oxford Inn. *Moderate.* Typical Best Western.

Rodeway Inn. *Moderate.* Swimming pool. Restaurant.

Holiday Inn. *Inexpensive.* Free airport transportation. Restaurant, bar.

Pascagoula
La Font Inn. *Moderate.* Large motel with excellent view of pool from spacious rooms. Family rates. Restaurant, bar. Pools. Play area. Pets welcome. Free airport transportation.

American Motor Inn. *Moderate.* New, with pool and restaurant.

Kings Inn. *Inexpensive.* Restaurant, cocktail lounge, entertainment. Pool and play area.

Travel Motor Inn. *Inexpensive.* Restaurant, cocktail lounge, entertainment. Free in-room coffee. Pool (heated).

Sardis
Gulf Trail Motor Lodge. *Inexpensive.* Restaurant, bar. Pool, play area. Pets allowed.

Holiday Inn. *Inexpensive.* Restaurant. Pool (heated). Play area. Pets welcome.

Starkville
University Inn. *Moderate.* Entertainment, dancing.

Best Western Motor Lodge. *Inexpensive.* Well-run medium-sized motel caters to families. Restaurant. Play area. Pets welcome.

Holiday Inn. *Inexpensive.* 1 mi. from Miss. State U. Restaurant, pool.

Tupelo
Hilton. *Moderate.* Hwys. 45 & 78, Atrium lobby. Restaurant, bar. Pool.

Holiday Inn. *Moderate.* Restaurant. Pool. Play area. Free airport transportation.

Tupelo TraveLodge. *Moderate.* Situated among many historical sites, this medium-sized motel offers an excellent jumping-off place for day trips. Pool. Restaurant nr.

Natchez Trace Inn. *Inexpensive.* Restaurant, bar, entertainment. Pool, play area. Pets welcome.

Ramada Inn. *Inexpensive.* Free airport transportation. Pools. Restaurant, bar, entertainment.

Rex Plaza. *Inexpensive.* This medium-sized motel offers all the facilities normally associated with larger operations. Restaurant, bar, entertainment. Pool.

Town House. *Inexpensive.* One of the better-run motels in the area.

Vicksburg
Anchuca and **Cedar Grove.** *Expensive.* Restored antebellum mansions, now bed and breakfasts. Superb.

Holiday Inn. *Moderate.* Restaurant, bar. Pool. Play area.

Best Western Magnolia Inn. *Inexpensive to Moderate.* Large dressing areas, tastefully decorated. Family units. Restaurant, bar, coffee shop. Play area.

Ramada Inn. *Inexpensive to Moderate.* Swimming pool. Restaurant.

Rivertown Inn Motor Inn. *Inexpensive.* Convenient location. Restaurant, bar. Pool. Pets allowed. Southern Tea Room.

West Point
Marshall. *Inexpensive.* Pleasing decor. In-room coffee. Restaurant, pool.

DINING OUT. Mississippi offers many traditional Southern specialties, as well as all the standard American favorites. Along the Gulf coast, be sure to try the shrimp prepared in the Creole manner, and hot gumbos or other seafood specialties. Among the Southern items to be found on many Mississippi menus: hush puppies, grits, country-style ham, and of course, Mississippi River catfish.

For other worthwhile restaurants, be sure to re-check hotel listings. Restaurants are listed in order of price category. Price ranges and categories for a complete meal are as follows: *Expensive:* $10 and up; *Moderate,* $6.50–$10; *Inexpensive,* $2.50–$6.50. For a more complete explanation of restaurant categories see *Facts at Your Fingertips* at the front of this volume.

Bay St. Louis
Annie's. *Moderate.* A coastal favorite for Creole-American menu.

Biloxi
White Pillars. *Expensive.* 100 Rodenburg. New Orleans-style seafood. Jambalaya, gumbo, trout Clemanceau and crabmeat Lorenzo are served in an enclosed patio setting. Family-owned. Elegantly restored mansion.

Baricev's. *Moderate.* 633 Central Beach Blvd. The small dock in the rear affords the owner some of the freshest seafood you can imagine. If you are a fish or shellfish fancier, be sure to stop here. Try the oysters and stuffed flounder. Overlooks the Gulf Bar.

The Factory. *Moderate.* A converted seafood factory that specializes in seafood. E. Beach Blvd.

Mary Mahoney's Old French House. *Moderate.* Magnolia Mall. This converted house and slave quarters features a lounge with live entertainment, a 24-hour La Cafe, and outdoor patio dining. Specializes in po-boy sandwiches for lunch and seafood for dinner. Family-owned.

Sea 'n' Sirloin. *Moderate.* West Beach Blvd. The stuffed sirloin is recommended, but you will find a wide selection of alternatives. Children's portions.

The Log House. *Inexpensive.* Dubuys Rd. Superior seafood.

Clarksdale
Delta Warehouse. *Moderate.* Nice surprise.

Ponderosa. *Moderate.* Steaks.

Columbus
Annie. *Moderate.* University Mall. Seafood and steak.

Possumtown Depot. *Moderate.* Converted R.R. Station.

Greenville
Does. *Expensive.* Superb food in dubious decor.

C & G Depot. *Moderate.* Converted train station in impeccable taste. Buffet at luncheon.

How Joy. *Moderate.* Chinese food a specialty.

Morrison's. *Inexpensive.* Cafeteria

Greenwood

Webster's. *Moderate.* Charming bar-restaurant. Barbecued oysters, trout florentine, prime ribs. Currently best dining in area.

Grenada

Monte Cristo. *Inexpensive.* Try the homebaked goods which add a delightful touch to the baked lobster and sirloins.

Three Lakes. *Moderate.* Greek salad, occasionally other Greek dishes.

Gulfport

Angelo's *Moderate.* European cuisine served in a semi-Old-World atmosphere, made even more pleasant by the large fireplace and view of the Gulf.

The Landing. *Moderate.* Lively hangout for a sporting crowd. Try weird but delicious French-fried vegetables.

Hattiesburg

Wagon Wheel Restaurant. *Inexpensive.* Good food and cheerful surroundings. Popular locally.

Jackson

Fishermans Wharf. *Moderate-Expensive.* Salty atmosphere.

Seafood Market. *Expensive.* Splendid decor.

Cerami's. *Moderate.* On the reservoir. First-rate Italian.

Cisco's. *Moderate.* Mexican.

Crechale's. *Moderate.* Jam-packed hole-in-the-wall. Great seafood and steaks.

LeFleur's. *Moderate.* A profusion of flowers and Creole cooking. What could be more appropriate to this area? You will enjoy the beef and shrimp dishes.

Silver Platter. *Moderate.* A dressy place that caters to patrons of arts.

Sundancer. *Moderate.* Lively. Top service. Splendid small menu. Best buy in town.

Palette. *Inexpensive.* In Art Museum. Delightful surprise.

Laurel

Parker House. A converted residence now serving Southern cuisine.

McComb

Yesterday's. *Moderate.* On National Register of Historic Buildings. Wine cellar.

Meridian

Weidmann's. *Moderate.* Special lobster and steak items, plus black bottom pie, make this a popular local dining spot. Children's portions.

Natchez

Broadway Station. *Moderate.* Converted railroad depot.

Carriage House. *Moderate.* Southern cooking.

Post House. *Moderate.* Oldest building in town. Charming addition to the historical scene, first-rate cuisine.

Cock of the Walk. *Inexpensive.* Catfish dinners only. Strawberry juleps.

Ocean Springs

Aunt Jenny's. *Moderate.* All you can eat of catfish and fried chicken.

Lagniappe. *Moderate.* Lagniappe is a Cajun word meaning "something extra." It describes this restaurant's Cajun and Lebanese cooking.

Sumi's. *Moderate.* Good Oriental food.

Trilby's. *Moderate.* Look over the display of Gulf Coast art and clocks while waifing for a delicious dinner. Creole menu and seafood as their specialty. Open for lunch and dinner. Closed Mon.

Oxford

The Gin Restaurant and Lounge. *Moderate.* A converted cotton gin.

Warehouse Restaurant. *Moderate.* Specialty: steaks. Closed Sun.

Pascagoula

Catalina. *Moderate.* First-rate seafood. Try the crab claws.

Tiki. *Moderate.* Strange decor but excellent seafood.

La Font Inn. *Inexpensive.* Try their seafood, soup and steak. Pastries made on the premises. Open for breakfast, lunch and dinner.

Starkville

Michaels. *Moderate.* In converted residence.

House of Kong. *Inexpensive.* Chinese cuisine.

Tupelo

Terrace. *Inexpensive-Moderate.* Despite location, serves good seafood.

Hunter's *Inexpensive.* Quiet, pleasant. Excellent shrimp.

Vicksburg

Maxwell's. *Moderate.* Lobster

Velchoff's. *Moderate.* Seafood.

Walnut Hill. *Moderate.* Lazy Susan roundtable.

NORTH CAROLINA

Tobacco and Textbooks

BY
JOHN PHILLIPS

John Phillips is a native North Carolinian living in Raleigh. He is on the staff of State Magazine *and is a member of the North Carolina Travel Council.*

North Carolina divides itself into three major geographical regions: the Coastal Plains, the Piedmont Plateau and western North Carolina. A visitor traversing the state from east to west moves first through the broad and deep Coastal Plain, swings onto the Piedmont Plateau and then climbs into western North Carolina with its chain of mountains.

A tour of North Carolina's Coastal Plain—about 25,000 square miles, including ocean beaches—can appropriately begin where the first English expedition to the New World landed: Roanoke Island.

Laying between the mainland and long barrier islands called the Outer Banks, Roanoke is a gateway to both. The approach from the north is via US 158 and the Dare County beach resorts of Kitty Hawk, Kill Devil Hills and Nags Head. From the west and south, main routes to Roanoke Island are US 64 and 264, converging before crossing Croatan Sound on William B. Umstead Bridge.

If you visit Roanoke Island between late June and early September, a pleasant way to study the earliest history of English-speaking people in America is to see "The Lost Colony" drama at Waterside Theatre (nightly except Sundays) in Fort Raleigh National Historical Site, near

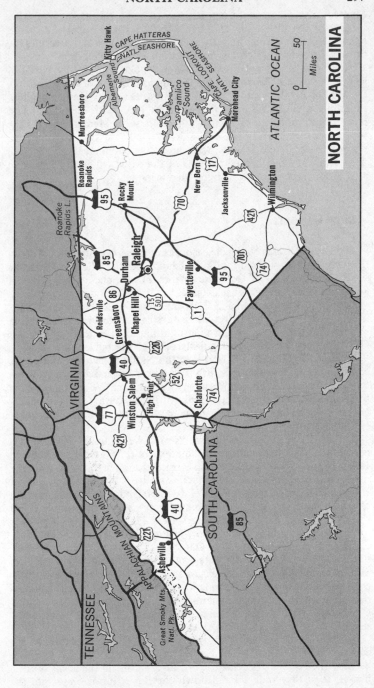

NORTH CAROLINA

ATLANTIC OCEAN

0 50
Miles

CAPE HATTERAS NATL. SEASHORE
Kitty Hawk
CAPE LOOKOUT NATL. SEASHORE
Albemarle Sound
Pamlico Sound
Morehead City

Murfreesboro

Roanoke Rapids L.

Roanoke Rapids
Rocky Mount
New Bern
Jacksonville
Wilmington

95
70
17
421
95
701
74

Raleigh
Durham
85
86
Reidsville
Greensboro
Chapel Hill
15 501
Fayetteville
1
220

VIRGINIA

40
52
High Point
Winston Salem
77
421
Charlotte
74

SOUTH CAROLINA

40
85

APPALACHIAN MOUNTAINS
22?
Asheville
Great Smoky Mts. Natl. Pk.

TENNESSEE

Manteo. The drama does not attempt to solve the mystery of what became of the little band of English settlers who disappeared, but it relates the story of their first few months on Roanoke and describes the dream of freedom which inspired them to leave England.

The birthplace of aviation is across Roanoke Sound from Fort Raleigh, giving Dare County another unique historical attraction. In 1900, the Wright Brothers chose the sand dunes near Kitty Hawk for glider experiments which led to their success, in 1903, with the world's first powered aircraft flight. Wright Brothers National Memorial marks the spot at Kill Devil Hills, site of the first flight. Year round visitors can study its interpretive exhibits, walk up to the Monument atop the tall dune and trace the marked patterns of the earliest flights. There is an airport for light planes at Wright Memorial.

Cape Hatteras

The Cape Hatteras National Seashore embraces seventy miles of ocean front between Nags Head (on Bodie Island) and the village of Ocracoke on the southern tip of Ocracoke Island. Focal point of the National Seashore is Cape Hatteras itself where the tallest lighthouse in the U.S.A. —208 feet—protects shipping from the treacherous Diamond Shoals. This lighthouse is open daily, and visitors can climb to the observation balcony. Of the six North Carolina lighthouses operated by the Coast Guard, this is the only one regularly open to the public.

Almost all of Ocracoke Island is in the National Seashore. There are comfortable accommodations for visitors near Silver Lake, port for the toll ferry from the mainland. Between Ocracoke and the central coast are the virtually uninhabited Outer Banks of Portsmouth, Core and Shackleford, destined for preservation in the natural state as the Cape Lookout National Seashore.

The development of seaside resorts and the National Seashore has ended more than two centuries of isolation for the Outer Banks between Kitty Hawk and Ocracoke. Roads, bridges and regular ferry service make the area easily accessible. Most impressive is the Herbert C. Bonner Bridge spanning Oregon Inlet to Hatteras Island. At the northern end of the Bridge is Oregon Inlet Fishing Center, where charter boats fish the Gulf Stream and other offshore waters. Hatteras Village is another important sport-fishing center. Sport-fishing craft are also based at Wanchese on Roanoke Island and at Ocracoke. The name "Gamefish Junction" is used to describe the waters off Cape Hatteras, where the Gulf Stream and cold northern currents meet and where northern and southern species of fish abound. During World Wars I and II, Cape Hatteras became known as "Torpedo Junction" because German submarines took a heavy toll of shipping in the area. Diamond Shoals has been feared by seamen as an area that claimed so many vessels it was called "The Graveyard of the Atlantic." Salvage operations were important to the early economy of the Banks. Nags Head, it is said, earned its name because the original residents used to tie lanterns on the necks of their horses; then they rode up and down the dunes luring ships into the shoals, where they were considered fair prey for salvage operations.

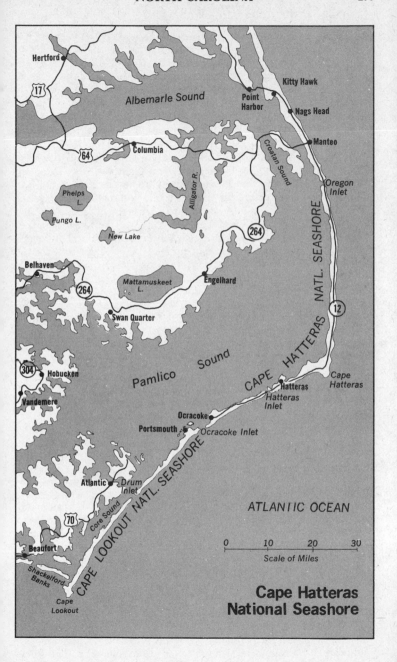

Cape Hatteras
National Seashore

Animals of the National Seashore

Shore birds and migratory waterfowl annually flock by the thousands to feed along the marshlands and beaches. Within the National Seashore is Pea Island National Wildlife Refuge on Hatteras Island. Here, in company with Canada geese, swans and wild ducks, over one-half the world's population of Greater Snow geese can be seen between early November and late January. The big white birds make Pea Island the southernmost point of their winter migration from Canada and the Arctic Circle. They arrive about mid-November, and begin their return flight shortly after New Year's. The Hatteras Island Highway, State 12, passes through Pea Island. From it there are good views of the geese feeding or circling overhead in symmetrical flight patterns. There are also observation platforms and a walkway atop a dike.

While it is possible for a visitor uninterested in history to enjoy the Outer Banks in any season, few people come here without feeling the impact of the past. It is evident in the accent of the older islanders' speech, and in the skeletons of wrecked ships, the exhibits and museums. Only a few minutes away from modern resorts, it is easy to sense the loneliness of being in a vast unknown territory, which must have been part of everyday life for the first settlers and seafarers who succeeded in establishing themselves on the Banks.

In early June, the International Blue Marlin Tournament brings affluent sportsmen to the Hatteras Marlin Club. The waters off Cape Hatteras regularly produce an abundance of very large billfish. In autumn, which shares honors with spring as a prime time for channel bass fishing, there are surf-casting tournaments at Nags Head and Hatteras.

The coast of Dare County abounds in pirate lore. A placid bay near Ocracoke Village is known as "Teach's Hole" because it was the hiding place of the pirate "Blackbeard" (Edward Teach), slain there in 1718.

The Central Coast

The Outer Banks swing southwest from Cape Hatteras, which is nearly thirty miles from the mainland, to outline the central coast of the state. Beaufort Inlet divides them from Bogue Island bordering Carteret County for some twenty-five miles.

This section of North Carolina includes a large peninsula formed by the Neuse and Oak Rivers and Pamlico, Core and Bogue Sounds. From Ocracoke it is reached by toll ferry docking at Cedar Island a few miles from the eastern terminus of transcontinental US 70. Carteret County is called the "Maritime Province" because of its maze of waterfronts.

The largest Carteret community is Morehead City, one of North Carolina's two ocean ports and the base for the state's largest fleet of charter boats that take sportsmen saltwater fishing. There are also "head boats" that carry large groups (at a fixed price per person) for trolling and bottom fishing offshore. The Blue Marlin Tournament, with accompanying festivities in early June, is Morehead City's largest annual event. Morehead is the gateway to resorts on Bogue Island via a drawbridge across Bogue Sound and the channel of the Intracoastal Waterway.

Beaufort is the county seat of Carteret. It appears today much as it did long ago when it was a principal port where seafaring men built neat, white residences in the Bahamas style. Settled in 1709, Beaufort is North Carolina's third oldest town.

Between Beaufort and the fishing village of Atlantic, US 70 heads through "down east" Carteret, where farming, fishing and boat building are the main occupations. Harkers Island is accessible from US 70 by highway and bridge. Except for the spectacular Cape Lookout Lighthouse with its black and white diamond patterned painting, a marina and some fishing camps, there is no development on Core Bank or Shackleford. There are motels on Harkers. You are likely to see large cabin cruisers or commercial fishing boats under construction on the premises of the islanders' homes.

Atlantic Beach was a resort as early as the 1870's, but in those days vacationers usually stayed in Morehead City and went by boat to the shore. In 1928 the first bridge to Bogue Island was built, and since then cottage and hotel-motel development has steadily increased. South of Atlantic Beach are the resorts and residential colonies of Emerald Isle, Pine Knoll Shores, Bogue Inlet and Salter Path.

North Carolina's seaside resorts are on narrow islands that have access to both ocean and sound. This makes for a kind of "have your cake and eat it too" situation; it is easy to enjoy sheltered boating waters and ocean surf as well.

A state park surrounds old Fort Macon on the northern tip of Bogue Island. There are swimming and picnic areas among the dunes and excellent surfcasting on the Park's shoreline. The Fort is a classic example of early nineteenth-century military architecture. It was seized by Confederate forces in 1861 and captured by the Union forces the following year. Transferred to the state as a park area in 1924, the Fort was called back into active service for a few years during World War II. It is a historic shrine today and houses a small museum.

The Southeastern Coast

Between White Oak River and New River, a large area of Onslow County is in the Camp Lejeune Marine Base reservation. You can drive through the reservation on State 172, linking up with State 24 from Morehead City and Jacksonville, the largest city near the base. Historic fishing communities of this area are Swansboro on the White Oak and Snead's Ferry near New River Inlet. State 172 intersects with US 17 a little farther south, and from it you can take a side trip to Topsail Island via State 50 & 210. Topsail, which is about thirty miles long and close to the mainland of Onslow and Pender Counties, has quiet seaside resorts at Surf City and New Topsail. There are uncrowded beaches for surf bathing or fishing, ocean-fishing piers and charter boats for sound and offshore fishing. Here, as at many other points along the Carolina coast, the Intracoastal Waterway channel is in a narrow sound separating island from mainland. For some three hundred miles in eastern North Carolina, this water route for pleasure craft and freight barges threads its way though a maze of rivers and sounds.

Two large resorts of southeastern North Carolina are Wrightsville and Carolina Beaches. Wrightsville spreads across an entire island and is reached from US 17 near Wilmington by US 74 & 76. It is one of North Carolina's oldest resorts. There are docks for charter and pleasure craft, plus ocean-fishing piers. Wrightsville and Masonboro Sounds, like Bogue Sound, are highly regarded for sailing. The surf along the southeastern beaches is usually gentle and considerably warmer than that along the Outer Banks.

Wilmington is a historic port, year-round recreational and historic center, and gateway to beaches and plantations. It is at the upper end of a peninsula formed by the Cape Fear River. Giovanni de Verrazano, navigating the mouth of the Cape Fear River, described the area as " . . . pleasant and delectable to behold, as is possible to imagine." The city is at the junction of US 17, 117, 74, 76, and 421. On the eastern banks of the Cape Fear opposite downtown Wilmington, the battleship *U.S.S. North Carolina* is enshrined in permanent moorings as a war memorial. Visitors may board the superdreadnaught daily and Sundays year round. From June until Labor Day a light and sound spectacular called "The Immortal Showboat," in honor of the ship's wartime nickname, is presented nightly. Spectators watch the hour-long show from a grandstand near the bow of the ship. The *U.S.S. North Carolina* earned twelve battle stars in the Pacific during World War II and was brought home for honored retirement in 1963.

Wilmington greets blossom time with the North Carolina Azalea Festival in early April. This is an extravaganza of pageants, parades, garden tours, art exhibits and concerts. Nowhere in North Carolina do azaleas bloom in such profusion as here and on nearby plantations. April is the month of peak color, dramatized by backgrounds of dogwood, pines, cypress and live oaks. Camellias bloom lavishly, too, from around Christmas until late March. Municipal Greenfield Park has a five-mile drive through azalea gardens bordering Lake Greenfield, and it is open all year. Zoning and planning have preserved old homes and buildings. The Cotton Exchange on the waterfront has been recently restored and is delightful with its shops and restaurants. The one-time headquarters of Cornwallis, the Burgin-Wright House, predates the Revolution. Historic Wilmington is a defined district in the city, and there are tours available.

On the highway to Wrightsville Beach are Airlie Gardens, situated on the grounds of an old plantation. Some fifteen miles south on State 133 to Southport is Orton Plantation. The Orton gardens feature formal and informal plantings of camellias, azaleas and other flowers. Orton Plantation, dating from 1725, personifies the popular concept of the antebellum South. The mansion with graceful white columns overlooks the Cape Fear River, and the approach is a sandy road winding through enormous trees and circling through the edge of the gardens. These gardens and Airlie gardens are open to visitors all year.

Fort Fisher and South

US 421 skirts Greenfield Park and continues down the Cape Fear peninsula to Carolina Beach and Fort Fisher. En route, it soars over a wide canal that connects the lower Cape Fear and Wrightsville Sound. Paradoxically, therefore, Carolina Beach has an insular location although it is actually North Carolina's only mainland beach. It more nearly resembles a city than any other North Carolina seashore resort, and it has an amusement area and boardwalk in addition to cottages, motels, shops, office buildings, and restaurants. It is also an important deep-sea sport fishing center, possessing numerous facilities for all types of fishing and pleasure craft.

South of Carolina Beach are the smaller resorts of Wilmington Beach, Kure Beach and Fort Fisher State Historic Site. At Fort Fisher, a museum displays ammunition, weapons and other artifacts brought up from the submerged wrecks of Confederate blockade runners close to shore. Several embankments and gun emplacements of the Fort have been marked. The largest land-sea battle in history, up to that time, took place at Fort Fisher in January, 1865. Below Fort Fisher, US 421 dead-ends at the Rocks, a breakwater built in 1875-81 to close the New Inlet and save Wilmington's harbor by insuring a sufficient depth over the main bar at the mouth of Cape Fear. There is automobile ferry service between Fort Fisher and Southport.

The Marine Resources Center is just south of Kure Beach on Federal Point, between the ocean and Cape Fear River. Here you'll find aquariums depicting typical North Carolina coastal marine habitats, lectures, films, field trips, and seminars.

Brunswick County is North Carolina's southernmost county and one of its largest. It extends from the Cape Fear banks near Wilmington to the South Carolina line. Its county seat is Southport near the mouth of the Cape Fear River. This gracious town, with its casual pattern of comfortable dwellings and tree-lined streets edged by a picturesque waterfront, is the home of the famed Southport Pilots Association. The Pilots go out in small cruisers to meet ocean vessels bound for Wilmington, and they guide them up the Cape Fear.

On the east side of lower Cape Fear River in Brunswick County, the town of Brunswick was founded in 1725. It was a flourishing river port until the American Revolution, when it was partly burned by the British. After the Revolution, the town never recovered, and it became extinct about 1830. Walls of St. Philip's Church and numerous house foundations remain. Also remaining are the massive works of Fort Anderson, a Civil War fortification erected by the Confederates; they have been improved for exhibit. There are historical markers in the area and trail-side exhibits, plus a visitor-center museum off N.C. Hwy 133, south of Wilmington.

Always closely identified with shipping and commercial fishing, Southport is a key point on the Intracoastal Waterway. It has a small boat harbor completed by the State Ports Authority in 1965. From Southport one may visit the nearby resorts of Caswell, Yaupon and Long Beaches.

Fort Caswell, constructed in 1825 and manned during the Civil, Spanish-American and both World Wars, is a religious assembly grounds operated by the Baptists of North Carolina. Many of its frame buildings are in use. Between Fort Caswell and Yaupon Beach is the Oak Island Golf Club. Yaupon Beach is a peaceful resort with good accommodations. Long Beach is somewhat larger. There are growing residential colonies, highly popular with retirees at Yaupon and nearby Tranquil Harbor. South of Oak Island are the smaller seaside resorts of Holden's Beach, Ocean Isle and Sunset Beach, each on its own sandy island and linked to US 17 by highways and bridges. All have fishing piers, motels and cottages. Near the bridge to Sunset Beach is Calabash, a tiny community so famed for excellent seafood that it has twenty thriving restaurants.

The inland communities of Brunswick County are small, primarily trading centers for the surrounding farms. Shallotte has inlet and river fishing. A residential and recreation complex about seven miles inland from Southport is Boiling Spring Lakes, situated in gently rolling countryside much like the famous Sandhills of North Carolina's southern Piedmont.

Large military reservations include Camp Lejeune (as noted in the Southeastern Coast Section), the U.S. Marine Corps Air Station at Cherry Point between New Bern and Morehead City, Seymour Johnson Air Force Base at Goldsboro and Fort Bragg and Pope Air Force Base near Fayetteville. Fort Bragg is the "Home of the Airborne" as well as the famous Special Forces "Green Berets."

Fayetteville is the county seat of Cumberland, and it is on the Cape Fear River, which is navigable from here to the Atlantic Ocean. Fayetteville dates from 1739 when Highland Scots settled it as Campbelltown. The city was named for General Lafayette. The old Market House in downtown Fayetteville was built in 1838 as a produce center on the site of Convention Hall, which had been destroyed by fire in 1831. George Herman Ruth ("The Babe") hit his first home run in professional baseball while training with the Baltimore Orioles here in 1914.

The largest town in the northeastern part of the state is Elizabeth City on US 17 and the Pasquotank River, the southeastern edge of the Great Dismal Swamp. The International Cup Regatta and the Craftsman's Fair are principal fall events. The Pasquotank and Great Dismal Swamp Canal form an alternate route of the Intracoastal Waterway, and Elizabeth City is popular with yachtsmen as well as motorists.

There are fine old courthouses of Georgian architecture at Hertford and Edenton (built in 1767). The Chowan County Courthouse, Cupola House, James Iredell House, St. Paul's Church and Penelope Barker House are open year-around. It was in Edenton on October 25, 1774, that a Tea Party protesting British taxes was organized by Mrs. Penelope Barker. The Tea Party Marker at Edenton Green is on the site. St. Paul's Episcopal Church is the state's second oldest church (1730's).

Washington is called "Little Washington" to distinguish it from the nation's capital. The earliest recorded mention of the name "Washington" for the town is dated October 1, 1776, making it the first town in the country to take this name. Washington contains many historic buildings. Located on the waters of the Pamlico at the junction of US 17 and 264, the town was the home of the De Mille family and the place where Edna Ferber was inspired to write *Showboat*. William C. De Mille was a celebrated nineteenth-century playwright. His son Cecil B. De Mille, the motion picture producer, was born in Washington. Edna Ferber visited the James Adams Floating Theatre at Washington to gather material for her book. Although the locale of *Showboat* was the Mississippi River, she used Beaufort County names and copied verbatim an inscription in St. Thomas Church at Bath.

Washington's tobacco warehouses are among the many eastern North Carolina sales centers where visitors are welcomed at auctions from

August until November. Others are in Rocky Mount, Wilson, Tarboro, Greenville, Williamston, Kinston, Goldsboro, Fayetteville, Lumberton, Whiteville and Smithfield. Check locally for information on sales hours. Wilson is the largest tobacco sales center in the state, leading the world in the production of flue-cured tobacco.

New Bern, a Colonial Capital

At New Bern, the first permanent colonial capital, the first state capitol building has been restored to its original elegance, and it is open (except Mondays) to visitors all year. Now known as the Tryon Palace Restoration, its gardens are on the site where Governor William Tryon supervised construction of a "seat of government and residence of the royal governor." Also at New Bern are the Fireman's Museum with horse-drawn fire equipment, the John Wright Stanly House of the 1770's and numerous other structures of classic Georgian architecture executed in brick and wood.

Among the most traveled routes through the Coastal Plain are US 17, 301, 421, 64, I-85 & I-95. Motorists in North Carolina can get off the beaten path to explore areas of unusual geographical or historical interest by using well-marked state roads connecting with the arterial highways. There is amazing variety to enjoy on the shunpikes of the Coastal Plains. In Tyrrell and Hyde Counties, State 94 runs north and south between US 264 and 64. It crosses Lake Mattamuskeet National Wildlife Refuge on a long causeway. Bird watchers enjoy seeing Canada geese and other waterfowl at their winter feeding grounds here, and there is excellent waterfowl hunting nearby. Accommodations and hunting guides are at Belhaven, Fairfield, New Holland and Swan Quarter. Another shunpike combines a free auto ferry from Currituck to Knotts Island with State 615 to Virginia Beach, Virginia. Accessible by State 55 and 111, southeast of Goldsboro, are Cliffs of the Neuse State Park and picturesque Seven Springs, which was once a famed watering place. There are motor roads into Croatan National Forest from US 70 southeast of New Bern; one of them terminates at a camping and picnic area on the Neuse River.

Turn off US 74-76 between Whiteville and Wilmington to visit Lake Waccamaw, where dark waters edged by cypress swamp offer boating, swimming and fishing. White Lake, so named because its crystal clear waters are on white sand, is just off US 701 in Bladen Lakes State Forest. Accommodations are plentiful. Pettigrew State Park, on Lake Phelps, is on a secondary road connecting with US 64 at Creswell. The Park is on portions of two early plantations, Bonarva and Somerset Place. The manor at Somerset Place is of Greek Revival Style, well-preserved. State-owned Lake Phelps has excellent fishing and is North Carolina's second largest natural lake.

Powerboat and sailing regattas are held in several communities on lakes or rivers; horse shows are annual events at Wilson, Enfield, Wilmington and Fayetteville. Benson, a trading center for rural Johnston County, celebrates harvest time each September with the annual Mule Day festival. The fourth Sunday in June signals the State Singing Convention, which brings hundreds of religious and folk singers and musicians to Benson's Singing Grove. The North Carolina Strawberry Festival is in May at Chadbourn. East Carolina University at Greenville has a summer theater on the campus, and Washington has a Summer Festival in early June.

Piedmont North Carolina

The Piedmont Plateau of central North Carolina begins at the fall line a few miles east of Raleigh and US 1 and rolls westward to the base of the Blue Ridge Divide. Within the 21,000-square-mile Piedmont are such distinctive geographical features as the Sandhills in the southeast, the Uwharrie and Sauratown mountains of the central area and large rivers. Principal lakes of the region—impounded along the Yadkin, Roanoke, Catawba and Pee Dee Rivers—offer excellent boating and fishing. The Piedmont has famous winter golf and riding centers, state parks and numerous all-year historical attractions. There are free tours of cigarette factories in several cities, and a wide choice of all-year accommodations.

Raleigh, the capital, is a good introduction to the entire state, and a convenient beginning for a tour of the Piedmont. It is on US 1 and two main east-west highways, US 70 and 64. One of the state's busiest airports serves Raleigh, Durham and Chapel Hill. Raleigh is the southeastern apex of the Research Triangle Park formed by North Carolina State University in the capital, the University of North Carolina at Chapel Hill and Duke University in Durham. The Sandhills resorts of Pinehurst and Southern Pines are seventy miles south of Raleigh.

In Raleigh, visitors can tour the historic Capitol (1840) and unusual Legislative Building, the North Carolina Museum of History in the Archives Building, the Museum of Natural History and the North Carolina Art Museum, which houses a multimillion-dollar collection of masterworks. This art museum is the first ever established with state funds in the U.S.A. All of these buildings are open free to the public.

The granite Capitol of Greek Revival architecture is on a six-acre square. Among the monuments on the square is an equestrian statue honoring the three Presidents born in North Carolina: Andrew Johnson, James K. Polk and Andrew Jackson. The Legislative Building, first structure ever built by any state for the exclusive use of its Senate and House of Representatives, was designed by Edward Durrell Stone and executed in marble and granite. The Capitol and Legislative buildings are open weekdays and also Saturday and Sunday afternoons. In the Capitol are the old Legislative Chambers, the permanent office of the Secretary of State and the office of the Governor. The North Carolina General Assembly convenes in the Legislative Building during January of each odd year. Visitors may observe the sessions from a gallery on the third floor.

About one mile from Capitol Square is the Andrew Johnson House, a tiny gambrel-roofed building where the 17th President was born. This historic shrine is located in Mordecai Park on Person St. and is open to the public. On N. Blount St., two blocks from the Capitol is the official residence of North Carolina's governors. This "gingerbread" mansion (1880's) has been restored recently and is adjacent to Historic Oakwood, a section where many homes of the same era have been restored. The Visitor's Center, 301 N. Blount St., is open daily and has information on points of interest.

Two miles W. of the Capitol is N. C. State University which is the agricultural and technical branch of the Consolidated University of N. C. with campuses at Chapel Hill, Greensboro, Charlotte, Asheville and Wilmington. The influence of N. C. State's noted School of Design is reflected in the newer buildings on campus and in the striking J. S. Dorton Arena on the State Fairgrounds a few miles south on Hillsborough St. This parabolic pavilion is used for livestock judging, rodeos and exhibits during Fair Week in October and for entertainment programs during the rest of the year.

America's Winter Golf Capital

In North Carolina's southern Piedmont the white sand and longleaf pine signify an area known as the Sandhills. Pinehurst and Southern Pines make the Sandhills the winter golf capital of America. Pinehurst is the home of the World Golf Hall of Fame.

There are 26 courses within a 15-mile radius of the Pinehurst-Southern Pines area, including Mid-Pines, Pine Needles, Knollwood, Whispering Pines, Seven Lakes and the Southern Pines Country Club.

"Top season" in the Sandhills resorts is from October through April, but year-round vacationing in the area is now on the upswing.

Horsemen as well as golfers discovered the Sandhills in the early 1900's. The oldest organized hunt in North Carolina, the Moore County Hounds, was established at Southern Pines in 1914. Today, the Moore County Hounds turn out in traditional splendor for fox and drag hunts between November and late March. Thoroughbreds and standardbreds are trained on Sandhills tracks, and riding is a major sport in the area. In April the Stoneybrook Steeplechase at Southern Pines is a big event.

April golf tournaments in the Sandhills are among the oldest in the nation—the North and South Invitation Amateur Championship for Men and the North and South Invitation Championship for Women. Some golf courses at each of the two resorts remain open through summer; all are open from October through April.

The Sandhills resorts are popular for year-round living as well as zestful vacationing. The subtropical gardens and renowned saltwater fishing of North Carolina's southeastern coast are within a few hours drive of Pinehurst and Southern Pines. In the immediate area are Gaddy's Wild Goose Refuge at Ansonville, Clarendon Gardens, crafts centers and the 57,000-acre Sandhills Wildlife Management Area with excellent field trial courses, deer hunting and fishing lakes. Dove, deer and quail hunting are within a short distance of the resort colonies. Pinehurst and the Sandhills Wildlife Management Area are settings for major field trials.

In May, Sedgefield, a suburb of Greensboro, hosts one of the South's oldest horse shows. The Sedgefield Hunt season is from Oct. until spring; visitors can arrange to ride here, as well as with other organized hunts in North Carolina.

Tryon, in the unique "Thermal Belt," is noted for its mild climate year round and enjoys year-round patronage—Northerners come here in autumn, winter and spring because of the equable climate at these seasons; Southern visitors find Tryon cooler than the lowlands in summer. Like Southern Pines and Pinehurst, Tryon has a growing colony of retirees.

Horseback riding is a major sport, with the Tryon Hounds offering fox hunting between October and spring, and the Block House Steeplechase and Tryon Horse and Hound Show prominent in March and April.

Charlotte is a bustling center of trade, manufacturing, transportation and communication. Its handsome Coliseum, Ovens Auditorium and Merchandise Mart form a complex where sports, cultural events, trade fairs and expositions are held. Named for Queen Charlotte of Mecklenburg, wife of George III, the "Queen City" is North Carolina's largest convention host and is readily accessible. The Mint Museum of Art has an excellent collection of paintings and other art works. Major events at Charlotte include the Festival in the Park, featuring arts and crafts, the Carolinas Carrousel with a parade on Thanksgiving Day, flower shows and tours of homes. Charlotte's residential areas are noted for fine homes and gardens.

Two educational and fun stops for families are Discovery Place, the nation's sixth-ranked "hands-on" science museum downtown, and Carowinds, the largest theme park in North Carolina, which is just south of the city on the North Carolina-South Carolina line.

On the Catawba River a few miles north of Charlotte is Cowan's Ford Dam, which forms Lake Norman. This lake covers more than 30,000 acres, and is the largest lake in the state. Duke Power State Park and many marinas and boat launching areas give access to the lake.

Morrow Mountain State Park near Albemarle, about forty-two miles northeast of Charlotte, has swimming, boating, fishing, hiking, camping and nature study. Here you can drive a scenic road to the top of Morrow Mountain, a distinctive feature of the Uwharrie Range. The Uwharries stretch across portions of four counties and include Uwharrie National Forest. Morrow Mountain State Park is on Lake Tillery, southernmost in the series of lakes along the Yadkin and Pee Dee Rivers.

Only a short drive from Morrow Mountain is Town Creek Indian Mound State Historic Site, on an area that was the ceremonial center and burial ground for a prehistoric tribe of Indians who lived on the lower Pee Dee. A stockade, a temple mound and other features have been restored here.

In the north central Piedmont, High Point, Thomasville and Lexington are focal points of North Carolina's large furniture industry. The Southeastern Furniture Exposition Building at High Point is the center of annual furniture markets, attended by buyers from all over America and foreign countries as well.

Greensboro, founded in 1808 as county seat of Guilford County, is named for General Nathanael Green who commanded Colonial troops in the Battle of Guilford Courthouse, which was fought just beyond the present city limits. William Sidney Porter, writer of short stories under the pen name "O. Henry," was born in Greensboro. The drugstore where he worked as a youth has been reconstructed in the Greensboro Historical Museum. Textiles have always played an important part in the life of Greensboro, and the first steam-powered cotton mill in North Carolina was built here in 1828. The city has tremendous textile operations today.

Guilford Courthouse National Military Park, on US 220 northwest of Greensboro, covers 150 acres with monuments, markers and a museum.

Here in March, 1781, Cornwallis won a victory over General Greene's American forces, but he was so weakened that the British surrender at Yorktown followed. The park is open year round. In spring, Greensboro, the park and surrounding countryside bloom with dogwood and redbud. During the entire year, the Greensboro War Memorial Auditorium-Coliseum is a center for athletic events, entertainment and cultural programs. Greensboro's Forest Oaks Country Club on US 421 S is the home of the famed Greater Greensboro Open Golf Tournament in April. This is one of the oldest stops on the PGA tour.

Winston-Salem, North Carolina's fourth ranking population center, is some thirty miles northwest of Greensboro and High Point. Winston-Salem is a major travel objective in its own right and a gateway to North Carolina's Blue Ridge Mountain vacationlands. It was two towns until 1913, when Winston (founded in 1849) was united with Salem (founded in 1766 by the Moravians).

Old Salem

Old Salem, in the heart of the city, is a treasury of time-mellowed buildings, reflecting—in architecture and arrangement—the middle-European heritage of its founders. The Old World charm which Salem has retained for two centuries has been enhanced with the restoration of more than thirty structures, some open as exhibition buildings and some in use as dwellings, shops or offices. Other buildings in Salem—among them Home Moravian Church (1800) and several units on the campus of Salem College—have been in continuous use since the late 1700's and early 1800's. The Brothers House, built on Salem Square in 1769 and owned and used by the Moravian Church until its restoration, is the setting for Moravian Candle Teas in early December. Visitors to the teas watch preparation of beeswax candles for the Christmas Eve Lovefeast services at the Home Church, and they are served traditional sugar cake and coffee.

Tours of Old Salem are held throughout the year. Exhibit buildings in addition to those previously mentioned are: Salem Tavern (1784); the Tavern Barn and Farm Museum; the Hiksch Tobacco Shop (1773), the oldest tobacco shop still standing in America; the John Vogler House built in 1819, the home of the village silversmith and clockmaker. Wachovia Museum, housed in the Boys' School (1794), has one of the largest collection of local antiquities in America. Old Salem is about six city blocks long by three blocks wide. As headquarters for the Moravian Church South, Salem is the setting for religious observances that have continued since the community's earliest days. In December, the many-pointed Moravian Christmas stars light Salem doorways. The Moravian Easter Sunrise Service, which opens on Salem Square in front of the Home Church and concludes in nearby "God's Acre," the Moravian Graveyard, has been held for nearly two hundred years. During the Moravian Easter Litany, the Church Band plays antiphonally. Just before Easter, the flat white gravestones of God's Acre are scrubbed clean, and fresh flowers decorate each grave. Visitors to Salem at Easter should plan to stroll through God's Acre on Good Friday or Saturday to watch the preparations, for Easter in God's Acre is like a vast outdoor flower garden.

Eight miles west of Winston-Salem, at Clemmons, is Tanglewood Park, a former country estate willed to the people of Forsyth County by Mr. and Mrs. William Reynolds. Tanglewood has golf, camping, swimming and tennis. In the center of the Park is the gracious manor house where visitors may dine.

At the western edge of Winston-Salem is Wake Forest University, opened in 1834 at Wake Forest, North Carolina, near Raleigh, and relocated on its present three-hundred-acre campus in the early 1950's.

Winston-Salem is the largest auction center for marketing flue-cured tobacco in the Old Belt. Auctions begin in September and continue until after Thanksgiving.

Two of North Carolina's state parks are located within 30 miles of Winston-Salem: Hanging Rock State Park and Pilot Mountain State Park. Near Wilkesboro, west of Winston-Salem on US 421, is the W. Kerr Scott Reservoir in the Blue Ridge foothills. The U.S. Corps of Engineers maintains campgrounds and boat launching facilities here. There are also powerboat races in summer.

Kerr Scott Reservoir is not to be confused with Kerr Lake, which is some 170 miles east near Henderson, and has an eight-hundred-mile shoreline extending into Virginia. Kerr Lake is impounded by the John H. Kerr Dam on the Roanoke River in Virginia. On the North Carolina shores of the lake are areas for picnicking, camping and boating. North Carolina's Kerr Reservoir Development Commission administers these recreational facilities. The Carolina Sailing Club sponsors regattas on Kerr Lake, the largest being the Governor's Cup in June. There is excellent fishing for bass, panfish and landlocked striped bass or "rockfish." The lake is used extensively by residents of the Triangle or Capital area. Farther east, north of Roanoke Rapids, is Lake Gaston, which offers facilities for boating and skiing.

Durham and Chapel Hill

Durham, only twenty-three miles from the capital, is a ranking industrial center, leading tobacco market of the Middle Belt and home of Duke University, one of the largest institutions of higher learning in the Southeast. The history of Durham is a fascinating chapter of the "American success story." Durham was only a small village when, in 1865, General W. T. Sherman received the surrender of General Joseph E. Johnston a few miles west at Bennett Place, a historic site open all year. Among the Durham County residents mustered out of the Confederate Army when the Civil War ended was Washington Duke, who walked 137 miles home to his farm to begin civilian life again. The Dukes, like most of their neighbors, grew tobacco. Washington Duke began grinding tobacco which he packaged and sold. By 1874, Duke and his three sons were established in Durham as manufacturers of smoking tobacco. Within a few years, they were producing cigarettes for domestic sale and export; the growth of the huge American Tobacco empire and other manufacturing enterprises began in their city. It has been said that James B. Duke did with tobacco what Rockefeller did with oil and Carnegie with steel. He endowed the University (formerly Trinity College), which bears his family name and is principal beneficiary of the Duke Endowment.

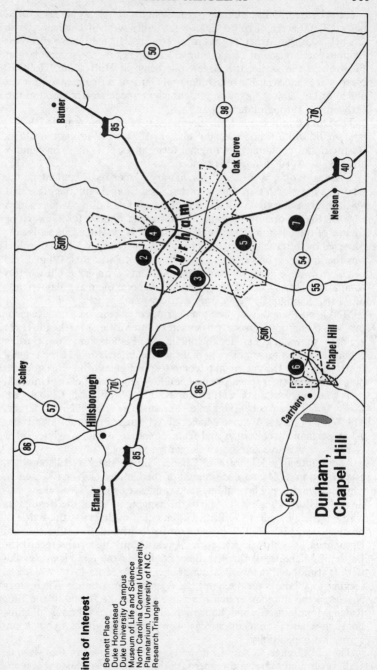

Durham, Chapel Hill

Points of Interest

1) Bennett Place
2) Duke Homestead
3) Duke University Campus
4) Museum of Life and Science
5) North Carolina Central University
6) Planetarium, University of N.C.
7) Research Triangle

Duke University has a Gothic West Campus and Georgian East Campus on 7,500 acres of rolling land a few miles west of Durham. Duke Chapel, a Gothic structure, has a spire rising 210 feet above the West Campus and houses an 18th century Flentrop organ, the second largest Flentrop in the world, the largest one being in Rotterdam, Holland. Nearby are the Sarah P. Duke Memorial Gardens with extensive formal and informal landscaping. The gardens offer a succession of blooms from early spring through late autumn.

The Duke family homestead, three miles north of Durham via US 501, is a small, white frame dwelling built in 1851 by Washington Duke. Restored and containing its original furnishings, it is open on Sunday afternoons, April through September.

Thomas Wolfe, who began his literary career as a student at the University of North Carolina, once described Chapel Hill as a place that "beats every other town all hollow." Situated on a hilltop at the eastern edge of the Piedmont Plateau, the town was named for New Hope Chapel of the Church of England. The site of New Hope Chapel is now occupied by the gracious Carolina Inn. The University of North Carolina was the first state university to open its doors to students. Chapel Hill has a growing colony of year-round residents who have chosen this community for its "stimulating serenity." Among them are playwrights, novelists, distinguished educators, scientists and artists.

Morehead Planetarium, first planetarium ever built on a college campus, was the gift of University benefactor John Motley Morehead. There are daily shows held here for the public. The Planetarium Rose Garden is built around a mammoth sun dial showing international time around the world. The U.S. astronauts come to the Planetarium for study in preparation for their space flights. The Old Well, symbol of the University, is a famous landmark on the campus. In the Monogram Club is Carl Boettcher's huge woodcarving of an "around the world" circus parade. The William Hayes Ackland Memorial Art Museum on the campus has a fine permanent collection and features special exhibits, while Coker Arboretum is a five-acre botanical garden nearby.

About fifteen miles north of Chapel Hill is historic Hillsborough, established in 1754 and once capital of the Colony of North Carolina, containing many public buildings and residences with historical associations. In Hillsborough is the site of the hanging of six of the Regulators whose uprising against the British culminated in defeat at the Battle of Alamance on May 16, 1771. Alamance Battleground, five miles south of Burlington, is a historic site open all year. Many historians regard the Battle of Alamance as the first major conflict of the American Revolution. It stimulated the westward movement of freedom-loving colonists, seeking new homes on the Southern Appalachian frontier. Their story is told in the outdoor drama *Horn in the West* at Boone in the Blue Ridge Mountains. Daniel Boone's trail to Kentucky began in Hillsborough where prominent citizens were partners in the company sponsoring his expeditions.

The old Orange County Courthouse with its Museum, the Masonic Hall, several churches and numerous other buildings of historical interest are open all year in Hillsborough. This is a place to visit at leisure for an insight into America's past. Only a short drive from contemporary hotels and motor lodges in the Triangle area, Hillsborough's accommodations are appropriate to the town's atmosphere of history—the Colonial Inn was built in 1781, and meals are available.

From the Piedmont Triangle area of High Point, Greensboro and Winston-Salem, I-85 and I-40 are the arterial routes toward the Southern Appalachians.

Western North Carolina, "Land of the Sky"

In 1794, French botanist Andre Michaux climbed Grandfather Mountain and sang the "Marseillaise," triumphantly believing he had discovered the highest point in North America. He hadn't, but there's such a "top of the world" feeling in surveying one's surroundings from promontories in western North Carolina that Michaux's enthusiasm is understandable. These Southern Appalachian Mountains—the Blue Ridge, Great Smokies, Blacks, Nantahalas and others—range in height from 5,000 feet to more than 6,000 feet. Their soft, rich tapestry of foliage is laced with tumbling streams and accented with massive rock outcroppings. Colors and visibility change constantly with atmospheric conditions and the seasons.

Mount Mitchell (6,684 feet) is the highest mountain east of the Mississippi River and one of the forty-nine peaks in North Carolina reaching 6,000 feet or more. Grandfather Mountain (5,964 feet) is the tallest peak in the Blue Ridge.

The Cherokee Indians were the first to explore and live in North Carolina. The haze that hangs over the high country was called "Sahkanaga" by the Cherokees, meaning the "Great Blue Hills of God." We know the area as the Great Smoky Mountains. Some 5,000 Cherokees live here today on their reservation adjoining the Great Smoky Mountains National Park and the Blue Ridge Parkway. Elsewhere in western North Carolina live descendents of the pioneers who began building homes in the mountains shortly before the Revolutionary War, and of settlers who came later from Virginia, Pennsylvania and other states.

Contrast is dramatic in most sections of the highlands. Hewn-log dwellings are reminders of the past. The present is here in twentieth-century architecture and culture. The future's pattern is indicated by the construction of superhighways, suburban residential areas, shopping centers and malls. There are cluttered country stores, sleek specialty shops, department stores and craft centers ranging from quaint to contemporary. The southern prong of the "Wilderness Road" crosses the Blue Ridge Parkway near the town of Boone. Each summer the outdoor drama *Horn in the West* tells the story of Daniel Boone and his fellow frontiersmen. At Asheville's Mountain Dance and Folk Festival in August and Mountain Youth Jamboree in March, you'll see natives of the area presenting traditional music and dances of the Southern Appalachians. At Fontana Village and other resorts you'll learn the intricate paces of Western-style square dances as well as those of local origin. It's a rare festival, fair or celebration in the mountains that doesn't feature at least one of the teams of clog dancers for which the region is noted. Traditional hymns are heard at the "Singing on the Mountain" at Grandfather Mountain on the fourth Sunday in June.

A Forest Kingdom

Western North Carolina's region is a huge "sample case" of vegetation, minerals and fauna as well as a fascinating complex of scenery. Botanists have classified over 145 varieties of trees and more than one thousand other plants in these mountains, and evergreen forests on higher peaks and slopes more closely resemble those of Canada than the Carolinas. In October the region is a riot of color when the hardwoods turn to crimson and gold accented by evergreens and the distant tones of blue which give the Blue Ridge and Great Smokies their names. There are two rules of thumb to remember in planning to see the autumn foliage parade. One is that color begins in the high elevations and moves down the slopes—the earlier your trip, the higher the places you should plan to visit. The other is that most generally distributed coloration usually occurs between October 10 and 25. In most areas below three thousand feet, it continues until November.

Spring comes later and lingers into June at elevations above five thousand feet. Its patterns of flowers and foliage, like those of autumn, vary according to altitudes, but they move upward. In April, small ground flowers decorate forest floors, while hardwoods assume tones of soft pink and pale green as their leaves unfurl. The snowy white of dogwood and silverbell appears in April and May. The "big three" of the mountain flower parade—laurel, flame azalea and purple rhododendron—begin blooming in late May and make their biggest displays in June. Tall white rhododendron blooms in late June; numerous wildflowers bloom all summer.

To natural advantages, the region has added varied accommodations, golf courses, swimming pools, riding stables, hiking trails, theme parks, festivals and sports events. There are summer theaters and two outdoor historical dramas, arts and crafts colonies, summer camps for boys and girls, religious assembly grounds and historical attractions. In a region of few natural lakes, huge power projects provide boating, fishing and water-skiing.

Snow-skiing is the growing winter sport. North Carolina is the southern-most state where skiing is possible extensively, and there are several ski resorts currently developed—Appalachian Ski Mountain at Blowing Rock; Beech Mountain and Sugar Mountain at Banner Elk; Hawk's Nest and Mill Ridge near Boone; Cataloochee near Waynesville; High Meadows at Roaring Gap; Sapphire Valley at Sapphire and Wolf Laurel at Mars Hill. North Carolina enjoys a mild year-around climate, but frequently natural snow is available. However, when Mother Nature won't cooperate, all the Tar Heel slopes are equipped with artificial snow-making equipment so that skiing may continue as long as the temperature permits. Skiing is enjoyed from December until early March.

Western North Carolina's resorts and towns are small to medium-sized, and its largest city, Asheville, is traditionally a resort as well as a county seat, trading center and gateway to the entire state. A chateau constructed by George W. Vanderbilt and a modest residence that was once a boarding house for "summer people" are two noted Asheville attractions. The chateau is Biltmore House, completed in 1895 in French Renaissance style. Biltmore House is furnished with antiques and art works from all over the world. Its Norman banquet hall is 72 X 40 feet, with a vaulted ceiling 75 feet high. The house is on a 12,000-acre estate and includes the Biltmore Dairy Farm. Residence, gardens and dairy are open to visitors year around. The original Vanderbilt holdings consisted of some 125,000 acres, including Mount Pisgah. Much of this acreage was deeded to North Carolina by Mr. Vanderbilt's widow, and it became the nucleus of the Pisgah National Forest.

Asheville's Famous Sons

The boarding house at 48 Spruce Street is the Thomas Wolfe Memorial, "Dixieland" in Wolfe's first novel, *Look Homeward, Angel.* Preserved as a literary shrine, it contains furnishings and personal possessions in use when Wolfe's mother opened the family home to paying guests. Pack Memorial Library nearby has the many different editions of Wolfe's books in various languages, together with correspondence, clippings and most books and articles written about Asheville's famous native son.

Thomas Wolfe and O. Henry are buried in Riverside Cemetery at Asheville. The marble angel which inspired the title of Wolfe's first novel is in Oakdale Cemetery at Hendersonville, twenty-five miles south of Asheville.

Asheville is headquarters for the Southern Highland Handicraft Guild and scene of the annual Crafts Fair in August. The Guild has a crafts center at 930 Tunnel Road (US 70) and also a downtown shop. The Guild operates a crafts center from May through October in the old manor house in Moses Memorial Park on the Blue Ridge Parkway. Artisans from many Southern states are Guild members, as are North Carolina's two noted crafts schools—Penland near Spruce Pines and the John C. Campbell Folk School at Brasstown. Guild centers, the two schools, the Fair and numerous crafts shops throughout western North Carolina are excellent introductions to the crafts of the region, and they have information about visiting individual craftsmen in their workshops or homes.

The Blue Ridge Parkway

A high-altitude route for pleasure travel between Shenandoah National Park in Virginia and the Great Smoky Mountains National Park entrance near Cherokee is the Blue Ridge Parkway. This is a scenic drive and offers varied recreational opportunities. It also illustrates the history, geology and culture of the mountains through such features as the Museum of North Carolina Minerals, pioneer dwellings, crafts centers, nature trails and exhibits. There are campgrounds, picnic areas and scenic overlooks. It should be emphasized that the Parkway is for optional travel, principally in spring, summer and autumn. Highest sections (in the Mount Mitchell area) and the entire seventy-five miles of Parkway west of Asheville may be closed from early November until mid-April due to bad weather. Snow and ice may also cause winter closure of some of the sections which are normally open all year. Other mountain highways are open all year, with the exception of the spur highway to Clingman's Dome in the Great Smoky Mountains National Park and a few U.S. Forest Service or privately built roads, which are not intended for through traffic.

The Cherokee Indian Reservation

Half of the Great Smoky Mountains National Park is within the state. US 441 is the transmountain highway through the Park; it enters North Carolina a few miles south of Franklin, links up with many other highways, and on the Cherokee Indian Reservation it meets US 19 and the Blue Ridge Parkway.

Cherokee is the largest town on the Reservation. Here the Indians relate their history through the outdoor drama *Unto These Hills* (late June through August). Oconaluftee Indian Village shows how the Cherokee lived two centuries ago. This is an outstanding attraction and is open from May through October. Baskets, pottery and other crafts produced in the village are sold at the Qualla Arts Cooperative and other shops of the area.

Cherokee's "Main Street" is lined with shops. Many of the mass-produced items come from manufacturing concerns operating on the Reservation and employing Cherokees. Among the numerous motels at Cherokee is the Boundary Tree, a tribal enterprise. Craftsmen and guides at Oconaluftee Village and actors in *Unto These Hills* wear traditional Cherokee costume, but the "chiefs" who greet visitors at most shops dress in Sioux-style feathers and buckskin. "Chiefing" has been a time-honored occupation for the tribesmen ever since visitors began coming to the Reservation; but the Eastern Band of the Cherokees has only one practical chief, who is elected by the tribe. Most Cherokees dress just like any other mountain people.

In the Park, one of the oldest uplands on earth, the Great Smokies Divide zigzags through from northeast to southwest for seventy-one miles along the North Carolina-Tennessee line for a few miles west of Cherokee. For thirty-six miles along its crest, the range maintains an altitude in excess of 5,000 feet. Sixteen peaks rise to more than 6,000 feet. Tallest is Clingman's Dome (6,643 feet). There's a paved road from US 441 to a parking overlook near the summit. From the overlook a hiking trail leads to the observation tower at the highest point.

At the Park entrance near Cherokee is Smokemont Ranger Station, with pioneer exhibits and farmstead showing how yesterday's settlers lived. In the Park are some seventy-five miles of paved roads, plus an equal amount of secondary roads, and over seven hundred miles of marked trails for hiking or horseback riding. There are short self-guiding trails at points of unusual interest like the evergreen "rain forest" on Clingman's Dome. Park campgrounds in North Carolina are at Deep Creek near Bryson City, Smokemont on US 441 and Balsam Mountain near Heintooga Overlook. Trout streams are open from May through August, but except for the fish that may be taken under special regulations, the Park is a sanctuary for every living thing.

For direct all-year travel between the Great Smokies and Asheville, US 19 and 19-23 can be used in combination with I-40. Waynesville, county seat of Haywood, is the largest city within twenty-five miles of the North Carolina boundary of the Great Smokies Park. The town is highly popular with travelers and seasonal residents because of its variety of accommodations, its golf course and its proximity to both the Parkway and the Great Smokies Park. Nearby is Lake Junaluska, a resort as well as a religious assembly, and Maggie Valley. Maggie Valley is 4,000 feet above sea level, with tall mountains on either side. For several miles along US 19, Maggie is intensively developed with motels, restaurants, shops and recreation facilities.

Square Dancing Areas

Canton, bypassed by a link of I-40 between Asheville and Waynesville, has one of the oldest and largest Labor Day celebrations in North Carolina.

Bryson City, on US 19 a few miles southwest of Cherokee, is a noted gateway to the Great Smokies Park and Cherokee Reservation. It is near the headwaters of Fontana Lake, which extends for some thirty miles along the southern boundary of the Park. Areas of Nantahala Forest also adjoin the lake, which is impounded by the highest dam in the TVA system. Main highways lead to the dam and Fontana Village resort from US 10 and State 28, which has views of the lake at several points, and State 129 through Robbinsville and the Lake Santeetlah area. Fontana Village—with lodge, cottages, boat docks, golf, swimming, tennis, square dancing, riding and other features—is the largest strictly resort community in the Great Smokies. The resort was developed from the community built to house the workers who rushed Fontana Dam to completion during World War II.

At the dam there are observation areas and a visitor center. Below Fontana, waters of the Little Tennessee River also form Lake Cheoah.

Lake Santeetlah, another nearby power lake, is surrounded by Nantahala Forest. Accessible by a loop road, which turns off 129 near Robbinsville and circles the lake, is Joyce Kilmer Forest, a 3,800-acre tract of virgin timber preserved as a memorial to the poet who wrote "Trees." There is a forest service campground near the entrance to the Forest; within the Forest are hiking trails. Snowbird Mountain Lodge is nearby.

The first transmountain wagon train in this century was initiated by North Carolina and Tennessee in 1957 to call attention to the need for a road across the mountains in the Joyce Kilmer Forest area. With the road assured, the wagon train continues as an annual event in other areas of southwestern North Carolina. Both Andrews and Murphy have been its destinations in the past, as well as Franklin. Sponsors of the wagon train say it will continue as a feature of the Fourth of July holiday season. In the Blue Ridge Mountain country north of Asheville, the citizens of Watauga and Wilkes counties staged a "Daniel Boone Wagon Train" in 1963. This wagon train has become an annual trip from North Wilkesboro to Boone, with overnight encampments enroute.

Near Spruce Pines, Burnsville and Bakersville is Roan Mountain, respectfully referred to as "The Roan." It rises to 6,285 feet on the North Carolina-Tennessee line and for nearly six miles never dips below 5,800 feet. The Roan has what has been called the world's largest natural garden of Catawba rhododendrons, and North Carolina's Rhododendron Queen is crowned here during the Rhododendron Festival in late June. On the Roan, reached by Highway 261 and a U.S. Forest Service road, is a recreation area of Pisgah National Forest. The rhododendron here is usually most colorful between June 15-25.

The origin of the name "Roan" is lost in legend, but Mt. Mitchell is named for the man who first measured its height and later lost his life while attempting to verify his findings. He was Dr. Elisha Mitchell, a professor at the University of North Carolina. His tomb is at the foot of the observation tower atop the mountain. The tower is in Mt. Mitchell State Park, and the Park was the first established of the state's parks. The Park is reached by a paved highway (State 128) which connects with the Blue Ridge Parkway.

Among the Blue Ridge Parkway recreational areas north of Asheville is Linville Falls, where the Linville River plunges into Linville Gorge. The gorge itself is a wilderness area in Pisgah National Forest. From several overlooks along the Parkway in this area, and from Wiseman's View on the rim of the gorge, are seen the mysterious Brown Mountain Lights which rise over a wooded peak in Burke County. They have never been explained by scientific theory or investigation. The dark of the moon in August is regarded as best for seeing this phenomenon.

Boone–Blowing Rock–Banner Elk

The visitor to the Boone-Blowing Rock-Banner Elk area finds himself in a section of North Carolina that offers many entertainment features, as well as beauty. Between Boone and Blowing Rock is one of the area's most popular attractions—"Tweetsie," a narrow-gauge train, so named because of its plaintive whistle. Tweetsie is located in a setting which includes a frontier-type village and amusement park.

Blowing Rock, adjacent to the Parkway and the eastern slope of the Blue Ridge Divide, is almost entirely a resort. The town is named for The Blowing Rock, a formation which takes its name from air currents which swirl upward around it. Golf and tennis are available at Blowing Rock and at nearby Boone, Linville and Newland. In 1962-63, the Boone-Blowing Rock-Banner Elk area became a winter sports center with the establishment of the following ski areas—Appalachian Ski Mountain, Beech Mountain, Mill Ridge, Hawk's Nest and Sugar Mountain. In this area, as in the Waynesville-Maggie Valley area to the southwest, skiing has given a lively new look to winter, with accommodations remaining open.

The Museum of North Carolina Minerals, on the Parkway at its junction with US 226, displays a sampler of the more than three hundred different kinds of gems and minerals found in North Carolina. Spruce Pines, six miles west of the Parkway, has a Gems and Minerals Festival in early August. "Rock shops" here and elsewhere in the mountains have information and equipment for collectors or "rockhounds." Franklin, a substantial community in southwestern North Carolina, is famous as a center of ruby making. The Cowee Valley and other localities nearby were once a source of commercially mined gems. Since the early 1950's, the ruby fields have been opened, and visitors can pay a small fee to "dig, find and keep." Findings often include sapphires as well as rubies.

Carl Sandburg's Home

Near Hendersonville on US 25 is Flat Rock, the home of the late Carl Sandburg. Mr. Sandburg's home has been appointed a National Historic Site. At the Flat Rock Playhouse, the Vagabond Players—North Carolina's oldest professional stock company—present plays from late June until Labor Day.

The area around Hendersonville and Brevard has over fifty percent of the summer camps for boys and girls. This is a multimillion-dollar industry for western North Carolina. Also in this area are several religious assembly grounds maintained by various denominations for summer conferences, study, retreats and recreation. Largest are Lake Junaluska (Methodist) and Montreat (Presbyterian) on US 70 west of Asheville. Evangelist Billy Graham lives at Montreat.

Near Brevard, US 276 enters the oldest section of Pisgah National Forest and crosses the Blue Ridge Parkway to link up with 23-19A and 19 at Waynesville to the west. The Cradle of Forestry in America, the site of the first forestry school in America, has a visitor center just off US 276. Beside the highway are Sliding Rock and Looking Glass Falls on the Davidson River. There are also Forest Service picnic areas and campgrounds along this route.

Pisgah National Forest covers 479,232 acres of western North Carolina, with its tracts of land widely scattered. Nantahala National Forest is comprised of 449,869 acres in southwestern North Carolina. Both have campgrounds, picnic areas, game management lands that offer hunting and trout fishing.

About eighteen miles west of Brevard and near the small community of Rosman on US 64 is the National Aeronautics and Space Administration Data Acquisition Facility, which tracks satellites. It is open to visitors daily and Sundays.

In the Sapphire country a little farther west, distinctive resorts along US 64 are Lake Toxaway, Sapphire, Cashiers and Highlands. Golf is one of the featured attractions. There are ski slopes at Sapphire Valley. The highest cliffs in eastern America are on Whiteside Mountain near Highlands. Highlands, four thousand feet above sea level, has been a summer resort for almost a century, and "summer people" greatly outnumber its year-round population.

Between Highlands and Franklin, US 64 negotiates the walls of Cullasaja Gorge and passes Bridal Veil Falls, Dry Falls and several Nantahala Forest recreation areas. You can drive an automobile under Bridal Veil and walk behind the waters of Dry Falls without getting wet.

The Nantahala Mountains rise sharply around Franklin. There is a Forest Service road to the top of Wayah Bald, where native pink and flame azaleas bloom in early June.

Southwest of Franklin, US 64 continues to the extreme southwestern corner of North Carolina, where the largest town is Murphy. Lake Hiwassee and Lake Chatuge offer fishing and boating and have resort developments on their shores.

North Carolinians say "from Manteo to Murphy" to describe the east-west extent of their state—it is over five hundred miles from one of these points to another. The entire trip can be made on US 64, although newer and wider highways cut down the driving time.

Two scenic approaches to Asheville and western North Carolina from the Piedmont are US 74 and I-40. After crossing the state from the coast via Charlotte in the southern Piedmont, US 74 approaches Asheville through Hickory Nut Gorge, where Chimney Rock and Lake Lure are noted features. Chimney Rock is accessible by a paved motor road and an elevator in the Rock itself. There are sports car hill climbs in spring and fall, and the Rock is open from March to November. As it nears the mountains, I-40 commands expansive views of the blue wall of the mountain ranges north of Asheville and then climbs the Eastern Continental Divide between Old Fort and Black Mountain.

PRACTICAL INFORMATION FOR NORTH CAROLINA

 FACTS AND FIGURES. The state was named for Charles I of England. Its nicknames are the "Old North State" and the "Tar Heel State." The state flower is the dogwood; the cardinal is the state bird. *Esse Quam Videri* ("To be, rather than to seem") is the state motto. Raleigh is the state capital, and the population of North Carolina is 5,082,059.

 HOW TO GET THERE. *By air:* Interstate airlines serving major North Carolina cities are: Piedmont, Delta, Eastern, United, US Air and Altair. Intrastate lines are: Wheeler, Sunbird, Mid-South and Atlantis. Limousine service available at all major airports.

By train: Amtrak trains go into Rocky Mount, Raleigh, Fayetteville, Hamlet and Southern Pines/Pinehurst. Southern Railway also has passenger service.

By car: A tourist is given a taste of "Tar Heel" hospitality at the state's lovely Welcome Centers located on I-95, I-85, and I-77 on the Virginia and South Carolina state lines and on I-40 on the Tennessee line. I-26 and I-77 come in from South Carolina.

By bus: Good service by Greyhound and Trailways.

 HOW TO GET AROUND. *By air:* See "How To Get There" section.

By car: North Carolina's state-administered highway system has more than 75,000 mi. of roads and bridges, all toll-free. I-26, I-40, I-77, I-85 and I-95, as well as US 17, US 19, US 64-264, US 70, US 220, US 221, US 258 and US 421 all have delightful rest areas with picnic tables and barbecues.

By ferry: The state operates toll-free ferries daily across Currituck Sound from Currituck to Knotts Island, Hatteras Inlet, Pamlico River, at Bayview, and Neuse River, at Minnesott Beach. Toll ferry service is available from Cedar Island to Ocracoke Island and Southport to Ft. Fisher. All state ferries carry automobiles. For ferry schedules write: Dept. of Transportation, Public Affairs Office, P.O. Box 25201, Raleigh, N.C. 27611.

By bus: In addition to Greyhound and Trailways, Seashore Transportation Co. operates within the state.

 TOURIST INFORMATION. For information regarding points of interest in the state and also information about camping, hunting and fishing write to the: N. C. Travel Division, Dept. of Commerce, Raleigh, N.C. 27611. Contact the Superintendent, Park Headquarters, Cape Hatteras National Seashore, Box 457, Manteo, N.C. 27954, for information about the Cape Hatteras National Seashore. The Public Affairs Office, North Carolina Dept. of Transportation, Raleigh, N.C. 27611, can supply ferry information and highway conditions bulletins. A pamphlet listing vacation events in North Carolina can be obtained by writing: "N.C. Calendar of Events," N. C. Travel Division, Dept. of Commerce, Raleigh, N.C. 27611.

Welcome Centers are located on I-95, I-85, and I-77 on the Virginia and So. Carolina state lines and on I-40 on the Tennessee line.

SEASONAL EVENTS. Festivals, fairs and other special events usher in spring and other seasons. A sampling follows of some of the better known annual events, listed in chronological order beginning with the spring months.

Late March: Annual *Old Time Fiddlers and Blue Grass Convention,* Mooresville, N.C. The state's oldest continuous fiddlers convention.

April: *North Carolina Azalea Festival,* Wilmington, features parade, garden tours, coronation of festival royalty, dances and concerts. The festival celebrates the blooming of millions of azaleas in and around this historic port city. *Greater Greensboro Open Golf Tournament,* Greensboro; and the *Stonybrook Steeplechase* in Southern Pines.

May: *Strawberry Festival,* Chadbourn; Sports Car Hill Climb, Chimney Rock; Men's and Women's North-South Golf Championships, Pinehurst; Hang Gliding Championship Competition, Grandfather Mtn., Linville; Hang Gliding Spectacular at Jockey's Ridge, Nags Head; "World 600" Grand National Stock Car Race, Charlotte; Marlin Tournament in Wrightsville Beach.

June: *Blue Marlin Tournament,* Morehead City; *International Blue Marlin Tournament,* Hatteras; *North Carolina Rhododendron Festival,* Bakersville and Roan Mountain. *"Singing on the Mountain,"* Grandfather Mountain, Linville, held on the fourth Sunday in June—begun as a family reunion in 1925, this is an all-day program of music and picnicking that draws thousands. Also in Spivey's Corner is the unusual *National Hollerin' Contest*—an event that has grown each year and has received national television attention.

July: Wagon trains—trans-mountain treks of horse-drawn vehicles and horseback riders end with Fourth of July parades at Franklin in southwestern North Carolina and Boone in the Blue Ridge Mountains. *Highland games* and the *Gathering of the Scottish Clans,* Grandfather Mountain, Linville—caber tossing, the Highland Fling, kilts, pipe bands. *Craftsman's Fair,* Asheville, a week-long event sponsored by the Southern Highland and Handicraft Guild, whose members display their finest products and demonstrate their skills.

August: *Gems and Minerals Festival,* Spruce Pine—displays of gems and minerals from North Carolina and other states, field trips for collectors. *Blowing Rock Horse Show,* Blowing Rock—Annual Mountain Dance & Folk Festival, Asheville.

September: *North Carolina Apple Festival,* Hendersonville; *State Championship Horse Show,* Raleigh, held in the J. S. Dorton Arena on the State Fairgrounds.

October: *North Carolina State Fair,* Raleigh—one of America's oldest and largest agricultural fairs, extensive exhibits and entertainment including the State Fair Folk Festival; *"National 500" Stock Car Race,* Charlotte; and *"American 500" Stock Car Race,* Rockingham. *Senior Men's and Senior Women's North-South Golf Tournaments,* Pinehurst; *Pumpkin Festival,* in Spring Hope.

The spring-through-autumn schedule of flower shows in North Carolina begins in February in Wilmington and Whiteville with *camellia shows.* The *Southeastern Flower and Garden Show,* at the Charlotte Merchandise Mart in February, features extensive horticultural exhibits and also room settings with living gardens created for this annual event. Raleigh and Kinston have *rose shows* in May; Hendersonville features the *Carolina Mountain Flower and Garden Show* in the summer.

NATIONAL PARKS. *Blue Ridge Parkway*—the motor road and its right of way are actually an elongated park for leisurely enjoyment of mountain country between Shenandoah National Park in Virginia and the North Carolina entrance to Great Smoky Mountains National Park. More than 250 miles of the Parkway have been completed in western North Carolina, where the road reaches its highest elevation (6,053 feet). There are over 100 scenic overlooks, and special recreational areas are open May through October. Except for stretches at the higher elevations, the toll-free road is normally open all year. Camper-trailers are permitted, but no commercial traffic. Maximum speed limit is 45 m.p.h., lower where posted. Pets are allowed—but only on leash or otherwise under physical, restrictive control.

Cape Hatteras National Seashore—America's first National Seashore, 45 sq. mi. on Outer Banks Islands of Bodie, Hatteras and Ocracoke, with 70 mi. of ocean beach for public use. Campgrounds, day-use centers of picnicking, surf bathing, nature trails, visitor centers and museums. Oregon Inlet Fishing Center (concession) has charter craft for deep-sea, sound or inlet fishing available spring through fall. *Pea Island National Wildlife Refuge* offers opportunities to observe shore birds and migratory waterfowl. There are up to 12,000 Greater Snow geese here between early Nov. and late Jan. There are 3 active lighthouses in the National Seashore. Cape Hatteras Lighthouse is open daily, and visitors can climb to the top. The state maintains highways through the park and operates free automobile ferries between Hatteras and Ocracoke Islands. There is also a bridge across Oregon Inlet to Hatteras Island. The northern entrance to the National Seashore is near Nags Head and is reached by US 158 and US 64-264 crossing to Outer Banks on bridges. The southern approach is from US 70 via a toll ferry between Cedar Island and Ocracoke.

Cape Lookout National Seashore embraces 58 mi. of shoreline between Ocracoke and Shackelford Banks.

Great Smoky Mountains National Park—800 sq. mi. shared equally by North Carolina and Tennessee. The main North Carolina entrance is on US 441 near Cherokee and the southern terminus of Blue Ridge Parkway. Oconaluftee Ranger Station, with Pioneer Exhibits and Farmstead, at the Park entrance, is open daily. Tent and trailer camping allowed at developed campgrounds; rough camping by permit from rangers. Pets must be kept leashed or restricted at all times. Marked hiking trails include 70 mi. of Appalachian Trailway along the crest of Great Smokies Divide. Livery stable concessionaires rent horses from June through Aug. Trout fishing mid-May to Sept. US 441 is the transmountain highway through the Park. At Newfound Gap on the North Carolina-Tennessee line, it intersects with a paved Park road to Clingman's Dome, highest peak in the Great Smokies.

Pisgah and Nantahala in the Southern Appalachians, *Uwharrie* in the Piedmont, and *Croatan* on the coastal plain are National Forests with a total area of over 1,124,000 acres, administered by the U.S. Forest Service. The forests are accessible by main highways, including sections of the Blue Ridge Parkway, and U.S. Forest Service roads. Developed recreational areas for picnicking, swimming, camping, stream and lake fishing, hiking trails, hunting in areas cooperatively managed by North Carolina Wildlife Resources Commission and the Forest Service. Pisgah and Nantahala contain the largest number of scenic and recreational features. In Nantahala National Forest is the *Joyce Kilmer Memorial Forest*. Headquarters for the National Forests in North Carolina are at 50 S. French Broad Ave., Asheville (P.O. Box 2750).

 STATE PARKS AND FORESTS. North Carolina's twenty-seven State Parks and two nature preserves range from mountaintop to seacoast. All except *Mt. Mitchell* and *Mt. Jefferson* are open year round, daily and Sun. Swimming areas and refreshment stands are open in about half of the parks from Memorial Day to Labor Day. Mt. Mitchell restaurant is open from May 1 to October 31. Vacation cabins (reservations advised mid-Apr. to Oct. 31) are found in two parks—*Morrow Mountain* and *Hanging Rock*—with tent-trailer camping in 12 of them. Campsites may be reserved for one or two weeks. Organized (group) camping facilities in two parks—*William B. Umstead*, with three sites in the Crabtree Creek Section and one in the Reedy Creek Section, and *Singletary Lake*. Youth camping (Boy Scout groups, etc.) facilities are available in several parks.

For more specific information write to any individual park, Dept. of Natural and Economic Resources, Division of State Parks, P.O. Box 27687, Raleigh, N.C. 27611 or call 919/733-4181. All State Parks are wildlife sanctuaries, and firearms are prohibited.

Boone's Cave—110 acres on Yadkin River, in Davidson County, reputed to be site where Daniel Boone spent a considerable amount of time. Undeveloped. Hiking, picnicking, fishing, nature study.

Carolina Beach—Formerly known as Masonboro State Park—15 mi. S. of Wilmington, at junction of Intracoastal Waterway and the Cape Fear River. A naturalist's delight. The Venus Fly Trap is endemic to this area. Year-round tent-trailer camping, fishing, boating, nature study, hiking & picnicking.

Cliffs of the Neuse—In Wayne Co., 14 mi. SE of Goldsboro of N.C. 111. Scenic, recreation, picnicking, swimming, tent, trailer & organized camping, boat rentals, fishing, hiking, nature study & museum.

Crowder's Mountain—16 mi. W of Gastonia in Gaston Co. Has facilities for picnicking, fishing, and hiking.

Duke Power—1,328 acres on Lake Norman, 10 mi. S of Statesville off US 21. Swimming, boating, picnicking, fishing, snack bar, 33 tent-trailer campsites, hiking, nature study.

Eno River—The park lies in Durham and Orange Counties. Undeveloped. Hiking available.

Fort Macon—on Bogue Island, opposite Morehead City and Beaufort, 4 mi. from Atlantic Beach, via US 70 and state road. Historic Fort with museum, bathing, beach, surf fishing, picnicking, snack bar.

Goose Creek—In Beaufort Co., 10 mi. E. of Washington; there is a boat launch, recreation, picnicking, fishing, hiking, nature study. Rough camping.

Hammocks Beach—on Bear Island, said to be one of the most beautiful and unspoiled beaches on the Atlantic Coast, 5 mi. SE of Swansboro via Rte. 24 and 2½ mi. free ferry (no vehicles). Memorial Day to Labor Day. Bathing, beach, fishing, picnicking, snack bar, hiking, nature study.

Hanging Rock—4,040 acres in Sauratown Mountains, about 32 mi. N of Winston-Salem via Rte. 89 & 66. Picnicking, lake swimming, fishing, rental rowboats, 6 cabins (Apr. to Oct.) 74 tent/trailer campsites, hiking, nature study, snack bar, observation tower.

Jockey's Ridge—At Nags Head in Dare Co. Site of the highest sand dune on the eastern coast. The park is undeveloped but offers hiking and nature study.

Jones Lake—in Bladen Lakes State Forest via Rte. 242, 4 mi. N of Elizabethtown. Picnicking, lake swimming, boating, fishing, snack bar, tent-trailer camping, nature study.

Kerr Lake—in Vance and Warren Counties, N of Henderson. There are boat launches, recreation, picnicking, refreshment stand, swimming, tent, trailer and organized camping as well as fishing and hiking.

Medoc Mountain—15 mi. SW of Roanoke Rapids in Halifax Co. Park is scenic and has tent and organized camping, picnicking, fishing, hiking and nature study.

Merchants Millpond—nature study, fishing, hiking, picnicking, boat launch are available at this facility 5 mi. NE of Gatesville in Gates Co.

Morrow Mountain—in Uwharrie Mountains on Pee Dee River, 7 mi. E of Albermarle. Picnicking, snack bar, swimming, 6 vacation cabins (mid-Apr. to Oct.), year-round 106 tent/trailer campsites, boating, fishing, hiking, museum, historic Kron House, nature study.

Mt. Jefferson—539 acres, including Mt. Jefferson, about 1 mi. W of Jefferson in Ashe County near US 221 and Blue Ridge Parkway in northwestern North Carolina. Picnicking, hiking, nature study.

Mt. Mitchell—1,469 acres, especially noted for its beautiful natural colors in autumn. The 6,684-ft. summit of Mt. Mitchell (highest peak in U.S. east of Mississippi River), with its 39-ft. observation tower, affords a magnificent view for many miles. 35 mi. NE of Asheville via Blue Ridge Parkway and then 5 mi.

to the peak. Tent camping, snack bar, restaurant, picnicking, museum, hiking, nature study. NOTE: Blue Ridge Parkway closes when icing develops on road during winter.

N.C. Zoological—5 mi. S of Asheboro, wild animals viewed in natural setting, picnicking, hiking, refreshment stand.

Pettigrew—17,360 acres, including 16,600-acre Lake Phelps, 9 mi. S of Creswell via US 64 and state road. Noted for freshwater fishing, boating, water-skiing, hiking, historic mansion and other buildings of Somerset Place Plantation. 13 tent/trailer campsites, picnicking and nature study.

Pilot Mountain—3,547 acres, including unique 5¼-mi. 300-ft. wide corridor to the Yadkin River Section, about 24 mi. N of Winston-Salem off US 52. Contains large quartzite monadnock rising 1,500 ft. above surrounding countryside, which the Indians called *Jomeokee* (the Great Guide). First phase of development now underway. Hiking, picnicking, nature study.

Raven Rock—In Harnett County, 6 mi. W of Lillington on US 421, then 3 mi. N by Rte. 1250. Outstanding 125-ft. rock formation on south bank, at "fall line" of Cape Fear River. Mountain-type trees and shrubs. Undeveloped. Picnicking, hiking, nature study, fishing in Cape Fear River.

(Theodore) Roosevelt Natural Area—a gift from family of our 26th President, to remain undeveloped in perpetuity, for nature and ecological studies. Six miles west of Atlantic Beach, 2 mi. E of Salter Path, on sound side of Bogue Island.

Singletary Lake—within Bladen Lakes State Forest, primarily for group camping. Boating, fishing.

South Mountains—Undeveloped park 13 mi. S of Morganton in Burke Co. Picnicking, organized camping, fishing and hiking are available.

Stone Mountain—5 mi. W of Roaring Gap, off US 21, about 8 mi. from Blue Ridge Parkway. Undeveloped. Picnicking, hiking, nature study. Oval-shaped granite dome over 600 ft. high, approximately 3 mi. in circumference at base.

Weymouth Woods—Sandhills Nature Preserve—"Natural Area" featuring longleaf pine and other sandhills flora and fauna. Hiking, nature study, museum.

William B. Umstead (Crabtree Creek Section)—12 mi. NW of Raleigh on US 70. Tent-trailer camping, organized group camping, picnicking, boating, fishing, hiking, nature study.

William B. Umstead (Reedy Creek Section) 10 mi. NW of Raleigh near Cary, off US 70-A & Rte. 54, also I-40. Picnicking, organized group camping, fishing, hiking, nature study.

 CAMPING OUT. There are many campgrounds in North Carolina, and visitors to the Tar Heel State can write to the N. C. Travel Division, Dept. of Commerce, Raleigh, N.C. 27611 for brochures listing these campgrounds.

 FARM VACATIONS AND GUEST RANCHES. There are two "dude ranches," located in the western part of the state, which have limited accommodations. For information write the Pisgah View Ranch, Route 1, Candler, N.C. 28715, and Cataloochee Ranch, Rte. 5, Waynesville, N.C. 28786.

 MUSEUMS AND GALLERIES. Historical: *Museum of the Cherokee Indian,* open year round and the *Oconaluftee Indian Village,* open May through Oct., Cherokee. Admission charge. *Greensboro Historical Museum,* 130 Summit Ave., Greensboro. Guided tours, lectures. Daily except Sun. and holidays. Free. *North Carolina Hall of History* in the Archives Bldg., 109 E. Jones St., Raleigh. Closed national holidays. Free. *Rowan Museum,* Salisbury. Historic houses, Indian relics. Open Tues. to Sun. Admission to the Town House and museum is free. Old Stone House: Admission charge. *Anson County Historical*

Society, 210 E. Wade St., Wadesboro. A general museum and historic homes. Open Wed., Sun. Admission charge. Shaw House: open daily Feb. to May. Free; House in the Horseshoe. Admission charge. *National Society of the Colonial Dames of America in the State of North Carolina,* 224 Market St., Wilmington. A historical museum in the Burgwin-Wright House and Garden (1771). Admission charge. *Wilmington-New Hanover Museum,* 814 Market St., Wilmington. Regional history museum. Closed Mon. and national holidays. Free.

Art: *Asheville Art Museum,* 152 Pearson Dr., Asheville. Closed Mon. and holidays. *William Hayes Ackland Art Center,* Columbia and Franklin Sts., Univ. of N.C., Chapel Hill. Closed holidays and third week of Aug. Free. *Mint Museum of Art,* 501 Hempstead Place, Charlotte. Sculptures and paintings from Italian Renaissance through 20th century. Closed national and city holidays. Free. *Duke University Museum of Art,* Durham. Closed Mon., national holidays. Free. *Weatherspoon Art Gallery,* University of N.C. at Greensboro. Closed Sun. during summer term; Sat.; major academic holidays; Easter vacation; Christmas vacation and between summer session and fall term. Free. *Greenville Art Center,* 802 Evans St., Greenville. Closed national holidays, July and Aug. Free. *The Hickory Museum of Art,* 3rd St. & First Ave., N.W., Hickory. Closed Aug. and holidays. Free. *North Carolina Museum of Art,* 107 E. Morgan St., Raleigh. Collections from classical periods to modern. Closed Mon. and holidays. Free.

St. John's Art Gallery, 114 Orange St., Wilmington. Collections of paintings, sculpture and special exhibitions. Closed holidays and Sat. and Sun. in summer. Free. *Southeastern Center for Contemporary Art,* 750 Marguerite Dr., Winston-Salem. Free. *Piedmont Craftsmen,* 936 W. Fourth St., Winston-Salem. An arts and crafts museum. Closed Sun. Free. *N.C. League of Creative Arts & Crafts* near Old Salem, Winston-Salem. Admission charge.

Special Interest Museums: *Colburn Memorial Mineral Museum,* 170 Coxe Ave., Asheville. Closed mid-Dec. to Jan. 2. Free. *Country Doctor Museum,* Vance St., Bailey. 18th- & 19th-century medical collections. Free. *Alphonso Whaling Museum,* Front St., Beaufort. Admission charge. *Hampton Mariner's Museum,* 120 Turner St., Beaufort. Free. Year around. Admission charge. *Morehead Planetarium,* E. Franklin St., Chapel Hill. Admission charge. *Discovery Place,* "hands-on" science museum, Charlotte. Admission charge. *Museum of the Cherokee Indian,* US 441, Cherokee. Open year around. Admission charge. *N.C. Museum of Life & Science,* 433 Murray Ave., Durham. Museum, life-sized natural history and space exhibits. Closed Mon. *Museum of the Albermarle,* Rte. 3, Elizabeth City. Old farming implements, Indian artifacts. Closed Mon. and holidays. Admission charge. *82nd Airborne Division War Memorial Museum,* Ardennes St., Fort Bragg, a military museum. Closed Mon. Free. *Schiele Museum of Natural History and Planetarium,* 1500 E. Garrison Blvd., Gastonia. Closed Mon. Free. *Natural Science Center,* 4301 Lawndale Dr., Greensboro. Closed holidays. Free. *Kings Mountain National Military Park,* Kings Mountain. Free. *Museum of the Sea,* Manteo. Free. *Bodie Island Visitor Center,* Manteo. Housed in c. 1872 Bodie Island Coast Guard Station and quarters. Free. *Ocracoke Visitor Center,* Manteo. Free.

New Bern Firemen's Museum, 421 Broad St., New Bern. Closed 1 wk. in July. Admission charge. *North Carolina State Museum, Bicentennial Plaza, Raleigh. Natural history indigenous to the state.* Free. *Rocky Mount Children's Museum,* Sunset Park, Rocky Mount. Natural sciences, geology, mini-zoo. *Museum of North Carolina Minerals,* Blue Ridge Pkwy., Spruce Pine. Closed Nov. to May. Free. *Nature Science Museum,* Reynolda Village, Winston-Salem. Free. Morehead Planetarium: Closed Sun. and major holidays. Admission charge.

HISTORIC SITES. *Thomas Wolfe Memorial,* 40 Spruce St., Asheville. Admission charge. *Historic Bath State Historic Site,* Bath. Admission charge. *Alamance Battleground,* 6 mi. S of Burlington on Rte. 62. This 1771 Battleground is the site of typical frontier dwelling (Allen House). Visitor Center, slide program. Tues. to Sun. Free. *Fort Fisher State Historic Site,* on US 421, 6 mi. S of Carolina Beach. Coastal defense fort that provided protection for Confederate blockade runners. Visitor center museum. Daily, all year. Free. *Somerset Place State Historic Site,* Creswell. Free. *Moores Creek National Military Park.* Near Currie, site of first battle of Revolutionary War in North Carolina. Monuments, markers, museum. Free. *Bennett Place State Historic Site,* Durham, has a visitor center and is open Sept. to May wknds., during June to Aug. Tues to Sat.; Free. The Bennett House is also open to visitors. *Historic Edenton, Inc.,* S. Broad St., Edenton. Free admission to Barker House Visitor Center Museum. Historic Houses are also open to the public: Cupola house (1725); Chowan county Courthouse (1767); James Iredell house (1759); and St. Paul's Episcopal Church (1736). Admission charge. *Market House,* Market Square, Fayetteville, open on a restricted basis. A square building with cupola, it is a rare example of the English form of town hall with open, arcaded ground floor surmounted by public rooms on the 2nd floor. *Guilford Courthouse National Military Park,* New Garden Rd. & Old Battleground Rd., Greensboro. Free. *Wright Brothers National Memorial.* Kill Devil Hill on US 158. Story of aviation and the Wright Brothers in reconstructed camp buildings. Daily, all year. Free. *Caswell-Neuse State Historic Site.* Kinston. Closed Mon. Free. *Roanoke Island Historical Park,* Manteo, has an Indian Village Museum and is located on the site that was selected for the first English colony attempt in America. Admission charge. *Carson House, Inc., Rte. 4, Marion. Open wkdays by appointment; wknds. 2 to 5. Admission charge. Town Creek Indian Mound State Historic Site,* Rte. 3, Mount Gilead. Closed Mon. Free. *Attmore-Oliver House,* 511 Broad St., New Bern. Closed on national holidays. Admission charge. *Stevenson House,* 611 Pollock St., New Bern. Admission charge. *Bentonville Battleground State Historic Site,* Newton Grove. Free. *James K. Polk Birthplace State Historic Site,* Pineville. Free. *Andrew Johnson Memorial,* Raleigh. Closed Sat. Admission charge. *The State Capitol,* Capitol Square, and the Legislative Building ("State House"), Jones St., in Raleigh, are open to the public and guides are available Free. *State Capitol,* Capitol Square, Raleigh, is open to the public. Built 1833-40, this building is one of the country's finest Greek Revival structures. *Fort Raleigh National Historic Site* on Roanoke Island (Highways 64 & 264). Exhibits illustrate the first English colonization attempts. In July and Aug. there are guided tours. Open all year. Free. *House in the Horseshoe State Historic Site,* Rte. 3, Sanford. Closed Mon. Free. *Brunswick Town State Historic Site,* 225 Pine Grove Dr., Southport. Free. *Zebulon B. Vance Birthplace State Historic Site,* Weaverville. Closed Mon. Free. *Bethabara Park,* on outskirts of Winston-Salem, first Moravian settlement in North Carolina, is open daily Easter-Thanksgiving. Free. *Old Salem,* Winston-Salem. Restored 1776 Moravian Congregational town. Seven buildings are open to the public: The John Vogler House (1819); Market-Fire House Museum (1803); Miksch Tobacco Shop and Garden; Salem Tavern; Single Brothers' House; Wachovia Museum; and Winkler Bakery. Craft demonstrations, guided tours, special holiday events. Combination or single admission tickets may be bought. *Duke Homestead* near Durham. 1852 ancestral Duke home. *Ft. Dobbs.* Near Statesville. Circa 1756. Named for Royal Gov. Arthur Dobbs. Visitor center. *Carl Sandburg Home* at Flat Rock. Home is open for visitors.

SPECIAL INTEREST TOURS. *Biltmore House and Gardens* Asheville. Admission charge. *Fontana Dam,* on Rte. 28 (between US 19 & US 129) is the tallest dam east of the Rocky Mts. The powerhouse lobby and balcony are open to visitors daily. A free incline railway operates daily carrying passengers from the overlook to the base of the dam. A panoramic view of the dam is a feature of this ride. *Cooleemee Plantation House,* on US 64, Fork. Visitors are welcome to walk through the grounds and garden May to Labor Day. Wed., Sat. and Sun. Admission charge. *Cowee Ruby Mines,* on Rte. 28, Franklin, are open during the daylight hours from Apr. to Oct. You may dig for rubies here. Other gem mines are the Hiddenite & Emerald mine at Hiddenite, and the Big Crabtree mine, at Spruce Pine. Rates depend upon the mine selected.

Chinqua-Penn Plantation House, Rte. 3, Reidsville. Closed Mon. *U.S.S. North Carolina Battleship Memorial,* moored on the west bank of Cape Fear River, Wilmington, is open daily. *Orton Plantation,* US 17 & Rte. 133, Wilmington, is open daily year round. Admission charge.

Rea House, Winston-Salem, open Tues. to Sat., including holidays except Christmas Day. Closed Mondays and from Jan. 2 to Feb. 1. Admission charge.

Pea Island National Wildlife Refuge, Manteo, is open weekdays. Closed wknds. and holidays. Free.

Tryon Palace Restoration, 613 Pollock St., New Bern. Admission charge. Tryon Palace. Admission charge. Tryon Gardens. Admission charge. Stanly House. Admission charge. Closed Mon.

 GARDENS. *Craggy Gardens,* 17 mi. NE of Asheville, on the Blue Ridge Pkwy., is just beautiful when the rhododendron is in bloom about mid-June. Open May to Oct. *Daniel Boone Native Gardens,* Horn in the West Dr., in Boone. Closed Nov.-Apr.; adult admission charged but children under 12 free, if accompanied by an adult. *North Carolina Botanical Garden,* Coker Hall, Univ. of N.C., Chapel Hill, is open daily. Free. *Sarah P. Duke Memorial Gardens,* on the campus of Duke University, in Durham, has a constant display of annuals, perennials and ornamental shrubs. Period of peak bloom is the month of April. Open daily. Free. *Clarendon Gardens,* Linden Rd., Pinehurst, is open mid-Sept. to Apr. Free. Closed Christmas week. *Elizabethan Garden,* Fort Raleigh National Historic Site on Roanoke Isl. Open daily. Admission charge but children under 12 free. Children under 16 must be accompanied by a parent. *Greenfield Gardens,* on US 421, are open daily. Free. The 185-acre park includes a lake, zoo, scenic boat rides, amusement park, as well as lovely gardens. The *Airlie Azalea Gardens,* on US 76, Wrightsville Beach, contain not only thousands of azaleas but also camellias and many rare plants. Open daily from the end of Mar. to end of Sept. During the blooming season (usually Apr.); children under 12 free.

 MUSIC. In North Carolina cities and towns, and on the University campuses, concerts of various types are scheduled at every session. In late winter and early spring, the North Carolina Symphony gives concerts on statewide tours; information about this is available from the Manager of the North Carolina Symphony, Memorial Auditorium, Raleigh, N.C.

Brevard Music Center is the home of the Transylvania Music Camp. It offers varied music concerts while the Camp is in session from July to mid-Aug. For further information write: Business Manager, Brevard Music Center, P.O. Box 592, Brevard 28712.

Mountain Dance and Folk Festival at Asheville, founded in 1927, is held in early Aug. It features instrumentalists, ballad singers and dancers from all parts of the Southern Appalachians. For information write: Asheville Chamber of Commerce, Asheville.

June Dance Week. Held in Brasstown and features clogging, traditional English, American and Danish dances. Contact John Campbell, Folk School, Brasstown, NC 28902.

 STAGE AND REVUES. North Carolina has a number of outdoor historical dramas playing during the summer months. Reservations are advised. *The Lost Colony,* Manteo, Mon–Sat., late June to Labor Day. *Unto These Hills,* Cherokee, Mon–Sat., late June to Aug. *Horn in the West,* Boone. Tues. to Sun., late June through Aug. *From This Day Forward,* Valdese. Early July through late August. *Strike at the Wind,* Pembroke. Thursday through Saturday nights, late June to mid-August. *The Liberty Cart,* Kenansville, Thurs.–Sun., mid-July through late Aug. *The Immortal Showboat,* sound-and-light spectacular at the *USS North Carolina Battleship Memorial,* Wilmington, at 8 nightly, June to Labor Day.

Summer theaters which present a different play or musical each week between late June and Labor Day are the *Flat Rock Playhouse,* Flat Rock; *Charlotte Summer Theatre,* Charlotte; *East Carolina College Summer Theatre,* Greenville; *Thomas Wolfe Playhouse,* Asheville, and the *Parkway Playhouse,* Burnsville.

 DRINKING LAWS. Local option under state control governs sale of alcoholic beverages. Distilled spirits are sold legally in package stores controlled by the N.C. Board of Alcoholic Control or "ABC." There are ABC stores in approximately half the coastal and Piedmont counties and in some cities and towns of the mountain counties. Some municipalities allow "mixed beverages" to be served in properly licensed restaurants. Under state law, no person under 21 years of age may purchase any alcoholic beverage containing over 14% alcohol.

 SUMMER SPORTS. Summer is tops for aquatic sports throughout the state and for trail riding and golf in the mountains.

Water sports: The surf bathing season begins in May and continues into late autumn. Except in very high mountain localities, swimming and water-skiing are also enjoyed from May to Sept. or Oct. In the mountains, they are best in June to Aug.

Bathing: While the greatest activity in boating and sailing is in summer, these sports extend to spring and fall in most sections of the state, and are year round along the coast. Lakes, rivers and sounds provide ideal environs for the use of pleasure craft and water skis. Marinas and public boat launching areas are numerous on lakes, rivers and coastal sounds. Along the 265 miles of Intracoastal Waterway in North Carolina, there are more than 80 marinas and other facilities for yachts and smaller craft. Detailed information about the Waterway in North Carolina is in the Southern Edition of the *Inland Waterway Guide,* published at 25 W. Broward St., Fort Lauderdale, Fla.

Fishing: The angler's choice in North Carolina ranges from mountain trout to blue marlin. Trout waters in the Blue Ridge and Great Smokies are open from April through summer. There is no closed season on any other species of freshwater game fish, or on the game fish taken along North Carolina's coast and offshore. Surf-fishing for channel bass is best spring through autumn; offshore fishing is prime between May and late autumn. The *Blue Marlin Tournament* at Wrightsville Beach is in late May; also a Blue Marlin Tournament at Morehead City and the International Blue Marlin Tournament at Hatteras are held in early June. No license is required for saltwater fishing. Charter craft, fully equipped for deep-sea, inlet or sound fishing, are available at Oregon Inlet near Nags Head, Hatteras, Morehead City, Wrightsville and Carolina Beaches, Topsail Island, Southport and several other points along the coast. Some 30 ocean-fishing piers are open from Apr. to Oct. They charge a nominal fee for fishing privileges, sell bait and rent tackle. For nonresidents, seasonal freshwater licenses are available—a five-day permit and a one-day permit. Either entitles the licensee to fish for all freshwater fish except mountain trout. The nonresident trout fishing license is required in addition to the regular fishing license or permit.

Golf is a year-round sport with over 300 courses open every month. Mountain courses, however, are at their best from May through Oct.; many are closed in winter. Caddies and electric golf carts are available at most courses. The "Sand-hills" of N.C. are famous for their courses and the #2 course at the Pinehurst C.C. ranks among the top ten of America's 100 greatest golf course. For a complete listing of North Carolina's golf resorts from the mountains to the coast, write for the pamphlet "N.C., Golf State U.S.A.", Travel & Promotion Division, Box 27687, Raleigh, N.C. 27611.

Horseback riding is at its best in the mountains during summer and year round throughout the state. It is most popular at the mid-south resorts of the Sandhills and in Tryon from autumn through spring. Horses for ring or trail riding are available at many mountain resorts, and there are riding concessions in the Great Smoky Mountains Park. Cataloochee Ranch, Waynesville, is headquarters each summer for a ten-day Great Smokies Trail Ride, sponsored by the American Forestry Association through its Trail Riders of the Wilderness Program. Stables that rent and board horses and give riding instructions are located near most of the larger cities. Riding with hounds on organized hunts enlivens the sports scene at Southern Pines, Tryon, Sedgefield, Charlotte and Raleigh from Oct. to Mar. There are spring steeplechase meetings at Southern Pines and Tryon.

Hiking: There are hundreds of miles of marked trails, including 200 miles of the Appalachian Trail, following the topmost mountain ridges through the Great Smoky Mountains Park and Pisgah and Nantahala national forests. The western part of the state has the greatest number of hiking trails. Spring, summer and fall are the best times to use them.

Tennis: is one of the fastest growing year-around sports in North Carolina. There are new courts currently under construction throughout the state. Some are membership clubs, and some are open to the general public. There are both indoor and outdoor courts: *Sugar Mountain* and *Beech Mountain* at Banner Elk, *Pine-hurst* resorts, the *Outer Banks Racquet Club* at Nags Head, *Tanglewood Park* in Clemmons, *Sapphire Valley,* Sapphire, and *Wolfe Laurel* near Mars Hill. Inquire locally for further information.

 WINTER SPORTS. Most sports are year round in many areas of the state, especially in the mid-southern regions. *Hunting* seasons begin in Sept. with dove shooting and continue through late winter. There is a varied pattern of open seasons on bear, boar, deer, small game animals, quail, ruffled grouse, marsh hens, ducks and Canada geese. Lake Mattamuskeet and Currituck Sound, near the coast, are famous for waterfowl hunting. Further information on current fishing and hunting regulations may be obtained from the North Carolina Wildlife Resources Commission, Raleigh.

Snow-skiing in the mountain areas starts, weather permitting, in Dec. and continues until early Mar. Ski areas in North Carolina include: Sugar Mtn., Beech Mtn., Hawk's Nest, Mill Ridge, Appalachian Ski Mtn. near Banner Elk, Blowing Rock & Boone; Wolf Laurel Ski Slope at Mars Hill; Fairfield at Sapphire Valley, Cataloochee, near Waynesville and Scaly, Scaly Mtn.

SPECTATOR SPORTS. The Charlotte Motor Speedway in Charlotte features NASCAR sanctioned late-model stock car races in May (World 600) and Oct. (National 500). The North Carolina Motor Speedway on US 74, between Rockingham and Hamlet, is the site for NASCAR races for late-model stock cars in Mar. (Carolina 500) and in Oct. (American 500). Motorcycle and sports car racing are done on the infield road course.

Golf: One of the country's major golf tournaments is the Greater Greensboro Open, held in April in Greensboro.

Boating: There are sailing regattas on Kerr Lake, near Henderson, Lake Gaston, near Roanoke Rapids, and other lakes, and on sounds in the vicinity of Kitty Hawk and Manteo. Powerboat races are featured on the Pasquotank River at Elizabeth City and on several inland lakes, including Lake Wheeler near Raleigh.

Horse races: Over 300 standardbreds are trained at Pinehurst during the winter. Harness-horse race matinees and time trials are featured here in spring. Betting is illegal in North Carolina, and there are no pari-mutuels.

College. North Carolina has six major colleges which play full schedules in nearly all intercollegiate athletics. Duke University at Durham, the University of North Carolina at Chapel Hill, North Carolina State University at Raleigh and Wake Forest University at Winston-Salem are all members of the Atlantic Coast Conference. Davidson College at Davidson & Appalachian State Univ. at Boone are members of the Southern Conference. East Carolina University in Greenville is independent. There are approximately 50 additional 4-yr. and junior colleges that participate in athletics on a smaller scale.

Hang gliding: The enthusiast of this new sport can watch the "daredevils" of today floating from the highest sand dune on the eastern coast (Jockey's Ridge at Nags Head) or from the lofty peaks of Grandfather Mountain at Linville, N.C. (The world Hang Gliding championships take place at Grandfather Mountain.)

SHOPPING. Shopping facilities are numerous and varied in North Carolina. The larger cities and towns have good department stores and specialty shops. In various sections of the state there are shops and centers that offer fine opportunities to purchase handicrafts or textiles—two products for which the state is noted. There are many large suburban shopping centers and malls in the major cities.

Outlet stores and malls featuring N.C. products flourish along highways near Burlington, Southern Pines, Greensboro, Raleigh, Eden, Kannapolis, Lexington, High Point and Thomasville. Write for *The Central N.C. Outlet & Discount Guide:* $2.00; P.O. Box 2550, Greensboro, NC 27402.

In addition to presenting the Craftsman's Fairs each year, the Guild operates 3 craft shops: *Allanstand,* 16 College St., and *Guild Crafts,* 930 Tunnel Rd., both in Asheville; the *Parkway Craft Center,* at the Moses Cone Memorial Park, Blowing Rock. When visiting the *Craftsman's Fair of the Southern Highlands,* which runs for five days in July at the New Civic Center, Asheville, you will be impressed by the variety of crafts offered for sale.

A *Flea Market* is held in Raleigh at the State Fairgrounds each Sat. & Sun. (except during the month of Oct.); also Charlotte has a Flea Market held the first weekend of each month at the Metrolina Fairgrounds. These are great places to shop, look or just pass the time of day.

WHAT TO DO WITH THE CHILDREN. Most North Carolina resorts cater to families and provide recreation for children. Among the many attractions which have a special appeal to youngsters, and are interesting to adults as well, are: The *USS North Carolina Battleship Memorial,* Wilmington. Visitors board a 35,000-ton super-dreadnaught, explore its hulk, and then see the ship's museum. The Memorial is open daily year round, and a sound-and-light spectacular tells its story nightly from mid-Apr. to Labor Day. *Tweetsie Railroad,* Blowing Rock, a 3-mi. scenic ride on a narrow-gauge railroad with steam locomotive. "Indian attacks" and a "train robbery" enliven the trip. There's a sky lift to an amusement park above the train station. Open daily June to Labor Day, Sat. and Sun. only from Labor Day to Oct. 31. There is a general admission charge; children under 5 free. *Gaddy's Goose Refuge.* US 52 nr. Ansonville. From 10,000 to 12,000 wild Canada geese can be fed by hand and photographed at close range between October and April. *Ghost Mountain Park,* Maggie Valley, US 19. Sky lift and incline railway to re-created Western town staffed by appropriately costumed "residents." "Gun fights" every hour. Stagecoach rides, blacksmith shop, soda shop, etc. Daily May to Oct. *Cherokee Indian Reservation,* US 19 and 441, at entrance to Great Smoky Mountains National Park. In summer there is the outdoor drama *Unto These Hills.* The *Oconaluftee Indian Village,* on US 441 in Cherokee, sponsored by the non-profit Cherokee Historical Association, displays how Cherokees lived 200 years ago. Guided tours daily; open mid-May to late Oct. Admission charge. *Grandfather Mountain,* Linville. Open Apr. to Nov. 15. Mile-high swinging bridge offers visitors breathtaking view of Blue Ridge Mountains and valleys. Building at crest of mountain houses US Weather Bureau Station, snack bar, gift shop. Live bears ("Mildred" and her cubs) can be seen in their natural habitat in a beautiful, newly completed "environmental compound."

Discovery Place, is an outstanding, nationally recognized "hands-on" science museum in downtown Charlotte. *Carowinds* theme park, 161 acres which straddle the North and South Carolina boundary line. This is the home of "Thunder Road," an exciting double roller coaster. The park is easily reached by I-77 ten mi. S of Charlotte and offers fun for everyone with rides, shows and exhibits. *The North Carolina Zoological Park,* located at Purgatory Mountain, a few miles south of Asheboro, south off US 64 onto Cox Rd. The Zoo is in its first stages of construction. It is open to the public as a primitive recreational area for daytime use. Picnicking, hiking and walking nature trails. For further information contact North Carolina Zoological Authority, Raleigh 27603. *Santa's Land,* on US 19, Cherokee, is open daily. Admission charge. *Frontierland,* on US 19, Cherokee, is open daily May to Oct. 31. Admission charge. *Cyclorama of the Cherokee Indian,* on US 19, Cherokee, is open 9 to 9 daily June to Labor Day; 9 to 5 Labor Day to Nov. 1 and Apr. to June 1. Admission charge; under 6 free.

Daniel Boone Railroad Park, off I-85 in Hillsborough. Amusement park open wknds, noon to dark from June to Labor Day. Closed rest of the year. A 2½-mi. train ride is also featured.

Three new *Marine Resource Centers* located in Fort Fisher, Manteo, & Atlantic Beach offer oceanographic and marine exhibits which are of great interest to coastal visitors and vacationers.

INDIANS. North Carolina is the home of the Eastern Band of the Cherokee Indians. Their reservation—the Qualla Boundary—covers 56,000 acres adjoining the Great Smoky Mountains National Park and has some 4,500 Cherokee Indian residents. The reservation is organized and governed under a charter issued by the state of North Carolina in 1889, and it is subject to regulations established by the tribe and the U.S. Government. The Cherokees are both U.S. and North Carolina citizens and enjoy full voting privileges. The largest community on the reservation is Cherokee, which serves as administrative headquarters for the reservation, and it is a famous year-around tourist objective.

HOTELS AND MOTELS. Travelers in North Carolina will find accommodations in all price ranges. National chains, such as Quality Courts, Holiday Inns, Ramada Inns, Howard Johnsons, Hilton Inns, Marriott Hotels, Sheratons, and the "Economy" motels such as Scottish Inns and Econotels are located throughout the state. Television, telephones, heat and air conditioning are standard equipment. Except for a few hotels in downtown locations, free parking is standard.

Subject to change these inflation-prone days, the accommodations listed are according to price catagories. Please note these are *average prices.* Coastal and mountain resorts have seasonal rates. Categories and price ranges based on double occupancy are: *Deluxe,* $60 up; *Expensive,* $50–$59; *Moderate,* $35–$49; *Inexpensive,* under $35. For a more complete explanation of hotel and motel categories see *Facts at Your Fingertips* at the front of this volume.

Asheboro

Holiday Inn. *Moderate.* Suites. Restaurant. Pool, golf privileges.

Sir Robert Motel. *Inexpensive.* Restaurant and pool. Open year round.

Asheville

Grove Park Inn. *Deluxe.* Macon Ave. To the massive native stone building of this distinctive resort completed in 1913, two wings have been added, one of them motel style and the other multistory with a ballroom. On the slopes of Beaucatcher Mountain, the Inn has terraced grounds overlooking golf course (guests may play), pool and tennis courts. Restaurants, gift shops. Open year-round.

Great Smokies Hilton. *Expensive.* 1 Hilton Inn Dr. Pool, golf course, indoor-outdoor tennis courts, restaurant and lounge. Seasonal rates.

Capri Motor Inn. *Expensive.* 29 Tunnel Rd. Pool, restaurant. Kitchenettes available.

Downtowner Motor Inn. *Moderate.* 120 Patton Ave. A high-rise motor inn convenient to stores, restaurant, City Auditorium, hotels. Pool, dining.

Holiday Inn. *Moderate.* At three locations: 201 Tunnel Rd. (Central); US 70E, Rt. 2 (East); US 19 at I-40 (West). Pool, golf privileges.

Howard Johnson's Motor Lodge. *Moderate.* 190 Hendersonville Rd. Restaurant, pool and playground.

In Town Motor Lodge. *Moderate.* 100 Tunnel Rd. Pleasant rms, many with a balcony, overlooking spacious grounds. Heated pool, play area. Restaurant nr.

Ramada Inn. *Moderate.* US 70 & 74, about 1 mi. E of center. Pool, dining rm., gift shop.

Sheraton Motor Inn. *Moderate.* Woodfin & Market Sts. Restaurant, pool, play area, golf privileges.

Atlantic Beach

Atlantis Lodge. *Expensive.* Secluded oceanfront location, 3 mi. from central resort area. Rms., kitchenettes.

Sea Hawk Motel. *Expensive.* Oceanfront. Attractive rms., many with refrigerators. Pool, beach. Golf privileges.

Fleming's Motel. *Moderate.* Comfortable accommodations. Excellent restaurant. Pool. Year-round. Seasonal rates.

Holiday Inn. *Moderate.* On the ocean. Some rms. with kitchenettes. Restaurant. Seasonal rates.

John Yancey Motor Hotel. *Moderate.* On ocean, pool, restaurant, golf privileges. Seasonal rates.

Ramada Inn. *Moderate.* Salter Path Rd. Good accommodations, restaurant, recreation. Seasonal rates. Open year round.

Banner Elk

Holiday Inn. *Moderate.* All services, located near ski resort at Sugar Mtn.

Belhaven

River Forest Manor. *Moderate.* Gracious old mansion, circa 1900; 600 E. Main St. Dining room features buffet smorgasbord. Antique furnished rooms. Sportsman's paradise. 25 rooms. Dock for boating enthusiasts.

Blowing Rock

Green Park Inn. *Deluxe.* A spacious white-frame resort hostelry adjoining the Blowing Rock Golf Course. Dining rm. Open year-round. Excellent dining.

Hound Ears Lodge and Club. *Deluxe.* An exclusive resort with its own golf course and ski slopes. Dining rm. Rms in chalets and main club building. Year round. AP.

Azalea Garden Motel. *Moderate.* Comfortable rms. on attractively landscaped grounds. Open mid-Mar. to end of Dec. Restaurant nr.

Hillwinds Inn. *Moderate.* Inviting, spacious rms. Barn Restaurant.

Yonahlossee Motel. *Moderate.* Restaurant, heated pool.

Appalachian Motel. *Inexpensive.* Attractive grounds with small lake. Year round. Restaurants nr.

Boone

Holiday Inn. *Expensive.* Color TV. Restaurant, pool.

Cardinal Motel. *Moderate.* Restaurant. Pool. Year round.

Center for Continuing Education. *Moderate.* Enjoy spacious rooms, beautiful view and excellent food. On Appalachian State Univ. campus and run by University.

Plaza Motel. *Moderate.* Pool. Year round. Kitchenettes.

Greene's Motel. *Inexpensive.* Comfortable place at a good location. Pool.

Brevard

Brevard Motor Lodge. *Moderate.* Pool. Year round.

Imperial Motor Lodge. *Moderate.* Pool. 26 rms. Year round.

Bryson City

Fryemont Inn. *Moderate.* Comfortable facilities, pool, restaurant. Season May through Oct.

Hemlock Inn. *Moderate.* A quiet, comfortable lodge with a secluded location off US 19. Restaurant. Season May to Nov. MAP.

Nantahala Village. *Moderate.* Pool, kitchenettes, restaurant. Well-maintained. Season April through Oct.

Bennett's Court. *Inexpensive.* Pool. Downtown location with restaurants nr.

Burlington

Best Western Inn. *Moderate.* Great lounge with live entertainment. Heated pool, near factory outlet stores & Elon College.

Holiday Inn. *Moderate.* Pool, restaurant. Display room offering information and maps for famed outlet stores in area. Within walking distance of outlet shopping park.

Ramada Inn. *Moderate.* Double-story motel. Restaurant, lounge with entertainment. Pool, play area. Near several outlet shopping malls.

Burnsville

Nu-Wray Inn. *Moderate.* On village square. A charming old inn with early American atmosphere. Meals served family-style are famous featuring Southern specialties (no Sun. night meal). Season Apr. through Dec.

Mtn. View Motel. *Inexpensive.* Open year round. Comfortable. Restaurant nearby.

Buxton

Cape Hatteras Court. *Moderate.* Pool. Restaurants and beach nr. Season Mar. to Dec. with lowered rates in spring and autumn. 15 cottages equipped for housekeeping.

Falcon Motel. *Moderate.* Hatteras Light opp. Spacious rms. Some kitchen units. Pool. Restaurant nr. Season from March to December.

Candler

Pisgah View Ranch. *Moderate.* Picturesque rural setting. Family-style dining, tennis court, square dancing, horseback riding. Popular with families. Open May to December.

Carolina Beach

Accordion Motel. *Moderate.* On ocean near business section and amusement area. Restaurant nr. Season: Mar.–Sept.

King's Motel. *Moderate.* Ocean front, kitchenettes, pool, restaurant. Year-round.

Cashiers

High Hampton Inn and Country Club. *Deluxe.* A distinctive resort facility with its own golf course, lake, riding, stables, and tennis courts. Dining rm., gift shop. Special program for children in summer. Season Apr. 1–Nov. 1. MAP.

Oakmont Lodge Motel. *Moderate.* All-year golf and tennis available. Kitchenettes.

Cedar Island

Driftwood Motel. *Moderate.* At Ocracoke Ferry landing on US 70 East. Dining room features local seafood.

Chapel Hill

Hotel Europa. *Deluxe.* Europa Dr. Elegant surroundings. Continental cuisine. Golf and tennis privileges. Nightly entertainment.

Carolina Inn. *Moderate.* Lovely Inn owned and operated by University of North Carolina. Restaurant features excellent buffet.

Holiday Inn. *Moderate.* Attractive rms. with color TV, pool, restaurant.

Charlotte

Radisson Plaza Hotel. *Deluxe.* Two NCNB Plaza, in downtown Charlotte. A new hotel offering excellent facilities. Heated pool. Reflections Restaurant features gourmet foods.

Adam's Mark. *Expensive.* At new civic and convention center. McDowell St. Restaurants and shops. Racquetball court.

Best Western. *Moderate.* At two locations: **Charlotte Airport** and **Coliseum,** Independence Blvd. Lounge, restaurants, pool.

Holiday Inn. *Moderate.* At five locations: 3815 N. **Tyron; Airport,** 2707 Little Rock Rd. & I-85; **Coliseum,** 2701 E. Independence Blvd.; **North,** I-85 at Sugar Creek Exit; **Woodlawn,** 212 Woodlawn Rd. Excellent facilities.

Howard Johnson Motor Lodge. *Moderate.* Three locations; **South,** 118 Woodlawn Rd.; 3931 **Statesville Ave.; Central,** 2400 Wilkinson Blvd.

Ramada Inn. *Moderate.* At three locations: **Coliseum:** 3501 E. Independence Blvd. **North:** 4330 I-85N; **I-77 S.** at Clanton Rd. Rms. are tastefully decorated. Pool. Restaurant.

Rodeway Inn. *Moderate.* Two locations; **Airport** and **Downtown,** 601 N. Tryon St. Comfortable and convenient.

Cherokee

Boundary Tree Motor Court. *Moderate.* On US 441 between village and entrance to Great Smoky Mountains National Park. Operated by Cherokee Indians. Pool and dining rm., snack bar, play area. Some rms. with kitchenettes, in stone buildings.

Cool Waters Motel. *Moderate.* Kitchenettes, pool, tennis privileges.

Craig's Motel. *Moderate.* Comfortable. Restaurant, pool.

Great Smokies Inn Best Western. *Moderate.* Acyuoni Rd. and 441 N. Nr. Great Smoky Mtns. National Park.

Holiday Inn. *Moderate.* Suites. Color TV. Restaurant. Trout fishing. Seasonal rates. Open year-round.

Newfound Lodge. *Moderate.* Dining rm., gift shop. Season Apr. to Oct.

Dillsboro

Jarrett House. *Inexpensive.* A comfortable inn built in 1890, well known for its dining rm. featuring Southern specialties, season Easter weekend–Oct. Limited handicapped facilities.

Durham

Sheraton University Center. *Deluxe.* Excellent facility. Nightly entertainment.

The Hilton Inn. *Moderate.* 8-story motor inn. Spacious rms. with color TV. Health Club.

Howard Johnson's Motor Lodge. *Moderate.* Double-story motor inn. Rms. have balconies or patios. Color TV. Restaurant, pool.

Ramada Inn. *Moderate.* At two locations: I-85 & Guess Rd.; Downtown I-40 & Duke St.

Carolina-Duke Motor Inn. *Inexpensive.* 2517 Guess Rd. Large motor inn with comfortable rooms. New steak & prime rib restaurant.

Downtowner. *Inexpensive.* Large, five-story motel with well-appointed rms. Color TV. Restaurant. Pool.

Edenton

Coach House Inn. *Inexpensive.* US 17. Pool, restaurant.

Elizabeth City

Holiday Inn. *Moderate.* Pool, lounge, restaurant. Golf and tennis privileges.

Fayetteville

Bordeaux Motor Inn/Convention Center. *Moderate.* Complete family recreation, bowling, skating rink, cinemas, restaurants. Shopping center.

Holiday Inn. *Moderate.* Pool, Copper Hearth Restaurant. Golf privileges.

Quality Inn-Ambassador. *Moderate.* Pool, golf package available. Pancake House.

Quality Inn Americana. *Moderate.* Pool, playground, TV. Adj. restaurant.

Ramada Inn. *Moderate.* 4-story motor inn. Color TV. Suites. Pool heated, play area. Restaurant.

St. James Inn. *Moderate.* Large motor inn with attractive rms. Color TV. Restaurant. Oyster bar in lounge. Sauna. Ice available on each floor.

Sheraton Fayetteville. *Moderate.* 301 Bragg Blvd. Suites, lounge, restaurant, and pool.

Flat Rock

Historic Woodfield Inn. *Inexpensive.* Historic inn near Flat Rock Playhouse. 21 rooms. Period decor. Excellent dining room but only evening meal served. Open all year.

Fontana Dam

Fontana Resort. *Expensive.* Lodge, cottages, riding, golf, planned recreation. Lodge open all year. Cottages: Apr. 1 to Thanksgiving wknd. Lower rates in winter season.

Franklin

"Poor Richard's" Summit Inn. *Inexpensive.* Year round. Comfortable spot with a good restaurant.

Quality Inn Town. *Inexpensive.* On the Little Tennessee River. Nicely furnished rms. Color TV. Restaurant nr. Pool.

Goldsboro

Holiday Inn. *Moderate.* Restaurant and pool. Year round.

Days Inn. *Inexpensive.* Comfortable, well-maintained. Pool, restaurant.

The Sir Motel. *Inexpensive.* W. Grantham St. at Hwy 70. Well-appointed rooms, excellent restaurant.

Greensboro

Greensboro Mariott Hotel. *Expensive.* 350 Regional Rd. at Airport. Luxury accommodations.

Americana. *Moderate.* I-40 at Rte. 68. Nr. airport. Restaurant, pool, golf privileges.

The Hilton Inn. *Moderate.* 2 locations 830 W. Market St. and at airport. Lovely rms. with color TV and balconies. Restaurant, lounge with entertainment, dancing.

Holiday Inn. *Moderate.* At two locations: **Four Seasons:** I-40 at High Point Rd.; **Airport:** I-40 & St. 68. Restaurant, pool.

Howard Johnson's Motor Lodge. *Moderate.* Three locations: North, I-85 at S. Elm St.; Coliseum, I-40 at High Point Rd. (heated pool, health club) & I-85 S. at Osborne Rd. TV, lounge.

Quality Inn Central. *Moderate.* 1000 W. Market St. Double-story motel. Color TV. Some efficiencies. Restaurant. Pool.

Ramada Inn. *Moderate.* I-85 & S. Elm St. Nicely furnished rms. Restaurant. Pool (heated), play area.

The Oaks Motel. *Inexpensive.* 1118 Summit Ave. Motel situated on lovely landscaped grounds. Restaurant, pool, and play area.

Smith's Ranch Motel. *Inexpensive.* 2210 Randleman Rd. Well-maintained motel. Color TV. Nr. restaurant. Pool, play area, shuffleboard.

Greenville

Holiday Inn Holidome. *Moderate.* Memorial Dr. Pool, tavern, excellent restaurant.

Ramada Inn. *Moderate.* Hwy. 264 Bypass. Near East Carolina Univ. & shopping center. Pool, live entertainment.

Harker's Island

Calico Jack's Inn. *Moderate.* Year-round. Dining rm., pool.

Harker's Island Fishing Center. *Inexpensive.* Small motel on Sound. Open year round.

Hatteras

Hatteras Marlin Motel. *Moderate.* Airconditioned, TV. Pool. Kitchenettes. Open year-round. Near charter boat docks.

Sea Gull Motel. *Moderate.* Nr. beach. Winter season. Kitchenettes. Restaurant nearby.

Henderson

Holiday Inn. *Moderate.* Near Kerr Lake. Rest., color TV, lounge, entertainment. Pool (heated).

Hendersonville

Dutch Inn. *Moderate.* Pool and restaurant. Year round.

Holiday Inn. *Moderate.* I–26 & US 64 E. Suites. Restaurant and lounge.

Ramada Inn. *Moderate.* I–26 & US 64 E. Pool, lounge, entertainment.

Briarwood Motel. *Inexpensive.* 1510 Greenville Hwy. Pool, picnic ground. Restaurant nr. Kitchenettes.

Hickory

Holiday Inn. *Moderate.* Centrally located with pool, coffee shop and restaurant.

Howard Johnson's Motor Lodge. *Moderate.* Inviting rms., lounge, restaurant.

Ramada Inn. *Moderate.* Delightful lounge, restaurant, pool. Some kitchenettes.

Hickory Motor Lodge. *Inexpensive.* Comfortable facilities. Pool, TV.

Mull's Motel. *Inexpensive.* Excellent restaurant. Pool. Racquetball court.

Highlands

Highlands Inn. *Expensive.* Old inn, recently refurbished with new addition. Season Apr.–Oct.

Skyline Lodge & Village. *Expensive.* Year-round. Restaurant, pool, golf & tennis.

Town House Motel. *Moderate.* Year-round.

High Point

Radisson High Point Hotel. *Expensive.* 135 S. Main St. New hotel with restaurant, lounge, pool, game room. Near Furniture Mart.

Holiday Inn. *Moderate.* 236 S. Main St. Convenient to business section. Good restaurant.

Trinity Inn. *Inexpensive.* I-85 and Hwy. 311 S. Good restaurant.

Hillsborough

Colonial Inn. *Inexpensive.* A small, pleasant inn built in 1759. Dining room features good Southern foods; ham, chicken, home-made breads.

Daniel Boone Inn & Campground. *Inexpensive.* Cafeteria, playground, antique music museum, "village" shops, ice-skating rink.

Jacksonville

Holiday Inn. *Moderate.* 701 Marine Blvd. Pool, lounge, restaurant.

Onslow Inn and Restaurant. *Moderate.* Convenient to Marine base. Two-story motel. Restaurant. Pool, play area.

Thunderbird Inn. *Moderate.* Pool, play area. Restaurant.

Town House Lodge. *Moderate.* Hwy. 17 N. Nicely furnished rms. Good restaurant. Pool.

Triangle Motor Inn *Inexpensive.* 246 Wilmington Hwy. Restaurant, pool.

Kill Devil Hills
(also see Nags Head)

The Sea Ranch. *Deluxe.* On the ocean. Spacious, attractive rms. Efficiencies. Restaurant. Beach, pool (indoor and outdoor), surf fishing, enclosed tennis courts. MAP, AP available.

Tan-a-Rama Motel. *Expensive.* Delightful efficiency apts., oceanfront. Open Mar.–Nov.

Cavalier Motor Court. *Moderate.* On ocean, nr. Wright Brothers National Memorial. Pool, play area. Housekeeping cottages and rms. with kitchenettes. Year round.

John Yancey Motor Hotel. *Moderate.* Oceanfront resort with pool. Dining rm., club lounge.

Kinston

Holiday Inn. *Moderate.* Restaurant. Pool.

Kinstonian Motel. *Inexpensive.* Pool, restaurant; convention/meeting facilities.

Laurel Springs

Bluffs Lodge. *Moderate.* Operated by National Park concessions. Small comfortable lodge. Good restaurant. Season May–Oct.

Laurinburg

Holiday Inn. *Moderate.* Restaurant, pool, play area.

Scotland Inn. *Inexpensive.* Golf and tennis privileges. Pool and restaurant.

Lexington

Holiday Inn. *Moderate.* Pool, restaurant.

Linville

Eseeola Lodge. *Deluxe.* Rustic 1892 inn with modern facilities. Dining room, pool, golf, riding. AP. Season early May to Sept.

Pixie Motel. *Inexpensive.* TV, restaurant.

Smoketree Lodge. *Inexpensive.* Open year-round. Restaurant. Small but comfortable.

Little Switzerland

The Chalet Motor Lodge. *Expensive.* Swiss-style chalet, lovely rooms, tennis, golf, pool, restaurant, lounge. Open May–Oct.

The Big Lynn Lodge. *Moderate.* Cottages & motel. Season mid-April–mid-Nov. MAP available.

Lumberton

Holiday Inn. *Moderate.* US 301-A, I-95 & Rte. 211. Restaurant, pool, color TV.

Howard Johnson's Motor Lodge. *Moderate.* Double-decker motor inn. Rms. have private balconies or patios. Restaurant. Pool.

Ramada Inn. *Moderate.* Lighted tennis courts, pool, restaurant, lounge.

Days Inn. *Inexpensive.* Comfortable motel. Pool, restaurant.

Maggie Valley

Cataloochee Ranch. *Deluxe.* Family ranch. Am. plan. Accommodations for 40 guests. Riding, tennis, fishing, swimming.

Maggie Valley Country Club & Motor Lodges. *Deluxe.* Year-round. Golf, pool, lounge, restaurant. Beautiful setting.

Holiday Inn. *Moderate.* Seasonal rates. Nr. ski slopes & tourist attractions. Restaurant.

Manteo

Elizabethan Inn. *Moderate.* Comfortable motel. Restaurant, pool, spacious grounds. Kitchenettes.

Duke of Dare Motor Lodge. *Inexpensive.* Pool, year round.

Morehead City

Buccaneer Motor Lodge. *Moderate.* 2806 Arendell St. Pool and restaurant. Year round.

Morehead Motor Inn. *Inexpensive.* 3300 Arendell St. Pool. Year round.

Nags Head
(also see **Kill Devil Hills**)

Cabana East. *Expensive.* Efficiencies, suites, Ocean and pool swimming. Open Mar.–Nov.

Holiday Inn. *Expensive.* On the ocean. Some kitchenettes. Restaurant, lounge with entertainment. Seasonal rates.

Sea Oatel. *Expensive.* Oceanfront, pool, restaurant. Open Mar.–Nov.

Carolinian Motor Hotel. *Moderate.* Oceanfront, pool, restaurant, lounge. Year round. Children's program in summer.

New Bern

Holiday Inn. *Moderate.* Restaurant, pool, year round. Golf and tennis privileges.

Quality Inn Palace. *Moderate.* Pool, play area, restaurant.

Ramada Inn. *Moderate.* Overlooking Neuse River. Rms. are nicely decorated. Color TV. Restaurant. Pool, play area.

Ocracoke

Harborside Motel. *Moderate.* Pleasant rms., some with kitchens, overlook the harbor. Dock & boat ramp available. Season Easter to Thanksgiving.

The Island Inn. *Moderate.* On Silver Lake harbor, in village. Dining rm. Jeeps, guides, and boats for hunters and fishermen. Open year round.

Pony Island Motel. *Moderate.* Restaurant. Year round.

Pinehurst

Foxfire Golf & Country Club. *Deluxe.* Year round, villas, tennis, Pool heated. MAP.

Pine Crest Inn. *Deluxe.* Restaurant, putting green, golf, bar, MAP.

Pinehurst Hotel. *Deluxe.* Distinguished resort. Six championship golf courses, 24 tennis courts. Excellent dining room.

Raleigh

Marriott. *Deluxe.* US 70 at Crabtree Valley. Indoor/outdoor pool, game room, lounge, two restaurants.

Raddison Plaza. *Deluxe.* Downtown, 420 Fayetteville St. Mall. Plush hotel near Civic Center.

Mission Valley Inn. *Moderate.* Avent Ferry Rd. & Western Blvd. At shopping center. Excellent restaurant and lounge. Live entertainment.

Hilton Inn. *Expensive.* Two locations: 1701 Hillsborough St. nr. State University: Pool, restaurant, club room. US 1 N: "Bowties" lounge; gourmet restaurant.

Holiday Inn. *Moderate.* At two locations: **Holidome:** US 1 N. Indoor pool, putting green. *Syd's* disco & lounge. Good restaurant. **Downtown:** 320 Hillsborough St. Top-floor dining & lounge offers vista of city.

Howard Johnson's Motor Lodge. *Moderate.* 2 locations: US 1, 401, and on Hwy. 70 W. at Crabtree Valley. Spacious grounds, restaurant, pool, play area.

Plantation Inn. *Moderate.* US 1 N. Restaurant, putting green, pool, fishing lake.

Ranch Motel. *Moderate.* US 70 W. Restaurant, color TV, pool. Near large shopping center.

Ramada Inn-Crabtree. *Moderate.* US 70 W. *Collonade Restaurant* rated one of top five of Ramada Inn restaurants in the world.

Sheraton Motor Inn. *Moderate.* 2 Locations: US 70 W & Creedmore Rd. at Crabtree Valley Mall; US 1 N. Good restaurants and entertainment.

Velvet Cloak. *Moderate.* 1505 Hillsborough St. Year-round pool, two restaurants, dance to live music nightly.

Research Triangle Park

Governors Inn. *Expensive.* Restaurant, club room, pool. Live entertainment.

Roaring Gap

High Meadows Inn. *Moderate.* Year round. Restaurant, pool, golf, ski slope.

Robbinsville

Snowbird Mountain Lodge. *Deluxe.* Mountaintop lodge, season late May to Nov. Excellent cuisine. No children under 12. AP.

Rocky Mount

Carleton House. *Moderate.* 215 N. Church St. Dining rm.

Holiday Inn. *Moderate.* 2 locations: I-95 N. and **Downtown:** 425 N. Church St. Pool, restaurant. Year round.

Howard Johnson's Motor Lodge. *Moderate.* Restaurant, pool, play area, putting green.

Ramada Inn. *Moderate.* Nicely decorated rms. Restaurant. Pool (heated), play area

Salisbury

Howard Johnson's Motor Lodge. *Moderate.* Pool, restaurant.

Holiday Inn. *Moderate.* Restaurant & pool.

Sanford

Holiday Inn. *Moderate.* Double-story motor inn. Suites. Restaurant, pool, golf privileges.

Palomino Motel. *Inexpensive.* Restaurant. Year round.

Sapphire

1896 Fairfield Inn. *Expensive.* Old mountain inn, cottages also available. Good dining room.

Sea Level

Sea Level Motel & Restaurant. *Moderate.* Attractive setting. Dining rm., boat docks. Year round.

Smithfield

Holiday Inn. *Moderate.* Restaurant. Pool, play area.

Howard Johnson's Motor Lodge. *Moderate.* Nicely furnished rms. Restaurant. Pool, play area.

Days Inn. *Inexpensive.* Color TV, pool, play area, gift shop. Tasty World restaurant.

Southern Pines

Mid Pines Club. *Deluxe.* Resort facility with 18-hole golf course. Dining rm. Rms. in main building and Golftel. Year round. FAP.

Pine Needles Lodges and Country Club. *Deluxe.* Resort with 18-hole golf course, pool, dining rm. Year round. AP.

Holiday Inn. *Moderate.* Restaurant, pool, golf privileges. Year round.

Howard Johnson's Motor Lodge. *Moderate.* Pool, restaurant, putting green, golf privileges. Year round.

Sheraton Motor Inn. *Moderate.* Pool, restaurant, club room.

Southport

Bald Head Inn. *Deluxe.* Lounge, restaurant. Season Mar.–Nov. Golfing.

Sea Captain Motor Lodge. *Moderate.* Kitchenettes, pool, restaurant.

Topsail Beach

Breezeway Motel. *Moderate.* Channel Blvd. On the inlet, restaurant, pool, lounge and pier.

The Jolly Roger Motel. *Moderate.* Oceanfront, rms., efficiencies. Year round.

Sea Vista Motel. *Moderate.* Ocean front, TV, efficiency apts., rooms. Nearby restaurant.

The Topsail Motel. *Moderate.* Rms., apts., cottages. Oceanfront. Year-round.

Washington

Holiday Inn. *Moderate.* Color TV. Restaurant. Pool.

Washington Motel. *Moderate.* Restaurant, pool. Year round. Golf privileges.

Waynesville

Waynesville Country Club Inn. *Deluxe.* Resort with 18-hole golf course. Dining rm. Seasonal rates.

Heath Lodge. *Moderate.* 900 Dolan Rd. Season late May through late Oct. Rustic mountain inn. Excellent dining. MAP.

Queen's Farm. *Moderate.* Dude ranch. Season May to Sept.

Oak Park Motor Inn. *Inexpensive.* Spacious, nicely furnished rms. Restaurant.

Williamston

Holiday Inn. *Moderate.* Color TV in very pleasant rms. Restaurant, pool, kennels.

Ross Motel. *Moderate.* Comfortable accommodations. Restaurant. Pool with service at poolside.

Wilmington

Best Western Carolinian. *Moderate.* Pool. Year round.

Carolinian. *Moderate.* Family atmosphere, pool, kitchenettes.

Holiday Inn. *Moderate.* Large motor inn. Restaurant. Disco featuring live entertainment.

Ramada Inn. *Moderate.* Double-story motor inn with nicely furnished rms. Restaurant, lounge with dancing and entertainment. Pool heated, play area.

Wilmington Hilton Inn. *Moderate.* Opp. battleship *USS North Carolina.* Pool, restaurant. Convenient to Historic homes and restored waterfront area.

Days Inn. *Inexpensive.* Restaurant, pool. Year round.

Wilson

Heart of Wilson. *Moderate.* Attractive, double-story motel. Restaurant, pool.

Holiday Inn. *Moderate.* Restaurant, pool.

Winston-Salem

Hyatt House. *Deluxe.* 300 W. 5th St. Downtown at Convention Center. Ice skating, pool, restaurant, lounge.

Hilton Inn. *Moderate.* Restaurant, pool, bar.

Holiday Inn. *Moderate.* At three locations: **Central:** 127 S. Cherry St.; **West:** Silas Creek Pkwy. & I-40.; **North:** N. Cherry-Marshall Expwy. Dining rm., pool.

Howard Johnson's Motor Lodge. *Moderate.* Pool, restaurant, nr. shopping.

Sheraton Motor Inn. *Moderate.* Pool, bar, cafeteria.

Tanglewood Motor Lodge. *Moderate.* Hwy. 158 W. off I-40. Manor House and motel accommodations. Golf, riding, pool. Restaurant, snack bars.

Wrightsville Beach

Blockade Runner Hotel. *Expensive.* Oceanfront. Restaurant, pool, play area, bar.

Silver Gull Motel. *Expensive.* At Pier. Restaurant nearby. Open year-round.

The Surf Motel. *Expensive.* Oceanfront efficiencies. Maid service.

 DINING OUT. The choice of good places to eat in North Carolina is extremely varied, including restaurants specializing in international cuisine, in several of the larger cities. Local specialties in Eastern North Carolina and a number of Piedmont localities include barbecued pork and chicken, fresh seafood, fried chicken and country ham. Hush puppies, made from corn meal batter and fried in deep fat, almost always accompany both fish and barbecue here. Grits is another Southern specialty widely served in North Carolina, usually with breakfast. There is also a wide selection of places which feature steaks and roast prime ribs of beef. The price range for restaurant meals in North Carolina is somewhat lower than in metropolitan areas of the Northeast. Restaurants are listed according to price category. Categories and ranges for a complete evening meal are as follows: *Expensive,* $20 and up; *Moderate,* $10-$20. For a more complete explanation of restaurant categories see *Facts at Your Fingertips* at the front of this volume.

Asheville

Weaverville Milling Company. *Expensive.* A few mi. N. of Asheville on Hwy. 19-23. A 1900's grist mill presents a rustic atmosphere for its patrons enjoying live entertainment and gourmet buffet dinners. Open nightly except Mon. All ABC permits. Reservations.

Big Freda's. *Moderate.* Hwy 70E at Oteen. Terrific food and entertainment. Sing-a-long with Freda.

Etowah Valley Golf Club. *Moderate.* On US 64 at Etowah between Hendersonville & Brevard. Dinner only. Elegance in dining.

Jareds. *Expensive.* Reservations suggested. Nationally known French restaurant. Crepes a specialty.

Mountaineer Steak House. *Moderate.* 148 Tunnel Rd. Daily 4 P.M. to midnight, specializing in steaks, rib roasts and beef kabob.

Bavarian Cellar. *Moderate.* Tunnel Rd. shopping center. German & Italian dinners. Continental sandwiches.

Beaufort
Clawson's Emporium Cookery & Saloon. *Moderate.* Good food served in 1890's atmosphere.

Belhaven
River Forest Manor. *Moderate.* Famous for its three-tiered buffet "groaning board." Great atmosphere.

Blowing Rock
The Farm House. *Moderate.* Overlooks the John's River Gorge. Features prime rib, country ham and served by college students who also "serve up" night-club entertainment. Open daily June to early autumn.

Sunshine Inn. *Moderate.* Open year-round. Bountiful home-cooked meals.

Boone
Daniel Boone Inn. *Moderate.* Family style restaurant offering country style steak, chicken, ham and biscuits.

Burnsville
The Nu-Wray Inn. *Moderate.* This old inn on Burnsville's Town Square is one of North Carolina's best known landmarks. Food served family style. No menus. Beef, chicken and hickory smoked ham presented in this "Southern-board" style. Breakfast, lunch, dinner. Season Apr. through Dec.

Calabash
There are 20 restaurants in this tiny fishing village. All are excellent and all are moderately priced.

Chapel Hill
Slug's At The Pines. *Expensive.* Charcoal steaks and Imperial crab are specialties.

Carolina Coffee Shop. *Moderate.* E. Franklin St. 1922 Chapel Hill landmark. Enjoy informal dining and excellent food. Closed Mondays.

Spanky's. *Moderate.* E. Franklin St. In heart of Chapel Hill. Lively night spot.

Charlotte
Epicurean. *Expensive.* 1324 East Blvd. Steaks, seafood are specialties featured in a very attractive setting. Beer & wine. Closed Sun. Chef-owned.

The Marker. *Expensive.* Sheraton Center. Excellent Continental offerings.

Slug's Tower Suite. *Expensive.* Jefferson First Union Towers. Enjoy a magnificent view from the top of the Towers and a delectable meal.

Silver Cricket. *Expensive.* 4705 S. Blvd. French Creole and nouvelle cuisine. Lunch and dinner.

Nakato. *Moderate.* 2501 E. Independence Blvd. Japanese Hibachi-style cooking.

Victoria Station. *Moderate.* Prime ribs and potable spirits. Enjoy good food in authentic railroad cars.

Gus's Original Forty-Niner. *Moderate.* Hwy. 49 E. nr. UNC at Charlotte. Lunch & dinner. American & Italian.

Boar's Head Restaurant. *Moderate.* 3101 N. Sharon Amity Rd. Salad bar, beef a specialty. Delightful lounge. Live entertainment.

Dillsboro

Jarrett House. *Moderate.* A comfortable old inn which has been in operation for more than 70 years. Country ham and fried chicken with fresh vegetables and hot biscuits are regional specialties found here.

Durham

Alexander's. *Expensive.* US 70W on Hillsborough Rd. A steak house and oyster bar with supper club atmosphere. Children's portions. Try the shore dinner for two.

Mr. Harvey's Bistro. *Expensive.* Excellent French cuisine; also other Continental dishes.

Sudi's. *Moderate.* Downtown Durham. Fun atmosphere and good dining.

Bullock's Bar-b-cue. *Moderate.* This is a specialty of the area. Worth trying.

Darryl's 1890. *Moderate.* Hwy. 15-501 halfway between Durham & Chapel Hill. Wonderful atmosphere, lunch and dinner. Excellent food.

Hartman's Steak House. *Moderate.* Dinner only. Specialty is steak, and noted for banana peppers and Hartman's cheese salad.

The Ivy Room Restaurant and Delicatessen. *Moderate.* Good food for whole family.

Land Lubber's. *Moderate.* 2226 Hwy. 54 East. Calabash-style seafood—the best west of the coast. Casual.

Fayetteville

Capt. Jim's Seafood Shack. *Moderate.* 2103 Owen Dr. Worth trying.

Flat Rock

Woodfields Inn. *Moderate.* Oldest continuously operated inn in the state. Southern fare, though beef Stroganoff & home-grown vegetables a specialty. Dinner only.

Goldsboro

Griffin's Barbecue. *Moderate.* 806 S. George St. Specializes in barbecued pork and chicken.

Greensboro

Brass Gate Restaurant-Holiday Inn Four Seasons. *Moderate.* Excellent food.

Darryl's 1808. *Moderate.* 2102 N. Church St. Lunch & dinner. Good sandwiches, steaks, pizzas in period restaurant.

Le Chateau. *Moderate.* Two locations: Friendly Shopping Center, 508 Teague St. Steaks cut to your desired thickness. Good salad bar.

The Pepper Mill. *Moderate.* I-40 at Guilford-Jamestown Rd. Varied menu, good food.

Greenville

Darryl's. *Moderate.* Good Italian and American dishes served in a delightful atmosphere.

The Gathering Place. *Moderate.* Dickenson Ave. Fine dining. Reservations requested.

Hickory

Mull's Restaurant. *Moderate.* Hickory bypass. A good variety of well-prepared foods in pleasant atmosphere.

High Point

The Depot. *Moderate.* Renovated R.R. depot. Fun atmosphere and good food.

Top of the Mart. *Moderate.* Good food. Great view.

Highlands

Highlander Restaurant. *Moderate.* Simple, tasty, homemade foods.

Hillsborough

The Colonial Inn. *Moderate.* 1759 Inn serving excellent Southern fare.

Kenansville

Country Squire. *Moderate.* Relaxing early American atmosphere. Menu varied, but beef is a specialty.

Kinston

King's Restaurant. *Moderate.* Barbecue is the specialty but the menu is varied.

Maggie Valley

Geisha Gardens. *Expensive.* Japanese Restaurant & Tea Room. Evenings by advance reservations only.

Manteo

Elizabethan Manor. *Moderate.* Family-type restaurant. Varied menu.

Marion

Crossbow International. *Expensive.* Restaurant is known statewide. A gourmet's delight. International cuisine.

Monroe

Friendship Inn and Hilltop Restaurant. *Moderate.* Nothing fancy but the finest of food.

Morehead City

Captain Bill's Waterfront Restaurant. *Moderate.* Seafood and steaks and "Down East" lemon pie are the specialties. Children's portions. Overlooks fishing fleet.

Mrs. Willis' Restaurant. *Moderate.* Just what the reader imagines, home cooked food. Very good.

Charter House. *Moderate.* Fresh seafood, slaw, and hushpuppies. Good wine list.

Nags Head—Kill Devil Hills

A Restaurant by George. *Expensive.* Great atmosphere. Excellent food.

Seafare Restaurant. *Expensive.* American cuisine featuring She Crab Soup and lemon chess pie. Dinner. Entertainment Sat. nights.

Dareolina Cove. *Moderate.* A popular restaurant with a varied menu including good seafood and steaks. Adjoins the Sea Oatel Motor Lodge.

Evans Crab House. *Moderate.* Located in Kill Devil Hills. Its crab dishes help make it one of the area's excellent restaurants.

Owen's Restaurant. *Moderate.* In Nags Head, good food in pleasant surroundings.

Spencer's Sea Food Safari. *Moderate.* Good coastal eating. Located in Nags Head. Highlights nautical decor and strawberry pie.

New Bern

Harvey Mansion Restaurant. *Moderate.* Features fresh seafood and other favorites. Enjoy delightful atmosphere of this restored 200-yr.-old mansion.

Henderson House. *Moderate.* Old, historic inn. Ever tried peanut soup? A specialty for lunch here. Lunch served Tues. through Sat. Dinner, Fri. & Sat.

Raleigh

The Angus Barn. *Expensive.* Raleigh-Durham Hwy. (US 70). Unique atmosphere and fine food in a spacious big red barn; collection of antiques and old farm tools. Steaks and rare prime ribs of beef are specialties. Open every night, reservations recommended.

The Charter Room. *Expensive.* Located in Velvet Cloak Inn. Reservations required. Not for those in a hurry. A dinner here is meant to be an experience.

The Scotch Bonnet. *Expensive.* In Mariott Hotel located at Crabtree Mall. Excellent gourmet dining. Reservations required.

Sisters Garden of Eating. *Expensive.* 6026 Falls of Neuse Rd. Creative cuisine served in one of the finest restaurants in city.

Balentine's. *Moderate.* 410 Oberlin Rd. Specializing in Southern food. Attractive cafeteria located in Cameron Village Shopping Center.

Barbecue Lodge. *Moderate.* Mini-city, Hwy 1 N. This is the place for barbecue, Brunswick stew, hush puppies.

Colonnade Restaurant. *Moderate.* Located in Ramada Inn-Crabtree. Fresh trout is a gourmet's treat. Internationally recognized.

Darryl's 1840 Restaurant. *Moderate.* Falls of Neuse Rd., **Darryl's 1849 Restaurant,** US 70 W., and **Darryl's 1906 Restaurant,** 1906 Hillsborough St. Fascinating decor and excellent food.

Joel Lane Restaurant. *Moderate.* Located in Mission Valley Inn. Very good food. Lovely setting.

Neptune's Galley. *Moderate.* Good seafood; steamed oysters in season.

Piccolo Italia. *Moderate.* On Hawthorne Rd. in Cameron Village. Small, intimate restaurant. Veal a specialty. Excellent.

Rocky Mount
Buck Overton's Barbecue. *Moderate.* Good pork barbecue.

Rosman
Red Lion Inn. *Moderate.* Reservations. Dinner only. Specialties: steaks, trout, homemade desserts. Season mid-Mar. to mid-Dec.

Shatley Springs
Shatley Springs. *Moderate.* Family-style meals. Features chicken & homemade breads. Seasonal.

Smithfield-Selma
French Country Inn. *Expensive.* Reservations only. Old colonial home is setting for excellent French cuisine. Located in small town of Selma.

Southern Pines—Pinehurst
Pine Crest Inn. *Moderate.* Dogwood Rd., Pinehurst. Features special dinner every night, also seafood, prime beef.

Spruce Pines
Beam's Restaurant. *Moderate.* Reservations. Patrons from far away come to Beam's to enjoy its Cantonese delicacies.

Tryon
Pine Crest Inn. *Moderate.* Attractive decor and atmosphere, delicious food. Open all year. Near business section of Tryon.

Mimosa Inn. *Moderate.* The dining room of this all-year resort inn is a charming setting, and the food is excellent. Unusual vegetable dishes and hot breads.

Waynesville
Heath Lodge. *Moderate.* Reservations required if not guest of Lodge. Lazy-susan tables laden with southern-style foods. Season May to Oct.

Wilmington and Wrightsville Beach
The Bridge Tender. *Expensive.* At Intracoastal Waterway drawbridge. On the waterway. Excellent seafood and steaks.

The Meditteranean. *Moderate.* On beach. Seafood and Italian. One of the best.

King Neptune. *Expensive.* One of Wrightsville Beach's most well-known seafood restaurants. Good dining.

Ballentines. *Moderate.* In Wilmington. Cafeteria with southern specialties.

Cortley's Old Fashioned Deli. *Moderate.* 316 Nutt St. in Cotton Exchange, Wilmington. Located in newly restored area of Old Wilmington waterfront.

The Cotton Exchange. *Moderate.* This is a restored waterfront area in Wilmington and houses several excellent eateries.

Dry Dock Seafood House. *Moderate.* 5215 Oleander Dr. Family restaurant; all-you-can-eat seafood buffet.

Stemmerman's Grocery. *Moderate.* Front & Orange Sts., Wilmington. Upstairs and Downstairs restaurants. Sandwiches to steaks.

Winston-Salem

Salem Cotton Company. *Expensive.* Located in restored manufacturing plant near Old Salem. Excellent dining. Reservations advised.

Berry's Restaurant. *Moderate.* Small and intimate. Specialties are crepes. Good wine list.

Darryl's 1913 Restaurant. *Moderate.* Brownsboro Rd. Food always good. Atmosphere fantastic.

Salem Tavern. *Moderate.* Old Salem. Specialty food served in an early 19th-century atmosphere.

Staley's Charcoal Steak House. *Moderate.* Steaks are the specialty. A variety of fish (flounder and trout) is also recommended. Chef-owned.

Valentino Restaurant. *Moderate.* Gourmet Italian cuisine. Very good.

Zevely House 1815. *Moderate.* Corner of 4th & Summit Sts. American & European dishes served in authentically restored oldest house in Winston-Salem. Casual atmosphere, excellent food.

SOUTH CAROLINA

Cradle of the Confederacy

BY
GEORGE DREHER

George Dreher was director of the South Carolina Travel Council for eight years and has traveled extensively throughout the South.

From the foothills of the Blue Ridge Mountains in the Up Country, to the sandhills of the Midlands, and on to the sparkling white sand beaches of the Low Country—South Carolina has a wide diversity of attractions to match the tastes of almost any visitor. Her history is preserved for all to see, but along with historic sites there are contemporary attractions, many designed for family entertainment.

Since the early 1960's South Carolina has been a leader of industrial expansion in the Southeast. The textile industry leads all others in the state and has created thousands of new jobs. Precision tool making, chemicals, and metal-working also thrive here.

But industrial expansion has not diminished the tradition most honored in South Carolina—Southern hospitality. The visitor's first evidence of this noted hospitality could well be found while stopping at Carowinds theme park, shared by North and South Carolina.

Just 13 miles north of Rock Hill and 10 miles south of Charlotte, North Carolina, on I-77, Carowinds theme entertainment park re-creates the culture and heritage of the Carolinas. It holds seven major historical areas, a narrow-gauge railroad which encircles the park, a modernistic monorail, and over a hundred rides. Camping is available.

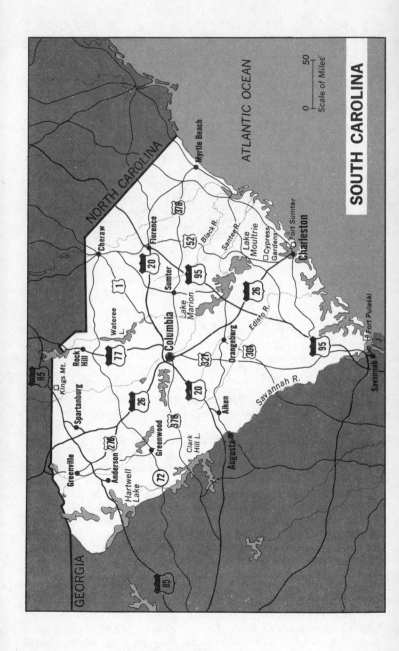

SOUTH CAROLINA

At Rock Hill the Catawba Indian tribes occupied 144,000 acres from 1652 to 1840, and the York County Historical Commission has placed eleven markers in the area. A major recreation center in Rock Hill is Joslin Park, named for A. O. Joslin of Providence, R.I., who established the world's largest bleachery here. Glencairn Gardens is a gift from Dr. Bigger, who started Glencairn as a hobby in a thickly wooded deer park next to his home. It reaches its peak in April, when thousands of red, white, and pink azaleas bloom. The Museum of York County, US. 21 and Mt. Gallant Rd., includes lifelike, mounted wild animals from various countries, a planetarium and a live-animal center. The restored Lansford Canal is a new attraction. Also here are Fort Mill, headquarters for Springs Cotton Mills, and Confederate Park.

From Rock Hill it is only a short drive west over State 161 to sites which have been termed "turning points" in the Revolutionary War—Kings Mountain and Cowpens. Kings Mountain National Military Park comprises 6 square miles and includes the battlefield and monuments, a museum with interesting artifacts and a diorama of the battle. Adjoining Kings Mountain State Park (6,141 acres) are family campgrounds and two summer youth camps. A dramatic battle was fought here on October 7, 1780, when outnumbered, ill-trained colonists conquered British troops to take the summit. The Visitor Center exhibits battle routes of the opposing forces, plus a scenic diorama.

A breechloading Ferguson rifle is also on display at the Center—invented by, and named after, the British major who fought and lost at Kings Mountain. Summers, there are "living history" demonstrations.

Leaving Kings Mountain, join State 216, turn left to I-85, and left again to Blacksburg. This quiet little town has new life these days, brought about by ultramodern textile mills. One, a Deering Milliken enterprise, was designed by Swiss engineers with watchmaker accuracy. An older established firm, a Chicago-owned mattress maker, is Burton-Dixie Corporation, at US 29 and State 5. The townspeople have conducted a clean-up campaign since the new mills were built—a vast change from when the place was called Stark's Folly because pioneers thought the land worthless.

Vineyards are another new commercial development. Growers sell Concord and Fredonia grapes through a cooperative. Not long ago these rolling hills were cotton fields.

A few miles southeast lies Cherokee Falls, formerly a popular Carolina watering spa. Cherokee Indians lived in these parts—farmers plowing their fields often find arrowheads and, sometimes, small pieces of pottery. The area has deposits of monazite, used in gas lamps, and thorium; limestone deposits are the best in the state, and gold prospecting has been resumed by Canadian interests near Smyrna.

Now drive to Gaffney on Routes I-85, US 29, State 18, 150 and County 82. It is a good idea to carry tire chains in upper South Carolina if you are traveling December through March, as snowfalls have increased in recent years. Late afternoon rain squalls prevail August through September. During spring, the woods blossom with dogwood and the Judas tree, with yellow jessamine, Carolina's state flower, and later, cowslips, wild azalea, violets of many kinds and woodbine. Thousands of peach blossoms cover the countryside like a delicate pink cloud. South Carolina is the largest peach producer in the South, and over half the state's peaches are grown within a 50-mile radius of Gaffney stretching toward the southwest.

This is old Cherokee and Creek Indian tribal country and was named for Captain Michael Gaffney, the first Irish settler. Besides being a great peach growing area, Gaffney is a pioneer textile manufacturing center. Limestone College, located here, is one of the oldest senior colleges in the South. In former days it was the Limestone Hotel, a watering spa for the horse-racing set from Charleston who spent summers here.

A visit to Sunny Slope Farms peach sheds near Gaffney, is pleasant in summer. Owned by the Ciggiano family, well known for their orchards in Italy, the farm handles 10,000 bushels of peaches a day from a 1,500-acre orchard.

Cowpens National Battlefield Site, 11 miles southwest on US 29 to junction State 110, marks a victorious battle over the British in 1781. You can follow a walking trail or auto-tour road to view battle sites. A visitor center displays paintings, carvings, weapons and maps relating to the battle. There are picnic sites and nature trails; an 1830 restored log cabin is open during summer.

On I-85, having departed either Gaffney or Cowpens National Battlefield site, drive west toward Spartanburg. The railroad overpass is the Clinchfield, an old and profitable coal-carrying line bringing tons of fuel daily from West Virginia, Tennessee and Pennsylvania mines to the atomic energy plant at Aiken.

You can find good local eating at numerous fish camps along this route. Most are open on weekends and specialize in catfish, catfish stew, some with trout, and hush puppies. Generally you are served all you can eat for a nominal sum. Bring your own liquor is the rule, although a few camps may have beer. Local people can steer you to the best fish camps down by the rivers, often via unpaved roads, which are worth negotiating for the whopping servings and warm hospitality.

Spartanburg, on I-85 and US 29, is the world's peach capital. The thousands of flowering shrubs, fruit trees and bulbs you will see blooming during spring and summer have been planted by local garden clubs.

Converse College for women, Wofford College for men, a junior college, General Hospital School of Nursing, two business colleges and the South Carolina School for the Deaf and Blind are located here. Converse was founded in 1890 and named for Marie Converse, the daughter of a textile leader. Each year a Contemporary and a Baroque Music Festival are staged, and faculty members present a Faculty Artist Recital Series. Converse also has an art gallery, a chamber orchestra, a Chorale, and an Opera Workshop that presents frequent programs. Wofford College is the home of the Black Music-Art Center, where exhibits of local and visiting artists are open to the public. The Spartanburg Music Foundation sponsors a symphony orchestra, Spring Music Festival, and the concert series.

A Center of Art and Industry

Art is actively promoted in Spartanburg by the Art Association, the Art Club, and the Artists' Guild. Traveling exhibitions, workshops, lecturers, and indoor and sidewalk exhibits designed to encourage local and regional artists are maintained.

The County Historical Association sponsors tours to landmarks of historical interest and lectures, and has restored Walnut Grove Plantation, the home of Kate Barry, Revolutionary War heroine. Interesting exhibits are on display in the regional museum, 501 Otis Blvd.

Spartanburg has become a textile and manufacturing center in recent years. At Chesnee (17 miles north on US 221), Spartan Mills opened a $25-million plant, and when Captain John Montgomery, the founder, dedicated his first mill he celebrated by serving roast turkey with all the fixings on a platform atop the chimney.

Spartanburg is named for the Spartan Regiment, formed in 1776. It was the Spartan Rifles under General Daniel Morgan who fought and won the day at the Battle of Cowpens.

Next is Greenville, thirty-one miles west from Spartanburg on I-85 or US 29. It was named in 1821 for General Nathanael Greene, a Revolutionary War hero.

Industrial engineering here centers around J. E. Sirrine & Co., US 29 bypass and US 276, whose leaders have blueprinted most of the major plants in the southeast. The firm's founders came from Connecticut to make wagons and buggies. The major mineral resource in the county is vermiculite. Seal fur auctions at the Memorial Auditorium are held in the fall, and they attract international buyers.

Bob Jones University, an interdenominational school at US 29 North on Wade Hampton Blvd., has a museum of sacred art containing European paintings from the thirteenth through the seventeenth centuries. Among them are works by Tintoretto, Titian, Veronese, Rubens, and Van Dyck. The collection is effectively displayed in a series of magnificent rooms including two Gothic chambers. A diorama depicts Biblical household scenes, and you also will see trees and herbs mentioned in the Bible. A second collection is on display in the ultra-modern Greenville County Art Museum, 420 College St., which also boasts the nation's most complete permanent collection of Andrew Wyeth paintings, along with other impressive collections of North American art.

On US 25 North visit Furman University's Baptist Museum. Although Baptist is the largest Christian denomination represented in Greenville, there are more than 185 churches of twenty-six different faiths in the city. One of the oldest is Christ Episcopal Church, built in 1829. It was designed by Joel Poinsett, for whom the Christmas Poinsettia is named.

Interesting historical spots in Greenville include the Rock House, Buncombe Road, home of Revolutionist Billy Young "That Terror to the Tories"; Batesville Mill at Pelham, first mill in Greenville County; Poinsett Bridge honoring Joel Poinsett; the old gun works, located where the railroad crosses the road to J. P. Stevens' Dunean Mill; White Hall, 310 W. Earle Ct., summer home of Henry Middleton, son of Arthur Middleton, signer of the Declaration of Independence, built in 1810; and the Shriners' Crippled Children's Hospital, on bypass 291.

Seven miles north of Easley on State 8 is Pickens, whose Historical Museum, Room 204, Pickens County Court House, displays pioneer and Indian mementoes. Pick up State 183 west and drive to its intersection with State 130, where the Duke Power Company's Keowee-Toxaway Visitors' Center has an audio-visual tour of the history of energy which includes a thunderstorm, a room of the planets, a working waterwheel, a reconstructed coal mine, and many other exhibits. The giant power project here has flooded archeological sites that have witnessed a visit by the Spanish explorer Hernando de Soto, settlements of the Cherokee Indians, and Fort Prince George, a wilderness outpost during pioneer days.

Clemson, southwest from Easley on US 123, is in the foothills of the Blue Ridge Mountains and the home of Clemson University, founded by Thomas Green Clemson, son-in-law of the South Carolina statesman, John C. Calhoun. The latter bequeathed most of his estate to the school, including his home, Fort Hill. Open to the public, the house contains many of its original furnishings, including a fine mahogany sideboard made of paneling from the officer's quarters of the frigate *Constitution*. In the parlor are a Duncan Phyfe sofa, once the property of General George Washington (the carved eagles on the back were said to be used as models for those on the first American silver dollar), and a marble-topped pier table, similar to one owned by James Madison in the White House. In the dining room is a sword of Colonel Ranson Calhoun, killed in a duel with Alfred Rhett of Charleston. An old spring house and Calhoun's office are in separate buildings. A Confederate one-cent postage stamp and $100 and $1,000 notes bore the statesman's likeness.

On the campus, near the agriculture building, stands Hanover House. It was built in 1716 as a plantation home; frame, with two huge chimneys of handmade brick, and named for the royal House of Hanover in England. In 1940 it was moved from the Low Country near Moncks Corner when the Santee-Cooper power dam was planned and given to Clemson for preservation.

Clemson's campus is bounded on the west by Hartwell Lake, where students and townspeople enjoy boating and waterskiing. In the Horticultural Ornamental Gardens on the campus, there's a teahouse (by the lake), a pagoda and a pioneer complex.

Oconee State Park (and area), via US 123, State 28 & 107, a restful retreat near Stump House Mountain, has a beautiful lake for picnicking or fishing. Musical names bestowed on many Oconee locations by the Indians are constant reminders of their way of life. Tamasee in Cherokee means "place of the sunlight of God." An old witch doctor buried a ruby-like gem, thought to have healing rays, in the vicinity—thus the name. The Tugaloo River in Cherokee means "two," an apt name, since the river converges with the Chattooga. One of the more comical is Coneross Creek, which means "the place where the duck fell off"—no doubt one of the many marsh ducks which can be found along the river's margins in autumn. Jocassee Valley means "place of the lost one." A daughter of a famous chief is said to have strayed in the valley and was never found. Keowee is "where the mulberry grows in bounteous stands." Near Fort Prince George, which stood on the Keowee River, several old mulberry trees are still standing. Oconee itself is derived from the Indian word Uk-oo-na, meaning "the water eyes of the hills." Waterfalls such as Whitewater Falls, Issaqueena Falls and High Falls, and countless others hidden away in dark precipices, abound in the area.

En route to Oconee you will pass by Seneca, named for the old Seneca Cherokee nation, and then through West Union and the Salem/Long Creek area. This is the center of a new apple industry, with a crop worth a half million dollars annually. Groucho Marx, the comedian, was one of the major owners. An apple festival, barbecue, square dance, golf classic and parade draws as many as 30,000 people each year. Walhalla is next on State 28, drawing its name from Norse mythology, meaning "beautiful garden of immortal heroes." There is a fish hatchery on State 107, one of the nation's largest, providing a million trout for restocking mountain streams in the Hartwell and Clark Hill Lakes area. The Chattooga River with a picnic area is nearby.

For Pendleton (and area), take US 76 and branch left on State 88. See the Old Farmer's Hall, oldest in the United States, with a post office on the first floor; the original banner carried by Wade Hampton's Red Shirts and the cannon used by the Red Shirt Company during the Civil War—it was last fired in celebration of Grover Cleveland's election as President. Near the cannon is a sun dial given the Farmer's Society by Col. Francis Huger, known as the liberator of the Marquis de Lafayette, from the dungeon of Olmütz.

Also visit the Old Stone Church and cemetery with its many historic graves. Of Presbyterian faith, it was founded in 1789. The building of rough field stone erected by John Rusk replaces the original log church two miles away. "Printer" John Miller, publisher of the famous *Junius Letters* in England, donated seventeen acres to the church and cemetery. The Calhoun Chapter of the United Daughters of the Confederacy erected an amphitheatre on the church grounds for Memorial Day meetings.

Among many historic homes in this section is Woodlawn, near the Old Stone Church—once the residence of a famous clergyman, the Reverend Jasper Adams. San Salvadore, on the Seneca River, was built by Major Samuel Taylor and named for a soldier killed by Indians on his place.

Pendleton Foundation for Historic Preservation has opened to the public Ashtabula House, three miles north on State 88. It holds antiques and relics, and the dining room and outside kitchen are restored.

Anderson, on US 76 and State 28 southwest from Clemson, is one of the state's five largest cities, named for General Robert Anderson, a Revolutionary War hero. It had one of the first hydroelectric plants in the United States and was nicknamed The Electric City. Power was derived from a plant at Portman Shoals on the Seneca River, now inundated by the Hartwell reservoir.

A textile center with fifteen large mills, Anderson produces cottons, synthetics, blends and plastics, and has also become known as the fiberglass center of the world. The city manufactures many allied products as well, from fiberglass fishing rods to garments. Good farmland—producing soybeans, cotton, pimientos, corn, wheat, oats, barley, hay, lespedesa, sorghum, peaches, pecans, apples and grapes—surrounds Anderson which justly endorses the local radio and TV call letters—WAIM—meaning: "Where agriculture and industry meet."

Hartwell Lake Reservoir, fifteen miles west of Anderson, has 960 miles of shoreline. Hernando de Soto, it is claimed, made an inland tour of the area in the 1500's, seeking gold. He found mussels instead and an Indian princess, who presented him with a strand of pearls. In 1965 the mussels reappeared in shoreline sands, and the pearl business may one day revive as a tourist interest. The area now has marinas and 3,500 boats. At Broadway Lake, a large residential section, national water-ski competitions are held, numerous boat-launching ramps, camping and picnic facilities are available, and navigation maps of the lake can be obtained free from the *Anderson Independent.*

The Hartwell Project is a multipurpose development comprising a concrete dam flanked by earth embankments, a reservoir and a power plant. Hartwell Dam operates in conjunction with the Clark Hill Project for the reduction of flood damages, generation of hydroelectric power—and also the regulation of river flow in the interest of navigation below Augusta, Georgia.

From Anderson, State 28 leads southeast to historic Abbeville, named for Abbeville, France, home of Dr. John de la Howe, an early settler here, schoolmaster, and founder of an industrial training school.

First Cry for Secession

On November 22, 1860, some three thousand persons gathered on Magazine Hill—now Secession Hill—to hear orators of the Southern cause and to choose delegates to a state convention. When the cry for secession went up in the South, the first formal voice came from Abbeville. A monument marks the event at the entrance on Secession Ave. Abbeville did not stop with lighting the fuse of secession. Many of its men fought in the War Between the States, and its women served in hospitals.

Death gasps of the Confederacy rattled clearly when President Jefferson Davis and his cabinet moved out of Richmond, Virginia, southward. On May 2, 1865, Armstead Burt invited President Davis and his cabinet to spend the evening in Abbeville, and it was decided that further resistance was useless. Jefferson Davis, President of the Confederacy, his full cabinet and six Confederate generals held their last formal meeting here. The government was disbanded, and cabinet members split up the next day to go their own way. The Burt House, now known as Stark House, with the room where the fateful decision was made, is kept much as it was that evening. Built more than 100 years ago by Squire Lesley, a lawyer from Ireland, and later purchased by Burt, it stands at the fork of State 28 and 20.

Many old churches and homes 150 years old are located in and around Abbeville. Trinity Episcopal, just off the square, one of the most visited, was organized October 16, 1842. There are historic names on the interior walls and tombstones. Organized in 1768, Upper Long Cane Church on State 20, two miles north of Abbeville, has a graveyard with veterans of ten wars. William Randolph Hearst's great-great-grandfather lived in the area before the Hearsts moved west to Missouri and California. Patric Noble's home—he became governor in the early 1800's—still stands. His son, Edward, was a signer of the Ordinance of Secession. Murals on the wall of the State Bank and Trust Co. depict historic people and incidents in and around Abbeville.

An unusual antique store, called Noah's Ark, lies just off the square. The contents change constantly and range from history books to iron bathtubs, old locks and keys to a church pew.

The Opera House was once one of the grandest in the Southeast. This showplace on the square retains some of its original majestic grandeur amidst fallen plaster, creaking hinged doors and gilded box seats. Show troupes came from up north in the 1900's and through World War II and performers paraded in the square before the 5 P.M. opening. Every show played to standing room only, with as many as 1,500 arriving by special train from other cities.

In front of the Opera House and City Hall is a monument to a World War II hero in France, Thomas Howie, "The Major of St. Lo."

From Abbeville, State 72 leads east to Greenwood, a diversified mill town. The late James C. Self built homes, churches, a fine hospital and other community buildings here. He had a strong interest in bells, and brought a bell foundry to Greenwood after hearing its bells in the Netherlands Building at the 1939 New York World's Fair. Each bronze bell is cast and turned by hand, the formula being handed down through the family.

The George Park Seed Co. in Greenwood is one of the nation's largest and even has its own post office to handle worldwide orders. The greenhouses and exhibit halls are open for inspection weekdays, and the gardens are open Sundays. Something is blooming from seed every day. The company is two miles from town; ask directions in Greenwood, as there are three ways to get there.

Two fine old homes, both on State 10 and open by appointment, are the Frazier Pressley House and Stony Point House. The first, at the end of a long cedar avenue, has square pillars, is octagon-shaped, and has a widow's walk on the roof. The second was begun by William Smith in 1825 and completed by his son, Joel Smith. The brick house was recently restored by the Donald Hawthorne family. On State 10 is Promised Land, a Civil War Federal Government Black relocation project of several thousand acres.

At Ninety-six, nine miles east on State 34, is the Old Star Fort occupied by Loyalist troops during the American Revolution.

From Greenwood to McCormick, follow US 221 south through Bradley, named for pioneer Irishman, Patrick Bradley. Turn right on State 10. Signs direct you to the Presbyterian Church with its old graveyard. One stone reads "Patrick Calhoun—in memory of Mrs. Catherine Calhoun aged 76 years who with 22 others was here murdered by the Indians the first of Feb. 1760." Continue on 10 to the Long Cane Creek covered bridge, one of three in South Carolina. State 10 runs into State 28; turn right, drive two miles to McCormick. The town was named for Cyrus McCormick of Illinois, inventor of the reaper. He owned thousands of acres in the county and gave most of the land on which the town is built. At the railroad station are the remains of a once-prosperous gold mining operation, the Dorn mine. Gold was discovered accidentally by hounds digging the creekside while on a fox hunt. The mine became the second largest in the state and yielded about a million dollars in gold.

Orators and Camellias

From McCormick, motor down State 28 onto US 221 and turn left at State 23 to Edgefield. You will be parallel to Clarks Hill Reservoir on your right, and a power dam. Named for a blacksmith, the area has good camping sites and fishing. Then through two villages, Plumb Branch and Parksville, to Modoc. Turn left on State 23 and drive to Edgefield, through pine seedling reforestation sections. This county claims more statesmen and politicians than any other South Carolina locality: orators, ten state governors, senators, congressmen and adventurers. The people here are individualists. Families enjoy famous old homes, sit on priceless chairs, eat from antique tables and pluck camellias from ancestral gardens.

In Edgefield pick up a "City of Edgefield Historic Map" from the *Edgefield Advertiser* newspaper, established in 1844 and located on the square. Have a meal at the Plantation House, also on the square. Visit Magnolia Dale on Norris St., surrounded front and side by magnolia trees planted 100 years ago. The museum on the second floor is filled with mementoes, photos and historical manuscripts. The house was given to the Edgefield Historical Society by the Kendall Company, of Boston. The Kendall Historical Map Room is at 900 Sumter St., Columbia.

Oakley Park is the Red Shirt Shrine Museum. Maintained by the Daughters of the Confederacy, it has many portraits, furnishings and interior decorations. On the second floor are maps, histories and clothes of bygone days. The house was built in 1835 by Daniel Byrd, descendant of the Virginia Byrds.

Many tourists go to Edgefield to check ancestral dates in five church graveyards. Trinity Episcopal, Simpkins at Wigfall, is one of the largest —Edmund B. Bacon deeded the land in 1836 for one dollar. Others are at Willowbrook Cemetery, the first Baptist Church, and Presbyterian Church on Church Street, Methodist at Norris Street, and St. Mary's Catholic on Bumcomb Street.

Edgefield has many historic private homes. Cedar Grove, US 25 North, was built in 1805 by the grandsons of Michael Blocker, one of the first Prussian families in America. It has handblocked wallpaper from Paris painted in pre-Revolutionary days, fine carved mantel moldings, and a double-deck piazza overlooking a terraced rose garden. The family cemetery is in the rear. The original Blocker Plantation house, built in 1775, was burned.

Pine House, on US 25, also known as Piney Woods Plantation, originally was the site of a tavern, on a one-thousand-acre grant, later inherited by Frances Van Swearingen Ezekiel McClendon in 1791. General Washington had a meal here, spent the night and changed horses. The tavern was across the road from the present Pine House. Carroll Hill, Bumcomb and Pickens Sts., was built by Chancellor James Parsons Carroll, signer of the Ordinance of Secession and representative in both branches of the legislature.

Halcyon Grove on Bumcomb St. was the town house of Governor Andrew Pickens, Jr., the son of General Andrew Pickens. It was later bought by Governor Francis Wilkinson Pickens, Minister to the Russian Imperial Court in St. Petersburg from 1858 to 1860. Pickens' beautiful third wife, the former Lucy Holcomb, was the toast of Russia. Their daughter, born in Russia, was named Olga Liva Lucy Holcomb Douschka Francesca Pickens. This young, beautiful American Joan of Arc, clad in red silk, stood beside Wade Hampton on the balcony of Oakley Plantation House as he rallied the crowd to the cause of the Confederacy with his spirited talk. The Pickens beauty mounted her horse, held the Red Shirt Banner high, and led 1,500 men in a triumphant parade. She is buried near her father in the Willowbrook cemetery. The tombstone reads only Douschka.

From Edgefield, State 19 runs southeast to Aiken, named for William Aiken, Sr., prosperous cotton merchant whose son became governor. The region is noted for sports in general and thoroughbreds in particular, with hundreds of events both for spectators and participants. Any Sunday afternoon, January through April, for instance, you can buy a ticket to one of the weekend polo matches. But if horses are not your cup of tea, then you'll find fine tennis courts or golf greens at your disposal. Quail and dove shooting and fishing are popular. Mayfield's Museum, on State 19N, exhibits Indian, early American and Confederate relics, including an Andrew Jackson collection.

Diapers—and H-Bombs

About 12 miles south is the AEC-Savannah River or H-Bomb plant. The Atomic Energy Commission property includes a 2,800-acre pond used as a cooling basin for water from plant reactors and for an ecology laboratory. The Commission also maintains a large technical film library. The AEC has increased production of Cobalt 60 for industry, medicine and research.

In the vicinity are mountains of creamy or grayish-colored kaolin mines. These are some of the largest and purest clay deposits in the United States, used for many things from wallpaper to glue, paints, or facial mudpacks. One of the newest industries in the area is the Owens-Corning Fibreglas plant.

It's time for a side trip. Graniteville lies five miles west of Aiken on US 1, and is an old textile community in the Horse Creek Valley. The Graniteville Company chain of textile mills which William Gregg founded in 1845 has grown to its present-day eleven plants; owns some fifteen thousand acres of land; and maintains a fine recreation center. The cloth shop, opposite St. Paul Espiscopal Church, is worth a stop to see and perhaps buy products from the mills.

A lover of people, Gregg gave five friends fifty acres each, with the stipulation that they would build homes in Graniteville and live there at least one season in the year. The iron grillwork from his own home, which burned, may be seen at the Grace Estate.

Johnston, nicknamed "The Diaper City," on State 23, 121, 191, is so called because the Riegel plant here produces 90,000 dozen diapers a week. Deering Milliken has a large woolen mill here. This textile and farming community grew from a depot on a main line railroad, the Charlotte, Columbia and Augusta. In recent years cotton crops have been replaced by peaches, grapes, pecans and livestock. The horse show is a major annual event.

From Aiken, I-20 angles northeast to Columbia, the state capital and a university city. The site was selected in 1786 when the Low and Up Country people wanted a Midland location for their state government. John Gabriel Guignard, surveyor general, laid out the city with lovely, wide streets.

The State House, a three-story granite building of Italian Renaissance style, was designed by John R. Niernesee, begun in 1851, but not completed until 1907. Bronze stars on the south and west facades mark scars made by Sherman's shells in 1865. On the first landing, north of the building, is a life-sized bronze statue of George Washington, his staff broken by Sherman's men. Inside the lobby is a life-sized plaster statue of John C. Calhoun, South Carolina's most distinguished statesman. It was used as a model for the marble statue in the Statuary Hall at Washington. On the landings of the wrought-iron stairway are two bronze plaques, one honoring South Carolina's signers of the Declaration of Independence: Thomas Lynch, Jr., Thomas Heyward, Jr., Arthur Middleton and Edward Rutledge. The other honors the state's signers of the Constitution; Judge Rutledge, Charles Cotesworth Pinckney, Charles Pinckney, and Pierce Butler.

The South Carolina flag, adopted in 1777, features a white palmetto tree and a crescent moon. The crescent was taken from the hats of the men who defended Fort Moultrie against the British. The palmetto, the state tree, is a variety of palm that grows along the Southeast Coast, and an ironwork replica of the tree stands in the Capitol grounds to honor the famous Palmetto Regiment which helped win the Mexican War of 1847.

A number of monuments to South Carolina's history stand in the hilltop park surrounding the State House in a setting of sweeping lawns, rose beds, old magnolia and oak trees, evergreens, and Chinese fan trees.

The twenty-eighth President of the United States, Woodrow Wilson, born in Virginia, lived in Columbia at 1705 Hampton St., now a museum.

For genealogists, the South Carolina Department of Archives and History is a storehouse of information. Early South Carolina was a melting pot for people of English, French, Scottish, Welsh, Eastern European, Swiss, and German stock. The American Revolution, Plantation Era and the War Between the States caused South Carolinians to migrate to all parts of the country.

Nowadays a balance of manufacturing, government, trade, services, banking, and agriculture goes to make up Columbia's economy. In fifteen years, some twenty-two different industries have opened, three in a 400-acre industrial park. A technical education center trains students in electronics, engineering, chemistry and related studies. Fort Jackson, outside the city, is one of the nation's largest infantry training centers, with a yearly average turnover of 23,000 recruits. Northwest of the city, via US 176 and State 213, the atomic electric generating station at Parr produces some 17,000 kilowatts.

The first week of April marks the Spring Festival, when tours of homes and gardens attract thousands. The city's fine new Riverbanks Zoological Park, 500 Wildlife Parkway, is one of the nation's most modern. Creatures roam freely in natural habitat areas—there are no cages or bars. There's also a huge, impressive aviary where birds fly about in settings which reflect their geographic origins.

Thirty-two miles northeast of Columbia on US 1 is the oldest inland town in the state, Camden. Dating from 1732, it was settled by Quakers from Ireland, who first named it Fredericksburg, then Pine Tree Hill—and finally Camden, honoring Lord Camden. Two great battles of the

Revolution were fought here—and in the Civil War the town was an important railroad center and storehouse, with a hospital for the wounded.

Headquarters of Cornwallis

Historic Camden is a restoration of the Revolutionary period. You can enter two restored log houses filled with museum exhibits and miniature dioramas; here even the soldiers' buttons are perfectly detailed. There is a model of the original town of eighty buildings, adapted from General Nathanael Greene's maps, and winding trails are lined with historic markers and restored fort sites.

When the British departed from Camden in 1781, they left remains of the old town wall and six surrounding forts, the Kershaw House where General Cornwallis headquartered and a large powder magazine. They also left swords, cannon balls, muskets and other valuable pieces of history that are on display. Trails cover much of the sixty wooded areas and you can go over them in an electric cart. Helpful guides will show you everything when you arrive and treat you to something the British never got in Camden at that time—real Southern hospitality.

Camden's fame now is its industry—DuPont built their first South Carolina plant here, in the 1950's—and sports. Fox hunting in the fall, winter stabling and horse training, plus the Carolina Cup Steeplechase, in March, are important.

At Sumter, US 76, 378, the Palmetto Pigeon Plant, founded by Attorney Wendell M. Levi, is the largest of its kind in the world, marketing 100,000 squabs a year.

From Columbia, drive south on I-26 about 41 miles to State 33, then west four miles, to Orangeburg and the fifty-five-acre Edisto Memorial Gardens. Acres of azaleas bloom in profusion, peaking in April, amid tall, moss-draped cypress, crab apple and flowering dogwood. The more than 6,000 rose bushes provide masses of color all summer. Orangeburg has golf, bird hunting and freshwater game fish in the numerous lakes and the Edisto River. A Federal Fish Hatchery, on 150 landscaped acres, breeds bass, redbreast, bream and other local fish. Salley Archives Building, on Middleton St., is open on request.

From Orangeburg take US 21 to its junction with US 17. Turn right for Yemassee, a wonderful area for flowers and vegetables. S. H. Kress and his brother, of dimestore fame, grew their bulbs at a plantation here.

Continue on US 17 through Sheldon. At Gardens Corner turn south onto US 21 to Beaufort, where British merchants once made forturnes in cotton and indigo. Browse around the old homes, built high for coolness, with spacious porches and old-fashioned gardens of camellias, jessamine, oleanders, and wisteria mingled with moss-bearded oak trees. Many of the houses were made of tabby, from crushed oyster shells, and some homes are open to visitors at azalea time in the spring. One is the home of Emily, unforgettable character in the novel *Sea Island Lady;* it has wide verandas, basement tunnel-porches and double front V stairs. Another interesting home is Verdier House on Bay Street, from which General Lafayette addressed the people of Beaufort.

The old arsenal built in 1795, now Beaufort Museum, contains several ancient cannons, an old steam fire engine, Indian arrowheads, Confederate money, stuffed snakes, alligator skulls, antebellum costumes and proclamations of the Secession. The Chamber of Commerce can furnish self-guided tour folders as well as a host of other information about the area.

The landscape here varies from high bluffs, densely wooded with subtropical growth, to sloping sandy beaches. Beaufort has one of the best natural harbors on the coast, with forty public boat landings, a yacht harbor and club. The South Atlantic Sailing Regatta is held during the annual Water Festival in July. Sailing and water-skiing are very much part of the scene. Crabbing and shrimping are big business in these sea islands, and one constantly sees small boats plying the waterways. The Atomic Age has not changed the quaintness and congenial tranquility of Beaufort.

The islands of Beaufort County include: Barnwell and Little Barnwell, named for John Barnwell, a Colonial hero from Ireland and a well-known Indian fighter, later known as "Tuscarora Jack;" Buzzard's Island named for its numerous buzzards; Bermuda Island, named by early settlers for their former home; Bull Island which recalls the Bull family of Colonial days, whose land grants extended from the Savannah to the Combahee rivers; Chisolm Island where Dr. Robert Chisolm grew and shipped olives until Federal troops destroyed his trees, using them for firewood; Coosaw Island, whose Indian name means Old Creek; and Fripp Island, which got its name from a family of planters who came from St. Helena in 1725 and recently has been developed by several South Carolina businessmen into a vacation paradise.

Most of Hunting Island is a state park, and is inhabited by many deer, raccoon and other game, with flocks of local and migratory birds and waterfowl. The beach has hard, smooth sand at low tide, and a width of four of five hundred feet. This palm-tree-lined resort overlooks St. Helena Sound, on the outer banks of the chain of sixty-four Golden Islands of Beaufort County. St. Helena Island was named in 1526 by Pedro de Quexos, a Spaniard who had set sail from Florida. He suddenly came upon the island and in prayerful gratitude he thanked his Saint, Elena, for leading him to such bountiful land.

Let's go on a side trip, from Beaufort to historic Port Royal, on State 281. Named by Jean Ribaut in 1562, when he expressed admiration for the wide sound and harbor, saying: "It is one of the greatest and fairest havens of the world, where without danger, all the ships of the world might anchor." Captain Robert Sanford sailed in here, with Dr. Henry Woodward, the English surgeon, who stayed as hostage while an Indian sailed back to England with Sanford. Woodward, then captured by Spaniards, was taken to the East Indies, where he was picked up in 1670 by an English vessel. He returned and went to Charles Towne where he introduced Madagascar rice to Carolina. During the Civil War, while the Confederates were concentrated in Charles Towne, Federal forces landed sixteen ships with 12,000 men at Port Royal. They kept possession of the Sound for the duration of the war.

Back into the car now, and off to Hilton Head Island on State 170 to the junction with US 278, then south and east. The island takes its name from British Captain William Hilton, 1663. Here at Hilton Head the golfer will find twelve beautifully sculptured public courses, including

Harbour Town, site of the famous Heritage Golf Classic in March. And he just may see an alligator basking in the sun at one of the water hazards. For the tennis enthusiast there are over 200 courts with the latest in surfacing. Boaters may rent power craft or sailing vessels. Or you can dock your own boat at one of the island's marinas.

Swimmers and sun lovers will delight in the warm, white sand that gently meets with the Atlantic. Bicyclists will find twenty-five miles of bike paths. And fishermen can try the island's inlets and bays or the challenge of the Gulf Stream for deep-sea fishing. For children there are day-long programmed activities directed by competent, professional staffs.

The environmentalist will find Hilton Head a haven. It is a managed development which incorporates the environment with recreational enjoyment. Hotel, motor inn and motel accommodations are plentiful, or the visitor may rent a villa-condominium.

Walk the History Trail

Leaving Beaufort backtrack on US 21 to Gardens Corner, turn right onto US 17, then north on State 3035, passing Green Pond and Ritter to Walterboro, a relaxing spot for fishing or golf, and bird hunting in season. Arrangements for guides with dogs can be made through the Chamber of Commerce, or hotel-motel management. The camellias here are a sight to see in fall and spring.

From Walterboro follow State 64 to Jacksonboro, then US 17 to Charleston.

The citizens of Charleston have achieved a happy balance between history and progress. A major seaport and diversified industry contrast with quaint streets and beautiful architecture. Historic homes and churches are visited annually by thousands from all parts of the country and the world. A walking tour, known as the History Trail, is marked with signs in the older part of the city. Guide folders are available at many hotels, motels, and restaurants, and at the Charleston Trident Chamber of Commerce Visitor Information Center, Arch Building, 85 Calhoun St.

Each spring thousands of visitors flock to enjoy the dazzling parade of color in Charleston's famous gardens and explore the scores of restored eighteenth- and nineteenth-century homes. Since 1977, they've also come for the twelve-day Spoleto Festival U.S.A., which features opera, theater, ballet, jazz and almost every other aspect of the arts.

When summer approaches, the face of Charleston seems to change. Summertime in Charleston promises the bouquet and beauty of lush oleanders, hydrangeas, hibiscus, roses, magnolia and the ever-favorite crape myrtle. Beautifully refurbished Cypress Gardens, Middleton Place Gardens and Plantation Stableyards and Magnolia Gardens all remain open all year for the enjoyment of children and adults alike.

In addition to Middleton's beautiful formal grounds and landscaped gardens (the oldest in America), the recently restored Plantation Stableyards offer an afternoon's trip back through time to the plantation life of the 1700's. Magnolia Gardens has a petting zoo with rare mini-horses. Nearby is Drayton Hall, considered the nation's finest untouched example of Georgian architecture.

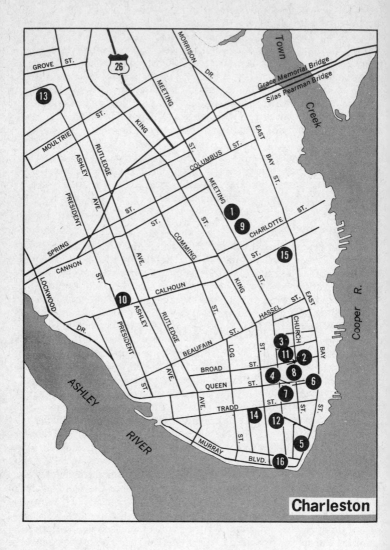

Charleston

Points of Interest

1) Charleston Museum
2) City Hall
3) Confederate Museum
4) Dock Street Theater
5) Edmondston-Alston House
6) French Huguenot Church
7) Heyward-Washington House
8) Hunley Museum
9) Manigault House
10) Medical University of South Carolina
11) Old Powder Magazine
12) Russell House
13) Sunken Gardens
14) Sword Gates
15) Visitor Information Center
16) White Point Gardens

Many other attractions are open throughout the summer that have particular appeal to young families with an interest in history.

Fort Sumter, where the Civil War began, can be reached by sightseeing boats departing from the Charleston Municipal Marina several times a day. Both the Fort Sumter cruise and Gray Lines's 25-mile Harbor of History Tour give the visitor a delightful boat trip and spectacular offshore views of Charleston's famous battery mansions.

Fort Moultrie on Sullivan's Island, another favorite attraction, is the site of the first decisive victory of Americans over the British during the Revolutionary War.

The Charleston Museum, oldest municipal museum in America, is now housed in a handsome new structure at 360 Meeting St. It has fine cultural, historical, and natural history collections, as well as decorative arts exhibits. Also displayed on the grounds is a full-scale replica of the first Confederate submarine, the *H. S. Hunley,* and other artifacts of the Civil War.

Charles Towne Landing, a beautiful state park, was built on the original 1670 landing site to commemorate Charleston's 300th birthday during South Carolina's Tricentennial Celebration in 1970. One of the most unusual parks in the country, Charles Towne Landing includes a theater and twenty-minute film showing the beauty of the Low Country; an Exhibit Pavilion whose outstanding exhibits and artifacts illustrate the first century of settlement; a Reception Center with gift shop, restaurant, and rental carts or bicycles; a 1670 Experimental Garden showing various crops grown by the early settlers; the original 1670 Settlement Site; the *Adventure,* a reproduction of a seventeenth-century trading ketch; the Animal Forest with animals indigenous to South Carolina in 1670, displayed in their natural habitat; and nearly one hundred acres of beautifully landscaped English-park type gardens with paths circling placid lagoons.

Other historic points of interest include the old City Market; the Confederate Museum; Old Slave Mart Museum and Gallery; Gibbes Art Gallery; the Old Powder Magazine, oldest public building in the city dating from 1713, and the Dock Street Theatre, reproduction of the oldest theater in America. Another permanent resident of this historic city is the aircraft carrier *Yorktown,* famed "Fighting Lady" of World War II, berthed at Patriots Point across the Cooper River in Mt. Pleasant. Planes, helicopters, ship models, weapons are displayed on board. Also here are the nuclear-powered submarine *Savannah,* destroyer *Laffey,* and submarine *Clamagore.* Nearby, on Long Point Road in Mt. Pleasant, is beautiful 738-acre Boone Hall Plantation, with original slave houses and ginhouse.

Also open to the public are some of Charleston's famous house museums—the Joseph Manigault House (1803), the Nathaniel Russell House (1809), the Heyward-Washington House (1770), the Thomas Elfe House (1760), the Edmonston-Alston House (ca. 1828), the Aiken-Rhett Mansion (ca. 1823–58), and the Calhoun Mansion (ca. 1876).

Those who prefer to simply walk or ride through the historic sections of Charleston may do so at their leisure by following the Walking Tour route or by taking romantic horse-drawn carriage tours. Also available are tape-recorded walking tours and bus tours. The Charleston Guide

Service offers well-trained professional guides who provide transportation and guided tours for individuals, families or larger groups.

Charleston County boasts four excellent beaches for sun bathing, surfing, or just building castles in the sand. Folly Beach, Sullivan's Island, the Isle of Palms, and Edisto all offer beautiful sandy beaches, featuring everything from amusement parks and fishing piers to family campsites, super-luxurious resorts and downright remote seclusion and privacy.

Travelers who pack a fishing pole will be delighted with the many varieties of fish abundantly pulled from freshwater and saltwater around Charleston. Surfcasting, pierfishing, deepsea fishing in the Gulf Stream, or plain old-fashioned cane-pole angling from a riverbank all provide sporting excitement for novice and veteran alike.

Twenty-three miles south of Charleston, on US 17 and State 20, Kiawah Island is being developed as a full-scale vacation resort. The island is being left in the natural state as much as possible, with accommodations, shops, and recreational facilities all within 7-minutes walking distance. For the nature lover, there is a 2,500-foot nature boardwalk through a sunken forest, and the island's forest, lagoons, creeks, and marshes are teeming with wildlife.

Seabrook Island, twenty miles south of Charleston on US 17 to State 20, then State 90, is another private resort and residential community. Its 2,042 acres have tidal creeks and marshes, massive sand dunes, moss-draped oakes, tall pines, and miles of sandy beach. The visitor may enjoy its excellent golf course and clubhouse while vacationing in oceanside villas, cottages, and lakeside treehouses.

Lake Moultrie and Lake Marion, thirty-five miles from Charleston on US 52 on the Cooper River and at the edge of the Francis Marion National Forest, are two of the most popular inland freshwater sports sections in South Carolina. They were created by a giant hydro-electric dam at Moncks Corner and Pinopolis and cover 171,000 acres of water and 450 miles of shoreline. World records in channel catfish (fifty-eight pounds) and black crappie (five pounds) are claimed. There's a striped bass hatchery nearby and many boat ramps.

Head north on US 52, thirty-two miles from Charleston, to Moncks Corner and Mepkin Plantation. This was once the Colonial home of Henry Laurens and passed through a succession of owners, including Clare Booth Luce, who gave it to the Trappist Monks.

US 17 shoots north from Charleston to McClellanville in Bull Bay, a migratory bird refuge. The place abounds in bird names—Duck Creek, Crow Island, Bird Island. The latter is a crescent-shaped strip of sand and grass and is home to many pelicans. The young pelicans consume 150 pounds of fish before they learn to fly—at the ripe age of two months. Their diet is principally menhaden, used commercially for processing into fertilizer. The sand dunes which stretch down the center of the isle keep the nests high and dry during tides. Other islands and parts of the mainland comprise a 60,000-acre refuge, occupying a fifteen-mile segment of the coast. There are two colonies of nesting waterfowl in the summer, 2,000 brown pelicans and 20,000 royal terns, so the sky is filled with the beautiful black and white, and brown and white birds. Near McClellanville is Hampton Plantation.

City of Ghosts and Plantations

Georgetown, north on US 701, is a city of memories, ghosts and fine plantations. Many prominent figures from pre-Revolutionary days and the Civil War were born, lived or visited here. Lafayette and DeKalb landed where Winyah Bay empties into the Atlantic. The waterway from Brookgreen to Georgetown was traveled by Theodosia Burr as she came to town to board the *Patriot*. Many legends are told of this beautiful daughter of the infamous Aaron. It is even said that she was captured by pirates and made to walk the plank, but who can believe that? Francis "Swamp Fox" Marion also lived here. On the mainland side of the bay, south of town, is Belle Island where Fort White, a sixteen-battery Confederate fort is in an excellent state of preservation.

McClellanville is a fishing center. Blues, mackerel, king mackerel (king fish), cobia, barracuda and dolphin are plentiful in season. Amberjack run up to sixty pounds.

US 17 leads to Pawley's Island, a quaint old island, a summer retreat for wealthy rice planters of the 18th and 19th centuries. Their charming plantations still grace the landscape. The beach and creek are the main attractions with fishing, clamming, crabbing, swimming, water-skiing, boating and hunting in season. A fishing pier boasts large catches; boats are available for rent or charter, either ocean-going or inland motoring. For children, there are a pavilion, bowling, miniature golf courses, and trampolines. And for the whole family, there's good eating at inns and restaurants in the area which feature fresh seafood. Continue on 17 to Brookgreen Gardens, which holds more than 350 works of American sculptors of the 19th and 20th centuries, displayed in a garden setting, and Huntington Beach State Park.

Sun Fun Capital

Myrtle Beach on US 17 is the focal point of the Grand Strand, first seen by Spanish settlers in 1526 and in the 1700s a focal point for English plantation owners. Today, it is a resort area that offers year-round vacation fun for the whole family. Accommodations are plentiful—more than 38,000 rooms—and the title "Camping Capital of the World" has been bestowed on the Strand, which contains some 15,000 campsites with more being added almost daily.

Spring and sports go hand in hand on the Grand Strand. The peak golf season runs from February through April. There's also a billfish tournament, stock car racing, horseshows and golf tournaments. Canadian-American Days, plantation tours, camellia shows, a folk music festival, and Fishing Rodeo, all provide a wide variety of pleasures between April and October.

The Sun Fun Festival in June kicks off the peak summer season at Myrtle Beach and the Grand Strand. With 55 miles of free public beaches and varied amusements and recreation for young and old, everything is in full swing throughout the summer.

Fall, the Indian summer season, offers the best in saltwater sports fishing along the Grand Strand. Ocean bathing is enjoyed until November, and major fall activities include the mid-October Arthur Smith King Mackerel Tournament—world's largest sportsfishing tournament of its kind—Indian Summer Days, Thanksgiving Holiday Fiesta, golf tournaments for amateurs and pros, and music festivals.

Winter is still playtime at Myrtle Beach and the Grand Strand. Christmas Holidays Festival, a January Jamboree and George Washington Days highlight the events schedule. The Myrtle Beach Convention Center offers inside entertainment, and golf is enjoyed throughout the winter.

Ten major annual festivals and other entertainment events are staged by the Greater Myrtle Beach Chamber of Commerce (P. O. Box 2115, Myrtle Beach 29577) and other groups to provide activity throughout the fall, winter and spring seasons.

PRACTICAL INFORMATION FOR SOUTH CAROLINA

FACTS AND FIGURES. Columbia, located in the geographical center of the state, is the capital. Population of the state is 3,121,820 (1980 Census).

The official state tree, the palmetto, has earned for the state its designation as the "Palmetto State." The state bird is the Carolina wren; the state flower, the yellow jessamine; the state stone, blue granite. The state animal is the white-tail deer, and the state fish is the striped bass. *Animis Opibusque Parati* ("Prepared in spirit and resources") and *Dum Spiro Spereo* ("While I breathe, I hope") are the state mottos.

HOW TO GET THERE. *By air:* Charleston and Columbia may be reached by direct flights of Delta, Piedmont and Eastern from out of the state. United also serves Columbia. There are direct flights to Greenville/Spartanburg on Eastern, Delta and USAir and to Myrtle Beach on Piedmont.

By car: Main routes coming into South Carolina include I-95 a multilane divided highway from Savannah, Georgia, into Hardeeville and continuing through the state and into North Carolina; I-20 from the Augusta, Georgia, area is also a main access to South Carolina; I-85, another multilane highway brings visitors into South Carolina from the northern part of Georgia. Main routes into the state from North Carolina include I-85, I-77 from Charlotte, N. C.; I-26 from Hendersonville; and I-95 from Lumberton into Dillon. US 17, a shoreline route, follows along from North Carolina through South Carolina and into Georgia. US 301 is another well-traveled route in and out of the state.

By bus: Trailways, Greyhound, Jefferson Lines, Inc., and Southeastern Stages, Inc. all go into South Carolina.

By train: Amtrak goes into Dillon, Florence, Kingstree, Charleston, Yemassee, Clemson, Camden, Columbia, Denmark, Spartanburg and Greenville.

HOW TO GET AROUND. *By air:* You can travel by air within the state on Delta and Eastern.

By car: I-95, I-20, I-26 and I-85 crisscross within the state and provide car travel. US 17, which runs along the shoreline, and US 301, an inland route, are also good. US 123, 321, 52, 78, 378 and State 72 are also in this category.

Car rental: Rental service is available at the Charleston, Columbia, and Greenville-Spartanburg airports. There are several rental firms operating in Orangeburg and Sumter.

By bus: Greyhound, Trailways, Jefferson Lines, Inc., and Southern Stages, Inc., have service within the state.

TOURIST INFORMATION. To obtain detailed information about South Carolina write: South Carolina Dept. of Parks, Recreation and Tourism, Edgar A. Brown Bldg., Suite 113, 1205 Pendleton St., Columbia, S.C. 29201.For information on South Carolina's two national forests, write U.S. Forest Service, P.O. Box 970, Columbia, S.C. 29202.To obtain information on the Grand Strand write: Greater Myrtle Beach Chamber of Commerce, P. O. Box 2115, Myrtle Beach 29577. Santee-Cooper Counties Promotion Offices, P.O. Drawer 40, Santee 29142, will supply information on the Santee-Cooper Lakes, the town, and nearby golf courses. The Hilton Head Island Chamber of Commerce, P.O. Drawer 5647, Hilton Head Island 29928, will send you complete information on what the island offers. For other resort island information, write: Wild Dunes Beach and Racquet Club, Box Y, Isle of Palms, S.C. 29451; Kiawah Island Resort, P.O. Box 12910, Charleston, S.C. 29412; Seabrook Island, P.O. Box 32099, Charleston, S.C. 29407; Fairfield Ocean Ridge Resort, P.O. Box 27, Edisto Beach, S.C. 29438; Fripp Island Resort, Fripp Island, S.C. 29920. Complete hunting and fishing information and regulations may be obtained from the South Carolina Wildlife and Freshwater Fisheries, Resources Department, Division of Game, P.O. Box 167, Columbia 29202. Charleston Convention Bureau, P.O. Box 834, Charleston, S.C. 29402, will advise you on deep-sea fishing and charter boats.

 SEASONAL EVENTS. Much of South Carolina's history and tradition is relived through the many and varied festivals and events held throughout the state. Tours of historic homes and events such as the Annual Foothills Arts and Crafts Guild Festival return the modern-day South Carolinian to the days when craftsmen used pegs instead of nails and country music was the only kind to be heard. South Carolina is also a home of such modern-day attractions as the Labor Day Southern 500 Stock Car Race at Darlington Raceway.

Among the regularly held events in South Carolina are:

January: January Jamboree, Myrtle Beach and the Grand Strand. Golf tournaments and awards, historic and garden tours, special sales, golf films, entertainment and package activity at hotels and motels. *Annual Georgetown Camellia Show,* Georgetown. Thousands of blooms are on display from many of the surrounding plantations, as well as from the entire state, North Carolina and Georgia.

February: Polo Matches, Aiken. Hard-riding professional and amateur polo players take to the field for some fast action every Sunday at 3:30 P.M. through April. The great international game has been played in Aiken for more than eighty years. Some of America's best polo players compete. Charleston's famous gardens—*Cypress* (open mid-Feb. to May 1), *Magnolia* and *Middleton Place Gardens and Plantation Stableyards* (both open all year) are noted for their colorful profusion of camellias and azaleas and for fine old live oak and cypress trees. Magnolia and Middleton Place are on State 61; Cypress on US 52.

March: Aiken Horse Trials, Aiken. A part of the competition in Aiken's Triple Crown. Some of the nation's finest thoroughbred horses, having wintered here, make their spring debut. *Annual Canadian-American Days,* Myrtle Beach and the Grand Strand. Folk Music Festival, parade, beach games, cruises, kids' days at amusement parks, historic tours, teenage parties, square dance, daily news from Canada, antique show, golf tournaments and awards, fishing, band concerts, tours of the Air Force Base, historic garden and industrial tours and a musical stage show. *Annual Spring Art Show,* Columbia, Mar. to Apr., presented by the Artists Guild of Columbia at the Columbia Museum of Art. *Charleston Festival of Houses,* Mar. to Apr. Afternoon and candlelight walking tours are offered. Magnificent private gardens and charming historic private homes are on display in this most historic city. The event is one of the highlights of touring the state's beautiful Low Country gardens in the spring. *Annual Carolina Cup Races,* Camden. An afternoon of forty-two steeplechase and flat races in late March or early April is sanctioned by the National Steeplechase and Hunt Association. It is a gala country blend of picnicking, renewing old friendships and racing at its best. The event is one of the earliest competitions for many thoroughbreds after an arduous winter training season. The feature race is the famed Carolina Cup, a 2-mile run over Springdale Course, one of the world's outstanding steeplechase courses.

April: Annual Sidewalk Art Show, Charleston. A display and sale of paintings and artwork by local and out-of-town artists at St. Philip's Church on Church St. This is a very colorful display in the historic section of old Charleston. *Annual World's Championship Landlocked Striped Bass Fishing Derby,* Santee and Cooper Lakes, Santee, Apr. to June. One of the world's largest freshwater fishing derbies, free to all participants. Striped bass, largemouth bass, crappie and bream division. Thousands of dollars in cash, trophies, motors and merchandise are up for grabs. *The Governor's Annual Frog-Jumping Contest.* The finest jumping frogs throughout the state compete in this dramatic contest held on Main St. in the little rural town of Springfield. Festivities also include marble shooting, horseshoe and yo-yo contest, greased pig chase, country music and dancing. Frog juice sold—10 cents a cup. *International Egg-Striking Contest.* The hardest-boiled eggs that can be found are paired in striking duels. Excitement builds with every strike of these rocklike eggs in a very colorful folk custom. Also in Springfield. *Rebel 500 Race,* Darlington. Top NASCAR stock car drivers test Darlington Raceway's 1⅜-mile oval for 500 miles. This is the second oldest race in NASCAR. *South Carolina Festival of Roses,* Orangeburg. "Miss South Carolina Queen of Roses" Beauty Pageant, rose contest with entries from all over the U.S., special show and banquet, country music, square dancing, special events for ladies and men throughout three days.

May: Annual Charleston Trident Fishing Tournament, Charleston, Berkeley and Dorchester Counties. The tournament is open to participants of all ages, free of charge. Anglers may enter the tournament by completing official entry blanks and having the entry certified at one of the numerous weigh stations. Entries must have been caught in the waters of these three counties. Offshore catches must be made in boats leaving from and returning to Charleston County. Thirty-seven species of eligible fish. Special surf, military and boat awards. *Iris Festival,* Summer, is held during the last week in May. *Spoleto Festival USA,* Charleston. The American counterpart to famed Spoleto, Italy, festival, with opera, ballet, modern and folk dance, arts, crafts, and theater. For information write Spoleto Festival USA, P. O. Box 157, Charleston 29402. Spoleto lasts from late May into early June.

June: Annual Sun Fun Festival, Myrtle Beach and the Grand Strand area. South Carolina's largest festival featuring Miss Bikini Wahine Pageant, crowning of Miss Sun Fun, two parades, Old-Fashioned Day on the Beach, National Turtle Race, South Carolina Baton Twirling Championship, archery shoot, beach games, street dances, historical excursions, treasure hunt, band concerts, fishing rodeo, golf tournaments and awards, arts and crafts shows, horse show, river cruises, watermelon eatin' contest, kids' day at amusements parks and a stock car race.

July: Mountain Rest Hillbilly Day, Mountain Rest Community. This tiny community comes alive with the pageantry of city slickers gone country: square dancing, clogging, greased pig chases and hootenanny. The twang of real hillbilly music sets the background for the enjoyment of mountain victuals served atop the beautiful Blue Ridge Mountain. *Beaufort Water Festival,* Beaufort. Parade, fishing tournament, golf tournament, beauty pageant, street dances, coronation ball, motorboat races, plays, shrimp boat parade with blessing of the fleet, and children's day activities.

August: Annual Foothills Arts and Crafts Festival, on the square in Pendleton. Exhibits, booths, artists at work in various media, crafts, demonstrations, etc.

September: Southern 500 Race, Darlington. Late-model stock car trials, parade and beauty pageant. All culminate in the annual Labor Day Southern 500, the granddaddy of all stock car races. Attendance is 75,000. *Branchville Raylrode Daze Festival,* Branchville. This festival takes you back to the days when railroads were king in this rural town. Festivities center around the railroad, which is part of the oldest line in the world, and the site of the first railroad junction. The firing up of an old steam locomotive with rides available adds reality to the event.

November: The Colonial Cup Races, Camden, feature the Colonial Cup $100,-000 International Steeplechase, which brings together the best in the U.S.A., with horses from abroad. The race is run over a special course covering 2 miles, 6½ furlongs with 18 jumps, none of which is repeated. *Chitlin Strut,* Salley. People from many areas of the Southeast come to this town to get their annual fill of chitlins, country music and dancing. Barbecue pork and chicken are available for those who don't crave the featured delicacy.

December: Annual Holiday Festival Golf Tournament, Myrtle Beach-Conway. Handicap tournament sponsored by grand Strand Area Golf Association at Quail Creek Golf Club.

 NATIONAL FORESTS. Cherokee Indians once roamed across the area now encompassed by Sumter National Forest. Colonial settlements followed, then the Revolutionary War, the Civil War and the bitter Reconstruction Period. All have left their imprint.

Named in honor of General Thomas Sumter, the "Gamecock" Revolutionary War hero, the Forest has three divisions—the *Andrew Pickens Division,* located in the Blue Ridge Mountains, and the *Long Creek* and *Enoree Divisions,* located in the rolling Piedmont section.

Visitors to the park can enjoy not only the facilities available there, but they may also visit such places as *Stumphouse Mountain Tunnel* and *Isaquenna Falls.* The tunnel, which stretches back some 1600 feet into solid granite, is the result of attempts to link Charleston with Cincinnati, Ohio, by rail. (The project failed.) Nearby is *Isaquenna Falls;* legend has it that a Creek Indian maiden escaped pursuit by leaping into the foaming falls and hiding on a small ledge.

The *Francis Marion National Forest,* located on the coastal plain north of Charleston, is named for a hero of the American Revolution, a general who was also known as the "Swamp Fox." Indians and Spanish and French explorers roamed the area, following the many waterways flanked by moss-covered gums and cypress and tall loblolly pines.

The American alligator, an endangered species, is found in the forest, as are many and varied forms of other wildlife.

The Forest is located on the Atlantic flyway of migratory birds, and in winter as many as 250 different bird species have been counted.

There are several public boat ramps and seven camping sites. The forest is divided into three Ranger Districts. The *Swamp Fox Ranger Station* and *Witherbee Ranger Station* are at Moncks Corner, the *Wambaw Ranger Station* at McClellanville. Spring fishing for bream and bass is excellent.

 STATE PARKS. Thirty-four state parks enhance the state with campgrounds, well-stocked lakes, nature trails and picnic tables. The parks are open all year during daylight hours. Concessions generally close Labor Day and reopen May.

Parks and locations are: *Aiken,* 16 mi. E of Aiken off US 78; *Andrew Jackson,* 8 mi. N of Lancaster on US 521; *Baker Creek,* 3 mi. SW of McCormick on US 378; *Barnwell,* 7 mi. NE of Barnwell on State 3; *Charles Towne Landing,* on SC 171 between US 17 and I–26 near Charleston; *Cheraw,* 4 mi. SW of Cheraw on US 1; *Chester,* 3 mi. SW of Chester on State 72; *Colleton Wayside,* 11 mi. N. of Walterboro on US 15; *Croft,* 3 mi. SE of Spartanburg off State 56; *Dreher Island,* 6 mi. SW of Chapin off US 76; *Edisto Beach,* 50 mi. SE of Charleston on State

174; *Givhans Ferry,* 16 mi. W of Summerville on State 61; *Greenwood,* 17 mi. E. of Greenwood on State 702; *Hamilton Branch,* 15 mi. SE of McCormick off US 221; *Hickory Knob,* 8 mi. SW of McCormick off US 378; *Hunting Island,* 16 mi. SE of Beaufort on US 21; *Huntington Beach,* 3 mi. S of Murrells Inlet on US 17; *Keowee-Toxaway,* on US 11 at Lake Keowee; *Kings Mountain,* 12 mi. NW of York on State 161; *Lee,* 7 mi. E of Bishopville off US 15; *Little Pee Dee,* 11 mi. SE of Dillon off State 57 *Lynches River,* 13 mi. SW of Florence on US 552; *Myrtle Beach,* 3 mi. S of Myrtle Beach on US 17; *N. R. Goodale,* 2 mi. N of Camden off US 1; *Oconee,* 12 mi. NW of Walhalla off Rte. 28; *Paris Mountain,* 9 mi. N of Greenville off US 25; *Pleasant Ridge,* 22 mi. NW of Greenville off US 25; *Poinsett,* 18 mi. SW of Sumter off State 261; *Rivers Bridge,* 7 mi. SW of Ehrhardt off State 64; *Sadlers Creek,* 13 mi. SW of Anderson off US 29; *Santee,* 3 mi. NW of Santee off US 301; *Sesquicentennial,* 13 mi. NE of Columbia on US 1; *Table Rock,* 16 mi. N of Pickens off State 11; *Woods Bay,* 2½ mi. S of Olanta on US 301.

 CAMPING OUT. South Carolina's commercial campgrounds and state parks are available from the mountains to the sea, offering to the camper the crisp air of the Blue Ridge Mountains or a quiet seaside beach. Camping fees at all state parks are $5.50–$9.50 a day per family for each site. Obtain permit from Park Superintendent before setting up camp. No advance reservations. One week maximum stay. For complete listing, write for booklet, "Mountains, Beaches, Lakes, and Other Places to Camp in South Carolina," S.C. Dept. of Parks, Recreation and Tourism, Edgar A. Brown Bldg., Suite 113, 1205 Pendleton St., Columbia, S.C. 29201.

All commercial campgrounds provide electrical and water hookups, showers and toilet facilities. Added attractions such as swimming and fishing are offered at the following campgrounds: *Lake Hartwell KOA Kampgrounds,* Rte. 3, Anderson; *Charleston's Kampgrounds of America,* US 78, Ladsdon 29456; *Wagon Wheel CG,* Dillon, 6 mi. N on US 301; *Swamp Fox,* on I-95 (Hwy 76, Exit 157), Florence; *Rocks Pond CG,* Eutawville; *Lake Murray Family CG,* State 1, Gilbert; *Lake Pines KOA Kampground,* Hardeeville, 2 mi. N. on US 17; *Apache Family CG,* Star Rte. 2, Myrtle Beach; *Lake Arrowhead CG,* Star Rte. 2, Myrtle Beach; *Lakewood Family CG,* US 17 S, Myrtle Beach; *Pirateland Family CG,* US 17 S, Myrtle Beach; *Sherwood Forest CG,* US 17 N, Myrtle Beach; *Birch Canoe Family CG,* Myrtle Beach, US 17 & 5th Aves.; *Holiday Inn Trav-L-Park,* Myrtle Beach, 9 mi. N off US 17; *Ocean Lakes Family CG,* Myrtle Beach, 5 mi. S. on US 17 at intersection of Rte. 375; *Pebble Beach Family CG,* Myrtle Beach, on Rte. 73 (S. Ocean Blvd.); *Ponderosa Family CG,* Myrtle Beach, 10 mi. N on US 17; *Springmaid Family CG,* Myrtle Beach, S. Ocean Blvd; *Riverside Family CG,* N Myrtle Beach, 2 mi. off US 17 on Little River Neck Rd.; *Sweetwater Lake CG,* 3½ mi. from I-26, just off US 21 near Orangeburg and St. Matthews (exit I-26 onto Rte. 22, proceed 2 mi. turn right onto Sweetwater Rd. and follow signs). *Harry's Fish Camp and CG,* Pineville, off Rte. 45; *Holiday Inn Trav-L-Park of Santee-Lake Marion,* Box 520, Sumter; *Shawnee CG,* P.O. Box 137, Santee; *Santee-Lake KOA Kampgrounds,* Rte. 3, Box 84, Summerton; *Woodland Park CG,* York, 8 mi. W on Rte. 5.

Camping areas and trailer stopovers are maintained also at the Francis Marion National Forest, rich in historical background; Cherokee Indians, colonial settlements, Revolutionary War battles and the War Between the States all left their influence on the forest areas.

TRAILER TIPS. The following trailer parks have hookup facilities for travel trailers: *Pine Acres Mobile Home Park,* Aiken, 1 mi. N on US 1; *The Windmill,* Bamberg, 12 mi. S on US 301 at jct. of State 64; *Rainbow Trailer Court,* 5020 Rivers Ave., 11 mi. NW on US 52, Charleston; *Crosby's Texaco,* Coosawhatchie, on US 17; *Esso Trailer Park,* Coosawhatchie, on US 17; *Johnson's Trailer Park,* 106 New St., 1 mi. N on US 301 and US 76, Florence; *Lockhaven Camper's Court,* 7 mi. S on I-95 at Interchange of State 403, Florence; *Munnerlyn's Trailer Park,* Rte. 4, 3 mi. N on US 301, Florence; *Rainbow Mobile Home Estates,* 3 mi. N on US 29, Greenville; *Fairway Trailer Park,* 1 mi. S on US 301, Manning; *Pine-View Mobile Home Park,* 10 mi. N on US 501, Myrtle Beach; *Carolina Wren Motel and Trailer Park,* 2 mi. N on US 301, Orangeburg; *Bennett's Trailer Park,* 3 mi. N of US 15, Walterboro; *North Walterboro Trailer Park,* Rte. 2, 3 mi. N on US 15, Walterboro; *Moore Mobile Manor,* 160 Oakwood Dr., Intersection of I-26 and US 378, West Columbia.

MUSEUMS AND GALLERIES. *Beaufort: Beaufort Museum.* Craven St. Donation requested.

Charleston: Charleston Museum, 360 Meeting St. at John St. The oldest municipal museum in the United States, now in splendid new quarters, houses exhibits of pre-Columbian Indian weapons and artifacts and South Carolina history and culture; it also contains exhibits of Confederate and Naval history with the focal point a replica of the Confederate States Submarine *Hunley,* which was the first submarine to sink a surface vessel. There are also planetarium shows. Admission. *Old Slave Mart Museum and Galleries,* 6 Chalmers St. Numerous artifacts of black life and history. Small admission charge. *City Hall Council Chamber,* corner of Broad & Meeting Sts. Portraits of many important leaders, including George Washington. Free. *Old Powder Magazine,* 79 Cumberland St. Built about 1713 near the city's outer wall, the museum is made of bricks cemented with oyster shell mortar. Mon. to Fri. Closed Sept. Small admission charge. *Charles Towne Landing Exposition,* 1500 Old Towne Rd. An exciting 300-acre exhibition park located on the site of the first permanent settlement in South Carolina. Features movies, exhibits and an Animal Forest with species indigenous to South Carolina in 1670 displayed in their natural habitat. Daily. Small admission charge. *The Confederate Museum,* 188 Meeting St., a military museum. Small admission charge. *Citadel Archives Museum,* The Citadel, a military museum. Free. *South Carolina Historical Society,* 100 Meeting St. Free.

Clemson: Fort Hill (Home of John C. Calhoun), Clemson University. Free. *Hanover House,* Clemson University. Closed Mon. Free.

Columbia: Columbia Museum of Art and Science, 1112 Bull Street, Italian Renaissance paintings from the famous collection of Samuel H. Kress Foundation; silver, miniatures, jewelry, pottery, and furniture from the historic heritage of Columbia and South Carolina are permanently displayed. Also exhibits of the sciences, natural history, art and history. Planetarium is also a feature here (small admission fee). Open Tues. to Sat. *Midlands Exposition Center, South Carolina State Historical Museum,* 1615 Blanding St. A general museum housed in 1820 Hampton-Preston mansion. Children free. *South Carolina Confederate Relic Room and Museum,* World War Memorial Bldg., Sumter at Pendleton. A history museum open Mon. to Fri.; by appointment only on Sat. Check for closing dates. Free.

Florence: Florence Museum, 558 Spruce St. A general museum. Closed holidays. Free. *Georgetown: The Rice Museum,* Front & Screven Sts. A history museum housed in the Old Market Bldg. (1835), located on the site of the Old Market. Small admission. *Greenville: Greenville County Art Museum,* 420 College St., has nation's largest collection of Andrew Wyeth paintings, other permanent North American collections, numerous changing exhibits, lectures, concerts.

Free. *Greenwood: The Museum,* 102–103 Main St. A general museum. Closed Christmas, Easter, and Thanksgiving. Free.

Lancaster: Andrew Jackson State Historical Park, 8 mi. N on US 521. The park contains a museum. Free. Open Mon.-Sat. *Rock Hill: Museum of York County,* Mt. Gallant Rd., 7 mi. NE off SC 161. One of the nation's finest regional natural history museums, its Maurice Stans African Hall has the world's largest collection of mounted African animals in environmental settings. Rte. 4, Box 211. Free. Closed Mon. *Spartanburg: Spartanburg County Regional Museum,* 501 Otis Blvd. Closed Mon. and national holidays. Free.

Art Galleries. *Charleston: Gibbes Art Gallery,* 135 Meeting St. Closed Mon., nat'l. hol. Free. *Clemson: Rudolph Lee Gallery,* College of Architecture, Lee Hall, Clemson University. Free. *Greenville: Bob Jones University Collection of Sacred Art,* at Bob Jones University. Closed Mon. and holidays. Free. *Sumter: Sumter Gallery of Art,* 421 N. Main St. Open daily. Free.

Special Interest Museums. *Florence: Florence Air and Missile Museum,* on US 301, 2 mi. N of Florence. Open daily. Admission. *Myrtle Beach: South Carolina Hall of Fame,* Myrtle Beach Convention Center. Astronaut Col. Charles M. Duke, Jr., a member of the Apollo 16 team that went to the moon in 1973, was the first member of the Hall of Fame. Open Mon. to Fri., *Guinness Hall of World Records, Ripley's Believe It or Not Museum. St. Matthews: Calhoun County Museum,* Railroad Ave., in the Calhoun County Library. Open Mon. to Fri. also by appointment. *Darlington: The Joe Weatherly Stock Car Museum,* at Darlington Raceway. Open daily May to Sept.; (except holidays) Mon. to Fri. the rest of the year. Closed Sat. and holidays. Free.

 HISTORIC SITES. Historic Camden, easily accessible from US 521 & 1, is a restoration of the Revolutionary period. When the British left Camden in 1781, they left behind swords, muskets, cannon balls and other valuable pieces of history. They also left remains of the old town wall and six surrounding forts, the Kershaw house which General Cornwallis used as his headquarters and a large powder magazine. Visitors can find out about the town, the people and the battles in two restored log houses filled with unique museum exhibits. Walk through the restoration site along winding trails lined with historic markers, take a bicycle tour or go on an electric cart. Closed Mon. Small admission charge.

Charleston, site of the first settlement and where the "first shot" of the Civil War was fired, is rich in historical sites. Its many and varied historic sites are listed in brochures which may be obtained from the Charleston Convention & Visitors Bureau, P.O. Box 834, Charleston 29402. *Fort Sumter National Monument,* in Charleston Harbor, may be reached by boats operated by Fort Sumter Tours from Municipal Marina throughout the year. Trips per day vary. Monument open daily. Free. Gray Line Water Tours has a two-hour water tour that passes fort; passengers do not disembark.

Many historic churches may be seen in Charleston: *First Baptist Church,* 61-65 Church St., the oldest Baptist congregation in South Carolina, the present church begun in 1819. *St. Michael's Episcopal Church,* S.E. corner of Broad & Meeting Sts. The first service was held Feb. 1, 1761. Its bells have crossed the Atlantic Ocean five times. George Washington and Marquis de Lafayette both worshipped here when visiting Charleston. *French Huguenot Church,* S.E. corner of Church & Queen Sts., site of three successive Huguenot Churches. The present edifice, begun in 1844, was designed by Edward Brickell White. Only Huguenot church in America adhering exactly to the liturgy of the French Protestant Church. *St. Philip's Protestant Episcopal Church,* Church St., north of Queen. The present building was begun in 1835. In its two cemeteries lie many distinguished South Carolinians, including John C. Calhoun. *St. John's Lutheran Church,* 10-12 Archdale St., one block west of King. *Beth Elohim,* 90 Hasell St., the nation's oldest synagogue in continuous use.

Historic homes open to the public for a small admission fee in Charleston are: *Nathaniel Russell House,* 51 Meeting St. *Joseph Manigault House,* 350 Meeting St. May 2 to Feb. 28, Tues. to Sun. Mar. to Apr. daily. *Heyward-Washington House,* 87 Church St. Open year round. *Thomas Elfe House,* 54 Queen St. Open year round. The *Arch Building* was constructed in the early 1800's and used as a "public house" for wagon masters and their helpers coming through Charleston.

Also in Charleston, the *Dock Street Theatre,* a restoration of the oldest playhouse in America, is open Mon. to Sat., Oct. to May.

Columbia, the capital of the geographical center of the state, offers the visitor much to see and enjoy. Stop at the State House, recognized as "one of the notable buildings of the world," and enter through the north entrance at the corner of Main and Gervais Sts. Bronze stars mark spots where shells from Sherman's army struck during occupation of the city in 1865. It's open weekdays and Sat. Just across from the State House, on Sumter St., is *Trinity Cathedral* (Episcopal), built in 1812. In the churchyard near the famous old "Governor's Oak" are graves of five South Carolina governors and other prominent citizens. And just down a few blocks on Sumter Street, you can enter the noted "Horseshoe" of the University of South Carolina.

Other historic points of interest include: *First Baptist Church,* 1306 Hampton St., built in 1859. The first Secession Convention met here on Dec. 17, 1860, but was moved to Charleston due to a smallpox epidemic. *Robert Mills Historic House and Park,* a restoration. This showplace of national architectural significance was designed by the famous Washington Monument architect, Robert Mills. The mansion was built in 1823 for the merchant prince Ainsley Hall. Closed Mon. Small admission charge.

Historic Pendleton grew from a crossroads of the Cherokee Trading Path to the Low Country and the Catawba Trading Path into Virginia. In existence since 1790, early Pendleton was described as "a grand center of society and trade, one of the foremost pioneer towns in the South." The Pendleton District historically comprised the present-day counties of Anderson, Oconee and Pickens in the northwesternmost part of the state. Included in the Pendleton District are such places as *Farmer's Hall (1826)* oldest such hall in the nation; beautiful *St. Pauls Episcopal Church* (1822) with its hand-pumped organ and slave gallery; and Hunter's Store building (1850), where many items of past eras are on display.

Cowpens National Battlefield Site, 11 mi. NW of Gaffney and 18 mi. NE of Spartanburg is a 1½ acre area with a monument to commemorate the battle. Free. *Kings Mountain National Military Park,* south of the town of Kings Mountain, off I-85, has a museum and visitor center. Park and headquarters building, open daily. Closed Christmas. Free.

TOURS. *By boat: Charleston: Gray Line Harbor Tour:* 2¼ hours. Daily. Tour departs from the Gray Line Pier. *Chattooga River Rafting Adventures,* Long Creek. Shoot the rapids on guided 7-hr. raft trip. All equipment and lunch furnished. Two-week advance reservations required. Wknds in May and Sept.; daily during summer months.

By bus: Gray Line Bus Tour of Historic Charleston. 2¼-hr. tours originate from the Francis Marion Hotel. Daily.

By train: Departing each morning and afternoon, the *Georgetown Historic Tour Train* provides guided tours of the original Old Georgetown. The train leaves the Chamber of Commerce building, located at 600 Front St. For further information, contact the Chamber of Commerce, Front St., Georgetown, S. C.

On foot: Charleston Walking Tours offers an interesting self-guided tour through old historic Charleston. Pamphlets may be obtained at the Charleston Visitor Information Center, 85 Calhoun St.

Others: Golden Leaves Tour, Table Rock State Park, cycling tour of the beautiful South Carolina mountain country takes place annually in Oct. Cyclists camp out Fri. night at the park, ride 60 mi. Sat. and 40 mi. Sun.

 SPECIAL INTEREST TOURS. *Trails:* Retrace the flight of the President of the Confederacy, Jefferson Davis, through South Carolina after the fall of Richmond in 1865. The *Jefferson Davis Trail* winds through small towns, farmland, forests and rolling hills removed from interstate travel. Much of the countryside on this Trail has changed so little since the nineteenth century that the visitor feels like he is going back through time.

Along the route the visitor will see "CS" signs keyed to a printed guide with special points of interest marked with numbered signs. Guide and sign numbers start at the northern border of South Carolina, where Jefferson Davis entered above Fort Mill.

Another tour which is distinctively signed is the *George Washington Trail.* When President Washington visited South Carolina in 1791, he followed the old King's Highway down the East Coast. This route is marked as the Coastal Section of the George Washington Trail from the South Carolina Welcome Center near Little River on US 17 to Savannah, where the President crossed over into Georgia. The Central Section of the Trail follows the route the President followed when he returned to South Carolina at the present town of North August. The Washington Trail is clearly marked with distinctive "Washington Coach" signs.

To obtain brochures which show the routings of both the Jefferson Davis Trail and the George Washington Trail write: South Carolina Dept. of Parks, Recreation and Tourism, Edgar A. Brown Bldg., Suite 113, 1205 Pendelton St., Columbia, S.C. 29201.

Georgetown has tours of *plantations and town houses* sponsored by the Women of Prince George, Winyah Episcopal Church. These annual tours are held in the second week of April. The plantations and houses, many over a hundred years old, are privately owned and are open to the public only at this time each year. Tours take a different route daily, showing plantations along the Black, Pee Dee, Santee, and Waccamaw rivers. Plantations dating back to land grants from King George II retain names of ancestral homes of the founders from England and Scotland. At some, original slave quarters are still intact, and vestiges of the once powerful rice-planting industry are in evidence. Rice was the chief means of support for many years in thousands of coastal areas. Indigo culture, too, had a brief span of prosperity. Several plantation homes are maintained, in whole or in part, in the style of antebellum hospitality and luxurious living. Histories of the houses and maps showing the routes for the day are provided. Tours are not conducted, and visitors provide their own transportation. Only small buses can go on the tours because of many low-hanging oak limbs. *Hopsewee Plantation,* 12 mi. S on US 17. Open Tues.–Fri., Feb.–Oct. Closed holidays. Fee.

Churches, the parishes of which were established more than two hundred years ago, are also open to visitors. Visitors have an opportunity to see many beautiful pieces of silver used in church services for decades. Box lunches and tickets are on sale at the parish house, Highmarket St.

Greenwood: Annual Greenwood County Historical Homes Tour (usually in April) is sponsored by the Greenwood County Chamber of Commerce. For more information contact the Greenwood County Chamber of Commerce, 518 S. Main St., P.O. Box 980, Greenwood, S.C. 29646.

Charleston: Boone Hall Plantation, on US 17 8 mi. N of the city at Mt. Pleasant. Small admission charge. *Charleston Naval Base Tour* is offered year round each Sat. and Sun. Enter the Base at South Gate off Spruill Ave. The ships on display are designated and can be boarded and inspected by visitors.

Pendleton: Tours conducted by the Pendleton District Historical and Recreational Commission during the year feature many of Oconee County's Apple

Orchards. In the spring at blossom time and in the fall during the harvest, special apple tours are conducted by PDHRC. For more information on these tours, write Pendleton District Historical and Recreational Commission (PDHRC), 125 East Queen St., P. O. Box 234, Pendleton 29670.

GARDENS. *Charleston: Middleton Place,* one of the world's outstanding landscaped gardens, is America's oldest. It was begun by the Middleton family in 1741, and completed a decade later. The first camellias planted in the New World were brought to Middleton by Andre Michaux, the botanist. They line pathways, their petals dropping to form pink, white and striped carpets. In spring, azaleas blossom across the landscaped terraces, around butterfly lakes and along formal walks. At the Plantation Stableyards, a variety of domestic animals and barnyard fowl, as well as artifacts, tools and farm implements have been assembled to tell the story of the economy which supported the self-contained plantation communities of the 18th and 19th centuries. Separate admissions for stableyards and garden (one fee) and Middleton House. Special group rates. Open daily all year. Rte. 61, 15 mi. N of Charleston toward Summerville or just off I-26, Summerville exit. *Cypress Gardens* might be described as "mysterious," with its lagoons of black water, in which centuries-old cypress trees grow. Its islands and banks are studded with flowers. Floral displays begin with the camellias and daffodils, giving way in early spring to multihued azaleas. Boat or walking tours may be taken through Cypress. Restaurant for lunch and tea. Special rates for groups and military personnel. Boat tour extra. Beautifully refurbished. Now open year round. Off SC 52, from I-26, 23 mi. N of Charleston. *Magnolia Gardens* is a fairyland of flowers. It has a special charm and a spirit that often has an almost hypnotic effect on visitors. No camera has ever fully captured its grandeur, nor can words adequately describe it. Growing in Magnolia Gardens are camellias so old that they are now trees, forming part of its collection of over 500 varieties. Live oaks, hung with shadowy shawls of moss, and gnarled cypress complement the thousands of azaleas, flowering bulbs and shrubs and the trailing yellow jessamine (official state flower). Admission. Special group rates. Open daily all year. Rte. 61, 10 mi. N of Charleston toward Summerville, just off I-26, Summerville exit. *Hampton Park* adjoins The Citadel (South Carolina's military college). It occupies a part of the grounds that were devoted to the Interstate and West Indian Exposition (1901-2), in which 31 states and territories participated. Hampton Park has gorgeous displays of azaleas and other flowers, a sunken garden, a pool, rose-bordered walks, pavilions, aviary, and zoo. Open all year. Free.

Summerville: The azalea gardens of Summerville, planted informally, rival Charleston's on a much smaller scale. One of the main varieties of azaleas growing along the banks of the streams is the "Pride of Summerville," a pleasing shade of pink. Tall trees drip festoons of gray moss. The *Summerville Municipal Gardens,* near junction US 17 and 78, off I-26, are open all year, but the best season is spring. Free.

Georgetown: Belle Isle Gardens, off US 17, 5 mi. S of the city, is a 5,000-acre expanse of landscaped grounds planted in azaleas and other flora. It occupies old rice fields of a plantation. Located here was Battery White during the Civil War. Open every day except Christmas, Nov. to Aug. Admission charge.

Murrells Inlet: Brookgreen Gardens, US 17, 18 mi. S of Myrtle Beach, is an outdoor museum of sculpture. The gardens contain more than 350 pieces representing the history of American sculpture from the nineteenth century. Sculpture in the gardens includes works by Anna Hyatt Huntington who, with her husband, developed Brookgreen. Across the highway is "Atalaya," former home of the Huntingtons. The castle-like home is a part of Huntington Beach State Park. Open daily except Christmas. Admission.

Orangeburg: Edisto Gardens, US 301, 21, in a city park just off I-26, were created less than 40 years ago from a dismal, swampy area extending along the banks of the North Edisto River. Tall cypress, crabapple and flowering dogwood are surrounded by plantings of azaleas which reach their peak in April. Edisto has 6,000 rose bushes, and its 110 varieties provide a veritable mass of blooms from early spring until frost. Open all year. Free.

Sumter: Swan Lake Gardens are so called because of their beautiful black Australian and white muted English swans that live on the lake. The gardens also are noted for their six million Japanese irises, which reach full bloom in late spring and are the focal point for an annual "Iris Festival." The festival is held the last week in May. Free.

Darlington: Williamson Park, located just off Spring St. on the northeast side of Darlington-US 52; SC 34, 11 mi. from I-20, is municipally owned. It is planted with hundreds of native shrubs and flowers, including azaleas, camellias and irises. Open all year. Free.

Hartsville: in *Kalmia Gardens of Coker College,* Rte. 151, 2 mi. W of the city, 12 mi. from I-95, both Up Country and Low Country flora are found. Kalmia is a 24-acre arboretum with over 700 varieties of trees and shrubs. The dominant species, from which the gardens take their name, is Kalmia latifolia, the mountain laurel. The pale pastels of the blossoms range from white to rose-colored and have purple markings within; the terminal clusters of blossoms remind one of pink parasols. Open all year. Free.

Columbia: The gardens of the *State House* are pretty in every season. To be seen on the beautifully planted grounds, both alive and as a cast-iron replica, is the palmetto (sabal palm), South Carolina's official state tree. One block of Senate St. to the rear of the building, is lined with living palmettoes. The replica, created by South Carolina's famous ironsmith, Christopher Werner—who also designed the sword gates at the Sword Gate House in Charleston—is so realistic that birds build their nests in the fronds in springtime. The tree was erected as a memorial to South Carolinians who died in the Mexican War. The small garden of the *Columbia Museum of Art,* 1519 Senate St., is located in the rear of the Science Museum. It contains more than 50 species of native South Carolina flora and some fauna. The garden is divided into three sections, representing South Carolina's Low Country, Midlands, and Up Country, with flora representative of all. Open daily except Mon. 10 to 5; Sun. 2 to 6. Free. The grounds of the *University of South Carolina* contain two beautiful small gardens. At the horseshoe of the old campus on Sumter St. is the *Memorial Garden* in the rear of the South Carolina Library. Borders in the garden are defined by clipped hedges of dwarf holly. Year round bloom comes from azaleas, roses, camellias, and other flowers. The other garden, reached through a small doorway in the old brick wall on Pendleton St., between Marion and Bull, is landscaped with a fountain and formal beds of floribunda roses, bordered by sasanquas and azaleas. It is beautiful in spring. Open all year. Free.

 STAGE AND REVUES. In Columbia the *Town Theatre,* 1012 Sumter St. is one of the oldest little theater organizations in the nation. It has been in continuous operation since 1919. Six plays are performed annually. In Charleston is the *Dock Street Theater,* opened in 1736. Original scripts, Broadway plays, Shakespearean and 18th century classics are performed. For list and dates of presentation write: Charleston Convention Bureau, P.O. Box 834, Charleston, S.C. 29402.

 DRINKING LAWS. Mixed drinks may be purchased in licensed restaurants, hotels and motels. Liquor is served in a miniature bottle, which the purchaser may mix or have mixed according to his taste. Liquor is sold by the bottle in state-licensed package stores. Hours of operation are from sunrise to sunset. No sales on Sundays, election days, New Year's Day, July 4, Thanksgiving and

Christmas. Wine and beer are available in most restaurants, or may be purchased in grocery stores. Legal drinking age is 21, 18 for beer and wine. Spirits may not be brought in from another state.

SUMMER SPORTS. *Swimming, golf, fishing, surfboarding*—they're all there in addition to a background of white sand, warm sun and blue sky on South Carolina's beaches.

The Grand Strand, with Myrtle Beach at its center, is a sparkling 55-mile strip of sand and surf stretching from the quaint fishing village of Little River to historic Georgetown. Known as the Sun Fun Capital, the Grand Strand offers fine public beaches, a mild climate and unpolluted waters.

For the *golfer,* there are 36 courses that add as much fame to the Strand as the white beaches. Unlimited accommodations, superb dining facilities, attractive prices and the largest variety of courses of any resort in America have all contributed to the designation of the Strand as "The Coastal Golf Capital of the U.S.A."

Harbour Town Links, Hilton Head Island, ranks among the second ten of America's 100 greatest; Dunes G. & B.C., Myrtle Beach, among the fourth ten; and Greenville Country Club among the second fifty, according to "Golf Digest." Also recommended are two located in No. Myrtle Beach; five in Myrtle Beach; two in Ocean Drive Beach; two in Charleston; 11 on Hilton Head Island; Wild Dunes, on The Isle of Palms; two in Aiken; and courses on Pawley's Island; Crescent Beach; Litchfield Beach; Fripp Island; Columbia; Santee; and Florence.

For the *fishing* enthusiast, the Strand offers many fishing piers. Or anglers can join the host of visitors surf-fishing. And charter boats for deep-sea fishing are available all along the Strand.

Charter boats for deep-sea fishing from Charleston provide rods, reels and bait.

South Carolina's streams, lakes and rivers offer the avid angler the opportunity to catch rainbow and brown trout in the mountainous areas of the western counties—Oconee, Pickens and Greenville. Or one may choose the Santee—Cooper Lakes, which are most noted for their nationally famous landlocked striped bass.

Charleston boasts four excellent beaches where *surf-bathing* and *water sports* are enjoyed. Folly, Sullivans Island, Isle of Palms and Edisto attract thousands of visitors each season. Attractive cottages are available by the week, month or season. The posh new 1,500-acre Wild Dunes Beach and Racquet Club, recently opened on the Isle of Palms, is the newest addition to the state's roster of fine coastal resorts.

Luxurious, beautiful Hilton Head Island offers the ultimate in accommodations, food, golf and subtropical beaches. There are 12 public golf courses on the Island, including the Harbour Town Golf Links where the annual Heritage Golf Classic is staged each spring.

Hilton Head offers a wide variety of fishing pleasures—a variety in both species and habitat. From the wide beaches for surf-fishing to the quiet saltwater lagoons, a fisherman will find a variety of catches. Also challenging are the bays and saltwater creeks and the warm Gulf Stream waters where big game fishing takes place.

Fishing boats and guided charter boats are available and fishing tackle is included in the charter boat rate.

WINTER SPORTS. *Hunting* in South Carolina is both a tradition and a sport. Alligators and all birds of prey are protected and may not be hunted. Deer, fox, mink, muskrat, oppossum, otter rabbit, racoon, skunk and squirrel may be hunted in season and within bag limits. Domestic game birds include the wild turkey, mourning dove, bobwhite quail, ruffed grouse, Wilson snipe, woodcock, marsh hen and duck.

SPECTATOR SPORTS. *Aiken: Polo* can be enjoyed each Sun. afternoon from March through part of April. Admission. *Beaufort:* the *South Atlantic Sailing Regatta* is held during the Beaufort Water Festival in mid-July.

SHOPPING. Handcrafted rope hammocks can be purchased at various shops on Pawley's Island on U.S. 17.The craft came from Africa and was practiced by ancestors of the craftsmen in the shop. Other handicrafts are also on display.

Basket weaving can be seen along US 17, north of Charleston. Numerous stands display this African craft.

In Charleston, *Historic Charleston Reproductions,* 105 Broad St., and *The Thomas Elfe Workshop,* 54 Queen St., have reproductions of Charleston furniture and accessories, porcelains, brass, china, lamps, crystal, silver, pewter. You'll also find woven seagrass and palmetto baskets at the *City Market.*

WHAT TO DO WITH THE CHILDREN. *Carowinds,* a magic-land theme park designed for family entertainment, is 85 miles north of Columbia. Follow US 21 N to Rock Hill and then I-77 to the park. On the border of the Carolinas, it's actually an "inter-state" park, shared by North and South Carolina. In 73 acres of excitement, Carowinds combines the thrills of over 100 rides and attractions with exhibits and settings that re-create the culture and heritage of the Carolinas. Plantation Square, Queen's Colony, Indian Thicket, Country Crossroads, Pirate Island, Frontier Outpost and Contemporary Carolinas are the theme areas that take you from yesterday to tomorrow. An authentic narrow-gauge steam locomotive encircles the park and a sleek monorail offers automated transportation. Brand new "Smurf Island" enchants the younger set. All rides, shows, exhibits and attractions are included in the price of a ticket. Camping facilities are available. Rock Hill offers motels and good restaurants. For rates and information: Group Sales, The Carowinds Corp., P.O. Box 15514, Charlotte 28210.

Keowee-Toxaway Visitors Center, north of Clemson and accessible from State Rtes. 130 and 183, is the focal point for visitors to one of the largest nuclear generating stations. The modernistic center uses colorful, animated displays and exhibits to take visitors on a magical trip through the history of energy. It is unique in that the displays involve the visitor in what is being seen. A working waterwheel, a thunderstorm and other reality exhibits create an environment not possible with static displays. Free.

Middleton Place Gardens and Plantation Stableyards, on State 61, 16 mi. north of Charleston and US 17 toward Summerville. At the Stableyards, youngsters can see domestic animals such as sheep, cows, pigs, horses, chickens, and peacocks, and take a ride in a mule-drawn wagon. Open daily, year-round. Admission charge.

Historic Camden, on US 521 in Camden, offers Revolutionary War museum exhibits, bicycle and electric cart tours, and a petting zoo for kids. Closed Mondays unless a holiday. Admission.

Also: A "family fun mecca," *Myrtle Beach* offers Guinness Hall of World Records; Magic Harbor family entertainment park, with rides, ice skating, water slide, games pavilion, country music and puppet shows; Ripley's Believe It or Not Museum, Wild Rapids and Water Boggan water slides; and Grand Prix, with racing on real race cars, bumper boats and go-karts. *Brookgreen Gardens* features a zoo completely stocked with local coastal animals and fowl. Open 9:30 to 4:45. *Charles Towne Landing,* 1500 Old Town Rd., Charleston, features an Animal Forest with animals native to South Carolina in 1670, displayed in their natural surroundings. Open daily. Admission; 5 and under free. *The National Fish Hatchery,* Lakeview Dr., Orangeburg, is open daily. Free. The *Walhalla Federal*

Fish Hatchery, in the Sumter National Forest, approx. 19 mi. NW on Rte. 107, Walhalla, is open daily. Free. *Riverbanks Zoological Park,* 500 Wildlife Pkwy., Columbia, has daily penguin and sea lion feedings.

 **HOTELS AND MOTELS.** You'll find an excellent selection of accommodations in this hospitable state. Facilities range from economy-priced motels to luxurious motor inns and hotels. Several of the idyllic sea islands dotting South Carolina's Atlantic coast are home to some of this nation's finest and most luxurious resort developments.

Accommodations are listed according to their category. Based on double occupancy, price categories and ranges are as follows: *Deluxe,* $70–$150 *Expensive,* $55–$70; *Moderate,* $35–$55; and *Inexpensive,* under $35. For a more complete explanation of hotel and motel categories see *Facts at Your Fingertips* at the front of this volume.

Anderson

Howard Johnson's Motor Lodge. *Inexpensive to Moderate.* US 76 and SC 28, jct. I-85. 10 min. from airport and downtown. Cocktail lounge and restaurant, pool, golf privileges.

Holiday Inn. *Moderate.* 3025 N. Main St. Restaurant, lounge. Color TV, pool, wading pool, playground.

Best Western University Inn. *Inexpensive to Moderate.* 3430 Clemson Blvd. Under 12, free. Pool. Pets. Café and lounge. Entertainment and dancing.

Thunderbird Motor Lodge. *Inexpensive.* 110 Sharp St. Free coffee in rooms. Pool.

Days Inn. *Inexpensive.* I-85 and SC 187. Pool, play area, gift shop, some efficiencies. *Tasty World* restaurant.

Beaufort

Best Western Sea Island Motel. *Moderate.* 1015 Bay St. Attractive motel facing the Bay has color TV, swimming pool, restaurants.

Ramada Inn. *Moderate.* 3127 Boundary St. Entertainment, cocktail lounge, restaurant. Swimming pool. Rooms for handicapped.

Budget Host—The Pines Motel. *Inexpensive.* Jct. US 21 & SC 170. Color cable TV, pool. Large landscaped grounds. Hot sandwiches, soft drinks on premises; near restaurants. Pets. A Budget Host Inn.

Lord Carteret Motel. *Inexpensive.* 301 Carteret St. Kitchenettes available. Refrigerators. Pets.

Camden

Holiday Inn. *Moderate.* I-20 Exit 92, 2½ mi N. on US 601 N, Lugoff, S.C. Color cable TV. Restaurant. Kennel. Pool (heated). Golf privileges.

Hampton Park Inn. *Inexpensive.* 322 DeKalb St. Color TV, dining room. Pool.

Mona Lisa. *Inexpensive.* 1011 W. DeKalb St. Pleasant rooms. Restaurant. Pets. Pool.

Charleston

Battery Carriage House. *Deluxe.* 20 S. Battery St. Delightful small luxury guest house has 10 beautifully furnished antebellum apartments, all with kitchen facilities. Color TV, continental breakfast, bicycles for touring city.

The Coach House. *Deluxe.* 39 East Battery. First floor of each unit has bedroom with queen-size canopy bed, kitchen, dining area; second floor has twin beds, living room with queen-size pullout sofa bed, and piazza overlooking harbor. Color TV and books on each floor. Continental breakfast. Dog house within dog yard.

The Elliott House Inn. *Deluxe.* 78 Queen St. 1861 structure houses 26 rooms, each with distinctive 18th-century style furnishings. Continental breakfast brought to rooms on silver trays or served *al fresco* in bricked courtyard. Sip wine by the fountain at twilight as St. Michael's Church chimes toll the hour. Courtyard jacuzzi, complimentary bicycles.

Indigo Inn. *Deluxe.* Pinckney at Meeting. In heart of historic district, Inn offers 18th-century ease, 20th-century comfort. Continental breakfast, daily newspapers are provided.

Lodge Alley Inn. *Deluxe.* Lodge Alley. Rooms, suites, and two-bedroom penthouse reflect Colonial ambiance. Oriental carpets, period reproductions, courtyard gardens. *French Quarter Restaurant, Charleston Tea Party Lounge* on premises.

Mills House Hotel. *Deluxe.* 115 Meeting St. Antique furnishings, glowing chandeliers give unusual charm and ambience to historic hostelry, reconstructed with all 20th-century amenities. Beautifully furnished lobby, guest rooms. Lounge, live entertainment, pool. Part of Holiday Inn system.

Planters Inn. *Deluxe.* 110 N. Market St. (Market at Meeting St.). This exceptional hostelry's 46 guest rooms and suites are magnificently decorated with opulent fabrics and furnishings, including mahogany four-poster beds and marble baths. Nightly extras ice, spare pillows, Italian chocolates. Guests' freshly polished shoes are delivered with complimentary newspapers in the morning. Concierge, 24-hour room service. In the heart of Charleston's historic district, the Planters Inn opens onto the 18th-century City Market.

Sheraton-Charleston Hotel. *Deluxe.* 170 Lockwood Dr., 1 blk. N. of U.S. 17. City's newest luxury hotel is elegantly furnished, has own concierge. Heated outdoor pool, jogging track, lighted tennis courts, golf privileges. Dining rooms, entertainment in lounge.

The Sweet Grass Inn. *Deluxe.* 23 Vendue Range. Eight distinctively furnished guest rooms in completely restored ca. 1800 house. Rooms complimented with fresh flowers and fruit. Free morning newspaper. Relax around open-hearth living-room fire or sun on the roof terrace on balmy days.

Swordgate Inn. *Deluxe.* 111 Tradd St. Several rooms available in small intimate inn off courtyard of 18th-century house. No credit cards.

Vendue Inn. *Deluxe.* 19 Vendue Range. Luxurious guest rooms feature canopied and poster beds. Oriental rugs, 18th-century furniture. Complimentary wine and cheese served in courtyard. Continental breakfast.

The Francis Marion. *Expensive.* 387 King St. This conveniently located land-mark hotel has been impeccably restored and refurbished. Extras, at no charge, include daily cocktail party with *hors d'ouevres* at the piano bar, a liqueur or cocktail nightcap, morning paper at your door, full breakfast in Cafe Marion or in-room Continental breakfast, and concierge service. A Ramada Hotel.

Best Western King Charles Inn. *Moderate to Expensive.* 237 Meeting St. Dining room, pool, cocktail lounge, entertainment, dancing. Color TV. Handicapped facilities.

Days Inn. *Moderate.* 155 Meeting St. Well-maintained, two-story motor inn. Dining room. Pool. Golf privileges.

Heart of Charleston. *Moderate.* 200 Meeting St. Pool, coffee shop, cocktail lounge.

Days Inn. *Inexpensive.* I-26 & W. Montague Ave.; 260 Hwy. 17 Bypass, Mt. Pleasant. Restaurants—ask about "Kids Eat Free" programs; senior citizen discounts.

Econo Lodge. *Inexpensive.* 5169 Rivers Ave.; 4500 Arco Lane; 2237 Savannah Hwy. Color TV. Pets. Retaurant adjacent.

Clemson

The Clemson House. *Moderate.* Hwys. 76 & 123. Operated by Clemson University.

Holiday Inn of Clemson. *Moderate.* US 123 and 76. Restaurant, lounge, pool. Color TV. On Hartwell Lake; marina, boating, fishing. Golf privileges.

Columbia

Columbia Marriott Hotel. *Deluxe.* 1200 Hampton St. at Main St. Indoor pool, whirlpool. 2 dining rooms, lounge.

Carolina Inn. *Expensive.* 937 Assembly St. Dining room. Pool. Pets. Entertainment.

Holiday Inn. *Moderate to Expensive.* Three locations. All have restaurant, pool, kennels. **Northwest:** US 1 jct. I-26. Free airport transportation. Live entertainment. Playground. **City Center:** 630 Assembly St. Live entertainment. **Northeast:** Jct. I-20 & US 1. Game room, in-room movies. Sauna, whirlpool, putting green.

Ramada Inn. *Moderate to Expensive.* US 378 at I-26. Spacious, comfortable rooms. Suites. Gourmet restaurant, nightly entertainment. Pool. Pets.

Best Western Inn. *Moderate.* Two locations: 4502 Devine St., I-26 and SC 302. Both have restaurants, lounges, pools. I-26 Inn has live entertainment, is near Riverbanks Zoo.

Howard Johnson's. *Moderate.* Two locations. Both have rooms with balconies or patios, restaurant, pool, play area. **North:** Bush River Rd., jct. I-26 and I-20; **West:** Knox Abbott Dr. & State St. Poolside service.

Quality Inns. *Moderate.* Two locations: I-10 at Broad River Rd.; I-20 at Two Notch Rd (US 1). Color cable TV, some kitchenettes. Pools, restaurants, lounges. Handicapped facilities.

Tremont Motor Inn. *Inexpensive to Moderate.* 111 Knox Abbott Dr. Coffee shop. Playground. Some refrigerators. Pool.

Days Inn. *Inexpensive.* Two locations: Jct. I-26, S.C. 302, I-20. U.S. 1. *Tasty World* restaurant. Pool.

Greenville

Hyatt Regency Greenville. *Deluxe.* 220 N. Main St. Brand new luxury hotel has stunning eight-story atrium lobby, two elegant restaurants, two unusual lounges. Entertainment.

Sheraton Motor Inn. *Moderate to Expensive.* 1001 S. Church St. A six-story motor inn with very attractive rooms. Restaurant. Pool. Golf privileges. Small pets.

Sheraton-Palmetto Inn. *Expensive.* 4295 Augusta Rd., at Jct. US 25, I-85. Dining room, dancing, entertainment. Color TV, pool.

Best Western Greenville Inn. *Moderate.* 2800 Laurens Rd. Dining room, cocktail lounge. Pool. Pets.

Golden Eagle Motor Inn (Textile Hall). *Moderate.* 540 Pleasantburg Dr. A large motor inn with inviting rooms. Dining room. Pool. Entertainment. Free local calls.

Holiday Inn. *Moderate.* Two locations: 27 S. Pleasantburg Dr., and I-85 at Exit 46. Both have dining rooms, entertainment, pools, color TV, kennels.

Howard Johnson's Motor Lodge Central. *Moderate.* Church and Augusta Sts. (downtown). Lovely rooms. Restaurant. Pool. Play area. Pets.

Howard Johnson's Motor Lodge (South). *Moderate.* Jct. US 25 and 291. Dining room. Pool. Private patios and balconies.

Ramada Inn. *Moderate.* 1314 S. Pleasantburg Dr. Pool. Dining room, lounge, color TV. Pets.

Quality Inn Colonial. *Inexpensive to Moderate.* Wade Hampton Blvd. Nice rooms. Restaurant. Pool with service at poolside. Play area. Small pets.

Quality Inn Comfort Inn. *Inexpensive.* I-85 at US 25. Pool, in-room movies; fishing, golf, horseback riding, tennis nearby. Ask about family, senior citizen, blue-ribbon, military programs.

Hilton Head Island

Adventure Inn. *Deluxe.* South Forest Dr. Golf privileges. Villas, cabanas, 2-story resort homes. Pool. Kitchenettes available. Pets.

Hilton Head Inn. *Deluxe.* Oceanfront. Beautifully furnished rooms with contemporary decor, also villas and cottages. Dining rooms, lounges, entertainment. Pool. Complete resort facilities of Sea Pines Plantation: superb golf, tennis, children's programs. Numerous vacation packages.

Hyatt at Palmetto Dunes. *Deluxe.* Oceanfront. Superb resort hotel has fine dining in elegant Hugo's lounges, live entertainment, pool. Golf, tennis, all resort facilities at neighboring Palmetto Dunes.

Mariner's Inn. *Deluxe.* Oceanfront in Palmetto Dunes. All rooms are ocean view. Health club, pool, sauna, game room, volleyball, golf and tennis privileges. Fine seafood dining at Pisces, casual fare at *The Custom House. Lounges, nightly entertainment.*

Marriott's Hilton Head Resort. *Deluxe.* Oceanfront, in Shipyard Plantation. Dramatically beautiful new luxury hotel has spectacular five-story atrium lobby, fine dining rooms, lounges, pool bar, bar, exercise rooms, saunas. Golf, tennis at adjacent Hilton Head Golf and Racquet Clubs.

Holiday Inn. *Expensive to Deluxe.* Large motor hotel with comfortable rooms. Ocean view. Restaurant, disco, lounge. Golf, tennis, marina privileges.

Sea Crest Motel. *Moderate to Expensive.* Golf privileges, putting green. Oceanfront. Pool (heated). Kitchenettes available.

Isle of Palms

Wild Dunes Beach and Racequet Club. *Deluxe.* Choice new 1,500-acre resort 12 mi. N.E. of Charleston offers accommodations in luxurious villas. Tennis center, championship golf course, swim center, 2½-mile beach, fishing and sailing at club's marina on IntraCoastal Waterway. Fine dining at Edgar's.

Kiawah Island

Kiawah Island Inn. *Deluxe.* US 17 South and SC 20, P.O. Box 12910. Oceanfront setting on lush, wooded island. Accommodations in inn and villas. Excellent dining rooms, lounge, entertainment. Golf, tennis, children's programs, pools, bicycling, sauna, complete resort activities. Numerous vacation packages.

Myrtle Beach
(All rates higher during May 1-Labor Day season)

The Breakers Golf and Beach Lodge. *Expensive to Deluxe.* 2006 N. Ocean Blvd. Golf privileges. Oceanfront. Tennis. 2 pools. Dining room. Entertainment. Kitchenettes available.

Ocean Dunes. *Expensive to Deluxe.* 74th Ave. N. Golf privileges. Oceanfront. Tennis. Pool. Dining room. Entertainment.

Sea Mist Resort. *Expensive to Deluxe.* 1200 S. Ocean Blvd. Large motel on the ocean. Some efficiencies. Three pools. Putting green. Tennis. Play area. Beach, surf fishing. Restaurant. Golf Package Plan available.

Captain's Quarters Motor Inn. *Deluxe.* 901 S. Ocean Blvd. Very inviting rooms, all with refrigerator and private balcony. Rooftop coffee shop. Pool (heated). Beach. Shuffleboard. Play area. Fishing. Golf privileges. Golf and tennis Package Plans available.

Myrtle Beach Hilton Hotel. *Deluxe.* Beachside, in Arcadian Shores. Luxury resort hotel has 14-story atrium lobby. Continental dining in elegant *Alfredo's,* lounges, entertainment. Shopping, social program, tennis, golfing on championship course. All rooms oceanfront.

Sheraton Myrtle Beach Inn. *Deluxe.* 7100 N. Ocean Blvd. Superb dining, dancing in Pinnacle Supper Club. Lounges, entertainment, tennis club, golf privileges. All rooms oceanfront.

Caravelle Resort Motel. *Moderate to Deluxe.* 6900 N. Ocean Blvd. Golf privileges. Oceanfront. Tennis. Pool. Dining room. Kitchenettes available.

Patricia Inn and Court. *Moderate to Deluxe.* 2702 N. Ocean Blvd. On the ocean. Kitchens available. Pool (heated). Dining room. Game room. Golf privileges. Tennis.

Quality Inn Seagull. *Inexpensive to Expensive.* US 17 S. at Pawleys Island. Only motel on Grand Strand actually on golf course. 2 mi. to Ocean, 20 mi. to downtown Myrtle Beach. Golf at 25 local courses; putting green. Dining room, lounge, entertainment.

The Driftwood on the Oceanfront. *Inexpensive to Deluxe.* 1600 N. Ocean Blvd. Oceanfront motel. Spacious, attractive rooms. Efficiencies. Coffee shop. Pool (heated). Beach and surf fishing. Golf package plans available.

Ocean Reef. *Inexpensive to Deluxe.* 601 S. Ocean Blvd. On the ocean. Spacious rooms with refrigerators. Some suites, efficiencies. Coffee shop. Pool (heated), 18-hole putting green. Shuffleboard. Play area. Golf Package Plan available.

The Beach House Motor Inn. *Expensive.* 6800 N. Ocean Blvd. Golf privileges. Oceanfront. Heated pool. Free continental breakfast. Kitchenettes available.

Holiday Inn. *Moderate to Expensive.* Three locations. **Downtown:** 6th Ave. S. & Ocean Blvd. Entertainment, tennis, oceanfront. **North:** 2713 Ocean Blvd. S., North Myrtle Beach. On the ocean. Restaurant, entertainment, fishing facilities. **Surfside:** on US 17 at Ocean Blvd. Golf Package Plan available. Kennels.

Pan-American Motor Inn. *Expensive.* 5300 N. Ocean Blvd. Coffee shop. Oceanfront. Attractive rooms open onto private balconies. Pool. Tennis, golf privileges.

St. John's Inn. *Moderate to Expensive.* 6803 N. Ocean Blvd. at 69th Ave. Rooms decorated in Spanish motif with view of the garden or the ocean. Restaurant, bar with dancing and entertainment during season. Pool (heated). Beach across the road. Shuffleboard. Golf privileges.

Jade Tree Motor Inn. *Inexpensive to Expensive.* 5308 N. Ocean Blvd. Coffee shop. Golf privileges. Oceanfront. Heated pool. Playground.

Jamaican. *Inexpensive to Expensive.* 3006 N. Ocean Blvd. Kitchenettes available. Refrigerators in many rooms. Balconies. Pool.

Swamp Fox Motor Inn and Restaurant. *Inexpensive to Expensive.* 2311 S. Ocean Blvd. Oceanfront. Spacious rooms with private balconies. Some kitchens. Three pools. Putting green. Shuffleboard. Play area. Beach, surf fishing. Golf Package plan available.

Cherry Tree Inn. *Moderate.* 5400 N. Ocean Blvd. Oceanfront motel. Kitchens available. Pool (heated). Golf privileges. Golf Package Plan available.

Dunes Village Lodge. *Inexpensive to Moderate.* 5200 N. Ocean Blvd. Oceanfront. Apartments available. Tennis. Golf privileges. Heated pool. Dining room.

Lakeside Motel. *Inexpensive to Moderate.* 6805 N. Kings Hwy. Pool, playground, putting green, lawn games. Own lake, fishing, boating. Picnic tables. Family-oriented. Restaurant nearby.

Ocean Spray Motel. *Inexpensive to Moderate.* 1304 S. Ocean Blvd. Family oriented. Pools; restaurant adjacent.

Seabrook Island

Seabrook Island Club. *Deluxe.* Luxurious accommodations in fully equipped villas and cottages on resort island. Beach Club and Island House—open to all guests—are centers for gourmet dining and leisure activities. Championship golf courses, tennis center, water sports, equistrian center, bicycling. Children's programs in season, many vacation plans.

Spartanburg

Holiday Inn of Spartanburg. *Moderate.* Jct. I-85 and I-26. Dining room. Pool. Playground. Kennels.

Howard Johnson's Motor Lodge. *Moderate.* I-85, SC 56 at Hearon Circle exit 72C. Very pleasant rooms. Pool. Play area. Pets permitted. Complimentary coffee. Restaurant.

Ramada Inn. *Moderate.* 1000 Hearon Circle. Coffee shop. Meeting rooms. Pool. Playground. Pets.

TraveLodge. *Inexpensive to Moderate.* 416 E. Main St. Inviting rooms. Restaurant nr. Pool (heated). Pets.

Spartanburg Motor Inn. *Inexpensive.* 578 N. Church St. Comfortable rooms. Pool. Free coffee in rooms. Restaurant adjacent.

Sumter

Holiday Inn of Sumter. *Moderate.* 226 N. Washington St. Golf privileges. Pool. Restaurant. Kennel.

Mt. Vernon Inn. *Inexpensive.* Broad at Washington St. Nicely furnished rooms. Pool. Dining room. Golf privileges.

DINING OUT. South Carolina's traditions include a reputation for good food, with its table fare varying over the distinctive geographical sections of the state. Menus vary from country ham and grits with red-eye gravy in the Up Country, to the renowned "she-crab soup" of Charleston. But throughout the state you'll find many restaurants serving good food at economical prices.

Restaurants are listed according to their category. The categories and price ranges for a complete dinner are as follows: *Expensive,* $20 and up; *Moderate,* $10–$20. *Inexpensive,* under $10. For a more complete explanation of restaurant categories see *Facts at Your Fingertips* at the front of this volume.

Anderson

Best Western University Inn. *Moderate.* 3430 Clemson Blvd. Tasteful room, varied menu. Entertainment in lounge adjacent.

Holiday Inn. *Moderate.* 3025 N. Main St. American cuisine. Favorite with local groups. Entertainment in lounge.

Charleston

Barbadoes Restaurant-Mills House Hotel. *Expensive.* Queen and Meeting Sts. Gourmet/Continental cuisine in elegant surroundings. She-crab soup and lobster Calhoun lead on list of superior dishes. Jacket and tie at dinner.

The East Bay Trading Company. *Expensive.* East Bay and Queen Sts. Stately brick structure, former warehouse, features seafood, Continental and native cuisine on three levels wrapped around skylight-topped atrium. Antiques, artifacts, lavish greenery lend a warm, serene atmosphere.

Perdita's. *Expensive.* 10 Exchange St. Continental cuisine served in Old World atmosphere. Children's portions. Small, elegant, low key, this is one of the South's best dining rooms. Reservations essential!

Silks. The Planters Inn. 110 N. Market St. *Expensive.* Taking its name from the collection of racing silks and equestrian paintings hung throughout the bar and dining room, Silks features imaginative grilled game, beef, lamb, and seafood entrees. A superb collection of American and imported wines fills an entire wall.

The Colony House. *Moderate to expensive.* 35 Prioleau St. Specialty: Low Country dishes, seafood. Baked pompano is a favorite.

Henry's. *Moderate.* 54 Market St. Rambling, unpretentious restaurant is a great local favorite. Ask to be seated in the bar!

Trawler Restaurant. *Moderate.* US 17N. Mt. Pleasant. Family dining. Specialties: fish stew and shrimp à la Newburg.

A.W. Shuck's, Charleston's Oyster Bar. *Inexpensive to Moderate.* 70 State St., in historic Market area. Specialties are stuffed shrimp. Shuck's Casserole.

Harold's Cabin. *Inexpensive.* Meeting St. Piggly Wiggly. In-the-know Charlestonians drop by for lunch, and you should, too. Ideal place to shop for take-home treats.

Lorelei. *Inexpensive.* Shem Creek, US 17N. Family dining. Specialty is seafood.

Columbia

Chandelier Room. *Moderate.* In Carolina Townhouse, 1615 Gervais St. Elegant decor. Beef and seafood specialties. Salad bar.

The Lion's Head. *Moderate.* 741 Saluda Ave. Beef specialties, children's menu. Lounge. Locally popular, reservations necessary.

Stadium Steak House. *Moderate.* 402 Blossom St. Beef and steaks only. Outstanding bar. Evenings only.

The Market. *Moderate.* 1205 Assembly St. Convenient to major hotels. Large dining facilities, with excellent service. Steaks, seafood (red snapper and lobster). Children's portions.

Morrison's Cafeteria. *Inexpensive.* US 176, Dutch Square Mall. Member of one of South's leading chains. Does own baking. Roast beef a specialty.

Winner's Circle Restaurant. *Inexpensive.* 1111 Green St. Home cooking featuring Southern specialties. Local favorite.

Greenville

Ye Olde Fireplace. *Moderate.* 291 Pleasantburg Dr. Children's portions. Exceptionally well-prepared steak and seafood. Entertainment.

Vince Perone's Restaurants. *Moderate.* 1 E. Antrim Dr. Unusual combination of two quite different dining establishments. The Lighter Side features deli items. The elegant Forum offers superb Italian, Continental, seafood specialties, extensive wine list. Also, cocktails, lounge, dancing. Great local favorite. Reservations advised in The Forum.

Capri's. *Moderate.* Good Italian food at four locations.

Charcoal Steak Houses. *Moderate.* There are five of them with low lights, carpets and combo, great favorites. All about the same price and type.

Morrison's. *Inexpensive.* McAlister Square, Pleasantburg Dr. Branch of popular cafeteria chain serves lunch and dinner.

Hilton Head Island

Fulvio's. *Expensive.* 33 New Orleans Rd. Continental dining with emphasis on Italian specialties.

The Captain's Table. *Moderate to Expensive.* Sea Crest Motel, Coligny Circle. Superb gourmet dining room specializes in Continental European cuisine, lobster dishes. Dinner only. Reservations requested.

The Boilers. *Moderate.* U.S. 278, 1 mi. from bridge. Fine fresh seafood. Family favorite.

Hudson's. *Moderate.* Shrimp Docks, Skull Creek. Superb fresh seafood from own docks. Local favorite.

LTFG (Looks Terrible, Feels Great). *Inexpensive.* Heritage Plaza, Pope Ave. Sandwiches, soups, salads. Lunch and dinner.

Myrtle Beach

Christy's. *Moderate to Expensive.* 2 mi. S. on US 17. Crab au gratin, lobster and prime ribs are specialties. Background music, entertainment, dancing.

Slug's Rib. *Moderate to Expensive.* U.S. 17 N. Superb restaurant serves only one entree—prime rib of beef.

Crab House. *Moderate.* U.S. 17 N. on Restaurant Row. All-you-can-eat seafood. Casual dress.

Rice Planter's Restaurant. *Moderate.* 6707 N. Kings Highway (US 17). Delightful large establishment, but amazingly rapid service. Specialties: crab fingers, shrimp creole, pecan pie. Children's portions.

Sea Captian's House. *Moderate to Expensive.* 3002 N. Ocean Blvd. Informal restaurant at the edge of the ocean. Own pastries. Specialties: grasshopper pie and seafood. Children's portions. Lunch and dinner. Closed Dec. & Jan. Also at Murrells Inlet.

Hoskins Restaurant. *Inexpensive.* On US 301. Main St. N. Myrtle Beach, Maritime decor. Seafood, steaks, and Southern fried chicken for the entire family.

Western Steer Family Steak Houses. *Inexpensive.* Two locations: 512 Hwy. 17 S., 8000 Hwy. 17 N. Steak and seafood platters. Children's menu.

Spartanburg

Four Seasons Steak House. *Moderate to Expensive.* 880 S. Pine St. Features beef and fresh seafood. Children's plates. Reservations advised.

Piccadilly Cafeteria. *Inexpensive.* 166 Westgate Mall. Popular locally. Usual cafeteria specialties plus home baked breads, desserts.

TENNESSEE

Walking Horses and Moving Music

BY
JUSTIN FAHERTY

Justin Faherty is a former executive of the St. Louis Globe Democrat, *the New York* Herald Tribune, *and the Bergen (N.J.)* Record. *He has written for newspapers on all 50 of the United States.*

Tennessee is a magnificent outdoor playground, with mountains, picturesque, man-made lakes impounded by TVA dams, and the Great Smoky Mountains National Park, for years the nation's most heavily visited national park.

The mountains, reaching heights of more than 6,000 feet, are a part of the Appalachians. Their natural beauty is preserved along the Tennessee-North Carolina border by the Great Smoky Mountains National Park and the Cherokee National Forest, which the sprawling 514,669-acre Park splits into two sections.

Many southbound visitors will head directly for the Great Smoky Mountains National Park via Gatlinburg, the charming resort community that abuts the park entrance. Others will prefer a more leisurely course. For the latter, US 421 southeast thirty-two miles to Mountain City will provide arresting views of the lake impounded by TVA's South Holston Dam and the dam itself. US 421 crosses the Appalachian Trail. Turning southwest at Mountain City on State 67, the scenic-minded will be rewarded with views of mountain-cradled Watauga Lake, another

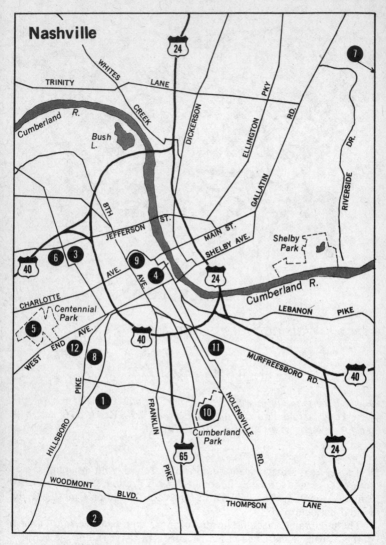

Nashville

Points of Interest

1) Belmont College
2) David Lipscomb College
3) Fisk University
4) Fort Nashborough
5) Greek Parthenon
6) Meharry Medical College
7) Opryland U.S.A.
8) Peabody College
9) State Capitol
10) State Fairgrounds
11) Trevecca College
12) Vanderbilt University

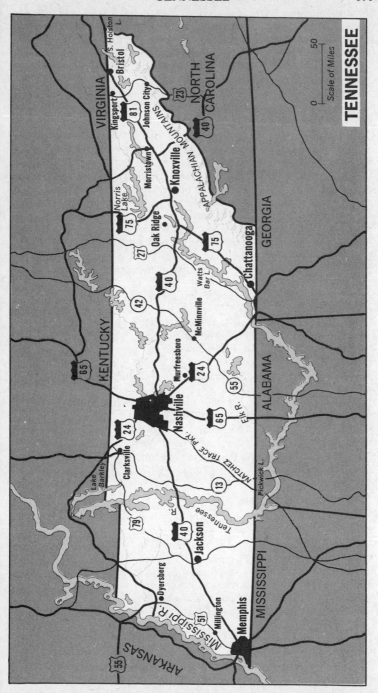

TVA impoundment, starting near Butler and continuing to the intersection with US 321. Proceeding on US 321, it is nine miles to Hampton. If you are here in early summer, turn south on US 19E and go thirteen miles to Roan Mountain. Atop the mountain marvel at the hundreds of acres of purple, rose-pink, and white rhododendron, which blossom between mid-June and early July.

From Roan Mountain return to Hampton, and then go six miles on US 321 to Elizabethton. It was here in 1772 that a group of settlers organized the Watauga Association and adopted a constitution—the first written document of its kind to be drawn up by freemen born on the American continent. A monument on the courthouse lawn commemorates the action.

It's nine miles from Elizabethton to Johnson City via US 321. Johnson City is a major burley tobacco auction market, as well as a railroad center. Two TVA dams are within easy driving distance, Boone and Fort Patrick Henry. Boone Dam, ten miles north, backs up a sixteen-mile-long lake. Fort Patrick Henry Dam, up the road, forms a ten-mile lake.

Tennessee Valley Authority lakes have a total shoreline of 10,000 miles, exceeding that of the Great Lakes. Fishing, boating, swimming and camping are permitted. Information is available from public safety officers at TVA dams.

Near Johnson City is one of Tennessee's oldest houses, Rocky Mount, seven miles northeast on US 19W, 411, and 11E. Those coming directly from Bristol on this multiple-number route will pass the two-and-a-half-story house, built in 1770 by William Cobb, a signer of the Articles of the Watauga. Twenty years later, when Tennessee became part of the territory of the United States south of the River Ohio, this house became Governor William Blount's headquarters and thus the new territory's first capitol.

South of Johnson City on US 411 and 11E is Jonesborough, oldest town in Tennessee, founded in 1779. The free state of Franklin was organized here in 1784 with John Sevier as governor. A twenty-one-year-old Andrew Jackson migrated here from North Carolina in 1788 to practice law for two years. Among the old buildings to see in this town is the Methodist Church, dating from 1845, at 215 W. Main Street.

Davy Was Born Here

On US 11E, near the little town of Limestone, is Davy Crockett Birthplace Park. On five acres along the Nolichucky River, the cabin where Crockett was born in 1786 has been reconstructed, a building for tourist information built, and pleasant picnic grounds provided. The limestone marker dates from the mid-1880's. Greeneville, twenty-two miles southwest of Jonesboro, was the home of Andrew Johnson, who became President following Lincoln's assassination. The city, founded in 1783, was named for Nathanael Greene, a general in the American Revolutionary War.

In downtown Greeneville, the town's most noted citizen is honored with the Andrew Johnson National Historic Site, containing his modest tailor shop and home and his burial place. Johnson's political career saw him successively as alderman, congressman, governor, senator, vice president, president, and then senator again.

From Newport, follow State 32 south to a junction with State 73, below Cosby, and then proceed southwest to Gatlinburg. This is real mountain driving, with hairpin turns and steep grades.

Visitors quickly see why the mountains got the name Great Smokies. A smoky blue mist is suspended above them much of the time. On clear days, it is possible to glimpse such famous peaks as Mt. Guyot (6,621 feet) and Mt. LeConte (6,593 feet).

Gatlinburg—Entrance to the Smokies

Gatlinburg lives for tourists. The attractive little city has a permanent population of approximately 3,000, yet it can accommodate 23,000 people per night in its several hotels and almost 150 motels. Crafts shops line its Main Street. As the western entrance to the Great Smoky Mountains National Park, it sees a major share of the park's more than 8,000,000 annual visitors.

Great virgin forests and wildflowers of incredible beauty cover the mountains, which have an altitude of 5,000 feet for thirty-six miles along the main crest. Sixteen peaks rise over 6,000 feet. The park is a glorious show of nature at any season, although some portions are closed in the wintertime. Summer and autumn are popular seasons.

From Gatlinburg drive southeast on US 441 to Newfound Gap for one of the most beautiful views of the park. For hikers or riders there are trails; the Appalachian Trail winds along the state line.

Among the attractions at Gatlinburg is the Sky Lift, a half-mile cable car ride up Crockett Mountain. There is skiing from mid-December through February at Ober Gatlinburg Ski Resort, and a double chair lift carries summer sightseers. In town, the American Historical Wax Museum features 120 historical figures grouped in appropriate scenes. In a more meditative vein, on River Road, there is Christus Gardens, where well-known incidents in the life of Christ are re-created by full-size wax models in a marble cloister.

New $10-million Gatlinburg Place on Airport Road offers a stunning IMAX film, "To Fly," along with a live musical program, "Pop Goes America," and an animated production, the "Backwoods Bear Jamboree."

Six miles north of Gatlinburg is Pigeon Forge, where visitors of all ages enjoy Silver Dollar City, a replica 1870's mountain community with working craftsfolk, along with thrill rides, oldtime music, and shows.

Old barns have a way of radically changing identities; one, on US 441, for years an old tobacco-curing barn, is now a pottery shop, Pigeon Forge Pottery. A second old building open to visitors is the Old Mill, which has been grinding away for at least 125 years.

If you follow State 73 west from Gatlinburg, you can take a short side trip to Cades Cove, a typical mountain settlement isolated from change until recent times. Many of the pioneer buildings remain or have been restored, and a meandering circle tour of the valley enables visitors to see the various points of interest easily. Cades Cove campground is a popular spot.

Return to State 73, proceed to the twin cities of Maryville and Alcoa. Maryville was a pioneer town. Sam Houston attended Maryville Academy (now Maryville College) here. Alcoa was founded in 1913 by the Aluminum Company of America.

En route to Knoxville, off US 129, you can visit the restored Sam Houston Schoolhouse, six miles northeast of Maryville. Houston, who taught at the school from spring until fall of 1812, later served as congressman from Tennessee and as the state's governor before moving on to Oklahoma and Texas.

Site of the gala 1982 World's Fair, Knoxville, on the Tennessee River, dates from 1786 and was named for Henry Knox, Secretary of War from 1785 to 1794. Catalyst for unprecedented downtown urban renewal, the 70-acre World's Fair site is being developed into an attractive permanent recreation area.

Antebellum Mansions

East Tennessee, mostly an area of small farms, was, in general, loyal to the Union. The siege of Knoxville in 1863 was a Confederate attempt to dislodge Union troops stationed there. After the war many of these Northern men returned to Knoxville to settle.

Knoxville grew rapidly and today is a city of varied industry, with textiles, marble, lumber and tobacco prominent in the economy. The University of Tennessee, TVA headquarters, and the Knox County seat are here.

Points of interest in the city range in time from territorial days to antebellum to modern. Knoxville's earliest link to the past is the Blount Mansion at 200 West Hill Avenue. It was built in 1792 for territorial governor William Blount.

Blount, a talented pioneer, was a member of the Continental Congress and the Constitutional Convention. He served under President Washington as a territorial governor and drafted Tennessee's first constitution. Upon Tennessee's admission to the Union he was elected to the United States Senate and served from Aug. 2, 1796 until his expulsion July 8, 1797. He was active in a plan to incite the Creeks and Cherokees to aid the British in conquering the Spanish territory of West Florida. During impeachment proceedings in Philadelphia, he was elected to the State Senate in Tennessee. When it convened, Dec. 3, 1797, he was chosen Speaker. He died in Knoxville, March 21, 1800, and is buried in the First Presbyterian Church Cemetery.

Attractions on the University of Tennessee campus include the Estes Kefauver Memorial Library, the Frank H. McClung Museum, and Neyland Stadium, home turf of the great Volunteer football teams. It has a seating capacity of 70,000.

The city's antebellum link is provided by Confederate Memorial Hall, 3148 Kingston Pike S.W., a beautiful mansion maintained by the United Daughters of the Confederacy.

Six miles northeast of Knoxville on Thorngrove Pike is the stately Ramsey House, built in 1797 by Francis Alexander Ramsey. Reputed to be the first stone house in Knox County, it is an excellent example of the finer homes that replaced log cabins in the late eighteenth century.

Top-Secret Town

Before heading south via US 11 to Chattanooga, visit Oak Ridge, once a top-secret atom bomb town. There are guided tours, demonstrations, and exhibits at the American Museum of Science and Energy on Jefferson Circle, conducted by the U.S. Atomic Energy Commission.

Nine miles south of Oak Ridge on State 95 is the Melton Hill Dam, a TVA dam finished in 1963. The dam forms a forty-four-mile-long lake and provides sufficient water for barge transportation to Clinton on the Clinch River, most upstream point on the TVA waterway system.

South on US 11, near Lenoir City, the motorist will come to Fort Loudoun Dam, another of the TVA constructions. There are docks and fishing facilities along the shore of its lake.

Continuing south, you pass through Athens and Cleveland. The latter is the gateway to three TVA dams that control the Ocoee River. If you're really adventurous, you can make arrangements in Cleveland with the game supervisor about hunting wild boar in the Cherokee National Forest.

US 11 leads on to Chattanooga, an attractive city set in the midst of steep mountain ridges. Great Indian trails joined here—the Great War Path over Lookout Mountain, the Shawnee Trail going north from Williams Island, and the Suck Creek Trail. Chattanooga became a Cherokee trading center, called Ross's Landing after the Scotch-Cherokees who were its operators. It was the starting point of the "Trail of Tears," when the Cherokees were forced in 1837 to move to lands west of the Mississippi.

In 1838, the name Ross's Landing was changed to Chattanooga, probably from a Creek word meaning "rock rising to a point."

Because of its strategic location, Chattanooga was an important prize in the Civil War; three battles were fought nearby, at Chickamauga Creek, Lookout Mountain, and Missionary Ridge. The eventual victory of Union forces in November, 1863, provided Sherman with a supply base for his Atlanta campaign.

South of the city, in Georgia, is the Chickamauga and Chattanooga National Military Park. Its nine separate parts include Point Park on Lookout Mountain, Signal Point on Signal Mountain, Missionary Ridge, Orchard Knob. Park Headquarters are just below Chattanooga in North Georgia, site of one of America's bloodiest battles—Chickamauga (34,-500 casualties in 3 days). Two thousand markers and monuments commemorate the men who died in these battles.

Civil War Battlegrounds

Chattanooga has a variety of attractions to offer the visitor. The movie *The Great Locomotive Chase* documented the role the locomotive *General* played in local Civil War history. Captain James J. Andrews, with twenty-one other Federal raiders, managed to seize the train near Marietta, Georgia, and move north along the track toward Chattanooga, destroying track and bridges as they went, while another Confederate engine, the *Yonah,* was gaining on them all the while. Andrews' raiders attempted to escape in the woods near the Tennessee line but all were captured.

In Chattanooga's beautifully preserved downtown Southern Railway Terminal, you can pay homage to its famed Choo-Choo and other vintage trains, browse through Victorian-era shops, and dine by gaslight in a huge 1,300-seat restaurant in the former lobby.

The top of Lookout Mountain, that "rock rising to a point," can be reached on what may well be the world's steepest incline railroad, overcoming a seventy-two per cent grade as it approaches the top.

You can also drive up Lookout Mountain via Lookout Mountain Road or Ochs Highway, reaching an elevation of 2,225 feet, some 1,700 feet above the city. The view is spectacular. It was here that the Battle Above the Clouds was fought in 1863.

Point Park, atop Lookout Mountain, offers a magnificent view of the Tennessee River's Moccasin Bend and the city below. The Ochs Memorial Museum and Observatory are located here.

Opposite the park, the Lookout Mountain Museum contains Civil War items, Indian relics, and dioramas. Nearby is Cravens House, built in 1856 and reconstructed on the original foundations.

If you've driven around the countryside, you have noticed many a farmer's barn with signs urging you to see Ruby Falls and Rock City on Lookout Mountain. These may be the two most heavily advertised sights south of the Ohio River. The twin caves of Ruby Falls-Lookout Mountain, on Lookout Mountain Scenic Highway, are deep in the mountains. An elevator takes sightseers 1,120 feet down to view the 145-foot fall of water. Colorful stalactites and stalagmites, many enormous, add to the interest.

The second attraction, Rock City Gardens, offers relief from concentrated museum sightseeing. In this naturally beautiful rocky setting, Fairyland Caverns and Mother Goose Village are sure to thrill young children.

"Confederama" is an unusual diversion located at the foot of Lookout Mountain, at 3742 Tennessee Avenue. It is an attempt to show, using miniature soldiers on a scaled-down battleground, the Chattanooga Campaign.

Nine miles north of the city, on US 127, is Signal Mountain, another high point giving a majestic view. Below is the Tennessee River, running through the "Grand Canyon" of the Tennessee.

Two Tennessee Valley Authority dams in the Chattanooga area are worth visiting. East on State 153 are Chickamauga Dam and Chickamauga Lake, the latter covering 34,500 acres and having 810 miles of shoreline. Booker T. Washington State Park borders this lake, as does Harrison Bay State Park farther north. Seven miles west, off US 41, is TVA's Nickajack Dam.

Farther northwest on US 41 is Monteagle. From July 4 to August 30, the Chautauqua Assembly shifts the emphasis in this charming Cumberland Mountain town from nature to art. Since 1882, concerts, art classes and lectures have made this a special place every summer.

Continuing westward, the suggested route is US 64 and 41A via Sewanee to Winchester.

Sewanee, six miles west, centers around the University of the South, with its handsome campus covering 10,000 acres.

From Winchester follow US 41A north to Tullahoma, site of the Arnold Engineering Development Center's giant wind tunnels and the University of Tennessee's handsome new Space Institute. Next town is Shelbyville. This is Tennessee walking horse country. Every year in late August-early September, the Tennessee Walking Horse National Celebration is held in Shelbyville. To the west, in Columbia, you can tour the fine old home where James K. Polk, our eleventh president, lived as a boy. The house was built by Polk's father, Samuel, in 1816, and has been restored by the Polk Memorial Association.

The Natchez Trace

Taking US 43 from Columbia southwest toward Lawrenceburg, you can make a side trip at Summertown on State 20 to the Meriwether Lewis Monument on the Natchez Trace, the old road which ran from Nashville to Natchez, Mississippi. Lewis, leader of the Lewis and Clark expedition, was mysteriously killed in 1809 near this spot at Grinder's Inn. His grave alongside the historic Trace (which has been converted into a national parkway) is marked by a symbolic broken column.

Returning to US 43, and turning westward on US 64 at Lawrenceburg, you reach David Crockett State Park, a 1,000-acre recreational area and another state memorial to the hero of the Alamo. Here Davy Crockett lived, served as magistrate, and operated a mill.

Four miles before you reach Waynesboro, there's a natural bridge, seven miles north of US 64 on a country road. The 41-foot long limestone bridge arches over a gurgling mountain stream.

Westward on US 64 is the little town of Crump, where a five-mile side trip south on State 22 leads to Shiloh National Military Park. Here in April 1862 one of the fiercest battles of the Civil War was fought. It became known as "Bloody Shiloh"; both North and South were shocked by the carnage. Markers and other materials graphically explain the action to the visitor.

Returning to US 64, continue west to reach Memphis, largest city in the state.

Modern Memphis

Memphis, capital of the mid-South and one of the South's largest cities, is a progressive, forward-looking metropolis mindful of the past. A visitor senses the contrast when he stands amid the Civil War relics in Confederate Park and looks at the downtown skyscrapers.

Before the white man came Memphis was one of the villages of the Chickasaw Indians living along the Mississippi River. Andrew Jackson, later president, was one of the founders of the city and is credited with naming it for the ancient Egyptian city on the Nile. The name means "place of good abode."

Late in developing, Memphis had only about 500 people when it was incorporated in 1826. Today the metropolitan area population is more than 800,000. A manufacturing, wholesale, and commercial center, it is the world's largest spot-cotton market, and the world's largest hardwood lumber center. There are numerous lumber mills and furniture plants. Cotton's status is evident in the unique row of cotton merchants on famous Front Street. An important event is the annual Cotton Carnival, which is held mid-May to early June. Memphis in May International Festival is a gala month-long celebration highlighted by visual and performing arts, food, films, and sporting events. A different nation is featured each year.

In PeeWee's Saloon on storied Beale Street, W.C. Handy blew those first lonesome notes and became the "Father of the Blues." And in a Memphis recording studio Elvis Presley launched the career that was to make him the "King of Rock 'n' Roll." Tourist attractions include the statue of Handy in Handy Park, and Presley's showplace home, Graceland. Portions of the mansion, along with its Meditation Garden, which includes Presley's grave site, are open to visitors. Reservations are suggested.

Brooks Memorial Art Gallery in Overton Park boasts outstanding collections of American and European paintings, as well as porcelain figurines. Also in the park, Memphis Zoo and Aquarium has over 2,000 animals, petting zoo, and children's amusement rides.

The Museum of Natural History and Industrial Arts, at 3050 Central Avenue, is housed in a former private home dubbed "The Pink Palace" because of its unique Georgia pink marble exterior. Among its natural history exhibits, the African collection is outstanding.

The Magevney House is the oldest pioneer home in Memphis and is located on Adams Street. Built in 1831, the house was originally owned by Eugene Magevney, an Irish-born pioneer schoolteacher.

Six miles south of Memphis on US 61 and 4½ miles west on Mitchell Road is Chucalissa, a prehistoric Indian village. This was one of the string of Indian communities along the Mississippi which disappeared between de Soto's visit in 1541 and the arrival of the French in 1673. The rebuilt village consists of grass-thatched huts and a great conical temple on a flat-topped mound. There are also an excavated cemetery and a modern museum.

North of Memphis on the Mississippi River bluffs is Meeman-Shelby State Park, consisting of 12,512 acres. It's located eleven miles west of Millington off US 51.

Recently opened on Mud Island in the Mississippi River is the $63-million Mississippi River Museum, the nation's only "riverama." It is a 50-acre complex dedicated to life on the lower Mississippi.

Casey Jones

From Memphis, drive northeast to Jackson on Interstate 40. Jackson was the home of John Luther "Casey" Jones, who rode into immortality on the "Cannon Ball Express" in the famous 1900 railroad wreck on the Illinois Central line at Vaughn, Mississippi. (The original version of the song that tells his story was written by Wallace Saunders, of Canton, Mississippi, Casey's engineer wiper.) The Casey Jones Home and Museum at Casey Jones Village, five miles northwest via US 45 bypass, displays an engine similar to the one he was piloting that fatal night, plus other nostalgic reminders of railroading in the good old days. You also can see his grave in the Jackson cemetery at Royal and Hardee streets.

Twenty-six miles northeast of Jackson via Interstate 40 is Tennessee's biggest state-owned recreational area: 46,000-acre Natchez Trace State Park, with three lakes. Not on the main tour route, but worth the trip.

By taking US 45 north from Jackson to Trenton and then State 104 west to Dyersburg, you're well on your way to the Reelfoot Lake area in northwestern Tennessee. First, however, at Trenton you can take a twelve-mile side trip to Rutherford, site of Davy Crockett's last Tennessee home. In 1822, Crockett came to West Tennessee, settling first in what is now Crockett County and then moving north to the Rutherford Fork of the Obion River. He lived there unti 1835, adding to his reputation as a bear hunter and serving three terms as a member of the U.S. Congress. Defeated in his last campaign for Congress, he moved to Texas, dying less than a year later in the Battle of the Alamo. The grave of Rebecca Hawkins Crockett, his mother, has been moved to the site.

Returning to Trenton, follow State 104 to Dyersburg; there change to State 78 and proceed north to Tiptonville, gateway to the Reelfoot Lake area. Unlike so many Tennessee lakes, this one was created, not by TVA, but by the earthquakes of 1811-12. The depression left by the quakes was gradually filled by the Mississippi River, making a lake of 14,500 acres. Weird shapes of the old forest emerging above the water give it a primeval kind of beauty. Below the surface, many species of fish have natural breeding grounds. Giant cypresses along the shore add to Reelfoot's fantastic appeal. Over 250 kinds of birds and other wild creatures inhabit the lake area, a winter home for many bald eagles. Reelfoot Lake State Park is south of the lake and Reelfoot Wildlife Refuge Area to the north.

Continuing east on State 21 to its junction with State 22, follow along the lake and then swing east through Union City to Dresden. Changing to State 54, continue to Paris, a growing resort area due to its proximity to Kentucky Lake on the Tennessee River, fourteen miles to the east. Formed by the largest of the TVA dams, Kentucky Lake is 184 miles long, extending south into Tennessee.

Pick up US 79 at Paris to proceed to Paris Landing State Park on Kentucky Lake. The 1,200-acre park is eighteen miles northeast of Paris and provides beautiful campgrounds and a lakefront resort lodge.

Leaving Paris Landing, US 79 skirts the southern border of Land Between the Lakes—an elongated strip of 170,000 acres flanked on the west by Kentucky Lake, formed by a Tennessee Valley Authority dam on the Tennessee River, and on the east by Lake Barkley, formed by a U.S. Engineers' dam on the Cumberland River. State 49, taking off from US 79, leads northward through Land Between the Lakes, which is being developed by Tennessee Valley Authority as a national demonstration in outdoor recreation development and conservation education. There are some developed family campgrounds, primitive camping areas, nature trails, and a variety of wildlife.

US 79 leads east to Fort Donelson National Military Park, one mile west of Dover. Here in February, 1862, General Ulysses S. Grant captured first Fort Henry and then Fort Donelson. When the Confederate commander requested a truce, Grant made his historic ultimatum: "Unconditional and immediate surrender." The victory was one of the early Union gains. The national military park contains the well-preserved fort and earthworks, as well as the Dover Tavern in which the surrender occurred.

US 79 from Dover to Clarksville skirts the southern edge of the Fort Campbell Military Reservation, the headquarters of the 101st Airborne

Division. Off US 79, four miles east of Clarksville—named in 1784 for Revolutionary War General George Rogers Clark—is Dunbar Cave Park, featuring a swimming pool as well as an underground guided tour.

At Clarksville, turn south on State 48, destination Dickson. For spelunkers, Ruskin Cave is twelve miles northwest of Dickson off US 70. There's a one-hour tour.

Just east of Dickson on the way to Tennessee's capital, Nashville, is Montgomery Bell State Park.

Attractions of Nashville

There are numerous things to see in and around the capital. The Nashville Chamber of Commerce, 161 4th Avenue N, Nashville, TN 37219, has an excellent detailed map listing the city and area attractions.

The settlement of Nashville was begun in 1779 under the leadership of James Robertson. In 1780 Robertson and a group of pioneers built Fort Nashborough on the west bank of the Cumberland River. This log stockade has been reconstructed at First Avenue North and Church Street, near its original location. Although surrounded by a modern city, the authenticity of the reconstructed blockhouses and cabins makes it easy to imagine the pioneers seeking shelter here from the Indians.

By the 1830's, the log construction of Nashville's public buildings began to be replaced by limestone and marble. On Charlotte Avenue between Sixth and Seventh avenues, the State Capitol, designed by William Strickland and finished in 1855, is an impressive example of Greek Revival architecture.

In 1862 the Capitol was renamed Fort Johnson, a stockade having been built around it when Union forces occupied the city. In December, 1864, the Confederates under General John B. Hood attempted to regain the city; they were unsuccessful, and Hood's army broke up.

Another local landmark that recalls ancient Greece is the full-scale reconstruction of the Greek Parthenon.

One becomes so accustomed to Tennessee's display of its love of Greek symmetry, that the Downtown Presbyterian Church, Church Street and Fifth Avenue North, seems even more of an oddity in this gracious Southern city. Here William Strickland deserted the Greeks in favor of the Egyptians. Although the church has been rebuilt twice since first constructed in 1816, it retains its Egyptian temple aspect in general structure and architectural detail.

It is not only because of its buildings that Nashville has been called the "Athens of the South." The city has also displayed a special interest in the arts and education. Vanderbilt University, chartered in 1872, is perhaps the best known of its many educational institutions. The George Peabody College for Teachers, Scarritt College, Belmont College, Meharry Medical College and Fisk University are among the other major colleges here. Some have their own collections of fine art.

Near Vanderbilt, at 1908 Grand Avenue, is The Upper Room. In its chapel on the second floor, of Georgian design, is a chancel which re-creates the room in Leonardo da Vinci's painting The Last Supper.

The fine Tennessee State Museum in the Polk Cultural Complex is highlighted by "Life in Tennessee" exhibits. The Cumberland Museum and Science Center on Ridley Avenue has displays of realistic animal homes from around the world and offers laser-light and planetarium shows.

Grand Ole Opry

Downtown on Fifth Ave. N. in this "Country Music Capital of the World," you can visit the former home of the Grand Ole Opry, Ryman Auditorium, now a museum. At the ultra-modern Opry House, 2800 Opryland Dr., about six miles from downtown, the famous "Grand Ole Opry" radio show is presented on stage each Friday and Saturday night. Opryland U.S.A. theme park, adjoining, showcases American music, sprightly live entertainment, food, crafts, rides, and family fun. Nashville's famous sound and some of its brightest stars are also highlighted at the Country Music Hall of Fame and Museum, 4 Music Square E., at the head of "Music Row," where more than half of all the nation's record singles are produced.

Nashville is a good base for further explorations into history. Southwest, off US 70S, is the estate of Belle Meade, once the site of the Dunham Station on the Natchez Trace. This imposing Greek Revival building, the "Queen of Tennessee Plantations," was constructed in 1853 by General William Giles Harding. Its stables were once famous for breeding some of the world's finest race horses.

If you return to Nashville by US 31, six miles south of town, off the highway, you will come to Travellers Rest. Andrew Jackson, Lafayette and Sam Houston are among those who have visited this house, a clapboard of two stories built in 1820.

One of the most popular attractions in the Nashville area is The Hermitage, the hauntingly beautiful home of Andrew Jackson. It is thirteen miles east of Nashville on US 70. The interior furnishings are the exact pieces used by Jackson and his wife, Rachel. And Rachel's garden is kept according to her design. The tombs of Jackson and his wife are at one corner of the formal garden, along with the graves of others close to the family.

Hendersonville is the home of Music Village, U.S.A., a still-developing entertainment complex featuring stage shows by top country musicians, exhibits, and refreshments.

Leaving Nashville on US 41, driving southeast, you'll reach Smyrna. Turn left on State 104 and go east one mile to the Sam Davis Home, boyhood home and burial site of the nineteen-year-old Confederate hero. A scout, he was captured by Union forces and hanged as a spy for refusing to betray the Union man who had given him information.

Farther south on US 41, about thirty miles from Nashville, is the 351-acre Stones River National Battlefield. This was the scene of the Battle of Stones River, which took place from December 31, 1862, to January 2, 1863, resulting in high casualties on both sides without giving either a real victory. The graves or markers of over 6,000 Union soldiers are in the twenty-acre cemetery.

A few miles farther and you reach Murfreesboro, capital of Tennessee from 1819 to 1825. On North Maney Avenue is Oaklands, one of the outstanding houses in Middle Tennessee. Built in three periods, it developed into a beautiful antebellum home. Prior to the Civil War, its guests included such personages as John Bell, presidential candidate against Lincoln in 1860, and Leonidas Polk, the bishop-general.

Driving east on US 70S, your destination is McMinnville and Warren County, which has more than 125 certified growers of fruit trees, shade trees, and other plants, making it one of the nation's largest centers for the production of nursery stock. There is excellent fishing in Center Hill Lake and other waters in the area. Cumberland Caverns, seven miles east of McMinnville, is described as one of America's largest caves.

Twelve miles northeast of McMinnville on US 70S is Rock Island. A dam here at the confluence of two streams and near where another comes in backs up all three.

At Sparta the route is north on State 42 to Cookeville, home of Tennessee Tech, and then nineteen miles to Livingston. Here a side trip may be taken to Dale Hollow Dam near Celina off State 52, with the route passing the entrance to Standing Stone State Park, which has swimming pool, fishing lake, restaurant and furnished cabins. Returning to Livingston, turn east on State 52 through Jamestown and Rugby Road, to the Junction with US 27. This rugged area is Tennessee's "upper Cumberland country." It has produced such sons as Sergeant Alvin C. York, reared at Pall Mall north of Jamestown and Secretary of State Cordell Hull, who grew up to the west near Carthage. Near Jamestown is another state park, Pickett.

After joining US 27, proceed north for a few miles to the intersection with State 63, then drive east to Caryville, gateway to the 1,500-acre Cove Lake Park, located two miles north on US 25W. South of Caryville on State 71 is Norris Dam, named for the Nebraska Senator, George W. Norris, who co-sponsored the legislation establishing the TVA. The dam was the first built by the authority; it forms a seventy-two-mile-long lake.

From Caryville follow US 25W north to State 63, and take the latter northeast to Harrogate and Cumberland Gap. Through the famous Cumberland Gap, hacked clear by Daniel Boone and other frontiersmen, flooded westward-bound settlers. In 1959, the Cumberland Gap area was dedicated as a national historical park covering thirty-two square miles in Kentucky, Tennessee and Virginia. The park contains approximately two miles of the Wilderness Road, Civil War fortifications and the Tri-State Peak from which all three states are visible. The visitor center is located near Middlesboro, Kentucky.

Continue the tour route by taking US 25E southwest to its junction with US 11W, and follow the latter highway to Rogersville. En route, by taking a side trip on State 32 to Morristown, you can visit the reconstructed Crockett Tavern and Museum. It was at this six-room tavern operated by his father that Davy Crockett spent his youth. On the wall of one room is the proverbial coonskin cap and rifle similar to Crockett's Old Betsy.

From Rogersville, continue east on US 11W into Kingsport, where, six miles south on US 23, is 1,500-acre Warriors' Path State Park on Lake Patrick Henry.

It's twenty-four miles from Kingsport to Bristol. This marks the end of your grand tour of Tennessee, encompassing the mountains, the blue-grass country and the Mississippi River, pioneer points of interest and

Civil War battlefields, the TVA and Oak Ridge—the old and the new. Tennessee can be a rewarding experience for anyone.

PRACTICAL INFORMATION FOR TENNESSEE

FACTS AND FIGURES. The state derives its name from *Tenassee,* the ancient capital of the Cherokee Indians. Its nickname is the Volunteer State. The iris is the state flower; the tulip poplar, the state tree; the mockingbird, the state bird. "Agriculture and Commerce" is the state motto. "My Homeland Tennessee" is the state song.

Nashville, population 455,700 (consolidated with Davidson County) is the state capital. The state population (1980 Census) is 4,591,120.

HOW TO GET THERE. *By air:* To Memphis and Nashville there are direct flights on *USAir, American, Delta, Eastern, Piedmont, Republic,* and *TWA.* In addition, *Ozark* has direct flights to Nashville; *Frontier, Texas International,* and *United* to Memphis. Knoxville may be reached on direct flights of *American, Delta, Eastern,* and *United;* Chattanooga on *Delta,* and *Republic;* Tri-City Airport on *Piedmont* and *Republic;* Clarksville on *Ozark;* and Jackson on *Republic.*

From Canada, Nashville and Memphis may be reached from Toronto on direct flights of *American. Delta* has service from Montreal to Chattanooga, Memphis, and Nashville. *USAir* has service from Toronto to Memphis and Nashville and from Montreal to Nashville.

By car: There are a number of interstate highways to bring the visitor into the state. I-65 runs from Alabama through Tennessee into Kentucky. I-55 comes from Mississippi into Memphis and out of Tennessee into Arkansas. I-40 comes in from Arkansas to Memphis, through Nashville and Knoxville and into North Carolina. I-81 comes in from Bristol, Virginia, to Bristol, Tennessee, and on to Knoxville. I-24 comes from Georgia up to Nashville. I-75 from Georgia to Chattanooga, up to Knoxville and into Kentucky.

By bus: There is good service into the state: Greyhound and Trailways; ABC Coach Lines, Arrow Coach Lines, Crown Transit Lines, Inc., Great Southern Coaches, Inc., Gulf Transport Co., Illini-Swallow Lines, Inc., Indiana Motor Bus Co., Jefferson Lines, Mid-Continent Coaches, Inc. Oklahoma Transport Co., Short Way Lines, Southeastern Stages, Inc., Southwestern Transit Co., Inc., Sunnyland Stages, T.N.M. & O. Coaches, Inc., and Wells Bus Line.

By train: Amtrak trains serve Memphis and Dyersburg from Chicago and New Orleans.

By boat: The *Delta Queen* and *Mississippi Queen* overnight river steamboats include Memphis in their cruise schedules.

HOW TO GET AROUND. *By air:* USAir, American, Delta, Ozark, Piedmont, Republic, Eastern, United, TWA, Allegheny Commuter, Capitol Air, Comair, Pan American Airlines, Skyways, Sunbird, and Tennessee Airways serve cities within the state.

By car: Tennessee has interstate highways criss-crossing the state. I-40 runs from Memphis through the middle of the state into North Carolina; I-65 divides the state and runs north and south; I-24, I-75 and I-81 complete the picture. US 51, 70, 79, 64, 45, 231, 431, 41, 27, 11 and 11W & 11E help visitors tour the state conveniently.

Car rental: Avis or Hertz cars may be rented in Chattanooga, Kingsport, Knoxville, Memphis and Nashville. In addition, Hertz has rental offices in Bristol, Jackson, Johnson City, Oak Ridge and Smyrna.

By bus: Greyhound and Trailways, as well as ABC Coach Lines, Brooks, Continental 5-Star, Great Southern Coaches, Gulf Transport Co., Illini-Swallow Lines, Inc., Jefferson Lines, Inc., Oklahoma Transport Co., Short Way Lines, Southeastern Stages, Inc. and Tri-State Bus Lines, Inc. serve some cities within the state.

By boat: For an unusual carefree vacation, consider renting a houseboat and cruise the beautiful Great Lakes of Tennessee at your own pace. Boats accommodate 6 to 8 persons and may be rented by the day or week. Contact: Chattanooga Area Convention Visitors Bureau, 1001 Market Street, Chattanooga 37402 for further information.

TOURIST INFORMATION. Fourteen welcome centers, conveniently located on the interstate highways entering Tennessee, are in operation 24 hours a day. Information about area attractions may be obtained, rest rooms and free pamphlets are available to visitors. For information and pamphlets on the state write Department of Tourist Development, P.O. Box 23170, Nashville, TN 37202. On request, this office will also provide specific information and pamphlets about camping, fishing, golfing, canoeing, events, wildflowers, the State Capitol, and other major sites of visitor interest. For complete information on facilities at any of the 49 state parks, natural areas and historic sites, write the Tennessee Department of Conservation, Division of State Parks, 2611 West End Ave., Nashville 37203. To obtain detailed information on the Great Smoky Mountains National Park, write Park Superintendent, Great Smoky Mountains National Park, Gatlinburg 37738. The Forest Supervisor, Cherokee National Forest, Box 400, Cleveland 37311, will supply information pertinent to the Cherokee National Forest.

Write Information Office, Tennessee Valley Authority, Knoxville 37902, for information about TVA activities. Recreation maps which show routes to all types of shoreline recreation areas, including public access areas and wildlife management areas are available for the various lakes in the Tennessee River system.

Public Information Office, Tennessee Department of Transportation, 106 Highway Building, Nashville 37219; Public Relations Department, Tennessee Game and Fish Commission, Ellington Agricultural Center, Nashville 37204; Tennessee Historical Commission, Room 422, State Library and Archives Building, Nashville 37202; and U.S. Corps of Engineers, P.O. Box 1070, Nashville 37202, are other helpful addresses.

Information on fishing and hunting and licenses may be obtained from the Tennessee Wildlife Resources Agency, Box 40747, Ellington Agricultural Center, Nashville 37402.

For city information, contact: Chattanooga Area Convention and Visitors Bureau, 1001 Market St., Chattanooga 37402; Gatlinburg Chamber of Commerce, Box 527, Gatlinburg 37738; Knoxville Area Council for Conventions and Visitors, Box 15012, Knoxville 37923; Memphis Convention and Visitors Bureau, P.O. Box 3543, Memphis 38103; Nashville Area Chamber of Commerce, 161 4th Ave. N., Nashville 37219; Pigeon Forge Dept. of Tourism, Box 209, Pigeon Forge 37863.

SEASONAL EVENTS. February: *National Bird Dog Field Trials.* Grand Junction, 3rd wk.

March: A *St. Patrick's Day celebration* takes place, complete with parades, costumes and games, Erin. The "Wearing O' The Green" at its best. *The Tennessee Pilgrimage* is arranged by the

Association for the Preservation of Tennessee Antiquities. Tours of historic Tennessee homes and other sites are featured in various Tennessee cities, 3rd. wk.

April: *Ramp Festival,* Cosby, paying tribute to this rare member of the onion family; public *Fish fry,* Paris, billed as the worlds largest. Tours of beautiful homes and gardens, concerts, antique shows and art exhibits are seen at the *Dogwood Arts Festival,* Knoxville. Naturalists gather to observe wildflowers that are native to the region at the *Wildflower Pilgrimage,* held the 3rd wk. at Gatlinburg. *Opryland American Music Festival,* Nashville, late April-early May.

May: *Memphis in May International Festival,* and *Memphis Cotton Carnival. Strawberry Festival,* Humboldt, with horseshows, parades, beauty contests, street dances and band contests. All held during the 1st wk. *Strawberry Festival,* Dayton. The *Franklin Rodeo,* Franklin, a full-fledged, action-packed Wild West rodeo. 1st wk. *Old Timers Day,* Dickson, is the highlight on the last Sat. Local people wear old costumes and ride in old buggies and wagons in parades. *Iroquois Steeplechase,* Nashville, thoroughbred horseraces, 2nd Saturday.

June: *Rhododendron Festival* atop Roan Mountain near Elizabethton. *International Country Music Fanfare,* in Nashville.

July: *Old Time Fiddlers Jamboree,* Smithville.

August: The *Tennessee Walking Horse National Celebration,* Shelbyville. Some of the finest horses complete in one of the nation's best-known championships.

September: *State Fair,* Nashville. Exhibits and competitions in all areas imaginable, from horse drawing to jelly. *Banana Festival,* in South Fulton, the 2nd week in Sept. The citizens celebrate their part as the main distribution point for all bananas shipped to the U.S. During Sept./Oct. there are other major fairs in the state: *Mid-South Fair* in Memphis.

October: *Craftsman's Fair* at Gatlinburg. *National Storytelling Festival,* Jonesborough. *Fall Color Cruise,* Chattanooga, last 2 weekends, featuring boating and driving along Tennessee River, music, dancing, festivities.

December: *Nashville Christmas Parade,* on Dec. 1. One of the biggest parades in the state, featuring more than 20 bands and 50 floats. *Cheekwood's Trees of Christmas,* Cheekwood Fine Arts Center, Cheek Rd., Nashville, displays various types of Christmas decorations used by people of foreign lands. *Maid of Cotton Pageant,* Memphis.

NATIONAL PARKS AND FORESTS. The famous *Great Smoky Mountains National Park* covers 514,669 acres of eastern Tennessee and western North Carolina. It is a land of mountains and vales, of waterfalls and cascades, in which over 130 species of trees stand tall in its woodlands. Unusual features of the park are the pioneer and mountaineer homes. An interesting, restored group of these is located at Cades Cove. Wildlife is abundant throughout the Park, as are flowering trees and shrubs, Hiking is one of the favorite pursuits here, and there are about 70 miles of Appalachian Trail, serviced by seven shelters spaced a day's walk from each other. There is a camping site at Chimneys, Tennessee, several modern tent and trailer camp sites within the Park, and hotels at nearby Asheville, Knoxville, and Gatlinburg. The park is open all year.

Tennessee's *Cherokee National Forest* covers 625,350 acres in a wonder-world of forests, streams, gorges and waterfalls. Its many lakes include 6,400-acre Watauga, 1,900-acre Parksville. Wildlife is abundant, including wild Russian boar, sometimes seen by campers. Other outstanding features of the Forest include the beautiful Tellico River, 5,000-foot Unaka Mountain. Trout fishing is excellent in many areas, but check regulations as fishing and hunting is only by special permit in some areas of the forest. Within this vast wilderness are 46 recreational areas and many camping sites.

STATE PARKS. Tennessee's state parks are among the nation's finest. There are 44 in operation. Accommodations range from campsites to suites in modern, motel-type inns. Furnished housekeeping cabins are available at weekly rates in 14 parks. There are swimming, boating, fishing, and 8 parks have golf courses. Many of the parks overlook lakes and have sandy beaches. All parks are wildlife refuges. Playing fields include tennis courts, baseball diamonds, and softball and badminton places. Hiking trails, bridle paths and horses are available at some. There are excellent restaurants and dining rooms, and convenient picnic places. The parks are popular, so reservations for overnight accommodations should be made well in advance.

TRAILER TIPS. Most of Tennessee's state parks and some of the state historic areas provide camping for tents or trailers or both. Camp sites are obtained on a first-come, first-served basis. For full information write Department of Tourist Development, P.O. Box 23170, Nashville, TN 37202. In several parks cabins are available from mid-May to mid-Sept. Rentals are mostly by the week and reservations should be made at the park of your choice.

Excellent camping and trailer facilities also are available in the Cherokee National Forest and the Great Smoky Mountains National Park in East Tennessee, the Tennessee Valley Authority's Land Between the Lakes recreation area in West Tennessee, and the Cumberland Gap National Historical Park in Northeast Tennessee.

MUSEUMS AND GALLERIES. Historical. Bell Buckle: *Junior Room Museum,* Webb School, a restored 1886 classroom on campus of prestigious preparatory school.

Benton: *Old Fort Marr,* an historic building (1813). Guided tours daily.

Harrogate: *Lincoln Memorial University* has Civil War exhibits and South's largest collection of Abraham Lincoln memorabilia.

Johnson City: *Carroll Reece Museum,* East Tennessee State University, a general museum.

Knoxville: *Frank H. McClung Museum,* University of Tennessee, a general museum. Closed holidays. *Students' Museum, Inc.,* 3816 Oakland Ave., a natural science museum and planetarium.

Memphis: *Chucalissa Indian Village and Museum,* 1987 Indian Village Dr. *E. H. Little Gallery,* Memphis State University Campus, a general museum. Closed during the summer and national holidays. *Memphis Pink Palace Museum,* 3050 Central Ave., was the palatial former home of Clarence Saunders, inventor of the self-service grocery. Its wide assortment of exhibits ranges from African big game trophies to an absorbing children's section.

Nashville: *Tennessee Agricultural Museum,* Ellington Center. *Tennessee Game Farm Zoo,* 18 mi. N.W. off I-24W, wild animals, including endangered species. *Tennessee State Museum,* 505 Deaderick St., superb "Life in Tennessee" exhibits. *Travellers' Rest Historic House,* off US 31 on Farrell Pkwy, is a general museum located in the 1790 home of Judge John Overton.

Vonore: *Fort Loudoun,* off US 441, a general museum with collections on agriculture, archeology, botany and artifacts from the Cherokee Indians.

Art Galleries. Chattanooga: *George Thomas Hunter Gallery of Art,* 10 Bluff View, housed in a 1904 home at the site of a Civil War battery guarding the Tennessee River.

Cowan: *Cowan Railroad Museum* in vintage small-town station, exhibiting grand era of passenger trains.

Johnson City: *Elizabeth Slocumb Gallery,* Department of Art, East Tennessee State University.

Kingsport: *Kingsport Fine Arts Center,* Church Circle St.

Knoxville: *Dulin Gallery of Art,* 3100 Kingston Pike.

Memphis: *Brooks Memorial Art Gallery.* Overton Park. Sculpture and paintings including the million-dollar Kress collection. *Dixon Gallery and Gardens.* 4339 Park Ave. French, American Impressionists, British landscapes and portraits.

Nashville: *George Peabody College Museum,* 21st Ave., an art museum. *Vanderbilt University Gallery,* 1801 Station B, 23rd at West End Ave. *Tennessee Botanical Gardens and Fine Arts Center,* Cheekwood, Cheek Rd., an art center and botanical gardens.

SPECIAL INTEREST MUSEUMS. Chattanooga: *Harris Swift, Museum of Religious and Ceremonial Arts and Library of Rare Books,* 526 Vine St. *Houston Antique Museum,* 201 High St. It houses a collection of 15,000 pitchers, china, copper and gold luster, as well as rare porcelains and furniture. *Hall of Presidents Wax Museum.* Foot of Lookout Mt. *Tennessee Valley Railroad Museum.* No. Chamberlain Ave., at the foot of historic Missionary Ridge. *Lookout Mountain Museum,* in Point Park on Lookout Mountain. Excellent Indian exhibits as well as armor and weapons from the Civil War. *National Knife Museum,* 7201 Shallowford Rd.

Gatlinburg: *American Historical Wax Museum,* on US 441.

Jackson: *Casey Jones Home and Railroad Museum,* US 45 bypass & I-40. A railroad museum in the former home of Casey Jones.

Knoxville: *Knoxville 1982 World's Fair Site* is now permanent recreation area. Its "symbol," 26-story Sunsphere, has a revolving restaurant, lounges, and observation decks.

Memphis: *Overton Park Zoo and Aquarium.*

Nashville: *Country Music Hall of Fame and Museum,* 4 Music Square E. *Nashville Parthenon,* Centennial Park. World's only replica of the famous Athenian temple. *Cumberland Museum & Science Center,* 800 Ridley Ave., in Ft. Negley Park. *RCA's Original Studio B,* corner Music Square W. and Roy Acuff Place.

Oak Ridge: *American Museum of Science and Energy,* Jefferson Circle, a science and technology museum.

Sewanee: *Fine Arts Gallery of the University of the South,* arts/crafts museum.

Pigeon Forge: *Smoky Mountain Car Museum,* US 441. *Silver Dollar City.* US 441. Replica 1870s mountain community.

HISTORIC SITES. Because of its geographical location, Tennessee was a Civil War battleground as well as one of the more important states in the westward movement of the pioneers. The names of Crockett and Boone echo through the rich history of the state.

A small park outside of Limestone, near Greenville, houses the replica log-cabin birthplace of *Davy Crockett,* while to the east of Morristown you will find *Crockett Tavern and Museum,* resembling a tavern once run by Davy's father. You will be intrigued by the fine collection of Early American tools on display. In the Rutherford area is a copy of the *Davy Crockett Cabin* in which he lived while serving in the Congress of the United States. Many of the furnishings in the house were actually owned by Davy, including a chair that he made himself.

Chattanooga: Lookout Mountain: *Cravens House,* reconstructed 1856 Civil War home.

Columbia: *Ancestral home of James K. Polk,* 301 W. 7th St. Closed Dec. 25. The rooms have been restored, and they contain many mementos of the life of the 11th president of the United States.

Dover: *Fort Donelson National Military Park and Cemetery,* off US 79, has earthworks, rifle pits from famed battle, military museum with many items from the Civil War.

Franklin: *The Carter House* is a grim reminder of the bloody Civil War battle of Franklin. Now fully restored, the house is furnished with some of the finest period furniture available.

Gallatin: *Cragfont.* The 1798–1802 home of General James Winchester of the Revolution and War of 1812.

Gatlinburg: *Cades Cove Open-Air Museum* in the Great Smoky Mountains National Park, a village museum on the site of a former pioneer community, preserved to show a way of life that has disappeared. The *Sugarlands Visitor Center,* also located in the Great Smoky Mountains National Park.

Greeneville: *Andrew Johnson National Historic Site,* Depot St., is open to the public, and contains many items from the life of this famous president.

Johnson City: *Tipton-Haynes Living Historical Farm,* Erwin Hwy. 19W. Historic buildings are open to the public: Tipton and Haynes house, Slave Quarter, Haynes Law Office.

Jonesborough: *Tennessee's oldest town,* still one of the most historic and picturesque communities in the South, has many buildings of note. On US 411, 8 mi. W of Johnson.

Kingsport: *1818 Netherland Inn, 1820 Exchange Place,* and *1852 Allendale* are open to the public.

Knoxville: *Blount Mansion,* 200 W. Hill Ave., 1792 office and mansion of Wm. Blount, governor of the territory south of Ohio, is open to visitors. There are several historic houses to visit in Knoxville. *Confederate Memorial Hall "Bleak House",* 3148 Kingston Pike. *Craighead-Jackson House,* 1000 State St. *General James White's home* (1786) and *White's Fort,* 205 E. Hill Ave., built by city's founder. *"Marble Springs"* Farm Home of Governor John Sevier, Neubert Springs Rd. *Ramsey House,* Thorngrove Pike.

Maryville: *Sam Houston,* hero of the Alamo, is remembered in Tennessee by the small schoolhouse north of Maryville where he once taught.

Memphis: 1870 *Fontaine House,* beautifully and restored and furnished Victorian mansion, 680-690 Adams Ave.; 1832, *Magevney House,* 198 Adams Ave.; 1852 *Mallory-Neely House,* 652 Adams Ave., all open to public.

Murfreesboro: *Oaklands,* N. Maney Ave., is open Apr. to Oct. *Stones River National Battlefield.*

Nashville: *Fort Nashborough,* 170 1st Ave. N. The 1780 log replica of Fort Nashborough, first settlement at Nashville, is open. *Belle Meade Mansion,* the "Queen of Tennessee Plantations," on Leake Ave. off US 70 (Harding Road). *The Hermitage* (1819), home of President Andrew Jackson, on Rachel's Lane; 12 mi. W of Nashville. *Tulip Grove* (1836), nearby home of Jackson's nephew and private secretary, may be visited on same admission.

Piney Flats; *Rocky Mount,* on US 11E, original U.S. Territorial Capitol, has a log house, smokehouse, blacksmith's shop, outdoor kitchen.

Shiloh: *Shiloh National Military Park* 10 mi. S.W. of Savannah, site of one of the crucial battles of the Civil War, contains markers and monuments to the fallen of both sides, many original emplacements are still clearly marked.

LIBRARIES. In *Nashville,* the Public Library of Nashville and Davidson County, 8th Ave. N. & Union, is a local history library and located on the site of former gardens of President James K. Polk. Collections of books pertinent to Nashville and the state of Tennessee as well as the Nashville Authors collection are available, plus many more.

TOURS. *By car:* Drive through scenic, historic 300-acres at *Reflection Riding* in Chattanooga. Historic details are noted; nature trails give the visitor relaxed enjoyment. Quiet pools reflect the majestic mountain towering above. Open daily. You can use your own car, set your own pace, and utilize a tape recorder and prerecorded commentary for a tour of the Great Smoky Mountains National Park. The history, geology, fauna and flora found in the park are presented on the tape which can be rented at Christus Gardens, Gatlinburg, and the Museum of the Cherokee Indian, Cherokee, N.C. It can also be purchased as a souvenir of your trip. You can get a magnificent view of the Great Smokies from the *Space Needle,* Airport Rd., just off the Pkwy., Gatlinburg.

By bus: Grand Ole Opry Tours, four hr. bus tour includes recording studios, homes of country music stars, backstage Grand Old Opry House visit. *Gray Line Tours,* Chattanooga, Great Smokies (from Gatlinburg, Knoxville), Memphis, Nashville.

By rail: The Incline Railway, America's most amazing mile straight up the side of historic Lookout Mountain, Chattanooga, offers visitors a thrilling view of the "Scenic Center of the South." *Autumn Leaf Special,* a steam train, takes you on a two-day excursion through the mountains of Tennessee in late Oct. Write: 7 Fairhills Dr., Chattanooga, Tenn. 37405; tickets on a first-come, first-serve basis.

By boat: The *Memphis Queen Line Riverboats,* Riverside Dr., foot of Monroe, provides visitors with a lovely 1½-hr. cruise on the Mississippi River. The *Delta Queen* and *Mississippi Queen* steamboats offer extended river cruises from Spring to late Fall, departing from Memphis. *Annual Fall Color Cruise and Folk Festival.* Two late Oct. weekends. Excursion and private boats ply "Grand Canyon of the Tennessee River" during peak of fall foliage. Sightseeing, dinner/entertainment, and champagne-brunch cruises on the Cumberland River are available to Nashville visitors aboard the *Belle Carol, Captain Ann, Nashville Showboat,* and *Music City Queen.* Dinner/entertainment and champagne brunch cruises available. Departs from 1 Ave. N., near Fort Nashborough May-Oct. Glass bottom boats explore *The Lost Sea,* a world inside a mountain, 5 mi. from Sweetwater on US 11.

By ski lifts: The double-chaired *Sky Lift* takes visitors from the main street, Gatlinburg, across the river and up the steep incline of Crockett Mt. The *Aerial Tramway* provides a delightful ride from Ober Gatlinburg Ski Resort lodge to the top of Mount Harrison.

SPECIAL INTEREST TOURS. *Bristol Caverns,* on US 421 SE, *Bristol,* is open mid-June to Labor Day.

Chattanooga: Ruby Falls, a natural waterfall 1,120 feet beneath Lookout Mountain in spectacular Lookout Mountain Caverns. Guided tours. *Canyon Land Park,* located atop Lookout Mountain, has chairlifts into the deepest gorge east of the Mississippi. Picnicking, fishing, hiking, swimming are also available to the visitor. *Rock City Gardens,* also atop Lookout Mountain, is a natural city of rocks. See seven states from Lover's Leap; cross Swing-'Along'-Bridge; *Fairyland Caverns* offer colorful scenes from fairytales in rock settings; *Mother Goose Village,* set in a cavern. *Sequoyah Caverns,* 35 mi. from Chattanooga, boasts one of America's prettiest caverns, featuring the Looking Glass Lakes. Daily. *The Confederama,* 3742 Tennessee Ave., is an automated presentation, in miniature, visualizing in lights, guns and smoking cannon the history of the area.

Ruskin Cave, off US 70 via Yellow Creek Rd., in *Dickson,* is open daily Apr. to Oct.

Christus Gardens, housed in a structure of native marble, on River Rd., *Gatlinburg,* depicts scenes from the life of Christ. Dioramas, life-size figures and narrative are inspiring.

Memphis: From the early days in America comes the *Chucalissa Indian Village,* south of Memphis on US 61. Here you may see the restored Indian Village and learn something of a long-forgotten way of life.

Wonder Cave, in *Monteagle,* just off US 41, has onyx formations and an underground river.

Nashville: The State Capitol, between 6th and 7th Aves. N. on Charlotte Ave. Free tours. *Opryland, U.S.A.* Lavish family entertainment complex in beautiful 110-acre park setting. Live performances, exciting rides, animal exhibits and craft shows. The *Upper Room,* 1908 Grand Ave. Free. Chapel has polychrome wood carving of Leonardo da Vinci's "The Last Supper," and world Christian Fellowship Window. The Upper Room Building is where the daily devotional booklet by the same name is published.

The *Old Mill,* just off US 441 in Pigeon Forge, a water-powered mill in operation since 1830, has guided tours daily except Sun. Apr. to mid-Nov.

Forbidden Caverns, on US 411, *Sevierville,* is open daily, June to Nov.

Tuckaleechee Caverns, Rte. 73, Townsend. Guided tours, 1 hr., through the caverns. Apr. to Oct.

 INDUSTRIAL TOURS. A tour is conducted by the *Tennessee Valley Authority* from its headquarters in Knoxville. The tour includes *Tennessee Valley Authority* dams, lakes, and steam-electric generating facilities in the Knoxville area. The address is Tennessee Valley Authority, Knoxville, 37902. *The George A. Dickel Distillery,* near *Tullahoma,* offers free guided tours Mon.-Fri. Closed holidays.

The Jos. Schlitz Brewing Co., 5151 E. Raines Rd. *Memphis,* welcomes visitors to tour the brewery and visit an authentic replica of a Mississippi River steamboat salon. Mon. to Fri. Tours on the half-hour. Free beer and pretzels.

Jack Daniel Distillery, State 55, *Lynchburg,* is the oldest registered distillery in the U.S., welcomes visitors to view the early art of making whiskey in Tennessee.

Pigeon Forge Pottery, just off US 441, *Pigeon Forge,* welcomes visitors to see craftsfolk transform local clays into finished products. Workshop demonstrations Mon. to Fri. Sales displays open daily.

The American-Saint Gobain Corp., Kingsport, acquaints the visitor with the making of plate glass for all use.

The Tennessee Eastman Co., also in *Kingsport,* takes you into the world of synthetics for home and business. Also of interest in Kingsport is the *Kingsport Press Inc.,* a large publishing firm.

The Century Electric Co. in *Humboldt* and *General Electric Co., Murfreesboro,* have tours which will inform you about electric motors.

The Kingston Steam Plant, just off I-40, *Kingston,* is one of the nation's largest steam-powered electric generating plants. The visitor balcony is open daily.

GARDENS. *Memphis Botanic Garden,* 750 Cherry Rd., in Audubon Park is open daily. Flowers, trees, exotic plants and wildflowers plus elaborate gardens give the visitor a panorama of beauty and solitude in a natural setting.

 MUSIC. Memphis is the home of the blues, while Nashville is the home of Grand Ole Opry and Opryland Theme Park. *Memphis:* The annual *Memphis Cotton Carnival Jazz & Blues Festival* is held the 2nd wk in May. Nashville: In June, *Country Music Fan Fair* with a large assembly of major Grand Ole Opry stars; in downtown Printer's Alley you can enjoy music ranging from country-western to pop and jazz in the *Carousel Club, Embers Showcase* and *Boots Randolph's Club.*

The well-known country music radio program *Grand Ole Opry* is presented every Fri. & Sat. night at the new Grand Ole Opry House. Sat. matinees mid-Apr.

to late Oct. Contact the Grand Ole Opry Ticket Office, 2802 Opryland Dr., Nashville 37214, (615) 889-3060, for schedules and advance ticket information. There are free musical concerts Sun. afternoons during July and August in the *Band Shell*, Centennial Park, Nashville.

To experience the country music stage shows & exhibits at Music Village, U.S.A., in *Henderson*, contact Music Village, U.S.A., Music Village Blvd., P.O. Box 819, Hendersonville 37077, (615) 824-4700.

DRINKING LAWS. Beer is sold in all counties; liquor may be purchased in retail stores in various counties, including Shelby (Memphis). Davidson (Nashville), Hamilton (Chattanooga), Knox (Knoxville), Maury (Columbia), Williamson (Franklin), Lake (Tiptonville), and Dyer (Dyersburg). Stores are open 8 A.M. to 11 P.M.; closed on Sun., election days, major holidays. Liquor by-the- drink is legal in Davidson County (including Nashville), Shelby County (including Memphis) and the municipalities of Clarksville, Oak Ridge, Knoxville and Chattanooga. By-the-drink sales: Mon.-Sat., 8-3 A.M.; Sun. from noon. Minimum age 19.

SUMMER SPORTS. With more than 600,000 acres of water and 10,000 mi. of shoreline, the state offers limitless opportunities for fishing, boating, water-skiing and other water sports.

Fishing: A wide variety of fish is found in the state—from bass and catfish to trout. Seventeen TVA lakes and 7 maintained by the U.S. Army Corps of Engineers offer excellent facilities. The Tenn. Game and Fish Commission operates 12 lakes, constructed and managed exclusively for the fisherman. Many state parks offer fishing. There is no closed fishing season in Tenn., except on trout in certain areas. On TVA and Corps of Engineers lakes, and the waters below them, the trout season is always open. There are almost 400 fishing docks and resorts on Tenn. waters. Public access ramps are plentiful and provide the fisherman an opportunity to explore most any body of water. Boats and motors can be rented at most docks and resorts; guides may also be available.

Non-resident fishing license fees are subject to change. Consult local authorities.

Canoeing: Tenn. was made to order for the canoeing enthusiast. You can shoot the rapids or float peacefully downstream on gentle rivers in the middle and western parts of the state. "Canoeing in Tenn." is available from the Tenn. Department of Tourist Development, P.O. Box 23170, Nashville, TN 37202.

Swimming, water-skiing and *boating* can be enjoyed on TVA's lakes.

Hunting: The state's naturally abundant woods, and its numerous wildlife preserves, offer a wide variety of game for the hunter. From Nov. to Apr. hunt clubs "ride to the hounds" and often entertain the *National Fox Hunters Ass'n.* In the 3rd week in Feb. the *National Field Trials Ass'n.* holds field trials for bird dogs on the Hobart Ames Plantation at Grand Junction.

Non-resident hunting license fees are subject to change. Write the Tennessee Wildlife Resources Agency, Box 40747, Ellington Agricultural Center, Nashville 37220, for up-to-date information. Permission, of course, is required to hunt on private and public lands.

Horseback riding: The most popular riding horse is the Plantation Walking Horse, bred largely in the rolling hills of Marshall and Bedford counties. This area is criss-crossed with bridle paths, and it is easy to arrange weekend or week-long trips through the countryside. There are 650 mi. of foot and horse trails in the Great Smoky Mountains National Park.

Golfing is very big in the state. The rolling land, plus native greens and mild climate make Tenn. a great place for golfers. The season starts in late Mar. and continues through and beyond Thanksgiving. There are 165 golf courses, the majority of which are of regulation size. Public courses welcome all visitors, while some private courses will admit visitors as well. "A Golfer's Guide to Tennessee," published by the Tenn. Department of Tourist Developement, P.O. Box 23170, Nashville, TN 37202.

WINTER SPORTS. *Ober Gatlinburg Ski Resort,* Ski Mountain Rd., on Mt. Harrison, operates daily from Dec. to Mar. Three rope tows and two double chair lifts are available. Ice skating is also offered here.

SPECTATOR SPORTS. *Memphis:* In mid-Dec. two of the nation's top college football teams play in the Liberty Bowl. The *Danny Thomas Memphis Golf Classic,* at the Colonial Country Club, is held for 4 days in May.

Nashville: NASCAR stock car racing. Music City 420 Winston Cup Grand National, mid-May; Busch 420 Winston Cup Grand National, mid-July. Both at Nashville International Raceway, Tennessee State Fairgrounds. On the 2nd Sat. in May, the *Iroquois Steeplechase* is held. Eight races are featured. *Longhorn Classic Rodeo.* Early August. Municipal Auditorium. Features more than 200 of the nation's top cowboys and cowgirls in six major contests.

The *Bristol International Speedway and Drag Strip,* on US 11E, in *Bristol,* features the Southeastern 500 during mid-Mar.; the Volunteer 500 in late July or early August. The IHRA All-American Drags are held for three days in mid-Aug. Mid-May is the time for Spring National Drags, held for four days.

Major college football, basketball, track and swim meets are on view at the University of Tennessee campus, Knoxville, where Southeastern Conference and intersectional rivals come to battle the "Vols."

SHOPPING. All along the mountain roads in East Tennessee you will find craft shops, where you may buy carved wooden pieces, fine handmade furniture, hand-woven cloth and rugs, patchwork quilts, pottery and other pieces of art made by the mountaineers.

Gatlinburg is a nationally recognized center for mountain crafts. You can see skilled artisans creating their handmade products in wood, leather, woven materials, metals, pottery and other art media.

Franklin is a unique village, filled with fascinating antique shops and unusual merchandise.

Overton Square, at Madison and Cooper, *Memphis,* has several unusual shops.

WHAT TO DO WITH THE CHILDREN. All of Tennessee's four major cities—Memphis, Nashville, Knoxville and Chattanooga—have parks and playgrounds. There are public swimming pools not only in the municipalities but also in many of the state parks. Exhibits in *Centennial Park* in Nashville include a locomotive, an airplane, and other items of interest to children. Swans swim placidly on a lake. And nearby is the reproduction of the Greek Parthenon.

Gatlinburg and nearby Pigeon Forge abound in commercial attractions. Among the more popular is the *Sky Lift* in Gatlinburg, which takes passengers to the top of *Crockett Mountain,* and *Silver Dollar City* in Pigeon Forge, featuring thrill rides, shows, and crafts demonstrations. *Tommy Bartlett's Water Circus* at Lake Gatlinburg in Pigeon Forge has water ballet, comedy, water-ski and helicopter-trapeze shows mid-May to mid-Oct. If the children tire of looking at bears in *Great Smoky Mountain National Park,* take them to the *Smoky Mountain Trout Farms* in Gatlinburg or Hempton and let them fish for trout. Everything is furnished. The *Fairgrounds Amusement Park* in Memphis is open daily. Games, rides and picnicking. *Opryland, U.S.A.,* 2802 Opryland Dr., a 110-acre entertainment park, is composed of five "towns" that highlight America's musical heritage. Rides, animal shows, craftsfolk demonstrating their arts, puppet shows, complete this fun treat. *Magic World,* on US 441, and *Porpoise Island,* at the foot of the Great Smoky Mountains, Pigeon Forge, are exhibits which appeal to children.

Dale Hollow National Fish Hatchery, in Celina, just off State 53, where rainbow trout are raised, has a Visitor Center.

There are outstanding museums of special interest to children in Oak Ridge, Nashville, and Memphis. Children and adults alike marvel at the interesting and informative displays relating to atomic power and radioactive isotopes at the *Museum of Science and Energy at Oak Ridge,* birthplace of the atomic bomb. The *Tennessee Game Farm Zoo,* 18 mi. N.W. of Nashville, has exotic animals from many countries, and a petting zoo where baby animals enjoy being cuddled. The *Memphis Pink Palace Museum* has a specially designed section where young people may operate educational exhibits. In the same building is the planetarium, also of interest to children. Also in Memphis, *Mud Island,* a themed entertainment complex centered around Mississippi life, offers monorail rides, a children's playground, picnic areas.

Fort Nashborough in Nashville is a replica of a frontier stockade. Here children can get an idea of what pioneer life was like.

Chattanooga offers a thrilling ride to the top of *Lookout Mountain* and back on the *Incline Railway,* one of the steepest in the world. Atop the mountain is *Point Park,* a museum with a collection of firearms, and other attractions, including *Rock City Gardens,* where youngsters especially enjoy *Fairyland Caverns* and *Mother Goose Village.*

Tennessee, with its many mountains and variable rock formations, has a number of intersting caves and caverns. Between Sweetwater and Madisonville on State 68 is the *Lost Sea,* a large underground lake. Visitors view it from glass bottom boats. Near McMinnville is *Cumberland Caverns,* with one of the Southeast's largest cave rooms. West of Gatlinburg is the *Tuckaleechee Caverns. Ruby Falls-Lookout Mountain Caves* are deep in *Lookout Mountain* near Chattanooga. Sightseers go down 1,120 feet on an elevator to view the 145-foot falls. *Wonder Cave,* five miles north of Monteagle, features an underground river. Other scenic caves and caverns include *Bristol Caverns* near Bristol, *Dunbar Cave* near Clarksville, which has an underground swimming pool, and *Jewel Cave,* 12 miles northwest of Dickson.

In Memphis, excursion rides on the *Mississippi River* are available aboard paddlewheel river boats, *Memphis Queen II, Memphis Queen III,* and *Belle Carol,* operating from the foot of Monroe Street. The trip takes one and one-half hours.

 **HOTELS AND MOTELS** in Tennessee run the full range from independent motor inns to virtually every major chain and system. As headquarters for the gigantic Holiday Inn chain, Memphis has eight of these establishments alone!

Listings are in order of price category. Based on double occupancy in peak season, without meals, price categories and ranges are as follows: *Expensive,* over $50; *Moderate,* $35–$50; *Inexpensive,* under $35. For a more complete explanation of hotel and motel categories see *Facts at Your Fingertips* at the front of this volume.

Bristol

Holiday Inn. *Moderate.* I-81 & US 11. Restaurant, taprooms for beer and setups. Pool, some live entertainment. Special weekend rates.

Chattanooga

Choo-Choo Hilton Inn. *Expensive.* 1400 S. Market St., in Terminal Station. Luxurious rooms in the Inn and restored Victorian-era railroad parlor cars, two dining rooms, three cocktail lounges. Indoor-outdoor pools, jacuzzi, ice-skating rink, tennis. Shopping in delightful boutiques at restored 1905 Southern Railway Terminal Station.

Holiday Inn. *Expensive.* Four locations. All have restaurant, lounge, pool. **I-124:** 401 W. M.L. King Blvd. Kennels; **South:** 2100 S. Market St.; **Southeast:** US 41 & I-75. Free airport transportation. Kennels.; **Tiftonia:** I-24 & US 41.

The Read House. *Expensive.* Broad and 9th Sts. Convenient downtown location in traditional hostelry, rooms in old and new sections. Pool, sundeck. Dining room, coffee shop, cocktail lounge, live entertainment. Free parking garage.

Sheraton Inn. *Expensive.* Two locations: 6710 Ringgold Rd., 407 Chestnut St. Restaurant, lounge with entertainment. Heated pool. Pets accepted.

Admiral Benbow Inn. *Inexpensive to Moderate.* 101 E 20th St., near I-24. Dining room, cocktail lounge, live entertainment, dancing. Pool.

Quality Inn: *Inexpensive to Moderate.* Two locations: I-75 and US 41; Dining room. Jogging track, tennis, basketball goal, game room. **Quality Inn Comfort Inn.** I-75 & TN 146 (Ringgold, GA). Dining room. Playground, fishing nearby. In-room movies.

Howard Johnson's. *Moderate.* Two locations; both with well-appointed rms., restaurant, pool, pets. **Downtown:** 100 W. 21st St.; **East Ridge:** 6616 Ringgold Rd.

Days Inn and Lodge. *Inexpensive.* 1401 Mack Smith Rd., near I-74 and US 41. Family restaurant. Pool, playground, souvenir shop.

Econo Lodge. *Inexpensive.* 6650 Ringgold Rd. Pool, restaurant, playground. Extra-large rooms, some with remote-control TV.

Shamrock Motel. *Inexpensive.* 5659 Brainerd Rd. Across from a regional shopping center. Family accommodations. Apartments available. Pool.

Clarksville

Holiday Inn. *Moderate.* US 41A and US 79. Dining room, cocktail lounge. Pets accepted.

Cumberland Gap

Holiday Inn. *Moderate to Expensive.* US 25E. Attractive motel back from highway. Dining rm. Heated pool, play area. Kennels.

Elizabethton

Camara Inn. *Moderate.* 505 W. Elk Ave. Pleasant rms., some with refrigerators. Restaurant, pool.

Franklin

Holiday Inn. *Moderate to Expensive.* I-65 and TN 96. Restaurant, pool, playground, pets.

Gatlinburg

Sheraton Gatlinburg Hotel. *Expensive.* Cherokee Orchard and Airport Rds. Lavish facility in contemporary design on brow of mountain overlooking town. Restaurants and coffee shop, entertainment and dancing, pools and poolside services. Laundry. Varied sports offerings. Inroom movies and free parking.

Brookside Motel and Ranch House. *Moderate to Expensive.* Roaring Fork Rd. Lovely landscaped grounds along mountain stream. Very attractive rms. Cottages also available. Restaurant opp. Heated pool.

Holiday Inn. *Moderate to Expensive.* 333 Airport Rd. Dining room, snack bar, game room, disco lounge, inroom movies, three pools with one inside.

Ramada Inn. *Moderate.* 756 Parkway. Nearby restaurant, indoor-outdoor pools, sauna, seasonal entertainment. Fireplaces in some rooms. Private club for mixed beverages.

Best Western. Locations include **Crossroads Motor Lodge,** *moderate to expensive,* in a downtown location on US 441, restaurant nearby, pool and some rooms with fireplaces; the **Fabulous Chalet,** *expensive,* Sunset Dr. Overlooks the Smokies, has heated pool and nearby restaurant, seasonal continental breakfasts, some fireplaces in rooms; **Twin Islands Motel,** *moderate to expensive,* in center of town on US 441, with restaurant, heated pool, fireplaces, balconies overlooking mountain stream; and **Zoder's Inn,** *moderate to expensive,* 402 Parkway, near downtown shopping, balconies overlooking stream, pool, restaurant nearby, some wood-burning firplaces in rooms.

Quality Inn Smokyland. *Moderate to Expensive.* In center of town, 727 Parkway. Pools for oldsters and youngsters, in-room coffee, refrigerators in some rooms, restaurants nearby.

Bearskin Motel. *Moderate.* 955 Parkway. Accommodations in either motel or rustic cottages. Efficiencies and kitchen units available. Pool, play area.

Mountain View Hotel & Motor Lodge. *Moderate to Expensive.* A vintage hostelry from early days, in center of town, 500 Parkway. Rooms in older building and new wings, dining room, pools for adults and kiddies.

Johnson City

Camara Inn. *Moderate to Expensive.* 2312 Brownsmill Rd. Restaurant, pool. Some in-room refrigerators, private club.

Holiday Inn. *Moderate to Expensive.* 2406 N. Roan St. Pleasant rms. Restaurant. Pool with service at poolside. Kennels.

Kingsport

Holiday Inn. *Moderate to Expensive.* 700 Lynn Garden Dr. Double-story motel. Restaurant. Pool. Kennel.

Best Western Camara Inn. *Moderate.* 805 Lynn Garden Dr. Inviting rms. Refrigerators. Pool; poolside service. Restaurant.

Tennessee Motor Lodge. *Moderate.* 1017 W. Stone Dr. Comfortable rms.; most have king-size beds. Restaurant. Pool with service at poolside, sauna.

Econo-Travel Motor Hotel. *Inexpensive.* 1704 E. Stone Dr. Inviting rms. Restaurant adj. Pets welcome.

Knoxville

Holiday Inn. *Moderate to Expensive.* Six locations, all with restaurants, lounges, pools. **Northeast:** 4625 Asheville Hwy. **West:** 1315 Kirby Rd. **World"s Fair Expo Site:** Henley Ave. at Clinch Ave. **Central:** 621 Dale Ave. **Airport:** US 129, Alcoa, TN.; **Northwest:** I-75 at Merchants Rd. (formerly Best Western of Knoxville).

Howard Johnson's. *Moderate to Expensive.* Two locations. Pools, restaurants. **North:** 118 Merchants Rd., N.W. **West:** 7723 Kingston Pike. North location has enclosed heated pool, carpet golf, game room.

Sheraton Campus Inn. *Moderate to Expensive.* 1706 W. Cumberland. Near the University of Tennessee campus. Very comfortable accommodations. Suites. Restaurant. Pool; poolside service. Pets.

Sheraton West. *Moderate to Expensive.* I-40 and I-75 at Cedar Bluff Rd. Spacious rms. Restaurant. Pool. Kennels.

Hyatt Regency Knoxville. *Moderate.* 500 Hill Ave. SE. A stunning contemporary modified pyramid reminiscent of Mayan-Aztec design, nine-story atrium lobby. Pool, shops, cocktail lounges with live entertainment and dancing, dining on lobby level and rooftop.

Best Western Cherry Tree Inn. *Inexpensive to Moderate.* 1500 Cherry St. Dining room, lounge, pool. One pet per room. Senior citizen discounts available.

Days Inn. *Inexpensive.* Lovell Rd. at I-40 and I-75, Concord, Tenn. Restaurant and pool.

Econo Lodge. *Inexpensive.* 2 locations: 6712 Central Ave. Pike; 1500 Cherry St. Both have pools, restaurants; cribs, rollaways, and free color TV.

Lebanon

Holiday Inn. *Moderate.* US 231S and I-40. Suites. Restaurant. Pool.

Days Inn. *Inexpensive.* I-40 and US 231S. Pool, restaurant. Senior citizen discounts.

Lenoir City

Red Carpet Inn. *Inexpensive to Moderate.* Jct TN 95, I-75. Well-maintained motel. Restaurant. Pool, play area. Pets.

King's Inn. *Inexpensive.* 3 mi. NW. on TN 95 Restaurant, pool, playground.

Memphis

Hyatt Regency Memphis. *Expensive.* 939 Ridge Lake Blvd. at I-240 Loop east of city. Contemporary high-rise, luxury rooms. Dining; lounge with entertainment and dancing; heated pool, shops, movies.

The Peabody Hotel. *Expensive.* 149 Union Ave. Famed landmark hotel has been magnificently restored to its original grandeur. Its "trademark," mallard ducks, still splash in the lobby pool and each afternoon march along a red carpet to the elevator to be whisked upstairs for the evening. Health club, heated indoor pool. 2 dining rooms, coffee shop, lounges, entertainment.

Sheraton Convention Center Hotel. *Expensive.* 300 N. 2nd St. Located downtown near Cook Convention Center and Mississippi River, has restaurant, cocktail lounge, outdoor pool, guest laundry.

Sheraton Airport Inn. *Expensive.* 2411 Winchester Rd., on grounds of International Airport. Restaurant, lounge, shops, pool, lighted tennis courts.

Holiday Inns. *Moderate to Expensive.* Memphis is the headquarters of this remarkable motel-hotel system. Flagship among the Inns in Memphis is the **Rivermont**, *expensive,* a high-rise contemporary tower overlooking the Mississippi River and the dramatic skyline of the city, with cocktail lounges, live entertainment, disco, gift shops, pools, restaurants and a gourmet roof-top dining room where music to accompany dancing and viewing are highlighted.

Other **Holiday Inns** in Memphis. *Moderate to Expensive.* I-40 at Macon Rd. and Sycamore View; **Midtown,** Union Ave. at I-240; Poplar Ave. at I-240; **Medical Center,** 969 Madison Ave.; Union Ave. at McLean Blvd; **Holiday City,** 3728 Lamar Ave; **International Airport** at 1441 E. Brooks Rd; I-40 & I-55; West Memphis, Ark. All have restaurants, lounges, pools and often feature live entertainment.

Ramada Inn. *Moderate to Expensive.* Five locations. All have inviting rms., restaurant, pool. **East:** 5225 Summer Ave.; **South:** I-240 at Mt.Moriah (2490 Mt. Moriah Rd.). Airport transportation available; **Southeast:** Lamar & Getwell; **Downtown:** 160 Union Ave; **Airport:** 1471 E. Brooks Rd.

Rodeway Inn. *Moderate to Expensive.* 2949 Airways Blvd. Very comfortable rms. Restaurant, lounge with entertainment. Pool.

Quality Inn. *Moderate to Expensive.* Three locations. All have tastefully decorated rms., restaurant, pool. **Airport:** I-55 at Brooks Rd. Entertainment. **East:** I-240 & Poplar. Indoor heated pool. **West:** 271 W. Alston Ave. Entertainment. Airport transportation available.

Sheraton Skyport. *Moderate to Expensive.* In the Memphis International Airport Terminal. Mini-rooms for overnight and between-flight naps. Convenient to restaurants, lounge, shops, airline and auto rental counters.

Admiral Benbow Inn. *Moderate.* 4720 Summer Ave. Inviting rms. Restaurant. Pool. Free airport transportation.

Howard Johnson's. *Moderate.* 3280 Elvis Presley Blvd. Pool, restaurant, playground, pets.

Days Inn. *Inexpensive.* Three locations: I-240/I-40 at 5301 Summer Ave.; I-55 at Brooks Rd.; I-55 at E. Shelby Dr. exit—1970 E. Shelby Dr. All have restaurants, facilities for handicapped. Children under 12 may eat free when accompanying adult is registered guest.

Murfreesboro

Holiday Inn. *Moderate to Expensive.* Jct. TN 96 and I-24. Restaurant. Heated pool. Kennels.

Howard Johnson's. *Moderate to Expensive.* Jct. US 231 and I-24. Pool, restaurant.

Ramada Inn. *Moderate.* Jct. US 231 and I-24. Well-appointed rms. Restaurant. pool.

Wayside Inn (Best Western). *Moderate.* Jct. I-24 and US 231S. Nicely decorated rms. Restaurant nr. Heated pool.

Quality Inn. *Inexpensive to Moderate.* Jct. I-24 and US 231S. Opposite shopping center. Restaurant, pool.

University Inn. *Inexpensive to Moderate.* 219 Broad St. Nicely furnished rms. Restaurant nr. Pool.

Days Inn. *Inexpensive.* I-24 at US 231 (Exit 81), 2036 S. Church St. Restaurant, pool, "Kids Eat Free" program, senior citizen discounts.

Nashville

Hyatt Regency Nashville. *Expensive.* 623 Union St. Located downtown, the luxury hotel features a stunning atrium lobby, gourmet dining room, revolving rooftop restaurant, cocktail lounges, live entertainment, dancing, shops.

Opryland Hotel. *Expensive.* 2800 Opryland Dr. at Opryland USA. Colonial design, lavish decor. Pools, dining room and restaurants, cocktail lounges with live entertainment and dancing. Boutique shopping.

Radisson Plaza Nashville. *Expensive.* 2 Commerce Pl. Striking contemporary design, downtown location. Two dining rooms, cocktails and live entertainment, heated indoor pool.

Maxwell House Hotel. *Expensive.* 2025 Metro Center Blvd. Convenient downtown location. Two dining rooms, swimming pool and saunas, lighted tennis courts, cocktail lounges with live entertainment.

Howard Johnson's Motor Lodge. *Moderate to Expensive.* At two locations. All have restaurant, pool. **North:** 2401 Brick Church Pike. Pets welcome. **West:** 6834 Charlotte Pike.

Best Western Drake Inn. *Moderate to Expensive.* 420 Murfreesboro Rd. Spacious, well-appointed rms. Some refrigerators. Restaurant. Pool

Congress Inn. *Moderate to Expensive.* 2914 Dickerson Rd. Comfortable rms Restaurant. Pool, play area. Color TV.

Holiday Inn. *Moderate to Expensive.* Five locations. All have restaurant, lounge, pool, kennels. **I-24:** 350 Harding Pl. Live entertainment; **North:** 230 W. Trinity Lane. Live entertainment; **Southeast:** 981 Murfreesboro Rd. Free airport transportation. Live entertainment; **Vanderbilt:** 2613 Wet End Ave. Live entertainment; **Briley Pkwy:** 2200 Elm Pk. at Briley Pkwy. Sauna, Holidome, Home Box Office. Near Opryland.

Quality Inn Parkway. *Moderate to Expensive.* 10 Interstate Dr. A 7-story motor inn. Restaurant. Pool. Pets accepted.

Ramada Inn. *Moderate to Expensive.* Four locations. All have pleasant rms. Restaurant, pool. **North:** I-65 at Trinity Lane. Pets welcome; **Capitol Hill:** 840 James Robertson Pkwy. Pets permitted; **South:** Harding Pl.; **Airport:** I-24 and I-40, Murfreesboro Exit.

Sheraton-Nashville Hotel. *Moderate to Expensive.* 920 Broadway. Spacious, nicely decorated rms. Restaurant, lounge with entertainment. Pool; poolside service.

Sheraton South Motor Inn. *Moderate to Expensive.* 737 Harding Pl. Very attractive rms. Restaurant, lounge with entertainment. Heated pool. Pets accepted.

Days Inn. *Moderate.* Color TV. Restaurant. Pool, play area. Pets welcome. At four locations: **Trinity:** I-65 and Trinity Lane; **Bell Road:** I-24 and Bell Rd.; **Plus Park:** I-24 and Murfreesboro Rd.; **Old Hickory:** I-40 and Old Hickory Rd.

Hilton Airport Inn. *Moderate.* No. 1 International Plaza. At Metropolitan Airport, 2-story motel with nicely decorated rms. Restaurant. Pool.

Comfort Inn. *Inexpensive.* 970 Murfreesboro Rd. Dining room. Senior-citizens program. Pool. Near golf, horseback riding, fishing.

Oak Ridge

Alexander Motor Inn. *Moderate.* 210 E. Madison. Nicely decorated rms. Restaurant. Pool.

Diplomat Motel (Best Western). *Moderate.* 206 S. Illinois Ave. Double-story motel with spacious rms. Restaurant nr. Heated pool, play area.

Rogersville

Hale Springs Inn. *Moderate to Expensive.* Opposite the Kyle House on Main Street of this charming historic east Tennessee town, which has been called the state's "best kept secret." Oldest continually running inn in Tennessee, built in 1824, the gracious hostelry has hosted Presidents Jackson, Johnson, and Polk. Eight overnight rooms are elegantly decorated with period antiques, oriental carpets. Canopied beds and fireplaces enhance the atmosphere.

 DINING OUT in Tennessee often means fresh Tennessee River catfish or such country specialties as ham withh red-eye gravy (sometimes made in Tennessee with coffee instead of water). Accompanying the meal may be hush puppies or home-baked biscuits, and desserts can include such Tennessee delights as pecan pie, blueberry pie, or fruit cobbler.

Restaurants are listed according to their price category. Categories and ranges for a complete dinner are as follows: *Expensive,* $20 and up; *Moderate,* $10–$20; *Inexpensive,* under $10. Not included are drinks, tax and tip.

Chattanooga

Green Room. *Moderate.* The Read House Hotel, Broad and 9th Sts. Elegant decor. Continental dishes, background music. They serve their own baked goods and ice cream.

Chattanooga Choo-Choo. *Inexpensive.* Choo-Choo Hilton Inn, 1400 S. Market St., in the Terminal Station. Spacious dining room under high dome of the 1905 era railway terminal, turn-of-the-century atmosphere. Steaks, chicken, seafoods. Cocktails.

Magic Seasons Family Restaurant. *Inexpensive.* 1305 Patten Rd.; take TN 58 & GA 157 5 mi. S.W. on Lookout Mountain. Informal, family-style restaurant encircles a large rock; children's menu.

Fehn's. *Inexpensive.* 600 River St. An entrancing view of the river from the tables near the windows. The varied menu gives you a wide selection of steaks and seafood. Chef-owned.

Gatlinburg

Open Hearth. *Moderate.* 1138 Parkway, on US 441. Very pleasant and friendly dining rm. with steak as their specialty. Background music.

Pioneer Inn. *Moderate.* 373 Parkway, on US 441N. Novel, unusual decor. Situated to provide dining on the river. Steaks, roast beef, chicken and flaming shish-kebab.

Ogle's Buffet Restaurant. *Inexpensive.* US 441 in center of town. Wide selections of salads, vegetables, meat dishes, desserts from buffet tables. Good mountain cookery is featured. Delightful for families.

Knoxville

Volador. *Moderate.* At Hyatt Regency Hotel, 500 Hill Ave. S.E. A rooftop dining room with superb views of the city and mountains. Continental specialties feature seafoods, lamb and duckling. Each Sunday there's a lavish brunch. Al fresco dining in season.

Regas Restaurant. *Moderate.* 318 N. Gay St. Informal service and excellent food. The seafood is superb. Save rm. for fresh strawberry shortcake.

Morrison's *Inexpensive.* West Town Mall. Cafeteria; member of excellent chain.

Memphis

Justines. *Expensive.* 919 Coward Pl. at East St. A superb resetoration of an old mansion, on attractive grounds, is the setting for excellent Creole and Continental cuisine. In the summer, terrace dining. Reservations recommended. One of the South's most famous dining rooms.

Four Flames. *Moderate to Expensive.* 1085 Poplar Ave. Enjoy superb dining in a charming antebellum house. American, Continental cuisine. Steak, seafood (New Orleans-style) are specialties here. Lounge with entertainment. Jacket and tie a must.

Grisanti's. *Moderate.* 1489 Airways Blvd. Steak, veal and delicious Northern Italian preparations are specialties. On display as the world's most expensive bottle of wine, purchased by the chef-owner a few years ago.

Pancho's. *Moderate.* Two locations: **Midtown,** 1850 Union and **W. Memphis,** US 70, just over the bridge. Mexican cuisine, char-broiled steaks. Businessman's Fiesta lunch served daily.

Britling's. *Inexpensive.* 5100 Poplar Ave., Clark Tower Mall. Buffet Clambake, whole Maine Lobster or N.Y. Strip Steak.

Britling Cafeterias. *Inexpensive.* There are three of these quality cafeterias with good food. Neat, clean, and inviting. Locally very popular. 20 Plaza Ave.; 4740 Yale Rd.; 4550 Poplar, in Laurelwood Shopping Center.

Monteagle

Jim Oliver's Smoke House Restaurant. *Inexpensive.* Sewanee Rd. (just off I-24, exit 134). Fabulous barbecue, fried chicken, country ham, steaks, ribs, catfish, and much more in attractive rustic setting. Adjacent trading post has specialty, handi-craft, antique shops.

Nashville

Hugo's. *Expensive.* In Hyatt Regency Hotel. 623 Union St. American, French and Continental specialties feature aged beef, lamb, veal and other menu choices in a posh atmosphere.

Julian's. *Expensive.* 2412 West End Ave. Classic French, chef owned, much flair.

Brass Rail. *Moderate.* 206½ Printer's Alley. Steaks, prime ribs and a variety of flambe preparations highlight the menu at this popular restaurant, situated in the downtown district and noted for lively night-time entertainment.

Mario's. *Moderate.* 1915 West End Ave. Continental menu, bar, background music, elegant decor. Specialty: Italian dishes. Chef-owned.

Morrison's. *Inexpensive.* One Hundred Oaks Shopping Center, Rivergate Mall, Hickory Hollow Mall. All are cafeterias, locally popular.

VIRGINIA

A State of Mind, A Way of Life

BY
RALPH DANFORD

Ralph Danford has been a travel writer for more than twenty years. A long-time resident of Virginia, he chose that state as his home after living in various places all over the globe.

Among several approaches to Virginia, all rewarding, one of the newest follows US 13 down the rural Eastern Shore and across seventeen miles of water via the Chesapeake Bay Bridge-Tunnel. The Bridge-Tunnel, which uses four man-made islands as stepping stones across the Bay, is a convenience and a show in itself.

On back roads off US 13 along the Eastern Shore are the quiet towns of Northampton and Accomack Counties. Across a series of bridges and causeways lies Chincoteague Island, scene of the annual pony penning during the last week in July. Firemen turn cowboy and herd wild ponies from Assateague Island across the channel to Chincoteague for auction on the carnival grounds.

The shaggy Chincoteague ponies, larger than a Shetland pony but smaller than a horse, are auctioned for the benefit of the island's volunteer fire department. Legend says that the ponies' ancestors swam ashore from a shipwreck in the 16th century or, alternately, that pirates put them on the island to graze.

The greater portion of Assateague is a national refuge for wildlife, including tiny Sika deer, scarcely three feet high. Native to Japan, they were released on the island in 1923 by a troop of Boy Scouts.

A visit to Assateague at any season affords spectacular displays of more than 250 kinds of birds. The winter features flocks of honking snow geese and whistling swans; spring brings sandpipers, plovers, curlews, and oyster-catchers; summer displays nesting colonies of egrets, herons, and ibises; and autumn offers migrating hawks and noisy flocks of ducks.

The Eastern Shore offers some of the best salt water fishing on the East Coast in the waters of Chesapeake Bay, and off the barrier islands along the Atlantic shore. The seafood industry is big business here with the local packers supplying the famous Chincoteague oysters to the finest restaurants in North America.

Tangier Island in Chesapeake Bay has the atmosphere of a fishing village of an earlier era. A unique English is spoken here by the natives. It resembles that of their ancestors, who settled the island in 1686. Until recently the island was relatively isolated. Access is by ferry from Reedville, Va. or from Crisfield, Md. Overnight lodging is available in a guest house.

Tidewater Virginia

Leaving the Eastern Shore, the traveler crosses the Chesapeake Bay Bridge-Tunnel into a metropolitan complex encompassing Norfolk, with the world's largest naval base; Virginia Beach, with a 28 mile stretch of public beach; Chesapeake, the gateway to Dismal Swamp; and Portsmouth, site of the country's oldest ship-repair yard. A neighborhood of Portsmouth, known as the Olde Towne Historic District, contains one of the largest collections of 18th- and 19th-century houses in the South. Directions for a self-guided walking tour can be obtained from the Portsmouth Historical Association. An interesting introduction to the Norfolk and Portsmouth skylines are the boat tours which operate from May through October and include the U.S. Naval Base, Norfolk, and its array of warships.

Norfolk and Tidewater Area

The first-time visitor to Norfolk may well be astonished at its variety. Long known as home port of the world's largest naval installation and as NATO's Atlantic headquarters, Norfolk plays host to an four-day Azalea Festival in late April that honors the alliance's member-nations.

One of America's outstanding art museums, the Chrysler, is located in Norfolk. It contains the collection of Walter P. Chrysler, Jr., and includes paintings and sculpture and a comprehensive glass collection with works representative of the history of glass-making from the early Chinese period through Art Deco.

Other features of artistic merit and historical interest in Norfolk are the Hermitage Foundation Museum, with its splendid Oriental collection and lovely grounds where you can picnic; the Adam Thoroughgood House, oldest standing brick home in America (1636); the Willoughby-Baylor House (1794); and St. Paul's Church (note the cannonball still embedded in the southeast wall) which survived a British bombardment

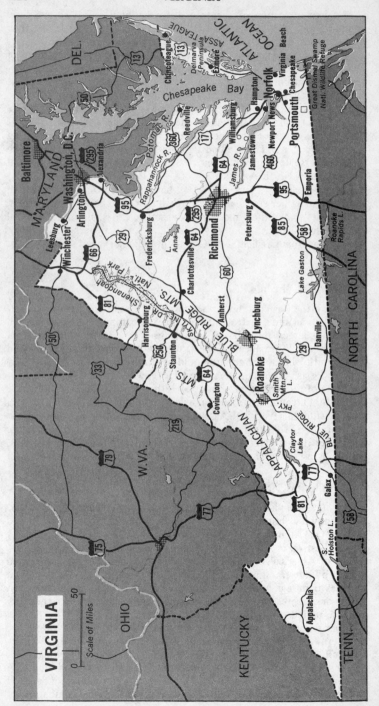

VIRGINIA

Scale of Miles
50
0

DEL.

ATLANTIC OCEAN

ASSATEAGUE

Chincoteague 13
Delmarva Peninsula
Exmore
13

Chesapeake Bay

Virginia Beach
Norfolk
Chesapeake
Hampton
Newport News
Portsmouth
Great Dismal Swamp Natl. Wildlife Refuge

Potomac R.
Reedville
360
Rappahannock R.
117
Williamsburg
Jamestown
James R.
64
Emporia
95
360

Baltimore

MARYLAND

Washington, D.C.
295
Alexandria
Arlington
95
Fredericksburg
295
Richmond
Petersburg
85
58
Roanoke Rapids L.

Leesburg
Winchester
66
29
L. Anna
64
Charlottesville
60
Lake Gaston

50

81
Harrisonburg
SKYLINE DR.
Shenandoah Natl. Park
Amherst
Lynchburg
Danville
29

33

Staunton
250
BLUE RIDGE MTS.
64
Covington
Roanoke
Smith Mtn. L.
BLUE RIDGE PKY.

219

APPALACHIAN MTS.

NORTH CAROLINA

79

W. VA.

Claytor Lake

77
Galax
58

77

81
S. Holston L.

75

OHIO

KENTUCKY

Appalachia

TENN.

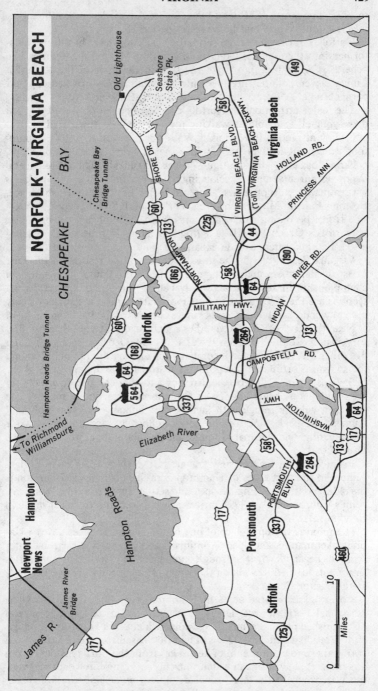

NORFOLK–VIRGINIA BEACH

CHESAPEAKE BAY

Old Lighthouse

Seashore State Pk.

Chesapeake Bay Bridge Tunnel

SHORE DR.

149

58

Virginia Beach

HOLLAND RD.

VIRGINIA BEACH BLVD.

(Toll) VIRGINIA BEACH EXPWY.

PRINCESS ANN

60

13

225

44

166

58

190

RIVER RD.

64

NORTHAMPTON

MILITARY HWY.

INDIAN

264

13

Norfolk

60

CAMPOSTELLA RD.

163

64

WASHINGTON HWY.

64

564

337

17

13

Elizabeth River

Hampton Roads Bridge Tunnel

To Richmond
Williamsburg

58

264

Hampton

Newport News

James River Bridge

Hampton Roads

117

Portsmouth

PORTSMOUTH BLVD.

337

460

James R.

17

Suffolk

125

0   10   Miles

in 1776. The house of Moses Myers, one of America's first millionaires, is a standout—hosts and hostesses in period costumes.

Norfolk's former courthouse, dating back to 1847, has been transformed into the General Douglas MacArthur Memorial Museum. The general is entombed in a crypt recessed in the floor of the Rotunda. Lining eleven galleries are mementoes, including his crushed cap and corncob pipe. A twenty-eight-minute film traces MacArthur's career.

The major attractions of Norfolk can best be seen on a well marked drive-yourself tour, plus a walking tour in the downtown area.

Newest attraction in Norfolk is Waterside, an exciting 80,000-square-foot waterfront festival marketplace that is home to scores of shops, galleries, bazaars, and boutiques—over 100 in all. There are several major restaurants, many specializing in seafood, as well as smaller cafes with romantic harbor views. Patterned after Baltimore's Harborplace, Boston's Faneuil Market, and New York's South Street Seaport, Waterside is fast becoming the focal point for a variety of city celebrations.

Norfolk's Ocean View Beach stretches along 15 miles of the Chesapeake Bay and offers a wide expanse of sand and a gentle surf.

Virginia Beach, one of the most popular seaside resorts on the East Coast, has combers high enough to attract the Atlantic Ocean surfing championship in July. Tucked away behind the beach and residential sections are the 2,700 acres of Seashore State Park, a melange of shady upland woods, sand dunes, and cypress swamps draped in Spanish moss.

Near the City of Chesapeake lies much of the Dismal Swamp, first surveyed by Colonel William Byrd II in 1728. George Washington and five other investors formed a company for digging ditches and draining the swamp. Fortunately for posterity, it resisted civilizing. In 1974 the U.S. Department of Interior, spurred by a lumber company's gift of fifty thousand acres, including Lake Drummond, set about making the swamp a wildlife refuge with facilities for human observers. July and August, the peak time for the pesky yellow fly, are not months for investigating Old Dismal. Inquire locally about boat tours to Lake Drummond.

From Norfolk, visitors may travel via the Hampton Roads Bridge-Tunnel to the port cities of Hampton and Newport News. Hampton is the oldest continuous English-speaking settlement in the New World. St. John's Church, built in 1728, prizes a set of communion silver made in London in 1618.

Hampton is the birthplace of one of the newest sciences. At the National Aeronautics and Space Administration's Langley Research Center America began its voyage through outer space. It was there the country's astronauts learned to walk on the moon. A space museum is open daily at the Visitor Center.

Covering sixty-three acres in Hampton, surrounded by a moat, is hexagonal Fort Monroe. During a century and a half, it held several distinguished prisoners, including Indian Chief Black Hawk and Confederate President Jefferson Davis. The brick casemate where Davis lived two years is now a museum of keepsakes from the Fort's history. From its ramparts the visitor can watch ships plying Hampton Roads and view the waters where the first ironclads, the *Monitor* and the *Merrimac*, clashed during the Civil War and changed the course of naval history.

In Newport News follow tour signs to the major points of interest, including the Mariners Museum, the War Memorial Museum of Virginia, Transportation Corps Museum at Fort Eustis, and the Newport News shipyards. From April through October a harbor cruise offers an enjoyable way of seeing the harbor area.

The Mariners Museum has an outstanding collection of miniature ships, marine paintings, figureheads, and relics from the sea. There is also an excellent marine reference library.

West on Interstate 64 from Newport News is the 23-mile Colonial Parkway connecting the information centers at Jamestown, Williamsburg, and Yorktown.

Jamestown

Jamestown, settled in 1607, was the first permanent English settlement in the New World. Start your tour at the visitor center operated by the National Park Service. Films and other displays in the museum provide background for a walking tour that includes the old church tower and the foundations of many of the original buildings. Also visit the glasshouse where craftsmen practice 17th-century glassblowing, one of the first industries of the colony, established in 1608.

A mile away from Jamestown—but not a part of it—is the Jamestown Festival Park, built by the Commonwealth of Virginia in 1957 and featuring Old and New World Pavilions. For the Old World Pavilion, tracing the settlers' origins in England, the British government provided costumed wax figures, guns, armor, coats of arms, and Captain John Smith's huge sea chest. The New World Pavilion interprets the settlers' contributions to American life, including the first representative assembly in 1619.

The Park also has a reconstructed stockade enclosing on an acre fifteen residences, a guardhouse, a storehouse, and a church. Moored at the James River dock are full-size reproductions of the tiny vessels—the *Susan Constant, Godspeed,* and *Discovery*—that brought the settlers to Jamestown in 1607, twenty years after the tragic failure to found a colony at Roanoke Island and thirteen years before the Pilgrims set foot on Plymouth Rock. What the settlers found when they landed at Jamestown is represented by an Algonquin Indian village, furnished with animal skins and primitive tools, similar to the one that housed Indian Chief Powhatan and his daughter Pocahontas. A look at the raw environment underscores the Indian girl's achievement in bridging the gap between her father's Stone Age culture and the Court of St. James.

Williamsburg

In 1699 the colonists moved their seat of government from Jamestown to Middle Plantation, which originated in 1633 as a palisade between the York and James Rivers. They renamed it Williamsburg in honor of King William III, and it served as the capital of a colony whose borders reached beyond the Great Lakes to the Mississippi River and encompassed the territory of eight of our present states. In 1780, during the Revolutionary War, the capital was moved to Richmond and Williamsburg lapsed into lethargy. The town slumbered so soundly that in 1912 it forgot to hold an election.

In 1926 John D. Rockefeller, Jr., set in motion the restoration of existing buildings and the reconstruction of others, including the Governor's Palace, the elegant residence of seven royal governors and the State of Virginia's first two governors, Patrick Henry and Thomas Jefferson. Original inventories guided the furnishing of the Palace and other exhibition buildings. Careful research also went into reviving one hundred acres of greens and gardens.

Always popular are the craft shops, including the bakery, the print shop, the blacksmith's forge, and the wig-maker's shop, tended by more than 100 craftsmen and interpreters. The staff that looks after Colonial Williamsburg more than equals in number its two thousand residents during the Colonial era.

In 1693 the College of William and Mary, second oldest in the United States, was founded in Williamsburg. It has been called "Alma Mater of a Nation" because of notable graduates including Presidents Jefferson, Monroe, and Tyler, and Chief Justice John Marshall. The nation's oldest classroom building is the Christopher Wren building, restored by Rockefeller to its original glory.

To set the stage for a journey into the 18th century the visitor should see the thirty-seven-minute color film *The Story of a Patriot,* at the Information Center and then roam the restored area. A walk down the main thoroughfare, with the College of William and Mary at one end, the restored Colonial Capitol at the other, will confirm Franklin D. Roosevelt's observation that it is "the most historic avenue in America."

Yorktown

Within a few minutes' drive is Yorktown and, overlooking the York River, the broad meadows where the combined French and American forces led by George Washington won the climactic battle October 19, 1781, against the British troops under General Cornwallis. This was the battle that ended the Revolutionary War and is sometimes referred to as "The victory that made a Nation."

In Yorktown is the home of Governor Thomas Nelson, who was serving with Washington during the siege. Sensing that American artillerymen were sparing his home, although British officers were quartered there, Nelson directed the cannon to fire upon it. Cannonballs are still imbedded in one wall.

Exhibits in the Yorktown Information Center trace the events of the three-week siege and the final assault on British redoubts. Among the displays are military tents used by Washington, dioramas of the battles, and a partially reconstructed British warship. From the Siege Line Lookout on the Information Center's roof deck, today's visitor has a view of the battlefield that Washington and Cornwallis would have envied. A self-guided tour by auto following the markers will include most of the historic sites.

Plantations and Historic Homes

Six miles east of Williamsburg on US 60 is Carter's Grove, operated by Colonial Williamsburg. The mansion was built in 1750 by the wealthy "King" Carter, and is considered one of the most beautiful in America.

Many famous Americans from Washington through succeeding generations have been entertained here.

A ferry at Jamestown takes the visitor across the river to the site of Smith's Fort Plantation. Remains of the breastworks, built in 1609 by Captain John Smith, are still discernible. In 1652 Thomas Warren built a brick house, now called the Rolfe-Warren House, on property he bought from Thomas Rolfe, the son of Pocahontas and John Rolfe. In the same area is Chippokes State Park, a plantation with a 350-year history that has retained its original boundaries and has continued through the centuries as a working farm.

No state has more plantation houses than Virginia, and State 5 from Williamsburg to Richmond, a winding, wood-lined road, has Virginia's greatest concentration of the great houses.

West of Williamsburg is the first in the procession of mansions, Sherwood Forest, the home of President John Tyler, who chose the name because he fancied himself a political Robin Hood. The dwelling, one of the longest private houses in America, extends three hundred feet and one room deep with a central portion of three stories.

Next is Belle Air, built in 1670, one of the oldest frame dwellings in America. Then appears Evelynton, a white-columned mansion named for Evelyn Byrd and standing on land once owned by her father, Colonel William Byrd II. Belle Air by appointment only; Evelynton closed to public.

The great Byrd himself—diarist, member of the Governor's Council, founder of Richmond, explorer—built and lived in neighboring Westover. In the center of the boxwood garden is Byrd's tomb, with the stately twenty-six-line epitaph he probably composed. It speaks of his being, among other things, "a splendid economist," a fair enough assessment of a planter who owned more than 179,000 acres.

Next in line is Berkeley, ancestral home of a signer of the Declaration of Independence, Colonel Benjamin Harrison, and two Presidents of the United States, William Henry Harrison and Benjamin Harrison. During the Civil War in 1862 while Federal troops were tenting in Berkeley's fields, General Butterfield composed the bugle call "Taps."

Shirley Plantation, last in the line on State 5, has been in the Hill Carter family for nine generations, since 1723. It was the home of Robert E. Lee's mother, Anne Hill Carter. The original furnishings, silver, and family portraits are still in the home.

The northern neck of Virginia, lying between the Rappahannock and Potomac Rivers, is noted for producing presidents and statesmen. James Madison came from King George County and George Washington and James Monroe from Westmoreland County, as did Robert E. Lee.

Stratford Hall, home of the Lees, gave the nation a host of public servants, including twelve members of the House of Burgesses and four Governors. Thomas Lee, who began building the house about 1725, was a Burgess who became President of His Majesty's Council. Two of his sons, Richard Henry and Francis Lightfoot Lee, signed the Declaration of Independence, the only two brothers to do so. Two other sons, Arthur and William Lee, represented the United States abroad as diplomats.

Also in the parade was Light Horse Harry Lee, Washington's cavalry leader, who, as a congressman eulogized his commander, was "first in war . . . peace . . . and the heart of his country." His son was Robert E. Lee.

Stratford Hall's massive proportions fit its destiny. Designed in the shape of a capital H and constructed of brick sent to Virgnia from England, the house measures ninety by sixty feet. It has four huge chimneys at each end. Its 1,500 acres today are worked as they were when Stratford was a showplace among Colonial plantations. The house is within sight of the Potomac River and only eight miles from Wakefield, the birthplace of George Washington.

The structure at Wakefield is an approximate reproduction of the Washington birthplace. The National Park Service built it of old brick on the site of the original, which burned Christmas day in 1779—the year Washington died. Many of the Washington family furnishings are among the early 18th-century antiques. Nearby is Monrovia, where President Monroe was born. Only the site remains.

Scattered throughout Virginia are many historic homes. South of Appomattox is Red Hill Shrine, the plantation and the last home of the great patriot, Patrick Henry, whose grave is also on this site. In Norfolk, visit the oldest standing brick house in America, the Adam Thoroughgood (1636), the Georgian-Federal Willoughby-Baylor House (1794), and the elegant Moses Myers House (1792), with hosts and hostesses in period costume. Near Leesburg are Oatlands and Morven Park. Sully Plantation in Chantilly is near Dulles Airport. And another presidential birthplace, that of Woodrow Wilson, is in Staunton.

Alexandria and Mount Vernon

The nation's most celebrated home, Mount Vernon, is in northern Virginia, fifteen miles from Washington, D.C., via the George Washington Memorial Parkway.

Between 1754 and 1799, Washington developed Mount Vernon into one of the period's finest estates, enlarging the house and expanding the acreage. The most striking feature is the high-columned piazza extending the full length of the house. Here tourists relax as if it were their own.

As a seventeen-year-old surveyor's apprentice, Washington drew the first map of his home town, Alexandria. He attended Christ Church on the corner of North Washington and Cameron Streets in downtown Alexandria and socialized with other patriots at Gadsby's Tavern, recently restored, on the southwest corner of Cameron and Royal streets. He was a member of the Friendship Fire Company, a volunteer corps.

Alexandrians insist proudly that their city offers as many buildings worth preserving as does Colonial Williamsburg. Still standing are eight hundred early buildings, many identified by bronze plaques, ranging from late Georgian and early Federal to Victorian.

Three miles west of Mount Vernon is Woodlawn Plantation, a wedding gift from George Washington to his adopted granddaughter, Eleanor Parke Custis, known as Nellie Custis, and his nephew, Major Lawrence Lewis.

Driving south, the traveler passes Pohick Church, the parish church for Mount Vernon, Woodlawn, and Gunston Hall, built in 1755 by George Mason, author of the Virginia Declaration of Rights. Gunston

Hall is a story-and-a-half brick house with a steep roof accented by pairs of tall chimneys at each end.

Fredericksburg

Fredericksburg, if it wished, could contest Alexandria's claim of being Washington country. At Ferry Farm, legends say, the boy Washington cut down his father's cherry tree and threw a silver dollar across the Rappahannock River. At Charles and Lewis Streets is the cottage Washington built for his mother, Mary. At 1201 Washington Avenue is Kenmore, the home of arms manufacturer Colonel Fielding Lewis, who married Washington's sister Betty. On Caroline Street is the Apothecary Shop of Hugh Mercer, where Washington worked while in Fredericksburg. And one of Washington's proteges, James Monroe, practiced five years in a law office at 908 Charles Street. The furnishings include the desk on which the Monroe Doctrine was signed.

Located halfway between the two warring capitals of Richmond and Washington, Fredericksburg was a frequent target for both sides during the Civil War. Few cities saw as much strife. From Marye's Heights Lee's strongly entrenched Army of Northern Virginia threw back repeated attacks of General Burnside's Federal troops on December 13, 1862. Fierce fighting also raged in the Battle of Chancellorsville, the Wilderness, the Spotsylvania Court House.

Richmond

The traveler has easy access to Richmond via Interstate 95, I–64 or US 1.

In Richmond the two most revered structures are the Capitol, designed by Thomas Jefferson, and St. John's Church, built in 1740–41. In the white frame church at 24th and Broad Streets Patrick Henry in 1775 made his liberty-or-death speech to the Second Virginia Convention.

Down the hill from St. John's is Richmond's oldest dwelling, the Old Stone House at 1914 East Main St., built about 1737. It has been dedicated as a memorial to poet Edgar Allan Poe, who haunted the environs for twenty-six years. The blood-red Raven Room contains forty-two somber drawings from Poe's poem on that bird.

The Valentine Museum at 1015 East Clay St. is devoted to the life and history of Richmond. In the rear is a garden, a peaceful retreat from the downtown's busy streets. Richmond's first residents, the Indians, get recognition in this museum.

In the far west end, at Grove Avenue and North Boulevard, is the state-supported Virginia Museum of Fine Arts. It pioneered in launching a fleet of artmobiles, traveling galleries to put art within reach of every hamlet.

At 818 E. Marshall St. is the house Chief Justice John Marshall built about 1790 and occupied until his death in 1835.

Richmond's newest attraction is a restored commercial area dating from the mid-1700's. Known as Shockoe Slip, it is becoming an entertainment center with a variety of restaurants and small shops.

Throughout the Civil War the North's rallying cry was "On to Richmond." Now at 3215 East Broad St. there is a headquarters for the

Richmond National Battlefield Park offering a road tour covering nine-ty-seven miles of battle lines, including Cold Harbor and Seven Pines.

Some 60 miles west of Richmond on Interstate 64 is Charlottesville, named in 1762 for Queen Charlotte, wife of George III. But it might just as well be called Jeffersonville, so thoroughly does Long Tom dominate the landscape and the intellectual atmosphere thereabouts.

Monticello

The domed mansion that is Monticello represents Jefferson's forty-one-year labor of love, of which he said: "All my wishes end where I hope my days will end—at Monticello."

The three-story building has thirty-five rooms but looks deceptively modest because twelve rooms are in the basement and a series of out-buildings, such as laundry, smoke house, dairy, stable, weaving quarters, and kitchen, is located inconspicuously beneath the long terraces ter-minating in two balancing chambers.

Always looking for labor-saving devices, he filled Monticello with unique features—tightly winding stairways, only twenty-four inches wide, to save space, a revolving door with shelves to serve dishes from the kitchen to the dining room in one sweeping motion, a dumbwaiter to bring wine from the cellar, a folding ladder to use in winding the cannonball clock that registers hours, days, and weeks.

Through a telescope on his mountain Jefferson watched the building of the University of Virginia, which he founded as "the last act of usefulness I can render." He designed the buildings, hired the faculty, and organized the curriculum. So well did he work that today students and faculty speak of "Mr. Jefferson" as if he were a living presence.

The Shenandoah Valley

West of Charlottesville the character of the land changes, and at times the independent temperament of the people seems to match the rugged terrain. The Blue Ridge Mountains form the great divide in Virginia. Wriggling along that range's backbone is the Skyline Drive, which runs 105 miles through Shenandoah National Park. At Afton the winding road changes its name to the Blue Ridge Parkway and continues 217 miles to the North Carolina border.

Beyond the Blue Ridge are the Allegheny Mountains and between the two ranges lies the Shenandoah Valley. At the head of the Valley, in northwest Virginia, is Winchester. Here sixteen-year-old George Wash-ington worked as a surveyor for Lord Fairfax. His headquarters at Cork and Braddock Streets is now a museum. Winchester is the site of the annual Apple Blossom Festival, which has a nationally televised parade featuring more than 50 floats and 80 bands representing 30 states.

The Valley offers an array of natural formations, the most renowned being Natural Bridge, off Interstate 81 and US 11, and twelve miles south of Lexington. It rears 215 feet above Cedar Creek and is ninety feet long and from fifty to one hundred fifty feet wide. Indians called it the Bridge of God. Thomas Jefferson, who bought it from King George III for thirty shillings, termed it "the most sublime of Nature's Work." Along the edge of the Valley are numerous caves. Luray Caverns is popular for its colorful formations and the unusual stalacpipe organ.

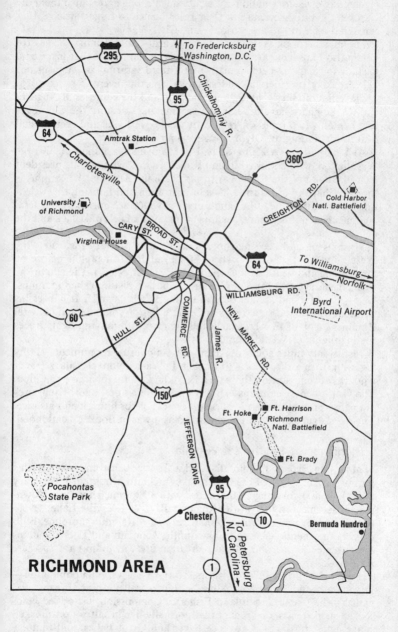

To Fredericksburg
Washington, D.C.

295

95

Chickahominy R.

64

Amtrak Station

Charlottesville

360

CREIGHTON RD.

Cold Harbor
Natl. Battlefield

University
of Richmond

BROAD ST.

CARY ST.

Virginia House

64

To Williamsburg

Norfolk

WILLIAMSBURG RD.

Byrd
International Airport

60

HULL ST.

COMMERCE RD.

James R.

NEW MARKET RD.

150

JEFFERSON DAVIS

Ft. Harrison

Ft. Hoke

Richmond
Natl. Battlefield

Ft. Brady

Pocahontas
State Park

95

Chester

To Petersburg
N. Carolina

10

Bermuda Hundred

1

RICHMOND AREA

Near the community of Mt. Solon are seven limestone columns rising high as a twelve-story building. Local residents long ago named them the Natural Chimneys because of their resemblance to huge furnaces that smeltered iron in the area prior to the Civil War.

The massive rock formations, set in a near circle against the side of a hill, also look like castle turrets and towers, an image that inspired a jousting tournament held annually on the third Saturday in August since 1821, making it America's oldest annual sporting event.

The cities of Harrisonburg and Staunton and the counties of Augusta and Rockingham have developed a regional park around the Chimneys that contains two miles of trails with scenic overlooks and recreational facilities including an Olympic-size swimming pool.

At Lexington is Washington and Lee University, named for George Washington, who endowed it, and Robert E. Lee, who was its president from the close of the Civil War to his death in 1870. On the campus is the Lee Chapel, built during his administration and housing the Valentine recumbent statue of Lee and a crypt in which are buried the General and members of his family. Visitors also may see Lee's old office and the college's museum.

Washington and Lee's neighbor is the Virginia Military Institute, "the West Point of the South," where Stonewall Jackson taught before he found fame and death as a Confederate General. VMI is the site of the research library and museum honoring another distinguished alumnus, George C. Marshall, Chief of Staff during World War II. It houses his personal papers and such relics as General Patton's helmet and General Rommel's map of El Alamein. A talking map with moving lights traces the highlights of World War II.

Just twenty miles south of Roanoke is an unusual monument—a tiny log cabin with a dirt floor—to Booker T. Washington, the black leader who was born in slavery there on a Franklin County tobacco plantation. The visitor center contains exhibits on his life and an audiovisual program interpreting his heroic quest for education for himself and his race. The reconstructed plantation is worked as it was in Booker's childhood.

Highlands of Southwest Virginia

Mountains, lakes, handicrafts, and a frontier spirit characterize this part of Virginia. One of the largest lakes is Smith Mountain Lake, forty miles long and covering 20,000 acres, with a 500-mile shoreline. Downstream seventeen miles on the Roanoke River is Leesville Lake, seventeen miles long and covering 3,400 acres with a 100-mile shoreline. Built in 1966 to generate electricity, the Smith Mountain and Leesville dams have created a vast and varied recreation area, including a 1,200-acre state park.

Fishing is a prime lure to visitors. To the usual Virginia population—largemouth and smallmouth bass, crappie, walleye pike, bream, and catfish—the Game and Inland Fisheries Commission has added landlocked striped bass, or "rock," that normally live in salt water, muskellunge native to the St. Lawrence River and Great Lakes, and rainbow and brown trout.

Moving deeper into southwest Virginia, where the Breaks Interstate Park joins Kentucky and Virginia, the visitor may see the largest canyon east of the Mississippi. More than five miles long and 1,600 feet deep, the gorge at one point nearly embraces the Towers, a pyramid of rock more than a third of a mile wide and nearly a half mile in length. The 2,670-acre park is seven miles from Elkhorn City, Kentucky, and 8 miles from Hayse, Virginia, on Ky-Va 80 off US 460.

Another impressive natural phenomenon is 100-foot-high Natural Tunnel, which curves 850 feet through rock and opens into a rockwalled chasm more than four hundred feet deep, six hundred feet in diameter, and three thousand feet around the rim. The tunnel is fourteen miles from Gate City. Natural Tunnel State Park has a visitor center open from Memorial Day to Labor Day.

Cumberland Gap

In the farthest southwest corner of Virginia is Cumberland Gap. Through that gateway in the Alleghenies passed the Wilderness Road, the main path of the immigrants who won the Northwest Territory and pushed the nation's boundary to the Mississippi River.

In 1750, leading a party of five men in locating an 800,000-acre grant for the Loyal Land Company in Virginia, Dr. Thomas Walker discovered the gap. He named the river nearby the Cumberland in honor of the Duke of Cumberland, son of King George II and Queen Caroline. Later the name was given to the gap as well.

Daniel Boone explored the pass and the rich land lying beyond it in Kentucky, and in 1775 he led thirty axemen in cutting the Wilderness Road two hundred miles from what is now Kingsport, Tennessee, to the Kentucky River.

By the end of the Revolutionary War in 1783 some 12,000 settlers had made their way into Kentucky, most of them by way of the Cumberland Gap. The pace of the westward movement quickened to a mass immigration and in 1792 Kentucky entered the Union with a population of 100,000. By 1800 the population was more than 220,000.

Cumberland Gap National Historical Park, covering thirty-two square miles, includes parts of Virginia, Tennessee, and Kentucky, and contains, along with the gap, a quarter-mile remnant of Wilderness Road, ruins of an early iron foundry, Civil War fortifications, the Tri-State Peak, and the Pinnacle, from which visitors can see several states formed when America was starting its westward expansion.

PRACTICAL INFORMATION FOR VIRGINIA

FACTS AND FIGURES. The state is named in honor of the Virgin Queen, Elizabeth I, of England. Because of the Colony's loyalty to the Crown, Charles II called it the Old Dominion. The first Constitution, adopted June 29, 1776, termed it the Commonwealth of Virginia. Chambers of Commerce have styled it the Mother of Presidents, for having had eight native sons in the White House; the Mother of States, because under the Royal Charter of 1609 Virginia's territory included the present states of Kentucky, Ohio, Indiana, Illinois, Wisconsin, Michigan, West Virginia, and part of Minnesota; and the Mother of Statesmen for having produced such distinguished offspring as Chief Justice John Marshall, George Wythe, who taught John Marshall at the College of William and Mary, and orator Patrick Henry. The American dogwood is the state flower; the oyster, the state shellfish; the cardinal, the state bird; the foxhound, the state dog. *Sic*

Semper Tyrannis ("Thus always to tyrants") is the state motto. "Carry Me Back to Old Virginia" is the state song. Lowest point: sea level, Atlantic Ocean. Highest point: 5,729 ft. Mt. Rogers, in Smyth and Grayson Counties, named for William Barton Rogers, state geographer and first president of the Massachusetts Institute of Technology. Speed limit: 55 mph, or as posted. Population is about 5,000,000, and the area of the state is 40,815 square miles. Virginia is in the Eastern Time Zone.

The Tidewater region, where much of America's history began, is a flat plain drained by four rivers, the lower Potomac, the Rappahannock, the York and the James, all of which flow into Chesapeake Bay. Richmond, the capital lies at the fall line separating this coastal plain from the Piedmont Plateau, roughly from Alexandria through Petersburg. The plateau rises into the Blue Ridge Mountains, these descend into a belt of valleys, caves and rivers bordered on the west by the Alleghenies.

The climate is generally mild. Spring comes early and swimming can last into October. The highly indented coastline totals 1500 miles. The western mountains are cool and pleasant in autumn, with vivid foliage displays and temperatures in the 50s and 60s.

HOW TO GET THERE. *By car:* I–95 parallels US 1 running north-south in the eastern portion of the state. I–95 passes through Washington, D.C., Richmond and Petersburg. I–81 parallels US 11 northeast-southwest in the western part of Virginia. I–64 is the major east-west route connecting Norfolk, Richmond, Charlottesville and Charleston, W. Va. The Chesapeake Bay Bridge Tunnel connects Cape Charles and Norfolk on US 13.

By air: Cities served by regular service include Bristol, Charlottesville, Danville, Lynchburg, Newport News (serving Williamsburg), Norfolk, Richmond, Roanoke, Washington, D.C. (two airports in N. Virginia).

By train: Amtrak serves Washington, Alexandria, Fredericksburg, Richmond, Petersburg, Culpeper, Danville, Manassas, Staunton, Lynchburg, and Charlottesville. Also direct service to Williamsburg and Newport News. Check with your nearest Amtrak office for any changes in cities served.

By bus: Greyhound and *Trailways* throughout the state. A wide selection of motor coach tours to and through Virginia from major cities in the Northeast. Consult your travel agent.

TOURIST INFORMATION. The Virginia Division of Tourism is located at 202 N. Ninth St., Suite 500, Richmond, Va. 23219. Tel (804) 786–4484. Nearly 600 travel leaflets are available at the highway information stations operated by the state.

SEASONAL EVENTS. *January:* Colonial Williamsburg starts the year with its *Annual Antiques Forum* in late January and early February. The Forum presents authoritative studies of Colonial furnishing, decorations and crafts. Check Colonial Williamsburg for dates and details. Also check at the appropriate locality for specifics on these Virginia events:

February: Alexandria has its annual *Washington's Birthday celebration* with banquets, balls and various ceremonies.

March: The *Highland County Maple Sugar Festival* in Monterey is the southernmost US maple sugar festival. Williamsburg, which almost always has something going, presents *Candlelight Concerts* in the Governor's Mansion throughout the month.

April: Early in the month is the *Williamsburg Garden Symposium* with lectures on horticulture and garden design and tours of the grounds. The last week of the month is *Historic Garden Week* all over Virginia. Norfolk has an *Azalea Festival* late in the month with parades and bands and tours and, of course, thousands of azaleas, all to honor the headquarters of the North Atlantic Treaty Organization. This festival is climaxed by the Coronation of the Azalea Queen, a vivid spectacle.

May: The *Shenandoah Apple Blossom Festival* at Winchester is one of the biggest annual events. The *Virginia Gold Cup Races* at Warrenton and the *Virginia Foxhound* show at Oatlands, near Leesburg, bring together horse lovers from across the nation. The hunt country also has steeplechases and a variety of fall events. May also features the *Virginia Beach Music Festival.*

June: Wolf Trap Park, in Vienna, is the first national park devoted to the performing arts. A schedule of the world's greatest classical and popular entertainment runs from June through August. Schedules and tickets available by writing Wolf Trap, Vienna, VA 22180. Norfolk has an annual *Harborfest,* each June. It is a salute to sailing ships of the world, culminating in a full-blown sea festival lasting all weekend. Also in June: the *Hampton Jazz Festival.*

July: This is a month of *bluegrass music festivals* at Martinsville, Narrows, Saltville, Dublin, Stuart, Middletown and Bristol. More detailed information is available through the Virginia Division of Tourism in Richmond. *Chincoteague Volunteer Firemen's Carnival* is in late July. The high point is when the little Chincoteague ponies swim the Assateague Channel. *Virginia Scottish Games* in Alexandria feature bagpipes, highland dances, Scottish athletic games, and Scottish foods.

August: The *Virginia Highlands Arts and Crafts Festival* takes place in Abingdon during the first two weeks. Along with the craft exhibits there are plays, demonstrations and classes. The *East Coast Surfing Championship* is held in Virginia Beach. Both professionals and amateurs compete in the two-day event. *Old Fiddlers' Convention* at Galax near the Blue Ridge Parkway. *Jousting Tournament* at Natural Chimneys is oldest continuous sporting event in America.

September. The *State Fair of Virginia* in Richmond is the big event this month. Over 700,000 people attend.

October: Many of the homes in the Waterford area have been preserved much as they were in the 18th and 19th centuries and open for tours during the *Waterford Homes Tour and Craft Exhibit.* The *Highland County Fall Foliage Festival* celebrates the beauty of the upland hardwood trees. For details write the Chamber of Commerce in Monterey. National Tobacco Festival in Richmond; Festival of Leaves, Front Royal; Nostalgiafest, Petersburg.

November: Winter is the oyster season in the Chesapeake and the *Oyster Festival* in Urbanna has a full schedule of festivities and lots of oysters to eat.

December: The *Christmas Walk* in Historic Alexandria takes place in the first days of the month. The walk is accompanied by bagpipe players. Christmas in Williamsburg, beginning on the 15th, recaptures the spirit of Colonial Christmas. Fredericksburg has many special events to celebrate the Christmas season.

 NATIONAL PARKS AND FORESTS. In Virginia's Appalachian mountains, including the Blue Ridge and Alleghenies, and such further subdivisions as the Massanutten and Shenandoah ranges, are more than 2 million acres of national and state forests and parks. Extending along the crest of the Blue Ridge from Front Royal south to Waynesboro is the Shenandoah National Park, featuring nearly 400 miles of foot trails, with elevations ranging from 600 to 4,000 feet. About 95 percent of the park is forested. The Skyline Drive, snaking through the park, provides 72 overlooks. From Hogback Overlook the visitor can see 11 bends in the Shenandoah River.

Virginia has two great national forests. The George Washington National Forest covers more than 1 million acres and contains the highest cascades in the Blue Ridge Mountains. The Jefferson National Forest, covering more than 600,-

000 acres, extends from the James River to the southwestern tip of Virginia, embracing Mount Rogers, the state's highest mountain. Camping, fishing, hunting, hiking, and an abundance of recreational opportunities exist in both of these National Forests.

On the Eastern Shore of Virginia is Assateague Island National Seashore Park, a favorite stop for migrating waterfowl as well as tourists. Just 15 miles northwest of Washington is Great Falls Park where the Potomac cascades over a series of falls, and churns through a rocky gorge. Also near Washington, adjoining the Quantico Naval Base, is the beautifully wooded Prince William Forest Park.

 STATE PARKS. Virginia's state parks are various and diverse. On or near the coast are *Seashore, Chippokes Plantation, York River, Westmoreland.* In the Piedmont are *Pocahontas, Bear Creek Lake, Goodwin Lake-Prince Edward, Holliday Lake, Occoneechee, Staunton River, Lake Anna, Smith Mountain Lake,* and *Fairy Stone.* In the mountains are *Douthat, Claytor Lake, Grayson Highland* (formerly Mount Rogers), *Hungry Mother, Sky Meadows,* and *Natural Tunnel.* Two other parks are being developed at *Mason Neck* in Northern Virginia, and *Caledon* on the Potomac River in King George County.

Low-priced vacation cabins may be rented in eight state parks for one-week periods between the Monday nearest May 1 and the Monday nearest October 1: *Clayton Lake, Douthat, Fairy Stone, Hungry Mother, Goodwin Lake, Prince Edward, Seashore, Westmoreland,* and *Staunton River* are the sites which have such facilities. Information on reservations and services may be obtained from the Division of Parks, 1201 Washington Building, Capitol Square, Richmond, Va., 23219.

 CAMPING OUT. Camping is permitted at all state parks from early April through late fall. except designated natural areas and historic parks. To reserve a campsite or cabin, at the Virginia State Parks use the Ticketron reservation system. Reservations may be made at some Ticketron offices or by mail to Ticketron, Box 62221, Virginia Beach, Virginia 23462. (804–490–3939, M–F, 10 A.M. –4 P.M.) Reservations handled all year for the camping season. The Division of Parks, 1201 Washington Building, Richmond 23219, administers the parks and publishes a pamphlet which describes each park and the facilities offered.

There are also camping facilities at the following areas: *Blue Ridge Parkway, Shenandoah National Park, Prince William Forest Park, George Washington National Forest,* and *Jefferson National Forest.*

 TRAILER TIPS. There are more than 300 commercial and 38 publicly owned campgrounds in Virginia. The publicly owned campgrounds, usually near national and state parks and recreation areas, charge a modest daily fee.All have dumping stations and all except Longwood at Kerr Reservoir have flush toilets. Almost all have hot showers. Water and electric hookups are available at Natural Chimneys, Breaks Interstate and Gatewood Lake. *Campgrounds in Virginia,* available from the Virginia Travel Council, 7619 Brook Rd., P.O. Box 15067, Richmond, Va. 23227, has a complete list of commerical and public campgrounds and trailer parks.

 MUSEUMS AND GALLERIES. Alexandria: The Torpedo Factory Art Center, where torpedoes were once manufactured. Here a variety of artisans work and display their wares. 105 N. Union St.; open daily 10–5.

Richmond: *The Virginia Museum of Fine Arts,* the nation's first state-supported museum, continues to be a pace-setter. It has a fleet of artmobiles touring the

Old Dominion, and the visitor may happen upon one of these portable galleries anywhere in the Commonwealth.

Valentine Museum reflects the history of Richmond and the life of its people. Source material for a vivid, accurate picture includes more than 20,000 photographs and the third largest costume department in the United States.

Edgar Allan Poe Museum has its home in the Old Stone House, Richmond's oldest residential building, and is filled with the melancholy poet's memorabilia and manuscripts. It succeeds in conveying a real sense of his time and mood.

White House of the Confederacy was built in 1817 and occupied by Jefferson Davis during the Civil War. The relics of both the battlefields and the home front give a graphic picture of the war.

The Science Museum of Virginia features a planetarium/space theater. It is located in the former Broad St. Station.

Newport News: *The Mariners Museum* displays figureheads, boats, ropework, marinescapes, ceramics, nautical and lighthouse equipment. An absorbing show for children.

Norfolk: *Hermitage Foundation Museum* in a landscaped park is located on the Lafayette River and contains a rare collection of Eastern art.

MacArthur Memorial Museum honors General Douglas MacArthur and traces his career with memorabilia and films.

Chrysler Museum contains a rich collection of European and American paintings and sculpture, as well as one of the world's great glass collections.

Big Stone Gap: *Southwest Virginia State Museum* contains exhibits tracing the region's history from frontier days to contemporary times.

Petersburg: *Quartermaster Museum,* on State 36 just inside Ft. Lee. Flags, banners, uniforms, insignia, and military mementos are featured in this unusual museum.

Williamsburg: *The Abby Aldrich Rockefeller Folk Art Center,* adjacent to the Williamsburg Inn is the largest collection of American primitive paintings and objects in the country. Given to Colonial Williamsburg by Mrs. John D. Rockefeller, Jr., it is housed in a charming 19th-century style building. The Christmas display of the old-fashioned tree and toys has become a tradition in Virginia.

 HISTORIC SITES. (See also the "Exploring Virginia" section, previously.) **Richmond.** Begin with *Capitol Square* and the state house designed by Thomas Jefferson. Inside is Houdon's famous statue of George Washington. From galleries in the Senate and House visitors may hear oratory from representatives who pride themselves on being members of the oldest continuous legislative body in the Western hemisphere.

Adjoining the Square, at 707 East Franklin St., is the house that was the residence of Robert E. Lee and his family during the Civil War.

Across the street from Capitol Square, at Grace and 9th Sts., is *St. Paul's Church,* where President Davis and General Lee worshipped, and where Davis received word that Richmond had to be evacuated, April 2, 1865. Open Mon. through Sat., 10 to 4, Sun. 1 to 4; services Sun. at 8 and 11.

At 818 E. Marshall St., within two blocks of Capitol Square, is the house built about 1790 by Chief Justice John Marshall. It was his home for 45 years. The original furnishings and family memorabilia impart a strong sense of the Chief Justice's personality. Open Tues.–Sat. 11–4. Sundays 1–4.

St. John's Church. Patrick Henry issued his liberty-or-death ultimatum in a plain, frame church at 24th and Broad Sts. on Church Hill. Among the graves in the churchyard are those of George Wythe, Jefferson's teacher and friend, and Elizabeth Arnold Poe, mother of the poet. Open 10–4, April–Nov.

Agecroft Hall. For visitors whose taste for history antedates Jamestown, there is at 4305 Sulgrave Rd. a mansion built in the 15th century in England. In the late 1920s it was disassembled and rebuilt in Richmond on terraced lawns overlooking the James River. Open Tues. through Fri., 10 to 4, Sat. and Sun. 2 to 5.

Appomattox. On April 9, 1865, retreating from Richmond and Petersburg, Lee's Army of Northern Virginia was surrounded at Appomattox Court House. After a final attempt to break the Federal lines, Lee met Union General Ulysses Grant in the home of Wilmer McLean and surrendered. Reconstructed *McLean House* is open daily 9–5:30 June 15 to Labor Day; 8:30–5 rest of year. Admission from April thru October is $1 per car, free remainder of year. Other buildings in restored village are Meeks General Store, the Woodson Law Office, Kelly House, county jail. Reconstructed courthouse contains a museum with audiovisual presentation.

Charlottesville: A tour of this area should begin with a visit to the Thomas Jefferson Visitors Bureau, located on route 20, just off I–64E. *Monticello,* the impressive estate of Thomas Jefferson, was designed and built by him between 1769 and 1809. The house contains unique architectural features, and many of Jefferson's personal effects. Open daily, March to October 8–5, rest of year 9–4:30.

Ash Lawn, the estate of James Monroe, designed by his friend, Thomas Jefferson. The house contains many of Monroe's belongings. Open daily March to Oct. 9–6, rest of year 10–5.

Michie Tavern Museum, near Monticello, is still an eating place as well as a museum of the 1700s when its guests included Jefferson, Monroe, Madison, and Lafayette.

University of Virginia, founded and planned by Jefferson. Free tours during school year.

Arlington: Arlington is a suburb of Washington, D.C., and contains the *Pentagon,* one of the world's largest office buildings, housing the Department of Defense. Free guided tours Mon.-Fri. 9–3. *Arlington National Cemetery,* the most renowned of all national cemeteries, contains the Tomb of the Unknowns and the graves of such famous people as William Jennings Bryan, Rear Admiral Robert E. Peary, John Foster Dulles, Gen. George C. Marshall, John F. Kennedy, and Robert F. Kennedy. The cemetery is open daily from 8 A.M. –7 P.M., April through September; 8–5 October through March. The Tourmobile operating from the Visitors Center is the best way to tour the cemetery.

On the brow of the hill overlooking the cemetery is *Arlington House,* the historic home of Mary Ann Randolph Custis. She and her husband, Robert E. Lee, occupied the mansion from the time of their marriage until the outbreak of the Civil War. Open daily, 9:30 A.M. –6 P.M., April through Labor Day; 9:30–4:30 the rest of the year.

Marine Corps War Memorial. At the north end of Arlington Cemetery is a 78-foot, 100-ton bronze reproduction of Joseph Rosenthal's famous photograph of Marines raising the flag on Iwo Jima.

Alexandria: Start a tour of this historic city at the Visitor Center located in Ramsay House, 221 King Street. Info on walking tours, events, maps, historic homes, antique shops, and restaurants. Also a 13 minute film on the historic sites.

Christ Church, Cameron and Washington Streets, completed in 1773. Both Washington and Robert E. Lee owned pews in this church. Open Mon.-Sat. 9–5; Sun 2–5.

Gadsby's Tavern, 134 N. Royal St. An 18th century inn frequented by Washington and other patriots. Now operated as a museum and restaurant. Museum hours Tues.-Sat. 10–5; Sun. 1–5.

George Washington National Masonic Memorial, King and Callahan St. Washington was the first master of the Alexandria Masons, and the museum includes Washington memorabilia. Open daily 9–5.

Old Presbyterian Meeting House, 321 S. Fairfax St. Built in 1774. Tomb of the Unknown Soldier of the American Revolution is in the cemetery. Open Mon.–Sat. 9–4, Sun. 12–5.

Stabler-Leadbeater Apothecary Shop, 107 S. Fairfax St. This pharmacy served George Washington and Robert E. Lee among other prominent Americans. The original furnishings, glass containers, and prescription records have remained in place from its founding in 1792. Open Mon.–Sat. 10–4:30.

Carlyle House, built in 1752, was General Braddock's headquarters and a meeting place during the French and Indian War.

Mount Vernon, 9 mi south via George Washington Memorial Parkway. George Washington's home from 1754 until his death in 1799, and one of America's most beautiful colonial estates. Open daily March to Oct. 9–5; Oct to March 9–4.

Woodlawn Plantation, 3 mi W. of Mt. Vernon. A gift from George Washington to Nellie Custis (Martha Washington's granddaughter) who married Maj. Lawrence Lewis (Washington's nephew). Mansion designed by the architect of the U.S. Capitol. Open daily 9:30–4:30.

Gunston Hall, S. via George Washington Parkway and US 1. The colonial estate of George Mason, the author of the Fairfax Resolves upon which our Bill of Rights is based. Open daily 9:30–5.

Fredericksburg: Visitors should stop at the Visitor Center, 706 Caroline St., to obtain complete information on the many attractions in and around this historic city. It is difficult for any Civil War buff to fight his way out of Fredericksburg, so thick were the engagements there. *The Fredericksburg and Spotsylvania National Military Park* embraces 5,600 acres and four battlefields; Fredericksburg. Chancellorsville, the Wilderness, and Spotsylvania Courthouse. The Visitor Center at Lafayette Blvd. (US 1) contains an electric map and Civil War relics. Open daily 9 to 5.

Near Sunken Road is a monument to the Angel of Marye's Heights, a 19-year-old Confederate, Sergeant Richard Kirkland, who, draped with canteens, made repeated trips onto the Fredericksburg battlefield to give water to wounded Federal soldiers.

Kenmore, the home of George Washington's sister, Betty Fielding Lewis, has superb plasterwork. Open Apr 1 to Oct 31, 9–5; remainder of year to 4. At the foot of Kenmore's formal garden is the home George Washington purchased in 1772 for Mary Washington, his mother. From here he left for his inauguration as President. Its hours coincide with Kenmore's.

In *James Monroe's Law Office* at 908 Charles St., the visitor may see the desk on which the Monroe Doctrine was signed. The office, where young Monroe practiced from 1786 to 1791, has become the repository for his papers, personal belongings, and furniture used in the White House. Open daily 9 A.M. to 5 P.M.

Petersburg: *Petersburg National Battlefield Park* commemorates a series of battles where the armies of Lee and Grant fought each other for 10 months until, gradually worn down, the Confederates had to give up the defense of Richmond.

During six days in July, 1864, Federal troops planted a mine that killed 278 men and ripped a 180-foot gap in the Confederate lines. The Confederates rallied, however, and threw back the Federal assault. The deep crater that resulted from the explosion is a focal point for battlefield tours. At the park entrance is a visitor center, with a museum featuring an electronic presentation, relics, models, and maps. Open 8 to 6 daily, Memorial Day to Labor Day; 8 to 5 the rest of the year.

Williamsburg: The city of Williamsburg encompasses the largest group of restored and authentically reconstructed 18th-century buildings in the world, and is the focal point for the Virginia Historical Peninsula. For your visit, the Colonial Williamsburg free publication *How to Enjoy Colonial Williamsburg* will prove invaluable. Check the current issue on arrival for the week's events.

Exhibition buildings and craft shops are open throughout the year. The buildings are attended by costumed, knowledgeable hosts and hostesses.

Holders of general admission tickets may purchase additional tickets to the Governor's Palace and Gardens for 20-minute carriage rides and for evening concerts and indepth tours. General admission ticket holders also may attend evening films and lectures at the Information Center and the introductory film, *The Story of a Patriot.*

The general admission ticket also covers the Tricorn Hat Tour for children during the summer, a 2½-hour expedition including the gaol (jail), bakery, palace maze, and bowling on the village green, all topped by the gift of a tricorn hat. General admission tickets also are necessary for a lanthorn (lantern) tour of selected craft shops by candlelight; concerts in the general courtroom of the capitol building on Sunday evenings, April through September; candlelight concerts by an orchestra in the Palace ballroom and supper room on Thursday evenings, April and May, September and October.

It is recommended you leave your car in the Information Center parking area and board the bus available to holders of general admission tickets. It stops at all major points of interest in the Historic Area and is within walking distance of everything else. The Information Center is adjacent to the Colonial Parkway. Follow signs after leaving I-64 at the Williamsburg exit. See the orientation film, *The Story of a Patriot,* shown continuously, special exhibits, bookstalls, restrooms, and the terminal for the bus. Foreign film viewers can listen, upon request, through earphones to the films' dialogue in French, German, Italian, Spanish, Japanese, Russian, and Portuguese. The *Capitol,* west end of Duke of Gloucester St. has been reconstructed, and furnished according to House of Burgesses inventories. Public gaol is on Nicholson St., north of the Capitol. It is a photogenic gem for the family, who want to record on film the spectacle of being locked in cells of former prisoners and pirates. *Raleigh Tavern,* north side of Duke of Gloucester St., is a reconstructed 18th-century hotel, restaurant, meeting place and stage coach stop. All furnishings are original to the period. *Brush-Everard House,* on the Palace Green, is a charming house, garden, and outside kitchen building of an 18th century merchant.

Governor's Palace, Palace Green, is the reconstructed residence and gardens of the Colonial governors. Escorted tours include the advance buildings and outbuildings. The Palace display of authentic furnishings from original inventories is worth the 30–40 minutes spent on the tour. *Wythe House,* Palace Green, was home of George Wythe, signer of the Declaration of Independence and founder of the Law School at the College of William and Mary. The *Magazine* on Market Square has an indoor display of 18th-century firearms and muskets which are fired periodically. A costumed militia and fife and drum corps carry out 18th-century drills and maneuvers complete with musket and cannon blast, twice weekly from late March through mid-October.

Check the location of the *Colonial Craft Shops* on a Colonial Williamsburg map. These shops are not to be confused with the contemporary Colonial Williamsburg Craft House which is located outside the historic area. Craftsmen and interpreters will explain trades and demonstrate 18th-century methods and skills. In the *Tarpley, Greenhow,* and *Prentis* stores you may buy the products. See *Spinning and Weaving,* corn meal being ground by wind power at the *Windmill,* furniture being turned at the *Cabinetmaker's Shop,* wigs being shaped at the *Wigshop,* wrought iron molded on a hand anvil at the *Blacksmith's.* Sample fresh gingerbread and cookies from the *Raleigh Bake Shop* oven, watch a book being bound at the *Printing Office* and *Book-bindery,* and mail a letter from the reconstructed first Virginia post office. The *Silversmith* displays patterns of flatware and clocks and will sell you charming jewelry made by hand in the 18th-century manner. Meanwhile, up the street the *Bootmaker* is sewing and mending and the *Milliner* will welcome you as she trims bonnets. The *Wren Building* on the campus of the College of William and Mary is open daily. The chapel, Great Hall, 3 classrooms, and convocation room may be seen. The rest is used for college activities, but the complex of campus buildings is open to the public. Stroll through the grounds.

Jamestown: Jamestown is where the first permanent English settlement in America was established, in 1607. *Jamestown Island.* Begin at the Visitor Center. Cross the footpath and bridge from the parking lot to the center. Orientation films, maps, and dioramas explain the historical significance of Jamestown. Next, follow the markers on a self-guided walk to the *Old Church Tower,* built in 1639. Its graveyard has tombstones bearing well-known family names. Built onto the Old Church Tower is the *Memorial Church,* a 1907 restoration. Nearby is the *Tercentenary Monument* erected in 1907 to commemorate the 300th anniversary of the colony's founding. Also in the vicinity are the *Pocahontas Monument* and the *Captain John Smith Statue.*

Overlooking the river you may visualize the landing of the *Susan Constant,* the *Godspeed,* and the *Discovery* (replicas of which are at Festival Park). Continue past the *Confederate Fort* (1861), circling along the river bank beyond the Old Church to view the foundations of Virginia's first *State House, Old Townsite,* and *New Towne.* The restoration reveals to viewers the first town plan by the white men on these shores and shows clearly the ancient complex of concentrated government, rural, and residential buildings. Also visit the Jamestown Festival Park, built to commemorate the 350th anniversary of the settlement of Jamestown. The Park includes a reconstructed fort and exact duplicates of the three small ships that brought the first settlers.

Yorktown: To understand the significance of the 18th- and 19th-century events which took place in the vicinity, stop at the National Park Service Visitor Center at the east end of the Colonial Parkway. Open daily except Christmas 8–6; winter months 8:30–5. View a 12-min. orientation film and exhibits there that trace the events of the three-week siege leading to Cornwallis' surrender and the victorious conclusion of the Revolution. Terms of the British surrender were drawn up at Moore House. Markers throughout the area explain the *Battle of Yorktown.* The *Monument of Alliance and Victory,* commemorating the French assistance in America's War of Independence, is on your way to the historic houses along Main Street. The large brick mansion with the high wall and ivy is the *Nelson House. Grace Church* (Episcopal), one block off Main St., is open for Sunday services. There is parking space behind the old *York County Courthouse.* The houses on Main St. are within easy walking distance. Also visit the Yorktown Victory Center for a history of the American Revolution and a film, "The Road to Yorktown," Connecting Yorktown, Jamestown, and Williamsburg is the Colonial Parkway, with historical markers that explain major events in this region.

COURTHOUSES. The courthouses of Virginia, historically and architecturally, are important to the visitor because they embody a concept of government and plantation life from the 18th century to the present which has played a vital part in the growth of the United States. An explanation of the Virginia county system will facilitate planning interesting side trips to include these government buildings. First of all, the visitor should know that there are no towns or townships in Virginia. Forty-one cities in the state are not part of the counties, although they may be surrounded by a county on the map. County seats are identified by the words "Court House" (or "C.H.") and this should not be confused with the individual building, known as the *courthouse* (one word), housing the county government offices.

The original exterior designs of the courthouses can still be seen, but the interiors have been renovated to comply with modern needs. Visitors are welcome within the buildings during normal business hours. *Charles City Courthouse* may be viewed while visiting the great plantations on the James River. The courthouses of *Gloucester, Mathews, Lancaster, New Kent* and *Surry* counties are all located in their espective county seats. *King William Courthouse,* on Route 30 between West Point and Route 301, is particularly beautiful, inside and out. This is one of the few courthouses where a guide will assist you. *Essex Courthouse* is in

Tappahannock and *King and Queen Courthouse* is 20 miles SE on Route 14. Middlesex Courthouse is in Urbanna, *Richmond County Courthouse* at Warsaw, *Northumberland* at Burgess and *Westmoreland* at Montross.

HISTORIC CHURCHES. Virginia's historic churches of the 17th and 18th century were usually located within easy riding distance of the great plantations. Many are beautiful, but all are important to American history for the role they played in the lives of the famous men who worshipped within them.

Williamsburg: *Bruton Parish Church,* Episcopal. Built between 1710 and 1715. Services regularly since the latter date. Frequent organ recitals and, during holidays, special choirs. Guides. Duke of Gloucester St. Services on Sun. 8:00 A.M. and 11 A.M. *Wren Chapel* of the College of William and Mary. Non-denominational. Open daily to visitors during the school term.

Hampton: St. John's Church, built in 1622, is one of the oldest churches in continuous use. The original communion silver dates from 1619.

Smithfield: St. Luke's (formerly Old Brick Church or Benn's Church) is one of the most beautiful small churches in the state. Built in 1632, and restored in 1887.

Yorktown: *Grace Church* (Episcopal) holds services at 11 A.M. each Sunday. Erected in 1697.

Jamestown: *Old Church Tower* (1640), the only remains of the old church where John Rolfe and Pocahontas were allegedly married. Easter Sunrise service nearby.

The many beautiful old churches are occasionally hard to find, but are well worth the effort involved. The following is only a partial list of famous churches, in alphabetical order, county-by-county. Charles City County is *Westover Church,* c. 1737, attended by two Presidents (Tyler and Harrison) and continuously used by the famous Byrd family of Virginia. Near Williamsburg, on US 60, is tiny *Hickory Neck* (Episcopal). Essex County: *Vauter's Church* (erected 1720–31) is on Route 17. In Tappahannock, *Beale's Memorial* (Baptist), built in 1728, has walls two feet thick. *St. John's* (Episcopal), erected in 1849, is known for its unique wooden Gothic construction. Gloucester County: about 10 mi. N of Gloucester Point on US 17 is *Abingdon Church,* 1755, where George Washington's grandparents worshipped in the original building (1655). *Ware Church,* c. 1700, is brick and sits in a grove of trees on Route 14, east of Gloucester Court House. James City County: *Olive Branch Christian Church* (Disciples of Christ) is a 19th-century edifice also on Route 17 below Yorktown.

King and Queen County: *Colonial Church,* erected 1729, still in use as a Methodist house of worship, at Newtown. *Mattaponi Baptist Church,* built before 1824, adjoins the burial ground of the Carter Braxton family (he was a signer of the Declaration of Independence). Route 14 at Stevensville. Lancaster County: *Christ Church,* 1732, one of the very early churches of the famous Carter family, built by Robert "King" Carter, who is buried here. Between Irvington and Kilmarnock on Route 3 (presently being restored by the NPS with its original furnishings): *St. Mary's White Chapel,* original building 1669, present one 1732–34. Architecturally unique as it departs from Church of England ecclesiastical laws.

New Kent County: *St. Peter's Church,* 1701–03, where George Washington and Martha Custis allegedly were married. Prince George County (on south side of James River): *Brandon Church,* a mid-19th-century version of the original edifice, was originally part of the Brandon Plantation. Original communion silver. Westmoreland County: *Yeocomico Church,* 1706, second building, constructed of oak. Mary Ball Washington, mother of George Washington, attended services here in the 18th century. Original communion silver and font.

MUSIC. Musical events and orchestral groups are enjoyed throughout Virginia. On a classical note, Alexandria, Arlington, Fairfax County, Norfolk, Richmond, Roanoke, and Newport News have regular symphony seasons. The Virginia Opera Theatre in Norfolk has a winter schedule.

The summer months are filled with country and bluegrass festivals, and a range that includes classical, jazz, and bands competing for honors.

One of the oldest festivals is at Galax, near the Blue Ridge Parkway, on the second weekend in August. It is the Old Fiddlers' Convention, with contestants of all ages playing the familiar mountain music native to the Blue Ridge area.

The Shenandoah Valley Music Festival in July appeals to the lovers of classical music. Performances are at Orkney Springs.

The annual Virginia Beach Music Festival in May brings together high-school bands from all over the United States competing in parade and concert presentations.

In June, the Hampton Jazz Festival at the Hampton Roads Coliseum brings together the big names in jazz today.

Slightly different, the songs and music of Colonial days can be heard on Sunday evenings between April and October at the Capitol in Williamsburg.

Northern Virginia's Wolf Trap Farm at Vienna is the nation's first national park for the performing arts. An outstanding summer program that includes opera, dance, symphony, popular and classical entertainers, a National Folk Festival, special children's programs, and other related activities contribute to the wide appeal of this indoor-outdoor park. Prior to performances many people bring picnic dinners to enjoy in the park. Box office info at (703) 255–1860 during the summer season.

STAGE AND REVUES. When Bob Porterfield was asking the General Assembly for funds for his newly created *Barter Theatre* during the Depressions, he told the legislators that Virginia wasn't getting enough after-dark entertainment. A suspicious state senator wanted to know what the showman meant by after-dark entertainment. "That, sir," retorted Porterfield, "is the kind of entertainment you can go home and talk about!"

Porterfield won his appropriation for the nation's first state-supported theater, which is still thriving at Abingdon and has a winter season at different locations in Virginia. Barter Theatre led the way for an ever increasing number of theatres.

One of the oldest of the supper theaters is *Swift Creek Mill Playhouse* at Colonial Heights south of Richmond. It claims to be the oldest grist mill in the country and certainly boasts the finest Sally Lund bread, small loaves baked from an original recipe. Equally distinguished is Hanover's *Barksdale Theater*, north of Richmond. The nightly buffet is generous and tasty.

Other theaters offering appetizing repertoires and menus are *The Richmond Barn Dinner Theater*, the *Cavalier Playhouse* in Norfolk, *Wayside Theatre* in Middletown, the *Hayloft Dinner Theater* in Manassas, *Mill Mountain Playhouse* in Roanoke, and *The Lazy Susan Dinner Theater* at Woodbridge. During the winter the *Virginia Museum of Fine Arts* in Richmond has a season of plays and musical entertainment. In Norfolk, the Chrysler Museum Theatre offers a variety of entertainment.

The Virginia Shakespeare Festival runs from mid-July to mid-August on the campus of William and Mary College in Williamsburg.

Southwest Virginia bills two colorful outdoor dramas. At the *June Tolliver Playhouse* in Big Stone Gap is *The Trail of the Lonesome Pine*, based on John Fox Jr.'s novel about the fiercely independent mountaineers around him. Radford is the production of *The Long Way Home*, the true story of a pioneer woman's escape from Indian abductors and her 43-day journey home on through the wilderness. A passion play is performed at Strasbourg during the summer season.

GARDENS. *Historic Garden Week in Virginia,* occurring the last week in April, embraces the two subjects—history and gardens—that intrigue Virginians most. For a free catalog for homes and grounds on public display write Historic Garden Week in Virginia, Garden Club, 12 E. Franklin, Richmond, VA 23219.

Nature's own garden presents a changing show along the Skyline Drive and Blue Ridge Parkway with white and violet splashes of rhododendron and mountain laurel in the spring and a coat of many colors in the autumn. At those seasons few motorists object to the slow pace of the traffic. Below the Blue Ridge in Charlottesville the University of Virginia has restored its gardens, including the plants along Mr. Jefferson's famed serpentine wall. Lexington has a Memorial Garden. In Tidewater hundreds of acres of jonquils blossom in Gloucester and Mathews Counties. Norfolk's airport is set amid azaleas. Each spring Norfolk stages an *International Azalea Festival* in the Gardens-by-the-Sea honoring the North Atlantic Treaty Organization. With a helping hand from Norfolk, Richmond has planted a beautiful display of azaleas in Bryan park, off I–95. Maymont Park also has lovely lawns, giant trees, and rocky bluffs above the James River, as well as an impressive Victorian mansion. Virginia's eastern shore is a kind of Garden of Eden with fruits, vegetables, and flowers. Most of the historic homes and plantations that are open to the public feature attractive gardens and grounds. The gardens of Walter Misenheimer (on State route 10, 21 miles E. of Hopewell) have been developed privately, but are open free to the public and are especially colorful during the azalea season.

SPORTS. *Swimming* in Tidewater is superb. The major rivers and their tributaries offer choice spots. Nearly all the state parks have beaches. Along the coast Virginia is belted by fine sand: Seashore State Park on the Chesapeake Bay and False Cape State Park on the Atlantic Ocean are outstanding. Visitors have free access to the full length of Virginia Beach, as well as Ocean View in Norfolk.

Tennis courts are available at most semi-private and public country clubs, usually near the larger cities. The major cities also have numerous public courts in parks. Many local schools also open their courts to visitors.

Golf is a big sport throughout the state, and is enjoyed during all seasons. A folder, *Golf in Virginia* available through the Virginia State Travel Service describes all courses that are open to the public.

Skiing. The Old Dominion's mountains offer moderate ski slopes: the Homestead at Hot Springs, Bryce Mountain near Basye, Massanutten at Harrisonburg, Cascades at Fancy Gap, and Wintergreen.

For the *Horse-lover,* northern Virginia hunt country that surrounds Leesburg, Middleburg, and Warrenton, is the scene of many notable equestrian events that attract a national audience. In May there are the Virginia Gold Cup at Warrenton and the foxhound show at the historic Oatlands estate near Leesburg. The oldest horse show in the U.S. is at Upperville in June. Other major events are the Deep Run Hunt meet in April near Richmond, and the Middleburg Hunt Races in the fall. The Blue Ridge bridle paths in the Shenandoah Valley are also popular.

The *Commission of Game and Inland Fisheries,* P.O. Box 11104, Richmond, nd local game wardens can supply you with a full set of game and fishing laws, hich should be studied, as the law is enforced rigorously throughout the state. ck hunting on the coasts and shotgun, rifle, and bow hunting in the western ions of the state are excellent. Hunting and fishing are allowed in the national ts, and the wildlife management areas with the proper credentials, in season.

Hunting is prohibited in the major national parks, along the Blue Ridge Parkway, and in the Williamsburg-Jamestown-Yorktown area. The use of dogs anywhere is very limited.

Hunting in Tidewater Virginia has been made more exotic by the introduction of the Iranian black-necked pheasant and the green pheasant from Japan, which thrive in this area. Native birds which abound are quail, duck, geese and turkey. (Turkey hunting allowed in most of the state.) Hunting license required; extra fee for bear, deer, and turkey hunting (season: mid-Nov. to early Jan.).

Fishing in Tidewater Virginia is excellent, and no license is required for salt water sport fishing. The season is year-round, and during winter, many fishermen use fresh water tackle to catch the ever-present striped bass (rockfish). Sea bass, bonito, dolphin, flounder, marlin, shad and speckled trout are only a few of the fish found readily here. Trophies and citations available to anyone catching big fish in the Virginia Salt Water Fishing Tournament, May 1–Oct. 31 (details at all harbors). Freshwater fishing requires a license, and an additional fee is charged for fishing in stocked trout waters. A permit is needed for fishing in the national forests. Several recommended public fishing spots include: Harrison Lake, Haynes Mill Pond, Piscataway Creek, Powell's Lake, Mattaponi River, Walker's Dam, Gardy's Pond, Cat Point Creek, Lake Anna, Smith Mtn. Lake, Lake Gaston, Chickahominy Lake and Kerr Reservoir. An excellent pamphlet on where and when to fish is available from the Commission of Game and Inland Fisheries.

DRINKING LAWS. In 1968, the state's General Assembly approved liquor-by-the-drink, the most radical change in the Alcoholic Beverage Control laws since their inception in 1934. The provisions permit "qualified establishments," meaning bona fide restaurants, not saloons, to serve mixed alcoholic beverages, subject to local option. Liberalizing of ABC laws apparently has caused no significant changes in the Commonwealth's cultural and social scene. Licensed establishments may serve mixed alcoholic beverages until 2 A.M.; most close at 1 A.M. or earlier. There are 250 ABC stores selling liquor by the package and 9,000 establishments selling beer and wine. Minimum age 21; 19 for beer.

WHAT TO DO WITH THE CHILDREN. In the belief that children are the most neglected segment of sightseers, curators at Jamestown, Williamsburg, and Yorktown have inaugurated special programs for their delight. At Jamestown children are encouraged to rummage through a chest containing clothes worn by a 9-year-old colonist with Captain John Smith. Groups are sent with maps to locate points of interest and mark their discoveries by pasting stamps in books. In Jamestown Festival Park children enjoy boarding replicas of the three sailing ships, exploring the triangular palisade, and climbing the ramparts. Festival Park has excellent facilities for picnics.

In the same sense of allowing children to participate in history, a costumed Williamsburg hostess will invite them to help straighten the Colonial furnishings in a disordered room. At Yorktown children tour the battlefield and then visit a simulated war room in the Visitors Center. There they may try on uniforms of British and American troops. The designer of the special events explains that the challenge is to bring the program directly into the child's experience.

In almost every historic shrine the alert adult may point out objects that delight a child's eye. At Monticello there is Thomas Jefferson's cannonball clock strung over the entrance. On the state's numerous battlefields are cannon and trenches good for climbing. At the White House of the Confederacy in Richmond is Robert E. Lee's sword. In Williamsburg children may sit briefly in the stocks for penitent wrongdoers. In Alexandria is a replica of the fire engine *Washington*. Langley Air Force Base has relics from man's first steps into space; the Norfolk Naval Station with its gray line of warships and the ship repair yard in Portsmouth the imagination. The western portion of Virginia is honeycombed with caves, underground wonderlands with colorful rock formations along Routes 11 and 340 and Interstate 81.

Two major theme parks that operate during the summer season are targets for the young set and popular with families. Near Williamsburg is the Old Country-Busch Gardens, featuring a touch of England, France, Italy and Germany. A Tudor name surrounds a version of Shakespeare's Globe Theatre. The Clydesdale horses are here, too. Sidewalk cafes and the French Follies contribute to the French atmosphere and the German village is complete with an antique carousel. North of Richmond, adjacent to I–95, is Kings Dominion, a fantasy land of rides, shows, and the wild animals of Lion Country. Roaming around the park are the cartoon characters of Hanna-Barbera. A replica of the Eiffel Tower provides an observation platform.

While in Norfolk, treat the kids to an ice cream cone at Doumar's. Abe Doumar was the inventor of the cone (1904), and the present-day Doumars still make the crisply delicious cones on the original (1905) equipment. In Norfolk's Gardens by the Sea, there's a train ride with botanical commentary. The Science Museum of Virginia in Richmond lets children get involved in many of the exhibits.

HOTELS AND MOTELS in Virginia span a wide range. Generally, accommodations west of the Blue Ridge are less expensive than those in the Piedmont and Tidewater areas. A competitive thrust, now extending along the East Coast to Texas, originated in Virginia with Econo-Travel Motor Hotels. There are more than 40 in that economical chain spread through Virginia.

Williamsburg offers a variety of prices for lodging. The Williamsburg Chamber of Commerce, for instance, will furnish visitors with an approved list of private homes offering rooms at quite moderate prices.

The price categories in this section, for double occupancy, will average as follows: *Deluxe*, $38 and up; *Expensive*, $28–$38; *Moderate*, $18–$28; and *Inexpensive*, below $18. For a more complete description of these categories see the Hotels and Motels section of *Facts at Your Fingertips*.

Abingdon

Martha Washington Inn. *Deluxe*. 150 W. Main St. Set back off the main street and opposite the Barter Theatre, this is an old-fashioned inn with a broad veranda. The rooms are furnished with antiques, including four-posters. Dining room is famous for southern dishes. Parlors are comfortable, home-like.

Alexandria

Old Town Holiday Inn. *Deluxe*. 480 King St. Colonial-style luxury hotel in heart of restored area. Indoor Pool.

Best Western Old Colony. *Deluxe*. First & N. Washington Sts. 18 blks. N of I–95 exits I–E, I–N. Color TV. Pool. Restaurant. 548–6300.

Holiday Inn. *Deluxe*. 2460 Eisenhower Dr. Color TV. Pool. Pets. Free National Airport van. 703–960–3400. Several others in area.

⸱e Guest Quarters. *Deluxe*. 100 S. Reynolds St. One and two bedroom suites ⸱h equipped kitchens. Hotel Service.

⸱dential Gardens Hotel. *Expensive*. Mt. Vernon Ave. & Russell Rd. Apts. ⸱ites with kitchens.

Appomattox

Traveler's Inn. *Moderate.* US 460 near State 24. Attractive, clean rooms. Call ahead as accommodations are scarce in heavy travel season. Air-conditioned.

Arlington

Arlington Hyatt at Key Bridge. *Deluxe.* 1325 Wilson Blvd. in Rosslyn. Indoor parking. 303 rooms, good dining facilities. 841-9595.

Best Western Rosslyn Westpark Hotel, *Deluxe.* One block to Metro subway to downtown Washington. Rooftop restaurant.

Sheraton National Motor Hotel. *Deluxe.* Near Pentagon at Columbia Pike and Washington Blvd. Pool, indoor parking, rooftop dining.

Stouffer's Concourse Hotel. *Deluxe.* Near National Airport on US 1 at 2399 Jefferson Davis Hwy. A full facility hotel. 979-6800.

Quality Inn Iwo Jima. *Expensive.* 1501 Arlington Blvd. on U. S. 50, close to Roosevelt Bridge. Pool, restaurant. 524-5000.

Basye

Bryce Resort. *Expensive.* 3,000-acre resort with facilities for skiing, 18 hole PGA golf course, tennis courts, lake, horseback riding.

Bedford

Peaks of Otter Lodge. *Expensive.* Blue Ridge Parkway at State 43 at the foot of Flat Top and Sharp Top Mountains. Rustic but comfortable. Country-style cooking. Park Rangers explain the habits of the tame wild animals that often mosey by. Dining room overlooks lake and patient fishermen.

Blacksburg

Marriott Inn. *Deluxe.* 900 Prices Fork Rd. Indoor and outdoor pools, putting green.

Sheraton Red Lion Inn. *Deluxe.* 900 Plantation Rd. Spacious grounds, tennis, pool, golf. Restful and unique.

Econo-Lodge. *Moderate.* 3333 S. Main St. Free in room movies. 951-4242.

Bristol

Skyland Motel. *Expensive.* On US 11, 19 & 59 ¼ mi. N of exit 5, I-81, at 4748 Lee Hwy. Color TV. Pool. Playground. Restaurant adj.

Econo Lodge. *Moderate.* 912 Commonwealth Ave. I-381 exit off I-81. Convenient location. 466-2112.

Buena Vista

Barnes Motel. *Inexpensive.* On US 60 at 617 W. 29th St. Pool and restaurant. 261-2156.

Cape Charles

Amerian House Motor Inn. *Deluxe.* On US 13 at Wise Pt., N end of Chesap Bay Bridge-Tunnel. Resort facilities. Private beaches, Pool. Playground. Obs tion lookout for Bridge-Tunnel. Seafood in restaurant.

Carmel Church

Ramada Inn. *Expensive.* Off I-95 on Rt. 207. Pool, suites, fishing lake. 448-2828.

Days Inn. *Moderate.* Off I-95 on Rt 207. Pool, restaurant. Near King's Dominion theme park.

Charlottesville

For information on **bed and breakfasts**—many in old and historic homes—contact Sally Reger, Guest Houses Reservation Service, P.O. Box 5737, Charlottesville, Va. 22905; 804-979-7264 or 804-979-8327, 1–6 P.M., M–F.

Best Western Cavalier Inn. *Deluxe.* Intersection of US 29 and 250. Near the Univ. of Va. Pool. Restaurant. 296-8111.

Holiday Inn North. *Deluxe.* US 29 & 250 bypass. Convenient to city, one of a complex of excellent accommodations at highway junction.

Best Western Mt. Vernon Hotel. *Expensive.* Jct. US 29 & 250 bypass. Quiet, high above the road, overlooking mountains. Fine restaurant.

Chincoteague

Mariner Motel. *Expensive.* Maddox Blvd. Largest in town. 336-6565.

Refuge Motor Inn. *Expensive.* Maddox Blvd. Pool, and Chincoteague ponies for petting. Overlooks wildlife refuge.

Culpeper

Econo-Lodge. *Moderate.* At US 15 & 29 Bypass. Near Germanna College and business district. 825-5097.

Sleepy Hollow Motel. *Inexpensive.* US 15 & 29 North on business route. Restaurant nearby. 825-8369.

Danville

Downtown Motor Inn. *Expensive.* 502 Main St. Heart of city. 793-5411.

Virginia Manor Inn. *Expensive.* On US 29 S. 729-3622. Pool, room phones.

Ford Motel. *Moderate.* S. on US 29 at 2660 W. Main. TV, room phones.

Doswell

Best Western Kings Quarters. *Deluxe.* I-95 & Rt. 30. Lodging at Kings Dominionn theme park. Low commercial rates off season. 876-3321

Fredericksburg

Howard Johnson's Motor Lodge. *Deluxe.* US 1, Massaponax exit from I-95, pool.

Sheraton Fredericksburg Inn. *Deluxe.* State 3 at I-95. Attractive rooms, balconies or patios. Pool, wading pool, tennis, golf.

Ramada Inn. *Expensive.* I-95 and Rt. 3. Pool. Near Civil War Battlefield. 786-1.

Thunderbird Motor Inn. *Expensive.* I-95 & Rt. 3E. (2205 Plank Rd.) Restaurant,

Front Royal

Quality Inn. *Expensive.* On Rt. 522 bypass. Good dining room in addition to usual facilities.

Cool Harbor Motel. *Inexpensive.* S of I-66 on US 340, 522. Pool. 635-2191.

Galax

Rose Lane Motel. *Moderate.* US 58 & 221. Spacious, gracious, set back on a hill from the highway. A good place to relax.

Hampton

Chamberlin. *Deluxe.* Off I-64 to Fort Monroe. Modernized, well-maintained hotel on the waterfront at Hampton Roads. Watch the world's ships glide by. Spacious rooms, terraces. Adjacent to Fort Monroe.

Sheraton Inn-Coliseum. *Deluxe.* 1215 W. Mercury Blvd. Indoor pool, many facilities.

Strawberry Banks Motor Inn. *Deluxe.* Exit 4 from I64. Overlooks harbor, some suites with fireplaces, pool, fishing pier.

Econo-Travel Motor Hotel. *Moderate.* Two locations at 1781 N. King St., and 2708 W. Mercury Blvd.

Harrisonburg

Econo Lodge. *Moderate.* Exit 64E from I-81. Honeymoon and whirlpool suites available. 433-2576.

Village Inn. *Moderate.* 5 mi S. on US 11. Pool, playground, restaurant.

Hillsville

Knob Hill Motor Lodge. *Moderate.* US 58 & 221. Superb views of beautiful countryside. Children and pets welcome.

Hot Springs

Homestead. *Deluxe.* Rt. 220, Warm Spring Valley. One of America's great resorts. Sports in season: skiing, skeet shooting, fishing in stocked trout stream, tennis, horseback riding, carriage drives, golfing on three 18-hole courses. Dance orchestra and movies every night.

Cascades Inn. *Deluxe.* 3 mi S of Hot Springs. The Homestead's slightly less expensive relation. Guests at Cascades may use the Homestead's resort facilities. MAP.

Irvington

Tides Lodge. *Deluxe.* Off State 3. A quiet, luxurious water place for knowledgeable gentry. Open Apr.-Dec. Heated salt-water pool. Dancing. All water sports, golf course, cruises on Inn's own yacht. Poolside service. 438-6000.

Leesburg

Sigwick Inn. *Expensive.* Intersection of Rt. 15 & 7 bypass. Located on 18-ho golf course with club house in hotel. Large pool, pleasant surroundings. 471-92

Lexington

Best Western Keydet-General Motel. *Expensive.* US 60 west. Quiet mo setting, comfortable surroundings. Restaurant.

Days Inn. *Moderate.* Near exit 53 of US 11 & I-81. Pool, playground. 463-9131.

Thrifty Inn of Lexington. *Expensive.* US 11A & US 11. Within easy distance of Washington and Lee University, V.M.I. and the George Marshall Research Library. 463-2151.

Luray

Luray Caverns Motel West. *Expensive.* On US 211 by-pass, opposite caverns. Full facilities. 743-4536.

Lynchburg

Holiday Inn South. *Deluxe.* US 29 Expressway at Odd Fellows Rd. Pool, restaurant.

Econo-Lodge. *Moderate.* US 29 Expressway at stadium exit. 847-1045.

Manassas

Olde Towne Inn Motor Lodge. *Expensive.* On State 28, Center & Main Sts. Coffee shop for breakfast, lunch. Pool. 368-9191.

Marion

Holiday Inn. *Deluxe.* Exit 17 off I-81, Jct. of US 11. 783-3193.

Quality Inn Virginia House. *Expensive.* I-81 at exit 17. pool, near state parks.

Middletown

Wayside Inn. *Deluxe.* US 11 near exit 77 of I-81 at 7783 Main St. Historic restoration of colonial inn with seven dining rooms. 869-1797.

Mt. Jackson

Best Western Mt. Jackson. *Expensive.* Exit 69 from I-81; pool, cafeteria and restaurant. 477-2911.

Natural Bridge

Natural Bridge Hotel and Motor Inn. *Moderate.* On US 11 at the famed natural wonder. Gracious, modern hotel has replaced classic structure which burned. The bridge is still there.

New Market

Quality Inn-Shenandoah Valley. *Deluxe.* Exit 67 off I-81; pool, sauna, dining room, cocktail lounge.

Shenvallee Lodge. *Expensive.* I-81 exit 67. Golf and other resort facilities.

Newport News

Holiday Inn. *Deluxe.* US 17 at 6128 Jefferson Ave., Pool, restaurant, airport transportation.

Best Western King James Motor Hotel. *Deluxe.* James River Bridge Circle and Jefferson Ave. All hotel services. Handy to Mariner's Museum, James River Country Club and Williamsburg.

Econo-Lodge. *Moderate.* 11845 Jefferson Ave. (Rt. 143 between I-64 & US 17). mins. from Colonial Williamsburg.

Inn. *Moderate.* US 17 at 6129 Jefferson Ave. Complimentary coffee.

Traveler's Inn Motel. *Expensive.* US 60 at 14747 Warwick Blvd. 3 mi E. of Ft. Eustis. Pool, restaurant. Some efficiencies.

Norfolk

Omni International Hotel. *Deluxe.* 777 Waterside Drive. First class in every respect. Cocktail lounge, award-winning restaurant, and a swimming pool. Entertainment. 622-OMNI.

Holiday Inn-Scope. *Deluxe.* 700 Monticello Ave. Pool. Airport bus. Meeting rooms. Dining rooms and coffee shop. Adjacent to Scope Coliseum. Within easy walk of Chrysler Museum. 627-5555.

Sheraton Inn-Military Circle. *Deluxe.* Virginia Beach Blvd. & Military Hwy. 15-story inn. Pool. Airport transportation. Enclosed in shopping mall. 461-9192.

Quality Inn-Lake Wright. *Deluxe.* On US 13 at 6280 Northampton Blvd. ½ mi. E of Jct. I-64. Pool. Restaurant, cocktail lounge, golf, dinner theater. 461-6251.

Econo Lodge. *Moderate.* 3343 N Military Hwy. Convenient to bases, convention center. 855-3116

Petersburg

Ramada Inn. *Deluxe.* I-95 Exit 3. Pool, restaurant. 1 mile from Ft. Lee.

Days Inn. *Moderate.* Exit 5 from I-95 at 2310 Indian Hill Rd. Dining room, pool.

Best Western American House Motor Inn. *Expensive.* 405 E. Washington St. The twin of the Cape Charles facility of the same name. Comfortable, colorful. Traditional decor.

Portsmouth

Imperial 400 Motel. *Expensive.* 333 Effingham. Pool, a few efficiencies.

Richmond

For information on **bed and breakfasts**—many in historic homes—contact Lyn M. Benson, Bensonhouse of Richmond, P.O. Box 15131, Richmond 23227; (804)-648-7560 or (804)321-6277.

Best Western Airport Inn. *Deluxe.* Opposite airport S of I-64. Full facilities. 222-2780.

Holiday Inn-South. *Deluxe.* West on US 60, 6346 Midlothian Tpk. Pool, restaurant.

Hotel John Marshall. *Deluxe.* Franklin & 5th Sts. Located within a half block of Richmond's department stores and shops.

Richmond Hyatt House. *Deluxe.* W. Broad at I-64, Brookfield. Indoor and outdoor pools; two restaurants. 285-8666.

Econo Lodge. *Moderate.* 1501 Robin Hood Rd. Comfort at low cost. 359-40

Roanoke

Howard Johnson's Motor Lodge-Troutville. *Deluxe.* Exit 44 on I-81. Full ties.

Ramada Inn. *Deluxe.* 8118 Plantation Rd. 6 mi. NW on 220 at I-81 exit 43. Heated pool. Free airport bus.

Roanoke Hotel. *Deluxe.* Wells Ave. & Williamson Rd. A handsome, rambling structure in Old English decor set on high, spacious, landscaped grounds within easy walking distance of the center of downtown. Heated indoor pool.

Econo-Lodge. *Moderate.* 6221 Thirlane Ave. (I-581 & Peters Creek Rd.), 563-0853, and at 3816 Franklin Rd. (Intersection US 220 & Rt. 419 across from Tanglewood Mall.) 774-1621.

Shenandoah National Park

Big Meadows Lodge. *Moderate.* At milepost 51 on Skyline Drive (20 mi S. of Jct. US 211). Variety of accommodations and activities. Reservations advised.

Skyland Lodge. *Moderate.* At milepost 41 on Skyline Drive. Motel and cottage rooms, dining room, tap room.

Springfield

Springfield Hilton. *Deluxe.* Off I-95 at Franconia exit, 6550 Loisdale Rd. Year round indoor pool, full hotel facilities.

Staunton

Hessian House Motel. *Expensive.* 10 mi S. at exit 55S on I-81. Well equipped units with patios or balconies, refrigerators, 2 pools.

Master Hosts Inn. *Expensive.* Exit 58 from I-81. Pool, restaurant.

Tyson's Corner

Best Western Tyson's Westpark Hotel. *Deluxe.* I-495, exit 10W on Rt. 7. Indoor pool.

Marriott Hotel. *Deluxe.* I-495, Exit 10 on Rt. 7 Convenient to one of the area's best shopping complexes.

Virginia Beach

Belvedere Motel. *Deluxe.* Ocean at 36th St. Glass doors opening onto private balcony. Heated pool, sun deck. Coffee shop.

Cavalier Hotel. *Deluxe.* Oceanfront at 42nd St. Pool, rooftop supper club. Family dining room. Tennis courts. Golf course privileges. 425-8555.

Diplomat Motor Inn. *Deluxe.* Ocean at 33rd St. Window wall and sliding glass doors open onto ocean veranda. Heated pool. Coffee shop. Golf.

Dunes Motor Inn. *Deluxe.* Oceanfront & 10th St. Heated pool. Guest bicycles. Game room. Dining room. Near fishing pier, tennis, golf. 428-7731.

Empress Motel. *Deluxe.* Oceanfront at 28th St. Pub, oceanfront balcony. Heated pool. Sundeck. Golf and beach club privileges.

Flagship. *Deluxe.* Atlantic Ave. at 6th St. Heated pool. Rooftop sun deck. Golf. Fishing. Tennis.

Sands. *Deluxe.* Atlantic Ave. & 14th St. Heated pool, lounge terrace. and golf club privileges.

Howard Johnson's Motor Lodge. *Deluxe.* Oceanfront at 38th. Balconies. Pool. Restaurant. Cocktail lounge. Meeting rooms.

Ocean House Motel. *Deluxe.* Atlantic Ave. at 31st St. Rooftop pool. Restaurant. Private balconies with ocean views. 425-7730.

Princess Anne Inn. *Deluxe.* 25th St. & Oceanfront. Dining room, coffee shop. Heated pool. Whirlpool, sauna. 428-5611.

Sea Gull Motel. *Deluxe.* Oceanfront at 27th St. Heated pool. Mini-refrigerator. HBO. 425-5711.

Seahawk Motel. *Deluxe.* 26th St. & Oceanfront. Pool. Restaurant. Jacuzzi. 428-1296.

Sheraton Beach Inn. *Deluxe.* Oceanfront & 36th St. Heated pool. Restaurants. Fresh seafood a specialty. 425-9000.

Thunderbird Motor Lodge. *Deluxe.* Oceanfront at 35th St. Dining room. Coffee shop. Pool. All oceanfront rooms, private balconies. 428–3024.

Triton Towers. *Deluxe.* 23rd & Oceanfront. Heated pool. Sun lounge. Coffee shop.

Windjammer Motor Lodge. *Deluxe.* Oceanfront at 19th St. Heated pool.

Carriage Inn. *Deluxe.* 1500 Atlantic Ave. Quiet central courtyard, pool and terrace. TV. Coffee shop. Near fishing piers, oceanfront marina.

Econo Lodge. *Moderate.* Oceanfront and 17th St. Comfortable rooms at reasonable cost. 428-4811.

Williamsburg

Best Western Patrick Henry Inn. *Deluxe.* York & Page Sts. Pool. Restaurant. Comfortable rooms. Pets. Airport bus.

Best Western Williamsburg Westpark. *Deluxe.* 1600 Richmond Rd. Yr.-round heated pool, bus to Info. Ctr. Pets.

Heritage Inn. *Deluxe.* 1324 Richmond Rd. Has restaurant and unusually large swimming pool. Accepts pets.

Holiday Inn, 1776. *Deluxe.* On US 60. Spacious grounds, tennis, par 54 golf. Similar accommodations at **Holiday Inn West,** 902 Richmond Rd.

Williamsburg Hospitality House. *Deluxe.* 415 Richmond Rd. Attractive Colonial decor. Pool, shuffleboard, bicycles. Shuttle bus.

Williamsburg Inn. *Deluxe.* Francis St. in historic area. Pool, golf, tennis, lawn bowling. (800)446-8956.

Howard Johnson's Motor Lodge. *Deluxe.* 1800 Richmond Rd. Pool, restaurant, attractive public rooms.

Merrimac Motel. *Expensive.* Rte. 143 East. Pool. Kitchenettes available.

Princess Anne Motor Lodge. *Expensive.* 1350 Richmond Rd. Comfortable rooms, tastefully appointed. Pool. 229-2455.

Quality Inn-Colony. *Deluxe.* Page & 2nd St. Pool. Restaurant. Snack bar. Other Quality Inns with high standards and *moderate* to *expensive* are: **Francis Nicholson,** Rt. 60, By-Pass Rd.; **Lord Paget,** 901 Capitol Landing Rd.; and **Mount Vernon,** 1700 Richmond Rd.

Ramada Inn-East. *Deluxe.* 351 York St., within two blocks of historic area. Pool. Restaurant. **Ramada Inn-West** on Rte. 60 offers similar accommodations.

White Lion Motel. *Deluxe.* 912 Capitol Landing Rd. Clean, attractive units, 18 with kitchens.

Econo Lodges #1 & #2. *Expensive.* 1408 & 1413 Richmond Rd.

Williamsburg Lodge. *Expensive.* S. England St. Set in beautiful gardens adj. to restoration area. Pool, golf, tennis, excellent food at moderate costs. Outstanding convention facilities.

Greenbrier Lodge. *Moderate.* 800 Capital Landing Rd. Playground, pool, fishing. English pub.

King William Inn. *Moderate.* 824 Capitol Landing Rd. Modern, quiet, central location.

Motor House. *Moderate.* Info. Center Dr. Inexpensive cafeteria, pool, meeting rooms. Adjacent to Information Center. (800) 446-8956.

Winchester

Best Western Lee-Jackson Motor Inn. *Expensive.* On US 50 & 522, exit 80 from I-81. Pool, lounge, restaurant, cable TV.

Quality Inn—Boxwood South. *Expensive.* US 11 S, exit 79 from I-81. Attractive grounds, full facilities.

Wytheville

Econo-Lodge. *Moderate.* Exit 23 off I-81 & I-77 to US 11 (E. Main St.). 228-5517.

Wythe Motor Lodge. *Moderate.* on US 11, exit 23 from I-81. Restaurant.

Yorktown

Yorktown Motor Lodge. *Moderate.* 3 mi. S on US 17. Room phones, and a pool. Restaurant adj. 898-5451.

 DINING OUT in Virginia can be as varied as the state's geography. US 460, from Petersburg to Suffolk, runs through peanut-and-ham country in Southside Virginia. It's as if the traveler is passing a smorgasbord all the way. On the coast, around Norfolk, Newport News, Northern Neck, and Eastern Shore, fresh seafood abounds. On the Peninsula, Colonial Williamsburg's seven dining facilities set an unflagging standard. The urban areas of Richmond and Northern Virginia stimulate fine cuisine. In unpretentious places in southwest Virginia, old-style Southern cooking is at its best—and at its best, it's unbeatable. Restaurant price categories are as follows: *Deluxe* $9–$12.50; *Expensive* $6.50–

$9; *Moderate* $4–$6.50; *Inexpensive* under $4. For a more complete explanation of restaurant categories refer to *Facts at Your Fingertips*.

Alexandria

Gadsby's Tavern. *Expensive.* 138 N. Royal St. Historic restored tavern of the colonial period.

Seaport Inn. *Expensive.* 6 King St. Seafood in a long-popular waterfront dining spot.

Taverna Cretekou. *Expensive.* 818 King St. Traditional Greek dishes served in bright Greek atmosphere.

Fish Market. *Moderate.* 105 King St. Excellent seafood. 836-5676.

Atlantic

Wright's Seafood Restaurant. *Inexpensive.* About 6 mi. from US 13 with a fine view of the bay and NASA's Wallops Island. Good, home-style cooking, with fresh seafood specialties.

Berryville

Battletown Inn. *Moderate.* Intersection of US 340 & State 7. A drawing card: chicken smothered in butter.

Charlottesville

Boar's Head Inn. *Expensive.* W. on Ivy Rd. US 250. Continental cuisine, prime rib, colonial atmosphere.

The Ivy Inn. *Expensive.* 2244 Old Ivy Road of US 250 west of Charlottesville. A popular seafood specialty; steaming kettle of clams, lobsters, shrimp, crab claws.

Michie Tavern. *Moderate.* Rte. 53, ½ mile below Jefferson's Monticello. Rustic structure was operated by Patrick Henry's father. One basic, tasty menu: Southern fried chicken, black-eyed peas, stewed tomatoes, cornbread and biscuits, choice of 4 salads. Open only for lunch.

University Cafeteria. *Inexpensive.* 1517 Main St. A favorite place for University of Virginia students. Clean, wholesome meals for the entire family.

Cheriton

Paul's Restaurant. *Inexpensive.* US 13. Don't be put off by the drug store counters out front. At the rear are booths, tables, and a varied menu, including fresh-baked pies and cakes and vegetables and fish from the neighborhood.

Chincoteague

Channel Bass Inn. *Expensive.* Seafood with a European touch. Modest rooms also available.

Fredericksburg

Allman's Pit Cooked Bar-B-Q. *Inexpensive.* A plain counter type roadside eatery known for very good barbecue.

Great Falls

L'Auberge Chez Francois. *Expensive.* 332 Springvale Rd., Great Falls, Washington's long-time favorite has moved to the country to an Alsatian inn. Dining here is an experience requiring reservations a week in advan family-owned restaurant—and superb!

Hampton

Mountain Jack's. *Expensive.* 1123 W. Mercury Blvd., 827-1012. The Peninsula's beef specialists. Also fresh seafood from the waters of Chesapeake Bay. Open daily for lunch, dinner.

Hanover

Hanover Tavern. *Moderate.* Rt. 301. Dining and theatre in historic stagecoach stop that catered to colonial leaders.

Jamestown

Mermaid Tavern. *Inexpensive.* Jamestown Festival Park. Clean, wholesome, tasty snacks.

Leesburg

Laurel Brigade Inn. *Expensive.* Rt. 7 Southern specialties. Parts of inn date from 1766. Also modest rooms at low prices.

Luray

Big Meadows Lodge. *Moderate.* On the Skyline Drive, 15 mi. north of US 33 crossing. Marvelous view from mountain ridge. Full-service restaurant and coffee shop. 999-2221. Same prices, hours, at **Skyland,** on Skyline Drive, 10 mi. south of US 211. Dining room, tap room. 999-2211.

McLean

Evans Farm Inn. *Expensive.* Rt. 123, E of I 495. Colonial atmosphere, extensive grounds, home-made desserts.

Tyson's Corner Magic Pan. *Moderate.* Lower level of Tysons Corner Shopping Center on St. 7 west of I-495; 790-8084. Very good entree and dessert crepes.

Middleburg

Red Fox Tavern. *Expensive.* US 50, in the middle of the hung country, a haunt for those who ride to the hounds. Restored building (c. 1728).

Norfolk

Esplanade. *Deluxe.* In the Omni International Hotel at 777 Waterside Dr. Excellent continental cuisine in a refined dining room overlooking the harbor. 622-OMNI.

Ships Cabin. *Expensive.* 4110 East Ocean View Ave., overlooking Chesapeake Bay. Seafood grill of grouper, swordfish, and bluefish; good broiled seafood plate.

Phillips Waterside. *Expensive.* In Waterside Festival Marketplace; 627-6600. Open 11 A.M. to 11 P.M., seven days a week. Cocktails, entertainment. Excellent seafood.

Purcellville

The Inn. *Expensive.* Rt. 7. Continental/American cuisine.

Richmond

⋯ilio's Capri West. *Expensive.* 1312 Gaskins Rd., 741-0621. Italian specialties, ⋯ home made pastries.

⋯ead Inn. *Expensive.* 15 mi. from Richmond at Manakin, Va. Virginia food, ⋯rn hospitality.

VIRGINIA

La Petite France. *Expensive.* 2912 Maywill St. 353-8729. The cuisine has a genuine French accent. A real treat.

Tobacco Company Restaurant. *Expensive.* 12th & Cary St. Victorian décor in restored historic area.

Morrison's Cafeteria. *Inexpensive.* Glenside Dr. & Broad St. off I 64. A popular chain with good variety.

Sally Bell's Kitchen. *Inexpensive.* 708 W. Grace St., 1 block off Belvedere St. A lively, always busy Richmond institution. Box lunches of spicy sandwich spreads, cheese biscuits, deviled eggs, fresh-baked tarts and cakes, all the makings of an elegant picnic. Take-outs only.

Roanoke
Hotel Roanoke. *Expensive.* Shenandoah Ave. & Jefferson St. A rambling Stratford-on-Avon structure offering old-style hospitality in a lofty dining room.

Smithfield
Colonial Inn of Smithfield. *Moderate.* 112 Main St. Southern cooking featuring, of course, Smithfield ham and fried chicken. Homemade pies and cobblers. Lunch and dinner. 357-3269.

Surry
The Surrey House. *Inexpensive.* Superb cooking with memorable specialties—peanut-raisin pie, peanut soup, apple fritters, crab cakes.

Syria
Graves Mountain Lodge. *Moderate.* Rte. 670 in Syria 10 mi. north of Madison on slopes of Blue Ridge. Country-style cooking and servings satisfy appetites whetted by mountain air. Open 12:30 to 1:30 P.M., 6:30 P.M. to 7:30 P.M., Sun. 6:30 P.M. to 7:30 P.M. Lodging in cottages motel-style units. 923-4231.

Tappahannock
Lowery's Restaurant. *Moderate.* On US. 17 in town. Seafood galore, from Rappahannock River and Chesapeake Bay. Open daily 7 A.M. to 9 P.M.

Virginia Beach
Three Ships Inn. *Expensive.* 3800 Shore Drive, between Chesapeake Bay Bridge-Tunnel and Lynnhaven Bridge. Early-settler decor, candlelit dinners by the fireplace or on patio. Gourmet dishes: shrimp Florentine, scallops Mornay, curries, crab imperial.

Wakefield
Virginia Diner. *Inexpensive.* US 460. For nearly 50 years this comfortable, unpretentious restaurant has been serving some of the region's finest food. Its ham and sausage biscuits are celebrated.

Warm Springs
Waterwheel Restaurant. *Expensive.* Gristmill Square. Fresh trout, quich Lunch and dinner.

Washington
The Inn at Little Washington. *Expensive.* Center on US 211, Dinner Wed.-Fri.; 5:30–10:30 Sat.; 4–9:30 Sun. Closed Jan.–mid-Feb.

White Stone

Windmill Point Marine Lodge. *Moderate.* 7 mi. east of White Stone on State 695. Fresh seafood, caught at the door.

Williamsburg

Williamsburg Inn. *Deluxe.* Francis St. Colonial Williamsburg's original dining place. A pleasing mixture of continental and regional cuisine ranging from frog legs Provencale to Virginia crab casserole. In a moderate-to-expensive range are menus at the **Cascades** on Information Center Drive and the **Williamsburg Lodge** on S. England St. An inexpensive Colonial Williamsburg dining facility is the **Motor House** cafeteria at the Information Center.

Christiana Campbell's Tavern. *Expensive.* Waller St. George Washington's favorite dining place in Colonial Williamsburg, specializes in seafood: Hampton crab imperial, chilled shrimp salad.

Josiah Chowning's Tavern. *Expensive.* Duke of Gloucester St. in Colonial Williamsburg. Specialties here include Brunswick stew and Welsh rarebit along with spareribs, prime rib and Chesapeake Bay crabmeat. Cocktails. Children's menus. Reservations are suggested.

King's Arms Tavern. *Expensive.* Duke of Gloucester St. in Colonial Williamsburg. Gracious dining with waiters in period costumes. Specialties are Virginia ham, fried chicken, English lamb chops and roast beef. Try the peanut soup. Cocktails. Children's menu. Call in advance for reservations and to check end of dinner hour, which can vary.

The above are all in Colonial Williamsburg. For reservations, toll-free, (800)446-8956. In Va.: (800)582-8976.

Chickahominy House. *Moderate.* 1211 Jamestown Rd. Ham biscuits, Brunswick stew, and buttermilk pie, plus antiques. Open 8:30 A.M. to 3:00 P.M. 229-4689.

INDEX

(The letters H and R indicate Hotel and Restaurant listings.)

FACTS AT YOUR FINGERTIPS
(See also Practical Information sections for each chapter.)

GEORGIA
Practical Information

LANGUAGE/30

For the Business or Vacationing International Traveler

In 25 languages! A basic language course on 2 cassettes and a phrase book . . . Only $14.95 ea. + shipping

Nothing flatters people more than to hear visitors try to speak their language and LANGUAGE/30, used by thousands of satisfied travelers, gets you speaking the basics quickly and easily. Each LANGUAGE/30 course offers:

- approximately 1½ hours of guided practice in greetings, asking questions and general conversation
- special section on social customs and etiquette

Order yours today. Languages available: (New) POLISH

ARABIC	GREEK	JAPANESE	RUSSIAN
CHINESE	HEBREW	KOREAN	SERBO-CROATIAN
DANISH	HINDI	NORWEGIAN	SPANISH
DUTCH	INDONESIAN	PERSIAN	SWAHILI
FRENCH	ITALIAN	PORTUGUESE	SWEDISH
GERMAN	TURKISH	VIETNAMESE	TAGALOG

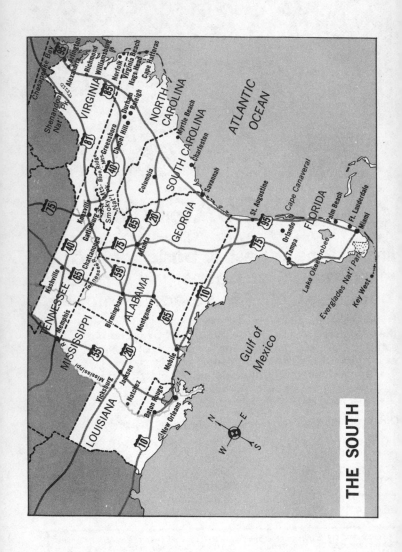

THE SOUTH